COURTROOM COMMUNICATION STRATEGIES

LAWRENCE J. SMITH

Member of the Louisiana and United States Supreme Court Bars

LORETTA A. MALANDRO, Ph.D.

President, Malandro Communication Inc. Tempe, Arizona

KLUWER LITIGATION LIBRARY

Kluwer Law Book Publishers, Inc.

New York, New York

Note: In this work, every effort has been made to use gender neutral language. Where clarity requires, however, the masculine pronoun has been used. The reader should note that it refers to persons of either gender.

Printed in the United States of America

90 89 88 87 7 6 5 4 3 2

Library of Congress Cataloging in Publication Data

Smith, Lawrence J.
Courtroom communication strategies

(Kluwer litigation library)
Includes bibliographical references and index.
1. Trial practice—United States. 2. Jury—United States. 3. Forensic oratory. 4. Persuation (Psychology) I. Malandro, Loretta A. II. Title. III. Series

KF8915.S59 1985 345.73'7 85–12550
ISBN 0–930273–07–9 347.3077

(Pub. 73079)

ABOUT THE AUTHORS

LAWRENCE J. SMITH practices in New Orleans, Louisiana, and received his J.D. from Loyola University. Mr. Smith is a noted legal author who served as Chairman of the Board of Editorial Advisors for the Association of Trial Lawyers of America's *The Anatomy of a Personal Injury Lawsuit*, 2d edition. He was Chairman of the Tort Law Section of ATLA and is a Board Certified Diplomat of the American Board of Professional Liability Attorneys. Mr. Smith is on the faculty of ATLA's National College of Advocacy and is a frequent lecturer on the subjects of medical malpractice and courtroom communication.

LORETTA A. MALANDRO is President of Malandro Communication Inc., a communication consulting firm in Tempe, Arizona. Dr. Malandro holds a Ph.D. from Florida State University in Communication Theory and Research. She has served as Vice-President of the Association of Trial Behavior Consultants and sits on its Board of Directors. Dr. Malandro was an Assistant Professor in the Department of Communication at Arizona State University and now serves as a trial consultant to lawyers across the nation. She is also author of several books and numerous articles in the area of communication research.

DEDICATION

To Ann, who will always be my everything,

To L.J. and Kathleen, who make everything worthwhile,

To Sid Bernstein, a true friend and teacher, whose continued support and encouragement over the years has so enriched my "process of becoming" that I am a better lawyer and a better person for having known him.

LAWRENCE J. SMITH

To my parents, who have created many possibilities and opportunities for me,

To Owen Marcus, for his effective subtle persuasion to explore new areas in my work and life,

To Debra, Ruth, and Pat for their true dedication and support in making this book become a reality.

LORETTA A. MALANDRO

ACKNOWLEDGMENTS

Both authors wish to thank Cheryn Heinen-Wall, whose massive research effort, along with great patience and diligence, made this text possible.

To Lanny Lindteigen, President of Performance Excellence, for his time, personal interviews, and invaluable contribution in discussing the application of the sophisticated communication techniques presented in Chapter 4.

To attorney Judy A. Gic, whose tireless efforts in editing Chapters 5 through 10 made it possible for the attorney-author to both author this text and practice law while maintaining his sanity.

To Debra Bolin of Malandro Communication Inc., and Patricia Gonzalez and Taryn Smith of Levy, Smith and Gennusa, a special thank you for the nights and weekends spent typing and proofing this work.

PREFACE

This is a book, the idea for which was conceived almost ten years ago, when the authors became aware of the need to merge the fields of law and communication in order to understand how and why jurors are persuaded in the courtroom. In the mid-1970's, a master trial lawyer from Phoenix, Arizona, Sam Langerman, presented a summation demonstration in a hypothetical wrongful death case which brought the audience of nearly 300 lawyers to the point of tears. He used method acting, making himself feel morose, and transferred that mood to those people in attendance. The videotape of that summation, however, did not have the predicted emotional impact on those viewing it. Emotion did not come across on the videotape. This experience underscored the fact that the impact of a verbal message is not merely what is said, but rather how it is said, and that this can even be affected by a person's physical presence.

Research in the areas of communication, psychology, and persuasion offered invaluable information to the authors in explaining how people are influenced and led by words, voice, and behaviors. We could find no published articles or works, however, which dealt solely with the subject matter of persuasive communication for attorneys. There are articles in the legal literature and other disciplines which deal with isolated issues such as posture and space and/or interpreting facial expressions, but nowhere was the subject of conscious and unconscious communication explored and presented in a comprehensive manner. Discussions with actors and actresses gave some insight into how method acting could be used to create mood transference, but nothing was available in concrete terms to teach lawyers nonverbal skills.

The authors decided to collaborate to bring two special areas of expertise—the law and communication research—together to explain the interrelationship of verbal messages with vocal cues, as well as the significance of the nonverbal portion of the messages. With this psychological framework, we would then be able to explain specific courtroom strategies such as increasing the credibility of a witness and using selected key words to embed certain ideas or facts into the unconscious minds of the jurors. We were no longer nibbling at the edges. The pieces began to come together.

Ultimately, we decided to organize this research material into four areas which now constitute the first four chapters of this book. This is the first time, to the knowledge of the authors, that anyone has collected the relevant psychological and communication research and collated them into one textbook for the legal profession.

A major focus of this text was an effort to take complex communication and psychological material and make it both intelligible and useable for trial attorneys. The method utilized by the authors to accomplish this objective was the development of basic communication principles. These principles were worked and reworked, defined and redefined, further simplified and further refined, until over fifty principles were reduced to the present twenty-one key communication principles.

The end result is four distinct chapters developing and detailing communication principles which deal with (1) how impressions are formed; (2) the persuasion process; (3) courtroom credibility; and (4) the decision-making process. There follow six chapters, Chapters 5 through 10, which apply these principles to both the pretrial process and to the courtroom itself.

Chapter 5 takes the trial lawyer from the initial interview up to the moment he walks into the courtroom with the client at his side. In this chapter, the latest thoughts in legal literature are combined with materials from communication and psychological literature to give the attorney the cutting edge in building rapport with the client and handling the case before trial.

The final five chapters deal with each phase of the trial process. These chapters take an in-depth look at what the latest literature has to say about what the verbal content of a trial attorney's message ought to be. In addition, the communication principles developed in the first four chapters are applied to teach the trial attorney not only how to engage the conscious mind, but to communicate with the unconscious. The attorney is taught to use psychological and communication principles so that he can subtly tap jurors feelings and emotions and thereby persuade jurors, not only by what he says but how he says it.

This text will teach the trial attorney when and how to use a message's inherent emotional content through each stage of the trial. The trial attorney will learn how to effectively communicate a client's message on all three communication levels—vocally, verbally, and nonverbally. He will also learn how to effectively pace a jury, as well as develop and anchor a case theme.

It is our belief that without a full understanding of the material contained herein, the trial lawyer is truly only half a lawyer. He may, on a hit-and-miss basis, sometimes instinctively come out with the right emotional message and communicate effectively. He does this, however, by the seat of his pants; he needs luck to win. On the other hand, if a trial attorney truly understands this material, he can control any courtroom situation.

Every experienced trial lawyer knows that jurors decide a case based on how they "feel" about the lawyer and his client, and then rationalize this finding with the evidence and the law. That is, the jurors real decisions are made on the unconscious level and then rationalized by the conscious mind. The complete trial lawyer, therefore, must know not only how to communicate with the conscious mind, but with the unconscious as well.

LAWRENCE J. SMITH
LORETTA A. MALANDRO
May 1, 1985

TABLE OF CONTENTS

Chapter 1
Impression Formation in the Courtroom

I. Communication Principles

II. Communication Techniques

IV. Appendix

Chapter 2
Persuasive Strategies in the Courtroom

I. Communication Principles

II. Communication Techniques

Chapter 3
Source Credibility in the Courtroom

I. Communication Principles

II. Developing a Courtroom Image

III. Communication Techniques

Chapter 4
Decision-Making Process of Jurors

I. Communication Principles

Chapter 5
Preparing for Effective Courtroom Communication

I. Initial Client Interview

II. Controlling Evidence Development Through Aggressive Discovery Techniques

Chapter 6
Selecting the Jury: A Two-Way Communication Process

I. Goals

II. The Means of Accomplishing the Goals of Voir Dire

III. Obtaining Information

Chapter 9
Cross-Examination: Controlling the Case

I. The Psychology of Control

II. Diminishing Credibility Through Mismatch

III. Listening to Witness' Answer; Observing Witness Reaction

Chapter 10
Summation: A Time for Motivating Jurors

I. The Function of Summation

Chapter 1

IMPRESSION FORMATION IN THE COURTROOM

IV. Appendix

KLUWER LITIGATION LIBRARY REFERENCES

JEANS, LITIGATION: Chapter 1, *The Relationship of Advocate and Client*; Chapter 2, *Mind Set of the Advocate*; Chapter 5, *Trial Preparation*; Chapter 6, *Voir Dire*; Chapter 8, *Direct Examination*; Chapter 13, *Cross-Examination*; Chapter 16, *Summation*.

JOYE & LOVETT, DRUNK DRIVING: THE TRIAL WORKBOOK, THE TRIAL SOURCEBOOK, THE TRIAL NOTEBOOK: Chapter 111, *Client*; Chapter 112, *Defense Witnesses*.

PREISER & PREISER, HANDLING SOFT TISSUE INJURY CASES: Chapter 10, *Psychology of the Trial*; Chapter 12, *Opening Statements*.

I. Communication Principles

§ 1.01 In general

Successful trial attorneys are successful communicators. Through years of experience and practice in the courtroom they have developed many communication skills on an unconscious level. This explains why many excellent trial attorneys can perform their "art," but have difficulty in describing precisely what makes them so good. They intuitively act in accordance with many underlying communication principles of persuasion. Throughout this book attorneys will identify behaviors and techniques which they have used effectively for years with little or no understanding of how and why they work. The purpose of this book is to provide a fuller understanding of persuasion in the courtroom.

Learning and developing new skills occurs in four stages:

Stage I: Unconscious Incompetence

Stage II: Conscious Incompetence

Stage III: Conscious Competence

Stage IV: Unconscious Competence

Many effective advocates operate at stage four in the courtroom: unconscious competence. They act and react correctly and unconsciously. Essentially the third stage of the learning process, which involves the conscious understanding of how and why a particular behavior works, has been skipped. By returning to stage three in the learning paradigm, the attorney will gain much more control over his use of communication strategies in the courtroom. Specifically the attorney will be able to (1) strategically use the techniques, (2) determine the appropriateness of a particular approach, and (3) analyze when and why specific techniques do or do not work. With this in-depth understanding of persuasion, litigation practice can have greater predictability for the serious student of persuasion. In addition, many inexperienced attorneys can shorten their learning curve in the courtroom by understanding the many communication factors that impact on jurors or judges.

There are three levels of communication which occur during the trial: verbal, vocal, and nonverbal. Unfortunately, traditional legal education does not adequately prepare attorneys in these three areas. Most programs in law school focus on the verbal aspect of communication. This includes the actual content of a message: facts, statistics, evidence, information, legal precedent, and testimony. Even in this area, however, the study is often limited to legal concerns and rulings. Rarely are the psychological factors which affect the structure and organization of the verbal message studied in detail. The other two areas, vocal and nonverbal, are learned through a trial and error process while practicing in the courtroom. The vocal area of communication includes voice qualities, pitch and rhythm, pauses, rate of speech and many other voice factors which affect both perceptions of credibility and the ability of the jurors to retain information. The nonverbal area of communication focuses on behaviors including space and distance, eye and facial behavior, movement, gestures, postural orientation, touch, personal appearance, and environmental surroundings.

The impact of verbal communication, which refers to the content aspect of a message and includes word choice, phraseology, and the logical structure of an argument, has been greatly overrated. Birdwhistle's research in the area of impression formation and decision making leads us to believe that verbal communication may account for as little as 7% of the actual impact of a message with vocal cues accounting for 38% and nonverbal behavior for 55%.[1] This does not mean, however, that the content of a trial is unimportant. The content of a trial is critical, but unless the attorney understands how to present a consistent message

---

[1] R. BIRDWHISTLE, KINESICS AND CONTEXT (University of Pennsylvania Press, 1970).

through all three channels, jurors will tend to believe the vocal and nonverbal messages first. In the practice of law, a trial attorney cannot afford to ignore behavioral research and what it says about how jurors make decisions in the courtroom.

The purpose of this chapter, *Impression Formation in the Courtroom*, is to (1) provide an understanding of the impression formation process,[2] (2) identify the ways in which jurors assemble information,[3] (3) present the six communication principles that operate in forming impressions,[4] and (4) focus on communication techniques that can be effectively used to create the desired impact of counsel, witnesses, and clients in the courtrooms.[5]

§ 1.02 Introduction to Communication Principles

Knowledge of the psychological and communication principles underlying impression formation are critical for attorneys in preparation for a trial. Pretrial strategy should focus on how to position the witnesses, client, and attorneys in the courtroom. The term "positioning" refers to the psychological strategy for connecting to the stereotypes that already exist in the minds of the jurors. Directing and controlling jurors' perceptions requires that the attorney understand how jurors process information and form impressions.

Your goal in any given case should be to remove those variables over which you can exert little control. If you do not have a high predictability of the jurors' response and/or perception, the variable should be eliminated or minimized. If you represent the defendant in a criminal case, for example, your client would be best advised not to wear red; not because we know how red will be perceived, but because we do *not* know how red will be perceived. Red is associated with passion, violence, blood, stimulation, fun, heat, and drama. As a color, red has both positive and negative associations. Although some jurors may have no association or a neutral association, the point is that the perception cannot be controlled. The key to pretrial preparation is limiting those areas over which you have little control of perceptions.

The following six communication principles can serve to guide the at-

---

[2] *See infra* §§ 1.47–1.86.

[3] *Id.*

[4] *See infra* §§ 1.02–1.08.

[5] *See infra* §§ 1.09–1.46.

torney in answering many questions regarding case strategy and the preparation of witnesses:

Principle 1: Communication is based on perception

Principle 2: People actively try to make sense out of their environment

Principle 3: Perceptions are organized and structured within a brief period of time

Principle 4: People use stereotypes to organize their perceptions

Principle 5: People tend to see others as similar to themselves

Principle 6: People attempt to maintain their original perceptions regardless of contradictory information

In this chapter, we will discuss the ways in which these six basic communication principles can be used effectively in the courtroom.

§ 1.03 —Principle 1: Communication is based on perception

Communication in the courtroom is based on the jurors' perception of their environment and the people in that environment. These perceptions differ from one person to the next because they are filtered through differing life experiences and exposure to others. Communication is not simplistic. We cannot assume that all people will respond the same way to the same person or to the same piece of information. For this reason, pretrial preparation should involve answering three basic questions related to perception:

1. What is already in the minds of the jurors and judge?
2. What will opposing counsel put in their minds?
3. What perceptions do you want the jurors and judge to have?

Without answering these three questions, the attorney's trial strategy loses its critical link to the jurors' model of the world. It is not enough to build a case that looks good on paper. There must be a carefully thought out strategy for translating the case into the minds of the jurors. The only way this can be done is through "linking to" the jurors' existing framework and belief system.

There are several methods for obtaining pretrial information about jurors. One method is through the use of a community attitude survey. Depending on how extensive the survey is, information regarding biases, stereotypes, and pretrial publicity influence can be obtained. A complete community attitude survey can be quite costly, ranging anywhere from fifty to eighty dollars per interview, but in many cases the information obtained is well worth the price.

Another survey method involves a jury pool analysis. At the time the jury pool list is released, researchers obtain additional information about potential jurors from two sources: (1) interviews and (2) observation. Interviews generally involve questioning friends, relatives, and neighbors to obtain information about political preferences, religious background, group affiliations, hobbies and so forth. Observation analysis provides information on the type of car, house, daily routine, and clothing preference of the individual. The data collected from both interviews and observations is meaningless unless interpreted in light of research findings to guide the analysis of the data. For example, if the data reveals that a potential juror is an artist then we can refer to the relevant social research to determine several personality traits representative of people in the creative areas. The research indicates that people engaging in full-time creative occupations, such as art, tend to have an egalitarian attitude. That is, they believe things should be equal and shared. In representing the defendant in a will contest case, you would want to eliminate this juror. The "share the wealth" attitude of a person in a full-time creative occupation would tend to be favorable to the plaintiff. This type of juror, for example, would tend to disperse the will inheritance between the plaintiffs and the defendants.

COMMENT: Behavioral trial consultants are often valuable in collecting, interpreting, and applying the data to a particular case. In this way, the attorney can be assured of a research-based interpretation of the information.

Both community attitude surveys and jury pool analyses offer valuable information about jurors. Particularly useful is the information which provides clues to jurors' perceptions and belief systems. Since we know it is difficult, if not impossible, to change people's beliefs, using existing perceptions can be very effective in persuasion. For instance, a juror's perception may be that "poor people commit crimes." If you are defending a person from a poor community in a criminal case, it will be important to create a picture of how your client differs from "poor" people. It will be an impossible task to attempt to alter the broad perception that "poor people commit crimes." Therefore, counsel needs to do three things:

1. *Acknowledge the existing belief system*. This does not mean to validate an existing belief as being correct, but it does mean to acknowledge that it exists. A comment in opening statement might be "I know that we often think of crime and poor people together. Perhaps it is due to a belief that the environment determines behavior."

2. *Link to the existing belief*. "Now my client has grown up in that poor type of environment. He's been exposed to a hard life."

3. *Build a new belief*. "But he's different. Ever since he was small, he has had a fervor for education. He reads classics from literature, sociology, science. . . . He has read more books than I have, and I read a lot."

Now the jurors are faced with a form of cognitive dissonance, i.e., an inconsistency between their beliefs and the attorney's statement about the defendant. Their belief that "poor people commit crimes" is not consistent with someone who reads educational books. Because the new information has been *linked to* their existing belief, jurors will be more likely to reduce the dissonance by agreeing with the attorney that the defendant is different. He is an exception to the rule.

Remember that our sixth principle of communication states that jurors attempt to maintain stereotypes despite contradictory information. This principle still stands when contradictory information is *not linked* to an existing perception. Let's assume the attorney presented the contradictory information in the following format:

> "My client is a young man who is dedicated to education. In fact, he has a fervor for education. He reads classics from literature, sociology, science. . . . He has read more books than I have and I read a lot."

Now the dissonance for jurors will increase. They will search for their existing belief and find that this new piece of information is incongruent with it. There is no link, no new logic to help jurors reduce the dissonance in favor of the defendant. Also there is no perceived similarity between the attorney and the jurors. The jurors may assume the attorney does not hold the belief that "poor people commit crimes." This perceived dissimilarity between jurors and attorney can result in jurors dismissing information before it is fully presented because it is outside of their perceptual framework.

Communication is based on perception, and perceptions control feelings. How jurors *feel* about a case determines how they will decide it. Therefore, the trial attorney should identify existing perceptions and then link to them throughout the trial.

§ 1.04 —Principle 2: People actively try to make sense out of their environment

In the courtroom, jurors select, organize, and interpret cues in order to ensure structure, stability, and meaning. An attorney needs to be aware of how jurors sort information. Exposure to jurors, especially during voir dire, is critical and the age old saying of "putting your best foot forward" takes on added significance.

Another consideration is that since jurors desire stability, there should be no surprises or major changes in personal appearance of witnesses and/or attorneys after the trial has begun. A subtle change, such as going from a suit to a sport jacket, is acceptable because it is consistent with the general framework and expectations of the jurors. A dramatic change in hairstyle, clothing style, or behaviors would irritate jurors and increase instability and uncertainty in their environment, resulting in discomfort. The only time a dramatic change would be appropriate is if the attorney wanted to regain the attention of jurors, perhaps in a long trial where they have become "too comfortable." A major change or shift may also be appropriate to emphasize emotional themes or intensify dramatic points.

Since jurors are actively trying to make sense out of their environment, it is important to present a (1) consistent and (2) congruent image of attorneys, clients, and witnesses. Consider the case of Patty Hearst. We can presume that her attorney, F. Lee Bailey, wanted to position Patty in the courtroom as a "victim," someone who was weak and easily influenced. To position Patty as a victim, clothing choices would be critical. Picture Patty Hearst entering the courtroom with wire-rimmed glasses, bouncy and curly hair, and well-fitting clothes in bright colors. Would she look like a "victim?" Most people would describe a person in the above attire as well-adjusted, liberal, and extroverted. We could assume that given this presentation of Patty Hearst, jurors would "make sense out of their environment" by deciding that she did not "look like" a victim, and, therefore, she was not one.

The following description depicts a more "victimized" Patty as she was described by a newspaper reporter during trial:

> As she entered the courtroom, all eyes locked on her. She was dressed in a coat at least two sizes too large. The collar was grotesquely broad and the sleeves so widely cuffed that they made her manacled hands look small and helpless. Her long hair hung listlessly on her shoulders and appeared deliberately lank. As she moved, her coat parted and one could catch a glimpse of the clothing that literally hung on her body. The neckline of her blouse sagged away from her thin neck, making it appear even thinner. The bow in her blouse was limp and tied low and, as it were, pulled the corners of her mouth down with it. Her skirt, simple and modest, fell slightly below her knees. She appeared to be a frail and vulnerable young woman, perhaps one who had suffered a great deal in the short span of her life.[6]

Courtrooms produce a form of "situational anxiety" for both jurors and witnesses. Both groups are generally unfamiliar with the courtroom environment and procedures. Jurors quickly try to reduce uncertainly about what will be happening in their environment. If a juror, for example, is forming a perception of an attorney who is very articulate, intelligent and persuasive, yet is dressed very sloppily with straggly hair the result may create a conflict for the juror. The information is incongruent—somehow it does not "fit" together. Uncertainty may be reduced by (1) deciding that the clothing is consistent with his articulate image, or (2) altering the first image by saying that he is not a good attorney. One way or another, jurors will reduce this uncertainty in order to increase their control and predictability over the environment.

It is important for attorneys to be especially aware of any inconsistent or incongruent messages which are presented. Jurors will act as "detectives" in analyzing the information and forcing it to fit their "picture" of what is occurring. In a rape case, for example, the prosecution may have selected a female juror whom they liked and felt fit their profile of an "ideal" juror. Their client, an attractive twenty-eight-year-old woman, created the perception, they thought, of a likable, respectable and victim-

[6] L. Malandro & L. Barker, Nonverbal Communication 74 (Random House, 1983). Copyright © 1983, Random House, Inc.

ized young woman. The female juror selected by the prosecution was a Seventh Day Adventist, and due to a conflict with the trial time and her religious beliefs, she was excused. She was overheard in the hallway commenting to another potential juror, "It's just as well I didn't sit on this case. I didn't like that young hussy anyway—she was wearing bright lipstick."

It takes just one juror to respond negatively to "one" variable to alter perceptions. Perhaps no one else would have noticed the lipstick or would have attributed it to the same association of "hussy". Bright lipstick, however, is not consistent with the image of a likable, respectable, and victimized young woman, particularly in a rape case. The history of lipstick is old. It was used in centuries past by "women of the night" and was, in fact, used to simulate the condition of a woman who was sexually aroused. Although we would not expect a contemporary person to have these associations, someone with a rigid religious background operates out of a different framework, and in most cases a traditional and somewhat "out-dated" model of the world. These are considerations which must be reviewed prior to the trial. Never underestimate the power of the jurors to notice what you might consider to be irrelevant information and cues.

Jurors have two specific tasks in reducing their anxiety and uncertainty in the courtroom:

Task 1. Jurors record the diversity of the data they encounter in a form simple enough to be retained by their limited memory.

Take 2. Jurors make assumptions beyond the actual data given in order to predict future events, and thereby minimize surprise.

The reduction of uncertainty occurs predominantly, and most exclusively, during the beginning of the trial. In addition, the information obtained by jurors through nonverbal channels (e.g., clothing, body movements, eye contact) and vocal channels (e.g., voice characteristics and quality) will outweigh the actual verbal content presented.

§ 1.05 —Principle 3: Perceptions are organized and structured within a brief period of time

What happens during the first part of the trial is difficult to reverse later. For this reason, trial consultants should not be hired halfway through the trial because their value and impact will be limited. Pretrial preparation and the first few days of trial (for the first 10% time period of any trial) is the time period which should receive the most critical attention.

The stages of impression formation in the courtroom are:

Stage 1: Voir dire

Stage 2: Opening statement

Stage 3: First witness testimony

Preparation for the first few days of trial should include a careful review of clothing choices, behaviors in the courtroom, postural orientation to jurors, eye contact with jurors, interaction with the judge, and the treatment of the official court family. Keep in mind that if any of the jurors lean towards authoritarianism they will pay particular attention to the cues of the judge since he represents to them the highest authority in the courtroom. Also, the same authoritarian juror will carefully observe the attorneys' displayed respect (or lack of it) to both the judge and the official court family. The court family will be viewed as an extension of the judge and, therefore, will require special attention.

Perceptual cues are organized and structured by jurors with or without interaction with the attorneys. As a result, facial expressions, posture, and displayed interest or boredom take on an increased significance.

§ 1.06 —Principle 4: People use stereotypes to organize their perceptions

Ethnic groups, religious groups, and corporate groups all share a commonality. They each have an implicit and often explicit "culture." Executives of IBM Corporation, for instance, have a traditional way of dressing in dark suits, white shirts, and wing tip shoes. They also have a culture in which conservatism is a trademark. To understand an IBM person, you must step inside his culture, see his world as he sees it. This is true of all subgroups. A subgroup can be identified within a given community. The culture in Louisville, Kentucky, is notably different from that of Manhattan; the belief systems, stereotypes, and biases come from a different base. Most people who live in a "sub-culture" for two years or more begin to assimilate many of the cultural patterns consciously or unconsciously. When analyzing jurors, a thorough review of the culture or cultures to which they belong is important. Knowing that a potential juror is an artist who has lived in Manhattan for five years provides important information. First, we have to understand "artists," their way of life, and belief systems. Are they egalitarian—striving to be fair and equal with everyone? Liberal? Do they have biases about big companies and corporations? Do they root for the underdog? Are they more tolerant of different types of people given their exposure in a large metropolitan area?

If you are accustomed to trying cases in Phoenix, Arizona, you will have a fairly comfortable feeling and expectancy of "Phoenix" jurors. If your next case is going to be tried in Yuma, Arizona, you will have a lot of homework to do. Yuma is a much smaller town, separated from all major cities. The quality of life is different, as is the sophistication level. A community attitude survey identifying patterns of thinking and preexisting stereotypes and biases would be very important. Another optional approach to the often costly community attitude survey is to assemble a mock jury in the trial area. A mock jury can be assembled by identifying preliminary characteristics of jurors you wish to seat. This may include certain educational background information, marital status, religious and/or political preferences. An employment agency can usually locate the "types" of people you are looking for. Assembling a group of six to twelve "mock" jurors and testing both your opening statement and the mock jurors' perceptions of witnesses and attorneys is invaluable.

COMMENT: Identifying stereotypes and the "culture" of jurors prior to the trial is critical. The case theme and strategy should utilize rather than avoid these stereotypes. Stereotypes are the jurors' means of organizing and sorting the information they receive. The insightful trial attorney will gain a decided advantage by building on stereotypes held by jurors rather than by ignoring them.

---

§ 1.07 —Principle 5: People tend to see others as similar to themselves

Jurors project their own thoughts and feelings onto others. A preliminary jury profile helps counsel understand how to "connect" to jurors. Demographic information, hobbies, and educational background all provide clues on the type of examples which can be used to link to the way jurors think. For example, if a juror plays baseball the attorney at some point could use a metaphor about "making a homerun." At the point at which he used this metaphor he should maintain eye contact with the juror who plays baseball. The eye contact and the selected phrase "connect" with the juror's way of processing information and creates a perceived similarity. Jurors are more likely to be persuaded when you work within *their* framework rather than yours.

All background information on jurors will help counsel to link to jurors' existing thoughts and beliefs. Jurors should be thought of by names rather than numbers. Often attorneys refer to jurors by numbers when talking to one another. This creates a detached attitude toward the juror and is a form of psychological distancing in the mind of the attorney. The way you think about a person can and will affect actual behaviors which will be manifested. Because attorneys are trying to link to the jurors in order to reduce psychological distance, jurors should be referred to by name. This can affect the behavioral cues of the attorneys which will indicate warmth, liking, and camaraderie with the jurors. Creating a psychological connection with jurors starts with how you "think" about jurors in your mind. Thought processes must be congruent with behaviors. For example, actress Mary Martin, in preparing for her stage performances would say to herself one hundred times "I love my audience, I love my audience." Then she would say another one hundred times, "My audience loves me, my audience loves me." This process of programming empathetic connections was reflected in her behavior toward her audience. As a man thinks, so he is. To increase the factors of likability and approachability of counsel, the trial attorney must think of jurors as individuals with unique and special characteristics.

Jurors feel they can increase the effectiveness of their predictions of another's behavior when they feel there is a similarity. To increase the momentum of the similarity principle, clothing choices, word usage, and behaviors should be similar to those of the jurors to a certain extent. If jurors are extremely casual in their clothing, it may be wise to avoid the high formality of the three-piece suit since the separation factor (or perceived differences) will increase. The goal is to create perceived homophyly (perceived similarity) between counsel, client, and jurors. Keep in mind, however, that matching clothing choices with jurors must also be tempered by the expectations jurors have of how an attorney "should" dress.

§ 1.08 —Principle 6: People attempt to maintain their original perceptions regardless of contradictory information

Stereotypes represent strong predispositions toward people and elements in an environment. When presented with contradictory information, jurors will attempt to maintain the stereotype using one of the following three methods:

1. Denying the existence of the disturbing element (e.g., information which is *not* consistent with their stereotype);
2. Placing the disturbing element in a context so as to render it harmless to the original stereotype;
3. Recognizing the incongruity, but maintaining the original stereotype anyway.

Given this tenacity to hold onto existing beliefs, counsel should understand the importance of connecting to an existing belief system rather than trying to alter or ignore it. If a preexisting belief structure of jurors is that "rich people do not commit murder," then a prosecutor will have to demonstrate motives and cause for why a rich person in this given circumstance would commit murder. The reason may have to be presented as an "exception" to the rule to allow jurors to hold onto their existing framework that "rich people do not commit murder." It is both difficult and unnecessary to attempt to change the entire belief structure of jurors regarding "rich people." The prosecution would stand a much better chance of success by persuading jurors that this "one" case and "one" individual represents an exception, a deviation from the norm. This allows jurors to reduce uncertainty and dissonance by holding onto their original belief structure.

II. Communication Techniques

§ 1.09 Developing a courtroom image

There is one compelling reason to develop a courtroom image: if you don't, the jurors will. Our second communication principle underscores the fact that jurors actively try to make sense out of their environment. One of the first things jurors do is collect information. The second thing they do is organize that information so that they can understand it and retain it for later use.

A well thought out courtroom image offers several important benefits:

(1) a single, directed image is selected, and (2) all elements that have an impact on the courtroom setting are presented consistent with the desired image (e.g., witnesses, visual aids, opening statement, and so forth).

Our reference to a courtroom image goes far beyond the concept of dressing witnesses and attorneys for court. The projection of an image in the courtroom is manifested and reinforced by all stimuli which enter into the jurors' perception. This includes behaviors, personal appearance, voice characteristics, word choice, relationship to others, and so forth. Our first communication principle says it all: Communication is based on perception. Everything which comes into the perceptual field of the jurors will affect the image of a witness, client, or attorney. Too often "image" is viewed only as personal appearance factors. Although these factors are important, they are only a few of the many factors that need to be considered in establishing an image.

The following sections provide techniques and strategies for developing a courtroom image based on the three channels of communication: verbal (e.g., word content, word choice, and phraseology); vocal (e.g., voice and vocal characteristics), and nonverbal (e.g., movement, gestures, appearance, eye and facial behavior).

§ 1.10 Establishing a strong image

A strong image or courtroom perception is established through three methods: consistency, repetition, and simplicity. A single method will not create a long-lasting or effective image. All three elements must be present for an image to work. At this point we need to clarify the broader concept of establishing an image. This is referred to as positioning. How you position a case in the courtroom determines how jurors make decisions. An image is a reflection of those variables that you have selected to position.

Positioning an image in the courtroom is what you do to the minds of the perceivers, in this case, the jurors. If we want the jurors to have the perception of our client as being trustworthy, likable, and responsible we must first consider (1) how the jurors perceive these traits and (2) their exposure to people who have these characteristics. This type of thinking literally forces us to view the world from their eyes. Too often in preparing the case for trial, counsel thinks in terms of how he would perceive a trustworthy person. This type of thinking will not produce the same results. The perception of "trustworthiness" differs with socioeconomic background, geographical location, and personal characteristics.[7] The only thing that matters in positioning a client as "trustworthy" in the courtroom is how the jurors identify the characteristics which constitute a trustworthy person. The net result is that we are constantly trying to link to how the jurors think. This concept cannot be repeated often enough. The psychological persuasion of another person depends on the extent to which information can be presented and linked to the way in which this individual thinks. This demands a "they" focus, not an "I" focus. How do they think? How will they perceive this? What prior experience do they have that will affect their response? An "I" focus asks, How do I project trustworthiness? What behaviors should I exhibit? How should I dress? The difference between an "I" and a "they" focus is considerable. A "they" focus utilizes communication and psychological principles of linking. An "I" focus renders decisions from a single, narrow, and incomplete perspective.

We define the concept of "positioning" in a similar manner to the way the word is used in the field of advertising. Millions of dollars are spent annually to create an image that will work in the marketplace. Keep in mind that an image is, once again, based on perception. IBM, for example, has a consistent image in the market. As a company IBM is viewed as conservative, reliable, and strong. Individuals within the company are viewed as wearing gray or navy blue suits, conservative ties, white shirts and wing tip shoes. By contrast Apple Computer is perceived in the marketplace as being innovative, different, and creative. The downside of this perception is that as a seven-year-old company they are also perceived as unreliable and unpredictable.

COMMENT: Much of the success of IBM has to be attributed to the position it created in the marketplace as a strong and reliable company. The image IBM projects results in a specific perception of the company and people. Even though the reality of the situation is changing with regard to dress behavior in IBM, the image persists because the perception persists. From this advertising model, we know that an image presented in the courtroom will result in a specific

---

[7] *See infra* §§ 1.48 *et seq.*.

perception. If the image is consistent and presented in a simple form, the perception will endure.

---

§ 1.11 Positioning a case

Positioning is the analysis of all elements of a case with regard to how they will be perceived by the jurors, judge, and opposing counsel. Positioning is a strategic way of thinking. It is "the way you build your case in the minds of jurors." This requires a different type of thinking than most attorneys engage in,[8] i.e., a "they" focus rather than an "I" focus. It is "outside-in" thinking. Most cases are approached from the perspective of what types of facts, testimony, and evidence are available and how can they best be organized. Taking a "they" focus approach requires considering how opposing counsel will approach this case, what is already in the minds of the jurors, and what preexisting biases, prejudices and concerns the jurors have. All decisions about a courtroom image made from a positioning concept provide a broader framework in which to view a case.

Positioning a case is essential for two reasons. In the courtroom there is (1) too much information (i.e., information overload) and (2) the information being presented is too complex. Too much information is presented by both parties, and as a result little is remembered. The only way to avoid this phenomenon is to select the information which has the best chance of getting through. The old debate model no longer applies. In this model, the debaters would stack as much evidence as possible behind a single point and often file box after file box would be carried into the debate room. Positioning, on the other hand, requires that you preselect information and focus only on that information which is most likely to be understood by the jurors.

This is one of the most difficult areas of preparing for trial. After months and, in many instances, years of preparing for a case, counsel must organize the information and often he attempts to present as much as possible. This shotgun approach results in a shotgun effect. Jurors will remember what they want to remember rather than what you want them to remember. There may be a considerable difference. To combat

---

[8] *See supra* § 1.10.

the element of information overload, you need to reduce the information supplied and focus the minds of the jurors.

Messages in the courtroom are too complicated. A good rule of thumb is: if they cannot be understood by a high school sophomore with a "B" average, then change them. Jargon, legal terminology, and eloquent sentence structure are not only unnecessary in the courtroom, they are a hindrance to communication. Consider the field of advertising. When was the last time you read an effective ad that required three or four readings before it was understood? Good advertising slogans like good courtroom messages are simple, direct, and can be understood on the first reading. Unfortunately, most messages in the courtroom require people to think too hard. The problem with a message that requires considerable thought is that you can no longer predict the outcome. Your goal should be to establish an image which you position with reasonable assurance that jurors will perceive your case in the way in which you want them to perceive it. If you do not have this predictability you are simply rolling the dice.

§ 1.12 —Positioning clients and witnesses in the courtroom

The single, most important question to ask prior to the trial is, "What perceptions do I want the jurors and judge to have?" The second question to ask is, "Do all case materials—evidence, theme, personal appearance factors, and other variables—support this perception?" Positioning the client and witnesses in the courtroom refers back to our concept of positioning an idea in the minds of the jurors. In other words, we want the jurors to have a particular perception of our client. To achieve this end, it is important to test perceptions rather than to rely on your own instinct.

To test for image perception in the courtroom a mock jury can utilize a five-step process in identifying perceptions: (1) identify the projected image of the individual, (2) identify the desired image, (3) identify the differences between the projected and desired image, (4) identify the external changes (e.g., personal appearance, behaviors) which need to be made, and (5) identify the internal changes (e.g., attitudes, beliefs) which need to be made. You can perform a simple test of image perception by utilizing a basic semantic differential survey in the form of an adjective checklist. As can be seen in Table 1–1 *infra*, semantic differential refers to a scale which measures responses to bipolar adjectives such as

Table 1–1
Sample of Semantic Differential Form for Assessment of Perceptions

Talkative:___:___:___:___:___:___:___:Silent

Attractive:___:___:___:___:___:___:___:Repulsive

Good-Natured:___:___:___:___:___:___:___:Irritable

Unqualified:___:___:___:___:___:___:___:Qualified

Expert:___:___:___:___:___:___:___:Inexpert

Gloomy:___:___:___:___:___:___:___:Cheerful

Unfriendly:___:___:___:___:___:___:___:Friendly

Composed:___:___:___:___:___:___:___:Excitable

Calm:___:___:___:___:___:___:___:Anxious

Active:___:___:___:___:___:___:___:Passive

Meek:___:___:___:___:___:___:___:Aggressive

Undependable:___:___:___:___:___:___:___:Dependable

Bold:___:___:___:___:___:___:___:Timid

Extroverted:___:___:___:___:___:___:___:Introverted

Unsophisticated:___:___:___:___:___:___:___:Sophisticated

Dishonest:___:___:___:___:___:___:___:Honest

Serious:___:___:___:___:___:___:___:Humorous

Insincere:___:___:___:___:___:___:___:Sincere

Liberal:___:___:___:___:___:___:___:Conservative

Spender:___:___:___:___:___:___:___:Saver

Thinks Like Me:___:___:___:___:___:___:___:Doesn't Think Like Me introvert/extrovert. Mock jurors are asked to complete the semantic differential form on their perception of the witness, client, and attorney.

To test the initial impact of a person (i.e., nonverbal behaviors only), have the individual walk into the room of mock jurors, sit down, and then stand up and walk out, all in approximately ten to fifteen seconds. This is enough time for the jurors to form their initial impressions. At this time they should complete their forms. During the initial walk through it is important that the individual avoid smiling and assume his normal "at rest" facial position. Most of the time jurors are watching what is referred to as "static" facial behavior in the courtroom. It is, therefore, important to understand how "nonsmiling" facial expressions are perceived. A second perception test involving the assessment of verbal and vocal impact is conducted by having the individual walk in again, sit down, and respond to a series of basic questions such as "what is your name?", "where do you live?", and so forth.

After the forms have been completed by the mock jurors they are summarized by totalling the responses to each bipolar set of adjectives. The summary will show one of several things: (1) there is no consistent perception of the individual, (2) there is a definite positive perception of the individual (e.g., warm, friendly, trustworthy), or (3) there is a definite negative perception of the individual (aloof, angry, pushy). This information provides you with a base from which to work. Sometimes a witness or client needs to receive this type of feedback before he is convinced that he is being perceived in a particular way. Obtaining the cooperation of your client or a witness in changing behaviors and personal appearance factors is essential.

COMMENT: At this point it is helpful to have a trial consultant work with you, since his skill enables you to assess quickly which characteristics are contributing to the overall image perception.

External factors which are analyzed include clothing style, fabric, and color; hair length and color; jewelry and artifacts; skin tone color; and many other factors. Don't be surprised if some jurors analyze these factors in a very detailed fashion. Additional behavioral factors which are considered include head angle, body position when standing and walking, movement of arms and hands, facial expression, and duration of eye contact. Often an individual may be sitting in a defiant position which results in his testimony being perceived as angry. By changing his body position, however, we can significantly alter this perception.[9]

Internal image changes refer to the attitudes and emotions of the individuals. This is a critical area in preparing a witness or your client for the courtroom. Without specific internal changes, the external changes may not last or will appear to be incongruent with the person's attitude. For instance, if you want a witness to be perceived as soft, approachable, and trustworthy, it is important to eliminate or neutralize attitudes of anger and resentment. If these attitudes persist they will, either consciously or unconsciously, be expressed through the person's nonverbal behavior. Given a contradiction between the verbal testimony of the witness and his behavior, the research indicates that people will give more weight to the behavior (e.g., if he doesn't look honest, he isn't).[10]

The first step in working with internal attitudes involves extensive questioning of the individual. This process is very much like that of a therapist/patient relationship. In the questioning process, the purpose should be to build rapport and to obtain complete information on what the individual is feeling. To do this, listening skills are important. Table 1–2 below lists the three critical stages of listening.

A client will disclose greater amounts of information and more accurate information about himself if counsel engages in responsive listening. Many people are anxious listeners. That is to say, they sit on the edge of their chair, they remain tense, and they appear as if they are going to interrupt at any moment. When these behaviors are apparent, the individual will reduce the amount of information to be disclosed. A responsive listening pattern involves using what is referred to as regulating behaviors such as nodding the head in affirmation, or saying phrases like "Yes, I understand," "Go on," "Tell me more." This listening pattern helps to elicit the feelings and attitudes of your client.

---

[9] *See infra* § 1.43.

[10] *See infra* § 1.65.

Table 1–2
Listening for Critical Information

Stage 1: Preparation for Listening
- Prepare to listen
- Know your own biases
- Avoid distractions

Stage 2: Listen Actively
- Take notes when appropriate
- Concentrate
- Be interested
- Be empathetic
- Delay judgment
- Listen with your eyes
- Listen for main points
- Listen for missing information
- Avoid interrupting

Stage 3: Listen Responsively
- Use listener responses
- Use paraphrasing
- Use regulating behaviors
- Ask for additional information
- Limit your own talking

It is important to have the client discuss and release any negative emotions, such as anger or resentment, prior to going to trial. If you can help your client fully express his anger, frustration, or resentment, the probability of these emotions surfacing at trial is greatly reduced. In other words, once an emotion is truly and fully expressed through yelling, crying, talking, or whatever it takes for the individual, the "emotional charge," as it is referred to in therapy, is gone. If the "emotional charge" of a client can be neutralized before trial, counsel will have greater control and predictability over (1) how the client will act and react to aggressive questioning tactics, and (2) how the client will be perceived by the jurors.

Cases in which you want to eliminate the emotional charge are those in which you want to demonstrate the client's responsibility and valiant efforts in coping with his tragedy. America loves a hero. So the client, who lost both legs in an accident and is no longer angry, will appear to be responsible and working out his life. The attorney can express anger at the injustice and the terror of the accident. The client should express sadness, which is a much more passive emotion than anger. This allows the jurors to feel two primary emotions: (1) anger at the injustice and (2) empathy for the client. This is a split-role perception. For this to be effective, the lines cannot be crossed. The attorney must be the only one who expresses anger. If the client begins to express anger, the impact will decrease and jurors will become confused about their response to both the client and the attorney.

COMMENT: Jurors will have greater empathy when the victim is no longer acting like a victim. We have greater compassion for the person who struggles to overcome his problems, who heroically moves forward in spite of obvious limitations. For this reason, the client can express sadness, but not anger. When a client expresses anger for his own situation, the natural response is to engage in avoidance behaviors—psychologically distancing oneself from the individual. On the other hand, an attorney can express anger for a client because he is one step removed. The response to an attorney expressing anger for his client's tragedy is received much more favorably by jurors. We can accept a third party calling our attention to an injustice.

Television and movies reinforce the hero/underdog relationship. Someone is always saving someone else. The American public is a hero-worshipping public. Further, the American public has little tolerance for people who do not try to better their own situation. The drama of the courtroom should parallel the drama to which people are exposed to on a daily basis. You should link to the existing ways of thinking when you are positioning your client and witnesses in the courtroom.

§ 1.13 —Positioning attorneys in the courtroom

How attorneys should look and appear in the courtroom has a lot to do with the geographical area in which the case is being presented. To maximize positive perceptions, an attorney's appearance should be consistent with the public expectation of what an attorney should "look like." There would be an obvious difference in clothing style for an attorney trying a case in Manhattan as compared to an attorney trying a case in Birmingham, Alabama. Styles and expectations should match. If the general public pictures an attorney in a conservative suit, the attorney should wear clothing that is consistent with these expectations. If counsel wears clothing that significantly contrasts with expectations, jurors will go through a period of uncertainty reduction in which they must adjust either their original expectations or their perceptions of counsel. In a state of uncertainty, jurors will most likely readjust their perceptions of counsel in a negative manner. Comments such as "he doesn't look like an attorney", "he must not to do very well", or "he doesn't have much respect for the courtroom" may be made by jurors.[11]

Matching clothing and personal appearance factors to general expectations is a form of "pacing." Pacing is the ability to link to an existing framework, the belief system of an individual, in order to build rapport and eventually lead the person to your way of thinking.[12]

Sections 1.16–1.32 offer more detailed information on perceptions of personal appearance factors. There are some attorneys who break all the "rules" in the courtroom. They wear dungarees, cowboy boots, and corduroy jackets. Those who do this with success have already altered the original expectation that jurors will have of them. Most jurors already have heard about the attorney and his success and, therefore, either expect something different or are at least willing to give the attorney more license to deviate from the norm. The more success an individual has, the more the public will tolerate variance from the norm. This is why famous personalities, artists, or geniuses often are described as having unusual characteristics or behaviors.

COMMENT: Inexperienced attorneys, as well as new trial attorneys, should not try to establish an individual or unique style until they have had a history of success and established a well-known name for themselves.

---

[11] *See infra* § 1.53.

[12] *See infra* Chapter 2, *Persuasive Strategies in the Courtroom.*

§ 1.14 —Positioning your case against opposing counsel

The saying "fight fire with fire" does not always work effectively with persuasion in the courtroom. When you are up against counsel whom you consider to have an argument as strong or stronger than you do, it is best to fight fire with water. Head-on confrontations can weaken your position. An example of what can occur as a result of a head-on confrontation with a strong competitor comes from the business world.

In 1969, RCA decided to compete with IBM in the computer market. Their strategy was to match IBM head-on and to announce that in a matter of years they would be number one in the market. Headlines read "RCA fires a broadside at #1" and "RCA goes head to head with IBM." President Sarnoff of RCA said it would not be long before they took over the market. Unfortunately for RCA, the result was a $250 million disaster. This demonstrated that strength, power, and money will not necessarily win a market. The most crucial thinking which was missing was that of positioning. The public saw IBM as the leader in the market. Their perception was that IBM was very strong. RCA's claim that it would take over the market within a matter of years was unrealistic with the public's perception of IBM's position in the market. In their advertising, RCA never acknowledged that IBM was strong or the leader.[13] Those companies that have acknowledged a competitor's obvious strength or that a competitor is the leader in the market have done well. For example, take the slogans "Avis tries harder" or "we're number 2." Everyone knows that the implied competitor is Hertz. American loves an underdog, but turns its nose up at those who are overtly aggressive and arrogant in their approach.

When opposing counsel has presented a strong argument, it is best to acknowledge this. Never be afraid to compliment counsel on an argument; this increases the jurors' perception of your credibility and trustworthiness. After all, they will know it is a strong argument. Your job is to recognize the strength of the argument and simultaneously point out the obvious weakness, the critical missing element, which undermines its position. When a head-on confrontation is used, such as attacking the case from every angle you can possibly conceive of, it intensifies the probability of losing. Back and forth arguments are difficult for jurors to sort and make it more difficult for them to judge the validity of each. Look for the hole and fill it. Concentrate on the one critical element that

[13] A. Ries & J. Trout, Positioning: The Battle for Your Mind 43–45 (McGraw-Hill, 1981).

is missing, the one erroneous premise or assumption. By focusing the jurors' attention on the missing information, they will process the input by saying, "they had a good case, it all made sense, but something was wrong, something was missing." This is a simple message for them to remember, and they will remember it. If you keep telling them that something is missing from your opponent's argument and back it up with a persuasive argument of your own, you will significantly reduce the effect of the opposition's case. For example, after a long emotional closing argument by the state in a rape/murder defense counsel might say:

> "The Prosecution has made a very fine argument. He has belabored the gruesome details of this young girl's rape and death. It is one of the strongest, most emotional arguments I have ever heard. But something is missing, something critical. He did not discuss the fact that there is clear and reasonable doubt about my client Jerry's guilt. There was no eyewitness, no physical evidence that linked him to this heinous crime that my opponent so brilliantly detailed in his argument. It was emotional. It was great. It was a blatant attempt to cover the fact that the only thing Jerry did wrong was to be walking on the same street where the poor girl's body was found."

A common question which is asked with regard to positioning against opposing counsel is, "if there is the potential of bringing up undesirable information, should we allow the other side to bring it up first, or should we present it?" Referring back to Principle 2 on uncertainty reduction and Principle 6 on a person's need to maintain his original perceptions, it is better for you to present the information first. In this way you can control the effect of primacy and direct the jurors to the perception you want them to have. Moreover, you also increase their perception of you as a trustworthy person. You were willing to admit a weakness or a flaw. This is the George Washington appeal, "Yes, father, I cannot tell a lie. I chopped down the cherry tree." Everyone loves honest George. The American public supports this form of integrity. By presenting the undesirable material first you can take the "wind out of your opponent's sails."

§ 1.15 Projecting a desired image

There are three basic factors to consider with regard to projecting a desired image in the courtroom. These factors include perceptions of (1) competence/expertness, (2) trustworthiness, and (3) dynamism. The perception of credibility (competence-expertness) is particularly important with expert witnesses and counsel. Credibility factors are associated with being an expert—an exclusive source of information. Perceptions of trustworthiness, on the other hand, become very important with regard to a client. Jurors are more likely to reward those people they like and trust. The third quality, dynamism, refers to the charismatic or dynamic quality of the individual. Attorneys who have a natural instinct toward drama or an ability to charm people have what we refer to as a dynamic quality. When an individual is dynamic, groups will listen for longer periods of time. The normal adult attention span is only about eighteen minutes. A dynamic individual who captivates and mesmerizes the jurors by his change of style and pace can easily triple this listening span.

Jurors do not listen continually in the courtroom. They tune in and out. The importance of keeping everything moving, interesting, and novel becomes clear. If you want jurors to really listen, you must develop dynamic qualities and also present the case in an interesting way. One way in which competence, trustworthiness, and dynamism is projected is through personal appearance factors. For example, the case of John DeLorean, charged with setting up a $24 million cocaine deal, offers an interesting example with regard to clothing choices. A week after her husband was arrested, Cristina Ferrare bought a somber, yet expensive designer wardrobe and cut off her shoulder-length hair. Reports supposedly claimed that she looked more like Joan of Arc in designer sackcloth than a *Vogue* fashion model with a well-publicized penchant for sables and jewels. She was dressing for acquittal. Cristina's instinct was correct, although her clothing choices were not. A better choice would have been conservative, tailored clothing of good quality. Designer clothing often evokes negative responses such as snobbish, pretentious, expensive, or socially-conscious. A more tailored, but feminine look creates more predictable and neutral perceptions such as "all-American," nice, neat, clean, and responsible.

It is important to provide specific guidelines for your client and witnesses about their personal appearance in the courtroom. Not all jurors will notice details about clothing, but is only takes one juror to make an observation which is later shared with others, to impact on the decision-making process.

§ 1.16 Personal appearance factors

A major factor in the initial assessment of an individual involves personal appearance. Personal appearance includes body shape and size, clothing, colors, fabric choice, style of jewelry, artifacts (e.g., eyeglasses, briefcase), hair length, hair color, hair style, perfumes, and colognes. Dressing an attorney, client, or witness for court involves the specific consideration of the type of case and the image you want jurors to have. Research indicates that definite perceptions are attached to personal appearance factors. The following sections will focus on specific considerations with regard to clothing, jewelry and artifacts, hair, and colors.

§ 1.17 —Clothing considerations for male attorneys

The general public's perception of how a male attorney should be dressed is as follows: a gray or navy blue suit, white shirt, tie, and polished shoes. In sum, a very conservative and professional look. This perception, however, will differ from one geographic area to another. The eastern region of the United States has greater expectations for a more formalized appearance which may involve the wearing of a three piece suit and/or a tie bar. The western United States allows for more freedom in dressing. In Arizona, some attorneys have substituted the bola tie (a string tie with a piece of jewelry) for the traditional tie. This approach may be very successful in Yuma or Winslow because in these areas people dress very casually and may not be accustomed to a formal suited look. However, this is risky when worn in the Phoenix and Tucson areas since they tend to have more cosmopolitan tastes.

This section offers general guidelines only. You should aim for the most "neutral" look that would be acceptable to jurors and judges in the courtroom. To begin with, a suit, rather than a sport jacket and pants, will result in a higher perception of credibility in most urban areas. A white shirt with a traditional collar, as opposed to a button down collar, will also be perceived as more credible. Conservative shoes such as wing tips or tie shoes rate higher than penny loafers. Socks should be nondescript and blend in with the rest of the attire. The total perception should be clean, neat, and professional so that the jury focuses its attention on the attorney's face. If their attention wanders anywhere else, then something about the clothing is competing with the total impact.

The tie can contrast with the suit, but should not be busy or have an unusual design that is distracting. The length of the pants should be appropriate (e.g., should break slightly on the top of the shoe). Pants that are too short or too long are very distracting and generally result in negative perceptions. The design of the suit should be limited to solids, tweeds, and small pinstripes. Avoid large stripes, plaids, and designs in the shirt and tie. There are too many perceptions associated with these patterns, and thus the predictability of the response to these patterns is too low. A conservative and professional look correlates with perceptions of high credibility.

Acceptable fabrics include wool, cashmere, and cottons. Men should avoid silk, velour or ultrasuede materials. Avoid raised or platform shoes. This gives others the impression that you are trying to be something you are not.

The above descriptions for male attire deal primarily with increasing the perception of credibility. There are some cases in which the attorney has ascribed credibility (i.e., an automatic perception of credibility and power) and what he really wants to work on is more approachability and likability from the perception of the jurors. In these cases, clothing factors can be changed that will alter the perception. For example, if you are more concerned with increasing approachability and likability, a sports jacket would be more appropriate than a suited look. A suited look will give you a more formal look while the sports jacket will give you a "down to earth," country-type of look. Rather than wearing a white shirt, a light blue shirt or a pink shirt tends to soften the image and give you a more approachable look. The fabrics you choose will also change. You should wear more touchable fabrics, such as a tweed. You can even wear a sweater vest, if that's appropriate and if you want to dress that informally in a particular region. If a sweater vest is worn, it should be a soft texture or fabric such as wool or cashmere. All of these changes in appearance will increase the perception of approachability. With regard to the sports jacket, a patterned sports jacket can be worn, such as herringbone or a small plaid. In the case of approachability factors you would want to avoid pinstripes. Pinstripes are associated more with formality and, hence, higher credibility. The colors to wear to increase approachability are in the brown and tan family. As you recall when we were talking about increasing credibility, the colors that are worn are from the gray and the navy blue family.

One instance in which the attorney would want to increase approachability would be if he already is seen as very powerful and needs to become more human and personable in the courtroom. Some attorneys already have a tremendous amount of power just by the nature of their voices, who they are, and their body sizes and stature. For these attorneys, the need is to reduce the possibility of intimidating the jurors.

COMMENT: Remember, those attorneys that need to establish credibility, such as younger attorneys, are advised to stay in the categories of the more conservative look such as the gray or navy blue suits which we described in the beginning of this section.

Male personal appearance factors will change with regard to credibility and approachability.[14] The underlying factor in making this determination is how people perceive you in a neutral state. In other words, are you perceived as a highly powerful or a low power person? Are you perceived as intimidating or friendly, trustworthy or untrustworthy? Understanding these original perceptions will tell us whether or not you already have credibility and if you need to increase approachability. The ultimate blend for an attorney is to have both approachability and credibility. This can be achieved by softening the appearance and presenting a combination image, for example, wearing a navy blue suit with a light blue shirt. This will help offset the hard, formal, corporate image and will help to personalize the attorney. This becomes of increasing importance when considered with Communication Principle 10: People are more easily influenced by people they like.[15]

§ 1.18 —Clothing considerations for female attorneys

There are perceptual differences of male and female attorneys based on expectations of jurors. Therefore, clothing considerations are an important factor in establishing both credibility and approachability for the female attorney. The most damaging look for a female attorney is the imitation-male look (i.e., pinstripe suit with tie). This is perceived as too hard and as an attempt to "look like a man." The perceptions associated with this look are not favorable in the courtroom or in a boardroom. Avoid extremes in clothing such as pants or a pantsuit. This dramatically reduces the perception of credibility for a woman, even when an

---

[14]*See infra* §§ 1.29, 1.30, which set forth in checklist form those important personal appearance factors which will increase the perception of credibility, as well as the perceptions of approachability and likability for male attorneys.

[15]*See infra* § 2.06, for discussion of this principle.

expensive pantsuit is worn. Avoid wearing ties similar to a man's. Bows and more traditional female "ties" can be worn. You should also avoid wearing tie tacs or male artifacts. A tie pin or other jewelry on the lapel of a jacket can be used. In short, anything that projects an imitation-male look should be avoided.

Where male attorneys can wear a three-piece suit, a woman cannot. A vest on a woman, whether it is a sweater vest or fabric vest, detracts from a professional look. On most women, it accentuates the chest area too much. This has a distracting effect. In all cases, attention is drawn away from the face. Always keep in mind that our final goal is to have full emphasis on the attorney's face, not on her clothing.

The most acceptable, professional look for a female attorney is a suit with a matching jacket and skirt, a blouse which buttons up to the neckline or has a high collar, slight ruffles or pleats, and closed toe shoes. The total look should not be hard or soft, it should be professional.

Let's examine the clothing in more detail. The perception of shoes is very important for a woman. They should be conservative, with little or no decoration. Simple pumps are the best choice. The heel should be 2½ inches or less. High heels in excess of 2½ inches on a woman creates a negative perception. Many women wobble on high heels and a wobbly person does not give the perception of being steady and solid. In addition, the higher the heel the more attention that is brought to the legs. It is important, however, not to wear shoes with a square flat heel. Avoid loafers or flats. These shoes are not perceived as attractive with professional suit attire. The shoes should have both closed toes and closed heels. This means no exposed toes or no sling back shoes with open heels. With exposed areas, too much attention is drawn to the foot. Further, many women move their toes in open-toe shoes causing another distraction. Simple, neat, plain, and conservative are the guidelines for shoes. Thus, avoid shoes with unusual designs, bows, or jewelry on them.

The suit should be classic, not fashionable or trendy. Trendy suit looks to avoid include Nehru jackets, jackets belted in the back, oversized jackets, and so forth. If you stay with classic suits and classic lines they will never go out of style. Also, you will minimize the possibility of unfavorable perceptions of your clothing choices.

The blouse a woman wears should come to the neck in the same way a man's shirt does. You should avoid scoop necklines or V-neck lines. Sweaters should be avoided altogether. They are perceived as a "secretarial" look and significantly decrease the perception of credibility. Slight ruffles, pleats and bows are fine. Again avoid the extreme of having too many frills.

Skirts should fall from just below the knee to two inches below the knee. Anything longer or shorter reflects trends in fashions. Avoid straight or tight skirts, as well as skirts with slits on the front, side, or back. Avoid flowing skirts or skirts that are too full. Wraparound skirts are acceptable as long as the skirt is secured at the wrap area to avoid the attention of interested observers who are waiting to see the skirt "unwrap." The most acceptable skirts are A-lines or slightly pleated.

Another consideration for women attorneys is the type of nylons worn. They should be professional and classic nylons. Avoid gray nylons, colored nylons, nylons with seams, nylons with any type of decoration, or nylons with any type of pattern in them. Once again, avoid the trends in nylons and stay with a classic look. Acceptable nylons are those of natural colors which match the skin tone of the individual.

COMMENT: The rule of thumb for a female attorney is to wear very classic and traditional clothing. Perceptions of both credibility and professionalism are much higher when this type of clothing is worn.

There are many instances in which a female attorney may want to increase the perception of approachability. In one particular case we know of, a lawsuit involving an ex-wife suing her husband for ownership of a business that they built together, the question was raised as to who should question the ex-wife on cross-examination. From the audio tapes and videotapes it was analyzed that the ex-wife, Laura, was very soft-spoken and responded well to men. She wore feminine clothing, was very petite, and appeared shy and submissive. The concern was who should question her during the trial—a male or female attorney. It was determined that it should be a female attorney since her comfort zone was clearly with male attorneys.

The next consideration was how should the female attorney dress for trial. Inasmuch as Laura looked and acted in a shy and submissive manner, it was known that in whatever manner the female attorney dressed a "perceptual contrast" would result. That is to say, the jury would compare the "image" of Laura and the female attorney due to their proximity to each other. Any image will be perceived as more extreme because of the contrast factor. Conservative clothing, for example, will appear to be much more conservative if a second person who is in the same visual field is wearing very sporty attire. If the female attorney dressed in the traditional attire of a suit (i.e., matching jacket and skirt) with a high collared blouse and closed-toe shoes, the appearance would be too harsh by comparison. The resultant image would be hard and aggressive and would appear as if the attorney was badgering a poor helpless little girl.

To avoid this perception it was suggested that the woman attorney dress in attire that would increase the perception of approachability. She wore a dress rather than a suit. In fact, the dress did not even have a jacket. She dressed in soft pastel colors. Her hair style was changed so that the hair framed the face area. This tends to soften the look and the lines of the face. By making these changes, the extreme in perceptual differences between the witness and counsel was avoided. The concern with perceptual contrast was heightened because of the fact that it involved a female attorney questioning a female witness.

There are still, unfortunately, stereotypes which damage the perception of credibility for a woman if she is seen as too hard or aggressive. It appears that these characteristics are perceived as threatening by many men and women. Whenever you consider dressing for approachability or credibility in the courtroom, you have to take into consideration the context of the entire trial. How are the jurors dressed? How do they expect counsel to dress? How will witnesses dress? How do you expect opposing counsel to dress? The psychological principle of perceptual contrast says that how a person is perceived is modified by others nearby. If you appear next to somebody who is very soft-spoken, you will appear to be even more formal and rigid if you are already dressed in a corporate or professional look. By contrast, if you were dressed in professional attire and you were questioning someone who was also dressed in professional clothing, neither one would be perceived in an extreme category because there is no apparent dissimilarity. Clothing must be considered in its entire context. That is why we must continually underscore the fact that these are only guidelines on the appropriate clothing to wear.[16]

---

[16] *See infra* §§ 1.31, 1.32, which set forth in checklist form those personal appearance factors which will increase the perception of credibility for a female attorney, as well as those factors which impact on approachability and likability.

§ 1.19 —Clothing considerations for clients and witnesses

As with clothing considerations for attorneys, we can only discuss general guidelines. Geographic considerations and how you want jurors to perceive the witness or client will result in differences in attire.

To increase credibility perception for expert witnesses, whether male or female, a suit should be worn much in the same manner as counsel. If the witness is already perceived as powerful and domineering you may want to soften the look by having him wear a sport jacket.

A woman generally should be dressed in "Sunday" clothing: a conservative dress with a jewel neckline or high collar. Fabrics which cling should not be worn. Guidelines which apply to a female attorney in terms of creating an image of "approachability" are also applicable here.[17]

To create a victimized look or a look of helplessness, the individual should wear oversized clothing (e.g., a jacket that is too large or sleeves that are too widely cuffed for the individual's size). This causes the body to look small and frail by comparison. A shirt or blouse that hangs off the shoulders a little bit with help create this look. Hair should be limp and straight. Avoid curly or wavy hair; it does not make the client or witness appear victimized. To create a submissive look for a woman, pastels and ruffles should be worn. Small prints and patterns are also effective.

Clothing alone will not change the perception. There will have to be a corresponding change in behavioral patterns. A female witness who is dressed submissively, for example, but places her arm on the back of a chair and stretches her legs out in a controlling manner will not be perceived as submissive. Remember, behavioral characteristics will override the clothing factors.

The way a witness or a client dresses in the courtroom can affect the entire case. Additionally, the spouses and family members of a witness or client will directly affect the perception of the witness. Even if a spouse or family member does not take the stand, his presence in the courtroom will be noted by jurors and is, therefore, of consequence in creating the overall impression. For example, in the John Jenrette case (John was a former Democratic congressman from South Carolina and was convicted in the Abscam bribery scandal), attorney Kenneth Robert-

---

[17] *See supra* § 1.18.

son asked Rita Jenrette to tone down her image after she came to a preliminary hearing in a tight low cut blouse. When she went out to buy a new wardrobe, one outfit had a demure white blouse tied at the neck with a schoolgirl bow but a tight skirt slit up the side. Her total appearance was incongruent and still emphasized an apparently "sexy" image. John wore the same suit everyday, one with a cigarette burn in it, looking totally down and out. Thus, while his counsel was apparently attempting to portray John Jenrette as totally broke, his wife still showed up with a $1,000 wardrobe. The jury looked at Rita as a sexpot which meant he either had money or the motive to get money. This is a good example of a perceptual contrast. Jurors will look at a spouse for additional information about the client. Then they will compare the dress and behavior of the spouse to determine if it supports the overall theme and information being presented by counsel.

In her autobiography entitled *Mo: A Woman's View of Watergate*, Maureen Dean goes into great detail discussing her color coordinated wardrobe for the nationally televised hearings of the John Dean Watergate trial. After her husband told her to dress like a wife, Maureen wrote, "I relied on my own fashion instincts, choosing a very high collared tan dress to wear the first day." One day she planned to wear a turban, but her husband suggested that that would not go well in middle America and he was correct. A turban does not represent a classical and traditional look; it is too high fashion and trend oriented.

COMMENT: It is important to coach your client and witnesses with regard to personal appearance factors. Witnesses do not have a good understanding of how much their clothing can affect the total impact in the courtroom. It is helpful to assist them step-by-step with their clothing. Something as small as wearing the wrong jewelry or too much makeup could make a significant difference in their overall image.

---

§ 1.20 —Jewelry and artifacts for male attorneys

There are different considerations with regard to jewelry, eyeglasses, and other artifacts that men wear in the courtroom. Although a man may not wear the amount of jewelry that a woman will, there are certain types of jewelry which should be avoided. To begin with, men should wear limited jewelry in the courtroom. Acceptable jewelry includes a wedding ring, a class ring, and a watch. Pocket watches, bracelets, and necklaces should be avoided. The reason for this is, once again, that the perception attached to this jewelry will vary and often it will create a negative perception. Bracelets and necklaces are not consistent with a classic, professional look for men.

Cufflinks, tie bars, and tie pins are acceptable if you are in an area where formality is expected. Avoid anything that sparkles such as a diamond. This becomes distracting from several perspectives: (1) the light will catch the stone, (2) the jurors will pay attention to the sparkling gem and, (3) the jurors will speculate on the cost of the object. The latter expectation may not always be favorable for you when jurors cnsider the cost of the item. Some people look at expensive items and translate it as, "This person is doing very well for himself." Other people view expensive items and say, "He thinks he's a hot-shot." In both cases, they are not paying attention to what you are saying. Remember, if you cannot control a perception, minimize or eliminate it.

Other jewelry which is important to avoid is anything that is garish. This means that you should avoid fancy belt buckles or anything that will compete with attention to the face. Once again, however, we have to qualify this by saying that this does not mean that wearing a bracelet or necklace in the courtroom is going to have a negative impact on the case. What we are simply saying is that there has been enough research done and evidence gathered to suggest that you cannot predict the perception that will be associated with this jewelry. Most of the perceptions that tend to be associated with a bracelet or a necklace on a man are not favorable in the context of the courtroom. Given these choices we simply recommend a very classic, conservative type of look that would be acceptable to anybody under almost any circumstance.

Eyeglasses are another important consideration; eyeglasses will generally increase the perception of credibility for both men and women. We use the word "generally" because some people who wear eyeglasses appear more distant and become less approachable to jurors. For the most part, eyeglasses have a positive perception. In a landmark study conducted by Thornton, the stereotypes of people who wear glasses were studied.[18] Subjects rated slides of people with and without glasses. Those with glasses were seen as more intelligent, industrious and honest than the non-spectacled individuals. Live models wearing glasses were also rated as more intelligent and industrious, but not more honest. A more recent study conducted by Hamid in a replication of the Thornton study was conducted in 1968.[19] Using magazine pictures of female figures wearing glasses he asked subjects to rate each figure. Wearers of glasses were often rated as religious, conventional, and unimaginative. Both studies indicate that glasses will correlate with a conservative perception providing that the glasses themselves are in fact conservative. These studies suggest that eyeglasses do in fact affect perception.

The male attorney should wear classical and conservative eyeglasses. On the other hand, he should avoid colored frames and round wire-rimmed frames. The reason for avoiding the round wire-rimmed frames is simply that they make the eyes appear smaller and closer together. This is perceived as a deceptive or dishonest look based on the stereotype that wide eyes mean innocence while small, beady eyes indicate deception. Also, the round wire-rim glasses may tend to date a person since they are associated with folk and rock musicians in the 1960's. The most popular frames are tortoise shell, brown, black, or gray rimmed, or conservative wire-rimmed. Whenever possible, avoid black rimmed eyeglasses; stay with the more neutral shades so that the color is not so stark or harsh on the face. As studies indicate, people wearing glasses are usually perceived as conservative, serious, and more intelligent. Glasses are an important part of the wardrobe.

When selecting glasses it would be beneficial to have a second or even third person with you to obtain their feedback on how the various frames change the perception. If your own vision is uncorrected except with glasses and you do not have contacts, you literally will not be able to see what the frames look like on you. When asking for feedback from another person, ask for specific feedback as to how you look in terms of such factors as credibility, believability, and approachability. What you are not interested in is whether you look fashionable.

The use of eyeglasses is also a very important factor in persuading others. Removing glasses at an appropriate time, for example, will often

---

[18] Thornton, *The Effects of Wearing Glasses Upon Judgments of Persons Seen Briefly*, 28 J. Applied Psychology 203–207 (1944).

[19] Hamid, *Style of Dress as a Perception Cue on Impression Formation*, 26 Perceptual & Motor Skills 904–906 (1968).

create a high impact because it will cause jurors to pause and listen to what you are going to say next. Removing the glasses at a time when you want to jurors to feel closer to you often increases the perception of approachability. Wearing glasses is only part of the entire impact that you want to create. How and when you remove your glasses can serve to anchor key points. This concept of anchoring will be discussed further in Chapter 4.[20]

Briefcases also enter into the perceptual field of jurors. They should be neat, classic, and professional. It is better to have a briefcase that is not bulky and overstuffed with papers so that it appears that you are well organized. Once again the perception that you want to create is that you are in control and that you know exactly what you are doing. Acceptable colors for briefcases are browns, blacks, grays and burgundy. If you have an opportunity to buy an orange briefcase, don't. It is as simple as that. Stay with conservative and classic looks.

§ 1.21 —Jewelry and artifacts for female attorneys

Jewelry, eyeglasses, briefcases, and handbags will make a difference in the overall perception that jurors will have of the female attorney. This section will focus on general guidelines for the wearing of jewelry and the use of artifacts in the courtroom.

Too much jewelry and no jewelry both have a negative impact. Too much jewelry is often seen as ostentatious; too little is viewed as too austere or cold. The rule of thumb for a female attorney is to wear no more than five points in jewelry. This point system refers to counting each piece of jewelry as one point. Earrings, for example, would count as two points. Thus, a woman wearing a ring, earrings, a watch, and a necklace would be wearing five points of jewelry. Any more than that and she may be distracting attention away from the case.

As with a male attorney, the jewelry should not have any sparkling stones. For example, if the wedding ring has a large diamond, then only the band should be worn. There are two perceptual problems if the wedding ring does have a large diamond: (1) it may be seen as too expensive or too rich and that could arouse envy, (2) it simply will distract attention because the light will catch it and the jurors will follow the movement of the light with the ring.

---

[20] *See infra* §§ 4.34–4.37.

COMMENT: As we've stated previously, the primary point is to focus the jurors' attention on the face of the speaker. Persuasion becomes much more effective when they are concentrating on facial and eye behavior. When too much or too flashy jewelry is worn, the tendency is to pay more attention to the jewelry and the sparkling nature of the gems than to the face and words of the speaker.

Earrings are another factor which should be considered with regard to appearance. For example, only post or clip-on earrings that are either small or medium-size should be worn in the courtroom. Dangling earrings should not be worn, as their movement can be very distracting and can reduce the image of professionalism. Dangling earrings are most often associated with nighttime or evening wear.

Necklaces should not fall below the upper chest area. When a necklace falls too low it pulls attention downward to the waistline or belt area because the necklace itself is pointing in that direction. When this occurs, it results in competition for facial attention. The impact that we are trying to project in the courtroom, especially for the female attorney, is a very classic and professional look.

The overall guideline in considering jewelry should be that complicated jewelry or jewelry that is too ornate or garish should be avoided. Do not wear your best pieces of jewelry in the courtroom, or anything that will be perceived as expensive. Also avoid anything that is considered high fashion. In other words, stay away from trends (the now-look); stay strictly with classic lines and classic looks. A pearl necklace, for instance, is considered a very classic piece of jewelry. It can be worn very well in the courtroom because it makes a very conservative statement. Pearls have a positive perception associated with them.

COMMENT: A female attorney should wear some jewelry, for the absence of any jewelry often creates a hard look. Jewelry should be used to soften the look, to compliment the clothing that is worn, and to constantly reinforce a classic, middle-American, professional look.

Eyeglasses constitute one of the most important artifacts used in the courtroom. Considerations for wearing eyeglasses parallel those of the male attorney.[21] The only exception is that a woman can wear a light colored frame (such as pale blue) if it is appropriate for her coloring and skin tone. Unusual or fashionable glasses should be avoided. Wider lenses are preferable to smaller lenses, because they open up the eyes while the smaller lenses cause the eyes to look small and closely spaced. Perceptual research indicates that eyes that are closely spaced together or appear to be small are associated with a higher degree of distrust. Those people that have a wide-eyed look or open-eyed look are considered to be more trustworthy, more likable, and oftentimes more innocent. The type of glasses that are worn actually restructure the facial features which in turn will affect the perception that you will create. As with jewelry and clothing, eyeglasses should not be trendy or fashionable. That means rhinestones, unusual frames, unusual or bright colors, and tinted eyeglasses should be avoided.

The reason for avoiding tinted eyeglasses is obvious. People cannot see your eyes. A commonly held stereotype is that if we cannot look a person in the eye, we cannot trust them. Thus, you should keep the facial area completely open and exposed so that people can see your eyes. Tinted glasses or glasses that change with the light source often cause a shaded look over the eye area. It is not the most favorable look to have. Tinted glasses should be used outside of the courtroom and a more conservative pair used inside.

Bifocals offer another challenge to the female (as well as the male) attorney. When bifocals are worn they often make the person appear harsh or condescending, especially when the person looks over the top of the glasses. If you are wearing bifocals, it is appropriate to point this out to the jurors so that they understand why you are tilting your head or looking a certain way. This is a good example of pacing the jurors. In other words, they will probably already be thinking about their perception of you and this will reduce their uncertainty.

Briefcases and handbags are other types of artifacts that enter into the

[21] *See supra* § 1.20.

perceptual field of jurors. For the female attorney, a briefcase will appear more professional than a purse. If possible, carry a small purse inside your briefcase. Your briefcase or purse, if you are using one, should appear professional. You should never have to search for anything. This becomes particularly important when we talk about perceptions of behaviors. You should always look like you know where everything is even at times when you do not. The briefcase should be clean, neat, and used. A brand new briefcase may give the impression of inexperience. A story involving Amelia Earhart helps us understand this perception. When she purchased her first leather jacket she wore it for thirty days and nights (even while sleeping) until it acquired a used look. Then she used the jacket for flying. She explained that had she worn a brand new leather jacket people would not trust that she was a seasoned pilot. A brand new briefcase may lead to the perception of a brand new attorney. This consideration with regard to briefcases applies more to the younger-looking attorney who appears to be the "new kid on the block."

COMMENT: Always keep in mind that whenever you wear jewelry, or carry a briefcase or handbag into the courtroom, you must try to minimize the possibility of a negative perception. Although you cannot predict precisely what perception will exist, you want to minimize any negative associations that might occur with a particular piece of jewelry or other artifact.

---

§ 1.22 —Jewelry and artifacts for clients and witnesses

Jewelry and artifacts for witnesses and clients will parallel the guidelines given for male and female attorneys.[22] Basically, jewelry and artifacts should be understated and limited. For the male witness they might be limited to a watch and possibly eyeglasses if the individual wears glasses. The female witness might be limited to wearing earrings and a conservative necklace (of medium or small size) or bracelet. For both males and females a wedding ring, class ring, or small conservative ring

[22] *See supra* §§ 1.20, 1.21.

can be worn. Generally, the same conservative guidelines that apply for male and female attorneys will apply for most witnesses in most cases.

There will be many instances, however, where you will want to position your witness or client in a specific way, such as, creating a "victimized" image. In the case of appearing victimized, the wearing of a significant amount of jewelry would not be appropriate. In these circumstances, the use of jewelry should be strictly limited. To present a client as submissive or helpless, use very small, fine, delicate jewelry. On the other hand, if you want a client to be perceived as tough, controlling, or dominant, the use of medium-sized jewelry will give a more definite statement or definite look.

COMMENT: Jewelry considerations for a witness or client must reflect how you want to position them in the courtroom. An important witness should not be left to make the jewelry selection choice on his own. Jewelry, to the juror-detective, offers many stereotypes which will affect the total perception of the individual.

---

§ 1.23 —Hair considerations for male attorneys

The overall image for the male attorney should be conservative and professional. This also applies to hair. A classic and conservative style has high predictability and thus value in reducing uncertainty for jurors in the courtroom. The shorter the hair, usually the higher the perception of credibility. Thus, hair length can make a considerable difference. As with other personal appearance factors, these differences can vary with regard to geographical location. The question that you always want to raise with regard to any personal appearance factor is "at what cost?" At what cost are you willing to wear your hair a certain way, knowing that you may be increasing the risk of a negative perception? This is not to say that a negative perception cannot be altered by behaviors—it just takes a lot more work.

An interesting study with regard to hair length was conducted by three researchers in 1972.[23] Subjects in two different classes were asked to rate

[23] P.A. Andersen, T.A. Jensen & L.B. King, *The Effects of Homophylious Hair and*

the credibility of a speaker who wore a different hairstyle when appearing before each class. For the first group the speaker had his hair combed so that it stood out from his head one and one-half inches and appeared quite long. This type was similar to that of many of the students in the class. For the second group, the speaker combed his hair flat so that it appeared short. The findings revealed that the short-haired speaker was rated significantly higher on the perception of competence and dynamism. One possible explanation for these findings is that males with long hair are perceived to be less mature when compared to males with short hair. More recent studies continue to support the fact that our culture still has more favorable attitudes connected with short hair than it does with long hair. Sideburns should be avoided since they often have a negative association attributed to them. Similarly, avoid any hair that covers the ears and hits the collar of the shirt or jacket. This usually will indicate that the hair is too long. Shorter hair also gives the appearance of a younger, fresher look; it appears cleaner and better styled.

With regard to hair style, trends and extremes should be avoided. If the hair is thinning it should be worn short. Credibility is lost by combing wisps of hair forward to cover up a balding area. Although a receding hairline does not have a negative perception, trying to cover up a receding hairline does. The same is true with wearing hair pieces or toupees. These should be avoided because they are perceived as an attempt to cover up something, and they indicate that the person is not comfortable with his own self-image and appearance.

COMMENT: To summarize, the hair style for men should be short and conservative; no trendy fashions or styles. Specifically, the hair should not cover the ears or come below the nape of the neck. Hair that is too curly may contribute to a perception of being frivolous. Straight or slightly wavy hair is seen as more professional.

Hair color is another variable that may have impact in the courtroom. Hair color with men, however, does not appear to have nearly as much

Dress Styles on Credibility and Comprehension (Paper presented to the International Communication Association) (April 1972).

impact as hair color with women.[24] There are some associations that go with hair color for men. For example, men with blonde hair are often perceived as being playboys, outdoor/sports oriented, or the California surfer-type; brown hair is seen as neutral or all-American; red hair is associated with temper; and black hair with seriousness. The only other stereotype that seems to stand out *clearly* for men is that gray hair is seen as more credible than other hair colors. Thus, men with partially or completely gray hair are perceived as more credible and experienced when compared to men without gray hair.[25]

Facial hair on men is probably the single most important factor with regard to hair considerations and their impact in the courtroom. There is contradictory information on facial hair, so once again the attorney should take a conservative approach. The most conservative guidelines suggest the avoidance of facial hair—beards, moustaches, and various combinations of both. There are many different perceptions with beards; some people like beards, some people do not. These perceptions change depending upon the grooming of the beard, the age of the individual, the style of the beard, and the geographical location in which the beard is worn. The male attorney must realize that there are more positive perceptions associated with clean shaven men then there are with men with beards.

When we examine the studies conducted on the research of beards, we see that there tends to be a difference in male and female perceptions.[26] For example, males view beards less favorably than females. A clean shaven male will stand further away from a bearded male. Females may see beards more favorably, but usually in terms of attraction rather than an increase in the perception of credibility. Bearded men may appear older and, therefore, more credible. Once again you have to weigh the costs and consider the variables that come into play: what type of beard is it?; what does the person wearing the beard look like?; does the beard enhance or detract from the total look?; is it appropriate given the geographical location?; are beards something that are often seen in the community and are they generally acceptable? All these questions have to be answered.

---

[24] *See infra* § 1.24.

[25] *See infra* § 1.24, for a discussion of gray hair on female attorneys, which creates a different perception.

[26] Freedman, *The Survival Value of the Beard*, 3 PSYCHOLOGY TODAY 36–39 (1969); Pellegrini, *The Virtues of Hairyness*, 6 PSYCHOLOGY TODAY 14 (1973).

COMMENT: The most conservative guideline to follow is to avoid wearing a beard. As can be seen above, the perceptions of a clean shaven face are neutral while the perception of a bearded individual will vary depending on any number of factors.

Negative perceptions do exist with regard to unusual types of beards such as the goatee, the beard and no mustache, bushy beards, and long sideburns running into a moustache. Anything that deviates from a classical look is going to be subject to some sort of perception. We cannot predict that this perception is always going to be negative, but we certainly cannot assure that it is always going to be positive. Therefore, extremes in a bearded look should definitely be avoided.

Moustaches also alter perceptions. Avoid handle-bar moustaches and moustaches that droop down at the corners. Moustaches that fall down at the corners create a hard look because they pull down the lines of the face. When this occurs it causes the person to look older and more severe. People look younger with shorter hair and moustaches which are kept short because this creates an image that pulls up the lines of the face. When wearing a moustache it is important that it does not cover the top lip. You do not want to have too much concealment with a moustache. Also, if you wear a moustache or beard in the courtroom, make sure you do not play with it. One of the most common problems that men with beards or moustaches have is that they are constantly touching it with their hands. That is distracting, especially if the behavior is performed repetitively. You should be aware that any behavior which is performed 40% of the time is perceived as being performed the majority of the time. The perception of the actual repetition of the behavior will be far greater, especially if it is an annoying behavioral pattern. Repetitious patterns often arouse a negative response in people. It is okay if a person scratches his chin once or twice, but it is irritating if he scratches his chin every half hour.

§ 1.24 —Hair considerations for female attorneys

There are two looks for the female attorney to avoid with regard to hair. These two extremes involve the little girl look and the hard masculine look. Neither look will increase the perception of credibility in the courtroom and both will undermine the power that a woman can have in the courtroom. The little girl look is often seen as too submissive and too childlike, and it reduces the perception of expertness and competence. The hard masculine look is seen as too much of an imitation male look and too hard or too belligerent, and it will often arouse feelings of competition and a "we'll show her" attitude. The overall image you should try to project is the professional, conservative, middle-American look. Trying to look like the all-American woman is probably the most appropriate rule of thumb for a female litigator.

Women are seen as more credible if their hair is shoulder length or shorter, or pulled up on top of their heads. Hair below the shoulder line is viewed as a little girl look or even as a sexy or romantic look, both of which are undesirable perceptions in the courtroom. The shorter hair length helps to pull up the lines of the face which results in a more youthful, professional look. Shorter hair focuses more attention on the eyes and creates the perception of having "big" eyes. There are a number of other reasons to avoid long hair. First, women with long hair have a tendency to run their fingers through their hair or play with their hair during the trial. This is referred to as preening behavior. It is akin to the same behavior men engage in with beards and moustaches. The bottomline is that it is distracting. Second, long hair often covers too much of the face; it falls forward and conceals the face. Third, long hair draws too much attention, particularly hair that is *very* long (e.g., below the mid-back level).

Hair pulled on top of the head also helps to pull up the lines of the face. On the other hand, long hair tends to be aging because it accentuates downward lines of the face. When the hair is pulled up on top of the head be careful that it is not pulled back too severely so that it creates a harsh look. In one antitrust case, the female attorney was a very attractive blonde. She pulled her hair back in a tight bun, wore a navy blue pinstriped suite, a white shirt, a tie, and closed-toe pumps. She appeared very hard and severe. Afterwards, jurors commented that they did not feel that she was very personable. She sacrificed approachability in an attempt to increase her credibility. You must remember that neither one needs to be sacrificed. By avoiding extremes, a balance can be maintained.

> **COMMENT:** If you like long hair, be prepared in your capacity as an attorney to pull it up on top of your head. Avoid braiding it or wearing a pony tail. These styles still give a long hair look. Long hair can only be concealed if it is worn up on top of the head.

Hair styles should be conservative and simple. Avoid bouffants or overly curly hair styles. If the hair is naturally curly, leave it alone. Hair styles can date an individual more than anything else. You can stay in style by sticking to classic cuts. Avoid extremes in hairdos such as trendy hairdos, unusual cuts, streaking, or coloring. The hair should be very well groomed and should frame the face. It is important that the hair be used to soften your look. If your hair is completely off your face you want to make sure that the look is soft enough. Remember that hair that falls on the forehead and the sides of the face tends to soften the overall look.

Hair color affects the perception of females more than it does males.[27] The media has a lot to do with implanting these perceptions into our minds. For example, blonde females are definitely associated with being spacey and frivolous, as well as "having more fun." This does not mean that the hair color has to be changed. It simply means that blonde females need to be aware of these stereotyped assessments so they can neutralize these perceptions with behavior and other personal appearance factors. Neutralizing factors include such things as using a low voice tone, wearing conservative eyeglasses, or wearing a classic suit. Thus, if a blonde female does not exhibit behaviors that reinforce the initial perception of "blonde," the original perception may be altered.

Black hair has a different association; it is usually seen as sultry and hard. You can look to television and movies to see the reinforcement of these characteristics, as for example, with Joan Collins and Linda Evans on *Dynasty*. Linda Evans is portrayed as the "good" woman and Joan Collins is the "bad" woman. Similarly, witches on television are almost

[27] *See supra* § 1.23 for discussion of hair considerations for male attorneys.

always cast with black hair, except on the few occasions where there have been "good" witches such as Glinda in *The Wizard of Oz* and Samantha on *Bewitched* (both have blonde hair).

Red hair is associated with sirens and is also seen as hot. In *Porgy and Bess*, there is a line that states that a "red headed woman can make a choo-choo jump off the track." Brown hair, surprisingly enough, has very few associations and that is probably one reason why brown hair is considered the most neutral of all colors. It is considered wholesome and all-American. It has neither good nor bad associations.

Gray hair for women is an entirely different category. A woman who is partially gray is not seen as credible as a woman with a full head of gray hair. Nor is a woman with gray hair seen to be as credible as a man with gray hair. This is because there is a difference in perceptions between men and women when it comes to age. Men are still perceived as more attractive and "better with age" than are women. This is quickly changing with role models of beautiful "older" women such as Jane Fonda, Sophia Loren, Joan Collins, and others.

Artifacts used in the hair will alter the perception. Avoid bows, flowers, barrettes, combs, and artificial hairpieces such as braids and falls. This will create a little girl look and will call more attention to the hair than the face. When the hair is worn up, pins which match the hair color should be used to secure the hair. Also, wisps of hair should not be falling down on the nape of the neck or on the side of the head. These wisps are often seen as a very romantic look and are more appropriate for evening wear than they are for the courtroom. The rule of thumb is to make it conservative, make it classic, and make it natural.

§ 1.25 —Hair considerations for clients and witnesses

For your client to convey a victimized look, the hair should be straight and worn down. Hair that is curly will make the person appear energetic. For the perception of credibility, the hair should be short, tailored, and professional. Neatness is an important consideration with both clients and witnesses.

In the case of witnesses, it is important for a male witness to be clean shaven. An attorney may choose to wear a beard, but this should not be a choice for a witness.

The guidelines for female and male attorneys with regard to hair considerations also apply to witnesses.[28] The only difference would be if you are trying to create a particular look for the witness, such as a victimized look as opposed to an expert witness look, or if you are trying to create a soft, submissive look. For example, in creating a soft, submissive look for a female client, have her use soft curls around the face and make sure her hair is a little bit on the longer side. You might want to put a barrette in her hair. All of this will serve to create more of a little girl look or a soft look. A loss of credibility will result, however, if the look is too young for the individual. In instances such as these, it is often important to have professional help in positioning the client or witness in the courtroom.

§ 1.26 —Makeup considerations for female attorneys

Our overall message with regard to clothing, jewelry, and makeup considerations is the same: be conservative, be professional, and be traditional. Although this message may be redundant, it works. If you avoid all extremes in any type of personal appearance factor you will convey a much more neutral image in the courtroom. We cannot guarantee a positive perception, but we can minimize factors which will lead to a negative perception.

There are many different perceptions with regard to makeup. Many religious groups such as Southern Baptists and Mormons have strong views against using any makeup. Your jury will most likely represent a combination of many different types of people so you want to avoid any extreme usage of makeup. Makeup also has a long history. Many years ago it was used to identify women of the night and was used primarily as a means of sexual allurement. Makeup in the courtroom should not be used to draw attention; it should be used to soften a look.

The purpose of wearing makeup in the courtroom is to soften the face, not so much to accentuate the eyes or lips. By softening the face, the person will appear very approachable and attractive. Attractiveness is a major variable in how well people are liked. People like people that they see as attractive.

There are certain colors to avoid when using makeup. For example, it is important to avoid hard colors such as black, and bright colors such as blue, green, or turquoise on the eyelids. The softer colors include the grays and browns. When using an eyeliner, a gray or brown will create a

---

[28] *See supra* §§ 1.23, 1.24.

much softer line than a black eyeliner. Eyeshadows which should be avoided include any that show a definite color such as blue, green, gold, or purple. It would be more advisable to stay with earth tone colors such as browns, beiges, and other neutral colors that give the face a natural look. Since makeup can "date" a person, be sure the application is appropriate and contemporary (without being extreme). Most department stores will provide a free lesson on the application of makeup. If you use this service, ask the professional to give you a daytime look. Check the makeup application by examining it in natural light to see whether or not it is appropriate. If there are harsh lines, or if you can see where one color begins and another ends, then chances are you have too much makeup on.

Lipstick is another personal appearance factor which should not be overlooked. One researcher studied the impact of lipstick in his study with six male students who interviewed six female students.[29] Following the interviews, the male students rated them according to personality perceptions. In these six interviews, three women were wearing lipstick and three women were not. The interviews were structured in such a way that each woman wore lipstick for three of her six interviews. The results were unanimous. The women who wore lipstick were perceived as more frivolous and more overtly interested in males. When asked on what basis the judgments were made, not one of the interviewers indicated that the presence or absence of lipstick affected his response. This suggests that some of our perceptions occur without a conscious awareness of the factors that are actually affecting the perception. In other words, we unintentionally receive a message from the source.

COMMENT: A note of caution should be added to interpreting some of the landmark but older research. The current dynamics of fashions might influence and alter many of these findings.

Extremes in lipstick draw attention to the lips. While bright lipsticks

[29] McKeachie, *Lipsticks as a Determiner of First Impressions of Personality*, 36 J. Soc. Psychology, 241–244 (1952).

do not belong in the courtroom, some lipstick should be worn because it will help give some color to the lips.

COMMENT: The absence of any makeup, for most women, usually makes them look too pale. You should avoid the extremes of heavy makeup and no makeup. The middle ground of using makeup to soften a look and to provide some type of color is most appropriate for the courtroom.

Another area of perception involves the use of makeup with eyeglasses. Researcher Hamid studied the perceptions of makeup cues in the presence and absence of glasses.[30] He had four women, all dressed similarly, serve as assistants during a class period. The first woman wore both makeup and glasses. The second wore makeup without glasses. The third wore glasses without makeup, and the fourth wore neither glasses nor makeup. At the end of the class period the students were asked to recall what each assistant wore and rate them on various personality traits. Although the women were wearing comparable clothes, the two who were wearing makeup were rated as wearing shorter skirts than the two without makeup. This same perception held true for the two without glasses. The perceptions of males and females differed with regard to the woman who wore glasses and makeup. Males perceived her as artistic, intelligent, self-confident, and sophisticated. They ranked her low in shyness, seriousness, and sentimentality. The females' perceptions of the same woman were remarkably different. Although they saw her as intelligent, they also perceived her to be both cold and conceited. Both the woman who wore glasses and no makeup and the one who wore neither glasses nor makeup were perceived as conservative and low in individuality. Finally, the woman wearing makeup without glasses was rated favorably on outward appearance but unfavorably in personality traits. Thus, we have a complication when makeup is worn with glasses. To avoid the negative trait associated with glasses and makeup, the female attorney should use a moderate amount of makeup with conservative glasses.

---

[30] Hamid, *Some Effects of Dress Cues of Observational Accuracy, Perceptual Estimate and Impression Formation*, 86 J. Soc. Psychology 279–289 (1972).

The colors used on the cheek area deserve special attention. Often cheek color is applied incorrectly and leaves a line on the face. This detracts from the overall professional image. Check the color in the sunlight and make sure it is applied correctly. Also have it checked by a professional. Remember, everything about your appearance has an impact in the courtroom.

Nail polish and the length of nails is also an important consideration. The nails are often scrutinized by jurors because the hands are used for gesturing. Nails that are too long on a female are perceived as claws. A female with long nails is often associated with a cat-like appearance. This tends to be a negative perception. Nails should be kept relatively short and they should not have any bright colors on them—no reds, oranges, fuchsias, or pinks. These colors draw too much attention to the hands and do not promote a professional image. Similarly, avoid stripes, decals, or any other ornamentation on the nails. Acceptable choices in nail polish include the light tones such as light pink, a natural tone, a buff color, or clear polish. It is also acceptable to go without nail polish as long as the nails are manicured and they look clean.

§ 1.27 —Makeup considerations for female clients and witnesses

Makeup considerations for female witnesses and clients should follow very conservative guidelines similar to those discussed for the female attorney in § 1.26. Basically, with regard to female witnesses and clients, a soft look should be created. Makeup should be used to create a natural, healthy, and attractive appearance. Counsel should always remember, however, that in a particular type of case the wearing of makeup may make a difference. In a rape case, for example, the plaintiff or victim should wear little or no makeup because the perceptions are much more dramatic and are too difficult to control.

§ 1.28 —Selecting colors for high impact

We have previously discussed the study of color psychology, which is quite complicated, in a number of these subsections dealing with specific personal appearance factors.[31] Following are some of the general factors with regard to colors that we feel again deserve your attention.

Colors which help to increase the perception of credibility tend to be in the conservative families of gray, navy blue, and white. This is why we

[31] *See generally infra* §§ 1.17–1.27.

recommend wearing suits which are gray or navy blue and present a very conservative image. On the other hand, when you want to increase the perception of approachability, the colors in the brown family—brown, tan, beige—are more effective. They do not, however, enhance the perception of credibility. It is important to note that they will not detract from credibility, but they will not increase the perception in this area. To soften a look, pastel shades can be used. This includes pinks, blues, and soft whites. At the same time, the softer shades in the pastel look increase the perception of approachability. If an individual is too overpowering and appears too strong, you can often use a softer shade in the shirt or blouse to tone down the overall image.

There is a difference between the use of solid colors and colors with a design pattern. Solid colors tend to have a more dramatic impact and create stronger statements. If you want to have a greater perception of power in the courtroom, you should wear solid colors, particularly around the facial area. For this purpose, avoid anything that has a distracting design, except for a tie that has a very small design pattern. With regard to a female and her clothing behavior, a solid suit with a solid shirt and a simple strand of pearls will create a "high contrast" look.

There are two colors that, because we cannot control the perception, should be avoided in the courtroom. The first color is black. Black is too harsh a color and very few people can wear black well. It is a color that is associated with many negative connotations such as death, evil, witches, and so forth. In one murder trial we saw a defendant who was dressed in a black shirt and black pants. It was difficult to understand why the attorney allowed the defendant to appear in the courtroom this way. Black, for obvious reasons, is an inappropriate color to wear when one is a defendant in a murder trial. The connotations associated with black tend to be consistent across cultures and are deeply embedded in our minds. Another color than can produce negative connotations is red. The color red is often associated with passion, violence, excitement, and blood. Once again we have color perceptions that are difficult to control. For this reason, it is advisable to avoid red in terms of clothing in the courtroom.

A new field which has emerged over the past ten years in the area of personal appearance is called color consulting. Many attorneys, both male and female, seek professional color consultants to assist them in choosing colors that are best suited for their skin tones and coloring.

Professional color consultants can be located through department stores; simply ask for their qualifications and background (most of them have been certified in this area). There is some validity for color consultants. There are definite colors that will cause the skin tone to look more sallow, or that will cause a person to look unhealthy, or that will actually detract from the total image of the person. When you are able to identify the colors that look best on you, you will see a marked difference in your overall attractiveness.

Studies which have been done on the changing of clothing color throughout the course of the trial provide some interesting data. It has been shown that if an attorney wears dark colored clothing during the beginning of the trial and progressively wears lighter colored clothing, the perception of the jurors tends to be that everything is going well for the attorney. If, on the other hand, the attorney wears a light colored suit and progressively moves to darker or more serious types of suits, the perception is that things must be getting tough and are not going as well for the attorney.

COMMENT: In serious injury or death cases, however, plaintiff's counsel may want to wear lighter colored clothing during his voir dire and opening statement when he is trying to establish rapport, but darker colors at the end of the trial when he has the widow or seriously injured plaintiff on the stand as well as when he is arguing damages in summation.

There are some important considerations with regard to choosing colors when utilizing demonstrative evidence. The most important consideration when preparing graphics and other visual aids is to be very consistent in the colors you choose. For example, if you are using demonstrative aids that are supportive of the evidence that you want jurors to believe, you should choose one neutral color (such as blue or green) and use it repeatedly. When you are utilizing such aids to present evidence which rebuts opposing counsel, you may want to use red or a bright orange color. This will call the jurors' attention to critical information and will serve to reinforce the serious nature of the material. The use of colors in graphics can anchor certain types of information if they are used consistently. For example, by using the color blue to present financial data and the color red to present evidence of an alarming nature, you will create a classical conditioning pattern. Everytime you use red, it will be associated with critical or serious information. Thus, you are using color to reinforce the way you want the jurors to perceive the information.

§ 1.29 —Checklist: Male personal appearance factors which increase the perception of credibility

1. *Clothing*
   ____classic, conservative clothing
   ____traditional two-piece suit (avoid three-piece suits, especially in rural areas; avoid trendy suits; avoid poor quality suits; avoid sports jacket)
   ____acceptable fabrics for suits include wools and wool blends (avoid silk, ultrasuede, or any other less traditional fabric)
   ____acceptable suit patterns include small pinstripes, solids, subtle and small plaids, subtle and small striped patterns (avoid all unusual patterns or very pronounced patterns)
   ____have suit pants and coat sleeves tailored to appropriate length (lengths which are too short reduce credibility; lengths which are too long project a look of being "overwhelmed" and "submissive")
   ____conservative tie (avoid unusual designs and patterns)
   ____solid long sleeved white shirt with classic collar (avoid open buttons and button-down collar)
   ____acceptable fabric for shirts is cotton (avoid silk and polyester shirts)
   ____conservative well-polished shoes (avoid casual shoes such as penny loafers)
   ____conservative leather belt (avoid unusual belt buckles and designs)
2. *Colors*
   ____acceptable colors for suits include colors in the gray and navy blue families (avoid browns, tans, beiges, and unusual suit colors)
   ____acceptable color for shirts is white (highest perception of credibility); light blue can also be worn (avoid shirts with designs and patterns; stay with solid colors)
3. *Jewelry*
   ____wear limited jewelry such as one ring, watch, tie bar or tie pin

(avoid bracelets, necklaces, pocket watch, extra rings, garish jewelry, and belts with large buckles or jeweled belt buckles)
____acceptable rings include wedding ring, class ring, or a conservative ring (avoid large, expensive, and sparkling stones as well as unusual rings)
____wear rings only on the ring finger of either hand (avoid rings on any other finger)

4. *Eyeglasses*
____eyeglasses, in general, increase the perception of credibility
____wear conservative frames (avoid round wire-rim frames and unusual colored frames; avoid black frames, acceptable frames include tortoise shell, neutral colors, some wire-rimmed frames; avoid all fashionable and trendy types of eyeglasses)
____wear clear lenses (avoid all tinted lenses and photo-sensitive lenses)

5. *Hair*
____short, conservative hair style (keep hair well-groomed and neat; avoid hair over the ears and hair hitting the collar area; avoid sideburns)
____classic, traditional hairstyle (avoid unusual or fashionable hair styles)
____use natural hair (avoid hair pieces and toupees; avoid combing hair to cover balding or thinning area; if hair is colored, have it done professionally)
____clean-shaven look (if beards and moustaches are worn they should be well trimmed and conservative; avoid all unusual looks including handlebar moustaches)

6. *Fingernails*
____nails should be short, well-groomed, and clean
____nails should be healthy and natural looking (avoid nail polish)

§ 1.30 —Checklist: Male personal appearance factors which increase the perception of approachability and likability

1. *Clothing*
____conservative clothing
____sports jacket (avoid two- and three-piece suits)
____acceptable suit patterns include tweeds, small plaids, and solids (avoid pinstriped suits)

——acceptable fabrics for suits include cashmere, wools, and wool blends (avoid silks, ultrasuede materials and other less traditional fabrics)

——acceptable fabric for shirts is cotton (avoid silk and polyester shirts)

——have suit pants and coat sleeves tailored to appropriate lengths (avoid lengths which are too short or too long)

——conservative or leather belt (avoid unusual belt buckles and designs)

——solid or subtle patterned long-sleeved shirt (short-sleeved shirt is acceptable only in very informal settings; button-down collar is acceptable; shirt can have small design, such as stripes)

——conservative, well-polished shoes (avoid shoes that are too casual; loafers are acceptable in informal setting)

2. *Colors*

——acceptable colors for suits include colors in the brown family—tans, beiges, browns (avoid gray and navy if jacket and pants match; gray and navy can be used for either jacket *or* pants)

——acceptable colors for shirts are light blue or light pink/rose (avoid white shirts)

3. *Jewelry*

——wear jewelry such as a ring and/or watch (avoid tie bar, tie pins, bracelets, necklaces, pocket watch, extra rings, garish jewelry, and belts with large buckles or jeweled belt buckles)

——acceptable rings include a wedding ring, class ring, or a conservative ring (avoid large, expensive, and sparkling stones as well as unusual rings)

——wear rings on the ring finger of left or right hand only (avoid rings on any other finger)

4. *Eyeglasses*

——eyeglasses are acceptable; they should be removed occasionally to increase perception of approachability

——wear conservative frames (avoid round wire-rim frames, unusual colored frames; avoid black frames; acceptable frames include tortoise shell, neutral colors, and some wire-rimmed frames; avoid all fashionable and trendy types of eyeglasses)

5. *Hair*

——short, conservative hair style (keep hair well-groomed and neat;

avoid hair over the ears and hair hitting the collar area; avoid sideburns)

____classic, traditional hair style (avoid unusual or fashionable hair styles)

____use natural hair (avoid hair pieces and toupees; avoid combing hair to cover balding or thinning area; if hair is colored, have it done professionally)

____clean-shaven look (avoid beards and moustaches)

6. *Fingernails*

____nails should be short, well-groomed, and clean

____nails should be healthy and natural looking (avoid nail polish)

§ 1.31 —Checklist: Female personal appearance factors which increase the perception of credibility

1. *Clothing*

____classic, conservative clothing

____traditional, two-piece suit with matching skirt and jacket (avoid pantsuits, trendy suits, poor quality suits, and suits with contrasting jacket and skirt)

____avoid three-piece suits (avoid all types of vests, either cloth or sweater vests)

____acceptable suit patterns include solids, subtle and small plaids, subtle and small striped patterns (avoid the classical pinstriped pattern; avoid all unusual patterns or very pronounced patterns)

____acceptable fabrics for suits include wools and wool blends; lighter weight spring and summer fabrics are acceptable (avoid fabrics which wrinkle, such as silk suits; avoid ultrasuede and other less traditional fabrics)

____acceptable fabrics for blouses are cotton and silk (avoid shiny and polyester blouses)

____bows and pleated blouses are acceptable (avoid male-looking ties; avoid ruffles)

____have coat sleeve length tailored to appropriate length (a sleeve length which is too long will result in the perception of submissiveness and being overwhelmed)

____skirt length should fall from just below the knee to two inches below the knee (avoid all extremes in skirt lengths such as above-the-knee and mid-calf lengths)

____if a belt is worn, it should be conservative and understated

____avoid all designer clothing and accessories

2. *Shoes*

____wear heels of 2½ inches or less (avoid high heels and flat heels)

____wear closed-toe and closed-heel shoes (avoid open-toe and sling-back shoes)

____wear classic and traditional shoes (avoid all designs, jewelry or bows on shoes; avoid unusual and fashionable shoes)

3. *Colors*

____acceptable colors for suits include colors in the gray, white, off-white, beige, and navy blue families (avoid browns and unusual suit colors)

____acceptable blouse colors include white (for the higher perception of credibility); light blue can also be worn (avoid blouses with designs and patterns; stay with solid colors)

4. *Jewelry*

____wear limited jewelry, up to five points; this may include earrings, a ring, a necklace, and a pin on jacket (avoid "male-type" accessories such as a tie bar or a tie pin; avoid bracelets that dangle, move, or make a noise; avoid garish jewelry and belts with large buckles or jeweled belt buckles)

____wear small- to medium-sized earrings (avoid all dangling and oversized earrings; select conservative earrings and avoid fashion trends)

____acceptable rings include wedding ring, class ring, or a conservative ring (avoid large, expensive, and sparkling stones as well as unusual rings).

____wear rings on the ring finger of the left or right hand only (avoid rings on any other finger; a ring on each hand is acceptable)

____wear a necklace that falls in upper chest area (avoid long dangling necklaces or necklaces with unusual designs and patterns; the most acceptable necklaces are conservative, such as a strand of pearls or a gold necklace)

____wear moderately-priced jewelry (avoid extremes in high-priced or low-priced jewelry; avoid costume jewelry)

____watches are acceptable and count as a piece of jewelry

5. *Eyeglasses*

____eyeglasses, in general, increase the perception of credibility

____wear conservative frames (avoid high fashion look in glasses; avoid round wire-rim frames; acceptable frames include tortoise shell, neutral or pastel colors, some wire-rimmed frames; wear wider, more open lenses as opposed to small glass lenses)

6. *Hair*
____conservative and classic hair style; wear hair shoulder length or shorter or pull hair on top of head (avoid long hair below the shoulder line or hair that is extreme in shortness and appears to be a male-imitation look)
____classic, traditional hair style (avoid unusual or fashionable hair styles; avoid bouffants, ponytails, and braids)
____hair should appear to be a natural color (avoid "colored" looks, such as bleached blond or streaked hair; keep coloring subtle)
____hair should be well-groomed and neat

7. *Fingernails*
____nails should be a moderate length, well-groomed and clean (avoid long nails; short nails are acceptable)
____nails should be healthy and natural looking (avoid colored nail polish, such as red and fuchsia; acceptable nail polish colors include clear, buff, and opaque colors such as light pink; avoid all decals and decorations on fingernails)

8. *Makeup*
____wear little to moderate makeup (avoid extremes of too much makeup or no makeup; makeup should look very natural in sunlight)
____wear soft colors (avoid eyeshadows with definite colors such as blues, greens, and purples)

§ 1.32 —Checklist: Female personal appearance factors which increase the perception of approachability and likability

1. *Clothing*
____classic, conservative clothing
____traditional, two-piece suit with contrasting skirt and jacket (for example, a solid jacket with a plaid skirt)
____dress with or without a jacket (dress should be tailored and conservative; absence of jacket reduces "authority" look)
____acceptable suit patterns include solids, subtle and small plaids, subtle and small striped patterns (avoid the classic pinstriped pattern)

——acceptable fabrics for suits include cashmere, wool and wool blends (avoid silks, ultrasuede, and other less traditional fabrics)

——acceptable fabrics for blouses are cotton and silk

——wear blouse with bow, pleats, slight ruffle or soft tie (avoid male-looking tie and blouses which are plain; a necklace can be substituted for a tie)

——wear blouses with jewel or normal neckline (avoid high-collared blouses)

——avoid all designer clothing and accessories

2. *Shoes*

——wear heels of 2½ inches or less (avoid high heels and flat heels)

——wear closed-toe and closed-heel shoes (avoid open-toe shoes and sling back shoes)

——wear classic and traditional shoes (avoid all designs, jewelry, or bows on shoes; avoid unusual and fashionable shoes)

3. *Colors*

——acceptable colors for suits include colors in the brown, gray, and blue family; a wider choice of colors can be used including pinks and roses (avoid gray or navy if jacket and skirt match; gray and navy can be used for either jacket or skirt)

——acceptable blouse colors include all pastels such as blue, pink, light rose, green, and so forth (avoid very bright colors and white blouses)

4. *Jewelry*

——wear limited jewelry, up to five points; this may include earrings, a ring, a necklace, and a pin on jacket (avoid "male-type" accessories such as a tie bar or tie pin; avoid bracelets that dangle, move, or make a noise; avoid garish jewelry and belts with large buckles or jeweled belt buckles)

——wear small- to medium-sized earrings (avoid all dangling and oversized earrings; select conservative earrings and avoid fashion trends)

——acceptable rings include wedding ring, class ring, or a conservative ring (avoid large, expensive, and sparkling stones as well as unusual rings)

——wear rings on the ring finger of the left or right hand only (avoid rings on any other finger; a ring on each hand is acceptable)

——wear a necklace that falls in upper chest area (avoid long dangling necklaces or necklaces with unusual designs and patterns;

the most acceptable necklaces are conservative, such as a strand of pearls or a gold necklace)

____wear moderately-priced jewelry (avoid extremes in high-priced jewelry and low-priced jewelry; avoid costume jewelry)

____watches are acceptable and count as a piece of jewelry

5. *Eyeglasses*

____eyeglasses, in general, increase the perception of approachability

____wear conservative frames (avoid high fashion look in glasses; avoid round wire-rim frames; acceptable frames include tortoise shell, neutral or pastel colors, some wire-rimmed frames; wear wider, more open lenses as opposed to small glass lenses)

6. *Hair*

____Soften the hair style, bring hair around the face in soft curls or waves (avoid severe hair styles, such as pulling the hair back too tight)

____conservative and classic hair style; wear hair shoulder length or shorter or pull hair on top of head (avoid long hair below the shoulder line or hair that is extreme in shortness and appears to be a male-imitation look)

____classic, traditional hair style (avoid unusual or fashionable hair styles; avoid bouffants, ponytails, and braids)

____hair should appear to be a natural color (avoid "colored" looks such as bleached blonde or streaked hair; keep coloring subtle)

____hair should be well-groomed and neat

7. *Fingernails*

____nails should be a moderate length, well-groomed and clean (avoid long nails; short nails are acceptable)

____nails should be healthy and natural looking (avoid colored nail polish, such as red and fuchsia; acceptable nail polish colors include clear, buff, and opaque colors such as light pink; avoid all decals and decorations on fingernails)

8. *Makeup*

____wear little to moderate makeup (avoid extremes of too much makeup or no makeup; makeup should look very natural in sunlight)

____wear soft colors (avoid eyeshadows with definite colors, such as blues, greens, and purples)

§ 1.33 Projecting confidence and power in the courtroom

Projecting confidence and power in the courtroom is another critical factor in a case. Messages are far more believable when they are presented by a source who is perceived to have both power and confidence. The important factors to consider with the projection of confidence are behaviorally manifested through the three channels of communication: verbal, vocal, and nonverbal. The following sections will discuss the projection of power and confidence through (1) controlling space,[32] (2) nonverbal cues,[33] and (3) vocal characteristics.[34]

§ 1.34 —Projecting confidence and power by controlling space

In American society, we equate the greater accumulation of space with status and dominance. For example, the more square feet you have in your house, the more cars you own, the higher you are up in a hotel or apartment building, or an aisle or window seat on an airplane offer greater space or visual access to more space. The more space an individual controls or occupies, the greater the perception of status. This explains in part why top executives have windows in their offices. It gives them a view of the outside which creates the illusion of more space and a larger office.

In the courtroom as well, status and space correlate. Those people that are seen as having greater power and confidence are people who have greater control and ownership of the courtroom. Men, by virtue of their size and stature, tend to have greater ascribed power. The taller a person is and the more space their body takes up, the more space they are perceived as "owning." Women, because they are usually smaller in stature, take up less space. As a result, women need to be even more conscious about expanding their personal spatial zones so they can increase the perceptions of power and control. There are four factors which project confidence with regard to space: (1) learning how to own and express ownership of space; (2) learning how to use gestures to control space; (3) staying physically exposed to the jurors, and; (4) avoiding invasion of territory that belongs to the jurors or the judge.

It is important to own the space that you occupy. This simply means that when you walk into a courtroom there should be no surprises. You

---

[32] *See infra* § 1.34.

[33] *See infra* § 1.35.

[34] *See infra* § 1.36.

should know the territory. Prior to going to trial, especially if it is an important case, you should walk around the courtroom and actually walk through the space. Know the territory so that when you walk in the courtroom, you are not walking in that space for the first time. Your behavior throughout the trial will display much greater confidence with this preliminary review of the space in which you will be working.

COMMENT: There is a definite difference when someone is walking in an area with which they are familiar. When you are familiar with an area you look and feel more confident. For this same reason, football teams go to see the field prior to the game when they are playing away from their home fields. They get very familiar with the territory. The same thing applies to the courtroom. Become familiar with the courtroom.

A second factor with regard to controlling space is the use of gestures. Many people recommend that an attorney's use of gestures in the courtroom should be limited and kept to a minimum. This is, we believe erroneous advice. Gestures in the courtroom should be natural. If your natural instinct is to use small and limited gestures, then you should follow that instinct. If, however, you are expressive and you tend to move your hands when you are talking, unless it is extreme and becomes very distracting, you should continue to gesture in a fashion natural to you. The more natural your gestures are, the greater the perception of trustworthiness and credibility. Moreover, when your gestures are more expansive and away from the body, you will create a larger personal bubble and, therefore, control more space. The more space you control, the greater the perceived dominance.

Gestures above the waist tend to have more impact in the courtroom, or in any speaking situation, than gestures below the waist. When the gestures are kept above the waist attention is brought up to the face, which is where we want to keep the focus. If you gesture below the waist you will most likely find that your hands move in a small manner below the beltline. Small movements below the waist will pull eye contact down to your hands, which is not the objective you want to achieve. Remember, keep the hands above the waist level for maximum impact.

A third element in projecting confidence with spatial behavior is maintaining an open body position with jurors. Avoid sitting behind tables, standing behind a podium, or standing behind anything or anybody that blocks you from having direct body orientation with the jurors. The reason for this is that when you remove barriers it increases immediacy. Immediacy, as we will discuss, is a series of approach behaviors.[35] An immediate person is one who is warm, approaches another person, leans towards another, and uses gestures in talking with the individual. In all cases, you want to minimize the distance—both physical and psychological—between you and the jurors. When we minimize physical distance, there tends to be a natural correlation in minimizing psychological distance. If you do have to use a podium, make sure that you move to the side of the podium so that the podium itself does not block you. This allows for greater contact and bonding with the jurors.

The fourth factor in projecting confidence is to avoid invading the jurors' (or judge's) territory. You never want to lean on the juror's box, as that is their territory. That becomes their personal space in the courtroom. The same is true of the judge's territory. Be cautious when leaning on the judge's bench; this can be perceived as an invasion of his territory. When you have invaded an individual's territory he will usually engage in a series of non-immediate behaviors which may include: leaning away from the source of discomfort, folding his arms across his chest, and pulling his head up and back.

COMMENT: The most important thing to remember when projecting confidence and power by controlling space is that when you move or stand in the courtroom you must project that you are in control. One of the most significant ways of doing this is through the manipulation of space. Above all, always act as if you belong exactly where you are.

---

[35] *See infra* § 1.38.

§ 1.35 —Projecting confidence and power through nonverbal cues

There is a difference between portraying confidence in the courtroom and being confident. Sometimes our level of confidence is lower than at other times, but in the courtroom an attorney must portray confidence throughout every aspect of the trial. Jurors will be watching for signs of your confidence level. One thing we do know about jurors is that they will look for behaviors that indicate whether or not an attorney has received what he wanted from a judge's rulings. During the course of the trial, jurors become confused with the jargon that is used. Even when hearing objections raised by counsel and listening to the judge respond with "overruled" or "sustained," jurors often become confused with the meaning.

Over several trials we observed the marked difference with which experienced and inexperienced attorneys raised objections. We watched the inexperienced attorneys stand up, raise their objection, and the judge would respond "overruled." When the judge responded "overruled," the young attorney would slump his shoulders forward, avoid eye contact, and drop his head much like a puppy dog. Jurors watch these behaviors and make assumptions, one of which is that the inexperienced attorney did not receive the ruling that he wanted from the judge. We observed the same process take place with our more experienced trial attorneys. The experienced attorney would stand up, raise his objection, and the judge would say "overruled." But here we noticed a critical difference. The experienced attorney stayed standing a moment longer, turned and looked toward his fellow counsel, gave a slight nod of approval, sat back down with a slight smile on his face, put his shoulders back and his chest out, and looked straight ahead. At this point, we noticed all the jurors were watching the attorney in awe. Although they did not understand exactly what happened, they were convinced of one thing: whatever counsel wanted, counsel got. What we learned from this is that to be perceived as confident, you must "act as if" you are confident. You must "act as if" the case is going well, even if it is not. Many of the perceptions that jurors form are based on observed behaviors. Jurors use nonverbal information to explain what is really occurring during the trial. The "act as if" technique helps to portray confidence through these powerful behaviors.

The way you stand, the way you walk, and the way you move will be subject to stereotypes. One of the most common stereotypes in our culture is the stereotype of identifying "winners" and "losers." It is very easy for a person to describe how they perceive a winner. "Winners" are consistently described as having good posture, keeping their shoulders back, holding their head high, maintaining direct eye contact, breathing deeply and evenly, using expansive gestures as opposed to gestures that are held close to the body, taking large steps when walking, controlling space, and "acting as if" they know what they are doing even when they do not. Herein lies a very important concept for those people that we call winners: they "act as if" they know what they are doing. In addition, our perception of winners is that they have a lower voice tone. They control their voices by using pauses effectively. You never feel that they are rushing because of nervous energy and you never feel as though they are talking too slowly. Winners always appear to know what they are doing. They appear to have a directed focus and they know where they are headed. "Winners" can be identified by their avoidance of what we call powerless speech.[36] Powerless speech includes the use of hedging words such as "like," "kind of," "perhaps," "maybe," and so forth. Winners speak using definite word choices.

An individual who portrays the characteristics of a "winner" will, in fact, be viewed as a winner. When our expectations and perceptions correlate with actual behaviors, we ascribe additional personality traits to the person. Therefore, an individual who "acts as if" he is confident will not only be viewed as confident but will be seen as having many other positive characteristics which are consistent with "winning" behavior. The operating principle is that people use stereotypes to organize their perceptions; it's quick, easy, and it reduces uncertainty.[37]

By contrast, a "loser" image also arouses definite stereotypes. The loser is commonly described as having poor posture, avoiding eye contact, angling the head downward, moving slowly or haltingly, appearing to be in a confused state, not speaking fluently and using "ahs," "ands," and other filler phrases, the chest cavity is collapsed, and shoulders are rounded forward. Many inexperienced attorneys display these behaviors, which reveal a lack of confidence, power, and direction. In addition, an individual who displays these behaviors increases anxiety and uncer-

---

[36]*See generally infra* §§ 1.79–1.85 for a discussion of perceptions of voice characteristics and qualities; *see specifically* § 1.85 for a discussion of powerful and powerless speech.

[37]*See infra* § 1.54.

tainty in others. We become relaxed listeners only when we feel that the speaker is in control.

There are two specific benefits you will derive from portraying confidence in the courtroom by using the "act as if" method. The first benefit that you will receive is that jurors will perceive you to be doing well in the trial. A great deal of their perception has to do with how you act and behave. Avoid showing anger or resentment, being upset with opposing counsel, or rolling your eyes. By maintaining neutral behaviors you will be in the controlling position. The second benefit to be derived from the "act as if" technique is that if you act confident, the jurors will respond to you as if you are, in fact, confident. By receiving their positive responses you will begin to feel more confident. Psychologically you will find that "acting as if" will assist you in developing specific attitudes, behaviors, and feelings. This phenomenon is often referred to as a self-fulfulling prophecy. You project a certain attitude which is reinforced by the response you receive, and you begin to develop the actual feelings associated with that attitude.

§ 1.36 —Projecting confidence and power through vocal cues

The voice level, tone and quality is a predictable indicator of anxiety. The lower the voice tone, the more credible it will be perceived. Lack of confidence in the voice tone is usually indicated when the voice pitch becomes high and strained. If the voice pitch becomes too rapid or too slow it indicates a degree of nervousness.[38]

The most important thing to do when portraying confidence with your voice is to take several deep breaths and to breathe very slowly and deeply. This will help relax the vocal chords and will keep them from tightening up. Slow, even breathing also helps to regulate the pitch of the voice. If you breath deeply, you will find that your vocal tone will stay lower. When you breathe from the thoracic cavity (upper chest), the vocal tone will become higher. Women experience this problem more commonly than men. The common response for women under stress is for the vocal tone to go up, while the common response for men under stress is that the vocal tone gets lower and louder.

To help maintain a smooth speaking voice, avoid drinking any icy drinks before you speak. Cold drinks tend to constrict the vocal chords causing them to produce a harsher sounding voice tone. In addition, if

[38] *See infra* §§ 1.79–1.85 for a discussion of perceptions of voice characteristics and qualities.

your voice sounds harsh to you, this may cause you to start to feel nervous tension. Also avoid dairy products such as cheese, milk, butter, yogurt, and ice cream, at least two to four hours before trial. Dairy products produce mucus and reduce proper articulation. Singers and professional speakers have known this for a long time and the best of them do not eat dairy products at all. It takes a lot more energy to project your voice and articulate properly after consuming dairy products. Also to be avoided is extremely hot soup or coffee as this can actually damage the vocal cords.

COMMENT: Since vocal qualities are listened to very carefully by jurors, it is important to practice portraying confidence with your voice. A course in persuasive speaking will assist the serious trial attorney in increasing the effectiveness of his voice. In these courses, instructors will analyze the voice and offer guidelines on how to utilize the voice for greater impact.

---

§ 1.37 Using rewarding nonverbal behavior in the courtroom

People respond more favorably when they feel that another person likes them. One of the ways that liking is indicated, and probably the most predominant way, is through nonverbal behaviors.

During initial interactions, nonverbal information is quickly perceived as rewarding or unrewarding. Specifically, the degree to which an individual is open and available for interaction is reflected in the overall dimension of nonverbal behavior.[39] For example, increased facial and vocal activity (speech volume and rate) communicate responsiveness. The face is often used to indicate comprehension and noncomprehension when others are speaking.[40] Nonverbal behaviors which communicate responsiveness are therefore regarded as rewarding, while those behaviors which communicate unresponsiveness are considered unrewarding. Table 1–3, *infra* at 74, provides examples of behaviors which are typically

---

39 A. Mehrabian, Silent Messages (Wadsworth Publishing Co., 1971).

40 A.E. Scheflin, Body Language and Social Order: Communication as Behavioral Control (Prentice-Hall, 1972).

perceived to be rewarding and unrewarding. Rewarding behaviors tend to promote open communication and increase likability and approachability. As would be expected, the unrewarding behaviors tend to close off communication and decrease likability and approachability. A "single" behavior is not necessarily perceived as rewarding or unrewarding. It is the "cluster" of several congruent behaviors or repeated behavioral patterns that create a particular perception.

In the courtroom there are many opportunities to use rewarding and unrewarding behaviors. For example, leaning back in a chair away from the jurors, draping the arm on the back of a chair, crossing the arms over the chest, or frowning may be viewed as unrewarding behaviors. They have the tendency to distance others. Other distancing behaviors include avoiding eye contact with the jurors or having very short or brief eye contact with the jurors.

Another form of contact jurors notice is the relationship between the attorney and his client. In this relationship, it is very important to exhibit rewarding behaviors. For example, if counsel engages in a series of nonimmediate behaviors with a client, such as leaning away from the client, avoiding eye contact with the client, putting books, or some other objects between himself and the client, or avoiding any type of physical contact with the client, it would most likely be perceived as a distant relationship. Specifically, the perception would be that counsel does not have a high regard or liking for the client. The perception of the jurors is likely to be that the attorney does not consider the client to be worthy of his attention or respect. As a result, the jurors may presume that the relationship between counsel and client is not a good relationship. Further, they may assume that if counsel cannot find some redeeming characteristics in the client, they will have a difficult time in doing so. It is, therefore, important for counsel to engage in a series of rewarding behaviors with the client. For example, maintain good eye contact with the client, lean toward the client when appropriate, act as though the client is a special friend, smile, and nod your head in agreement with the client.

In the case of a client of the same sex, it is appropriate to touch the client. Touching him or her on the shoulder or a touch on the elbow show that you are not afraid to have contact and that this person is an important person. This demonstrates psychological closeness. On the other hand, counsel must be careful when dealing with a member of the opposite sex, particularly if he or she is attractive. In this instance, it would be more appropriate to avoid touch/contact behavior because it could be perceived as a more intimate relationship. The type of touch, the length of the contact, and the location of touch make a difference in perception.

One of the most common problems that occurs in the courtroom is that when attorneys receive what they view to be negative feedback from the jurors (such as scowling, leaning away from the attorney, or crossing arms) they engage in a reciprocal behavioral response of avoidance. The common reaction of anyone when they feel that they are receiving a negative response or are being rejected is to pull away and to avoid contact. Nobody wants to be rejected. What needs to happen in the courtroom is exactly the opposite. The moment the attorney starts to receive negative behavior of any kind from a juror, the attorney then needs to pay particular attention to using rewarding behaviors. For example, give that juror more eye contact, more attention, and talk directly to him whenever possible.

It is important to inject a note of caution here. Reading body movements, as well as eye and facial behaviors of jurors, is extremely difficult and often produces unreliable information. It is not unusual to see a juror cross his arms and we cannot, categorically, say that this means anything. They may be covering up a spot on their shirt, they may be cold, or it may simply be a comfortable position. It is not a fair assessment to say that the juror exhibiting these behaviors is displaying negative feedback or is in disagreement with counsel. Likewise, jurors who nod their heads, smile at you, and take notes (if allowed) when you are talking may not necessarily be indicating that they like you or your case. Trial consultants who work specifically in the area of nonverbal communication can assist in analyzing the classes of nonverbal behaviors which occur. For example, an expert in the area of nonverbal communication would analyze eye and facial behavior, body movement behavior, distance, and touch. These variables would be analyzed as a "cluster" of behaviors and the consultant would pay particular attention to congruent and incongruent patterns. Further, the expert would examine "baseline" behaviors which are the normal behaviors that a person exhibits when he is not under stress or experiencing situational anxiety. The expert would then look for deviations in these behavioral patterns. This description of the process of analyzing nonverbal behaviors indicates the more complicated nature of the analysis rather than the popular book approach of reading "body language." The superficial analysis of nonverbal cues in the courtroom is not only unreliable, but can be dangerous.

The behaviors that the attorney exhibits with the judge constitute another area that deserves attention. Many jurors will look to the judge as an indicator of how to act and react in the courtroom. Therefore, the relationship between counsel and judge becomes extremely critical. Those jurors who have a more authoritarian personality pattern will develop an even greater reliance on the judge for indicating how they should behave. Most jurors look to the judge as a signpost and, in so doing, actually observe the relationship between counsel and judge. It is important to keep that relationship smooth and professional. Treat the judge with respect and high regard. This relationship should also be extended to the official court family. Give them eye contact and exhibit rewarding facial behaviors such as smiling.

It is difficult to identify your own behaviors as rewarding or unrewarding during the course of a trial. One method of identification is to have a colleague sit in the courtroom and observe your behaviors. An observer can provide you with a more accurate assessment as to how you respond in voir dire, during your opening statement, and while conducting cross-examinations. This type of feedback is extremely helpful in identifying unconscious behaviors which may have an impact on the overall perception others have of you.

Table 1–3
Rewarding and Unrewarding Nonverbal Behaviors

Rewarding Nonverbal Behaviors	*Unrewarding Nonverbal Bahaviors*
Keeping hands loose and open	Closing hands into fists
Using the palm up when talking	Using the palm down when talking
Keeping the upper torso and loser torso open (no crossed arms or legs)	Crossing legs away from another person and/or crossing arms over the chest
Leaning toward the other person	Leaning away from another person
Keeping a socially acceptable distance (1½ to 3 feet)	Keeping a far distance (a distance greater than 3 feet)
Standing or sitting in front of objects so they do not serve as a barrier	Sitting or standing behind objects (e.g., desk, table, chair)
Unbuttoning suit jacket	Keeping suit jacket buttoned

Rewarding Nonverbal Behaviors	*Unrewarding Nonverbal Bahaviors*
Steady postures and absence of nervous movements	Nervous, abrupt movement patterns such as foot movement, moving back and forth in small circles, nervously tapping object on desk, constant change of postural orientation
Use of facial concentration and evaluation gestures (such as head nods, stroking the chin)	Nonexpressive facial cues (using a "poker" face)
Smiling when appropriate	No smiling; frowning
Standing at an appropriate distance when talking to a seated individual	Standing or towering over a seated individual, forcing them to "look up to you," and increasing their discomfort by invading their personal space
Using an object (e.g., pen, pipe, eyeglasses) to point or gesture rather than your finger	Pointing finger at individual
Nodding head to show recognition, understanding, or agreement	Offering no verbal or nonverbal signs of recognition, understanding, or agreement
Maintaining good eye contact	Staring (over eye contact) or avoiding eye contact (under eye contact)
Listening without interrupting	Interrupting (verbally and nonverbally by appearing overly anxious to talk)
Maintaining positive body orientation toward individual	Turning away from the person, looking back over your shoulder, turning your back
Focusing on the person visually and audibly when he is talking	Listening or talking to the person without looking at him
Using a firm handshake	Loosely clasping hand; clasping hand too hard; not shaking hands
Maintaining a level head tilt; tilting the head to the left or right	Tilting the head upward and back so that the eyes "look down" at the individual

§ 1.38 Projecting likability and approachability in the courtroom

Within a very short time period, people decide whom they like and whom they trust. This reinforces Communication Principle 3: "Perceptions are organized and structured within a brief period of time." Some people simply look more likable and approachable than others. The purpose of this section is to identify those behavioral cues which tend to promote likability.[41] This will lead us into a very important principle which will be introduced in Chapter 2, Principle 10: "People are more easily influenced by people they like." Likability is a factor that affects the total perceptions formed by jurors. Simply stated, people are more willing to support and agree with those people they like; people buy people.

There are several behavioral cues which tend to promote likability. One of the first cues that we can identify is the projection of greater immediacy. Immediacy, as we defined earlier, is considered an approach behavior.[42] People who are immediate tend, in all ways possible, to reduce the physical and psychological distance between themselves and another person by behavioral cues. One example of immediacy would be through the use of gestures. When a person gestures toward another person it is referred to as an "abbreviated approach behavior." It is a form of reaching out to touch the person without making actual physical contact. When using gestures to create greater immediacy and approachability, make sure your body orientation is openly facing the jurors. At the same time, keep the palms up when gesturing as opposed to speaking with the palms down. When gesturing with the palms down, a more formal environment is created. Palms held up tend to project the nonverbal message of "I want your help," and "I want to work with you."

COMMENT: You should experiment with this in a setting outside the courtroom and notice the difference in the response that you get just by reversing the position of the palms.

---

[41] *See supra* §§ 1.16–1.32.

[42] *See supra* § 1.34.

Another cue which is important to avoid if you want to increase likability and approachability is pointing your finger. If you point your finger at anyone, it becomes an intimidating cue. There is actually a physical response in the body. The adrenalin flow becomes much higher and people respond as if they are being attacked. Thus, be careful to drop this gesture when talking with the jurors. If you have to point, then soften the pointing gesture by using an object instead of your finger. For instance, you may point with a pencil or take your glasses off and point with the end of the glasses. On the other hand, pointing your finger is a very effective gesture when used to focus negative attention on opposing counsel and his client.

Greater immediacy can also be expressed through facial behavior.[43] Your facial behavior should be responsive when the jurors are responsive. For instance, if the jurors laugh at something that takes place in the courtroom it would be to your advantage to also laugh. This increases the perception of similarity between you and the jurors.

Another behavioral cue that tends to increase likability and approachability is a relaxed body posture. People who are perceived as having higher status tend to have a more relaxed body posture. This may be in direct contradiction to what most people think. Most people assume that if you have an upright posture, with shoulders back in a squared military style, you will have greater status. However, just the opposite is true. A person with an asymmetrical stance (i.e., more weight on one foot than another) evincing a relaxed style will be perceived as having greater status. This is also a higher immediacy cue. People are seen as more approachable and likable the more they become "real" in the eyes of another person. Relaxed body postures tend to do this.

To increase the perception of immediacy, as well as enhance likability and trustworthiness in the courtroom, you will want to maintain "soft" facial and eye behavior. This means being able to respond with your face as opposed to keeping it stoic throughout the trial. You should respond in accordance with the jurors' responses to events they find interesting. Use rewarding facial behaviors whenever possible, such as smiling or nodding in agreement to a comment you want to support.

A second behavioral cue used to increase likability is the voice. We know that credibility increases with a lower voice tone. Likability and trustworthiness tend to increase with a softer voice tone or a voice tone

---

[43] *Id*.

that is easy to listen to. Consider the voice tone of a good therapist: melodic, rhythmic, and almost hypnotic in cadence. The vocal tone should not be harsh. In a subsequent chapter we will discuss the process of anchoring vocal tones—using a different voice tone for different types of statements and emotional appeals.[44]

A third characteristic in projecting likability is smiling. Smiling is considered one of the most highly rewarding behaviors. When you smile genuinely, people tend to like you more. Rewarding behaviors will help to increase immediacy and warmth and, therefore, increase likability in the courtroom.

COMMENT: One belief that we have about smiling is that people who smile are less likely to reject us. Whenever possible, the trial attorney should respond by smiling appropriately to naturally occurring humor in the courtroom.

A final approach in increasing likability involves mental preparation and thinking of the jurors as friends. One common problem that frequently occurs in the courtroom is that jurors are often thought of as numbers on a diagram. It is to your benefit, however, to think of the jurors as friends from next door that you would talk to on a conversational level. When you think of jurors in this manner, you will find that the way you talk to them will be much different. Think of jurors in terms of their names. Learn their first and last names. When you think about them inside and *outside* the courtroom, think about Bob Jones or Mary Smith as opposed to thinking about a number. This will make a corresponding difference in the behaviors which you project.

§ 1.39 Handling objects in the courtroom for maximum effect

The way in which you touch an object will affect the perception that jurors will have of your regard for that object. For example, if you use a book as demonstrative evidence and you touch the book lightly and put it down as though it was an unimportant document, it will, in fact, be perceived as an unimportant document. There are times when you are displaying pieces of evidence or pointing to a chart when you want to

[44] *See infra* Chapter 2, *Persuasive Strategies in the Courtroom*. *See also infra* § 1.81.

convey the importance of the document. To do so, handle the object with care and touch it for a moment longer than usual. When you read important information from a book or document, handle the book carefully, hold it for a second longer than usual, and then place it slowly and easily on a table as though it is the most valuable object in the courtroom.

On the other hand, if you want to show disdain for information contained in a document, hold it away from your body and put it down as soon as possible—thus indicating a nonverbal display of dismissal. Treat the document as something you would throw in a wastebasket.

When you are using visuals and overheads, the same types of behaviors can be applied. When you are referring to your overheads, do so in a manner that indicates that they are important, valuable, and prepared especially for the jurors. When you refer to opposing counsel's overheads or graphs, however, refer to them with short and abrupt gestures, touching them or hitting them lightly. Nonverbally dismiss these graphs as inaccurate and unimportant. You can increase this perception by turning your back to the document or blocking the view. When referring to opposing counsel's document, use limited eye contact. Do not use his graphs as a focal point. If you do, then the jurors will too.

§ 1.40 Touching people in the courtroom

The United States is considered to be a noncontact culture. Therefore, touching others must be done with care and discrimination. The use of touch, however, usually indicates a positive relationship between two people. For example, touching your client can be perceived as a highly rewarding behavior providing there are no external considerations such as touching a very attractive client.[45] The most neutral places in which to touch your client are the shoulder area and the elbow. Research indicates that people respond to touch and that we have a greater liking for those people who touch us. It is a very old form of contact, and most people need touch as a form of reassurance and comfort. Touch is a display of immediacy and will generally be perceived as indicating psychological closeness between you and your client.

Touch in the courtroom can also be used in a controlling manner. For example, the elbow can be used as a form of leverage in controlling and directing the movement of another person. By holding the elbow of a

---

[45] *See supra* § 1.37.

person you can literally lead them where you would like them to go. When you take a person's elbow and steer, you will find that they will walk in the direction in which you are leading. This can also be done while shaking hands with a person. Grab their elbow at the same time and use it as a steering mechanism. Politicians have used this technique for a long time. When faced with a long line of people with whom to shake hands, they will shake hands, grab the elbow of the person, let go of their hand, and then use the elbow to steer the person to the side so they can move on to the next person. Remember, the person who initiates touch is the person perceived to have greater power.

Another form of touch is the use of abbreviated approach patterns as we discussed in § 1.38. Abbreviated approach behaviors include gestures which reach toward another person but do not actually make physical contact. Abbreviated forms of touch can be used effectively with jurors in creating a bond. These behaviors include gesturing toward the juror, keeping the palm up, and using wide gestures to include all the jurors when speaking. In every way possible, you must try to decrease the distance (both physically and psychologically) between you and the jurors.

§ 1.41 Avoiding negative image factors

In a recent anti-trust litigation case, a key witness for the defense had a habit of tilting his head upward so that it appeared that he was looking down his nose at the attorneys and jurors. Posttrial interviews with jurors revealed that they perceived the witness as arrogant and condescending. As a result, several jurors had little recall of what the witness had said. This selective perception created what is referred to as a "listening bias" and resulted in a loss of credibility for the witness. Behaviors influence listening patterns of jurors.[46] Words seldom overcome a negative nonverbal perception of an individual. The following sections will identify behavioral patterns which are frequently perceived as (1) ar-

---

[46] *See infra* §§ 1.42–1.45. *See also* Cone, *Techniques for Developing Juror Empathy*, 19 TRIAL 54 (July 1983): "We all can remember the client who laughed nervously at inappropriate times during the testimony, who smiled at the most ghastly times, or who showed no visible emotions when describing the horrible types of pain or intensities of mental distress fortunately spared most of us. . . . We can remember the jury's inadequate response in terms of its verdict on such occasions."

rogant,[47] (2) hostile,[48] (3) submissive or lacking in confidence,[49] or (4) aloof and insensitive.[50]

At this point, it is important to keep in mind that it does not make any difference whether these behaviors are intentional or not. The point that we are focusing on is perception. The entire thrust of this chapter is not on what nonverbal behaviors mean to the source, but how they will be perceived by the receiver. Herein lies a great difference. To coach a witness, use videotape feedback and analysis. Change behaviors, postures, and head angles so that your witness can actually see the differences in his behaviors. When you change the behaviors of a person, the psychological factors also tend to change. For example, if you can get a witness to sit in a relaxed posture and tilt their chin downward, they will have limited success in being able to project arrogance. Remember that emotions are directly related to the body position. Change the body position and you change the expression and the feeling of emotion.

§ 1.42 —Avoiding projection of arrogance

The projection of arrogance is exhibited through a number of behavioral factors. The first thing to keep in mind is that when arrogance is projected—whether by an expert witness, the attorney, or the client—there usually is a negative response. Most people do not like arrogant people. There are several behavioral cues that indicate arrogance: head tilt, speech patterns, and emphasis on key words.

The head tilt can be critical in projecting arrogance. A common head position that many people hold is to tilt their head upward so that the chin is up and the eyes are looking down. Although it may not be intended as arrogant, the look is often perceived as such. Jurors cannot determine intention so they deal with perception. If the head is pulled back and away from the shoulders with the chin held up, you have a perception of arrogance. You can change this perception by changing the head angle, tilting the chin down, and bringing the eye contact more level with the listener.

A second pattern that is often perceived as arrogant is speech that is drawn out. This means speech patterns that draw out or enunciate

[47] *See infra* § 1.42.

[48] *See infra* § 1.43.

[49] *See infra* § 1.44.

[50] *See infra* § 1.45.

words in a particular way to give them emphasis. For example, take the phrase, "I already answered that." Reread this phrase and now put the emphasis on the word "already." When you do that, you will hear a much more arrogant statement which says, "Didn't I already tell you that? Weren't you listening to me?"

Other factors which support the perception of arrogance are unrewarding nonverbal behaviors. For example, the witness sits back in his seat, crosses his arms, leans back, tilts the head up, and looks down his nose. These behaviors are often perceived as arrogance.

Videotaping your witnesses and client prior to trial is very effective in helping them identify undesirable behaviors. A good way to do this is to have your witness or client experiment holding his head in several different positions. This will give you a clear idea of how he looks and what kind of image he is projecting just by changing the tilt of the head.

§ 1.43 —Avoiding projection of anger and hostility

When people project anger, they engage in an attack or fight pattern. The initial response to any type of anger or threat is a "fight" or "flight" response. The first response results in sitting forward on the edge of a chair, clenching both fists and the jaw, and pushing the head forward. The second response is drawing back with no perception of pulling away. Both responses are negative responses that should be avoided. There are several things that you can do to help a witness avoid these patterns of anger. First, you can coach the witness to breathe evenly and deeply. When a person is experiencing any anger or form of hostility, he tends to breathe in short, shallow breaths in the upper thoracic cavity. As a result, his speech pattern tends to become quicker and more abrupt and he begins to feel angry. If you can get the person to sit back in his chair, breathe slower, relax the facial muscles, and unclench the hands, two things will happen. First, the individual will no longer give the projection of being angry; secondly, he will no longer be able to experience the feelings of anger that he was experiencing in the fight position. It is very difficult, if not impossible, to experience a particular emotion if you do not have the corresponding body state.

COMMENT: You can try this experiment on yourself. Sit in a position that you would be in when you are angry and upset and speak in the voice tone that accompanies this position. Then try to repeat the same verbal message, but sit in a position that is very relaxed with the shoulders slumped forward. Most people will find that they cannot achieve the same degree of anger in their voice. Your body posture effects not only the representation of information, but how you experience emotional states.

---

§ 1.44 —Avoiding projection of submissiveness and lack of confidence

Lack of confidence and submissiveness is portrayed through what may be called "shrinking" behaviors. "Shrinking" behaviors are behaviors that literally result in the person taking up less space. These behaviors include holding the hands on the lap in a clasped fashion, keeping the legs and feet together, and pulling the shoulders in and forward. In essence, a person engaging in "shrinking" behaviors will take up as little room as possible. For example, he will never put his hands on the back of a chair. On the other hand, he will tilt his head downward or to the right or left, and his eyes will be looking up toward another person. When people engage in such submissive behaviors, they automatically relinquish power.

There are times, however, when you may want a witness to behave submissively. When you want an individual to appear very humble or to create a victimized look, encourage the use of "shrinking" behaviors. People who engage in "shrinking" behaviors look as if they need to lean on another person or object. The general response to "shrinking" behaviors is to help the individual if you, in fact, like him. "Shrinking" behaviors are usually perceived as "endearing" types of behaviors and can generate an empathetic response.

§ 1.45 —Avoiding projection of insensitivity and aloofness

Behaviors of insensitivity and aloofness are very close to those behaviors that indicate arrogance. They generally are behaviors of dismissal. These behaviors include leaning away from the other person, avoiding extended eye contact, and dropping the voice at the end of sentences. When an individual projects behaviors of insensitivity and uncaring on the witness stand, he is often perceived as a cold person.

Another indication of insensitivity and aloofness is the dismissal of questions and people as unimportant by using the voice tone to project a condescending attitude. Witnesses and clients can be alerted to this type of behavior by tape recording them during a pretrial rehearsal. Let them listen to their voices and to how they sound when they respond to questions. In most cases, they will notice the negative perception they have created with their voice tone. If they do not, reverse roles and allow them to question you. Using their voice tone, respond to the questions and then play the tape back. A role reversal such as this will often jar any witness into "hearing himself for the first time."

§ 1.46 Coaching witnesses for trial

It is important to coach witnesses for the courtroom. Often it will be their first appearance in the courtroom and they will be experiencing a high degree of situational anxiety. In the previous sections, we have discussed several ways in which you can prepare a witness for the courtroom. First, you can use videotape analysis and allow the witness to see how he looks on videotape. Many people do not have a good perception of how they appear to others and have never seen themselves on videotape. Second, a mock jury can also be assembled to provide the witness with direct feedback on how he will be perceived in the courtroom. Additionally, the use of a social scientist can assist you not only in coaching the witness, but in identifying which specific behaviors have to be altered.

Another effective strategy for preparing witnesses for trial is to actually take them to the courtroom and allow them to sit both in the witness stand and the jury box. This helps to reduce situational anxiety and stress, and allows them to focus on how jurors will be watching them throughout the trial.

As we mentioned earlier, it is important to counsel witnesses with regard to both clothing and behavior. The most important message you want to get across to all witnesses is that everything they do in the courtroom—the words they speak, the movements they make, and the clothing they wear—will be perceived and interpreted without creating hostility or rejection. Everything will have an impact. It is most critical for them to understand how important their behaviors and attitudes are to winning the case. It is imperative that they comprehend that facts and evidence are only part of the final formula that is used by jurors in rendering their decision.

III. General Overview of Impression Formation Process

§ 1.47 Introduction to Communication Principles in impression formation

Research in the area of impression formation is extensive. For the purpose of this chapter we have identified six major principles which provide the groundwork for understanding how impressions are formed in the courtroom. The principles are:

Principle 1: Communication is based on perception

Principle 2: People actively try to make sense out of their environment

Principle 3: Perceptions are organized and structured within a brief period of time

Principle 4: People use stereotypes to organize their perceptions

Principle 5: People tend to see others as similar to themselves

Principle 6: People attempt to maintain their original perception regardless of contradictory information

By understanding these six principles, attorneys can make important decisions regarding the image they want their clients, witnesses, and themselves to present in the courtroom. More importantly, these concepts provide the basis for understanding how people will be perceived, and they suggest ways in which these perceptions may be altered.

The six principles of impression formation are fundamental and basic to the trial lawyer. A thorough understanding of these principles will provide the basis for counsel to approach his case with a fuller awareness of the elements that contribute to the final decision-making process of judges and jurors.

§ 1.48 Impression formation in the courtroom

One of the most significant areas of concern for attorneys is the period during which impressions are first formed. Impressions of other people, regardless of their validity, establish the basis for further communication. It is not uncommon to hear a comment such as "He looks like a law student," or "She looks like a successful attorney." Comments such as these tell us that people form their impressions based on limited information. Researchers ask the question: "What perceptual information, such as appearance, voice, or behaviors, enter into these stereotypic appraisals?"

More specific questions can be asked with regard to impression formation in the courtroom. For example, "How does the physical attractiveness or unattractiveness of a litigant affect the outcome of a trial?" "Does the prosecution have a 'homecourt' and territorial advantage?" "Can we identify deception based on nonverbal behavior patterns?" "How can the credibility of a witness be established?" "Does seating arrangement affect jurors' perceptions of counsel?" The answers to these questions will affect both the attorney's preparation for trial and, more importantly, the final outcome of the case.

Communication is based on perception. This is our first and most fundamental principle. We live in a society where people are bombarded with so much information each day that they have learned to use shortcut techniques to make decisions. One of these shortcut techniques is to judge people based on initial perceptions of their appearance, background, and behavior. Once we have made these initial decisions about an individual, all further communication is filtered through this arrived-at perception. If we decide that a person "looks like a law student," then we will proceed to treat that perception as if it were an actual fact. We will respond to the individual as though he actually was in law school; that is, we might assume that he is an intellectually capable, academically motivated, and career-oriented person. It makes little difference whether the initial perception is correct. People treat the perception as accurate and make decisions from this base of information.

The importance of understanding impression formation in the courtroom is well illustrated by the much publicized Pulitzer divorce trial, where Judge Harper claimed that the demands of Roxanne Pulitzer, thirty-one, on her husband, Peter Pulitzer, fifty-two, were exorbitant. The judge wrote that he felt sorry for Peter Pulitzer when he saw "the embarrassment, the painful hurt, and the frustrating concern exuding from his doleful eyes and aging face." At the same time he wrote, "the wife nonchalantly sat at the table doodling on a note pad as though unconcerned." Later in the trial the judge added that he was "somewhat relieved when the wife finally broke into tears indicating that she was, after all, capable of human emotion and concern."[51]

Judge Harper's observations offer an example of the type of nonverbal information which affects the decisions of judges and jurors alike. Accurate or inaccurate, all observations and facts are subject to a personal selection process by which an individual (1) selects those specific items to which he will attend and (2) attaches significance to those items based on his own experiences.

What would have happened during the course of the trial if Peter Pulitzer displayed "anger through snapping and fiery eyes" rather than "doleful eyes with an aging face"? Would the outcome have been different if Roxanne either had cried earlier in the trial, appearing submissive and victimized, or had listened intently rather than "doodling on her note pad?" Perhaps so! Research indicates that all factors, characteristics, and behaviors of the attorney, client, and witnesses can have a great influence on the ultimate outcome of a trial. Words, stories, testimony, charts, graphs, and expert witnesses are only part of the final formula by which judges and jurors render their decisions.

Again, communication is based on perception. Any element that enters the perceptual field via sight, sound, or movement has a potential impact on the outcome of a trial. Al Cone, past President of the Association of Trial Lawyers of America, wrote in *Trial* magazine:

> "One factor that can create a wide range in the verdict for the same injury in the same type of accident is the jury's perception of the nature and characteristics of the plaintiff.
>
> "Please note the word 'perception' above. Often the plaintiff may be a totally admirable person, fully worthy of the warmest feelings of admiration and approval of the jury, but because of a failure of presentation of his or her personality, the jury may not warm up to or emphathize with the plaintiff, and therein lies a tale of woe for concerned plaintiff's counsel."[52]

§ 1.49 —The process of perception

The process of perception incorporates verbal, vocal and nonverbal variables in reaching a perceptual judgment.[53] We are conscious of other

[51] *See* TIME, January 10, 1983, at 24.

[52] Cone, *Techniques for Developing Juror Empathy*, 19 TRIAL 54 (July 1983).

[53] Vocal communication focuses on "how" something is said rather than "what" is said. Vocal variables include voice tone, pitch, inflection, intonation, and rate of speech.

people and events in the world around us through our senses of sight, sound, smell, touch and taste. We assemble information about other people by observing physical appearance, indications of social role and class, actions, voice, gestures, and any other cues which may be meaningful to us. From these assorted cues an integrated, unified and fairly detailed "picture" of the other person is formed. We feel we know what he is like—what his attitudes, needs, and feelings probably are. From this "picture," we predict what our future interactive behaviors with that person will be.

The process of "person" perception involves the three phases of collecting, sorting and cataloging information. We (1) select those people to whom we plan to pay attention; (2) organize and structure the perceptual cues we receive, imposing consistency and stability; and (3) attach meaning to our perceptions.

Human perception is a selective and constructive decision-making process. There is little question that jurors are active rather than passive observers in the courtroom. In a world full of competing stimuli, jurors will select information based upon their own needs, desires, sets, and past experiences. Communication researchers Berger and Calabrese describe the process this way:

> When we receive a stimulus from outside ourselves, internal stimuli are mobilized. This is how our past experiences, attitudes, and beliefs become involved in the perceptual act. These internal stimuli give us an expectancy set, the learned patterns of meaning that we already hold. These enable us to organize our perceptions into meaning quickly.[54]

When the object of our selective perception is another person, we are generally motivated to observe him carefully because we feel we must somehow be able to make sense out of him. This motivation is based on a need to (1) reduce the uncertainty about that person, (2) predict his actions, and (3) adapt our own behavior accordingly. We also want to determine what he, in turn, expects of us.

There are several identifiable stages in the area of "person" perception.

The nonverbal message system includes body movements, postural orientation, eye and facial behavior, touch, seating arrangements, personal appearance, and body structures and types.

[54] Berger & Calabrese, *Some Explanations in Initial Interactions and Beyond: Toward A Developmental Theory of Interpersonal Communication*, 1 HUM. COM. RESEARCH 100 (1975).

Stage one involves the organization and structure of the perceptual cues. During this stage, behavior is organized into meaningful categories. Stage two involves identifying the person as a causal agent, that is, as someone who is responsible for his actions. During this stage, we decide whether or not a particular observed behavior is more than likely intentional. When a person performs a certain behavior or speaks in a certain manner intentionally, we attach meaning to that conduct and form impressions about the type of individual with whom we are dealing. Any deviant action is even more meaningful to us because it violates socially expected norms of appropriate conduct. More importantly, we make the assumption that these deviant behaviors are intentional; that is, the person is deliberately performing these behaviors to elicit a specific response or to make a statement about himself.

The third stage of "person" perception involves seeing other people as similar to ourselves. We project our own thoughts and feelings onto others. Further, we assume we can empathize with certain people because we have felt that way ourselves. We also feel we can increase the effectiveness of our predictions of the other person's behavior since we see this person as similar to ourselves and we know what our own responses would be to a given situation. This supports Communication Principle 5: People tend to see others as similar to themselves.[55]

We have a tendency to attempt to impose consistency on our perceptual judgments. We prefer to work from a more stable data base so that the likelihood of accuracy of our predictions about people will be increased. As a result, personal generalizations and stereotypes are developed which lead us to attach great importance to initial observations. As Buckhout states in *Scientific American*:

> Perception and memory are decision-making processes affected by the totality of a person's abilities, background, attitudes, motives and beliefs, by the environment and by the way his recollection is eventually tested. The observer is an active rather than a passive perceiver and recorder; he reaches conclusions on what he has seen by evaluating fragments of information and reconstructing them. He is motivated by a desire to be accurate as he imposes meaning on the overabundance of information that impinges on his senses, but also by a desire to live up to the expectations of other people and to stay in their good graces. The eye, the ear and other sense organs

---

[55] *See infra* § 1.55 for a further discussion of perceived similarity.

are therefore social organs as well as physical ones.[56]

How do jurors use the perceptual process? Consider the following. After a two-week trial, the plaintiff who sustained a back injury received a small monetary award. The attorneys for both the plaintiff and defendant were surprised by the small amount of money awarded to the woman. Posttrial jury interviews revealed that one of the more influential jurors pointed out to the other jurors that the plaintiff had been wearing open-toed shoes. Further, the juror observed, the color of the plaintiff's toenails changed three times during the course of the two week trial. If her back was in such bad shape, how was she able to bend over to paint her toenails?, the juror asked. The jurors ultimately answered that question in rendering their decision.

Whether or not the logic makes sense, the perceptions do. The jurors were operating as "detectives," assimilating important visual information to add to the evidence. It is certainly a powerful reminder that we cannot control the meaning that is attached to a particular stimulus, such as painted toenails. When the meaning cannot be controlled, the stimulus should be eliminated or minimized.

§ 1.50 —What motivates jurors to form impressions

One of the major motivating factors for jurors to form impressions quickly is described in Principle 2: "People actively try to make sense out of their environment." We select, organize, and interpret stimulus cues such as environmental surroundings, colors, behaviors, and personal appearance. We do this to ensure that we have three basic factors operating in our lives: structure, stability, and meaning. Nowhere is this more evident than in the courtroom. In an alien and usually unfamiliar environment, jurors attempt to organize the stimuli to (1) create a day-to-day structure, (2) have reasonable stability, and (3) give meaning to what they are hearing and seeing during the trial.

For example, in one case an attorney mentioned that his daughter had given him a ring which only fit on his "pinky" finger. He had worn this ring for a while, but was concerned whether it was appropriate to wear it during trial. The answer to this question can be determined by reviewing the first two principles. First, "communication is based on perception." We know immediately that a ring of any kind on any finger will enter into the perceptual field of most people. The second principle, "people

---

[56] Buckhout, *Eyewitness Testimony*, 231 Sci. Am. 24 (1974).

actively try to make sense out of their environment" suggests that rings along with other personal appearance factors will be "perceived" and interpreted."[57]

Rings offer symbolic information in our culture. A ring worn on the ring finger of the left hand usually indicates some relationship attachment such as engagement or marriage. Jurors actively look at attorneys and their clients to determine marital status, and then apply their perceptions and beliefs about single and married people. Married people are viewed much more favorably than single people. For instance, people who are married tend to be perceived as solid, stable, community-oriented, responsible, and conservative. Single people, by contrast, are often seen as unstable, spenders, unpredictable, not as responsible, more liberal, and less serious.

A "pinky" ring does not have the single perception that a wedding ring has. The individual wearing the pinky ring could be perceived in several different ways. He might be viewed as liberal, homosexual, trendy, or normal. These are only a few of the possible perceptions. The important consideration is that the perceptions of a "pinky" ring worn by a male attorney cannot be controlled. Factors over which you have limited perceptual control should be eliminated or minimized. Rings other than engagement, wedding, or class rings open the doors to speculation about the individual wearing them. Therefore, it is advisable to avoid wearing non-traditional rings in the courtroom.[58]

Jurors are motivated to form impressions in order to make sense out of their environment. To do this jurors engage in two tasks:

Task 1: Jurors simplify the information they gather.

Task 2: Jurors make assumptions beyond the actual data given in order to (a) predict future events, and (b) minimize surprise.

Human perception is a selective and constructive decision-making process. Any behavior, event, or environmental surrounding that is observed in the courtroom has the potential of influencing the decision-making process.

---

[57] *See supra* §§ 1.16–1.32 for a further discussion of personal appearance factors.

[58] *See supra* § 1.20.

§ 1.51 —The time period in which impressions are formed

Impressions are formed within four to six minutes in a face to face encounter. Televised and video perception formation ranges between thirty to forty-five seconds, while perceptions of a telephone interactant are formed in less than thirty seconds. This introduces Communication Principle 3: "Perceptions are organized and structured within a brief period of time."

The process of impression formation in the courtroom occurs over four periods or stages: (1) the first visual observation of the courtroom, client, and counsel; (2) voir dire; (3) opening statement; and (4) testimony of the first witness. During the first visual observation of the courtroom surroundings the perception is formed predictably very quickly—within four to six minutes. This time period is very similar to the perceptions formed in any social setting.

According to two communication researchers, four minutes is the average time during which strangers in a social setting interact before they decide to part or continue their encounter. In other words, the four-minute barrier is the minimum break-away point—the socially acceptable period that allows you to move on to another conversational partner.[59]

The first stage of impression formation in the courtroom relies primarily on nonverbal cues: the personal appearance of the attorney and client, eye contact, facial expressions, movements, seating positions, smiling behavior, touch, and breathing patterns.

The second impression stage occurs during voir dire. Although the explicit purpose of voir dire may be to determine which prospective jurors to eliminate for cause or based on peremptory challenges, the implicit purpose is equally as important. During voir dire, the attorney must establish rapport with the jury and exhibit important characteristics such as honesty and objectivity. The foundation for the trial is built on this "perceived" information about counsel and/or witnesses. Even in federal court where the attorney may not be actively involved in questioning potential jurors, the jurors are still observing and collecting important information about counsel.

Jurors see themselves as "detectives in the courtroom." They identify their role as a modern Sherlock Holmes, in which their task is to uncover

---

[59] L. ZUNIN & N. ZUNIN, CONTACT: THE FIRST FOUR MINUTES (Ballantine Books, 1972).

information by observation and inference. Sherlock Holmes, in fact, said it best: "There is great power in the observation of trifles." The critical time for an attorney to attend to the trifles in a trial is during the first four stages of impression formation. Although jurors may not have the remarkable powers of observation displayed by Sherlock Holmes, they do watch carefully.

During the opening statement and the testimony of the first witness, jurors continue to collect information based on the content of what they hear, the voice qualities, and the nonverbal behaviors of the individual.

It is important to provide specific guidelines for your client and witnesses about their personal appearance in the courtroom. Not all jurors will notice details about clothing, but it only takes one juror to make an observation which is later shared with others, to impact on the decision-making process.[60]

COMMENT: Principle 3 states that "perceptions are organized and structured within a brief period of time." It is important to remember that the most critical stages of impression formation occur in the courtroom from the first visual contact through the testimony of the first witness.

---

§ 1.52 —The primacy effect

In forming initial impressions of others, we tend to place the greatest emphasis on information we receive first about a person. The primacy effect, as this is called, supports our third communication principle: "Perceptions are organized and structured within a brief period of time." This "order effect" has been demonstrated in classic experiments by Solomon Asch[61] and A.S. Luchins.[62] Asch presented subjects with lists of traits about people and then asked the subjects to write a full impression of the person. He discovered that unified impressions of people are

---

[60] *See supra* §§ 1.16–1.32.

[61] Asch, *Forming Impression of Personality*, 41 J. Abnormal & Soc. Psychology 258–290 (1946).

[62] Luchins, *Primacy-Recency in Impression Formation* in 1 The Order of Presentation in Persuasion 33–61 (Yale University Press, C. Hovland et al., eds. 1957).

formed based purely on scanty information. In fact, the subjects went beyond the adjectives given and expanded upon what they thought the person was probably like. Asch also found that traits presented earlier tended to be more important in the formation of the overall impression. For example, if a person was described as "intelligent, industrious, impulsive, critical, stubborn, and envious," he was perceived more positively than a person who was described as "envious, stubborn, critical, impulsive, industrious, and intelligent."[63] The simple relocation of the word "intelligent" from the first position to the last position significantly altered the perception.

Luchins, in his experiment on the primacy-recency effect in impression formation, presented subjects with two paragraphs about "a boy named Jim."[64] He wanted to determine whether the order in which the paragraphs were read would influence the subject's perception of Jim's personality. Luchins found that the order in which the paragraphs were read did, in fact, affect perceptions of the personality sketch written about Jim. The experimental findings confirmed that the majority of subjects who read the paragraphs in Experiment 1 perceived Jim as an introvert, while those who read the paragraphs in reverse order in Experiment 2 viewed Jim as an extrovert. Luchins confirmed the existence of a primacy effect: the information presented first is most decisive.

Luchins then went one step further to determine whether the primacy effect always exists. He found that if people were warned not to make snap judgments before reading the paragraphs or if they were given simple arithmetic problems to do before reading the second paragraph, the primacy effect was reversed or eliminated completely.[65] It is important to keep in mind, however, that a primacy effect often prevails and that the information presented first is very decisive. These findings serve to underscore the importance of the first impression from the initial client interview all the way to the courtroom.

When applying the primacy principle to the courtroom it is not surprising to find that jurors have a much better recall of the beginning and the ending of trials. The primacy/recency controversy continues over which has greater impact—the information presented first or the information presented most recently. In the courtroom, both the beginning

---

[63] *See* Asch, *supra* note 61.

[64] *See infra* § 1.87.

[65] Discussed in S.L. Tubbs & S. Moss, Interpersonal Communication 80–82 (Random House, 1978).

and the ending of a trial are critical. Both stages have a significant impact on how the jurors will perceive stimuli and retain information. Posttrial research reveals that jurors retain little information presented during the middle of the trial. Even more emphasis can be placed on the influence of the primacy effect because the first part of the trial is novel for jurors. At this point they are stimulated and alert to new input and information.

Once a first impression is formed, jurors tend to assimilate new information on the basis of the judgments they have already made. Jurors feel a need to remain consistent in their perceptions, therefore, negative information concerning a positive first impression will most likely be discounted in some way by the perceiver. This is not to say that more recent information does not have an effect on jurors' perceptions but clearly the first impression, the effect of primacy, is a very strong force in impression formation. Considering the power of first impressions in shaping our opinions about others, an attorney who wishes to make a particular impression should attempt to do so from the beginning of his contact with an individual.

§ 1.53 —Shortcut approaches to decision-making used by jurors

Our second and third communication principles explain in part the shortcut approaches used in decision-making today. The need to reduce uncertainty, increase predictability, and organize perceptions in a short period of time has resulted in a new form of decision-making. Rather than a slow, analytical approach where all pieces of evidence are thoroughly weighed and considered, single pieces of evidence are being used for quicker decisions.

As mentioned previously, first impressions are formed by jurors during the first few days of the trial. After that point, little new information is used to alter the initial perceptions. Jurors actively engage in ways in which to reduce their experience of "situational anxiety" (a tension created by unfamiliar surroundings) by quickly making initial decisions. First, jurors become visually familiar with their surroundings: where they are seated, where the judge is seated, the layout of the courtroom, and the courtroom procedures. Then they become familiar with the "people" in the environment: what they look like, how they act, what they sound like, who they remind them of, and so forth. The following are examples of some of the conscious and unconscious questions which jurors ask and answer for themselves in order to reduce uncertainty about an attorney: Is the attorney married? Does he have children? How old is he? Is he trustworthy? Is he interesting? Is he honest? Is he likable? Is he someone I could approach? Could I talk to him on a one-to-one basis? Is he arrogant? Is he experienced? What type of personal life does he have? Is he intelligent? Is he rich? What types of books does he read? What type of car does he drive? What hobbies does he have?

We live in a society that is easily the most complex and rapidly changing social and physical environment that has ever existed. It is easy to understand why "certainty" and "predictability" are highly valued items. Dr. Robert Cialdini, the author of *Influence: How and Why People Agree to Things*, explains why shortcut decision methods are being used more today than ever before.

> Because of remarkable technological advances, information is burgeoning, choices and alternatives are expanding, knowledge is exploding. In many areas of science, existing knowledge is estimated to double every five to ten years—and this accumulation is likely to continue as 90 percent of all scientists who have ever lived are alive and working today. Closer to home, things are changing quickly, too. The evidence shows that we have more social contacts but shorter personal relationships; we uproot and move more frequently to residences that are built and torn down faster than ever; we travel more frequently and rapidly but stay for less time; in stores, shops, and showrooms we are confronted with an array of diverse options among styles and products that were nonexistent last year and may well be so again next year. Novelty, turnover, and acceleration are the modern bywords of civilized existence.
>
> In this avalanche of change and choice, people have had to adjust. One of the most fundamental adjustments has come in the way they make many of their decisions. People no longer have the time, energy, nor capacity for analyzing carefully all the pros and cons of the majority of decisions that face them. There is too much information, too much stimulation, too many alternatives to deal with. Instead, they must often revert to a simpler, shortcut approach.[66]

This shortcut approach to decision making and the increasing need of people to decrease uncertainty has been capitalized on by many institutions in our society. For example, regardless of where you are, when you

---

[66] Cialdini, *Instant Influence: Twenty-first Century Selling,* MALANDRO COMMUNIQUE NEWSLETTER (March 1984).

walk into a McDonald's you know you can order a Big Mac with "special sauce, lettuce, cheese, pickles, onions, on a sesame seed bun." And not surprisingly, it tastes just like the Big Mac you get at the McDonald's in your local neighborhood. McDonald's is counting on this—no surprises, no changes, no substitutions. By maintaining predictability, McDonald's is assured of increasing the comfort level of most people. In our fast-moving and stressful environment, people want less change, not more. People want to reduce uncertainty and increase predictability. It works—in advertising with the public, in marketing restaurant and hotel chains, and in the courtroom with jurors.

COMMENT: Thus, the shortcut methods used in decision-making have two common characteristics: (1) they rely on single pieces of evidence as indicators of a trend and (2) they utilize stereotypes and generalizations as a means of organizing the data. This introduces Communication Principle 4: "People use stereotypes to organize their perceptions."

§ 1.54 —The use of stereotypes and personal generalizations

The word "stereotype" was originally a printer's term for the plate that printed the same image over and over again. In our perception of people, we all have a need to reduce uncertainty and to impose order and stability on the perceptual cues we receive from myriad events and people with whom we come in contact. It is virtually impossible to handle the sheer number and complexity of perceptual cues bombarding us at any given time. As a result, people use shortcut methods to try and make sense out of the world around them. Stereotyping is a method that allows people to do just that.

Research findings in nonverbal communication indicate that people can draw very accurate conclusions about another person with regard to demographic characteristics, such as age, sex, race, and socioeconomic status as well as some personality variables. We cannot say categorically, however, that *all* stereotypes are accurate. It is important to keep in mind that although some stereotypes may be quite valid, stereotypic judgments can have damaging effects on further communication. The following story of an elderly club member who was attending a distinguished public dinner in London illustrates how judging another person based on stereotypes can result in an embarrassing and somewhat humorous social situation.

> "[He] was disconcerted to find himself seated next to a silent Chinese. Wanting to be courteous, however, he leaned toward him and asked tentatively, 'Likee Soupee?' The Chinese looked at him briefly, nodded, but said nothing and the conversation lapsed. However, it appeared that the Chinese was a foreign guest of some note, for as coffee was served, he was called upon to say a few words. He rose, bowed and made a fifteen-minute speech in impeccable English about the sociological significance of the European Common Market. Amid polite applause, he then sat down, turned to his abashed English neighbor, and after the briefest of pauses, asked softly, 'Likee Speechee?' "[67]

People tend to organize and sort data through the use of stereotypes and personal generalizations which have formed over time from personal experiences. These stereotypes are sometimes justified and sometimes not. Generalized perceptions based upon noninterpersonal stimuli also play a role in preconceptions and impressions of others. Personal interaction with one person, for example, often has an impact on the impression of another person when the second person is perceived to be similar to the first. In other words, we frequently determine what a person from the desert Southwest is like based upon generalizations we have drawn from experiences with other residents of the Southwest. Personal generalization is a necessary process because it saves time in reaching a meaningful picture of the other person, especially if he is perceived to be similar to others we have already encountered. Stereotyping is a necessary "shortcut" method used by people to organize an abundance and overflow of information.

Consider the hypothetical case involving a defendant from the Arab community. Without knowing any other facts, we know that a major issue will be the perception of the defendant and stereotypes which extend to the general class of Arab people. The location of the trial and the exposure of the people in the community to Arabs will account for many preconceived notions. A community attitude survey should be conducted. If the survey reveals that the community members believe Arabs to be rich, manipulative, and basically untrustworthy, several decisions

---

[67] D. Bloodworth, The Chinese Looking Glass (Farrar, Straus & Giroux, 1976).

about the case will hinge on this information. The decisions may involve considering a change of venue, establishing a low profile image for the defendant, and/or acknowledging existing stereotypes and presenting the defendant as an exception (e.g., someone outside the "general" class of Arabs).

COMMENT: Given a case which involves a major and unknown perceptual judgment about the defendant or plaintiff, it is valuable to conduct a community attitude survey. A well-designed and executed survey can identify preexisting attitudes, biases, and beliefs about a person or class of people.

As stated previously, a stereotype is a perceptual shortcut, a fixed impression of an individual based upon what we know about the groups to which we infer he belongs.[68] These groups may be more like us (Catholic vs. Protestant) or less like us (hippie vs. retired). We constantly make judgments about people based upon what we believe to be true about their reference group. Stereotyping, although generally considered a negative process, is a fact which attorneys cannot afford to ignore. Stereotypes extend to social groups (such as the perceptions of a member of the Kiwanis Club or of the Junior League), ethnic groups (e.g., a native American or a black), and physical cues (we know how a successful person dresses; a blonde woman who giggles is perceived to be of below average intelligence). We also find that information about a person's attitudes influences our perceptions of that person. If we know a woman supported the Equal Rights Amendment, we infer she must therefore hold certain other attitudes.

Jurors not only use stereotypes in the courtroom, they rely on them. The complexity and amount of information presented necessitates a shortcut method for collecting and organizing data. Stereotypes offer this method. This is both good and bad news for trial attorneys. The bad news is that clients, witnesses, and even counsel will be subject to the detective-like scrutiny of jurors. The good news is that you can identify

[68] S.L. TUBBS & S. MOSS, INTERPERSONAL COMMUNICATION 75 (Random House, 2d ed. 1981).

and create the image you want to present using the research on stereotyped perceptions. For instance, if you want to increase the perception of credibility of an expert witness you can do so by utilizing the stereotype of how people expect experts and authorities to look. This includes wearing conservative glasses, a white shirt and tie, short hair, a gray or navy suit, limited jewelry (e.g., a watch and a wedding ring). In Part II of this chapter, we explored specific communication techniques for presenting a desired image in the courtroom.

§ 1.55 —How jurors look for similarities

Communication Principle 5 introduces the concept that "People tend to see others as similar to themselves." This process is referred to as "perceived homophyly" or perceiving the sameness in others. There is a built-in comfort level when we perceive another person to be like ourselves. This relates back to our principle on uncertainty reduction and the attempt to make sense out of our environment. If we notice that other people have similar traits and attributes, then we have a better idea about how we would expect them to behave and think.

The first determination people make about another person is whether they are alike in some way. We focus on similarities first, rather than on differences. In jury selection, for example, we are apt to look for a prospective juror in the same age group as our client in an attempt to match up certain similarities.

An effective approach during trial is to maximize the perception of similarities between jurors and clients, jurors and witnesses, and jurors and counsel through the use of clothing, word choice and vocabulary, and movement behaviors. This approach is referred to as "pacing"—a communication technique for matching the behaviors of another person to increase the perception of similarity and, hence, rapport. The natural instinct is to look for similarities between oneself and another person. By matching the movements of another person, dressing in a similar manner, or talking with the same rhythmic pattern of speech, the perception of similarity will be increased. Specific communication techniques for pacing jurors, judges, witnesses, and opposing counsel will be discussed in a later chapter.[69]

---

[69] *See infra* Chapter 2, *Persuasive Strategies in the Courtroom*, discussing Communication Principle 9, "People are more easily influenced by others they perceive as similar to themselves"—where the relationship between similarities and persuasion will become more evident.

§ 1.56 —Maintenance of original perceptions

Once an initial perception is formed, will additional information alter this perception? Principle 6 answers this question: "People attempt to maintain their original perceptions regardless of contradictory information." This was demonstrated by Haire and Grunes in their study of the perceptions of a hypothetical working man.[70] For the first group of subjects the working man was described as someone who: "works in a factory, reads the newspaper, goes to movies, average height, cracks jokes, strong, and active." For the second group he was described with the same adjectives, but with the addition of the word "intelligent." After reading the descriptive lists, the subjects were asked to write a paragraph describing the type of person they perceived this working man to be. The second group experienced more difficulty in writing their paragraphs because of the inclusion of the word "intelligent." For many of these subjects, intelligence was not consistent with their stereotype of a factory worker. However, their original perceptions remained unchanged. Rather than altering the original perception they used one of the following methods to deal with the contradictory information:

1. Denial of the existence of the disturbing element:

   > "He is intelligent, but not too much so, since he works in a factory."

2. Placing the disturbing element in a context so as to render it harmless to the original stereotype:

   > "He is intelligent, but doesn't possess the initiative to rise above his group."

3. Recognizing the incongruity, but maintaining the original stereotype anyway:

   > "The traits seem to be conflicting. . .most factory workers I have heard about aren't too intelligent."[71]

The inability to perceive areas of differences among people and the encouragement of self-fulfilling myths about other people are two undesirable effects of stereotyping.[72] When we only see people in the context

---

[70] Haire & Grunes, *Personal Defenses: Process Protecting and Original Perception of Another Personality*, 3 HUM. REL. 403–412 (1950).

[71] *Id.*

[72] B. PATTON & K. GIFFIN (eds.), INTERPERSONAL COMMUNICATION IN ACTION 117–119 (Harper & Row, 3d ed. 1981). *See also supra* § 1.54, *The use of stereotypes and personal generalizations*.

of the groups to which we infer they belong, we do not allow for differences among people. Clearly, the occupation "factory worker" is insufficient to draw any conclusion as to the individual's intelligence. We are forced into categorical thinking of "allness," and we miss the continuum of behaviors and attitudes that truly represent the differences among people. Unless we consciously maintain open minds, we are susceptible to thinking of people in an either/or posture. Either he is dependable or undependable, liberal or conservative. The many differences that lie between the two opposites are missed.[73]

This dichotomized approach also tends to give rise to a phenomenon known as the "halo effect." If we decide a particular stereotype is a good one, then we tend to portray other behaviors of our stereotyped person as good also. What we are in effect doing is oversimplifying our perceptions.[74] A juror, for example, might decide that a defendant is a "good person" because the defendant testified that he attended church regularly. The perceptual stereotype of a "good person" would then be extended by the juror to the behaviors of the defendant in other areas. The juror might even go so far as to ask, "How could a good person who attends church regularly commit murder?" The strength of the stereotype will influence the answer to this and other questions.

Stereotyping also causes us to participate in self-fulfilling myths about others. "If we perceive a person as untrustworthy and treat him/her as such, we tend to make the person less trustworthy."[75] Thereafter, our perception of the lack of trustworthiness is reinforced resulting in our treating the individual as even less worthy of trust. Although some stereotypes have a basis in fact, it is important to remember that stereotypes are overgeneralizations, shortcut perceptual processes, and their accuracy must be evaluated in light of the specific individual in question.

As our fourth communication principle states: "People use stereotypes to organize their perceptions." Stereotyping in the courtroom is common, and we cannot overemphasize that attorneys need to ask and answer several pretrial questions: (1) How will the jurors perceive the client? (2) How will the jurors perceive the witness? and (3) How will the jurors perceive the attorney? These were the three primary questions that had to be raised in a will contest case. From a legal standpoint, the case was simple. From a human one, it was more complicated. It involved a

---

[73] *Id*. at 118.

[74] *Id*.

[75] *Id*.

wealthy man who died, leaving the bulk of his $5 million estate to his second wife of 12 years with whom he had had a daughter. His five children by his first wife were contesting the will, claiming they should have had a greater share of the estate. The plaintiff's counsel's strategy in court was to paint the second wife, whom we will call Sarah, as a cunning, manipulative woman who had threatened to leave her husband—a man who was deathly afraid of being alone—if he did not amply provide for her in his will.

Sarah's defense counsel did not believe she was any of those things. On the contrary, they believed she had been a devoted wife and a loving mother who deserved every cent her husband left her. Trouble was, she did not look the part.

She wore her shoulder-length bleached-blonde hair brushed back from her face in a style that made her appear hard and brassy. She used little makeup, which caused her fair features to fade into her bleached hair. At 5 feet 9 inches tall she had a taste for severe-looking ultrasuede suits, furs, and boots. Sarah, 35, who was a dentist in a Southeastern city, wore braces on her teeth creating what her lawyer thought might be perceived as a "jaws" look.

The preliminary question raised was, "Does the defendant 'look like' a cruel, manipulative, and cunning woman?" After reviewing videotapes of the defendant and then meeting her in person, it had to be concluded that based on commonly shared stereotypes she could be cast by jurors as cold, aloof, and hard. One of the major areas of consideration was the hard look created by her bleached-blonde hair.

There is a long history of associations and stereotypes for blonde hair dating back to ancient Rome when there were few natural blondes. The state decided to make blonde hair a badge of sin. The wicked "ladies of the evening" were licensed, taxed, and required by law to wear yellow wigs or to dye their hair blonde as a mark of their profession. Messalina, the third wife of Emperor Claudius, threw a wrench in the works when she began wearing a blonde wig. Soon many other women in Rome, aside from the "ladies of the evening," began wearing blonde wigs. The Roman men were distraught and complained that they no longer could tell a lady from a prostitute by the color of her hair.[76] Many centuries later, the German poet Goethe warned of the fair-haired beauty:

---

[76] L. Malandro & L. Barker, Nonverbal Communication 61 (Random House, 1983). Copyright © 1983, Random House, Inc.

> Beware of her fair hair for she excels
> All women in the magic of her locks;
> And when she winds them around a young man's neck,
> She will not ever let him free again.

Another common, but unfortunate, association for women who have blonde hair is the "dumb blonde" image. Perhaps the "dumb blonde" image was a spinoff from the frenetic post-World War I period when the most frivolous of the flappers were also the most likely to experiment with the new platinum blonde bleaches. Anita Loos summarized the image of blondes in the title of her 1925 book, *Gentlemen Prefer Blondes, But Gentlemen Marry Brunettes*. From 1925 until now, the perception of blondes has remained fairly consistent.[77] In November 1969, the *London Daily Mail* quoted a well-known psychologist as saying:

> If a man is serious about a girl he wants her to be natural. Anything artificial does not appeal to a serious thinking man who values quality. Generally speaking, a man prefers a blonde for a mistress and a brunette for a wife. Brunettes have more integrity.

It is unlikely that any of the jurors in the will contest case knew the history of blonde hair. Nevertheless, contemporary perceptions, which have in part a historical base, indicated that bleached blonde hair ranked low on perceptions of credibility and likability, and high on perceptions of frivolity and hardness. The defendant's total projected image had several questionable elements with the bleached blonde hair being only one of them. The jurors' perception of any unfavorable aspect of the defendant's appearance could easily result in reinforcing opposing counsel's attempt to stereotype her as manipulative and cunning.

As a result Sarah's hair was dyed to a softer, more natural shade of blonde. Then it was cut and styled to show more of her face, creating a softer and more trustworthy image. Light makeup was applied to add softness to her face and to reduce the hard angular lines. For the first day of trial Sarah wore a pastel dress with a bow. At her attorney's recommendation, Sarah had her braces removed before the court date. The result was that she appeared as a warm and loving mother rather than a hard and manipulative woman. The jury found unanimously in her favor.

Because the visual image of a person creates such a strong perception, it is difficult to portray an opposite image through testimony. In other

[77] *Id*. at 62.

words, if the individual looks and behaves as a soft-spoken, sincere person, it will be much more difficult to convince jurors that he is ruthless and cunning. Given contradictory information, a strong visual image can have a powerful and overriding effect. Even if the jurors had knowledge of Sarah's appearance prior to trial, her actual physical appearance in the courtroom to which the jurors would be exposed on a day-to-day basis would have greater impact.[78]

Jurors operate on stereotypes of witnesses and attorneys; attorneys operate on stereotypes of jurors. There is little question that stereotypes play a major role in the trial process. A detailed analysis of existing beliefs and biases during pretrial preparation will assist counsel in identifying how perceptions will most likely be formed. Arnolds and Sannito, in *Trial Diplomacy Journal*, comment:

> Even the simplest personality is too complex to be adequately understood on the basis of the type of questioning that can usually be done during voir dire. Recognizing the limitation built into the voir dire procedure, therefore, one must play the odds. If a juror walks like a policeman, talks like a policeman and associates with policemen, one must assume he is not the reincarnation of Roger Baldwin. Except in those cases where an overwhelming "hunch" dictates otherwise, one must rely to a large extent on stereotypes. The question is, what stereotypes? Is it true, for instance, that law enforcement-types vote to convict more often than do other jurors?[79]

§ 1.57 Impression formation theories

The theoretical models of impression formation provide the empirical and logical support for the six communication principles. We have selected only those theories which are well recognized in the fields of communication and psychology, and which we believe apply directly to the courtroom.

The four models we will review include (1) trait association theory, (2) private theory of personality, (3) attribution theory, and (4) uncertainty reduction theory.

Here we must admit our academic bias. We feel that understanding the theoretical models can assist the attorney in making many decisions

---

[78] *See supra* §§ 1.16–1.32.

[79] Arnolds & Sannito, *Jury Study Results Part II: Making Use of the Findings*, 5 Trial Dipl. J. 14 (1982). This article first appeared in Trial Diplomacy Journal, Vol. 5, 1982.

beyond what we can reasonably address in this book. The following descriptions serve as summaries rather than as in-depth reviews of the theories. The references provide the interested reader with direction in areas he may want to pursue further.

A brief description and operational understanding of the theories will assist in the analysis of a case and in making strategic decisions about courtroom image. These theories offer insight into "how" and "why" jurors process information. Understanding the conceptual and theoretical framework of impression formation allows counsel to develop guidelines which can be applied on a case-by-case basis for the selection of jurors, witness preparation, and other important factors in the impression formation stages of a trial.

§ 1.58 —Trait Association Theory

Asch's work on stimulus traits in 1946 eventually lead to the development of the trait association theory.[80] He felt that when a person (the perceiver) identified "traits" in another person (the stimulus person), the perceiver would then, in response to his impression of the stimulus person, make further inferences about that person. According to Schneider, Hastorf and Ellsworth, "Asch believed that it was the intervening impression that made it possible for the subject to generate new information. It was then a two-step process: stimulus traits—impression—response inferences."[81]

Bruner and Tagiuri theorized that the intervening impression may not be formed at all.[82] They believed that inferences about another person could be based solely on the perceived traits. Some traits just seem to be "right" with other traits. For example, in completing the following sentence, "John is bright, eager and (thin, fat)," "thin" seems to "go with" the other characteristics. We do not draw an intermediate impression before choosing "thin."

In their *Handbook of Social Psychology*, Bruner and Tagiuru state:

> ". . .what kinds of naive, implicit 'theories of personality' do people work with when they form an impression of others? We know from

---

[80] Asch, *supra* note 61.

[81] D. Schneider, A. Hastorf & P. Ellsworth, Person Perception 156 (Addison-Wesley, 2d ed. 1979).

[82] Bruner & Tagiuri, *The Perception of People* in 2 Handbook of Social Psychology (Addison-Wesley Publishing Co., G. Lindzey ed. 1954).

> the Asch studies that such terms as 'warm' and 'cold,' when introduced into a description of personality, alter the apparent quality of certain other traits. In 'everyday personality theory' we would ask, what kinds of inferences is a person led to by knowledge that another person is 'warm'? A study of inferential relations between attributes of personality is necessary if we are to understand common sense personality theory and the way in which certain forms of knowledge about another person come to influence drastically the total impression formed."[83]

We all have an "implicit theory of personality," a sense of which characteristics go with which other traits, although we may not be able to articulate it. They "seem" right and logical to us, while others "seem" wrong and illogical. Bruner and Tagiuri argue that this perceived interrelationship among traits represents a naive, common sense theory of personality.

To understand how jurors process information it is important to study the dimensions underlying these "perceived" trait relationships. What traits do jurors link together? How about "lean and mean," "fat and lazy," "blonde and dumb"? The system of rules which tells us which characteristics go with which other characteristics, such as "John is bright, eager and thin" constitute our own trait associations and our implicit theories of personality.[84]

§ 1.59 —Private Theory of Personality

Over years of getting to know the people in our environment and having those people get to know us, we each develop a "private theory" of what people are like. We may have particular things we look for while evaluating the other person, things that to us are meaningful clues to reaching a conclusion about the other person. Researchers Kretch, Crutchfield, and Livson call this our "private theory of personality." Their description of this theory comes from their early work on cognition and the organization of perceptual cues:

> "One factor that determines the content we tend to select (in order to fill in a sketchy impression) is our general notion of 'what goes with what' in people. This notion in fact constitutes a private theory of personality that each of us has and that determines, to a consider-

[83] *Id*. at 649.

[84] *See infra* § 1.88.

> able extent, how we judge others. This private theory is almost never stated or examined and is therefore referred to by psychologists as an 'implicit theory of personality'."[85]

Jurors tend to be confident of their abilities as amateur psychologists. They engage in detective work by assembling additional information and by then using trait associations to expand their information pool. Once again this reminds us of the importance of controlling and pretesting perceptions in the courtroom.

§ 1.60 —Attribution Theory

The Attribution Theory, first postulated by Heider, is the general process of determining the causes of behavior. This theory examines how an individual explains the reasons for his own behavior and the behavior of others. It is an inferential process adopted in order to make accurate causal attributions and is based on how well the perceiver understands himself and his environment.

Heider couched his theory in "common sense" terminology, calling it a theory of "naive psychology."[86] He attempted to explain what the lay person *perceives* to be the cause of behaviors rather than the scientific causes of behaviors. We seek to simplify our understanding of behaviors by making assumptions of general causes.

There are two general types of attribution: reactive and purposive. "Reactive attribution" is when the perceiver feels another person's behavior is relatively unconscious and therefore unintended. This type of attribution does not yield much information about the person and our "naive psychologist" does not give as much attention to these behaviors. The assumption is that unconscious behavior tells us less about the type of person with whom we are dealing than conscious and intentional behavior.

The second type of attribution is much more meaningful. "Purposive attribution" is when the perceiver decides the behavior of another was intended. Through the attribution process, he now attempts to infer why this behavior occurred. This process depends upon how well the perceiver heeds the perceptual cues and how well he understands his own

---

[85] D. KRETCH, R. CRUTCHFIELD & N. LIVSON, ELEMENTS OF PSYCHOLOGY 801 (Alfred A. Knopf, Inc., 2d ed. 1969).

[86] Heider, *Social Perception and Phenomenal Causality*, 51 PSYCHOLOGICAL REV. 358–74 (1944).

thoughts and feelings. It is the perceiver's internal state that is responsible for the attribution.

The Attribution Theory is based on three assumptions.[87] First, people try to determine the causes of behavior. They seek informational cues from their environment and knowledge of similar past experiences to understand why, for example, that person was so angry that he threw his change on the floor of the restaurant. Second, people assign causes to behavior systematically. The perceiver will look for cause-effect relationships if there appear to be any, and the perceiver will assign the most likely cause to the effect (behavior) he has witnessed. Perhaps our angry customer has been observed arguing with the waitress. The perceiver will most likely attribute the cause of the money being thrown on the floor to the altercation with the waitress. Third, the attributed cause affects the perceiver's own feelings and behavior. In our example, the perceiver may decide he does not want that waitress to serve him. It is the perceiver who adds meaning to the observed situation.

We use attribution processes when we want to understand why a person behaved as he did in a particular situation. We make sense of the behaviors by assuming the behaviors were caused by the purposes and intentions of that person. The Attribution Theory tells us that jurors will establish cause and effect links if the attorneys do not. In some cases, counsel may not be able to prove a cause and effect relationship. By presenting the evidence in a particular order, counsel can lead jurors to establish in their own minds the cause and effect relationship that counsel may be unable to demonstrate in the courtroom.

§ 1.61 —Uncertainty Reduction Theory

When strangers meet for the first time they experience a high level of uncertainty about what to expect from the other person and about what the other person expects of them. The need to reduce uncertainty involves two types of predictability: proactive and reactive. In the case of proactive predictability, the individual is able to predict another's actions before they occur. In the case of retroactive predictability, the behavior of another can be explained after it occurs. People experience a greater degree of comfort when they feel they can both predict and explain the actions of another.

Researchers Berger and Calabrese posit that the primary concern of

---

[87] F. Heider, The Psychology of Interpersonal Relations (Wiley, 1958).

strangers is to reduce the level of uncertainty and increase their ability to predict the behavior of others in any given transaction. People do not like uncertainty and are motivated to reduce it as quickly as possible.

Further, this theory contends that a reduction in uncertainty will be the result of an information gain concerning the other person. Berger and Calabrese state:

> Given the high level of uncertainty present at the onset of the entry phase, as the amount of verbal communication between strangers increases, the level of uncertainty for each interactant in the relationship will decrease. As uncertainty is further reduced, the amount of verbal communication will increase.[88]

In the courtroom, we know that jurors have a primary need to reduce uncertainty in order to increase comfort. Therefore, anything that counsel can do to provide jurors with additional information, such as wearing a wedding ring, helps to reduce uncertainty. This is discussed more fully in Part II of this chapter, which explores specific communication techniques that can be employed by counsel to present a desired image to the jurors.

§ 1.62 Accuracy in forming impressions

How accurate are jurors and counsel in their initial judgments of others? Not surprisingly, the answer to this question is that some people are far more perceptive and accurate than others. The following three subsections will focus on (1) the accuracy of initial perceptions, (2) individual differences in accuracy, and (3) how jurors deal with contradictory information. Researchers Tagiuri and Petrullo explain the many facets of person perception:

> In order to behave appropriately, we may have to assess a person's traits, his intentions, feelings, attitudes, capacities, his role-related behavior, the situation in which the behavior occurs. We may have to "know about" what a policeman is likely to do in the role of policeman, or we may have to evaluate a temporary state, such as anger, or the intention to help. In forming an impression, there is always a purpose—although at times weak—and the impression may vary with the purpose.[89]

---

[88] Berger & Calabrese, *supra* note 54, at 101–102.

[89] PERSON PERCEPTION AND INTERPERSONAL BEHAVIOR xiii (Stanford University Press, R. Tagiuri & L. Petrullo eds., 1958).

Our ability to form accurate impressions of others involves our ability to assemble and integrate a complex array of perceptual cues. We must take into account those cues which add understanding to the particular perceptual stimulus at hand. There are three major elements for the perceiver to consider: (1) the situation in which the person to be judged is involved; (2) the perceived person apart from the perceptual situation; and (3) the perceiver himself (for it is the perceiver who attaches meaning to stimuli).[90] Perceptions of people differ for the simple reason that different people respond to different aspects of a person.

In order to be as accurate as possible in the impression formation process, we must feel an event is important and significant to us. "Insignificant events do not motivate a person to bring fully into play the selective process of attention."[91] This raises the issue of saliency: the more important we perceive an event as being, the more carefully we attend to it, and thus the more likely we will be to make an accurate judgment.

Additionally, the longer the period of observation of the stimulus person or event, the greater the likelihood of increased accuracy in perception. Shorter exposure times produce less reliable information and recall.[92] Also, the absence of distractions will allow the opportunity for more accurate judgments. Crowds, fast movements, poor lighting all are contributors to errors in perceptual judgment.[93]

The situation in which perceptual cues are observed exerts a subtle influence on the perceptual process. Some perceptual contexts are evidentially easier to evaluate than others. It is usually safe to assume, for instance, that people in the student union are affiliated in some way with the university. The degree to which we share similar backgrounds and experiences with the stimulus person will increase the likelihood of our forming an accurate impression.[94]

One of the most valuable skills for a trial attorney to have at his command is the ability to form accurate impressions during a short period of time. Through formal communication training an attorney can dramatically increase his ability to read and respond to external stimuli. This is one of the most highly valued skills of trial consultants, particularly dur-

---

[90] *Id.* at xiii–xiv.

[91] Buckhout, *supra* note 56 at 25.

[92] *Id.*

[93] *Id.*

[94] Tagiuri & Petrullo, *supra* note 89, at xi.

ing voir dire: the ability to accurately analyze verbal, vocal, and nonverbal cues of potential jurors.

§ 1.63 —Accuracy in perceiving people

How accurate are we in the judgments we make about the people around us? Just as we can have differing perceptions about the quality of a movie we have seen, so too, do we differ in our perceptions of other people. Since the process of person perception is an ongoing internal process, few people realize that they are constantly making judgments about other people. Tagiuri and Petrullo comment:

> Regardless of the degree of skill which an adult may have in appraising others, he engages in the process most of the time without paying much attention to how he does it.[95]

Even fewer people realize that their evaluations could be wrong. We make our judgments quickly, and those judgments become internalized. The fact that three eyewitnesses can describe the same object person in three different ways underscores the phenomenon that people differ in their perceptions of others.

Accuracy in person perception has been a concern of social psychological research for the past thirty years.[96] What are the qualities of an accurate perceiver? How accurate is this perceiver in different contexts, receiving different stimulus cues, or perceiving persons unlike himself? No one picture of the ideal perceiver has emerged, notwithstanding a number of efforts to determine the optimum qualities.[97]

We are, however, often able to make accurate perceptions of another person. Researchers have learned that accuracy in person perception depends on a number of interrelated factors.[98] One of the most important elements is how well we know the person we are observing. This critically affects the accuracy of our perceptions of him: the more information we already possess about the stimulus person the more likely we are to have observed that person under differing circumstances. The greater the exposure to the person, the more information perceivers have upon which to base their judgments of that person.

---

[95] Tagiuri & Petrullo, *supra* note 89.

[96] Taft, *The Ability to Judge People*, 52 Psychological Bull. 1–23 (1955).

[97] Schneider, Hastorf & Ellsworth, *supra* note 81.

[98] Patton & Giffin, *supra* note 72; and Ellsworth, *supra* note 81.

Accuracy is also higher when we are judging those who are like ourselves. When the stimulus person is from the same background or occupation, or has the same educational experience as the perceiver, perceptual validity increases. This supports the fifth communication principle: "People tend to see others as similar to themselves." Whenever possible jurors will look for similarities between themselves, counsel, and witnesses. The greater the perceived similarities, the greater the chance for jurors to develop an empathetic response to the client.

The quality of cues given out by the stimulus person also affects the accuracy of our perceptions. Some cues (both verbal and nonverbal) are very clear: a hearty handshake accompanied by a warm smile and a cheery "hello" are easier to evaluate than cues that are subtle, ambiguous, or contradictory. Some people are more "up front" and we can "read them like a book" since they possess attributes that are easier for us to evaluate, simply because we are more used to seeing and interpreting those attributes.

Although we are remarkably successful in our perceptions of others, Patton and Giffin, in their review of the research on accuracy in person perception, urge caution in the perception process because:

1. Much of the behavior of others that can be observed is trivial or incidental and is not valuable for drawing conclusions regarding personality or intentions.
2. The observable behavior of others is often neatly designed to mislead or deceive us.
3. Their actions are often determined by external factors beyond their control and not by internal states, personalities, or intentions.[99]

We can increase our abilities as accurate perceivers if we concentrate on (1) behavior that could have one or, at the most, very few possible reasons to explain it and (2) behavior that deviates markedly from widely accepted social norms. When we examine the research in this area it becomes apparent that jurors, as a group, will not necessarily form the same perceptions of counsel or witnesses. Given this fact, the focus needs to be on minimizing negative areas of perception. Jurors will influence one another, however, in their observations. The extent to which we can direct the jurors' attention to particular qualities of an individual will increase the likelihood that they will share similar perceptions.

---

[99] Patton & Giffin, *supra* note 72, at 115.

The ability to perceive others accurately involves the observation of different stimuli and the translation of those stimuli into a meaningful picture of the other person. While assembling research and experience to accurately assess behavior is the domain of the social scientist, the application of this material in the courtroom is invaluable for attorneys.

§ 1.64 —How individuals differ in accuracy of perception

Individuals differ in their ability to perceive stimuli and translate those stimuli into a meaningful picture of the other person. Accuracy in perception tends to increase with the age of the perceiver.[100] However, it is the experiences and the learning derived from those experiences that tends to account for the increasing accuracy of perception with age.[101]

Intelligence and maturity also account for differences in individual accuracy in perception.[102] Generally the more intelligent person is also better able to make accurate perceptual judgments. Related to this idea is the concept of "cognitive complexity."[103] Perceivers who are more cognitively complex have more dimensions (or categories and concepts) available in their evaluative repertoires. They are better able to make distinctions among various types of stimulus cues. In addition, they differentiate more precisely and tend not to group people together as much. The ability to have and use a greater number of concepts for describing people generally makes them better at accurate perceptions of stimulus persons. Accuracy in selecting jurors plays a critical role in trials. The identification of various traits and demographic background on jurors provides predictive information on how jurors will engage in decision-making. In the trial of American Indian Movement members accused of the murder of two FBI agents, for example, the defense accepted three engineers and one accountant on the jury for a very specific purpose. Researchers Bonora and Krauss report:

> "The defense assumption was that jurors who would take a strong analytical approach to the evidence would tend to discount that part of the prosecution's evidence which was based on innuendo and an appeal to the prejudice against AIM which existed in the commu-

---

[100] J.A. DeVito, The Interpersonal Communication Book (Harper & Row, 2d ed. 1980).

[101] Patton & Giffin, *supra* note 72.

[102] DeVito, *supra* note 100.

[103] Crockett, *Cognitive Complexity and Impression Formation* in 2 Progress in Experimental Personality Research (Academic Press, B.A. Maher ed. 1965).

nity. In the deliberations, three of the four jurors who were typed as analytical took the lead in establishing a methodical approach to reviewing the evidence. They also saw to it that the standards of reasonable doubt and burden of proof were consistently applied to the evaluation of all of the evidence. Each of them came to the conclusion that the prosecution simply had not been able to meet the burden of proof and persuaded the other jurors to accept their position."[104]

Another area where individuals differ is in their level of authoritarianism. Considerable research has been conducted on the authoritarian dimension of personality.[105] Generally it has been found that the less authoritarian a person is, the better able he is to make accurate judgments of other people. People low in authoritarianism "are less rigid in their expectations, judging more from what they know about the person and assuming less that he or she is like themselves."[106]

How can we determine the authoritarian level of the individual? A person high in authoritarianism would agree with the following five statements (while a low authoritarian would disagree):

1. Police should not hesitate to use force to maintain order.
2. The right to private property is sacred.
3. Obedience and respect for authority are the most important virtues children should have.
4. If people worked hard at their jobs, they would reap the full benefits of society.
5. Every person should have complete faith in a supernatural power.[107]

In addition, a person high in authoritarianism would probably disagree with the following three statements (while a low authoritarian would most likely agree);

---

[104] NATIONAL JURY PROJECT, JURYWORK: SYSTEMATIC TECHNIQUES, 203 (National Jury Project, B. Bonora & E. Krauss eds. 1979).

[105] The interested reader will find a discussion of early research on authoritarianism in R. BROWN, SOCIAL PSYCHOLOGY (Free Press, 1965).

The various scales used to measure authoritarianism can be found in ROBINSON & SHAVERS, MEASURE OF SOCIAL PSYCHOLOGICAL ATTITUDES (University of Michigan Press, rev. ed. 1973).

[106] Tubbs & Moss, *supra* note 65, at 81.

[107] NATIONAL JURY PROJECT, *supra* note 104, at 203–204.

1. People ought to pay more attention to new ideas, even if they seem to go against the American way of life.
2. If it weren't for the rebellious ideas of youth, there would be less progress in the world.
3. The findings of science may someday show that many of our most cherished beliefs are wrong.[108]

Nonverbal cues can also help identify those jurors higher in authoritarianism. High authoritarians tend to sit more rigidly and fold their arms across their chests more often than low authoritarians.[109] Other nonverbal behaviors can help alert the trial lawyer to higher degrees of authoritarianism in a juror. Based on their study, Bonora and Krauss concluded:

> Because they tend to be submissive to authority figures, observing the juror's relationship to the judge during voir dire is useful. The high authoritarian can be expected to be more deferential than most, to hang on to the judge's words, to be quick to modify statements in accordance with the answers the judge seems to want, and, in general, to make an effort to win the judge's approval. The frequent use of "sir" may also be an indication that a juror is particularly respectful of authority.
>
> At the opposite extreme, it is rare to find people who are openly disrespectful. Look for indications that a venireperson is not overawed by the judge's authority. Look for the person who responds thoughtfully to the judge's questions and who does not automatically respond to the judge's cues as to the appropriate answer.[110]

If we are able to ascertain the level of authoritarianism in a potential juror, we can also make some predictions about the probable attitudes that juror holds. For example, if we feel a particular juror is a high authoritarian, we could predict that he would most likely:

—believe that verdicts affect one's own insurance premiums

—believe that money should not be given for pain and suffering

—believe that large verdicts are never justified no matter what the amount of the injury

—have a high respect for authority

---

[108] *Id.* at 204.

[109] *Id.*

[110] *Id.* at 204–205.

—be submissive to authority figures

—accept the status quo

—conform more to group pressure

—be influenced by the status of other individuals.[111]

In the courtroom, knowing the level of the juror's authoritarianism is helpful because we can predict that the high authoritarian juror is inclined to:

—be prejudiced against minority groups

—be for capital punishment

—believe the defendant should take the stand

—believe an indicted person is probably guilty

—believe that police statements are true.[112]

Other factors that play a role in the accuracy of an individual's perception are:

(1) the ego of the perceiver[113]—the more objective a person is about himself, the more insight he tends to have into the behavior of another person;[114]

(2) stress—in times of stress we tend to be less reliable in our perceptual judgments than when we are not under stress;[115]

(3) fear;[116]

(4) the physical condition of the observer;[117]

(5) the observer's "expectancy" state—i.e., what he expects, wants, or needs to see.[118]

Most of what has been learned about jurors' perceptions has been through research using the "mock jury." Psychologist Frederick comments:

---

[111] *Id.* at 204.

[112] *Id.*

[113] Schneider, Hastorf & Ellsworth, *supra* note 81 at 227.

[114] Tubbs & Moss, *supra* note 65, at 81.

[115] Buckhout, *supra* note 56, at 25.

[116] Loftus, *The Eyewitness on Trial*, 16 TRIAL 30–35 (1980).

[117] Buckhout, *supra* note 56, at 25.

[118] *Id.* at 25–26.

"This paradigm involves the presentation of experimentally developed case materials or trial transcripts to subjects, usually college students, who in turn render a verdict in the case as if they were jurors. Simulated or mock jurors, therefore, refer to subjects who have participated in such a procedure.[119]

§ 1.65 —How jurors make decisions with contradictory information

The process of impression formation involves the study of how people combine various pieces of information into a meaningful, organized, and structured view of another person. Not all of the information concerning the other person is consistent. For example, the observer may note that the person is friendly, kind, and smiles often at people he knows but is rather abrupt with strangers. Does this mean the person is unkind? Abrupt? Contradictory? Everyone projects conflicting perceptual cues at times, and we have all been aware of receiving conflicting information from the same person. This conflicting information is assimilated into a stable, overall picture of the person to produce a general judgment through the resolution of the contradictory information.

Inconsistencies in personal perceptual cues can be resolved in either of two general ways. First, we may resolve such inconsistencies through "relational tendency."[120] In this method, the perceiver either changes the meaning of the inconsistent information so that it is compatible with other information, or the perceiver looks for new traits in order to resolve the inconsistencies.

The second method for dealing with contradiction is "linear combination."[121] In this approach, the general impression of the stimulus person is considered to be an additive combination of pertinent information taken from stimulus characteristics. Thus, those characteristics that add up to a higher score are taken to be the more accurate and take precedence in the impression.

It appears that people differ in their tolerance for contradiction or in-

---

[119] Frederick, *Jury Behavior: A Psychologist Examines Jury Selection*, 5 Ohio N.U.L. Rev. 572 (1978).

See infra Part IV, *Appendix*, § 1.89, *Mock jury research studies*, which sets forth a number of criticisms of mock juries, as well as analyzes over 600 questionnaires returned by jurors after their deliberations.

[120] Schneider, Hastorf & Ellsworth, *supra* note 81, at 175–180.

[121] *Id*. at 175.

consistencies during impression formation and also differ in their ability to resolve those contradictions.[122]

Some people deal with inconsistent information by discounting it (reducing the impact of information by weakening or disregarding it). A subject will actively discount material that is contrary to the preponderance of information he has concerning a person. Thus, if most of the perceptions are positive and a negative trait is presented, generally the negative trait will be discounted and the overall impression will remain a positive one.

Another way to deal with inconsistent information is to ignore the contradiction (for all practical purposes, the contradiction was never heard). Consider the following example reported by Vinson:

> In a recent, well-publicized murder trial, the jury acquitted a wealthy defendant of first-degree murder, disregarding the testimony of three eyewitnesses. When later interviewed, jury members described an astonishing conclusion. Many of them, particularly the opinion leaders, felt that rich men do not commit murder or behave the way the defendant was alleged to have acted. The jurors' basic belief, that rich people do not commit murder, remained unshaken despite the testimony of three witnesses. The jurors rejected the testimony that contradicted their structure of belief.[123]

Jurors may also rationalize away the contradiction by minimizing the importance of the contradictory material. This may be accomplished by making excuses for the contradiction or attributing the contradiction to circumstances that were not germane to the situation. Vinson offers us another example of how jurors deal with contradictory information:

> In one recent case, much scientific and technical data were presented to show that bacteria had been introduced into a patient's body through the implantation of an artificial heart valve. The patient had died from a massive pulmonary infection. During posttrial interviews, jurors indicated that they had attached little weight to expert testimony on behalf of the plaintiff. . . . They believed that the level of competence in the medical community would ensure that the heart valve was properly sterilized and inserted. They also

---

[122] *Id*. at 188–190; *see also* Crockett, *supra* note 103.

[123] Vinson, *Psychological Anchors: Influencing the Jury*, 10 LITIGATION 24 (1982). Reprinted with permission from 10 LITIGATION, No. 4, at 24 (Summer 1984). Copyright © 1984, Section of Litigation, American Bar Association.

> believed that the standards of the medical products industry were sufficiently high so that no defective heart valve could have been manufactured. . . . Some argued that even if the device had not been sterile, the patient should have been able to fight off the infection and that no such product could be expected to be 100 percent safe.[124]

The above example introduces Communication Principle 6: "People attempt to maintain their original perceptions regardless of contradictory information."

As discussed earlier, our perceptions of other people involve verbal, vocal, and nonverbal dimensions. Many times the verbal message and the nonverbal signals accompanying the message (e.g., gestures, tone of voice) are contradictory. For example, a person may be telling us how glad he is to see us but his vocal tone is one of annoyance, he avoids eye contact with us, and his hands are fidgeting as he attempts to back out the door. Research has shown that given a contradiction in the verbal and nonverbal signals, the nonverbal signal will be chosen by the perceiver as the more accurate indicator of the person's true message.[125] Nonverbal messages are considered to be harder to fake because, although we may be glib with words, we are not so adept at masking our feelings nonverbally. Additionally, since over 90% of a given message is transmitted nonverbally and vocally while less than 10% of the message comes from the actual verbal content, most of our informative cues are nonverbal, and we, as perceivers, give the nonverbal elements their requisite weight in resolving the contradictory signals.[126]

§ 1.66 Perceptions of multiple parties

Are groups (multiple parties) perceived and adjudicated differently from individuals by a group of observers (jurors)? This question raises some important factors to be considered by counsel in cases involving multiple party plaintiffs and multiple party defendants.

Given the complicated nature of information processing and perception, jurors faced with the task of adjudicating under conditions of multiplicity will need to process a complexity of information. Knowledge of how they process this information will bear on the attorney's strategy in

---

[124] *Id.*

[125] M.L. Knapp, Nonverbal Communication in Human Interaction 22 (Holt, Rinehart & Winston, 2d ed. 1978).

[126] Birdwhistle, *supra* note 1.

preparing his case and witnesses. What is known about the process of impression formation of groups is that is differs from the perception of a single individual.[127]

General responses and attitudes regarding groups provide interesting results. In one study, it was shown that the mere classification of people into groups evoked a negative bias in observers for no apparent reason. In addition, the study revealed that when a group was presented without member individuation, which means the perceptual separation of each member as an individual, it assumed an "out-group" identity and became the object of discrimination and negatively biased judgments. Whenever individuals were identified separately there was a significant lessening of discrimination and negative bias.[128] The "built-in" biases about groups complicate the multiple party cases. There are several operative principles, however, which can be applied to control and direct group impression formation.[129]

As a general rule, if you are representing a plaintiff in a situation where multiple plaintiffs are seeking damages, it is important to individualize your plaintiff and to distinguish him from the other member of the group. Likewise, where multiple defendants are involved, you may want to avoid grouping all of the defendants together. This can be accomplished, for example, by physically separating the parties in the courtroom to achieve a subsequent psychological separating of parties in the minds of the jurors. When no attempt is made to individuate or separate the parties, jurors will ordinarily engage in a process called cognitive averaging.[130]

§ 1.67 —How jurors perceive multiple parties

People cluster data and identify a generalized or overlay image for a group. This is referred to as cognitive averaging. Rosnow and Arms reported that group impression formation is a function of cognitive averaging. In other words, both positive and negative characteristics were averaged by observers in order to establish a middle ground. Individual

---

[127] B. Catchings & V. Waldron, *Trial Behavior Under Conditions of Multiplicity: Strategies for Litigation Involving Multiple Parties* (Paper presented to the Association of Trial Behavior Consultants, Second Annual Conference, Chicago, Illinois) (October 9, 1983).

[128] Wilder, *Reduction of Intergroup Discrimination Through Individuation of the Outgroup*, 36 J. PERSONALITY & SOC. PSYCHOLOGY, 1361-1374 (1970).

[129] *See infra* §§ 1.67–1.70.

[130] *See infra* § 1.67.

characteristics were displayed by a cognitive mean which is similar to the cognitive averaging concept.[131]

A subsequent study found that observer impressions of a group were influenced by the worst member—that is, the cognitive average was weighted more heavily by the influence of the member most negatively perceived. Less extreme members were virtually ignored. When observers did not average, they used the most negative member as the sole basis for judgment.[132]

These results suggest that a group of three to four attorneys representing multiple parties should remove, if at all possible, any person who would represent an extreme in terms of negative impression formation. For instance, in a case where a group of attorneys are representing several clients, and all attorneys are perceived positively except one, jurors will heavily weight the averaging process based on the attorney who is perceived negatively. The group is brought to its lowest common denominator by the most negative extreme member.

Another way to combat this impact is to present those who have the most positive impact first, down-playing any person in the extreme category. An extreme negative perception may be the result of physical unattractiveness, arrogance, an unpleasant voice, annoying behaviors, or any combination of behaviors that enter the jurors' perceptual field. Therefore, clients or attorneys with abrasive personality characteristics that will be construed as negatively extreme by the jurors should be avoided as much as possible to avoid contamination of the group impression.

The same factors hold true for multiple defendants whether in a criminal or civil case. In the criminal setting, for example, if one defendant is simply an "accessory" then the defense counsel should attempt to individualize his "less guilty" defendant from the main culprit. This technique has been employed successfully in a number of major criminal trials, including in the defense of some of the Watergate defendants. Jacob A. Stein of Washington, D.C., represented Kenneth Parkinson, a lawyer for the Republican Party's effort to re-elect President Nixon. Stein made sure that he and Parkinson sat alone at a table that was sepa-

---

[131] Rosnow & Arms, *Adding Versus Averaging as a Stimulus Combination Rule in Forming Impressions of Groups*, 10 J. Personality & Soc. Psychology 363–369 (1968).

[132] Leon, Oden & Anderson, *Functional Measurement of Social Values*, 27 J. Personality & Soc. Psychology 301–310 (1973).

rate and apart from the table at which Haldeman, Ehrlichman and their cohorts sat.

§ 1.68 —The primacy effect with multiple parties

The client who takes the stand first is likely to determine how the members of the group will be perceived. The perceived similarity of the group may be contingent upon who is selected to represent the entire group.[133] Once again the primacy effect is operative: the individual who represents the group first will establish the manner in which the group as a whole will be viewed. Since jurors tend to see group members as similar, those who will portray the most desirable image should take the stand first. The jury would likely generalize their image to the entire group. Principle 5 tells us that jurors tend to see others as similar to themselves. This principle has implications for groups. Jurors will perceive group members as similar to one another based on their impressions of the first members they observe. From this point they will use cognitive averaging.

Similarly, those attorneys who represent a particular party first, create a strong primacy effect for other counsel. The best advice is to put your best foot (or attorney) forward.

§ 1.69 —Perception of responsibility of multiple parties

Attribution studies reveal that the classification of individuals into groups has an effect on the attribution of responsibility: i.e., that individuals acting alone were held more responsible for their actions than those acting in groups.[134] Additionally, a survey of court records in the state of Virginia revealed that judges consistently assigned longer sentences to defendants acting alone than to those acting in groups of two or more.[135] Thus, the research shows that group members are held less responsible than individuals for their behavior and will be judged less severely than those individuals acting alone.[136]

The research goes one step further to suggest that common behavior among people is attributed to situational causes while unique behavior is

---

[133] Catchings & Waldron, *supra* note 127, Wilder, *supra* note 128.

[134] Catchings & Waldron, Trial Behavior Under Conditions of Multiplicity: Strategies for Litigation Involving Multiple Parties (Presentation to Ass'n of Trial Behavior Consultants, 2d Annual Conference, Chicago, Illinois) (October 1983).

[135] *Id*. at 319–320.

[136] Catchings & Waldron, *supra* note 127.

attributed to the properties of the agent performing the behavior.[137] Given this information, for example, it would be advantageous for counsel for a group to present the uniformity of actions among litigants. The best approach would be to depict the multiple group claiming injuries as having uniformly engaged in actions that precipitated their personal harm. Applying the common behavior principle, the uniformity of their actions would likely affect a juror diffusion of responsibility and a situational attribution. Simply stated, jurors would shift responsibility from the clients to other causes.[138]

§ 1.70 —Separating your case in a multiple party dispute

Let us hypothetically assume that you are involved in an antitrust case with four defendants, and the judge ruled that the case would not be separated but would be tried as a multiple party case. Further, he ruled that counsel could not sit at separate tables in the courtroom. Given these parameters we know that the jurors will engage in cognitive averaging, and the four defendants will be treated as one in the minds of the jurors. Antitrust litigation is complicated, involves long hours in the courtroom, and has a decided tendency toward being boring for jurors and attorneys alike. There is little doubt that the jurors will not actively work to separate the defendants, witness testimony, and opening statements. They will average. It is easier, quicker, and reduces uncertainty.

Methods for separating multiple parties include any consistent application of behavioral changes that will be perceived differently and favorably (or at least as neutral) from the other counsel. For example, if all counsel members are using yellow legal pads, the attorney wishing separation in the minds of the jurors should use white legal pads. If the height of the chairs can be changed, they should be made higher. This slight elevation separates the party visually from others. (It would not be appropriate to lower the chairs because there is a negative bias toward shorter objects, things and people.) Clothing distinctions can easily be made. For example, if other counsel is wearing very conservative gray and navy blue suits, the counsel wishing separation can wear brown suits with blue shirts instead of white shirts. Postural orientation can be more relaxed to obtain separation of parties. Counsel should avoid conferring with other attorneys in front of the jurors, and avoid any common group behaviors.

---

[137] Kelly, *Attribution Theory in Social Psychology* in NEBRASKA SYMPOSIUM ON MOTIVATION 208 (University of Nebraska Press, D. Levine ed. 1967).

[138] Catchings & Waldron, *supra* note 127.

If the entire group displays "concern," counsel should adopt another attitude, perhaps one of neutrality to continually underscore that he is not a member of the group. These methods are effective only if: (1) They are used in the beginning of the trial (primacy effect); (2) They are applied consistently; (3) The separating or individuating behaviors are associated with positive (or neutral) perceptions of the jurors; (4) The separating or individuating behaviors are clearly different and distinct from the other parties.

§ 1.71 Special factors affecting impression formation

Jurors engage in several primary areas of impression formation. We know that jurors visually perceive a great deal of information throughout the trial and attach meaning to their observations. Primary areas for jurors' perceptions include (1) attractive/unattractive individuals, (2) personal space, territory, and crowding, (3) environment and seating arrangements, (4) voice characteristics and qualities, and (5) touch behavior.

§ 1.72 Perceptions of attractive/unattractive people

As the studies in the Appendix at the end of this chapter indicate, society is biased toward attractive people.[139] Therefore, it behooves trial lawyers to assist their clients in the choice of wardrobe, hairstyle, make-up, and any other factors which can increase the perceptions of attractiveness. Factors such as extreme neatness and cleanliness help to offset the negative impact of an unattractive client. In addition, attorneys need to examine their own personal appearance for the courtroom since likability of attorneys is largely a function of perceived attractiveness.[140]

§ 1.73 Perceptions of territory, personal space, and crowding

The ways in which an individual uses space communicate a variety of messages to those around him. The use of space communicates status, dominance, affection, and the nature of relationships. The courtroom represents a fascinating study in the use and control of space. The judge, for example, occupies the highest territory in the room. Since height increases the perception of status, the judge will receive automatic deference. In addition, whenever we are forced to "look up to another person" (i.e., tilting the head back and raising the eyes), the result is that

[139] *See infra* § 1.90.

[140] *See supra* §§ 1.16–1.32.

we feel more submissive and hence tend to fulfill that role. The rules concerning the occupation of space and movement differ from courtroom to courtroom. The chance for greater persuasive appeal exists more when movement and, therefore, control of the space, is permitted. Sections 1.74–1.76 will explore the perceptions of territory, personal space, and crowding. An awareness and understanding of the influence and impact of territory, personal space, and crowding can increase an attorney's communication effectiveness.

COMMENT: The study of space, called proxemics, is of importance to the trial lawyer in three specific areas: (1) territory, (2) personal space, and (3) crowding. Territory refers to fixed spatial zones such as desks, walls, and objects. Personal space is defined as the constantly changing spatial needs that each individual has; specifically, personal space is the invisible "bubble" of space which surrounds each person. Considerations of crowding arise when examining the behavior tendencies when these spatial zones are violated.

---

§ 1.74 —Perceptions of territory

It is not only in the animal kingdom that we find territory marked off by boundaries. We also attempt to define and mark off that area which we consider to belong to us. Fences built around personal property or bushes planted on property lines illustrate how people in our society identify what belongs to them. Territoriality of humans is defined as the continuous association of a person or group with certain places.[141]

In the courtroom, territory is clearly defined. The judge occupies the highest and usually the largest space. Jurors are given a "box" which constitutes their territory. When an attorney leans on the jurors' box he is invading their space. Unless the jurors have a very positive regard for the attorney, this could have a negative impact. Counsel is often restricted to a prescribed spatial area. In some courts, attorneys are lim-

[141] Edney, *Human Territories: Comment on Functional Properties*, 8 ENV'T & BEHAV. 31–47 (1976); *see also infra* Part IV, Appendix, § 1.91.

ited to sitting behind the counsel table when asking questions. Other courts restrict counsel, when asking questions, to standing behind a podium. When possible such spatial restrictions should be avoided. The podium acts as a barrier between counsel and the witness and the jury and does not allow the use of the full body movements in communicating. If the podium is optional, it generally should not be used. Where it is mandatory, try to work from one side or the other of the podium so the view of the body is not blocked. Whenever possible avoid all physical barriers that separate you from the jurors.

Counsel must remember, however, that people respond with varying degrees of hostility when their territory is invaded. Thus, counsel should exercise caution when invading the territory of the jurors by leaning on or placing objects on the jury box. The same caution applies to the territory occupied by the judge.

§ 1.75 —Perceptions of personal space

Everyone has an area surrounding his body which is viewed as personally belonging to him. This is our personal space and is referred to as our personal "bubble." Personal space varies with each individual, culture, and the circumstances in which the person finds himself.

There are four categories of personal space according to researcher Hall: intimate distance, casual-personal distance, socio-consultive distance, and public distance.[142] Each of these distances is dependent upon the type of relationship the individuals have. The intimate distance ranges from zero to eighteen inches and is used by individuals who are interacting on a personal level. Casual-personal distance occurs when the parties are one and one-half to four feet apart and is used during conversations and discussions with friends. Socio-consultive distance is used primarily when the parties are discussing impersonal topics and standing from four to eight feet apart; this tends to be the range for more formal business discussions. When giving a speech, the speaker is usually within the public distance, ranging from eight feet to the limits of the audience's visual or auditory fields.

It is important to maintain the appropriate distance in communication. The speaker who discusses an informal topic with an acquaintance but within the acquaintance's intimate distance is violating the norm for the

[142] E.T. Hall, The Silent Language (Doubleday, 1959).

appropriate use of personal space. The receiver's judgment of the communicator will be affected by this violation of personal space norms.

Use of personal space can communicate how we feel about a person. When we like someone, we tend to stand closer to that person.[143] Conversely, if we do not care for someone, we tend to widen the distance between ourselves and the other person. This pattern of approach-avoidance behaviors becomes particularly important during the trial. Often counsel will perceive a particular juror to be responding negatively. The natural reaction is to engage in an avoidance behavior and increase the distance between yourself and the perceived hostile party. However, the perception itself of the juror may not be accurate. Additionally, the increased distance will reinforce the feeling of separation and dissimilarity for both parties. Similarly, if counsel is unhappy with his client, the clearest indicator will be the distance he puts between his client and himself.[144]

§ 1.76 —Perceptions of crowding

When a person becomes concerned about the spatial limitations around him, he experiences the psychological state of crowding. We all need a certain amount of space and when that space is not available, we feel restricted and, at times, trapped. Our language reflects this aversion to being restricted when we tell an acquaintance to "stop crowding" us.

Crowding can be the result of stimulus overload, behavioral constraint, or surveillance.[145] When so much is happening around the person that he cannot process all the stimuli, he becomes tired and confused and tries to escape from the situation. Stimulus overload is often found in residents of large cities. One way to cope with this type of crowding is for the individual to isolate himself and put himself outside of all of the commotion.

Behavioral constraint results when one invades another's personal space and restricts that person's movements. According to Greenberg and Firestone, surveillance can also create behavioral constraint.[146] Even

---

[143] Mehrabian, *Significance of Posture and Position in the Communication of Attitudes and Status Relationships*, 71 PSYCHOLOGICAL BULL. 359–373 (1969).

[144] *See infra* § 1.92.

[145] Malandro & Barker, *supra* note 76, at 231–232.

[146] Greenberg & Firestone, *Compensatory Responses to Crowding: Effects of Personal Space Intrusion and Privacy Reduction*, 9 J. PERSONALITY & SOC. PSYCHOLOGY 637–644 (1977).

if a person is not sure he is the object of surveillance, the mere fact that he thinks he is being watched can result in behavioral constraint.

When personal space is violated and crowding results, the intent of the invading person can have an impact upon the manner in which he is perceived.[147] For example, if a person invades your personal space for the purpose of rewarding you, you will perceive that person more positively than you do a person who has not invaded your territory. If someone invades your space for the purpose of reprimanding you, your feelings toward the invading party will be intensified and will be more negative. The purpose behind the invasion of your personal space is an important consideration in how that invasion (and resultant crowding) will be perceived.

Crowding is a psychological condition. Attorneys must be careful not to intrude on the jury's personal space or to invade the territory around the testifying witness unless they understand the possible repercussions such violations will have. The perceptions of the jury will be affected by considerations of territoriality, personal space, and crowding.[148]

Density is a physical situation where crowding is a psychological condition. Density refers to the number of people in a given space.[149] If there are too many people to be accommodated in a given space, crowding may be the result if the people perceive the situation as being one of spatial restriction.

§ 1.77 Perceptions of environment and seating arrangements

Our surroundings have an impact on us. They influence how happy we are, how much work we are able to accomplish, and how comfortable and secure we feel. Do you have a particular chair you always like to sit in? Do you have a favorite room in your house? A place where you work more efficiently or study better? The environment in which we find ourselves does have an effect on us: it can stimulate (or depress) us; arouse our curiosity (or dull our senses); encourage (or discourage) us.

What are the important factors to consider when analyzing the environment and its impact on us? There are six factors that shape our perceptions of surroundings: (1) formality, (2) warmth, (3) privacy,

---

[147] Burgoon, *A Communication Model of Personal Space Violations: Explication and an Initial Test*, 4 HUM. COM. RESEARCH 129–142 (1978).

[148] *See infra* § 1.34.

[149] Malandro & Barker, *supra* note 76, at 233.

(4) familiarity, (5) constraint, and (6) distance.[150] The way in which we perceive our environment affects our communication messages as well as our behavior. The following paragraphs will briefly examine these six perceptual frameworks:

(1) Formality is the first way in which we perceive our environment. It has been said that "[t]he greater the formality, the greater the chances that the communication behavior will be less relaxed and more superficial, hesitant, and stylized.[151]

(2) A warm environment is conducive to feeling comfortable and at ease. We like being in a setting where the overall impression, created through the use of colors, carpets, draperies, and lighting is enjoyable and inviting.[152]

(3) When our surroundings provide us with privacy, we feel more secure and conclude that it is less likely our conversations will be overheard. We communicate in a less formal, more intimate way, with our messages structured for a particular person rather than for a group.

(4) Familiarity with our surroundings makes us feel more comfortable and secure because we know what the norms governing the environment are. We like to be in familiar surroundings and the fast food chains, for example, have capitalized on our preference for the familiar.

COMMENT: It is important to understand that a juror feels very uncomfortable in the unfamiliar surroundings of the courtroom. He has, in all likelihood, never been in a courtroom before, much less served on a jury. Thus, the juror's anxiety level is high and will affect his perceptions of what occurs in the courtroom.[153]

---

[150] M.L. Knapp, Nonverbal Communication in Human Interaction 87–89 (Holt, Rinehart & Winston, 2d ed. 1978).

[151] *Id*. at 87.

[152] Malandro & Barker, *supra* note 76, at 184.

[153] Vinson, *Psychological Anchors: Influencing the Jury*, 8 Litigation 21 (1982).

(5) Any environment possesses a degree of constraint. The intensity with which an individual perceives constraint is directly related to the space available and the privacy of this space during the time he is in the environment.[154]

(6) Power and status can be communicated by distance. For example, the closer a subordinate's office is to the decision-maker, the more power and status the subordinate himself is perceived to have.[155]

For a more in-depth discussion of the various studies that have been conducted to determine how people respond to various aspects of our environment, *see infra* Part IV, *Appendix*, § 1.93.

§ 1.78 —Perceptions of spatial arrangements and seating behavior

Where you sit makes a difference; it communicates a message to those around you. What is your perception of the person who sits at the head of the table during a corporate board meeting? Power is where you sit and is based on a need for psychological control and protection.[156] Seating behavior preferences can be traced back through history:

> In ancient times, seating choice was a matter of self-protection and survival. When a power figure sat at the head of a round table, for instance, it was very important where the next power figure was placed. One natural choice today might be to put the next most powerful individual to the right, based on the concept of "right-hand" person. This method was not used in ancient times for the simple reason that it was easier to stab to your left with the dagger in your right hand than to stab to your right, again with the dagger in your right hand. It was therefore prudent to place a powerful

---

[154] Knapp, *supra* note 150, at 88; with regard to how much constraint our environment exercises over us, Knapp observed:

> There is a difference between temporarily confining environments and permanently confining ones. A trip across country in a car is temporarily confining, while a trip in jail is of a much more constraining and permanent nature.

[155] Knapp, *supra* note 150, at 87; the importance of understanding the factors which influence our perceptions of the environment was summarized by Knapp as follows:

> Once we have perceived our environment in a certain way, we may incorporate such perceptions in the development of the messages we send. And, once that message has been sent, the environmental perceptions of the other person have been altered. Thus, we are influenced by and influence our environments.

[156] M. Korda, Power! How to Get It, How to Use It (Random House, 1975).

> guest to your immediate left, since in that position he could not stab you, while you were excellently positioned to kill him. The person on your immediate right would be someone of no risk or importance to you.[157]

The shape and size of the table used in conferences and meetings has an impact on the communication. For example, a round table represents unity and the perception that all parties are equal. There are certain status demarcations, however, even with a round table. Comparing the round table to the face on a clock, it has been found that the highest power position is at twelve o'clock. Power moves clockwise around the table, with the least powerful person sitting at the eleven o'clock position.[158]

Equality of participants is symbolized at a square table. Each party has an equally sized side of the table and also has separate edges. If the attorney wants to promote equality in interactions among the parties, the square table is an excellent choice because all four people are seated an equal distance from each other and direct eye contact is possible from all four positions.

The rectangular table, with its two longer and two shorter sides, is used most often in conference rooms and board meetings. The shorter side at the front of the room is generally considered to be the "head" of the table and this seat is reserved for the person with the most power and status. This person also is the one likely to lead the meeting, thus this seat is often referred to as representing dominance or leadership within the group.[159] At the family dining table, the father usually occupies this position and directs the dinner activities. In trial deliberations, the jury foreman would most likely be the one to sit at the head of the rectangular table.

§ 1.79 Perceptions of voice characteristics and qualities

How often have you heard someone complain, "It's not what you said but how you said it"? That statement is especially true when applied to the courtroom.

---

[157] L. Malandro & L. Barker, Nonverbal Communication 192 (Random House, 1983). Copyright © 1983, by Random House, Inc. Reprinted with permission.

[158] M. Koneya & A. Barbour, Louder Than Words . . . Nonverbal Communication (Charles E. Merrill Publishing Co., 1976).

[159] Knapp, *supra* note 150.

> The lawyer says, If the judge and jury hear me and know what I am talking about, that is all I need to understand of the voice.
>
> How little he is impressed with the fact that the voice is the vehicle for the conveyance of his thought, and that is is not so much *what* is said as *how* it is said.
>
> Many a juror has considered a man's argument weak, because his voice and manner were against him; while, on the other hand, a lawyer, understanding the power of the human voice, has completely won the hearts of the jurors by appealing to their sympathies.[160]

Voice characteristics or paralanguage is an important consideration for attorneys. Paralanguage is the vocal aspect of speech, the study of all cues in oral speech other than the content of the words spoken.[161] Vocal variables include voice tone, pitch, loudness, and rate of speech as well as pauses, dialects, vocal segregates (vocalizations such as uh-uh and shhh), and vocal characterizers (such as laughing and yawning).[162]

Jurors form impressions of the parties, their attorneys, and others during the court proceedings based in part on perceptions of voice characteristics and qualities. When listening to others speak, jurors form impressions of the speaker's personality, credibility, likability and competence based on vocal and nonverbal cues.[163] For example, anger expressed through subtle vocal shifts by witnesses and attorneys is easily identifiable by jurors. Therefore, attorneys wanting to project the best possible image to the jury should develop their voice for maximum impact and high drama in the courtroom.[164]

COMMENT: Although we do form impressions of another's personality characteristics based on vocal cues, this

[160] Wauman, *The Voice: How to Train It—How to Care for It* (1889), quoted in Cooper, *The Impressive Voice in the Courtroom*, 69 Trial 53–55, 69 (1979). Reprinted with permission from Trial (July 1979). Copyright © 1979, Association of Trial Lawyers of America.

[161] Malandro & Barker, *supra* note 76, at 276.

[162] Trager, *Paralanguage: A First Approximation*, 13 Stud. in Linguistics 1–12 (1958).

[163] *See, e.g.*, O'Barr & Conley, *When a Juror Watches a Lawyer*, 3 Barrister 8–11, 33 (1976).

[164] *See infra* Part IV, *Appendix*, § 1.94, for a discussion of vocal cue studies.

does not mean that the stereotype is accurate. Listener judgments are often in error, as is the nature of stereotypical perceptions.[165] The important point is that the listener does ascribe certain attributes to the speaker: impressions are formed based on voice characteristics and qualities.

In the following pages we will discuss the vocal and nonverbal variables of rate (or speed of speech), pitch, loudness, pauses, dialect and social status, and the relevance of these factors to the courtroom. Courtroom considerations of powerful speech versus powerless speech in impression formation will also be examined.

§ 1.80 —Speed of speech

The rate of delivery used by the attorney in the courtroom has an impact on the impression he makes with the jury. Peskin notes that "the faster talker is generally more favorably regarded by his listener. In addition, the listener tends to learn from the fast talker."[166] A speaker with a faster rate of delivery is more persuasive and is also seen as more intelligent, knowledgeable, and objective.[167] This does not mean that an attorney should rush through his presentation, going as fast as he possibly can. What it does mean is that, given the listener's ability to comprehend about 350 words per minute (the average speaking rate is between 125 and 190 words per minute), a faster rate of delivery will enhance the attorney's credibility with the jury.[168] A brisker, faster delivery leaves the juror with the impression of the attorney as confident, in control, and capable.

---

[165] J.A. DeVito, The Interpersonal Communication Book 299–300 (Harper & Row, 2d ed. 1980).

[166] Peskin, *Nonverbal Communication in the Courtroom. Part 3: Chronemics*, 3 Trial Dipl. J. 4 (1980).

[167] Miller, Maruyana, Beaver & Valore, *Speed of Speech and Persuasion*, 34 J. Personality & Soc. Psychology 615–624 (1976).

[168] M.L. Knapp, Essentials of Nonverbal Communication 208 (Holt, Rinehart & Winston, 1980).

> . . . people who speak rapidly or in a standard accent are perceived as more competent than people who speak slowly or with an unusual accent.[169]

Addington found that the combination of rate, pitch and vocal quality led to a perception of greater credibility for the speaker.[170] On the other hand, a rate which is too rapid (i.e., over 300 words per minute) could cause jurors to lose track of the argument or just quit making the effort to listen. Moreover, Goldman-Eisler found that an increase in the speed of speech and the inhibition of breathing (e.g., labored breathing) is a sign of anxiety arousal.[171]

Another interesting finding in voice perception is that people tend to talk longer to persons they like.[172] In voir dire, therefore, the observant attorney may be able to tell who the potential juror likes and, perhaps, with which side of the case the juror feels more at ease.

Counsel should also be aware that in a study of follow-up questionnaires completed by actual juries, the amount of verbosity was a predictor of which juror would most likely be elected foreman. Sannito and Arnolds state:

> The most prominent trait perceived by jurors in the 62 forepersons who were studies (30 percent females and 70 percent males) was *verbal productivity*. Seventy-nine percent of the 550 jurors saw the foreperson as either "talkative" (37 percent), "one of the most talkative" (36 percent), or the "most talkative" (5 percent) person compared with the others.
>
> Also, 79 percent of those questioned said the foreperson was either the first, second, or third person to speak at the start of the selection process.[173]

---

[169] Andrews, *Exhibit A: Language*, 18 PSYCHOLOGY TODAY 30 (February 1984).

[170] Addington, *The Relationship of Selected Vocal Characteristics to Personality Perception*, 35 SPEECH MONOGRAPH 492–503 (1968).

[171] Goldman-Eisler, *Speech-breathing Activity—A Measure of Tension and Affect During Interviews*, 46 BRIT. J. PSYCHOLOGY 53, 60–62 (1955).

[172] Howeler & Vrolijk, *Verbal Communication as an Index of Interpersonal Attraction*, 34 ACTA PSYCHOLOGICA 511, 514 (1970).

[173] Sannito & Arnolds, *Jury Study Results: The Factors at Work*, 5 TRIAL DIPL. J. 7 (1982).

§ 1.81 —Voice pitch

Voice pitch is also a meaningful courtroom cue. The pitch, or highness or lowness of the vocal tone, is a good indicator of emotionality. Sannito explains this effect:

> To evaluate how sure a witness or potential juror is in what they tell you, listen to their vocal pitch as they complete their answer. Those who finish with a *rising pitch*, as if asking a question, are uncertain of the statement they are making. When we finish an answer with a rising intonation, we are wondering if our reply is acceptable, which means we don't know!. . .People who are confident, signal their certainty by punctuating their sentences with a lowered pitch. How they end any one statement will determine how much weighting to give their answer.[174]

He then goes on to show the application of voice pitch patterns in the courtroom during voir dire:

> First, try to notice the pitch pattern of each person during jury selection. If they typically end their statements with a lower pitch, they are probably confident, self-assured, and definite in their thinking. In other words, the odds are they won't buckle under pressure. He/she believes in his/her own opinion.[175]

When cross-examining a witness with increased pitch, the attorney should get tougher. By keeping the pressure on, the witness is more likely to become increasingly uncomfortable with a resultant drop in credibility in the eyes of the jury. The lawyer should also make sure his own witnesses have an appropriate pitch level so as to avoid damaging his own credibility with a "high, questioning voice."

Pitch can also be used by the attorney to highlight his own presentation. By changing pitch levels appropriately, the lawyer can attract the juror's attention, generate interest, and make his point in a manner that will more likely be remembered by the juror. Several researchers have concluded:

> Variety and animation through the effective use of paralinguistics gives the human voice its needed flexibility. Flexibility of voice increases listener interest, reveals the speaker's personality, helps to

---

[174] Sannito, *Nonverbal Communication in the Courtroom*, 6 TRIAL DIPL. J. 27 (1983).

[175] *Id*. at 27–28.

> clarify the speaker's thought and most importantly it conveys emotional values.[176]

Emotions (anger, sympathy, solemnity) can also be expressed through changes in pitch. We use the voice as a behavioral indicator of various moods and emotional states. It is not unusual to find a witness saying exactly what you wanted him to say, but destroying the impact by the tone of his voice. Attitudes are projected through the voice and most sensitive listeners will recognize them.

§ 1.82 —Loudness

Loudness is another vocal and nonverbal cue that attorneys can use effectively. Volume can be used to create an appropriate atmosphere for the attorney's presentation. "By dramatically *lowering* his voice, the trial lawyer can work to create a warm, friendly, almost, private club-like atmosphere."[177] When voice tones are lowered, jurors typically respond by leaning forward and increasing their attention to hear what is being said.

The trial lawyer should be aware that loudness is related positively to perceived credibility.[178] A word of caution is in order here: loudness is not akin to screaming and shouting at the maximum decibel level. Volume that conveys the impression that the attorney is in control, is confident, and knows what he is doing will increase perceived credibility for the lawyer. On the other hand, the attorney must keep in mind that anger and contempt are also expressed through increased vocal volume.[179]

§ 1.83 —Pauses

Using the pause to highlight important points in the presentation of the case can be an effective vocal and nonverbal device in the courtroom. Pauses refocus jurors and draw their attention back to the case. Peskin explains:

> The pause should be a purposeful interval of silence giving the jury time to digest the concept it has just heard. The pause serves to

[176] Peskin, *Nonverbal Communication in the Courtroom. Part 4: Paralinguistics*, 3 Trial Dipl. J. 8 (1980).

[177] *Id*. at 9.

[178] Sannito, *supra* note 174, at 28.

[179] Costanzo, Mackel & Costanzo, *Voice Quality Profile and Perceived Emotion*, 16 J. Counseling Psychology 267–270 (1969).

punctuate what the speaker has said, as periods and commas set off words into thought groups in written communications. Pauses cannot be too long or too frequent or else they may suggest to the jury that there has been a blank space, or a lapse in your thinking. Such a distraction is as annoying as the vocalized "uh" or "er" and must be avoided.[180]

Effective speakers use pauses to punctuate what they are saying. A controlled and deliberate pause can have a very great impact on jarring the attention of the listeners. To become effective in using pauses, you need to practice. For many people pausing is not natural. Pauses are best used directly before and after your critical points. In this way they anchor your most important information.

§ 1.84 —Dialect

Dialect is another area where vocal characteristics are used as cues to form an impression of a person. School teachers, for example, were more likely to judge children as culturally disadvantaged if the teacher detected a dialect or indications of nonstandard English.[181] Bradford, Ferror and Bradford found that Chicanos who had a noticeable accent when speaking English were rated lower on ability, intelligence, and success.[182] Individuals who speak with an accent were found to be perceived as having less social status.[183]

Studies of witness credibility in the courtroom have found the same results: an accent, regional dialect, or nonstandard English usage resulted in decreased credibility of the witness.[184] Defendants who spoke in complete sentences and grammatically correct English were acquitted more frequently than defendants who did not have a proper command of the English language.[185] Conley, O'Barr, and Lind observe:

---

[180] Peskin, *supra* note 176 at 9.

[181] Williams, *The Psychological Correlates of Speech Characteristics: On Sounding 'Disadvantaged'*, 13 J. SPEECH & HEARING RESEARCH 472–488 (1970).

[182] Bradford, Ferror & Bradford, *Evaluation Reactions of College Students to Dialect Differences in the English of Mexican-Americans*, 17 LANGUAGE & SPEECH 255–270 (1974).

[183] Mulca, Hanley & Prigge, *Effects of Phonological Speech Foreignness Upon Three Dimensions of Attitude of Selected American Listeners*, 60 QUARTERLY J. SPEECH 411-420 (1974).

[184] *See, e.g.*, H. GILES & P.F. POWESLAND, SPEECH STYLE AND SOCIAL EVALUATION (European Monographs in Social Psychology, No. 7, London Academic Press 1975).

[185] Parkinson, *Verbal Behavior and Courtroom Success*, 29 COM. EDUC. 22–32 (1981).

> . . . lower social-status witnesses, by virtue of the way they speak, may have less credibility and thus a lesser chance of a fair hearing than do higher-status witnesses.[186]

§ 1.85 —Powerful and powerless speech

The use of "powerful speech" has an effect on the impressions that are formed of a witness at trial. Perceptions of a witness' competence, intelligence, likability, and believability are a result of the vocal cues of powerful or powerless speech.

In an experiment based on a segment from an actual trial involving a collision between an automobile and an ambulance, researchers Conley, O'Barr, and Lind altered the testimony to reflect the power modes. Note the following example:[187]

Q. Approximately how long did you stay there before the ambulance arrived?

A. [Powerless]: Oh, it seems like it was about, uh, twenty minutes. Just long enough to help my friend, Mrs. Davis, you know, get straightened out.

[Powerful]: Twenty minutes. Long enough to help get Mrs. Davis straightened out.

Q. Now how long have you lived in this town?

A. [Powerless]: All my life, really.

[Powerful]: All my life.

Q. You're familiar with the streets?

A. [Powerless]: Oh, yes.

[Powerful]: Yes.

Q. You know your way around?

A. [Powerless]: Yes, I guess I do.

[Powerful]: Yes.

The powerless answer is a tentative answer. It is characterized by hedges, vocalizations, and when spoken orally, a rising intonation. The

---

[186] Conley, O'Barr & Lind, *The Power of Language: Presentational Style in the Courtroom*, 6 DUKE L.J. 1375–1399 (1978).

[187] *Id*. Reprinted with permission. Copyright © 1978, Duke University School of Law.

powerful answer is direct, concise, and sure. Goodman and Loftus explain:

> Powerless speech is characterized by instances of (a) hedging ("I think," "it seemed like," "kind of," "sort of,"); (b) hesitation ("well," "uhm," "er"); (c) overpoliteness ("yes, sir," "please, sir"); (d) overuse of adverbial intensifiers such as "very, very," "surely," "definitely." A powerful speech style is one which omits these features.[188]

Voice characteristics and qualities do have an impact on impression formation in the courtroom. The attorney must understand the wide-reaching implications of vocal and nonverbal variables. Goodman and Loftus summarize for us:

> . . .when preparing for trial, attorneys should do more than simply rehearse the content of the testimony. Just as many attorneys might advise their clients to dress neatly for court appearances, they might also advise them to clean up their speech. The manner in which the witness imparts the testimony has a tremendous impact on jurors. Enhanced credibility can be achieved by encouraging the witness to observe a few stylistic guidelines while testifying. Witnesses should be coached to speak in straight-forward, grammatically correct sentences. They should use a powerful, not a powerless, speech style.[189]

§ 1.86 Touch behavior

Physical touch is an important aspect of communication. Mehrabian concludes that, "Even when it contradicts postures, positions, and words, it still determines the total impact of a message."[190]

The importance of physical contact in human communication can be seen in the care of infants. Babies who are held and cuddled grow and thrive; infants who are deprived of human touch are slower in their development. Touch is considered to be so important in infant development that parents of premature newborn babies are encouraged to hold their babies through special sleeves in the isolettes.

---

[188] Goodman & Loftus, *Social Science Looks at Witness Examination*, 20 TRIAL 56 (1984). Reprinted with permission from TRIAL (April 1984), Copyright © 1984, Association of Trial Lawyers of America.

[189] *Id*. at 57.

[190] A. MEHRABIAN, SILENT MESSAGES 6 (Wadsworth Publishers, 1971).

As our children grow, society teaches us that we should touch them less. By the time children are about ten to twelve years old, a significant decrease has occurred in touching behavior. In a study conducted by Dr. Ann Cain, forty-four percent of those surveyed said that their pets received more physical attention than did family members.[191]

American culture is considered to be a "noncontact" culture.[192] We have developed highly organized norms for the use of physical contact and, overall, we are taught to use touch sparingly and carefully. When members of our society do touch other members, the physical contact is regarded as highly meaningful to the person who has been touched.

Our language reflects the fact that we consider touch a meaningful way in which to communicate. We may observe that we were "touched by his thoughtfulness," or that, in times of crisis, we "feel for her."

We "ask permission" to touch another person and likewise we "give permission" to be touched. Helping a person across the street allows us to touch them as we guide or support them. Circumstances of our encounter with another person may affect our perceptions of the appropriateness of physical contact. We are more likely to allow another person close to us in a crowded elevator than we are standing in a supermarket check-out line.

We express approval and liking for another person through use of tactile communication. Avoidance of touch can communicate disrespect, dislike, or disapproval as well as refusal. Withdrawal of physical communication also communicates negative attitudes and disagreement.

We can communicate a variety of emotions through touch. Smith found that detachment, mothering, fear, anger, and playfulness could be communicated by individuals whose hands were touching but who were physically separated by a screen.[193]

Tactile communication is a meaningful and important way in which we communicate with each other. In the courtroom the use of touch generally serves to define the nature of a relationship. When counsel

---

[191] Kaleina, *More Than Other Folks, Pets Get Loving Strokes*, The Arizona Republic, March 3, 1979, at C–2.

[192] Malandro & Barker, *supra* note 76, at 252.

[193] A.I. Smith, Nonverbal Communication Through Touch 1–45 (Ph.D. dissertation, Georgia State University, 1970).

touches his client in a soothing, supportive manner he creates the perception of a bond between himself and the client.[194]

IV. Appendix

§ 1.87 Luchins' experiment on the primacy-recency effect in impression formation[195]

Try the following experiment with a colleague. Read the following paragraphs about Jim under Experiment 1 only and then write a brief description of Jim. What type of person is he? What are some of his personality characteristics? Then have a colleague follow the same procedure by only reading the paragraphs for Experiment 2.

Experiment 1: A Boy Named Jim

> After school Jim left the classroom alone. Leaving the school, he started on his long walk home. The street was brilliantly filled with sunshine. Jim walked down the street on the shady side. Coming down the street toward him he saw the pretty girl whom he had met on the previous evening. Jim crossed the street and entered the candy store. The store was crowded with students, and he noticed a few familiar faces. Jim waited quietly until the counterman caught his eye and then gave his order. Taking a drink he sat down at a side table. When he had finished the drink he went home.
>
> Jim left the house to get some stationery. He walked into the sunfilled street with two of his friends, basking in the sun as he walked. Jim entered the stationery store which was full of people. Jim talked with an acquaintance while he waited for the clerk to catch his eye. On his way out, he stopped to chat with a school friend who was just coming into the store. Leaving the store, he walked toward school. On his way out, he met the girl to whom he had been introduced the night before. They talked for a short while, and then Jim left for school.

---

[194] *See supra* § 1.39; *see also infra* Part IV, *Appendix*, § 1.96.

[195] Reprinted with permission from 1 C. Hovland, The Order of Presentation in Persuasion 33–61 (Yale University Press, 1957). Copyright © 1957 by Yale University Press, Inc.

Experiment 2: A Boy Named Jim

Jim left the house to get some stationery. He walked into the sunfilled street with two of his friends, basking in the sun as he walked. Jim entered the stationery store which was full of people. Jim talked with an acquaintance while he waited for the clerk to catch his eye. On his way out, he stopped to chat with a school friend who was just coming into the store. Leaving the store, he walked toward school. On his way out he met the girl to whom he had been introduced the night before. They talked for a short while, and then Jim left for the school.

After school Jim left the classroom alone. Leaving the school, he started on his long walk home. The street was brilliantly filled with sunshine. Jim walked down the street on the shady side. Coming down the street toward him, he saw the pretty girl whom he had met on the previous evening. Jim crossed the street and entered the candy store. The store was crowded with students, and he noticed a few familiar faces. Jim waited quietly until the counterman caught his eye and then gave his order. Taking a drink he sat down at a side table. When he had finished the drink he went home.

Before we present Luchins' results, answer the following questions:

In Experiment 1, did you perceive Jim primarily as an introvert or an extrovert?

In Experiment 2, did your colleague perceive Jim primarily as an introvert or an extrovert?

Luchins found that the order in which the paragraphs were read did affect perceptions of the personality sketch written about Jim. The experimental findings confirm that the majority of subjects who read the paragraphs in Experiment 1 perceived Jim as an introvert, while those who read the paragraphs in reverse order in Experiment 2 viewed Jim as an extrovert. Luchins confirmed the existence of a primacy effect: the information presented first is most decisive.[196]

§ 1.88 Trait Association Theory test

The following is an experiment which has been used to test trait associations. Read the directions for Test 1 only and complete the identifi-

---

[196] *See supra* § 1.52.

cation of adjectives which best describe the individual. Then ask a colleague to do the same for Test 2 and compare the results.

Test 1

Directions:

Here is a list of characteristics that belong to a particular person that you have been asked to create in your mind. Read them carefully and try to form an impression of the kind of person described.

Intelligent—Skillful—Industrious—Warm—Determined—Practical—Cautious

Select from the following list those traits which best describe the picture of the individual you have formed in your mind. Underline one adjective in each pair.

1.	Generous	Ungenerous
2.	Shrewd	Gullible
3.	Unhappy	Happy
4.	Irritable	Good-natured
5.	Humorous	Humorless
6.	Sociable	Unsociable
7.	Unreliable	Reliable
8.	Popular	Unpopular
9.	Important	Unimportant
10.	Ruthless	Humane
11.	Good-looking	Unattractive
12.	Persistent	Unstable
13.	Frivolous	Serious
14.	Restrained	Talkative
15.	Self-centered	Altruistic
16.	Imaginative	Unimaginative
17.	Strong	Weak
18.	Dishonest	Honest

Test 2

Directions:

Here is a list of characteristics that belong to a particular person that you have been asked to create. Read them carefully and try to form an impression of the kind of person described.

Intelligent—Skillful—Industrious—Cold—Determined—Practical—Cautious

Select from the following list those traits which best describe the picture of the individual you have formed in your mind. Underline one adjective in each pair.

1.	Generous	Ungenerous
2.	Shrewd	Gullible
3.	Unhappy	Happy
4.	Irritable	Good-natured
5.	Humorous	Humorless
6.	Sociable	Unsociable
7.	Unreliable	Reliable
8.	Popular	Unpopular
9.	Important	Unimportant
10.	Ruthless	Humane
11.	Good-looking	Unattractive
12.	Persistent	Unstable
13.	Frivolous	Serious
14.	Restrained	Talkative
15.	Self-centered	Altruistic
16.	Imaginative	Unimaginative
17.	Strong	Weak
18.	Dishonest	Honest

Only one word has been altered in the list of characteristics presented in both Test 1 and Test 2. In Test 1 the word "warm" was used; in Test 2 the word "cold" was used. Now compare the different trait associations with the adjective pairs in Test 1 and Test 2. The majority of subjects who have completed this test show a marked difference in the words they select depending on whether the characteristic "cold" or "warm" appeared. "Warm" seems to go with generous, happy, humorous, and popular, while "cold" is associated with unsociable, shrewd, self-centered, and unimaginative. This reaction supports both Asch's work and the concept of trait association theory. Human perception, association, and experience lead us to believe that certain characteristics just "seem" to go with others.[197]

[197] *See supra* § 1.58.

§ 1.89 Mock jury research studies

The mock jury paradigm is not without its critics. For example, Gerbasi, Zukerman, and Reis have questioned the ability to generalize mock jury research. Among their concerns are the fact that most mock jury research takes place outside of the actual courtroom setting and presents the case to the mock jurors via taped sequences or written reports.[198] Would the mock jurors respond to a live courtroom presentation in the same manner that they respond to the research setting?

Gerbasi et al. also criticize mock jury research because the activities asked of the mock jurors are not the same as those asked of an actual juror. Actual jurors must assess guilt or innocence and then render a verdict (and perhaps impose a sentence). In much of the mock jury research, guilt is already established in the case and the researcher is interested in how the mock juror evaluates other variables (such as the defendant's attractiveness).

For example, in a recent civil case involving a baby who had been badly burned when a large aircraft crashed into its home and where liability was not an issue, seven mock juries were used to predict a potential verdict for this horribly damaged child. Since liability was not a question, the only issue presented to the mock juries was the amount of the verdict. The mock juries' awards ranged from $14 million to $32 million. The actual verdict, however, was only $10.9 million. Perhaps this indicates that mock juries tend to be more liberal than those physically confined in the courtroom who know that they have actual responsibility to make an award.

Additionally, the decision-making process used in mock jury research is not the same as in actual trial situations. Jurors in the actual courtroom setting make their decisions as groups through the group decision-making process. Much of the mock jury research asks the mock jurors to make an individual (isolated) decision.

Another criticism of mock jury research is that subjects are usually college students recruited for the study. This raises other questions: How representative are college students of the population as a whole? Would the results of the study have been the same if the subjects were drawn from an actual jury pool?

Although the criticism leveled against mock jury research studies is

---

[198] Gerbasi, Zuckerman & Reis, *Justice Needs a New Blindfold: A Review of Mock Jury Research*, 84 Psychological Bull. 323–345 (1977).

plentiful, there are some interesting conclusions about juries and jurors that result from this type of research. Trial lawyers should be aware of the results that have been produced using the mock jury paradigm, while bearing in mind the possible limitations inherent in this type of research.

Sannito and Arnolds, under the auspices of the *Trial Diplomacy Journal*, have analyzed over 600 questionnaires returned by jurors upon completion of their deliberations. On the basis of these responses, the following summary was made:

A. The most prominent traits of the foreperson, in order of importance, were *verbal productivity*, *warmth*, and *confidence*. Of lesser importance were word usage, intelligence, and dominance.

B. *Skill* and *likability* of the attorneys were the best single predictors of initial and final verdict. Attorneys' dress was insignificant.

C. *Likability of the victim* significantly affected juror decisions in a criminal case. A likable complaining witness increased the chances for conviction and an unlikable one made acquittal more likely.

D. The more *attractive* defendants had a better chance for acquittal than the less attractive ones in criminal cases.

E. Secretaries convicted at an alarming rate.

F. High frequency of conviction was also found for jurors in precision occupations, such as engineers, programmers, machinists, bankers, bookkeepers, and accountants.

G. Irish, especially Irish women, were significantly more conviction prone than any other ethnic group studied. Seventy-four percent of the Irish in the study convicted compared with only 46% of the Germans. In general, courtroom stereotypes are risky.

H. Women convicted slightly more than men (60% to 53%) and women with degrees were significantly prone to convict more than acquit.

I. Jurors with small families and whose spouses have college degrees tended to convict, while those with larger families and less educated spouses were more likely to acquit.

J. A *leaderless jury* was more likely to acquit than one with a strong and appealing leader.

K. The degree to which jurors have an antiauthoritarian attitude, called the *defense factor*, was far and away the best predictor of acquittal.

L. The authoritarian disposition was an excellent predictor of conviction. We are calling it the *prosecution factor*.[199]

§ 1.90 Additional studies regarding perceptions of attractive/unattractive people

"Society is biased against uglies," says researcher Heckenmueller, "and somehow attractive people tend to be more persuasive or wield more influence than plain people."[200] Society recognizes and identifies its attractive members from an early age. According to Algozzine, teachers interact less frequently and less positively with the unattractive child.[201] With the unattractive individual, the nonverbal responses include behaviors of avoidance (e.g., reduced eye contact, greater distance from the person) as well as the verbal response of singling out the "misfit" through namecalling or other forms of ridicule.

Attractive people, according to researchers Berscheid and Walster, are rated higher on a wide range of socially desirable evaluations such as success, personality, popularity, sociability, and persuasiveness.[202] In studying the effect of attractiveness on persuasiveness, Mills and Aronson had one woman made up to look both attractive and unattractive at different times. In the unattractive guise, she wore loose-fitting clothing, her hair was messy, her make-up was conspicuously absent, a trace of a mustache was penciled on her upper lip, and her complexion was oily. Independent observers rated her as less persuasive than when she appeared attractively attired.[203]

Dion, Berscheid, and Walster reported that subjects predicted beautiful people would have more fulfilling lives, happier marriages, and more prestigious occupations.[204] Attractive women seem to receive deferential treatment when compared with their less attractive counterparts. Attractive women are more successful in changing attitudes of male stu-

---

[199] Sannito & Arnolds, *Jury Study Results: The Factors at Work*, 5 TRIAL DIPL. J. 8 (1982). Reprinted with permission.

[200] Heckenmueller, *Researchers Say Society Biased Against Uglies*, Tallahassee Democrat, November 9, 1972.

[201] Algozzine, *What Teachers Perceive—Children Receive?*, 24 COM. Q. 41-47 (1976).

[202] Berscheid & Walster, *Beauty and the Beast*, 5 PSYCHOLOGY TODAY 42–46, 75 (1972).

[203] Mills & Aronson, *Opinion as a Function of the Communicator's Attractiveness and Desire to Influence*, 1 J. PERSONALITY & SOC. PSYCHOLOGY 73–77 (1965).

[204] Dion, Berscheid & Walster, *What is Beautiful is Good*, 24 J. PERSONALITY & SOC. PSYCHOLOGY 207–213 (1972).

dents,[205] have more dates,[206] and are given lighter sentences in court cases.[207]

Attractiveness is an important consideration in the jury's perception of the defendant, plaintiff, or witness. Most of the research in this area has been conducted through laboratory simulations, but the implications for the attorney are many and worthy of examination.

Kalvin and Zeisal asked judges who had presided over actual criminal cases whether they would have rendered the same decision their juries had reached.[208] The results of the survey indicated that in those cases where the judge and jury disagreed on the verdict, 11-14% of those disagreements could be attributed to the impression made by the defendant. Landy and Aronson deduce that:

> These results seem to indicate that an attractive defendant can move the jury to be more lenient than the judge would have been, i.e., acquit rather than convict. Conversely, an unattractive defendant can presumably move the jury to be more severe than the judge would have been, i.e., convict rather than acquit.[209]

Research on attractiveness/unattractiveness can be categorized in two areas: (1) social attractiveness (character traits and behavioral traits accepted by society) and (2) physical attractiveness.

In a seminal study which has generated much research in the area, Landy and Aronson investigated the effect of the character of the parties on the jury's verdict.[210] The researchers reasoned that a socially successful (and thus attractive) person would be viewed more favorably by the jury than a person described to the jury as less successful (and, therefore, less attractive). The subjects in the study were presented with a case involving a negligent homicide by reckless operation of a vehicle in which the defendant was described as either an attractive or an unattractive person in terms of his social characteristics. The attractive defendant was described as follows:

---

[205] Widgery & Webster, *The Effects of Physical Attractiveness Upon Perceived Initial Credibility*, 4 Mich. Speech. J. 9–15 (1969). *See also* Mills & Aronson, *supra* note 203.

[206] E. Berscheid & E. Walster, *Physical Attractiveness* in 7 Advances in Experimental and Social Psychology 157–215 (Academic Press, L. Berkowitz ed. 1974).

[207] H. Sigall, *Psychologist Proves Good Looks Helpful*, Associated Press Release (1974).

[208] H. Kalven, Jr., & H. Zeisel, The American Jury (Little, Brown, 1966).

[209] Landy & Aronson, *The Influence of the Character of the Criminal and His Victim on Stimulated Jurors*, 5 J. Experim. & Soc. Psychology 146 (1969).

[210] *Id.*

> Sander is a sixty-four-year-old insurance adjuster who has been friendly with everyone and was known as a good worker. Sander is a widower, his wife having died of cancer the previous year, and he is, consequently, spending Christmas Eve with his son and daughter-in-law. When the incident occurred, Sander's leg banged the steering column, reaggravating a gun shot wound which had been the source of a slight limp and much pain. Sander's traffic record shows he has received three tickets in the past five years, two of which were moving violations.

The unattractive defendant was described as follows:

> Sander is a thirty-three-year-old janitor. In the building where Sander has been working as a janitor for the past two months, he was not known by many of the firm employees, but was nevertheless invited to join the party. Sander is a two-time divorcee, with three children by his first wife, who has since remarried. He was going to spend Christmas Eve with his girlfriend in her apartment. The effect of the incident on Sander was negligible; he was slightly shaken up by the impact, but suffered no major injuries. Sander has two misdemeanors on his criminal record in the past five years—breaking and entering and a drug violation. His traffic record shows three tickets in the same space of time.[211]

Defendants of attractive character were assigned shorter prison terms (nine years) than those defendants who were described as unattractive (twelve years).

As we can observe from the descriptions of the attractive or unattractive defendant used in the Landy and Aronson study, there are many factors used in the manipulation of attractiveness (such as age, occupation, marital status, and injury). Other research followed the basic idea used by Landy and Aronson, but attempted to separate the effects of some of the factors.

Sigall and Landy attempted to determine the effect of attractiveness in terms of personal likability and not as a function of sympathy for the defendant because of injury suffered.[212] The defendant was described as "loving and warm" (attractive) versus "cold and unapproachable" (unattractive). The "loving and warm" defendant received a prison sentence

---

[211] *Id*. at 148.

[212] Sigall & Landy, *Effects of the Defendant's Character and Suffering on Juridic Judgment*, 88 J. Soc. Psychology 140–150 (1972).

almost three years shorter (6.52 years) than the "cold and unapproachable" defendant (9.22 years).

The study of socially desirable characteristics and the effects of those characteristics on sentencing by mock juries was conducted by Austin, Walster and Utne.[213] Male and female mock jurors sentenced a defendant in a purse snatching case. The defendant was described as having only taken the victim's purse or has having beaten the victim as well as having taken the purse. In the process of attempting to escape the police, the defendant was said to have suffered either no harm, moderate harm, or excessive harm. Results show that the defendant who beat his victim was punished more severely than the defendant who only snatched the purse. Also, the more severely hurt the defendant in the escape attempt, the less severe was his sentence.

In describing the defendant in a simulated negligent homicide by operation of a vehicle case, Kaplan and Kemmerick varied trait characteristics.[214] The negatively described defendant was found to be the most blameworthy and was given the harshest sentence while the positively described defendant was treated less severely in his sentencing.

Attractiveness and race of the defendant were studied by Nemeth and Sosis.[215] The sentence imposed was found to be a function of the attractiveness of the defendant and the characteristics of the jurors. Here again, attractiveness of the defendant affected his sentence with the more attractive defendant receiving a lesser punishment. Attractiveness in this experiment meant "a likable, middle-class, upstanding citizen with no criminal record" while unattractiveness referred to "a working class citizen who has had marital difficulties and has a criminal record." They found that the race of the defendant had no substantial effect.

Reynolds and Sanders also report research that affirms the importance of the social attractiveness of the defendant.[216] The effect of social attrac-

---

[213] W. Austin, E. Walster & E. Utne, *Equity and the Law: The Effect of a Harmdoer's "Suffering in the Act" on Liking and Assigned Punishment* in ADVANCES IN EXPERIMENTAL SOCIAL PSYCHOLOGY (Academic Press, L. Berkowitz & E. Walster eds., 1976).

[214] Kaplan & Kemmerick, *Juror Judgment as Information Integration: Combining Evidential and Nonevidential Information*, 30 J. PERSONALITY & SOC. PSYCHOLOGY 493–499 (1974).

[215] Nemeth & Sosis, *A Simulated Jury Study: Characteristics of the Defendant and the Jurors*, 90 J. SOC. PSYCHOLOGY 221–229 (1973).

[216] Reynolds & Sanders, *Effect of Defendant Attractiveness, Age and Injury on Severity of Sentence Given by Simulated Jurors*, 96 J. SOC. PSYCHOLOGY 149–150 (1975).

tiveness has been found to be lessened when the jury as a group discusses the case. In one study, jurors were individually asked to sentence the attractive and unattractive defendant (here defined as high status and low status).[217] (Individual jurors gave longer sentences to low status defendants but when the jurors met as a group of 4 to 6 jurors the sentences rendered by the group were less severe for the low status individual. (The discussion phase did not affect the sentence of the high status individual).

Similarity of attitudes also appears to generate a perception of defendant attractiveness for the juror. Griffin and Jackson presented mock jurors with different attitudinal orientations of a defendant.

> *Version A*: He is described by the psychologist as a person with a firm belief in God, a strong allegiance to the American way of life, and as a person who feels that men cope with stress and financial matters better than do women. Further, the social worker characterizes him as a person who enjoys sports, dancing, and involvement in current social problems such as promoting the cause of public school racial integration. It was ascertained that he has no previous criminal record with the exception of one minor traffic violation.
>
> *Version B*: He is described by the psychologist as a person with a firm belief that there is no God, a negative opinion concerning the American way of life, and as a person convinced of the superiority of women in adjusting to stress and handling financial matters. Further, the social worker characterizes him as a person who does not enjoy such activities as dancing and sports, but is involved in current social problems such as a campaign to prevent public school racial integration. It was ascertained that he has no previous criminal record with the exception of one minor traffic violation.[218]

The more dissimilar the attitudes of the defendant and the juror, the more likely the defendant was to be found guilty and the longer his prison sentence. In addition, the defendant was found to be less attractive to the juror than a defendant with attitudes similar to those of the juror.

Physical attractiveness has been studied and found to exert an influ-

---

[217] Izzett & Leginski, *Group Discussion and the Influence of Defendant Characteristics in a Simulated Jury Setting*, 93 J. Soc. Psychology 271–279 (1974).

[218] Griffin & Jackson, *Simulated Jury Decisions: The Influence of Jury-Defendant Attitude Similarity-Dissimilarity* 1 Soc. Behav. & Personality 1–7 (1973).

ence on juror's perceptions.[219] Efran demonstrated the impact of physical attractiveness through an experiment concerning cheating on a university examination.[220] Physically unattractive cheaters were judged guilty more often than attractive cheaters and they were also given harsher punishments. In other words, Efran found the defendant's attractiveness to be negatively correlated with the assessment of guilt and the severity of punishment. He found that the "physically attractive defendants were judged with less certainty and given less severe recommended punishments."

An interesting study of physical attractiveness was conducted by Sigall and Ostrove. For the purpose of the experiment a female defendant was used. The researchers hypothesized that "an attractive defendant would receive more lenient treatment than an unattractive defendant when the offense was unrelated to attractiveness; when the crime was related to attractiveness, the attractive defendant would receive relatively harsh treatment."[221]

When the crime was burglary (unrelated to the physical attractiveness of the defendant), jurors would impose more lenient sentences on the attractive defendant. However, when the crime was a swindle it was seen as related to attractiveness; the defendant was perceived as having used her attractiveness to help perpetrate the crime. Jurors imposed harsher sentences on the attractive defendant when the crime was a swindle. Thus the attractive swindler and the unattractive thief were given longer sentences than the unattractive swindler and the attractive thief. It appears that attractive people are viewed as "better" than unattractive people. When an attractive individual, however, deliberately takes advantage of her attractiveness, she is especially disliked.

Stephan and Tully found that physically attractive plaintiffs in a personal injury case recovered more often and received higher monetary awards than did unattractive plaintiffs.[222] Friend and Vinson found that

---

219 *See* Berscheid & Walster, *supra* note 206, for overview of physical attractiveness research up to 1974.

220 Effran, *The Effect of Physical Appearance on the Judgment of Guilt, Interpersonal Attraction, and Severity of Recommended Punishment in A Simulated Jury Task*, 8 J. Research in Personality 45–54 (1974).

221 Signall & Ostrove, *Beautiful but Dangerous: Effects of Offender Attractiveness and Nature of Crime on Juridic Judgment*, 31 J. Personality & Soc. Psychology 410–414 (1975).

222 Stephan & Tully, *The Influence of Physical Attractiveness of a Plaintiff on the Decision of Simulated Jurors*, 101 J. Soc. Psychology 149–150 (1977).

mock jurors were very much aware of the physical attractiveness of the defendants.[223]

In addition, Cash and Duncan recently found that physical attractiveness stereotyping is as prevalent among black American college students as among whites.[224] For both groups, the highly attractive individual is perceived as having a more socially desirable personality and as having greater potential for the future.

§ 1.91 Additional studies on perceptions of territory

Like animals, humans have an affinity for "home." "Man's home is his castle" is as true for the human psyche as the homing instinct is for the spawning salmon. "People use their homes to display and assert their individuality," says Irwin Altman, a psychologist at the University of Utah.[225] In his studies of how people use environment to communicate their needs, Altman stresses that personalities and culture are expressed through the home and its territory.

He cites the example of the Nubian tribe in Egypt who were forced to relocate when the Aswan High Dam was built in the 1960's. The Nubians had been accustomed to living in hamlets of 100 to 200 people where their homes could house relatives, friends, and animals. Altman reports:

> Elaborate decorations on the interior and exterior of their homes contained commonly understood symbols like plates over the front doorway welcoming strangers and stars of Islam. The Nubians' new houses, after the move, were inappropriate to their lifestyles. The walls were so low that there was not room for plates and religious signs; the windows were so large they invaded the Nubians' sense of privacy; and the quarters were too cramped for family visits. There were health problems, mortality problems, women could not go out, there was no place to put their animals and not enough storage. . .They had to give up their sense of identity. And the whole Nubian culture changed forever.[226]

Unlike animals who defend their territory (often attacking and fighting

---

[223] Friend & Vinson, *Leaning Over Backwards: Jurors' Response to Defendants' Attractiveness*, 24 J. Com. 124–129 (1974).

[224] Cash & Duncan, *Physical Attractiveness Stereotyping Among Black American College Students*, 122 J. Soc. Psychology 71–77 (1984).

[225] Altman, *Decor, Appearance of Homes, Provide Clues about Residents*, The Arizona Republic, April 29, 1984, at S–2.

[226] *Id*. at S–2.

an intruder), humans adhere to social norms which discourage the defense of territory. For example, McAndrew studied the reactions of college students when their places were taken at library tables.[227] In McAndrew's study, students were asked to help answer a questionnaire. While the students were away, another student's belongings were put in the subject's place. Upon returning and finding that his space had been taken, not a single subject demanded his place back. Instead, every subject found a new place to sit.

We can usually identify those spaces that are "off limits" or that are taken in particular instances. Students in a college class sit in "their own" seats even without a seating assignment. Children know how to interpret books piled on an "empty" seat on the school bus. We all know the signs of territoriality and we usually respect those signs and find space of our own.

Exactly what is "territory"? Researchers have defined it both as a function of size and as a function of the use to which it is put. Scheflen categorizes territory by size, beginning with the "spot," the smallest territory and moving up to the "region."[228] The "spot," is a small space where we may put a drinking glass or our elbow (as on the arm of a chair). We may find ourselves jockeying for control of the spot when we are in a movie theatre and someone else's elbow is attempting to take our spot on the armrest. A "cubit" is an 18-inch space which may be combined with other cubits to form a "K-space," which is the area an individual usually occupies. A "location" is the space around the person and a "module" is a row of locations (a module would be the checkout line in a supermarket, for example). A "region" is an area the size of a room which several people can occupy; the region has a "nucleus" at its center.

Status and power can be communicated through how much territory we occupy. An important person in a corporation has a correspondingly large office space while the "gopher" usually works out of a cubby hole-sized closet. If we know a person who owns a summer home at the beach, a retreat in the mountains, or a riverfront cabin we will afford him the status and importance in proportion to the territory he controls.

---

[227] McAndrew, Ryckman, Harr & Solomon, *The Effects of Invader Placement of Spatial Markers on Territorial Behavior in a College Population*, 104 J. Soc. Psychology 149–150 (1978).

[228] A.E. Scheflen, *Micro-territories in Human Interaction* in Organization of Behavior in Face to Face Interaction 159–174 (Mouton-Aldine Publ., A. Kendon, R.M. Harris, & M.R. Keys eds. 1975).

Territory can also be classified according to the uses to which it is put. Altman identifies three types of territorial uses: primary, secondary, and public. Primary territories include those territories over which a person has exclusive control, such as clothing and toothbrushes. Secondary territories are generally associated with the owner, but are not the exclusive property of the owner, such as the regular parking space at the office. Finally, public territories are those territories open to everyone, such as the public library or the city hall.[229]

Certain factors influence territoriality such as the more desirable the territory the more likely it is to be invaded by others seeking that territory. Shafer and Sadowski studied territoriality of tables in a barroom and discovered that the most desirable tables were those that were in the midst of the social interaction.[230] These tables were most likely to be invaded. The "best seat" on the school bus or the "best spot" to study in the library will be taken the moment the occupant vacates it.

We attempt to communicate to others that we occupy a space by leaving "markers"—our coats, books or other personal belongings. By leaving these items in the space, the implicit communication is, "Keep out. Someone is sitting here." It appears to make a difference if these markers are male or female markers. Feminine markers (such as a purse or a sweater) are less effective in "saving a place" than are briefcases and jackets which are perceived to be more masculine markers.[231]

The intensity of territorial invasion makes a difference. It is one thing to have a person who is sitting right next to you flow over into your space on the library table and quite another for them to peer over your shoulder at you.[232]

§ 1.92 Additional studies on perceptions of personal space

We tend to give more personal space to those people we perceive as having more status and authority than we possess. Dean, Willis, and Hewitt found that subordinates in the Navy gave their superiors more space than they did their fellow subordinates. The more superior the

---

[229] I. Altman, THE ENVIRONMENT AND SOCIAL BEHAVIOR (Brooks/Cole, 1975).

[230] Shafer & Sadowski, *An Investigation of Territorial Invasion in A Barroom Environment*, 38 SOCIOMETRY 408–419 (1975).

[231] *Id.*

[232] Krail & Leventhal, *The Sex Variable in the Intrusion of Personal Space*, 39 SOCIOMETRY 170–173 (1976).

officer, the more space he was accorded.[233] Superiors in this same Navy study did not discriminate among various status levels of subordinates.

It also appears from research that deviant members of our society have a need for greater personal space.

> The research related to pathology and deviance supports the notion that the boundaries of personal space represent "body-buffer zones" used to protect people from emotional and physical threats. Individuals with more serious personality problems see others as threatening and therefore need more space for protection. A current television public-service message suggests that most violent prisoners were abused physically as children. It appears that in response to their physical abuse as children, these prisoners developed larger personal space needs than most people. As a result, their space is more likely to be invaded by others with smaller needs, thereby causing them to feel "attacked." Thus they are more likely to respond in a pathological or deviant manner.[234]

§ 1.93 Additional studies regarding perceptions of environment

We respond to various aspects of our environment such as our environment's overall attractiveness, as well as the colors, lighting and sounds of our surroundings.

Not surprisingly, we respond favorably to an attractive environment and negatively to an unattractive one. Maslow and Mintz, in a famous study of the effects of an attractive, average, and ugly room on subjects' perceptions of photographs found that subjects in the attractive room gave significantly higher scores to the pictures.[235] In addition, subjects in the ugly room reported fatigue, headaches, sleepiness, irritability and hostility, while those in the attractively decorated room said they felt pleasure, enjoyment, energy in their environment.[236]

Table 1–4 identifies the symbolic meanings and specific moods associ-

---

[233] Dean, Willis & Hewitt, *Initial Interaction Distance Among Individuals Equal and Unequal in Military Rank*, 32 J. PERSONALITY & SOC. PSYCHOLOGY 294–299 (1975).

[234] Malandro & Barker, *supra* note 76, at 231.

[235] Maslow & Mintz, *Effects of Esthetic Surroundings: I. Initial Effects of Three Esthetic Conditions Upon Perceiving "Energy" and "Well being" in Faces*, 41 J. PSYCHOLOGY 247–254 (1956).

[236] Mintz, *Effects of Esthetic Surroundings: II. Prolonged and Repeated Experience in a "Beautiful" and "Ugly" Room*, 41 J. PSYCHOLOGY 459–466 (1956).

ated with colors in the environment. Colors play a major role in the perception of both people and environments.[237]

Table 1–4
Color in the Environment: Moods Created and Symbolic Meanings

Color	*Moods*	*Symbolic Meanings*
Red	Hot, affectionate, angry, defiant, contrary, hostile, full of vitality, excitement, love.	Happiness, lust, intimacy, love, restlessness, agitation, royalty, rage, sin, blood.
Blue	Cool, pleasant, leisurely, distant, infinite, secure, transcendent, calm, tender.	Dignity, sadness, tenderness, truth.
Yellow	Unpleasant, exciting, hostile, cheerful, joyful, jovial.	Superficial glamor, sun, light, wisdom, masculinity, royalty (in China), age (in Greece), prostitution (in Italy), famine (in Egypt).
Orange	Unpleasant, exciting, disturbed, distressed, upset, defiant, contrary, hostile, stimulating.	Sun, fruitfulness, harvest, thoughtfulness.
Purple	Depressed, sad, dignified, stately.	Wisdom, victory, pomp, wealth, humility, tragedy.
Green	Cool, pleasant, leisurely, in control.	Security, peace, jealousy, hate, aggressiveness, calm.
Black	Sad, intense, anxiety, fear, despondent, dejected, melancholy, unhappy.	Darkness, power, mastery, protection, decay, mystery, wisdom, death, atonement.
Brown	Sad, not tender, despondent, dejected, melancholy, unhappy, neutral.	Melancholy, protection, autumn, decay, humility, atonement.
White	Joy, lightness, neutral, cold.	Solemnity, purity, chastity, femininity, humility, joy, light, innocence, fidelity, cowardice.

Even our language reflects how colors communicate both emotionally and physically. We have "black days" and "blue Mondays." We can

[237] Reprinted with permission from J.K. Burgoon & T. Saine, The Unspoken Dialogue: An Introduction to Nonverbal Communication 110 (Houghton Mifflin, 1978) Copyright © 1978 by Houghton Mifflin Company. Used by permission.

"see red" and we are "green with envy." Madison Avenue knows which colors appeal to consumers and products are marketed in those colors: red and white toothpaste containers, red and yellow cereal boxes.

The use of color in the school environment has been studied by Ketcham.[238] Over a two year period he studied the impact of color on school improvement variables such as language aptitude, safety habits and social ability. Ketcham found that the students in the school that used dynamic colors in the environment also showed the most improvement in the variables studied. In the school painted in dynamic colors the corridors were painted yellow, northern exposure classrooms were a pale rose, classrooms with a southern exposure were painted in shades of blue and green, and green chalkboards were used to reduce glare. This use of color was found not only to be more pleasing to the students, it also stimulated learning. Ketcham contrasted the results with his dynamically painted school to a school that was left unpainted and to a third school that was painted in the traditional color scheme. The unpainted school showed the least student improvement and the traditionally colored school showed the next best student achievement level.

Lighting can also make a difference in environment. General Electric markets its "soft white" light bulbs to create a more relaxed and inviting environment. We all know of softly lit restaurants where we feel at home and want to linger over dessert. Likewise, being in a room with glaring lights may give us a headache, make us feel fatigued, and prompt us to leave as soon as possible. We can imagine the old television scene where the policeman interrogates the accused under a single, dangling, glaring light bult and we can empathize with how uncomfortable the accused must have felt.

Researchers have found that verbal behavior differs depending on the lighting in the room. Gergen, Gergen, and Barton placed some subjects in a darkened room and another group of subjects in a lighted room.[239] Subjects were told they could do whatever they wanted to do for an hour. Each room contained four male and four female subjects, was ten feet by twelve feet, and had padded floors and walls. In the lighted room, the researchers found that the subjects carried on a continuous line of con-

---

[238] H. KETCHAM, COLOR PLANNING FOR BUSINESS AND INDUSTRY (Harper & Row, 1958).

[239] Gergen, Gergen & Barton, *Deviance in the Dark*, 7 PSYCHOLOGY TODAY 129–230 (1973).

versation while in the darkened room the subjects rarely spoke after about thirty minutes.

The effects of colored lighting have also been studied.[240] Interestingly, subjects who perform tasks in red lighting appear to have reactions that are 12% faster than subjects who perform the same tasks in a regularly lighted room. Subjects who performed in the green lighting situation were slower in performing the tasks. Also, red lighting tended to cause the subjects to overestimate their judgments of time, length, and weight while subjects in the green lighting situation tended to underestimate time, length and weight tasks. Not surprisingly, Thompson found that fatigue of subjects rises in direct proportion to the dimming of the perceptual field.[241]

Another factor which affects our perceptions of the environment are the types of sounds we hear. An audio recording which is becoming increasingly popular with new parents contains the sounds a baby hears in the womb. Playing this record in the newborn's nursery lulls the baby into a restful sleep. Adults respond to sounds as well. A loud sudden sound can startle us and make our hearts "skip a beat." A change in the surrounding noise level will undoubtedly attract our attention and make us more aware. Silence, the absence of sound, is meaningful as well. Silence in a conversation can communicate disapproval, confusion, or disinterest. If we have just met a person, silence in a conversation can make both people very uncomfortable.

A final factor affecting our response to an environment is music. Music is often used to soothe and create a mood. Some radio stations advertise themselves for the atmosphere they try to create, calling themselves "easy listening" and "music for your memories." Music can lift or depress our spirits; it can remind us of happy or sad times. Music, according to researcher Mehrabian, has a more immediate effect on our arousal level and feelings of pleasure than several cups of coffee.[242] And, finally, music is also used by business establishments to create a desired response in the clientele, as Malandro and Barker observe:

> . . . it is important to realize that music is often used to evoke a particular response. . . . For example, various types of merchants use music in an attempt to increase the desirability of their products.

---

[240] R. Birren, Color Psychology and Color Therapy (University Books, 1975).

[241] J.J. Thompson, Beyond Words: Nonverbal Communication in the Classroom (Citation Press, 1973).

[242] A. Mehrabian, Public Places and Private Spaces 50 (Basic Books, 1976).

They use music to create an environment that will elicit a particular response from the customer. A supermarket may raise the volume of music to stimulate more purchases in a short period of time. A softly lit restaurant uses soothing music to match the intimate atmosphere. A disco uses flashing lights and music that is loud and has a repeated beat to produce excitement. Each of these businesses uses a different type of music in order to produce a special environment—an environment that will sell their products.[243]

§ 1.94 Vocal cue studies

Vocal cues also allow us to identify and recognize an individual. In a famous example, Bruno Hauptmann, the alleged kidnapper of the Lindbergh baby, was identified by a witness who said he recognized Hauptmann's voice. However, three years had elapsed since the witness first heard the kidnapper's voice and the veracity of the identification was questionable. In studies of voice recognition, McGhee found that accuracy drops off dramatically after about three weeks, and after five months accuracy in voice identification is only about 13%.[244]

Researchers have examined how accurately subjects perceive demographic characteristics from vocal cues. One of the first researchers to explore the accuracy of these impressions was T.H. Pear.[245] Pear asked over four thousand subjects to judge the vocal cues of nine speakers. He found that subjects reliably identified the sex and general age of the speaker and were also able to recognize the occupations of actor and clergyman.

Nerbonne discovered that listeners could accurately discriminate between male and female speakers and between black and Caucasian speakers.[246] He also found that subjects accurately perceived the age range of the speakers and were able to detect dialectal regions of the country as well as general educational levels of the speaker. Subjects assessed age accurately in a study conducted by Davis.[247] Lass et al. reported that

---

[243] Reprinted with permission from L. Malandro & L. Barker, Nonverbal Communication 192 (Random House, 1983). Copyright © 1983, by Random House, Inc.

[244] McGhee, *The Reliability of the Identification of the Human Voice*, 17 J. Gen. Psychology 249–271 (1937).

[245] T.H. Pear, Voice and Personality (Chapman and Hall, 1931).

[246] G.P. Nerbonne, The Identification of Speaker Characteristics on the Basis of Aural Cues (Ph.D. Dissertation, Michigan State University, 1967).

[247] P.B. Davis, An Investigation of the Suggestion of Age Through Voice in Interpretative Reading 69 (M.A. Thesis, University of Denver, 1949).

96% of the listeners accurately identified the sex of the speaker and 76% of the listeners were able to recognize the sex of a speaker who was whispering.[248]

Vocal cues can also aid in determining the socioeconomic status of the speaker. Harms showed that listeners were able to classify correctly speakers as having high, medium or low social status; they also attached higher credibility ratings to high status speakers.[249] Moe, in a replication of the Harms study, established that vocal characteristics are meaningful indicators of socioeconomic status.[250]

The voice also transmits cues about the emotional state of the speaker. Research in this area generally holds the content of the speech constant or else uses a content-free message (such as reciting the alphabet). Reviews of studies on content-free speech indicate that judges can consistently identify the emotion expressed and can also estimate its strength. Researchers, however, have been unable to identify the exact vocal cues that convey individual emotions.[251]

Davitz and Davitz retained message content and found that active feelings such as anger and joy were expressed with a loud voice, a high pitch and a fast rate.[252] Despair or boredom were conveyed with a relatively quiet voice, low pitch, and slow rate. Reardon concluded that listeners were more accurate in identifying negative expressions of emotions than positive ones and that anger was the most easily identified emotion.[253]

The evaluation of vocal characteristics goes beyond simply identifying demographic characteristics of an individual or the emotions of the speaker. We also make judgments about an individual's personality

---

[248] Lass, Hughes, Bowyer, Waters & Broune, *Speaker Sex Identification from Voiced, Whispered and Filtered Isolated Vowels*, 59 J. ACOUSTICAL SOC. AM. 675–678 (1976).

[249] Harms, *Listener Judgments of Status Cues in Speech*, 47 QUALITY J. SPEECH 164–168 (1961).

[250] Moe, *Listener Judgments of Status Cues in Speech: A Replication and Extension*, 39 SPEECH MONOGRAPHS 144–147 (1972).

[251] Scherer, Koiwunaki & Rosenthal, *Minimal Cues in the Vocal Communication of Affect: Judging Emotions from Content-Masked Speech*, 1 J. PSYCHOLINGUISTIC SPEECH 269–285 (1972).

[252] Davitz & Davitz, *Nonverbal Vocal Communication of Feeling*, 11 J. COM. 81–86 (1961).

[253] Reardon, *Individual Differences and the Meanings of Vocal Emotional Expressions* 21 J. COM. 72–82 (1971).

characteristics based on the cues in paralanguage. Table 1–5 summarizes the research findings on the stereotyped judgments that listeners make.[254]

Table 1–5
Simulated Vocal Cues and Personality Stereotypes

Simulated Vocal Cues	*Speakers*	*Stereotyped Perceptions*
Breathiness	Males	Younger, more artistic
	Females	More feminine, prettier, more petite, more effervescent, more high-strung, and shallower
Thinness	Males	Did not alter listener's image of the speaker; no significant correlations
	Females	Increased social, physical, emotional, and mental immaturity; increased sense of humor and sensitivity
Flatness	Males	More masculine, more sluggish, colder, more withdrawn
	Females	More masculine, more sluggish, colder, more withdrawn
Nasality	Males	A wide array of socially undesirable characteristics
	Females	A wide array of socially undesirable characteristics
Tenseness	Males	Older, more unyielding, cantankerous
	Females	Younger; more emotional, feminine, high-strung; less intelligent
Throatiness	Males	Older; more realistic, mature; sophisticated; well adjusted
	Females	Less intelligent; more masculine; lazier; more boorish, unemotional, ugly, sickly, careless, inartistic, naive, humble, neurotic, quiet, uninteresting, apathetic. In short, "Cloddish or oafish" (Addington)

[254] M.L. Knapp, Essentials of Nonverbal Communications 208 (Holt, Rinehart & Winston, 1980), as adapted from Addington, *The Relationship of Selected Vocal Characteristics to Personality Perception*, 35 Speech Monographs 492–503 (1968).

Simulated Vocal Cues	*Speakers*	*Stereotyped Perceptions*
Orotundity (Roundness of tone)	Males	More energetic, healthy, artistic, sophisticated, proud, interesting, enthusiastic. In short, "hardy and aesthetically inclined." (Addington)
	Females	Increased liveliness, gregariousness, esthetic sensitivity, and "increasingly proud and humorless" (Addington)
Increased Rate	Males	More animated and extroverted
	Females	More animated and extroverted
Increased Pitch Variety	Males	More dynamic, feminine, aesthetically inclined
	Females	More dynamic and extroverted

§ 1.95 Additional studies on powerful and powerless speech

The differences in powerful and powerless speech has a definite impact on the impressions that are formed of the speaker. As Table 1–6 indicates, when the witness was a female speaking in a powerful style, the average jury award to her was over $29,000. When a man testified in a powerless way, the award was only $19,000. This suggests that the way in which a witness gives testimony can affect the monetary award to the plaintiff.

Parkinson attempted to verify the results of this laboratory research by examining transcripts from thirty-eight criminal trials. The results of his analysis indicate that successful prosecutors used language differently from prosecutors who lost cases.

> . . . prosecution attorneys who secured convictions spoke longer, asked more questions referring directly to the witness, and made more indicative statements than did their less successful counterparts. Prosecution attorneys who failed to secure convictions used more polite forms, more hyper-correct grammar, and more conditional statements than did those who succeeded in securing convictions.[255]

---

[255] Parkinson, *Verbal Behavior and Courtroom Success*, 29 Com. Educ. 22 (1981).

Table 1–6
Powerful and Powerless Speech

Mean ratings given to female and male witnesses who spoke in a powerful versus a powerless mode. Higher values indicate a rating in the direction of a particular characteristic. Ratings of zero to eleven were possible.[256]

Characteristic	Female Witness Powerful Speech	Female Witness Powerless Speech	Male Witness Powerful Speech	Male Witness Powerless Speech
Competent	8.61	6.85	8.44	6.18
Intelligent	8.57	5.77	7.80	6.18
Likeable	8.48	6.54	8.52	7.23
Believable	9.70	7.88	10.24	8.86
Amount of Damages	$29,608	$22,730	$25,319	$18,909

In addition, successful defense attorneys used more abstract language (perhaps in an effort to distance the accused from the crime), more legal jargon, and more ambiguous language.

The speech of defendants in the trial transcripts examined by Parkinson also produced generalizable conclusions:

> . . . defendants who used more markers of courtesy or deference, spoke in more grammatically complete sentences, and used more polite forms were most often acquitted. Unsuccessful defendants, those who were convicted, made more references to themselves in their testimony.[257]

In another study of powerful and powerless speech Bradac, Hemphill and Tardy studied the effects of power modes on judgments of victims and villains. Their conclusion, based on their pilot study, is consistent with the results of O'Barr et al., and Parkinson.

> The pilot study showed that hedges, intensifiers, polite forms, and deictic phrases produced judgments of low power, and the absence

---

[256] *See* O'Barr & Conley, *When a Juror Watches a Lawyer*, 3 BARRISTER 8–11, 33 (1976). Reprinted with permission from BARRISTER MAGAZINE, published by the Young Lawyers Division of American Bar Association. Copyright © 1976, American Bar Association.

[257] *Id*. at 31.

of these forms coupled with short or one-word replies produced judgments of high power. Furthermore, the high-power style produced attributions of relatively high competence, and this style produced perceptions of higher communicator attractiveness than did low-power style.[258]

§ 1.96 Additional studies on touch behavior

Andersen and Leibowitz found that variables of sex, age, and religion seem to have an effect on our amount of touching behavior.[259] For example, men are more likely to touch women than other men; women are more likely to touch men than other women. As both men and women get older, their tendency to touch members of the opposite sex decreases. Likewise, older married people touch members of the opposite sex less. Protestants appear to engage in touching behaviors less than non-Protestants.

Messages of status and emotion are communicated through tactile communication. In the following list, which of the people in each pair do you feel would be more likely to touch the other person first?

Nurse	Doctor
Lawyer	Secretary
Employee	Boss
Student	Professor
Male	Female
Younger	Older

If you chose the person with the higher status in each pair (doctor, lawyer, boss, professor), you have selected the person who is most likely to initiate touching behavior.[260] If you chose the male over the female and the older person over the younger person, you have again selected the person most likely to initiate contact.[261] The important point is that the person who initiates physical contact generally controls the

[258] Bradac, Hemphill & Tardy, *Language Style on Trial: Effects of "Powerful" and "Powerless" Speech Upon Judgments of Victims and Villains*, 45 W. J. SPEECH COM. 334 (1981).

[259] Andersen & Leibowitz, *The Development and Nature of Touch Avoidance*, 3 ENVTL. PSYCHOLOGY & NONVERBAL BEHAV. 89–106 (1978).

[260] A. MEHRABIAN, SILENT MESSAGES 6 (Wadsworth Publishers, 1971).

[261] N.H. HENLEY, BODY POLITICS: POWER, SEX AND NONVERBAL COMMUNICATION (Prentice-Hall, 1977).

interaction.[262]

Henley concluded that we expect higher status persons to touch us more than we touch them; we expect dominant persons (or those trying to assert their dominance) to touch more.[263]

The handshake is an important way by which we communicate with each other through touch. Malandro and Barker explain:

> In Western culture the handshake is an expected formality, particularly when a personal bond is absent or weak, or when there has been a long separation. The handshake is a modification of the primitive gesture of both hands that indicated no weapons were being concealed. Later this became a greeting of a hand-to-chest gesture, known as the Roman salute. During the time of the Roman empire, men grasped each other at the forearms instead of the hand. The modern handshake takes many different forms and serves basically as a gesture of welcome; the palms interlock, signifying openness, and the touching itself signifies oneness.[264]

Our handshake reveals our relationship with another person. We may vary the intensity of our grip or even the grip itself depending upon who it is we are greeting. For example, you may shake hands with a stranger much differently than you shake hands with a good friend. Fraternities and sororities, as well as some of the cultural or ethnic groups in our society, vary the traditional grip of the handshake to communicate their special relationship with each other. Societal norms governing handshakes have been changing as well; it is now rather expected that a female will give as well as receive a firm handshake from a male, especially in the business environment.

The "body guide" is another way in which physical contact is communicated. By simply placing your hand on the back of another person you can guide that person in a particular direction, whether it is to negotiate a crowded room or to cross a busy street. A hand placed on the elbow accomplishes the same purpose. Both of these "body guides" allow the person who is guiding to communicate his superiority over the other person. Morris observes:

> Even between spouses, it (the body guide) is an expression of mo-

[262] Malandro & Barker, *supra* note 76, at 258.

[263] Henley, *supra* note 261, at 107.

[264] Reprinted with permission of L. MALANDRO & L. BARKER, NONVERBAL COMMUNICATION 260–261 (Random House, 1983). Copyright © 1983, Random House, Inc.

mentary dominance, an act of taking charge of a situation. Used by a wife towards a husband, it presents a pseudo-motherly tie-sign to on lookers. Used deftly by a male, it imparts a master air to his actions. Used unwisely it can quickly become pompous and patronizing.[265]

We also communicate emotions through physical touch. We may hug a friend we have not seen in a long time or we may kiss him/her on the cheek. The kiss on the cheek as a signal of welcome has been used so often that it has become an expected way to signal welcome to your guests. (How many of Johnny Carson's female guests *do not* kiss him on the cheek?)

Heslin and Boss found that 60% of subjects observed at an airport used touching to communicate a greeting or a farewell.[266] Touching behavior in farewell appeared to be more emotionally intense than greeting behavior, and understandably so.

---

[265] D. MORRIS, MANWATCHING: A FIELD GUIDE TO HUMAN BEHAVIOR (Harry N. Abrams, 1977).

[266] M.K. KNAPP, NONVERBAL COMMUNICATION IN HUMAN INTERACTION (Holt, Rinehart & Winston, 2d ed. 1978), as cited from HESLIN & BOSS, NONVERBAL INTIMACY ON ARRIVAL AND DEPARTURE AT AN AIRPORT (Purdue University 1976) (unpublished manuscript).

Chapter 2

PERSUASIVE STRATEGIES IN THE COURTROOM

KLUWER LITIGATION LIBRARY REFERENCES

JEANS, LITIGATION: Chapter 2, *Mind Set of the Advocate*; Chapter 6, *Voir Dire*; Chapter 8, *Direct Examination*; Chapter 13, *Cross-Examination*; Chapter 16, *Summation*.

PREISER & PREISER, HANDLING SOFT TISSUE INJURY CASES: Chapter 10, *Psychology of the Trial*; Chapter 11, *Selecting the Jury*; Chapter 12, *Opening Statements*.

I. Communication Principles

§ 2.01 Introduction to persuasion

The study of persuasion is both fascinating and complicated. The courtroom provides an ideal setting for observing the principles of persuasion in action. People who are skilled in persuasion tend to have a high awareness of the behavioral cues of others, as well as their own. This high sensitivity or awareness allows the persuader to become something of a chameleon. What we mean is that the persuader changes and adapts his behavior to fit the appropriateness of the person or persons he is persuading. The more flexible a person is, the more powerful he is at persuading others. Effective trial attorneys represent persuasion at its best. They are masters at adapting their style and behavior to fit the differing circumstances of each case.

One important aspect of persuasion is the study of influence: how and why people agree to things. The way in which people are influenced has changed dramatically over the past decade. The advent of the high tech era has resulted in an accelerated influence process. People now use shortcut methods to make their decisions. Where once thorough logical analysis was used, quick and immediate decisions are now being made. The decisions are sometimes based on single pieces of evidence, which are in turn used to indicate a general trend. Generally speaking, Americans no longer wait until all the evidence is in. Rather, they move at top speed to assimilate the characteristics of a person. In this chapter we will explore the six short-cut techniques for influencing others: (1) reciprocity, (2) commitment and consistency, (3) social proof, (4) liking, (5) authority, and (6) scarcity. We will attempt to reframe the attorney's point of view with regard to how he can influence others.

§ 2.02 Summary of Communication Principles

The six Communication Principles we present in this chapter provide a frame of reference for understanding the role of persuasion and influence in the courtroom. Each principle highlights a fundamental motivation for people to be persuaded or to seek a change in behavior. The need to be consistent, for example, is a motivating force in formulating beliefs and attitudes. The logical presentation of information by counsel linked to the preexisting beliefs of the jurors is a strategy for maximizing the need of jurors to be consistent in their beliefs. Sections 2.03–2.08 offer a summary of the six principles of persuasion.

§ 2.03 —Principle 7: People feel obligated to repay others regardless of whether they like the gift or the giver

In American society's current avalanche of change and choice, people have had to adjust. One of the most fundamental adjustments has come in the way they make many of their decisions. People do not identify, collect, and weigh each piece of information in a decision-making situation. They no longer have the time, energy, or capacity for analyzing carefully all the pros and cons of most decisions. There is too much information, too much stimulation, and too many alternatives to deal with. People are forced to revert to a simpler, shortcut approach. They try to pick out one reliable piece of information and respond automatically to it. In the courtroom, this means that a single piece of evidence can become the stimulus which produces an entire series of decisions. The reciprocity principle can cause individuals to select or overemphasize certain pieces of evidence because they feel obligated to repay others regardless of whether they like the gift or the giver.[1]

One question people ask themselves before agreeing to another's request is, "Do I owe this person something?" If the answer is yes, they frequently reply affirmatively to the request when they would have other-

[1] R. Cialdini, Influence: How and Why People Agree to Things (William Morrow & Co., 1984).

wise declined. They may agree to repay a larger favor than the one they received. This pressure to give back to those who have given something first accounts for the remarkable success of the Hare Krishna solicitors. They give people in public places an unsolicited gift (usually a flower) and then ask them for a favor (a contribution). This "benefactor-before-beggar" tactic accounts for much of the funding of the Krishna's 108 centers worldwide.[2]

The principle of reciprocity is a very powerful principle. It engages people on many levels. For example, if you receive unsolicited gifts, cards, or special favors, or someone goes out of his way for you or spends extra time with you, these all create various forms of obligation. Your automatic tendency, whether or not you like the gift, is to reply and obligate yourself by giving that person something. Several major corporations, realizing the tremendous power of obligation, restrict their employees from receiving gifts of any kind from vendors or companies during the holidays or any other time of year. If a vendor gives the employee a gift, an employee may lean toward giving that vendor business simply because he feels obligated. Thus, these corporations have a policy that when the employees receive such gifts, they are usually given to charities and a note is sent back to the vendor informing him of the fact that the company has a policy that employees cannot receive gifts.

In order for the principle of reciprocity to work there are several factors that need to be considered. First, the person must know about the favor or gift, otherwise there is no obligation. If you take care of something or help someone, but never let him know it, he would not feel obligated to you. If a person is going to obligate someone, he has to tell him what he has done for him. For example, if you have gone out of your way to spend time with a person, you need to let him know that you have rearranged your schedule in order to meet with him. This is what sets up the obligation. Additionally, never advise the receiver that he owes you a favor in return. Simply imply that you did this for him because he is valued and special. Since most people feel obligated on the basis of reciprocity, they need not be told that they are obligated.

In application, the principle of reciprocity is most clearly seen in the negotiation setting. The rule of give and take is exactly what negotiation is based upon. In the negotiation setting, the reciprocation principle can be set in motion by giving in on minor points, as for example, the location of the meeting. This can set up a series of obligations. Let the other

---

[2] *Id.*

side know that you are giving in on the location, then they will "owe" you one. In the courtroom, on the other hand, we do not see the reciprocity principle operating as much because its application is not as direct in that setting.

There are many ways in which an attorney can employ reciprocity to obligate a business client. If you genuinely do extra things for a client—or your secretary or staff does them—let the client know about the extra effort. Clients are given attention in many different ways: e.g., returning their phone calls promptly or sending them a courtesy letter telling of the progress of the case.

The most important thing to keep in mind about the principle of reciprocity is that it is powerful and automatic. The moment you do something for another person he begins to feel obligated, regardless of whether he likes you or whether he likes what you have given to him.

Because of the power of this principle, you need to consider the flip side of the coin. Not only can a person obligate others, but keep in mind that others can obligate you. It is very important to look at the principle of reciprocity in terms of the extent to which you allow others to obligate you in specific settings. By recognizing the power of reciprocity, you can refuse to become committed to settings, situations, and people when it is not to your advantage.

§ 2.04 —Principle 8: People have a need to be consistent

After committing themselves to a position, even in some trivial way, people are more likely to agree to perform behaviors that are consistent with that position. People more easily decide to comply with a request (to buy, to donate, to vote, or to consent) if they have already done something that is consistent with the request. For example, in one Cancer Society charity drive, it was found that homeowners who had previously gone on record as supporting the Cancer Society (by accepting and wearing a small lapel pin for a day) were nearly twice as likely to give a monetary donation a week later when the charity drive began. It is important to recognize, however, that not all small initial commitments are equally good at producing consistent future behavior. They are most effective when they are active, public, and freely made.[3]

People have a need to be consistent for a very simple reason. They want to avoid cognitive dissonance. Cognitive dissonance is simply a sit-

[3] *Id.*

uation where there is conflicting information. When an individual experiences conflicting information, he quickly tries to reduce the dissonance by making the information consistent. For example, jurors may expect counsel to dress and behave conservatively. If they see that counsel is dressed in a nonconservative manner they will do something to reduce this dissonance. Most likely the dissonance will be reduced in a negative way for counsel. They will perceive the attorney to be incompetent and not representative of their expectations of legal counsel. They reduce dissonance by saying that this attorney is not exemplary of what they consider to be a good legal professional. When dissonance is reduced, it is changed to become consistent with the primacy information. This reinforces one of the principles we previously discussed: that people will attempt to maintain their original perceptions regardless of contradictory information.[4]

In order to engage the principle of consistency, we must first obtain a commitment. Once we receive that commitment, there are three factors which should be added to make a very powerful form of commitment. The commitment should be active, public, and freely made. An active commitment refers to a timely commitment, one that is made now, not a commitment that was made in the past. Secondly, if a verbal commitment can be made in front of other people (a public commitment), it will have much greater power. And if a commitment is both public and in writing it will have even greater power. On the other hand, simple nonverbal public commitments (a simple nodding of the head) will have the least amount of power. The third factor is that the commitment must be freely made. It must be noncoerced. The person must feel that he had a choice in making the commitment. Once he makes that choice, he will feel obligated to be consistent to the commitment. This is so, even if a person commits to a very small thing. You can then build on that commitment. In negotiation and selling this is referred to as building a series of yes responses. The person who agrees on one issue then becomes inclined to agree on other issues. It is easier to get an agreement on small issues, such as "Isn't it a nice day out?" or "Don't you enjoy what you are doing?" These rudimentary questions asked on a one-to-one basis can obtain the initial commitment. It does not matter what the original agreement is. As one builds the yes responses, the items can have larger and larger stakes. Illustratively, in obtaining commitments during voir dire, an attorney can build on small commitments. Counsel should ob-

---

[4] *See supra* § 1.08.

tain early on small commitments from the jurors to be fair at trial, to be impartial, and to try to put aside all other prejudices. These are all examples of building a small base and proceeding from that point on.

The commitment and consistency principles apply throughout the trial. Verbal agreements to particular attitudes and behavioral beliefs during voir dire constitute a commitment from the juror. Properly structured voir dire questions will illicit the desired response. This commitment constitutes a public commitment in front of the juror's peers. It is also taken down by the court reporter. Counsel can repeat the commitment, which increases its effectiveness. If counsel obtains a commitment from a juror such as, "Even though I have served in a similar case before, I will put aside all biases," the attorney can paraphrase by saying, "Okay, Mr. Jones. What I understand you to say is that your biases, to the best of your ability, will not enter into this case." This way counsel obtains two commitments to the same concept. The repetition of the person's verbal commitment also reinforces the message. The juror's peers hear the commitment once again. A commitment should always be anchored.[5] Anchoring is locking in behavior so that attention can be called to it quickly and easily. One form of anchoring is simply to paraphrase, as we did in the above example, so that attention is called to it again. Thus anchoring serves to lock in the commitment so that people will not forget it.

Another form of commitment in the context of a trial might be in the form of nonverbal commitments: jurors responding by nodding their heads or leaning forward. However, we urge caution in interpreting any of these behaviors because they do not always mean that that individual is in agreement with you. A person may lean forward because his back is sore or he may simply want to change positions. It is one area to look at, but it should never be considered as the sole form of commitment within the courtroom. It must be put into context. Additionally, try to use word commitments. During opening, closing, cross-examination, or whenever possible, remind the jurors of earlier commitments they have made. During the closing statement you should go back to the original commitments made by jurors on voir dire. To strongly reinforce their prior commitments, phrase them as closely as possible in the way the jurors phrased their initial commitments on voir dire. By doing so, it becomes a form of pacing.[6] It will link more closely to the words they

[5] *See infra* Chapter 4 for a discussion of the technique of anchoring.

[6] *See infra* Part II, *Communication Techniques*.

spoke and the commitments they made. It will also serve as a stimulus to remind them of what they said previously.

COMMENT: Given that people have a need to be consistent with their commitments, build upon that need. Remind them about their need to be consistent and the earlier commitments they made. Capitalizing on commitments in this manner can be very effective, particularly during your closing argument.[7]

---

§ 2.05 —Principle 9: People are more easily influenced by others they perceive as similar to themselves

People are more easily influenced to perform an action or hold a belief when they see others taking the same action. People decide what is appropriate conduct for themselves in a particular situation by viewing how others are acting. It is for this reason that advertisers love to include the words "fastest growing" or "largest selling" in their product descriptions. They do not have to say directly that the product is good; they only need to say that others think so. Research indicates that a person is influenced most by the actions of others who are similar in age, sex, background, and so on.[8] Simply stated, people are more easily influenced by others they perceive as similar to themselves.

The principle of similarity is very powerful because it operates upon the need to reduce uncertainty. In Chapter 1, we discussed research which indicated that people have an ongoing need to reduce uncertainty and increase predictability about an individual.[9] In every case we seek to increase predictability, particularly in unfamiliar settings such as the courtroom. Similarity is based upon the need to increase predictability so that the individual can feel more in control of a situation.

When we believe that we are similar to another person or he is similar to us, we tend to justify his behaviors and actions or to explain why he

---

[7] *See infra* § 10.17, for a discussion of how to drive voir dire commitments home in summation.

[8] CIALDINI, *supra* note 1.

[9] *See supra* § 1.54.

behaved or did something in a particular way. We presume that we know how he thinks. Our empathetic response is greatly increased. We assign to him properties and characteristics which we believe we have in ourselves. On an unconscious level, we go out of our way to help him. We feel that he should be given a break because if we were in a similar situation we would want the benefit of the doubt.

During the trial, therefore, it is important for counsel to maximize the perception of similarity.[10] We want the jurors to perceive the witnesses, the clients, and most importantly, legal counsel as being similar to them. By maximizing similarity in any way we can, we stand a greater chance of influencing the judgment of jurors. The most powerful technique for maximizing the perception of similarity is pacing and leading. In order to have the highest form of impact, similarity must be matched on all three channels of communication—verbal, vocal, and nonverbal.

§ 2.06 —Principle 10: People are more easily influenced by people they like

This is probably one of the easiest principles to understand. Most of us recognize that psychologically we will give more favors and respond more favorably to people we like. The attraction principle, even in terms of physical and psychological attraction, is discussed in Chapter 1.[11] People give all sorts of breaks and considerations to others who are physically more attractive. Attractiveness is just one variable in the area of likability. In essence, people "buy" people. We tend to "buy" those personalities and personal attributes we like. This factor is external to evidence and proof. When we are presented with the same evidence from two different sources, with one source having greater appeal to us than another, we tend to move toward the source that has greater likability and allow it to influence us more easily. This is often an unconscious response. When we perceive someone to be attractive, we often give him many rewarding or nonverbal behaviors. We reinforce him with words and acknowledge him with nonverbal behaviors such as smiling.

We find this type of influence factor operating in the courtroom. For example, if attorneys are liked we will attribute to them many favorable traits. We will listen to them more attentively. On the other hand, if an attorney is not liked it is harder for him to influence jurors. As stated

[10] *See infra* Part II of this chapter, *Communication Techniques*, for an in-depth discussion of this point.

[11] *See supra* § 1.38.

above, we would much rather respond favorably to people we like. We make it harder for people we dislike to influence us. Listening and attention go down dramatically; we turn them off. Professional salespeople have known this for years. That is why they spend a great deal of time just building rapport with their customers. Similarly, when an attorney meets with a client for the first time, building rapport with the client may take up the largest part of the interview.

§ 2.07 —Principle 11: The perception of credibility increases with the perception of authority

People are more willing to follow the suggestions of someone they perceive to be a legitimate authority. How do people decide who constitutes an authority in a given situation? They do so on the basis of two features of authority: knowledge and trustworthiness. Demonstrating knowledge can usually be accomplished by showing evidence of superior training, skill, or information (e.g., "Babies are our business" and "Makers of award winning spirits since 1841"). Establishing trustworthiness is trickier. One device that advertisers have used successfully to convey trustworthiness is to first mention a small drawback in their product and then describe its outweighing advantages. For example, Avis advertises: "We're number two, but we try harder," and Listerine claims, "It's the taste you hate three times a day."[12]

American society is very responsive to authority. Anybody that wears a uniform tends to generate a mechanical response from us. It is frightening to realize that people automatically respond in a positive way to anyone wearing a uniform. In many cases, crimes have been committed by people wearing official uniforms. For example, moving van company's "employees" are able to steal a houseful of furniture because the neighbors see the movers in official-looking uniforms. The neighbors legitimize the actions taking place because they see the uniforms.

Authority in the courtroom is represented primarily by the judge because of his position of power and control of space. As previously discussed, when you control territory and space you will be perceived as having greater power.[13] At the beginning of the trial, counsel may be assigned initial credibility simply because he is part of the dynamics in the courtroom. The greater the perceived authority of the individual, the

---

[12] CIALDINI, *supra* note 1.

[13] *See supra* §§ 1.73–1.76.

greater the possibility of influencing the jurors in their decision-making process.

In order to convey authority, it is important to project confidence in all three levels of communication: verbal, vocal, and nonverbal. An authority is seen as someone who knows what he is doing. Competence has to be conveyed very clearly to jurors, otherwise counsel will lose his initially perceived authority. If counsel does not work to maintain the perception of authority, the authority itself can be lost.

It is equally important for expert witnesses to develop a perception of authority. Expert witnesses have to have a certain amount of authority or the jury will not give them expert status. If expert witnesses are not perceived to have expert status, the weight of their testimony will be negligible.

§ 2.08 —Principle 12: People are more easily influenced when they believe the source to be scarce and valuable

People try to seize those items and opportunities that are scarce or dwindling in availability. This desire to want things more as they become unavailable accounts for the success of the "deadline," "limited number," and "can't come back later" sales tactics. It also explains why a portable TV might be bought by an individual simply because he was told that it was the last one left. Even though the individual may not have wanted the portable TV, the scarcity factor compelled the person to buy it. Research indicates that people want a scarce item even more when they are in competition with others for it.[14]

Advertisers have known for years that if they position a product as being scarce and valuable that more people will buy it. When they say it is a limited offer or it is only available today, people tend to reevaluate and think more about purchasing the object. Likewise, an expert witness who is considered to be scarce (hard to get) will be considered to be more valuable. Thus, counsel should reveal when an expert witness has traveled a far distance to testify. If jurors are made aware of this information, they will then treat the expert testimony as being more valuable. This reinforces the old aphorism: "Prophets are never honored in their own land." Even a speaker who goes from one area of our country to another, or an international speaker who comes from a foreign country to speak in the United States, will initially be given greater authority

---

[14] CIALDINI, *supra* note 1.

because he is perceived as being more scarce and valuable and his time with us is limited.

Information can be treated this way also. Information can be presented as being scarce and valuable by saying to the jurors, "Only [you] know this" or "this is the first time this information has been released." When you let jurors know they are dealing with scarce or valuable information, two things will happen. First, their attention will be called to the information that is being presented. Secondly, the information will be anchored in their minds, which means that they will recall it easier. Since we know that jurors do not listen to all the information presented, that their minds tend to wander throughout the course of the trial, and that the normal adult attention span is eighteen minutes, anything you can do to call their attention back to information previously presented will assist you in your case.

II. Communication Techniques

§ 2.09 Maximizing the perception of similarity

People are more easily influenced by others they perceive as similar to themselves. This is Communication Principle 9, which we presented general background information on *supra* § 2.05. We are much more easily influenced by people that we perceive as being similar to ourselves for two very important reasons. First, when we perceive a similarity, we know that the person is somewhat predictable. This creates an immediate reduction of uncertainty. The more predictable a person's behaviors and the less stress we experience in understanding that person, the more likable he becomes to us. The second reason we are more persuaded by others similar to us is because we believe that they view the world as we do. For example, if a salesperson walked into a Fortune 500 office wearing jeans and a T-shirt, he would find it very hard to persuade them to buy his product, simply because the perception of similarity would be so low he would not be perceived as credible. Similarity is an indicator to us that it is appropriate to proceed with some basic assumptions. We perceive people as being similar (Principle 5) and we are more influenced by them if they are (Principle 9).

Maximizing similarity increases the bond of rapport between individuals. The most critical step in persuading and influencing another person is building rapport. Even veteran salespeople sometimes forget the importance of this step. You cannot sell anyone anything until rapport has been established. Rapport, then, is not a prelude to persuasion, but is the actual first and critical step in the entire influence process. Once rapport has been established a window is opened. This window offers a passageway for linking to the preexisting attitudes and beliefs of a person. Your skill in "opening a window" is basic to your ability to persuade.

The goal in any interaction with either an individual or a group is to maximize the perception of similarity. Keep in mind that our fundamental communication principle is that communication is based upon perception. We cannot maximize actual similarity; the best we can do is maximize the perception of similarity. We can maximize similarity by increasing the perception of similarity on both the conscious and unconscious levels. The most persuasive way of maximizing similarity is on the unconscious level. The goal of an expert persuader is to engage the conscious mind while communicating to the unconscious mind. The reason for this is that we are more persuaded by unconscious influences than we are by conscious behavior. This goes back to the demonstrated fact that "actions speak louder than words." We feel a stronger sense of persuasion when it does not involve the direct, conscious use of words, but rather the more subliminal and unconscious messages contained in vocal cues and nonverbal behavior.

The conscious ways in which most people maximize similarity with others are easily recognizable. For example, talking about common interests such as running, discussing common goals, working on a cooperative project, engaging in a common profession, or living in a similar geographical region. Discussing these similarities with another person constitutes a conscious effort at matching. In any interaction that a person has with another person, they immediately move towards any similarity or common bond. Although the conscious techniques for maximizing similarities are influential, we tend to reduce the impact of conscious behaviors. We suspect that conscious behaviors could be manipulated. We never quite trust the conscious words as being real. We do not know if someone is telling us the truth or simply what they want us to hear.

As previously indicated, the most powerful way to maximize similarity is through unconscious methods. People who are naturally in rapport with one another truly like each other, and tend to have imitative behaviors. In other words, if one person stands with his arms crossed, the other person will unconsciously match this behavior by also crossing his arms; if one person talks fast, the other person will increase his rate of speech; if one person eats very slowly, the other will tend to slow down his rhythmic pattern. These are not consciously manipulated behaviors. For the most part, they are simply behaviors that occur as a result of one person liking the other and unconsciously adapting his behaviors.

The importance of understanding this behavioral pattern is clear. In situations of rapport with another party we unconsciously adapt and match his behaviors. On the other hand, if we are with people that we do not like we unconsciously mismatch. Thus, it is possible to deliberately and consciously match or mismatch the behaviors of another person in order to increase perceived rapport or dissonance.

Matching the behaviors of others is one aspect of pacing techniques. In order to establish rapport, it is important to know how to pace an individual. Pacing involves matching the way in which an individual approaches a situation in order to establish a common bond. Pacing behaviors are subliminal and outside of conscious awareness. The exception to this is if an individual is obvious and deliberate in each matching action. When effectively pacing another individual the resulting perception will be that there is a common bond, a shared similarity, and excellent rapport. In a subsequent section,[15] we will discuss self-monitoring skills as a characteristic of an effective persuader. High self-monitors generally tend to be very good pacers. They look to others to judge behavioral appropriateness in a particular situation and then they match their behaviors to fit the specific environment or person with whom they are interacting.

Because each client is different and the courtroom setting is constantly changing, the need for pacing is obvious. Every communication with a person is unique. People have different characteristics, behavioral traits, and attitudes which must be adapted to on a unique and singular level. When you treat people as a group rather than differentiating on an individual level, at best you will have a hit-or-miss effectiveness in establishing rapport and persuasion. The best way to communicate with people is by pacing their individual behaviors and adapting to them on a one-to-one basis. Succinctly stated, pacing refers to our ability to match the rhythmic patterns in the vocal, verbal, and nonverbal channels of another person.

In order to insure the effective use of pacing techniques, there are two other areas that need to be considered: (1) the basic rules of a relation-

[15] *See infra* § 2.66.

ship;[16] and (2) how we absorb behaviors or unconsciously imitate behaviors of another person.[17]

§ 2.10 —Basic rules of a relationship

In order to fully understand and appreciate the use of pacing, it is essential to understand the basic rules of a relationship. Unconsciously we tend to pace people we like and to mismatch behaviors of people we do not like. In a relationship that is effective, solid, and balanced there are four basic rules which we implicitly follow:

1. There is a basic reciprocity in the interaction;
2. Self-disclosure tends to occur at the same rate;
3. Comfort is maintained by an established equilibrium;
4. Each interaction has a shared rhythm.

The first basic rule of the relationship states that there is a basic reciprocity in interactions. This means that in every working relationship there is a balance. Those relationships that are imbalanced eventually disintegrate. The principle of reciprocity (Principle 7) states that we feel obligated to repay others for gifts or favors. This principle also applies to relationships. If someone does something for us in a relationship, we then feel obligated to return the favor. Understanding the nature of reciprocity is fundamental to appreciating the philosophy of pacing. The very act of pacing creates a balance in a relationship. A gift, a card, flowers, a special kindness, interest in the other person, or doing special favors all engage the principle of reciprocity. Relationships that survive have a basic reciprocity: both people attempt to match their partner.

A healthy relationship is one where self-disclosure tends to occur at the same rate. Thus, if one person gains information power over another, the latter may begin to feel uncomfortable. For example, if you meet someone for the first time and he begins to disclose great amounts of information about his personal life and what he likes to do, and you offer no information about your personal likes and dislikes, he will eventually begin to feel a distrust. In fact, he should. Except in a therapeutic relationship where we do not expect the other person to reciprocate, we expect others to self-disclose.

Self-disclosure can be used effectively in the courtroom. It is often

---

[16] *See infra* § 2.10.

[17] *See infra* § 2.11.

used by the attorney in his opening or closing statement where he reveals how he feels. It might even be a remark as simple as, "I know how I feel about this, and I know that you would feel the same way." When an attorney or witness self-discloses in the courtroom a bond is created with the jurors. As a result, liking and trust increase. This self-disclosure, however, must be real and genuine. There is a collective consciousness which exists among groups which gives them tremendous insight into whether a person is "real" and "sincere." Manipulated or false behaviors and emotions will not only inhibit rapport, but will destroy credibility and trust.

The third basic rule of a relationship is that comfort is maintained in the relationship by an established equilibrium. This tells us that relationships, like all other aspects of human interaction, are subject to the concept of uncertainty reduction.[18] When we have certainty in a relationship, we have a fixed comfort level. In essence, an equilibrium has been established. This equilibrium tells us that the relationship is moving along smoothly and that it is a workable relationship for both people.

The final basic rule of a relationship is that each interaction has a shared rhythm. This is the rule that underlies the technique of pacing. Every relationship establishes a rhythmic basis. If you spend time with a person year after year, you will find that you have not only established a rhythm with one another but you have adapted to one another to compensate for changes in the other person's rhythm or style. When arguments occur in a relationship, they are generally a result of a mismatch of behavioral and rhythmic patterns. For example, one spouse may be in a very energetic mood and ready to go out to dinner. The other spouse may have returned from work very lethargic and tired and wants to do nothing but sit at home. The basic rhythm patterns are obvious. One is fast and one is slow. If neither one compromises, an argument will usually result.

When we have rapport with another person, we are in sync with him. Another way of stating this is that when we have rapport with another person, we are pacing him and he is also pacing our behaviors. Human beings are very susceptible to picking up behaviors from another person. The fact that we actually do absorb behaviors from another person, which is to say we unconsciously imitate their behaviors, tells us that pacing is a powerful, unconscious, and active process.

---

[18] *See supra* § 1.61.

Most successful people are very good at pacing the behaviors of others. Successful people who pace, for the most part, are not aware of their behaviors. They are operating at an unconscious level. If trial lawyers can recognize how pacing works, then they can strategically use it to build rapport in the courtroom and with their clients. Trial lawyers can also use their knowledge to decrease rapport in a relationship. This will cause the relationship to dissolve or create the appearance of dissonance, as for example, between the opposing party's witness and the trial lawyer, and hopefully the jury, so as to discredit the witness.

§ 2.11 —Absorbing behaviors

If you spend a great deal of time with another person you run the risk of unconsciously absorbing his behaviors. People constantly receive sensory stimuli from hearing a voice, feeling a touch, and visually observing movements of those with whom they have contact. Your internal video camera is on and it records everything that is happening around you. As you record imprints of other people they are played back in your mind and, in a very real manner, you are teaching yourself their behaviors. Therefore, it is good advice to surround yourself with only those people whose behaviors you do not mind catching.

Have you ever called a friend and talked to his roommate in error thinking it was your friend? How about two sisters who sound identical on the telephone? Have you spent time with a person who has a particular facial expression or perhaps a gesture that drives you crazy only later to note, much to your dismay, that you have imitated the same behavior? Perhaps you have gone with your spouse, boyfriend, or girlfriend to meet his or her family. Soon you are seeing and hearing a duplication of your friend's behavior. The entire family talks a particular way, sits a certain way, and even eats in the same manner.

We observe, imitate, and adopt behaviors and actions of others. For example, children imitate behaviors from television, movies, and important people in their lives (e.g., their parents). We absorb behaviors and imitate others at two levels, conscious and unconscious. Who you surround yourself with will make a difference in what you become. Further, if we absorb and imitate behaviors of those people we like and respect we are pacing them, entering their world. On the other hand, those people we do not like and respect we simply do not pace.

The process of absorption is so subtle that an individual does not notice when it occurs.[19] That is why there is considerable research in the area of spousal imitation. If you live with a spouse for more than 10 years, you begin to imitate and pick up his or her behaviors. Many people say that spouses start to look like one another. This does not mean that they have the same type of hair or body structure, but it does mean they have the same imitative patterns. They may focus their eyes the same way, smile the same, or use similar gestures. All of these are unconsciously imitated. The most dramatic example of absorbing behaviors can be viewed in a family relationship where children imitate their parents. Without knowing it, the children unconsciously pick up the cues of the parent. The parent may sit a certain way and the child begins to copy this behavior. Imitation is the sincerest form of flattery because we do not pace or imitate those people that we do not like. When a child imitates a parent, that is usually a positive comment about the relationship between the child and parent. The child who imitates a parent has a healthy respect and liking for the parent.

In addition, the status of an individual will make a difference in terms of imitative behavior. The higher the status, the more likely the behavior will be copied. Consider the trend set by movie stars and models. Their impact on the fashion industry is most notable. The movie *Flashdance* starring Jennifer Beals brought a new wave of dancing and torn off-the-shoulder-type clothing. John Travolta ushered in disco in *Saturday Night Fever*. The stars from *Dynasty* and *Dallas* continue to influence hairstyles and fashions for thousands of men and women.

We also use imitation behaviors as a means of group identification. When we want to be a part of a group or be accepted by a group, we pace the group's clothing choices. For example, a street gang wears identical jackets with their insignia; a fraternal organization conveys their identification with a pin; member status in a conservative corporation is marked by wearing gray or navy blue suits with white shirts; a judge wears a robe. Because of the high visual impact, pacing clothing is one of the strongest links to building rapport with another person or group.

---

[19] D. Morris, Manwatching: A Field Guide to Human Behavior 18–21 (Harry N. Abrams, 1977). Anthropologist Morris refers to contagious behaviors as absorbed actions.

> "Absorbed actions are those behaviors which are unconsciously copied from other people. As a species, we are strongly imitative and it is impossible for a healthy individual to grow up in a community and not become infected with its typical action pattern."

Maximizing the perception of similarity is based on the fact that we need to engage the conscious mind while communicating to the unconscious mind. The most effective way to maximize similarity is through the unconscious mind by pacing the behaviors of another person. The fact that we already "absorb" behaviors effortlessly from others reinforces the existence of unconscious pacing.

§ 2.12 —Pacing techniques

The concept of pacing is not new. It has been used for years in a therapeutic context where therapists pace the patient to establish rapport and build a bond of trust.[20] Studied by researchers under many different names, pacing has gathered much more interest in recent years. The phenomena of pacing has been referred to as interactional synchrony,

---

[20] For the interested reader, the following books are recommended in the areas of neurolinguistic programming and Ericksonian hypnosis:

R. Bandler & J. Grinder, Frogs into Princes (Real People Press, 1979).

R. Bandler & J. Grinder, Patterns of the Hypnotic Techniques of Milton H. Erickson, M.D.I. (Meta Publications, 1975).

R. Bandler & J. Grinder, Reframing: Neurolinguistic Programming and the Transformation of Meaning (Real People Press, 1982).

R. Bandler, J. Grinder & V. Satir, Changing with Families (Science and Behavior Books, 1975).

R. Bandler & J. Grinder, The Structure of Magic (Science and Behavior Books, 1975).

L. Cameron-Bandler, They Lived Happily Ever After: A Book About Achieving Happy Endings in Coupling (Meta Publications, 1978).

R.B. Dilts, J. Grinder, R. Bandler, J. DeLozier & L. Cameron-Bandler, Neuro-Linguistic Programming I (Meta Publications, 1979).

F. Farrelly & J. Brandsma, Provocative Therapy (Meta Publications, 1978).

M. Feldenkrais, The Elusive Obvious (Meta Publications, 1981).

J. Grinder & R. Bandler, The Structure of Magic II (Science and Behavior Books, 1976).

J. Grinder & R. Bandler, Neuro-Linguistic Programming and the Structure of Hypnosis (Real People Press, 1981).

J. Grinder, J. DeLozier & R. Bandler, Patterns of Hypnotic Techniques of Milton H. Erickson, M.D. II. (Meta Publications, 1977).

S.R. Lankton, Practical Magic: A Translation of Basic Neuro-Linguistic Programming into Clinical Psychotherapy (Meta Publications, 1980).

M. McMaster & J. Grinder, Precision: A New Approach to Communication (Precision Models, 1980).

V. Satir, Making Contact (Celestial Arts, 1976).

shared rhythmicity, relatedness, matching, mirroring, contacting, tracking, echoing, shadowing, congruency, interactional equilibrium, reciprocity norms, analog matching, positioning, posture sharing, and mirror-like matching.

Early research was based on the premise that when people are in rapport with one another they tend to match each other with verbal, vocal, and nonverbal cues. The verbal channel of communication comprises the content aspect of the message which includes word choice and phraseology. The vocal aspect includes voice characteristics, pitch, tone inflection, intonation, and other vocal qualities. The vocal channel refers to how something is said rather than what is said. Finally, the nonverbal channel of communication includes body movement and gestures, eye and facial behavior, touch, distance, clothing, and environmental factors. Matching another person or group of people in one or all channels of communication creates an extremely powerful unconscious connection.[21] These three channels of communication provide a wealth of information on how an individual thinks. The highest quality of information available is behavioral. When you focus on the behavior of an individual, you have the necessary information to understand how he processes information. In essence, how he thinks and how he sees the world.

Pacing is based on the premise that there is a rhythm to everything in the universe. We have biological rhythms, sociological rhythms, psychological rhythms, and so forth. An underlying beat exists. When you are out of pace with yourself, there is a lack of synchrony. You feel out of balance and the rhythm is gone.

One's ability to connect to the beat of another person is at the heart of persuasion. When you are connected to another person, you will have greater rapport. After having established rapport we have the potential to lead the other person to the point of persuasion. If one does not pace an individual or group, it is impossible to persuade them. People are not persuaded when they do not feel a link or bond between themselves and the persuader. Pacing, therefore, is essential to being able to persuade.

People speak different languages, and every subculture (e.g., engineers, attorneys, blue collar, white collar, athletes, etc.) can be identified in the way in which its members communicate. Your effectiveness in matching another person's model of the world will determine your success in establishing rapport, power, and persuasion. Pacing defined is simply your

---

[21] *See infra* §§ 2.23–2.36.

ability to connect with what already exists in a person, organization, or in a culture. The caveat for the trial attorney is that his matching with some subculture group must be subtle. An attorney should match the verbal content of any subculture group only minimally. If the attorney brings his choice of words too far below his normal verbal fluency he will be perceived as either consciously trying to curry favor, or deceitful, or incompetent. This caveat does not apply to nonverbal matching because, when properly performed, it takes place on an unconscious level.

§ 2.13 Understanding how rhythmic patterns influence behavior

Beats and rhythms exist in everything we do. The study of rhythmic patterns and their influence in the persuasion process has been of particular interest to advertisers and retail merchants. For example, research in American business indicates that supermarket shoppers spend almost 40% more cash when slow tempo music, rather than thumping disco, is played in the background. Slower music induces shoppers to meander down supermarket aisles taking more time to make purchases.

Understanding rhythmic patterns and their pervasive nature in relationships and environments provides a look at why pacing techniques work. Sections 2.14–2.18 present information on how rhythmic patterns influence behavior. Specifically, the effects of (1) musical rhythms, (2) breathing rhythms, (3) interaction rhythms, (4) group rhythms, and (5) individual rhythms will be explored.

§ 2.14 —The effects of musical rhythms

Research has shown that the beat of music can produce a corresponding change in our heartbeat, brain waves, and blood pressure.[22] When we

---

[22] Lozanov has conducted considerable research in the area of contemporary physiology and psychology. His writings include:

Lozanov, *The Nature and History of the Suggestopedic System of Teaching Foreign Languages and its Experimental Prospects*, 1 SUGGESTOLOGY & SUGGESTOPEDIA J., No. 1 (1975); *Suggestology and Suggestopedia* (Address to the Second International Conference on Suggestive-Accelerative Learning and Teaching, Iowa, 1977) (Videotape) (Iowa State University, 1977); *Suggestopedia in Primary Schools*, 1 SUGGESTOLOGY & SUGGESTOPEDIA, No. 2 (1975).

Lozanov & Balevsky, *The Effect of the Suggestopedic System of Instruction on the Physical Development, State of Health, and Working Capacity of First and Second Grade Pupils*, 1 SUGGESTOLOGY & SUGGESTOPEDIA 3 (1975).

G. LOZANOV, P. BALEVSKY & R. TRAHSLIEV, BASIC TRENDS AND METHODS OF are out of sync, music can always put us back into a particular rhythmic state. You have probably noticed this phenomenon whenever you play music. If the music is fast, it tends to make you move faster. If the music is slow and peaceful, it will tend to cause you to relax. This is another common example of absorbing behaviors and rhythms, not only from other people, but from environmental situations. Researchers also report that rhythm and pace of verbal content affects learning.[23]

The idea that music can and does affect your body and mind is not new. We have been singing lullabies to babies for years. For centuries, people sang sea chants and harvesting songs to ease their labor. From Asia to the Middle East to South America, people have used music to carry them into unusual states of consciousness.

The fact is simple: human beings absorb rhythmic patterns and experience corresponding physiological changes. If you want people to move quicker, play a faster beat. Likewise, if you want them to slow down, play a slower beat. When you want to get people excited, you can do so by raising the pitch of your voice, moving your arms more, or standing up instead of sitting down. All these are behaviors that are very much akin to speeding up the beat of music. When you increase your behavioral rhythm pattern, you will influence both the psychological and physiological responses of your listeners. Therefore, when we listen to a motivational speaker, we expect the speaker to be dynamic. If we listen to a eulogy, we expect the speaker to be more subdued. Both are trying to elicit a specific outcome. Both outcomes are directly related to the behaviors which they manifest.

§ 2.15 —The effects of breathing rhythms

Pacing the breathing patterns of another person can be very effective in establishing rapport and creating an essential link for persuasion. Breathing is directly related to the emotional state that a person is experiencing. When a person is very upset or under stress, his breathing tends

---

OUR EXPERIMENTAL SUGGESTOLOGICAL INVESTIGATIONS (Institute of Suggestology, Bulgaria, 1969).

[23] OSTRANDER, SCHROEDER & OSTRANDER, SUPER LEARNING (Dell Publishing, 1979). *See also* R. Benitez-Borden & D. McClure, Toward a Theory for Research of Learning in an Altered State of Consciousness (University of Iowa, 1974) (unpublished monograph); Benetez-Bordon, McClure & Schuster, *Foreign Language Learning via the Lozanov Method: Pilot Studies*, 1 J. S.A.L.T. 1 (Spring 1976); Benitez-Bordon & McClure, *The Effects of Suggestive Learning Climate, Synchronized Breathing and Music on the Learning Retention of Spanish Words*, 1 J. S.A.L.T. 1 (Spring 1976).

to occur in their upper chest cavity. Someone who is angry also breathes in the upper chest. On the other hand, when a person is relaxed, lethargic, or in a mild state of depression, his breathing drops to the lower abdominal cavity.

To have true empathy for another person involves your ability to experience what that person is experiencing. One method of doing this is to imitate and emulate the breathing patterns of the individual. Pacing breathing patterns is a very powerful way of connecting with a person. First of all, the act of breathing is automatic and pacing an individual's breathing causes a very subconscious and subliminal link to occur. Secondly, synchronistic breathing is a very powerful way to create a common bond with an individual since it is directly related to his emotional state. For example, it is impossible to experience a true state of depression and breathe rapidly in the upper chest area. Likewise, a real state of anger cannot be experienced by breathing very deeply and slowly. This information is invaluable when preparing a witness for trial. If you have a witness who is angry and upset, teach him how to slow down his breathing pattern. If you can prompt him to breathe deeply, slowly, and evenly, he will not experience this anger. Remember that all emotional states are manifested physically. If you change the breathing behavior, you change the emotional state.

You can pace an individual's breathing pattern by carefully observing the rate at which he breathes. This can be done by watching the rise and fall of the shoulder area or by simply watching the chest cavity. It is easy to discern whether a person is a rapid, shallow breather or a very heavy, slow breather. Breathing patterns reveal the person's emotional state, as well as the fundamental rhythmic pattern of the person. They offer valid evidence about how quickly an individual responds to different events and stimuli. Most importantly, pacing breathing patterns will assist in creating an emotional and empathetic bond with another person. It is perhaps the most powerful of all the pacing techniques.

§ 2.16 —The effects of interaction rhythms

Early research has explored the extent to which we maintain a rhythmic dance in a conversation with another person. Researchers Condon and Ogston reported that the body of the listener was found to dance synchronously with the speaker. This is a description of pacing: a shared pattern between the listener and speaker.[24] When the speaker would lean back in the chair, the listener would sit in a similar manner. When the arms were crossed by the listener, the speaker would imitate the same position. The most remarkable thing was that this imitation was unconscious and neither the speaker nor the listener were aware of the match. They also analyzed sound films of social interaction to examine the interrelationships of the movement in the listener and found it was rhythmically coordinated with the speech and movements of the speaker. Apparently we are also influenced by very subtle features of a listener's behavior.

Even though we are unaware of the movement patterns when we are in a conversation, the listener is moving while the speaker is both moving and speaking. This movement may not be a gross or large movement, but a minute movement such as moving the hands, the head, or blinking.

Synchronization of movements in interaction is important because it is a means by which is created the delicate coordination which causes expectancy to occur among participants. To move with another person is to show him that you are with him in intentions and expectancies. Coordination of movement in interaction is of great importance since it provides one of the ways in which two people signal whether or not they are open to one another. Synchronizing is particularly important at those points where a relationship is being established and/or where it is ending.

People also synchronize with others by a flash reaction rather like a reflex. The synchronization seems to be instantaneous. One can theorize that this explains why pacing almost never reaches the level of conscious awareness. When synchrony occurs between two people, the internal experience at that moment is a feeling of great rapport. The individual feels that he is really getting through to the other person though the conversation may actually be completely trivial. On a subliminal level, people either connect or disconnect.

It is important to note, that synchrony does not imply or demand that one match the exact attitude and behaviors of another person. Rather, it implies that one must pace the degree of intensity and feeling of the other's behaviors. In other words, you do not have to display anger with an angry person, but you must display intense concern.

Posture sharing may also reflect listener attention. When people are in

---

[24] Condon & Ogston, *Sound Film Analysis of Normal and Pathological Behavior Patterns*, 143 J. NERVOUS & MENTAL DISEASE 338–347 (1966).

sync with one another, they tend to sit in the same posture.[25] Unconsciously, people communicate to one another that they are seeing eye-to-eye.

§ 2.17 —The effects of group rhythms

In 1976, two researchers examined postural sharing as a nonverbal indicator of group rapport.[26] Since posture sharing occurred on a one-to-one level, their experiment raised the question as to whether it would occur in a group. Would individuals in a group pace one another?

A systematic observation and question format were used to investigate the relationship between posture sharing and self-rapport. A pattern of significant positive correlations revealed that the greater the amount of mirroring and matching postures evidenced by students in regard to the teacher, the higher the ratings of involvement. Conversely, a significant negative relationship was found between the amount of mismatched posture displayed and reports of interest. The students were constantly telegraphing their attitude about the instructor through a match or mismatch of their postural behavior.

§ 2.18 —The effects of individual rhythms

Human beings are very regular in their patterns of listening and speaking. A person's conversational rhythm is one of his more stable and predictable characteristics. It reveals a lot about how he relates to other people. People have their own unique and individual rhythmic patterns which are developed from early childhood.

The man who discovered interaction rhythms and invented not only methods of measuring them, but also a computer called an interaction chronograph to analyze them, is anthropologist Dr. Eliot Chapple.[27] Chapple believes that our rhythmic patterns are partly innate. He postulates that an individual's future interaction rhythm is first manifested by

---

[25] DAVIS, INSIDE INTUITION (McGraw-Hill, 1973).

[26] *Id.*

[27] E. CHAPPLE, CULTURE AND BIOLOGICAL MAN (Holt, 1970); E. CHAPPLE & L. SAYLES, THE MEASUREMENT OF MANAGEMENT (Macmillan, 1961); E. Chapple, *The Standard Experimental (Stress) Interview as Used in Interaction Chronograph Investigation*, 12 HUM. ORG. 23-32 No. 2 (1953); E. Chapple, *Toward a Mathematical Model of Interaction: Some Preliminary Considerations* in EXPLORATIONS IN MATHEMATICAL ANTHROPOLOGY (M.I.T. Press, P. Kay ed. 1970); E. CHAPPLE, ET AL., PRINCIPLES OF PROGRAMMED INTERACTION THERAPY (In preparation).

how active or inactive he is as a baby. However, before the rhythm becomes set at the age of three or four, experience can change it considerably.

From earliest childhood, an individual's basic rhythm affects his relationships with people. It is easy to see that throughout life it is important to find people who's interaction rhythms compliment our own. Chapple believes that finding the perfect listener, experiencing that sense of relaxation, and being able to talk or not talk when one wants to is one of the greatest pleasures in life, but is actually hard to come by. Most of the people we meet operate at tempos that do not mesh with our own. Whenever two people meet who have not yet established a comfortable relationship, there is a period of groping for a common rhythm.

Everyone has their own particular basic rhythm, such as an upbeat tempo when they are feeling particularly good. Most people vary their rhythm within a certain range. For example, a man may habitually operate at one rhythm with his wife or good friends, and at quite another rhythm with his employer. The secondary rhythms occur at random, but surprisingly, when computer analyzed, they appear to be mathematical multiples of the basic beat, a doubling or a halving for example. Some people are very flexible and have a lot of subrhythms available; others are not. These are the compulsive talkers and individuals who speak seldom and almost grudgingly.

Interaction rhythms help to explain some of the paradoxes of human relationships such as why people who appear to have everything in common just cannot seem to get along while people who apparently have nothing in common get along beautifully. For example, one of the ways a husband and wife may be mismatched is in their basic interaction rhythms. This is not always obvious during their courtship, since at that time both are very attentive and eager to adjust. As a result, both people are pacing one another during the beginning of the relationship. After a while, the adjusting phase is over and the natural pace emerges. This is, in lay terms, called that period in the marriage when "the honeymoon is over." It is at this point that the longevity of a relationship can be gauged. It is true that people do not have an isolated relationship with others, but instead live in the midst of a whole system of relationships. Thus, rhythmic imbalance at any one point may be compensated for by rhythmic balance at others. This provides an excellent explanation for relationships having balance and imbalance simultaneously. The important thing to note is that tolerating rhythmic imbalance in a relationship requires that we have rhythmic balance in another part of the relationship or in another relationship altogether. Rhythmic patterns influence behavior on many levels.

§ 2.19 Using pacing and leading techniques in the courtroom

Successful trial attorneys have two very specific abilities of which they may or may not be consciously aware:

1. The ability to pace an individual or group;
2. The ability to adapt behaviors to people or situations.

Both behaviors require a "they" focus rather than a "we" or "I" focus. Most people focus on internal states such as "What am I feeling?" "What should I say next?" "How should I sit?" "What should I write?" "How shall I approach him?" An individual who has developed an external awareness will ask what is on the other person's mind, what is he feeling, what do they want to achieve, what is he revealing through his nonverbal behaviors, what is important to him?

Being "they"oriented is a critical skill for a top executive, salesperson, entrepreneur, and particularly a trial lawyer. "We" or "I" people tend to believe that with proper motivation, anything is possible. The successful "we" believers reach their goals in spite of their internal focus. "They" people usually see things more clearly because their focus is on the other person, the competition, or the environment. "They" people seek out the weaknesses and strengths of others in order to maximize their communication. "They" people also attempt to understand how others think and process information so they can adapt their approach to the individual.

The concept of pacing and leading is fundamental to a trial. Most successful trial attorneys unconsciously pace and lead witnesses, jurors, and judges. The application of this method can be used for two specific purposes: (1) to increase rapport and the fluency of communication, and (2) to decrease rapport and the fluency of communication.

COMMENT: Once a person has been paced effectively, counsel should be able to lead him to the desired point of view or outcome. Remember, the ability to be effective at pacing and leading techniques rests on an understanding of rhythmic patterns and how they operate at all levels.

Pacing specifically involves linking to an individual's perception and experience of the world. When a person perceives you as being similar to himself, the chance of persuading him is much greater. In order to link to another person, the first stage is to gather information about how that person thinks and how he experiences the world. People experience the world through their senses. The first is kinesthetic which is through feelings; the second is auditory which is through hearing; and the third is visual which is through seeing. People tend to have one dominant system that overrides the others. This means that a kinesthetic person focuses on how he "feels" about things, a visual person focuses on what things "look" like, and an auditory person focuses on what things "sound" like. In all cases, it is important for the attorney to pace and adapt to each one of these types of systems used by an individual in order to maximize rapport. In order to diminish rapport, you simply mismatch the system that is being used.[28] Section 2.20 will focus on how to gather information about people in order to pace them effectively.

§ 2.20 Determining how a person processes information

Understanding how a person processes information is a critical key to persuasion. The way people think and compile information tells the persuader how to present information in order to convince another person. There are two methods by which to understand how people process information. The first method is through the use of predicates. Predicates refer to the verbs, nouns, and adverbs which people use when speaking. In § 2.21 *infra*, we will discuss the use of predicates and how they help to identify whether an individual is kinesthetic, auditory, or visual. A second method that provides additional information in determining how a person processes information is through analyzing eye movement patterns and gaze directions. This will be discussed more fully *infra* § 2.22.

§ 2.21 —Use of predicates

People pick up information through their senses: what they see, what they hear, what they taste, what they feel, and what they smell. In

---

[28] *See infra* § 2.41.

American culture, we predominantly rely upon three methods for assembling information. Of the five senses, the three methods that we rely on are: feeling, seeing, and hearing. Throughout this chapter, we will be discussing these methods as follows:

PRIMARY REPRESENTATIONAL SYSTEMS

Kinesthetic (feeling)
Visual (seeing)
Auditory (hearing)

These three systems, which we refer to as representational systems, tell us how a person experiences the world—whether through things that he feels, sees, or touches. Illustratively, if an individual who is predominantly visually-oriented went to buy a car, his first instinct would be to examine the cars in terms of how they look. Being a visual person, he would look at the color, the lines, and the shape of the cars. The final decision would rest on whether the car "looked" like the right car for him. On the other hand, the kinesthetic person, whose feelings are dominant, would get in the car to determine how it feels. His concerns would be different: "Does the car feel right? Does it hold the road? Does it turn the corners right? Do the gears shift the right way? Does it handle well?" Contrarily, the auditory person would listen to how the car sounds. He would listen to the purr of the engine, as well as the sounds the car makes when it turns the corners or accelerates at high speeds. He would also want logical and factual information about the car. Counsel should be aware that although most people have a primary representational system, they also develop a secondary representational system. This means, for example, that they may initially gather their information from what they see and secondary information may then come from what they feel.

It is important to understand the differences in how kinesthetic, auditory, and visual individuals think and experience the world. One way to identify the visual, kinesthetic, and auditory person is through the selection of words. The way we experience the world is often expressed in our language. Table 2–1 offers examples of different types of predicates used for the three different representational systems. Study the following table and try to identify whether there is one particular class of words that you use more than another. Once you become familiar with these words, it will be very easy when talking to an individual to begin to identify the way in which he thinks and which representational system he relies most heavily upon.

Table 2–1
Examples of Visual, Kinesthetic, and Auditory Predicates

	Visual Predicates		
Focus	Graphic	Watch	Colorful
Bright	Illustrate	Vision	Glimpse
Show	Color	Brilliant	Look
Pretty	See	Evident	Notice
Envision	Picture	Sketch	Sight
Draw	Hazy	Oversight	Shining
View	Peek	Clearly	Hidden
Clear	Imagine	Perspective	Notice
	Auditory Predicates		
Listen	Ringing	Compliment	Pardon
Hear	Resonate	Loud	Sound
Discuss	Yell	Silent	Request
Declare	Told	Shout	Whispering
Implore	Call	Talk	Quiet
Acclaim	Assert	Noisy	Ask
Harmony	Profess	Orchestrate	
Petition	Noise	Address	
	Kinesthetic Predicates		
Feel	Terrified	Hunger	Contact
Pressure	Burdensome	Doubt	Nurture
Hurt	Firm	Shocking	Emotion
Get the point	Tense	Heavy	Graceful
Experience	Touchy	Touch	Sensual
Longing	Pushy	Concrete	Weighty problem
Wait	Shatter	Irritated	

The representational system becomes important to the attorney because if he doesn't match the individual's representational system, he may find that the individual is much less responsive to what is being said.

A summary of the way the kinesthetic, auditory, and visual person thinks is as follows:

Individual With Primary Visual Representational System:
"It looks good to me."

Individual With Primary Kinesthetic Representational System:
"It feels good to me."

Individual With Primary Auditory Representational System:
"It sounds good to me."

COMMENT: Successful attorneys, intuitively and unconsciously, often match the representational system of another person. This is another example of pacing. Pacing is a skill that is used most frequently by those people who have high self-monitoring scores. Our attempt in this chapter is to outline the specific ways in which attorneys can pace an individual to increase rapport and to ultimately lead the individual to a desired behavioral or attitudinal change.

---

§ 2.22 —Eye movement patterns and gaze direction

Eye movement patterns and gaze directions tend to correlate with how a person processes information. If you observe eye movement patterns, it will provide you with a second indication of how a person thinks. Are they visualizing an object, are they feeling an emotion, or are they having internal dialogue within their own mind?

A right-handed individual who looks up to his right will generally be constructing a visual image. Thus, if you are describing the scene of a crime, the visual person will actually be picturing it with you when their eyes move up and to the right-hand corner. When a right-handed person looks up to the right, they are constructing a visual image. If they are looking up to their left, they are usually remembering a visual image. They may be recalling a time in their life when they sat on the ocean front or when they were in a crowded room.

When the eyes move across and at an even level to the right, we find that most people are constructing a dialogue. They are thinking about what they are going to say or what would be appropriate to say under a particular circumstance. They may actually be having a dialogue with another person in their mind. When the eyes of a right-handed person move across and level to the left, it is usually a memory of an auditory experience. This may be an experience of hearing the waves crashing on the rocks or an experience of hearing different types of music. When the right-handed person's eyes move down to the lower right, the person is usually experiencing an emotion or other bodily sensations. When the eyes move down to the lower left, they are usually listening to their own internal dialogue or "talking to themselves."

When observing a left-handed person, simply substitute a mirror-like image.

Observing eye movement behavior patterns will often give you correlative information with the predicate system. Thus, if the person has a visual predicate system and he moves his eyes continually to the upper right or left, it tells you very strongly that he relies on visual information and will be most easily persuaded through the matching of this system. Similarly, if a person uses many of the kinesthetic words such as touch, get a handle on, or get in contact with, and he tends to look down to his lower right, we can safely conclude that he understands information through the kinesthetic process.

COMMENT: The trial attorney must appreciate the fact that eye movement patterns which occur with jurors, such as looking away from counsel, is not an indicator that the jurors are not interested. It may be a more reliable indicator of how they are processing the information.

Identifying predicate usage and eye movement behavior provides important clues in identifying whether an individual is predominantly kinesthetic, visual, or auditory. Pacing or matching an individual involves speaking that person's language, using similar voice patterns, and using similar movements. This means pacing an individual on a verbal, vocal and nonverbal level. Therefore, the kinesthetic (feeling) individual should be paced on three levels: verbal, vocal, and nonverbal. The same applies to the visual (seeing) and auditory (hearing) individuals. These techniques will be discussed in the following sections.[29]

§ 2.23 Pacing verbal communication

Match the way an individual talks and you will literally be speaking the same language. Successful salespeople listen carefully to the customer's needs, then use the words of the customer to sell them on benefits. For example, if a customer says he is interested in "more efficiency in office systems," then this should be used as the key phrase by the salesperson when responding. An example of a mismatch would be if the salesperson responds with "so, you are interested in getting everything more organized." People choose phrases and words for a reason. Listen carefully to what they say, and you will be able to speak their language.

Another good example of verbal pacing occurs when the salesperson finds out that his customer likes to hunt. Before you know it, he has hours worth of hunting stories to tell. Or he finds out that the customer is a Roman Catholic and the next thing you know, he is telling him about having lunch with the cardinal. These are examples of pacing strategies which are oriented to pacing the person on a conscious level through common interest or common behaviors.

In addition to matching word choice and key phrases, verbal pacing also involves matching predicate systems. As we discussed *supra* § 2.21, a predicate system refers to the class of words that people use. Basically, to establish rapport, you should choose the adverbs, adjectives, and verbs the person uses and which indicate his major representational system.[30]

COMMENT: Ordinarily, the adult vocabulary includes the usage of about 1,000 words per day. This tells us that most people repeat many of the words that they use. People also tend to repeat key phrases and key words. This represents the way in which they understand information. As we've discussed, pacing verbal language or information means that we identify key words and phrases of the individual. By identifying key words and phrases, we identify the primary representational system they use. We can then begin to match it. This creates the perception of speaking the same

[29] *See infra* §§ 2.23–2.36.

[30] *See supra* § 2.21, Table 2–1 for a listing and classification of the key words.

language as the other person. In addition, it underscores Communication Principle 9 which is that people are more easily influenced by those people whom they perceive as similar to themselves. Maximizing similarity on the verbal level is a powerful way in which to create rapport with another person. People listen to other people who speak the same language. Sections 2.24–2.27 will provide specific methods for matching verbal communication.

---

§ 2.24 —Pacing key words and phrases

Every profession, company, and class of people has its own jargon. The type of words that are used in any profession tells us the way in which they order information. The legal profession uses words and phrases such as "aforementioned," "prior to," "pursuant to," "hereinafter," and so forth. To build rapport with an attorney, for instance, you should use similar language. Likewise, teenagers have a completely different vocabulary which might include such words as "awesome," "outrageous," or "for real." Therefore, it is more effective when talking to a teenager to utilize his language structure rather than trying to impose your own language structure on him.

IBM is a good illustration of a corporation that has its own language. Their language includes such words as "net," "escalate," and "pitch." The word "net" is equivalent to "bottom line." However, if you are talking to an IBM person and they say "net it out for me," you will be much better off by responding with "this is how I'd like to net it out" rather than "the bottom line is." This gives a parallel construction in using the language that the other person uses.

COMMENT: The most critical thing for a successful communicator to remember is not to impose his own language on another person.

If you listen carefully to another person, you can clearly pick out the key words and phrases that he uses. In order to pace this individual, pay attention to those words that are important to him. Listen for the phrases that he uses over and over again. When you respond to him, use his phrases in your language. This is matching a person in terms of his verbal communication. In some situations, it may be helpful to take notes when talking to an individual. Write down the specific phrases he uses and then use that information as reference material when preparing a report or proposal to be evaluated by that person.

§ 2.25 —Pacing the visually dominant individual

Pacing the visual individual means understanding his predicate system and using the same words he uses. If he says, "Take a look at this," you might respond by saying, "Let's focus on this." When you use the same predicate system as another person, your chance for rapport increases dramatically. An example of how to use a matching predicate system with a witness is presented in the following question-and-answer material. When you read the transcription, you will notice that the attorney used visual words in response to the visual words that were used by the witness. It is much easier to lead a person to your point of view if you speak his language.

Q. You are headed north to where?

A. To Mendota. *See*, after I unloaded, I called in and asked them for a load and I told them I was unloading. They told me I had a load of cantaloupe to *look* up at Mendota.

Q. Now, you called every morning, didn't you?

A. Right.

Q. According to their instructions, did you report to anybody at anytime on the phone that you had trouble with the brakes on the tractor in the trailer, or any other trouble with that tractor or trailer?

A. It's not *clear* to me, I just don't recall.

Q. Now, I've got a new map here, and I'm going to *focus* up here, it *looks* like Mendota. Is that about the way that you went up? Put the *look* on that. It's part of a California map that I took out of a book.

A. Yes, that *looks* like it.

Q. Okay, and you got up there and did what, if anything?

A. I first reported in and told them I was there, you know, *looking* for my load.

Q. Sure, I *see*.

A. And there was, I forget how many trucks I *saw* ahead of me, there was four or five or so trucks up ahead of me, because it was pretty busy. After I reported in, I told them it was my turn, to come out and get me. I told them to *look* for me in the McAdams truck.

Q. While you were up there, how long were you in Mendota?

A. I can't exactly say right now.

Q. Did you leave in the *dark*?

A. As I *picture* it, it was still *daylight* when I left, just around *daylight*.

Q. In the summertime just about *dusk*—when it is getting *dark*—would that be about a good estimate?

A. It was right before *dark* came. If I remember *clearly*, I think I pulled out right before it got *dark*.

Q. How many thousand pounds of cantaloupe did you have?

A. Let me *see*. I believe it was 39,000, something in there.

Q. Okay. Will you *look* at this map and *show* me the route you took from Mendota? Take this red pen, if you can, down through California, and here is an Arizona map, across into Arizona, if you can *show* me.

A. *See*, I'm not exactly *clear* how I went because I can't *picture* which route I took.

Q. I *see*. I'll *show* you my map and you tell me if my map *looks* correct. Now, how does my map *look* to you?

A. It *looks* okay. I know I took 180, I came down through Bakersfield. From Bakersfield, I went across 40.

Q. Okay, and then getting into Arizona, how does that *look* to you?

A. Right, I took 40 all the way across Arizona.

Q. Does my map *look* to be correct?

A. It *looks* right to me.

The example of matching the predicate system with the witness underscores several things. First of all, the witness used a dominant visual predicate system and the attorney matched it. The underlined words in the transcript illustrate the consistent matching of predicate systems. A second observation is that the attorney also used the same style of language of the witness. The attorney talked in more of a lay language with the witness rather than using legal jargon. There is no question that greater rapport can be built when one matches both the style of language and the predicate system that another person uses. This is a good example of not only matching the predominant representational system, but also of matching the actual verbal style and syntax of the individual.

§ 2.26 —Pacing the auditorily dominant individual

Pacing the auditory individual requires the same type of process as used in pacing the visual individual. Learn the predicate system used by the auditory person and use those same types of words in your language structure. Before you can lead a person you need to match the way that person speaks and thinks. The auditory person will have internal dialogues. He will think about things in a logical order. To maximize the perception of similarity with the auditorily dominant person, use his language and listen carefully.

§ 2.27 —Pacing the kinesthetically dominant individual

In pacing the kinesthetic individual on a verbal level, use the types of words that a kinesthetic individual would use such as "touch," "handle," or "get in contact with." When a kinesthetic person hears these words being used, he will translate it as if you are speaking the same language as he is. The translation goes even a step further. Not only are you speaking his language, but this will increase his perception that you feel things the same way he does. Once a person perceives that this similarity exists, the chances of influencing him is much greater. A kinesthetic person, particularly because he operates by his "gut level response," will want to know that you feel things in a similar manner. If you respond to a kinesthetic person by using logical and ordered language, he will not be able to "sense" your ability to empathize, and therefore, his trust of you will diminish.

§ 2.28 Pacing vocal communication

People have a wide variety of speaking styles. Some are soft while others are loud and abrasive; some talk in long sentences while others in very short, abrupt sentences. Vocal pacing involves listening to how a person talks and matching his rhythm and inflection. If a person talks with very short, direct, and bottom-line statements, you should be cued to use the same style. By the same token, an individual who is a rapid speaker will have greater rapport with someone who matches his rapid speaking style.

People talk at different rates with varying rhythms and different tones. In all cases, the way a person talks tells you how quickly or how slowly he tends to process information. Some people are very deliberate and methodical in their thinking. They present information in much the same manner. Those people that talk "bottom line" and "net" tend to be highly visual, and visual people tend to talk at a faster rate.

When you present information to people in a manner similar to the way they speak, their comprehension in understanding that information is much greater. Sections 2.29 and 2.30 set forth specific ways in which you can pace the vocal communication channel.

§ 2.29 —Pacing vocal rate

Inasmuch as there are individual rate differences in speech patterns, it is important to note how quickly a person speaks. The normal rate of speaking is between 125 and 200 words per minute. With a naturally slow speaker, however, communication improves through the use of a slower language pattern. It is well documented that salespeople in New York City who move to Atlanta have a very difficult time in building rapport with their customers. The primary reason they experience difficulty is that their speech pattern is much more accelerated than the native Georgian. As a result, there is limited listening. It is not that the Georgian cannot comprehend what the transplanted New Yorker is saying, it is simply that the Georgian is not predisposed to receiving information that quickly. They do not present it that quickly themselves. They live in an environment where information is presented at a much slower rate.

While pacing the vocal rate of others, be sure to listen not only to how quickly they speak but at what point they begin to slow down. When a person slows his vocal pattern, he is probably accenting information or becoming contemplative about particular information. Pacing this person would mean that if he speaks slowly, then you should speak slowly; if he speaks fast, then you should speak fast.

§ 2.30 —Pacing vocal characteristics

There are three specific vocal characteristics to consider in pacing: (1) sentence patterns, (2) pauses, and (3) degree of expression.

The sentence pattern of an individual will vary. He may use long sentences, short sentences, abrupt sentences, or run-on sentences. When pacing an individual, follow the same sentence pattern that he uses. If he talks in very short, clipped sentences, make sure that your sentences are equally as short. If he asks you questions, make sure that you ask questions. Psychologists have closely examined and studied the dialogue that takes place between two interactants. The results show that when one interactant talks in run-on sentences with no reciprocal questions while the other interactant talks in much shorter sentences and does ask questions, both interactants will evaluate the rapport between them as very low. This tells us that people want a basic reciprocity in communication. This is one of the basic rules of a relationship, discussed *supra* § 2.10.

People may feel that a conversation is imbalanced. By imbalance we mean that one person spends considerably more time "talking" while the other person gains information power over another. When this occurs, both people lose the perception of rapport. The best communicators listen and talk equally. The other person will cue you as to whether or not he wants to answer questions or whether or not he wants to talk about himself. To be a sensitive listener helps to establish rapport.

The use of pauses is another cueing technique that can be used in an interaction. When an individual pauses in the middle of a thought, it is very important for the listener not to interrupt the thought at that point. The pause used by that individual is an indication that he is gathering information and assembling thoughts. Pacing requires that you allow the individual to assemble his thoughts. It also gives you an opportunity to integrate the information. Equally important, if the individual uses pauses, is for you to use pauses also.

The degree of expression communicated by a person in his vocal language gives you another cue as to how to pace that individual. Some people are very expressive with a wide pitch range. They can express various emotions, from excitement to sadness, through the voice. Other people have a very monotone and flat vocal expression which does not express emotions. The person who is generally very expressive with his voice in terms of emotional patterns should be paced by the communicator in an equally expressive manner. A true mismatch occurs when you have an expressive individual who is very animated with his vocal qualities talking to a person who is more cerebral and keeps the voice at a very slow monotone. For example, we are all familiar with the individual who comes home from work extremely excited about what is going on. His spouse responds in a flat voice tone, "Well, that's nice." At this point, the expressive individual becomes very frustrated with the conversation because there is no reciprocity in expression. Similarly, if a person is talking to someone with a monotone voice and who tends to talk very matter of factly, the communicator should match those characteristics in order to be much more persuasive. To respond in an animated, *expressive* way would run counter to the way that person thinks.

§ 2.31 Pacing nonverbal communication

Nonverbal pacing is the matching of body orientation, gestures, movements, touch, and distance factors in other people. When you are in rapport with another individual, you will automatically look like him in the way you sit and move. If you pace someone nonverbally, you follow his body rhythms. If the other person is anxious and moving around a great deal, you need to match the same intensity by also moving around or by facial expressions. It is important to remember, however, that you do not have to use the exact behavior of an individual. Hand movements, for example, can match foot movements; head nods can match the speaking pattern. These are all examples of pacing the general state of the individual.

People express their emotional tendencies through gesturing and movement patterns. To effectively match this, it is very important to observe how people talk with their hands. Then, when it is your turn to talk, use the same types of gestures. If a person is breathing slowly, slow your movements down also. To the extent that you are able to match the individual on the nonverbal level, you will increase rapport. The ability to adapt and have high flexibility in your behavioral responses to another individual is the key to persuading others.

Pacing can only be done successfully by those attorneys who have an adaptive nature and a genuine "they" focus. This shows up in many excellent trial attorneys, who have the ability to shift their ideas and their way of thinking. By practicing pacing skills, you can really increase your degree of flexibility and adaptation.

Pacing the nonverbal communication cues of another individual is at the heart of pacing behavior and establishing rapport. The nonverbal communication of the individual is generally expressive of internal and unconscious emotional states that the individual is experiencing. In order to maximize the perception of similarity, you must pace the nonverbal cues. For example, if an individual is a nonmovement-oriented person, it would be important in a conversation with him to sit equally as still. Basically, he is expressing the way in which he processes information. This is what makes him most comfortable. A person will indicate through nonverbal behaviors many of the emotional states that he experiences. He tells you whether he is fast or slow, whether he likes to reflect, or move quickly. All of this can be picked up through the nonverbal cues. When these cues are paced on a subtle level, it will not be observed by the other person. Sections 2.32–2.36 will discuss pacing the nonverbal behavior of an individual with regard to (1) gestures and movement, (2) touch, (3) postural orientation and distance, (4) eye movement and facial cues, and (5) personal appearance.

§ 2.32 —Pacing gestures and movement

Pacing gestures and movement offers the most fundamental cue of nonverbal pacing. Kinesthetically-oriented people tend to engage in a great deal of movement. You will find that when they talk they have to move; when they are thinking about something they may have to walk around. They have a hard time sitting for a long period of time. To pace a kinesthetic individual, if he walks or paces, you should also stand and move around. If you remain seated, the rhythm of the interaction will be thrown off. What is most important in establishing rapport is that the rhythms are mutual and occur at the same time. If you are walking with somebody who walks fast and you are walking at a slower rate, one person or the other will be put into an uncomfortable position. Remember, the most powerful communicator is the most flexible one. If you are the person engaged in the persuasion process, then you want to make sure that you are the one doing the adapting to the other individual. If gestures are used a lot by the other individual, then when you talk use an equal amount of expression with gestures.

Generally speaking, the auditory person will not use as much movement and will prefer to sit quietly when they are talking. This should cue you to slow your movements down. If you move around and shift in your seat you will begin to make him feel very uncomfortable. Remember, behaviors are absorbed. Therefore, if you move around a lot the auditory person will start to absorb your behaviors which will not be natural to him. Consequently, he will find the interaction to be uncomfortable. People will often comment on the nature of interaction as being a good one, one with chemistry, or one that clicked. What they are really referring to is that the rhythm of the interaction matched. Whether we discuss this consciously or not, an individual should realize that there is an unconscious perception of similarity to another person, and therefore, we must think in a like manner.

The visually oriented person usually moves and gestures. If the individual leans back in his chair, the pacer should also lean back. If he leans forward, the pacer should come forward with him. When a person starts to lean forward, he is cueing you that his interest is picking up or he has something very important to say. When he leans forward that becomes a tip for the pacer to give him equal attention and interest at the same time. For example, if you are having lunch with an individual who has been eating during the course of the conversation but suddenly puts down his fork to make a particular point, at that moment you should do the same. Give him the same intensity of expression and attention for which he is cueing you at each particular moment in time.

§ 2.33 —Pacing touch behavior

The research that has been done in the area of touch behaviors tells us that people usually have a higher regard for people by whom they are touched.[31] If you are with an individual who likes to touch a great deal, this becomes a cue that he would like to have you touch him back. Unless there is a great status differential, you should do so. Touch is a powerful communicator. A touch-oriented person (this is often the kinesthetically oriented person), not only touches individuals, but he also touches paper, documents, holds onto a coffee cup, and likes to have things in his hands. To pace a touch-oriented person, if he is holding something in his hands, hold something in your hands at the same time. Although this sounds very obvious, it is very subtle. It will communicate rapport with the unconscious and will not be perceived by the other person unless the imitation behaviors are overly obvious that they cue the individual.

§ 2.34 —Pacing postural orientation and distance

Postural orientation will tell you whether an individual is engaging in an exclusion or inclusion process. When people want to exclude others from a conversation, for example, they may turn their shoulder to the person being excluded. Hence, the phrase "getting the cold shoulder." On the other hand, when a person wants to include another in a conversation, he tends to have full body orientation—i.e., he turns toward the individual. Counsel should be aware that there are other reasons why postural orientation may shift. Thus, another reason for exclusionary posture may be to have a casual conversation. A casual conversation is

[31] *See supra* §§ 1.40 & 1.86.

best set up by a side-to-side posture. Front-to-front postural orientation, however, increases formality.

The distance that an individual keeps from another is also another clue about their relationship. If an individual allows another person into his personal territory or personal bubble (eighteen inches or less in North American culture), he is allowing that person to influence him at a deeper level. An individual who comes closer to another is cueing that person that he likes him. To pace him, the person should maintain the close distance. The common reaction, however, is to engage in a flight pattern when someone approaches us. We generally take a step backwards or we move out of that spatial zone. If you are with a person who likes close distances, in order to pace him you need to match that behavior.

COMMENT: Observing the postural orientation of people tells you about their relationship to formality, informality, distance, territoriality, and most importantly, tells you about their relationship to you.

---

§ 2.35 —Pacing eye movement and facial behavior

Eye movement and facial behavior are generally expressive of attitudes and emotions of a person. If an individual uses a number of rewarding nonverbal cues, particularly smiling, it is important that the person doing the pacing also match those cues. There is nothing as incongruent as a conversation taking place between a person using many rewarding nonverbal cues (such as nodding his head and smiling) and a person using limited nonverbal cues or encouragers. Eventually the conversation will slow down and end. As indicated throughout this work, when there is a mismatch in the cues the conversation will generally come to a halt. Pacing is effective only if you show the other person the same type of attention and cues that you are being shown. The philosophical underpinnings of this is that people communicate those things they want for themselves. If an individual tells you "thank you" or "sends you lots of cards or notes," he is telling you that is the type of attention he would like from you. If someone smiles at you a great deal, he is indicating to you that he would like the same rewarding nonverbal cues from you.

Consciously or unconsciously people are always telling others what they want back. It is the astute observer and the skilled communicator who is able to perceive those behaviors and then feed them back.

With regard to facial and eye behavior, if you are speaking with an individual who tends to move his eyes to the upper right or left just when it is your turn to talk, move your eyes in the same direction. Now you are instituting a visual phenomena. If he moves his eyes down to the lower right, the sign of a kinesthetic, then when you are speaking on that type of issue move your eyes to the lower right also. Again, we are talking about pacing and following the behaviors of another person. When pacing is working well, you will find that it occurs simultaneously. There is neither a follower nor a leader. Both people tend to automatically pace one another. Once this phenomena is achieved, we say that the relationship is clicking or that it has natural rapport.

§ 2.36 —Pacing personal appearance

In Chapter 1, we discussed many of the personal appearance factors that affect perceptions of credibility and approachability. When dealing with an individual, pacing his personal appearance becomes another link for creating similarity. This is particularly important with clients and witnesses. When you want a client and witnesses to have rapport with the jurors, you should keep in mind how they are dressed and what demographic regional factors must be taken into consideration. For example, in a trial taking place in the metropolitan area of Manhattan, jurors have the expectation that an attorney will dress in a three-piece pinstriped suit. It is best to pace that expectation. Pacing not only involves pacing the actual physical phenomena of another person, but also pacing their expectations.

§ 2.37 Direct versus complimentary pacing

There are two different types of pacing techniques which can be used: direct versus complimentary. So far the text has covered only direct pacing, which involves matching the actual cues and behaviors of another. Direct pacing is a direct mirror image of the other person. Complimentary pacing is matching the general mood, emotional state, and intensity of the individual rather than his direct behavioral patterns. There are some circumstances in which you want to use only complimentary pacing. For example, if a person is very angry and you match his behaviors by being equally as angry, the result usually is an escalation of the anger that he is experiencing. Complimentary pacing is very effective when the state that you are matching is a highly negative state.

We have previously defined pacing as linking to the unconscious mind of another person. This allows us to understand why both direct and complimentary pacing are equally effective. Pacing really means to pace the emotional tone or experience that the individual is having. It is showing him behaviorally that you are experiencing similar qualities to what he is experiencing. One might argue that simply replicating the movements, behaviors, and breathing patterns of another person is an outward display of those characteristics and not a direct display of a similar emotional state being experienced. The interesting thing that happens, however, is that if you do duplicate the patterns of another person you will, in effect, begin to experience some of the similar states that he has. If you hold your body in a collapsed position (thoracic cavity collapsed, head and eyes going down to the lower right, breathing very shallowly), chances are you will usually experience a depressed emotional state. Thus, by matching, not only are you empathizing with the person externally, but you will, in fact, begin to empathize with that person on an internal level.

When the body assumes a particular posture it affects the types of sensations you can have. You can experience this by sitting in different postures and recognizing the various emotional states that seem to correspond with each posture. Pacing must then be defined as pacing a person's overall emotional tone. When we do this, we have to ask several questions about the individual. First, how important is the state or the experience to the individual at this time? Secondly, what type of intensity is he experiencing? Thirdly, what is his attention focused on? The answers to these three questions will give you a key to the person and how much focus you need to put in these relative areas also.

Using complimentary pacing means to identify the state that the individual is experiencing and finding a complimentary state that would support, not only his experience, but lead him out of that state. The intensity, rather than the actual behavior, is matched in complimentary pacing. If you do not match the "intensity" of the individual experience, the result will be a mismatch. This, in part, explains why a husband/wife argument can get out of hand if one spouse is angry and the other spouse acts nonchalant and says "Don't worry about it, it's really not a problem."

COMMENT: It is very important to keep in mind that complimentary pacing does not mean the pacer has to be experiencing that exact same state, but it does mean that the pacer has to be experiencing the exact same intensity. Intensity is the key word.

Another situation in which complimentary pacing is effective is with an individual who is depressed or lethargic. Obviously the person doing the pacing would not match the actual state of depression, but one would want to slow down personal behaviors and pay attention to the person. Keep in mind that the entire purpose of matching an individual is not only to build rapport, but to eventually lead him to a new behavioral state. So, in the case of the depressed person, one matches his behavior slowly. Once rapport has been established, the person pacing the individual can then begin to change the pace and he will find that the depressed person will follow the new pace. This all occurs on a very unconscious level and it requires that the pacing be accurate and subtle.

Direct versus complimentary pacing offers two different strategies to pace an individual. It really makes little difference which strategy is used as long as you are always pacing the overall emotional tone or experience that the other person is having. When you walk into a crowded room, you can immediately pick up the type of atmosphere that is there. People automatically begin to adapt to the atmosphere in the room. This is called pacing the environment. It is important to keep in mind that pacing occurs on individual and group levels.

A good way to practice your pacing techniques is to use direct and complimentary pacing in everything that you do. Every time you meet and speak with a group of people, pay attention to the emotional tenor and tone and adapt your behaviors. Every time you speak to an individual—whether it is the postman, another attorney, or your spouse—watch their behaviors, listen for their emotional tone, and change your behaviors to match theirs. The skill of pacing is acquired very quickly if you practice it regularly. However, the courtroom should not be the place to practice pacing. It needs to be an ongoing activity. This way you can truly develop and refine the skill of pacing. If you are a high self-monitor, you will probably find it easier to use the pacing skill because chances are you are using it already. On the other hand, if you are a low self-monitor, you will have to work a little harder at observing others' cues and then adapting yourself to those types of behaviors.

§ 2.38 Pacing on multiple levels

Pacing another person is a pervasive strategy. In order to be effective in pacing another person, an individual should pace at as many different levels as possible. If an individual is talking to a person who speaks very quickly and he matches him by also speaking quickly, is he not pacing him correctly? Although the answer is yes, he is not going to influence him nearly as effectively if he uses only one channel of communication. By pacing a person on multiple levels, an individual should create a more profound ability to lead the person and, therefore, influence his behavior. Thus, in order to pace effectively the pacer must simultaneously pace in all three channels of communication: verbal, vocal, and nonverbal.

When you are pacing an individual, you may find yourself becoming extremely self-conscious. As you try to pace an individual's gestures, you may find it very difficult to pace his breathing pattern, to pace his eye and facial movement behavior, and to identify whether he is kinesthetic, auditory, or visual all at the same time. While it is very complicated in the beginning, it becomes a simpler strategy the more you use it. The best way to start practicing pacing on multiple levels is to choose one level to begin with. For example, one day pay attention to verbal pacing. Pay attention to all the words. Another day focus on vocal pacing and pay attention to matching the vocal tones of another individual and so on. If you will build your repertoire of skills in each of these areas, you will find that you will quickly be pacing on multiple levels without even being consciously aware that you are doing this.

We are now dealing with level three of the learning process which is conscious competence.[32] At this point, you know what you have to do to make pacing an effective communication strategy, but you will have to do it consciously. To do any behavior consciously is the first step to learning that behavior, but it is also the stage of feeling awkward and self-conscious. By the time you reach level four which is the stage of unconscious competence, that behavior or the skill of pacing will become so ingrained in what you are doing that you will pace automatically without effort or conscious knowledge that you are pacing another individual.

---

[32] *See supra* § 1.01.

The other important value to this is that you will begin to recognize when a communication transaction is ineffective and be able to identify whether pacing was or was not used effectively.

Pacing on multiple levels requires particular attention to pacing the entire gestalt of the person. In other words, to pace his entire experience and overall emotional tone. The more similar you become to a person and the more in tune you become with what he is feeling, the more he will see you similar to himself. This also increases the subtle effect of pacing. When a person is effectively pacing another individual, he automatically does it on multiple levels.

§ 2.39 When to pace

Pacing is not a skill to be used randomly or selectively. It is a pervasive communication skill that should be used all the time in every situation. The only time it should not be used is if you are trying to (1) decrease rapport or (2) decrease credibility. If that is your purpose then you need to mismatch, rather than pace, communication behaviors.[33] In every other situation, you would want to use pacing skills. It is very unlikely that you will be able to influence another individual without first pacing his behavior. Four stages occur in the pacing process:

1. acknowledging the state the other person is experiencing;
2. treating that experience as valid;
3. empathizing with the individual;
4. gently leading him to a new state.

The first stage of pacing involves actually acknowledging the state that another person is experiencing. Too often, the focus of many people is concentrated on themselves—"what am I going to do, what should I say." The first stage of pacing requires a high sensitivity to people. This should be an ongoing process. When we say that you should pace all the time, we literally mean that. Your sensitivity to other people should be so high that you are continually paying attention to what they are experiencing. Before you can give anyone a new experience or lead them to a new behavior, you have to first understand where they are coming from.

The second stage of pacing requires you to "treat that experience as valid." Many times an individual will say something to us and we will simply disallow it. For example, someone might say, "I really don't like

---

[33] *See infra* § 2.41 for a discussion of mismatching and its application.

coffee." We might say to that person, "What do you mean you don't like coffee? Everybody drinks coffee; coffee is great." In a case such as this, we are saying that the person's opinion or presumption is not valid. This is a common error that many salespeople make. Unless you pace the individual and link to his frame of reference, the chance of persuading him is very low indeed.

The third stage of pacing involves empathizing with the individual. In other words, you will have to match either through direct or complimentary pacing the experience that he is having. This will demonstrate to him, both on a conscious and unconscious level, that you are speaking the same language.

The fourth stage of pacing focuses on gently leading the individual to a new state or behavior. In § 2.40 *infra*, we will discuss when and how to lead an individual. The important point to recognize is that leading an individual to a new state (which is commonly defined as persuasion or influence) very rarely, if ever, occurs prior to the other three stages.

Illustratively, Alcoholics Anonymous is successful because the individuals who are teaching the new behaviors and are helping other people kick the habit of alcohol are exalcoholics themselves. Consequently, they acknowledge the state they are in, they validate it as a true state, and they empathize from a very internal level because they have been there before. Only after they have done those three things will they try to lead the person to a new state.

COMMENT: The most effective trial attorneys are good pacers. They are continually engaged in the process of pacing and leading.[34] The state of pacing should be an ongoing state used both in your personal and professional life. There are very few circumstances under which you would not want to pace another individual.

---

[34] *See infra* §§ 2.45–2.48 discussing the pacing of jurors, clients, witnesses, and the judge.

§ 2.40 When to lead

The purpose of pacing is to establish rapport and then to lead a person or a group to a new experience, behavior, or response. Once an effective pace has been established, you can lead the individual to a new behavior. Pacing and leading, therefore, work hand in hand as a behavioral approach to persuasion. When you have effectively paced an individual, you can test your ability to lead. For example, stand in the hallway talking to an individual pacing the verbal, vocal, and nonverbal channels; then begin to move toward another location and notice whether he follows you. If he does, the pacing has been effective. If he does not, you may need to pace longer. It is interesting to note that when rapport is well established between individuals, a third party can no longer identify who is pacing and who is leading.

The point at which you want to lead in any interaction is after you have established a solid base of rapport and can identify that the pacing has been effective. As indicated above, effective pacing can be identified by testing a new behavior: do something different and see if the other person follows your lead. If the individual still stays in his own pace, he simply is cueing you that he is not ready to move on. This is very important information. When an individual is not ready to move on there is no point in trying to give him new input or new information, because he will not integrate it at that time. Pay attention to the pace and move from that point.

COMMENT: Remember, leading an individual involves a very subtle switch between pacing and leading behaviors. When you are pacing an individual, you are constantly adapting to his state and his behaviors. When you begin to lead an individual, you begin to institute new behaviors.

---

§ 2.41 When to mismatch

When you are out of sync with another person and when the common link is not present, the result will be a multiple behavioral mismatch. When a relationship is waning, the first indicators are behavioral. Patterns and rhythms change, usually on several levels. This results in an observable mismatch. On an unconscious level, we tend to pace those people we like, evaluate highly, and prefer. We tend to mismatch those people we dislike, evaluate negatively, or do not prefer. At the times when we most need to establish rapport, we unconsciously pull away or mismatch. For example, an argument between a husband and wife, a misunderstanding between a manager and subordinate, a traffic ticket received from a police officer are situations of avoidance and subsequent mismatch. In each situation, the natural response is to be right and to fight back.

There may be situations, however, in which you would want to mismatch an individual. These situations would have to encompass either (1) the desire to decrease rapport with an individual or (2) to decrease the credibility of an individual. When you mismatch behaviors of an individual, it will cause the conversation to become less fluent. It will change the rhythm pattern of a conversation. The conversation itself will appear awkward and the interaction stilted or stiff. Another common phenomena that occurs in a mismatch is that the pacer can put the other person in a state of situational anxiety. This will usually result in a decrease of fluency in his speech patterns. Lack of fluency reduces the perception of credibility. Therefore, if counsel is cross-examining a witness and deliberately mismatching the behaviors of the witness, we can predict that the witness will experience some situational anxiety, a loss of fluency, and hence, a loss of perceived credibility. The loss of fluency is usually characterized by hedges such as "um", "oh", "I don't know", and so forth. These types of filled pauses are perceived as low in credibility by the jurors.

Mismatching means exactly what the words say. When you want to mismatch an individual's behavior, you simply assume the opposite of his behavior. You use contrasting behaviors. If you are talking with a kinesthetic person and you want to mismatch him, then use visual predicates. If you are talking to an individual who does not move when he speaks, then you should move around a great deal. This is sure to increase his anxiety and decrease his comfort level. Whenever you mismatch an individual, you increase the uncertainty that that person has in dealing with you in an interaction. When you increase uncertainty, the result is a relationship that no longer has reciprocity or balance.

§ 2.42 How to regain rapport when it is lost

When rapport is lost in an interaction, it can usually be attributed to one of two reasons: (1) there has been a temporary mismatch of the behavioral cues of the individual or (2) there has been a miscalculation as to the actual experience that was going on. In order to regain rapport, you need to recalibrate your perception of the mental state which the other person has been experiencing. Your perception may not have been correct in the original instance and, therefore, rapport was not established because of the lack of accurate information.

There are two steps that must be taken in order to recalibrate to an individual. The first step is to ask questions and listen to the individual's responses. This allows you time to test the actual state he is experiencing and how he behaviorally expresses that state. Try to increase your own sensory awareness of his vocal, verbal, and nonverbal cues. The second step is to begin pacing again. At this point, very slowly begin the pacing process all over. The entire point of regaining rapport is to recalibrate and check your premise.

§ 2.43 Pacing in one-to-one and group interaction settings

There is a difference between pacing an individual and pacing a group. When pacing an individual, you are using discrete behaviors. You are analyzing very precise behaviors of one person in the verbal, vocal, and nonverbal communication channels. When pacing a group, you are looking at an overall tendency the group is manifesting. It requires a greater awareness and greater skill to pace a group. Professional speakers probably offer us the best example of the ability of people to pace groups. Using their awareness level and sensitivity, they follow the group's emotional state. A good speaker uses general group response as a guideline for where he goes and how he leads the group from one step to the next. Your most persuasive speakers are always extemporaneous speakers. Extemporaneous speaking allows for a built-in mechanism for the speaker to adapt the presentation to the group as he begins to lead the group. The following sections will discuss various applications of pacing individuals and pacing groups.[35]

§ 2.44 —Pacing an individual

To begin developing your pacing skills, the easiest place to start is by pacing an individual. This will allow you to focus on one person and slowly increase the channels of communication in which you pace him. You can begin by pacing the verbal channel, then increase to the vocal channel until you are pacing the individual on multiple levels which include the verbal, vocal, and nonverbal channels. After the pace has been established, you can test his behavior to see if he is ready to be lead into a new state by instituting new behavior and watching his behavioral response. If he responds favorably and tends to follow your direction, then the pacing step has probably been established sufficiently and you can move on to leading the individual.

§ 2.45 —Pacing jurors

Pacing jurors offers us the example of pacing a group. When a professional speaker paces a group, the group represents a collective consciousness. Each group tends to have a particular emotional tenor, a state, or a response that they experience collectively. If there is humor used, the majority of the group will respond and laugh to the humor. If it is a serious conversation, the majority of the group will respond to the seriousness of the situation. Group participants pace each other. As a result, they develop a collective way of responding. If one person laughs in the group, the entire group tends to respond in kind. That is why a group can be influenced as a single body.

To pace a group, the first step is to identify the collective consciousness of the group. One way to do this is to look for any signals or signs of the overall, emotional state in the environment. Is it a serious setting, a formal setting, what are the circumstances that have brought the people together, what is their purpose there, how do they perceive their role, what type of self-image do they have? These become very important questions; particularly, when we ask what self-image does the individual have? Their self-image will determine the type of response that they expect in the environment.

You pace a group much in the same way that you pace an individual. Simply put, you should adapt to the vocal, verbal, and nonverbal cues of

[35] *See infra* §§ 2.44–2.48.

the group as a whole. When you cannot determine in a group whether there are kinesthetically, auditorily, or visually dependent people, you will need to use multiple language in your system (i.e., kinesthetic, visual, and auditory predicates).

To individualize your communication to a group, try to identify specific traits that particular individuals have and as you speak, be sure that you talk to a particular individual and try to match his state. For example, if you can clearly identify a member in your group that is visual, then when you use visual predicates maintain eye contact with that person. At that moment, you will be using his language and you will create a particular type of bond.

By the time a professional speaker has finished talking, whether it is for thirty minutes or an hour, he will experience a tremendous loss of energy. This is due to the fact that he has been constantly tuned into present time, his focus has been on the audience, and he has been continually adapting to a changing audience response.

An effective trial attorney will experience this same state. After the trial is over, he usually experiences a state of exhaustion simply from the intensity and concentration that must occur in the courtroom. The more you concentrate on other people, their responses, their reactions, and their perceptions, the more you will feel drained. The good news is that the feeling of exhaustion is a behavioral key to the fact that you have psychologically prepared and adapted yourself for that group very effectively.

When pacing jurors, there are several things to remember. Pace the group as a whole. It is very difficult to try to pace individuals in a jury setting because a trial lawyer usually does not have enough information at his disposal. Use multiple channels for pacing the jury. Use a multiple predicate system. Make sure your stories are full of sensory descriptions so that you appeal to all different types of individuals in the group.

Another element to consider when pacing jurors is that if you do receive a negative feedback or response from an individual, use that to pace him even more. Remember that we have an instinctive flight response to anyone when we receive a negative response pattern. We try to avoid them, avoid eye contact, and move further away. When you receive a negative response simply use complimentary pacing. Move a little bit closer and give a little more eye contact, slow down the speech pattern, and become more empathetic in your vocal patterns. With this technique you can usually lead someone out of a negative response state. There is one important caveat to remember. It is important to avoid stereotyping single nonverbal cues of jurors. Single cues alone are not accurate indicators of the state a juror is experiencing. You must pace the behaviors that jurors have and lead them into new behaviors, without allowing yourself to be trapped in stereotypes.

§ 2.46 —Pacing clients

In order to be successful in the practice of law you not only have to create but to maintain clients. The extent to which you can develop rapport with clients has a lot to do with future business. Those attorneys that are good at building rapport tend to generate lots of business simply on a referral basis. That tells us a lot about their ability to work with people.

Pacing is a very useful tool when building a client relationship. In pacing clients, it is important to consider three things: (1) how the public selects an attorney, (2) the expectations the client has of the attorney, and (3) what attorney behavioral characteristics clients tend to like and dislike. The first factor to consider is how the public selects an attorney. According to recent research, more than 80% of those persons who had employed a lawyer did so on the basis of word of mouth. The attorneys were not selected at random or on the basis of nonpersonal sources of information.

In this age of high tech development, the need for high touch (people) skills has increased more than ever. Even with the advance of technology, people still buy people. When they are looking for an attorney, they are looking for someone that can understand their needs, empathize with them, and create a bond of trust and rapport. It is not that legal skill is unimportant, but given that a basic level of competence does exist, clients are still going to choose an attorney who they perceive will genuinely care about them.

The second factor to consider is the expectation the public has of the attorney. What does the public expect the attorney to behave like, look like, and act like? An individual may have many predispositions when he walks into an attorney's office. To the extent that the attorney meets these expectations, he is pacing the new client. Generally speaking, clients expect the attorney's office to be formal and the attorney to be wearing a jacket when they walk in. If they are greeted by a very informal office setting and the attorney is sitting in a short sleeved shirt, this would result in a nonpacing situation or a mismatch. Keep in mind that pacing has to do not only with behavioral traits, but also with environments and expectation levels.

The third factor to consider when discussing the pacing of clients is what specific things do clients generally like and dislike about attorneys. Ordinarily, clients dislike attorneys who project:

(1) a superior attitude;

(2) boredom or indifference;

(3) impatience or nonpersonal behaviors;

(4) rudeness, brusque, or hurried behaviors.

On the other hand, individuals report they do like attorneys who project:

(1) friendliness;

(2) professional appearance;

(3) efficiency;

(4) courtesy and personal behaviors;

(5) noncondescending behaviors.

In communication research, this is referred to as person and nonperson behaviors. If the attorney demonstrates that he is giving a client 100% of his attention, he will be using what we call person behaviors; behaviors that show that you care about the person and that he demands your full attention. Attorneys must remember that the client's decision is going to be based upon an instinctive feeling as to whether or not he believes rapport could be sufficiently established. Therefore, pacing a client should involve the use of person behaviors. Very few people want to be treated as an object or as something of little importance. Person behaviors involve stroking an individual and increasing his perception that he is being given 100% of you. These behaviors include the following:

Greeting others

Engaging in conversation

Using good eye contact

Using animated facial expressions

Displaying sincere interest in others

Keeping a normal to close distance

Removing any barrier between you and the other person (e.g., a desk)

Using expressive vocal cues

Immediate body orientation

Avoiding interruptions (e.g., phones and other people)

When an individual receives person treatment he feels as if he has been valued by the attorney—i.e., the attorney has really listened to what he had to say. This is a form of general pacing: pacing the individual in terms of his expectations and needs.

A form of mismatching an individual would be to give him nonperson behaviors. That would decrease his value based on your behaviors. Nonperson behaviors include the following:

Ignoring others

Avoiding eye contact

Avoiding conversation

Using a nonimmediate body orientation

Using neutral facial expression

Keeping a normal to far distance

Keeping objects and barriers between you and the client (e.g., a desk or books)

Using a monotone vocal cue

Displaying a lack of interest

Not listening

Acting hurried

Taking phone calls

Looking at papers

Interrupting the individual

Another consideration in pacing clients is the frequency with which the attorney talks and the frequency with which the client listens. In the beginning of an interaction with a client, the sole purpose should be that of obtaining information. Obtaining information is very difficult to do when the attorney is doing all the talking. During the first stages of interaction with a client, therefore, the attorney should talk no more than 30% of the time while listening 70% of the time. This is a rule that is often violated by attorneys. They attempt to tell the individual everything they can do without finding out the details of what the individual wants or needs.

Even when you know what the individual wants and even if you would like to tell him right away what he needs, you will not be pacing the individual. People want to be able to tell their story from their perspective. Only by telling the attorney the story, will the client have a reasonable sense of assurance that he is dealing with him personally. Even if the attorney accurately knows what the client is going to say, he should allow him to say it.

As this conversation progresses, the ratio between speaking and listening can change. At some point, the listening factor may go down to 30% while your speaking goes up to 70%. This will only occur in the interaction with the client when you have information to present. Talking with him about what he can expect, the types of things that might go wrong in the case, the fees involved, and so forth. This will be the information-giving period. At all points throughout the interaction with a client, it is important to continually pay attention to his changing state and mood. He will cue you when you need to listen more. The most common problem with attorneys in working with clients is that they do not listen enough; consequently, their focus is on themselves rather than on their clients.

Another consideration in pacing clients is to show empathy. Even though you may have dealt with many divorce cases that sound similar to the one your client is describing for you, it is probably the first and only time this person is going to go through this experience. Therefore, it requires that you treat his experience as unique and new. It is very easy to get into the habit of saying, "Oh, I've heard this before," or "This certainly isn't new," and responding in a mechanical fashion. A client will pick up these cues and will feel that you cannot truly empathize with him. This case is very important for the client. It is occurring at the very center of his world. For the attorney, it is probably only one case among many. However, at that moment, it must appear to the client that his case is the only case you are working on. In order to achieve this perception the attorney has to pace the client's verbal, vocal, and nonverbal cues and allow him time to fully express himself.

The value of building rapport with a client in the beginning of the interaction is that you will not have to do your homework later. If rapport is built in the beginning, you will find that when the client calls up with a question and your secretary attempts to respond to him that he will be much more willing to accept a secondary source. If rapport has not been fully established and you have not created a full sense of confidence in him by showing personal concern for his case, he will continually demand your attention by asking for you personally to get back to him.

The establishment of sufficient rapport in the beginning saves time in the end. Although it may mean more time with the client in the initial meeting, the attorney will save time from this point on. The first meeting is the most important and critical meeting that an attorney can have with his client. This discussion coincides with the rule of primacy as set forth in Principle 6: People attempt to maintain their original perceptions regardless of contradictory information. What you establish first will be believed by the client. Establishing the proper first impression can make it easier for you and your associates to deal with the client in the future.

§ 2.47 —Pacing a witness

There are three strategies to consider with regard to pacing a witness. The first strategy is to match the behavior of the witness in order to demonstrate that a relationship exists and increase the witness' comfort level. The second strategy is to match the behavior of a witness in order to lead him to the desired behavioral response. The third strategy is to mismatch the behavior of a witness in order to decrease his fluency and hence decrease the perception of credibility. Each of these strategies will create a different communication interaction with the witness and will certainly create a different perception of the witness by the jurors.

Matching the witness to demonstrate that a particular relationship exists will occur with your own witnesses. An attorney should be careful to pace his own witnesses. This causes them to be perceived as being very comfortable when they are in front of the jurors. By matching the behavior of your witness you will find that not only will the witness feel comfortable but you will also increase the comfort level of the jury. As a result of increasing their comfort, the jurors will be more receptive to what the witness has to say. This will increase their perception of credibility of the witness. There is no circumstance that we can think of in which you would want to mismatch your own witness' behavior. Matching your witness requires that you do some homework before the trial to get to really know your witness. Make sure you spend enough time before trial to establish rapport with the witness. Put him on videotape, spend time questioning him, spend time talking to him and, particularly, spend time listening to him and you will create a better relationship.

The second strategy in pacing a witness is to match the behavior of the witness in order to lead him to a new behavior. This is most often done with witnesses called by opposing counsel. You may start by questioning your opponent's witness in such a way that you match his behavior. This will create a rapport and easy fluency between yourself and the witness. As you match the behavior of the individual, he will begin to drop his defenses. As a result, he will start to feel that you are more similar to him. When you finally arrive at the point of asking critical questions, the opposing witness will already be in a state of wanting to please you or wanting to say yes. This is a form of communication entrapment; you can lead him to the types of answers you want him to give. It is a very easy process to lead him once rapport has been established.

The third strategy in pacing witnesses is to mismatch the behaviors of the witness. Mismatching behaviors should only be applied when questioning the opposition's witness whose credibility is subject to attack. Mismatching, as we have discussed previously, is the use of opposite behavioral cues to decrease fluency. By mismatching, the witnesses will engage in a form of weak speech by using many hedging words. The bottom line is that the opposing hostile witnesses will lose credibility in terms of perception by the jurors. When witnesses are mismatched, they may also become quickly confused on the witness stand.

§ 2.48 —Pacing the judge

Pacing the judge requires consideration of three very important factors. The first factor is what is the self-image of the judge? How does he perceive himself with regard to the trial? The second factor involves the consideration that the judge is very instrumental in influencing jurors. The third factor is to remember that the official court family is the extension of the judge, therefore, court personnel should be treated in a similar manner as the judge himself.

The self-image of the judge is one area that the attorney must understand. It is essential information in pacing the judge. Most judges have a self-image of being important. They insist on being treated with respect. This is built into our system of law. We put the judge at a higher elevation level, we look up to the judge, all information is controlled by the judge, and the judge is the person who renders the final decision. Therefore, it is understandable why the self-image of the judge would be that of being important and being treated with respect. In order to pace that self-image it is important to use the behavioral characteristics that show the judge that you agree with this self-image. This will mean making sure that your vocal tones show deference and respect, your clothing is appropriate, and your behavior is well-mannered. Avoid being antagonistic toward the judge at all costs. There is very little to gain by antagonizing the judge; it certainly does not win points in the eyes of the jurors.

Jurors look to the judge as the marker of the trial. They look to the judge to give them indications of whether or not their behavior is appropriate. Are they doing the right things? Are they considering the right information? Is the information even important? Particularly, those jurors who lean towards authoritarianism will follow the judge's lead.

The way the attorney paces the judge will visibly show the jurors his relationship to the judge. The jurors will have a natural respect for the judge. It is important, therefore, that the attorney continually pace the judge by demonstrating respect and consideration. This simply means that with the judge, as with anyone else, the attorney paces the judge's verbal, vocal, and nonverbal cues. When you approach the bench, pace the judge by using behaviors similar to his. Allow the judge to assume a dominant position while you assume a more subordinate position. This does not show a lack of power. It simply shows a supportive position allowing the judge to reside in the power position. This increases the attorney's position of strength and persuasion.

The third consideration is that the official court family is an extension of the judge. For that reason, court personnel should be treated with exactly the same behaviors. The jurors look at the official court family as part of the team. They consider them as being influential in their decision-making process. They are in contact with the official court family, who in turn are in contact with the judge. All behaviors the attorney uses for the judge would also be appropriate pacing behaviors for the court family. It is very important not to treat anyone in that family with lack of respect. Do not treat them as subordinates. Treat them at least at the level of peers and, hopefully, at the level of being in the management side of the court system which means that you will put them in the superior position.

Pacing the judge and the official court family means that the attorney is going to use primarily complimentary pacing techniques to allow them to feel as though they are in the power position and the position of control. This enhances the attorney's ability to persuade from two perspectives. First, it will increase their perception of the attorney's credibility. Secondly, it will increase the perception that the attorney has a favorable relationship with the judge. This will also help the attorney with jurors since they will be more favorably disposed towards someone who has won the judge's approval.

If the attorney does not have a favorable relationship with the judge, dissonance will result in the minds of the jurors. In other words, they like and respect the judge, they want to like and respect the attorney but if the attorney does not like and respect the judge, it forces them to make a choice. Do not force jurors to make these types of choices. Pace the judge. Show the jurors that there is a favorable relationship that exists, and that you have respect for the court as they do. When jurors are forced to make a choice between judge and counsel, counsel usually loses.

Sometimes counsel is faced with a highly volatile judge who is prejudiced against either the attorney personally, the client, or the nature of the case. In that situation, the attorney should use complimentary pacing. He should match the judge's intensity and mood, but in the opposite direction. If the judge talks fast, with an angry tone, and expresses negative comments about counsel, his client, or his cause, the attorney should talk slowly and in humble terms. Soon the jurors will perceive that the attorney is doing all he can to be nice to the judge and to talk to the judge. The more humble and fair the attorney appears, the more hostile and unfair the judge appears. Eventually the jurors may perceive that the judge is taking unfair advantage of the attorney, his client, or cause. As the complimentary pacing is applied, the jurors perception of the judge's hostility is increased by the comparison.[36] At some future point, the attorney's humble attitude and apparent helplessness (as opposed to the hostile judge) will cause a sympathetic response from some jurors. If the jurors were now forced to choose between the attorney and the judge under these circumstances, the attorney would at least stand a chance of winning.

§ 2.49 Pacing and leading to create a mood transference

Transferring a mood in the courtroom is the process of leading jurors to experience a particular emotional state. This state might be a state of anger, empathy, or pity. Or, the attorney may want the jurors to view

[36] *See supra* § 2.37 setting forth the difference between direct versus complimentary pacing.

everything in a very logical, detached type of perspective. In almost every instance, the attorney is probably trying to counter the emotional state that opposing counsel is attempting to create.

It is very important that you understand how to create a mood or emotional state that jurors experience in the courtroom. Your opening statement and closing argument, as well as everything that has transpired in the courtroom, has to support the way you are trying to lead the jurors. Keep in mind that these are not individual strategies to be used by themselves, but to be used collectively. The following sections discuss how to transfer feelings, factual information, and visual information.[37]

§ 2.50 —Transferring a feeling

Before we can understand how to transfer a feeling, it is important to understand what behavioral cues tend to go along with a person experiencing a particular feeling. When you want jurors to experience the state of extreme empathy, the trauma of a tragedy that has taken place, the deep emotional feeling and concern for a family that lost a loved one, then you must not only display certain behavioral cues, but you must lead the jurors to use these cues themselves. If you have already established rapport with the jurors, when you use these behaviors they will begin to pace you. Of course, this is the true test of your being able to lead the jurors. If you want jurors to experience a particular state as you are presenting your opening or closing statement, for example, you need to use those behaviors (vocal, verbal, and nonverbal cues) that correspond with the particular drama that you are trying to create. Too often trial attorneys will deliver a very emotional argument in terms of the verbal content and not use the correct vocal and nonverbal behaviors. If the verbal content is in itself emotional, but the vocal and nonverbal behaviors are not, the attorney will not be able to transfer an emotional state to the jurors. Given a contradiction between vocal and nonverbal behaviors and verbal content, jurors will believe the behaviors. Therefore, your behaviors will nullify the effect of the emotional story or picture that you are trying to paint.

For example, to convey a feeling of empathy for a tragic emotional experience of your client you will want to utilize the following behaviors:

A slower voice tone

A lower voice tone

[37] *See infra* §§ 2.50–2.52.

Extremes in vocal patterns from soft to loud

Dropping the eyes to lower right

Using left-handed gestures and hand movements that pull the eyes of the jurors down to their lower right

Using a slower movement pattern

Using a slower breathing pattern

Using dramatic pauses

Beginning with the first item on the list, it must be recognized that a slower voice tone correlates with a depressed emotional state. When a person is experiencing a feeling, his voice pattern tends to become slower and his vocal tone tends to drop lower. This is the way we express concern.[38]

By using extreme vocal tones of going from soft to loud, you will be able to create the drama that is associated with feeling. This means being able to develop the voice so that it will go through all ranges and all types of pitch patterns. An individual can best process kinesthetic information when the eyes are dropped down to the lower right. It increases the jurors ability to experience what you are describing. You must remember that if you are not genuinely feeling the effect that you want to create, it will be impossible for jurors to feel that same state. You need to bring about the particular behavioral state by feeling the emotion you wish to transfer. Drop your eyes down to the lower right, collapse the upper chest cavity as though you have sighed, and let out your air. These are the appropriate nonverbal cues to use to create a feeling of tragedy.

The next step is to make sure the jurors start to process the information on a kinesthetic or feeling level. To do this, use left-handed gestures. Keep the gestures low enough so as to pull the jurors' eye contact down into their lower right hand corner. When done properly, they are in the mood to process kinesthetic information. Therefore, you want to deliver your most important and dramatic lines when their eyes are in this position. Save this type of motion and gesture for the key points.

Slower movement patterns are also indicative of conveying an emotional state to jurors. To convey the tragedy, therefore, you do not want to be fast or flip. Rather, you want to be slow and draw it out when describing it.

A very critical consideration with the kinesthetic transference of mood

---

[38] *See supra* §§ 2.21, 2.27.

is the use of a slower breathing pattern. When a person is feeling emotional, he usually breathes from his abdominal cavity, there are more pause patterns, and he tends to sigh. In order to convey and transfer this feeling, you will need to use the same behaviors.

The other feeling that counsel may want transferred in certain very limited situations is when counsel is trying to instill anger on the part of the jurors. In other words, arousing their feelings so that they are angry at an injustice that has taken place. Anger has several other behavioral characteristics that go with it. In order to transfer or display the characteristics of anger, the following behavioral patterns must occur:

A fast vocal tone

Usually a higher vocal tone

Louder vocal tone

Eyes moving straight across

Direct eye contact

Gestures that are midwaist to upper level

Gestures that are firm and definite

Quicker movement patterns

Decisive movement patterns

Dramatic pauses

The sense of conveying anger has an altogether quicker movement pattern. When a person is angry, he tends to breath in his upper chest area, so his breathing pattern is very different. He moves at a different rate. In order to motivate people to become angry, both the attorney's speech patterns and movement patterns must be quicker. To convey anger, you have to come forward and be aggressive in your behaviors. Do not be afraid to point, as long as you are pointing at opposing counsel or his client. Never use the pointed finger at your own people.

The best way to practice the transference of a kinesthetic feeling is to first take the feeling that you are trying to convey and put yourself in the same body position and state of mind. Before going into the courtroom, you should experience whatever state you are trying to convey on a personal level. For example, to convey the feeling of anger, practice being angry. Practice feeling the emotional state yourself and try to perceive behaviors that you have in that state. Observe yourself. When you are unhappy, notice what you do. When you are happy or carefree, notice your behaviors. Also become a watcher of people and study basic human nature. You will notice the behaviors that people use in displaying anger or passion or empathy are very similar. All you have to do is understand those behaviors, use them, feel the state, and then transfer the mood to the jurors.

§ 2.51 —Transferring factual information

There are times when you want to convey to jurors that the information being presented is just factual. The last thing the attorney wants to do is lead jurors into an emotional state. In order to do this, you need to follow several behavioral cues. These cues include the following:

Keeping the eyes level

Keeping the breathing pattern even

Using a moderate rate of speaking

Avoiding extremes in vocal tones

Keeping all behaviors in moderation

If you want jurors to treat information as a matter of fact, you must treat it as a matter of fact. The behaviors you use for transferring factual information to jurors are very nondescriptive and moderate. The eyes stay at an even level, neither moving up or down, just appropriate eye contact. Breathing tends to be even so jurors will not see an extreme in the breathing patterns. The one risk that is run in transferring factual information is that it can become boring. Thus, when you do transfer information that is factual, you will want to break it up by emphasizing key points or making something more exciting simply to maintain the attention of the jurors.

§ 2.52 —Transferring visual information

In many types of cases, there is a need to describe a picture, scene, or event for the jurors. This definitely involves the transfer of visual information. Some jurors will pick up these visual pictures very quickly because they will be visually oriented. Other jurors who are kinesthetically or auditory-oriented will need the attorney's help in obtaining the transfer of information. Behavioral cues used to transfer visual information include the following:

Using quick vocal tones

Breathing in the upper chest

Keeping the eyes moving up to upper right or left

Using gestures that are above the waist and expansive

Pointing up to a chart

Maintaining a fast pace

Using these behavioral cues is most appropriate when the attorney is telling a story. If the attorney asks the jurors to picture or focus on some object, he should pick up his rate of speech, pull his hands up and get the jurors' eyes moving to the upper right and left.

COMMENT: Remember, what you are trying to do with the eye movement pattern behaviors of the jurors is to keep their eyes in the quadrant corresponding to the state you want them to experience. When you want them to have an emotional feeling, you want their eyes going down to the lower right. When you want them to have an auditory or more factual type of feeling, you want the eyes level. To visualize or picture a particular event, you want the eyes moving to the upper left or right. To do this, you need to point up.

One way of getting jurors to visualize information is through the use of charts or graphic displays. With the proper use of a chart, the attorney can induce the proper eye movements. If you want the jurors to be assisted in visualizing or seeing what you are saying, make sure that you are using hand motions to pull their eyes up. Point to the uppermost part of the chart, or to the top of the screen. This will pull their eye contact up. Try to keep the chart high enough so that when you point to it you are pointing in an upward direction. If you want the jurors to visualize an event, you should never pass out material to them. When they are looking at such material, their eyes are looking down.

III. General Overview of Persuasion and Influence

§ 2.53 Introduction to Communication Principles which apply to persuasion

There are many principles which could be introduced in the area of persuasion. For the purpose of our inquiry into the role of persuasion in the courtroom we have identified six salient principles. These include:

Principle 7: People feel obligated to repay others regardless of whether they like the gift or the giver.

Principle 8: People have a need to be consistent.

Principle 9: People are more easily influenced by others they perceive as similar to themselves.

Principle 10: People are more easily influenced by people they like.

Principle 11: The perception of credibility increases with the perception of authority.

Principle 12: People are more easily influenced when they believe the source to be scarce and valuable.

Each principle represents a specific body of research. The essence of each principle is its inherent logic. Properly applied, each principle provides the attorney with new skills, and an important new frame of reference for viewing persuasion in the courtroom. This chapter is an attempt to reframe the attorney's point of view with regard to how he can influence others.

§ 2.54 What is an attitude?

Attitudes are defined as "a learned predisposition to respond in a consistently favorable or unfavorable manner with respect to a given object."[39] Attitudes are formed as a result of beliefs which are acquired over time. Beliefs are defined as "the information that a person has about

[39] M. Fishbein & I. Ajzen, Belief, Attitude, Intention and Behavior 5 (Addison-Wesley, 1975). The analysis in this section follows the general theoretical approach of Fishbein and Ajzen.

other people, objects, and issues."[40] The information upon which beliefs are based may be fact or opinion, or may come from direct observation or from outside sources. The basis of the information upon which we form beliefs is unimportant to the ultimate understanding of persuasion. The information source for establishing beliefs may be valid or invalid, accurate or inaccurate. What is important is that beliefs are formed from selected perceptions. In Chapter 1, we learned that communication is based on perception. With this understanding it is essential to realize that an individual has a belief, which for him, is absolutely valid. All perceptions are, therefore, both uniquely individual and valid for the person.

Beliefs, in turn, determine a person's attitude toward an object. For example, an individual may have favorable beliefs about church. The individual will then tend to have a favorable attitude about church. Based on these favorable attitudes, the individual may intend to go to church on Sunday mornings. If he follows through on his intention, the resulting behavior will be to actually get in the car and go to church. This offers us a brief description of the relationship among beliefs, attitudes, intentions, and behaviors. These four elements surface in all persuasive paradigms.

Understanding the formation and characteristics of attitudes is at the core of persuasion. Why and how people process information is directly related to their beliefs in attitudes. Any attempt at modifying an individual's behavior must first recognize the attitudes held by the person. Behavioral modification seems to occur most often following a shift in basic attitudes and beliefs. At this point we need to clearly define our beliefs about "changing attitudes." Attitudes can be expanded, altered, and modified—but they are rarely totally discarded. In the short period of time available to the trial attorney in the courtroom, it may be unrealistic to assume that he can change a person's attitude. At best, he can influence a juror's thinking patterns so that the individual will be permissive enough to allow for (1) an exception to his basic belief, or (2) a shift in his frame of reference. In both cases the persuader will need to acknowledge the existing attitude and build on it.

The characteristics of attitudes provide a broader understanding of their role in persuasion. Some characteristics of attitudes are:

—formed as a result of the learning process;

---

[40] R. Petty & J. Cacioppo, Attitudes and Persuasion: Classic and Contemporary Approaches 7 (William C. Brown Co., 1981).

—organized and relatively stable;

—powerful;

—predispositions or reaction tendencies;

—dominant or latent;

—at times not readily apparent.

Attitudes also vary in intensity and have two main components: (1) a *cognitive* and (b) an *affective* dimension. The cognitive aspect refers to a set of beliefs or more rational appraisal of the attitude object, while the affective component refers to an emotional or feeling response toward the person or object.[41]

Understanding the function of attitudes in the persuasion process is important for the attorney. Communication scholars Taylor, Buchanan, and Strawn stressed that if an attorney has demographic information about his jurors, he can draw some generally valid conclusions about the juror's attitudes and behaviors. Their conclusions are as follows:

1. *Attitudes predict behavior*. If I am an economic conservative, I am not likely to give money away in the form of a large, punitive verdict.
2. *Human attitudes can be measured by scales*. You have probably participated in some of these by picking a number between one and ten to represent your attitude about a subject, with one being the least favorable and ten the most favorable.
3. *Once people's attitudes about a subject are quantified, the numerical expressions can be compared statistically to other such expressions*. You have seen the commercial that states, "Four out of every five doctors recommend. . . ."
4. *People's attitudes can be correlated with observable behavior and other demographic features*. For instance, Republican or Democratic party registration can be correlated with both the likelihood of getting a plaintiff's verdict and the size of the verdict in a civil case.
5. *Groups of demographic features will emerge as not only positively correlated with an attitude, but as positively correlated with each other*. Note the relationship between a juror's sex, race, and the final verdict. These correlations give additional strength to the prediction that persons having a given group of demographic features are likely to have a

[41] W. Brembeck & W. Howell, Persuasion 129–130 (Prentice-Hall, 1952).

certain attitude about a fact or argument.[42]

Since attitudes are a learned predisposition it is reasonable to conclude that attitudes reveal important information about how an individual thinks and behaves. Altering existing attitudes is a skill which is essential for the advocate. Using attitudes as predictive information about jurors offers a valuable source of information.

§ 2.55 What is persuasion?

When we talk about persuasion we are referring to the complex process by which we attempt to influence others. Our attempts to influence others fall into one of three categories: (1) an attempt to influence an individual to believe as we believe by incorporating our beliefs into his preexisting attitudes; (2) an attempt to influence a person to believe even more strongly in his own preexisting attitudes; and (3) a direct attempt to change or modify a person's behavior by changing his preexisting attitudes. The modification of behavior is usually the desired outcome in the trial process. For example, the prosecutor not only wants jurors to agree that the defendant is guilty of the alleged act, he wants jurors to act on this conviction by rendering a verdict of guilty.

Authors in legal journals have defined persuasion in the courtroom in a fairly consistent way. For example, both Costopoulos[43] and Grandoff[44] set forth the following definition of persuasion:

> Persuasion is defined as "an act of influencing the minds of others by arguments or reasons, by appeals to both feeling and intellect; it is the art of leading another man's will to a particular choice, or course of conduct."

Persuasion, in its purest form, is an act which produces specific behavioral outcomes. There are three types of persuasion which take place during the course of a trial: (1) attitudes formation, (2) attitude reinforcement, and (3) attitude and/or response changing.[45]

Persuasion as attitude formation is the first type of influence that may occur in the courtroom. Theoretically, jurors will be participating in the

---

[42] K. TAYLOR, R. BUCHANAN & D. STRAWN, COMMUNICATION STRATEGIES FOR TRIAL ATTORNEYS 62–63 (Scott, Foresman and Co., 1984). Copyright © 1984 by Scott, Foresman and Company. Reprinted by permission.

[43] Costopoulos, *Persuasion in the Courtroom*, 10 DUQ. L. REV. 384 (1972).

[44] Grandoff, *The Lawyer as Persuader*, 52 FLA. B.J. 763 (1978).

[45] TAYLOR, BUCHANAN & STRAWN, *supra* note 42, at 4.

trial proceedings having formed no attitudes about the case prior to the trial. It is counsel's job to influence the juror's formation of attitudes by providing information about the nature of the case. Once the jurors have this information, they will begin to process it to form opinions and attitudes about the trial proceedings. This constitutes the first stage of persuasion. Through the process of gathering information the jurors will form attitudes upon which they will eventually base their verdict.[46]

It is unrealistic, however, to expect that jurors come to the trial devoid of attitudes, preconceived opinions, and even stereotypes. Therefore, the second type of courtroom persuasion involves attitude reinforcement. "Certain constitutional and legal concepts—the right to a fair trial, presumption of innocence, reasonable doubt, preponderance of evidence, maintenance of an open mind, right of a defendant not to testify—are inherent in the trial process."[47] The trial attorney will want to reinforce these particular attitudes in the minds of the jurors so that his client will be given fair consideration by the jurors.[48] In addition, counsel will want to reinforce any attitudes which are favorable to his client. One method of reinforcing attitudes is referred to as anchoring. This will be explored more fully in Chapter 4.

The third type of persuasion involves attitude and/or response changing. This type of courtroom persuasion is one that typically occurs in every trial. The attorneys representing the various sides make open efforts to influence the jury's attitudes or, if necessary, to change the jury's (or particular juror's) mind. As communication scholars Taylor, Buchanan, and Strawn so aptly state: "The strategy in the case is aimed at changing the beliefs and attitudes of the jury in the defendant's [or plaintiff's] favor. This is the classic meaning of persuasion—to induce change from one set of attitudes and behaviors to another."[49]

§ 2.56 Persuasion as influence

We are constantly influencing people in everyday transactions. As a population we are strongly influenced by both print and visual media

---

[46] *Id.*

[47] *Id.*

[48] The term "fair" is used as a general description. It is the premise of the authors that it is difficult, if not impossible, for jurors to put aside preexisting stereotypes and biases. It is, therefore, the task of counsel to identify the preexisting attitudes in order to build them directly into the persuasive strategy.

[49] TAYLOR, BUCHANAN & STRAWN, *supra* note 42, at 4.

from billboards to television. There is such an overabundance of information available that people have unconsciously developed shortcut decision-making strategies.

These shortcut strategies reflect a great need for people to quickly reduce uncertainty and to build a consistent perception of both people and objects which surround them. The six basic strategies by which people are influenced are: (1) reciprocity, (2) commitment and consistency, (3) social proof, (4) liking, (5) authority, and (6) scarcity. Each strategy can stand by itself or be used in conjunction with the others. The most important factor to remember is that these strategies were not developed by individuals, they have evolved in our society. That is, these strategies are a result of the need to reduce the overload of information received daily.

The courtroom is no exception in the influence process. The abundance of information and nonverbal stimuli which occurs in the courtroom creates the need to use shortcuts. From the advocates point of view it is important to understand the process of influence from two perspectives: (1) to utilize the influence strategies as a form of persuasion, and (2) to avoid being trapped by the influence attempts of others.

§ 2.57 —Reciprocity

The process of reciprocation is explained by sociologist Alvin Gouldner as giving benefits to those who give benefits to you; a favor for a favor; obligation and repayment.[50] There is little question that the concept of reciprocation is deeply ingrained in our society, as it is in all societies.[51] As psychologist Robert Cialdini notes in his book, *Influence: How and Why People Agree to Things*, reciprocation is an overpowering rule in interactions. "The rule," Cialdini observes, "possesses awesome strength, often producing a 'yes' response to a request that, except for an existing feeling of indebtedness, would surely have been rejected."[52] Reciprocation is such a pervasive phenomenon that it can be stated as Communication Principle 7: People feel obligated to repay others regardless of whether they like the gift or the giver.

How does reciprocation function in persuasion? If the persuader can

---

[50] Gouldner, *The Norm of Reciprocity: A Preliminary Statement*, 25 AM. SOC. REV. 161–178 (1960).

[51] *Id*.

[52] R. CIALDINI, INFLUENCE: HOW AND WHY PEOPLE AGREE TO THINGS 32 (William Morrow and Co., 1984).

induce a sense of indebtedness and obligation in his listener, he will increase the possibility that the listener will repay him or return the favor in a manner desired by the persuader. Reciprocation is powerful; when someone does us a favor, we feel obligated to repay the favor. We are continually obliging and repaying others. For example, if your car breaks down and your neighbor gives you a ride to work which is ten miles out of his way, suddenly you are obligated. Unless you pay for the gas or offer a favor in return, you will feel indebted—as if you owe him. In fact, a common expression used when someone does a favor for us is, "I owe you one." And indeed we do. We do not like to be in a position where we are obligated. We want to repay the favor as quickly as possible in order to reduce our sense of indebtedness.

Reciprocation operates whether we like the giver or not. We "owe" him and a disliking of the individual must be overwhelmingly powerful before we are willing to risk the label of "welcher" by deciding not to repay the favor. "The power of the reciprocity rule," Cialdini explains, "is such that by first doing us a favor, strange, disliked, or unwelcome others can enhance the chance that we will comply with one of their requests."[53]

We attempt to control the areas where a sense of indebtedness for a favor may create harmful conflicts of interest. Thus, political campaign donations are restricted in dollar amount—we do not want our politicians to "owe" too much to their big contributors.[54]

In the area of bargaining and negotiation, concessions are a primary consideration: when to offer a concession, how large of a concession to offer, and so on. The rule of reciprocity is clearly operational in these settings. Underlying the willingness to make a concession is the negotiator's knowledge that the other party will, in turn, offer his own concession. Chertkoff and Conley discovered that the more often one party gives ground, the more frequently the second party also makes concessions.[55]

Concessions, of course, must be made carefully in order to be effective. Effective concessions should meet the following four requirements:

1. The original request must be rejected by the person;

---

[53] *Id*. at 41.

[54] *Id*. at 37–38.

[55] Chertkoff & Conley, *Opening Offer and Frequency of Concession as Bargaining Strategies*, 7 J. PERSONALITY & SOC. PSYCHOLOGY 185–193 (1967).

2. The original request should be large enough so that its rejection will be perceived by the target person as irrelevant for making self-attribution;
3. The original request should not evoke in the target person resentment, anger, or hostility;
4. The second request must be unambiguously smaller than the first one.[56]

We should not, however, overlook the positive value of reciprocation in our society. Without the knowledge that when we give something away the receiver will feel obligated and indebted to pay us back, the exchange of goods, services, and information in our society would be severely limited. In fact, society has established sanctions to insure that repayment is made. Those members who renege and "take advantage" of others by failing to repay the debt are viewed negatively by society and may even be ostracized by their peers.

We are not proposing that the rule of reciprocity be engaged in in the courtroom. Its application would understandably be prohibited since attempting to do "favors" for jurors would constitute an unethical influence attempt. The positive value of utilizing reciprocity rests in negotiations and with clients. Negotiations with other attorneys, for instance, embody the basic procedure of give and take. Moreover, in establishing a strong client relationship, the sense of obligation is often used. For instance, if a client asked you a legal question which required a considerable amount of research on your part for which no monetary compensation was requested, a feeling of indebtedness could be created. Here we use the word "could" because the feeling of indebtedness will be directly related to how the information is presented. If the client is not informed by you as to the amount of work which was required they may not feel obligated. To utilize the rule of reciprocity it is important to explicitly inform the client of two things: (1) there was a considerable amount of work and (2) the client is not being charged for the work. Once this sense of obligation has been created, you can exchange it for another favor. You may have a busy schedule one day and need to reschedule the client to another day. This is a different type of favor, but nevertheless, it is an acceptable request. Most likely, the client will respond agreeably in deference to the favor that you have already performed.

---

[56] Even-Chen, Yinon & Bizman, *The Door in the Face Technique: Effects of the Size of the Initial Request*, 8 EUR. J. SOC. PSYCHOLOGY 135–140 (1978).

Reciprocity, the principle of give-and-take, is used on a daily basis by children and adults alike. "I owe you" and "you owe me" make up the fundamental operation of the theory of exchange in our society. Avoiding being trapped by the principle of reciprocity is equally as important as utilizing the concept. Whenever you accept a favor or a gift from another person, you place yourself in a position of being obligated. It may appear to be a small favor or an inconsequential gift, but the results are the same. If you accept it, you set the stage for obligation in which you must repay the giver in kind or risk the negative perception of being "ungrateful."

§ 2.58 —Commitment and consistency

The need to be consistent with things we have already done or said is, as social psychologist Robert Cialdini states, a "nearly obsessive desire of every human being."[57] This relates to Communication Principle 8: People have a need to be consistent.

The desire to be consistent in itself is strong and even stronger if an individual makes a public commitment (whether verbal or written). Not only does he know what he has said, but he has a host of witnesses who will serve to remind him. Thus, when questioning jurors during voir dire, it is important to elicit public commitments from them that will be heard by yourself and others. Then, during closing argument it is very effective to refer to those earlier commitments to reinforce the jurors' need for consistency.[58]

One application of the principle of consistency can be seen in the persuasive technique commonly referred to as "foot-in-the-door." As communication scholars Burgoon and Bettinghaus explain:

> The major assumption underlying the foot-in-the-door technique is that a powerful predictor of future compliance is past compliance; that is, a person who has been induced to comply with a small request is more likely to comply with subsequent, larger demands.[59]

Like the door-to-door salesman, if you can get your foot in the door, you stand a much better chance of selling your goods. If you can get the

---

[57] CIALDINI, *supra* note 52, at 66.

[58] *See infra* § 10.17, for an explanation of how to use commitment and consistency in summation.

[59] Burgoon & Bettinghaus, *Persuasion Message Strategies* in PERSUASION: NEW DIRECTIONS IN THEORY AND RESEARCH 155 (Sage Publications, M. Roloff & G. Miller eds. 1980).

individual to make a small commitment, the chances are much greater that he will comply with a larger request in the future.

In two often-cited studies from the *Journal of Personality and Social Psychology*, researchers Freedman and Fraser examined the foot-in-the-door technique.[60] In one experiment they discovered that people who complied with an initial small request from an individual were much more likely to comply with a later, larger request made by the same individual. The second experimental condition is even more interesting, because it revealed that people tend to comply with a second request even if the person making the request is not the same person who made the first and smaller request. Other communication researchers have replicated the results found in the Freedman and Fraser study.[61]

The need for consistency has been discussed in several of our communication principles. Consistency and reduction of uncertainty are the two primary motivators for Principles 2, 4, and 6 presented in Chapter 1. In reviewing these principles it becomes clear that the use of stereotypes in impression formation, as an example, provides a consistent way in which to view the world. Inconsistency creates high uncertainty. Most people want their private and public world to be both predictable and consistent. In reviewing Principles 2, 4, and 6, consider the influence of the need to be consistent as an underlying motivator to perform certain behaviors:

Principle 2: People actively try to make sense out of their environment. ("A place for everything and everything in its place." An environment that makes sense is one which is consistent.)

Principle 4: People use stereotypes to organize their perceptions. (Stereotypes invoke consistency by using a general category in which to catalog an entire class of people, objects, or behaviors.)

Principle 6: People attempt to maintain their original perceptions regardless of contradictory information. (This is an attempt to maintain

---

[60] Freedman & Fraser, *Compliance Without Pressure. The Foot-in-the-Door Technique*, 4 J. Personality & Soc. Psychology 195–202 (1966).

[61] *See, e.g.,* Pliner, Hart, Kohl & Saari, *Compliance Without Pressure: Some Further Data on the Foot-in-the-Door Technique*, 10 J. EXPERIM. SOC. PSYCHOLOGY 17–22 (1974).

consistency in one's beliefs, thereby, resolving any form of cognitive dissonance.)

Obtaining a public commitment, verbal or written, is the first major step in getting an individual to maintain consistency in his future actions. Trial attorneys use this principle by obtaining a minor commitment or acceptance of a point by jurors during voir dire. Once the groundwork for this acceptance has been laid, counsel will then ask for a larger commitment which is predicated on the earlier, smaller commitment. The attorney might say, "If you accept *X*, then it follows that you must accept *Y*." To remain consistent jurors can be influenced to accept *Y*. Excluding voir dire, counsel cannot ask jurors to make a public commitment. However, jurors can and should be asked to commit to various actions or beliefs in their mind. By building on the need to be consistent, arguments can be presented in a "smaller then larger" order of request.

§ 2.59 —Social proof

Social proof (or social validation) is the process by which a person determines the appropriateness of his behavior by observing how other people, whom he believes to be similar to himself, behave in the same situation. We, in effect, look for evidence and cues in our environment upon which to base our actions. In this way we answer questions as varied as what to wear to the Heart Association fund raiser or how to react in an emergency situation. We look for social evidence to guide us. This leads us to Communication Principle 9: People are more easily influenced by others they perceive as similar to themselves.

The more people we find engaging in a particular activity or possessing a particular belief, the more likely we are to be influenced by social proof. Similarly, uncertainty prompts us to seek social validation for our actions. "In general, when we are unsure of ourselves, when the situation is unclear or ambiguous, or when uncertainty reigns, we are most likely to look to and accept the actions of others as correct."[62] Most jurors experience uncertainty in the courtroom because the setting is new to them and they are unsure of what behaviors are appropriate and expected. Whenever possible, counsel should point out how others similar to them have behaved in order to invoke the influence of the social proof principle. Used appropriately, social proof can influence the type of decisions jurors render.

---

[62] CIALDINI, *supra* note 52, at 129.

We determine behavioral appropriateness by watching those people who are most like us perform. We then use the actions of others to decide on proper behavior for ourselves, *especially when we view those others as similar to ourselves*.[63] The communication principle involving social proof is a powerful one. Whether the choice is one of what clothes to wear or what behavior is appropriate in the courtroom, the fact that other similar people are performing that behavior will increase the likelihood that we will comply in a like manner. In rendering a verdict, jurors are often influenced by social proof within the context of the jury itself. Jurors are more easily influenced by other jurors whom they perceive both to be similar to themselves and to have authority and credibility.[64]

§ 2.60 —Liking

Whether or not we like someone will influence the degree to which we allow him to influence us. Liking is defined by psychologists Berscheid and Walster as "the affection we feel for casual acquaintances."[65] We like some acquaintances more than others; some acquaintances we do not like at all. Generally, the more we know about the person as an individual, the more we are inclined to like them.

Derived from the preceding analysis is Communication Principle 10: People are more easily influenced by people they like. The degree to which you can identify with the juror and allow him to know you increases the probability that the juror will like you. Self-disclosing information about yourself through words or actions will allow jurors to feel a greater identity with you. Something as simple as wearing a wedding ring or laughing at a humorous event discloses information about an individual. When we like an individual we try to reward him in every way possible.

In the courtroom, liking is an important quality to consider for both attorneys and witnesses. In a survey of 600 actual jurors conducted for *Trial Diplomacy Journal*, researchers Sannito and Arnolds found that likability was a key factor in persuasion. They reported that the best

---

[63] *Id*. at 142.

[64] *See infra* Chapter 3 for a further discussion of the influence of authority and credibility in the courtroom.

[65] E. Berscheid & E. Walster, Interpersonal Attraction 176 (Addison-Wesley, 2d ed. 1978).

single predictors of initial and final verdict were the skill and likability of the attorneys.[66]

Likability of the victim is also an important consideration in a trial. Sannito and Arnolds conclude:

> How the victim came across influenced the jury's decision about the defendant. When the jury liked the complaining witness, the defendant's chances of going free were substantially reduced; conversely, when the jurors strongly disliked the victim, they tended to acquit the defendant.[67]

There are four factors which tend to increase the likability of an individual: (1) perceived similarity, (2) physical attractiveness, (3) cooperative endeavors, and (4) proximity. The process of increasing likability involves greater personalization of an individual. Perceived similarity increases the personalization of an individual because predictability is higher. When we feel that an individual is similar to ourselves, our assumption is that we know how he will behave. Physical attractiveness is a means of personalization because we attribute many positive personality traits to those people we find physically attractive. Working with another person on a cooperative endeavor also affords us the opportunity to get to know him better. Finally, our proximity to another person increases the likelihood that we will get to know him better. The following paragraphs will explore each of these four factors in relation to liking.

The first factor that influences liking is perceived similarity. Communication researchers Griffin and Jackson examined similarity of attitudes and found that when jurors perceive a similarity of attitude between themselves and the defendant, their perception of defendant attractiveness increases. The more dissimilar the attitudes of the defendant and the juror, the more likely the defendant was to be found guilty and the longer his prison sentence.[68]

Physical attractiveness is a second factor associated with liking. We tend to favor persons who are attractive. This factor is discussed extensively *supra* Chapter 1. Physical attractiveness exerts a definite influence on juror's perceptions. Using a female defendant, researchers Sigall and Ostrove hypothesized that "an attractive defendant would receive more

---

[66] Sannito & Arnolds, *Jury Study Results: The Factors at Work*, 5 Trial Dipl. J. 8 (1982).

[67] *Id*. at 9.

[68] Griffin & Jackson, *Simulated Jury Decisions: The Influence of Jury-Defendant Attitude Similarity/Dissimilarity*, 1 Soc. Behav. & Personality 1–7 (1973). *See also supra* § 1.55.

lenient treatment than an unattractive defendant when the offense was unrelated to attractiveness; when the crime was related to attractiveness, the attractive defendant would receive relatively harsh treatment."[69] They reported that when an attractive individual was perceived as deliberately taking advantage of her attractiveness she was especially disliked.

Our third factor, cooperative endeavors, also promotes liking among people. It is the act of cooperation which influences liking. In other words, it does not seem to matter whether the participants anticipate success based on their cooperation. Moreover, as articulated by communication scholar DeVito: "If individuals in a cooperative enterprise do not have a positive regard for each other at the beginning, they will probably develop mutually positive feelings. If such positive feelings are already present, they will probably increase."[70] The application of DeVito's observation to the jury group is unmistakable. The jurors are engaged in a cooperative endeavor which is to render a verdict. Therefore, they will most likely emerge from the jury room with a positive regard for each other.

Finally, proximity or geographic closeness to another person also increases the probability that we will like that person. Proximity provides us with the opportunity to get to know the other person, to gain some information about him. We tend to like people we know because we can better predict their behavior, and perhaps because of this they seem less frightening to us than complete strangers.[71] This reinforces, once again, the need for uncertainty reduction which forms the basis of Communication Principle 2. The result is a circular process: liking increases predictability and predictability increases liking.

§ 2.61 —Authority

Authority is another factor that influences us in a persuasive situation. We respond automatically to those people we perceive to have authority. There is little question that authority is a powerful motivator. Our society relies on a system of authority to conduct its business. We teach our children early to obey adults, respect authority, and to do what they are

---

[69] Sigall & Ostrove, *Beautiful but Dangerous: Effects of Offender Attractiveness and Nature of Crime on Juridic Judgment*, 31 J. Personality & Soc. Psychology 410-414 (1975).

[70] J. DeVito, The Interpersonal Communication Book 440–441 (Harper and Row, 2d ed. 1980).

[71] *Id*. at 433.

told. Adults are not immune themselves, however, from the influence of authority over them.[72]

Another implication of authority is that we place great stock in our "expert" figures. An experiment recently reported in *Psychology Today* recounts the study done at the University of Illinois at Chicago, by criminal justice scholars Steven Balkin and Pauline Houlden.[73] The researchers gave their subjects the following scene:

> A deserted street in Chicago's business district at 10 o'clock on a weeknight. You can see only one figure. Are you scared?[74]

The subjects were then given a description of a member of one of 25 occupations as the figure in the scene. The subjects reported they felt safest when the lone figure was a uniformed police officer, firefighter, or soldier.

Communication Principle 11 states that the perception of credibility increases with the perception of authority. Power, importance, and status are conferred on authority figures. In the courtroom, the judge is the primary authority figure and consequently he can greatly influence the jurors by his behavior and responses to both witnesses and counsel.

Communication scholars Taylor, Buchanan, and Strawn recall an incident where an obviously tired and impatient judge told an attorney that his witness' testimony was repetitive of earlier testimony from other witnesses. In fact, this witness was expressing the opposite view from earlier testimony. The attorney immediately filed a motion for a mistrial citing that "the judge had departed from his stance of neutrality and had, in effect, agreed with his opponent. The jury, he charged, would be strongly influenced by the judge's actions, much to the detriment of his client."[75] The motion for a mistrial was granted.

The courtroom itself is filled with symbols of authority. The following list, compiled by Taylor, Buchanan, and Strawn, shows how pervasive authority symbols are in the courtroom.

1. The judge's station is elevated above all others in the courtroom.
2. In an era when expensive materials are not used even for important

---

[72] Milgram, *Behavioral Study of Obedience*, 67 J. ABNORM. & SOC. PSYCHOLOGY 371–378 (1963).

[73] Meer, *Uniform Guide to Public Safety*, 18 PSYCHOLOGY TODAY 8 (1984).

[74] *Id*. at 8.

[75] TAYLOR, BUCHANAN & STRAWN, *supra* note 42, at 8.

offices, rare and valuable wood is likely to be found somewhere in a courtroom.

3. Flags, the symbol of governmental authority and power, are often found in the courtroom.
4. The authority of the jury is presented by a special area (box) in which they are comfortably seated, generally elevated above the floor of the courtroom.
5. The witness stand is isolated from the areas reserved for other trial participants and is usually located somewhere close to and beneath the judge in full view of the jury.
6. An architectural barrier generally separates the arena for the drama of the trial from the spectators' seats.
7. Lawyers and their clients seated at tables in front of the judge are isolated from the other trial participants and from each other.[76]

The basic human response to authority is automatic and instinctive. Most people defer to authority figures allowing them to influence both their behaviors and decisions. Jurors particularly seek out authority figures in the courtroom to guide their responses. This explains, in part, the success of the "act as if" technique discussed in Chapter 1. If counsel "acts as if" he is confident and in control even when his internal feelings do not correspond to this state, he will be perceived to have greater authority. As a result, the believability of what he says is greatly increased. The same opening statement could be presented with two different vocal tones: one strong and authoritative and the second weak and questioning.[77] People will listen more attentively and will be more influenced by the authoritative voice. To increase the perception of credibility, first increase the perception of authority. As we discussed in Chapter 1, this can be done through changes in personal appearance, voice, and behavioral cues.

Increasing the perception of authority is also critical with expert witnesses. The common belief about experts is that they are confident and very knowledgeable. The expectation held by the general public is that a true expert is, in fact, an authority. An expert witness who exhibits characteristics which contradict these expectations will most likely suffer a loss of credibility in the eyes of the jurors. When expectations are not

---

[76] *Id*. at 13.

[77] *See supra* § 1.85, discussing powerful versus powerless speech.

met or are contradicted by the nonverbal behaviors of an individual, the verbal message will either be dismissed or its importance greatly reduced. For this reason the selection and preparation of an expert witness is critical. The important question is "Does the expert look and sound like an expert?" Our first and the most fundamental principle, "Communication is based on perception," operates at all times. It is worth repeating that all events which occur in the courtroom are filtered through individual perceptual processes and are, therefore, subject to multiple interpretations. The bottom line is that it does not matter what you intend to say or do in the courtroom—what really counts is how it is perceived by others.

§ 2.62 —Scarcity

Another strong impact on the persuasive process is the effect of the scarcity of the item or information in question. For example, the Cabbage Patch doll craze hit the market in time for the 1983 Christmas rush. Cabbage Patch dolls, with their pudgy cheeks and wide, staring eyes (their look, says a *Newsweek* article, "can be approximated in the adult face by sucking in both lips and puffing out the cheeks") are considered ugly by some.[78] But, no matter how you view the doll, the Cabbage Patch doll is a bonanza for Coleco Industries and is an example of Coleco's shrewd advertising policy: overpromote and undersupply. As *Newsweek* pointed out, "On top of all their cuddly charms, the Cabbage Kids now have the lure of the unattainable."[79] The Cabbage Patch fad is an illustration of Communication Principle 12: People are more easily influenced when they believe the source to be scarce and valuable.

Not only does the scarcity phenomenon apply to items and products, it also applies to information. In one of the experiments conducted during the University of Chicago Jury Project, researcher Dale Broeder reported an interesting psychological phenomenon.[80] Broeder, using people who were actually serving on juries at the time of the study, taped mock trials based on an actual court case. The case involved a middle-aged female stenographer who was injured when the car in which she was a passenger crashed into the defendant's car.

Broeder set up three experimental conditions. In the first, the jury was told that the defendant had no insurance and there was no objection

---

[78] *"Oh, You Beautiful Dolls!"*, 102 NEWSWEEK 78 (December 12, 1983).

[79] *Id*. at 5.

[80] Broeder, *The University of Chicago Jury Project*, 38 NEB. L. REV. 744–760 (1959).

raised to this information. In the second experimental condition there was a disclosure that the defendant had insurance, and there was no objection raised by defense counsel. In the third condition, it was disclosed that the defendant had insurance and defense counsel objected. As a result of the objection, the judge instructed the jury to disregard that information.

The results of the study are very interesting. Broeder concluded:

> Where the defendant disclosed that he had no insurance the average award of all verdicts was $33,000. Where the defendant disclosed that he had insurance but there was no objection the average award rose to $37,000. Where, however, the defendant said he had insurance and there was an objection and an instruction to disregard, the average award rose to $46,000—$13,000 more than when the defendant said he was not insured and $9,000 more than when he said he was insured but where there was no objection or instruction to disregard.[81]

Broeder's results can be explained in the following way. When the jurors were told they could not use the information, the information became more valuable to them. Ruling the information inadmissible made it scarce and unavailable to the jurors. In fact, the inadmissible ruling made it more valuable because it had now become information that had previously been available and now was denied to them. Consistent with psychologist Jack Brehm's psychological reactance theory, the jurors reacted against the restriction of the information and valued it even more.[82]

In a more recent study conducted by psychologists Wolf and Montgomery, testimony from a police undercover agent was either ruled admissible, inadmissible without an admonishment to disregard, or inadmissible with an admonishment to disregard the testimony.[83] When jurors were told to disregard the testimony (admonishment condition), they were more likely to desire to be allowed to consider the testimony than were jurors who had not been admonished to disregard the information. Wolf and Montgomery also explained the results in terms of Brehm's psychological reactance theory. When you instruct individuals that they cannot use particular information, you have informed them of

---

[81] *Id.* at 754.

[82] J. Brehm, A Theory of Psychological Reactance (Academic Press, 1966).

[83] Wolf & Montgomery, *Effects of Inadmissible Evidence and Level of Judicial Admonishment to Disregard on the Judgments of Mock Jurors*, 7 J. App. Soc. Psychology 205–219 (1977).

both the importance and the value of the information. The result is predictable: they will use the information. When you call attention to information which you want ruled inadmissible, you will focus the jurors attention on the testimony. It is worth considering whether you want to run the risk of making the information more valuable or scarce by asking for the judge's ruling on it.

§ 2.63 Theory of power of groups in persuasion

Individual behavior often changes when a person becomes a member of a group. The impact of this factor for the attorney is obvious: once an individual juror begins deliberating with the other jurors, he is no longer an individual. He has now become a member of a group: the jury. The implication of this factor in the decision-making process of the jury is the subject of Chapter 4. It is important to note here, however, the power of groups in the persuasion process.

Groups have been described, by communication scholars such as Cartwright and Zander, as having a homogenizing effect on individuals.[84] In other words, groups exert pressure on an individual to conform to the group, thus producing a homogeneous outlook among group members. Group pressure can be very powerful and difficult for an individual to resist.

Psychologist Solomon Asch conducted a series of well-known experiments on the impact that a group has on an individual. Asch discovered that even when subjects knew that the group choice was in error, their individual decision matched that of the group. They conformed to group pressure of majority opinion and yielded even when they knew the group's decision was wrong.[85]

§ 2.64 Characteristics of an effective persuader

Persuasion is both an art and a learned skill. Some people seem to have a natural ability to convince people to behave in a certain way. Successful salespeople, actors, politicians, and trial attorneys share a common characteristic: they tend to be high self-monitors. A high self-monitoring individual uses external cues from the environment and from people to determine how he will respond. The high self-monitor devel-

---

[84] D. Cartwright & A. Zander, *The Nature of Group Cohesiveness* in GROUP DYNAMICS (Harper & Row, D. Cartwright & A. Zander eds., 3rd ed. 1968).

[85] S. ASCH, SOCIAL PSYCHOLOGY (Prentice-Hall, 1952).

ops a "they" focus and subsequently finds it much easier to pace individuals and to link to their frame of reference.

Sections 2.65–2.67 will examine three characteristics of an effective persuader: (1) the use of high self-monitoring skills, (2) the ability to develop source credibility, and (3) the use of nonverbal cues in persuasion.

§ 2.65 —Source credibility

The study of credibility is so intrinsically bound to the study of persuasion that an entire chapter is devoted to this topic.[86] Clearly credibility is one of the primary characteristics of an effective persuader. Credibility in the courtroom is of special importance since jurors expect attorneys and judges to be competent.

Speech communication scholars such as McCroskey have generally defined speaker credibility as the receiver's attitude toward a source (speaker) at a given point in time.[87] Important to this definition is the understanding that a speaker's credibility rests with the *audience's perception* of him. As has been pointed out, "credibility and like terms do not represent attributes on communicators; they represent judgments by the listeners. . . ."[88] An attorney may be the most upstanding member of his community, but if his jury in a particular case perceives him as untrustworthy or sneaky his word will be questioned.

Credibility is a multi-dimensional concept. Communication researchers such as Berlo, Lemertz, and Mertz discuss credibility as consisting of three dimensions: (1) competence, (2) trustworthiness, and (3) dynamism.[89] Expertise (or competence) is the skill, knowledge, and judgment of the communicator on an issue.[90] A source rated high in expertise would be considered qualified, skilled, informed, authoritative, able, and

---

[86] *See infra* Chapter 3, *Source Credibility in the Courtroom*.

[87] J.C. McCroskey, An Introduction to Rhetorical Communication (Prentice-Hall, 1972).

[88] C. Sherif, M. Sherif & R. Nebergall, Attitude and Attitude Change: The Social Judgment-Involvement Approach (W.B. Saunders Co., 1965).

[89] Berlo, Lemert & Mertz, *Dimensions for Evaluating the Acceptability of Message Sources*, 33 Pub. Opin. Q. 563–596 (1969).

[90] D. Zimbardo, E. Ebbesen & C. Maslach, Influencing Attitudes and Changing Behavior 98 (Addison-Wesley Publishing Co., 2d ed. 1977).

intelligent.[91] Trustworthiness is "motivation to communication without bias."[92] An individual rated high in trustworthiness is regarded as, among other things, just, fair, and ethical.[93] Audiences judge a person's dynamism by factors such as how forceful, emphatic, bold, or active he is during the communication.[94] Fluency of the presentation has been found to be a factor in a listener's evaluation of a speaker's credibility. Fluent speakers were rated more dynamic and also more competent than less fluent speakers. The fluent speaker was also judged to be more trustworthy.[95]

Word choice and language also affect a person's credibility. As we discussed previously,[96] powerful speech influences the credibility of the speaker. An attorney using powerful speech is more likely to be perceived as intelligent, likable, and believable. All characteristics and behaviors expressed through the channels of verbal, vocal, and nonverbal communication have an impact on credibility.

Thus, attorneys who are seen as highly credible (in terms of their audience's perceptions of expertise, trustworthiness, and dynamism) are more likely to be able to influence their audience—the jury. As researcher Berkowitz concluded in his book *Social Psychology*:

> . . .highly credible communicators can produce greater opinion changes than less credible sources. Much of this change probably occurs because the audience members are engaged in a rational attempt at problem solving. They want to arrive at the best possible evaluation and believe that the credible speaker or author, because of his expertise, knows what is right. Therefore, his opinion is accepted.[97]

COMMENT: In summary, the attribution of credibility to an

[91] E. BETTINGHAUS, PERSUASIVE COMMUNICATION 106 (Holt, Rinehart and Winston, 1968).

[92] ZIMBARDO, *supra* note 90, at 98.

[93] BETTINGHAUS, *supra* note 91, at 106.

[94] *Id*. at 107.

[95] Miller & Hewgill, *The Effect of Variations in Nonfluency on Audience Ratings of Source Credibility*, 50 Q. J. SPEECH 36–44 (1964).

[96] *See supra* § 1.85.

[97] L. BERKOWITZ, SOCIAL PSYCHOLOGY 54 (Scott, Foresman and Co.).

individual is perception oriented. As Principle 1 states, communication is based on perception. Ascribed credibility is a function of how others perceive an individual.

---

§ 2.66 —Self-monitoring

Self-monitoring is the degree to which people are concerned with how they express themselves in various situations. Some people are very conscious of the requirements of a social or business situation. As a result they are very aware of their own behavior in those situations. These people try to match their actions to the requirements of each given situation. Years of research have been conducted to identify the behavioral and occupational differences of the low and high self-monitors. Psychologist Snyder, the most well-known researcher in this field of inquiry, has reported his experimental findings in *The Journal of Personality and Social Psychology* and *Advances in Experimental Social Psychology*. According to Snyder, the high self-monitoring individual is "one who, out of a concern for social appropriateness, is particularly sensitive to the expression and self-presentation of others in social situations and uses these cues as guidelines for monitoring his own presentation."[98]

People vary in their concern with how they are presenting themselves to others. There are striking and important differences in the extent to which people can and do control their self-presentation. The strategies and techniques a person uses to control the impression he conveys to others is referred to as "impression management." Some people engage in impression management more often—and with greater skill—than others. Professional actors, as well as many trial lawyers, are among the best at it. The following self-monitoring test will provide you with insight into your skills in this area.[99]

Assessing Your Self-Monitoring Skills

Directions: The following statements concern your personal reactions to a number of different situations. No two statements are exactly alike, so

---

[98] Snyder, *The Self-Monitoring of Expressive Behavior*, 30 J. PERSONALITY & SOC. PSYCHOLOGY 526–537 (1974).

[99] The Self-Monitoring Test was developed and tested by Mark Snyder, Department of Psychology, University of Minnesota. Reprinted with permission of the author.

consider each statement carefully before answering. If a statement is TRUE or MOSTLY TRUE as applied to you, mark it as true. If a statement is FALSE or NOT USUALLY TRUE as applied to you, mark it as false.

True False

— — 1. I find it hard to imitate the behavior of other people.

— — 2. My behavior is usually an expression of my true inner feelings, attitudes, and beliefs.

— — 3. At parties and social gathering, I do not attempt to do or say things others will like.

— — 4. I can only argue for ideas which I already believe.

— — 5. I can make impromptu speeches even on topics about which I have almost no information.

— — 6. I guess I put on a show to impress or entertain other people.

— — 7. When I am uncertain how to act in a social situation, I look to the behavior of others for cues.

— — 8. I would probably make a good actor/actress.

— — 9. I rarely seek the advice of my friends to choose movies, books, or music.

— —10. I sometimes appear to others to be experiencing deeper emotions than I actually am.

— —11. I laugh more when I watch a comedy with others than when alone.

— —12. In a group of people I am rarely the center of attention.

— —13. In different situations and with different people I often act like very different persons.

— —14. I am not particularly good at making other people like me.

— —15. Even if I am not enjoying myself, I often pretend to be having a good time.

— —16. I'm not always the person I appear to be.

— —17. I would not change my opinions (or the way I do things) in order to please someone or win their favor.

True False

— —18. I have considered being an entertainer.

— —19. In order to get along and be liked, I tend to be what people expect me to be rather than anything else.

— —20. I have never been good at games like charades or improvisational acting.

— —21. I have trouble changing my behavior to suit different people and situations.

— —22. At a party I let others keep the jokes and stories going.

— —23. I feel a bit awkward in company and do not show up quite as well as I should.

— —24. I can look anyone in the eye and tell a lie with a straight face (if for the right end).

— —25. I may deceive people by being friendly when I really dislike them.

SCORING: Give yourself one point (1 point) for each of the following questions to which you responded False: 1, 2, 3, 4, 9, 12, 14, 17, 20, 21, 22, and 23. Now give yourself one point (1 point) for each of the remaining questions that you answered True: 5, 6, 7, 8, 10, 11, 13, 15, 16, 18, 19, 24, and 25.

COMMENT: The self-monitoring survey which you just completed measures how concerned you are with the impression you make on others, as well as your ability to control and modify your behavior to fit the situation. If you scored 16 or above, you tend to be a high self-monitoring individual; if you scored 7 or below, you tend to be a low self-monitoring individual. If your score is in the range of 8 to 15 you will have traits of both the high and low self-monitors, but without a strong preference toward one end of the scale or the other.

High and low self-monitoring individuals differ greatly with respect to their adaptation skills and how they are viewed by others. High self-monitors are "concerned with the situational and interpersonal appropriateness of their behaviors."[100] They are especially sensitive to social cues and are careful to monitor those cues in order to determine what the appropriate behavior is in a particular circumstance. High self-monitors are particularly skilled at pacing an individual, group, or situation. Pacing, as we discussed, is the ability to link to a person's emotional state through the matching of verbal, vocal, and nonverbal cues. This was discussed more fully in Part II of this chapter. Because high self-monitors rely on the cues of others to determine their own actions, they naturally and instinctively pace people. It is not surprising to find that high self-monitors are better able to communicate and understand emotional states. Their sensitivity to people allows them to tap in very quickly to what a person is experiencing.

In addition, high self-monitors actively invest cognitive time and effort in attempting to read others. High self-monitors will most likely find this book to be of special interest, not because it provides new information, but because it explains skills and strategies they have used for years. In reading others, high self-monitoring individuals are better able to detect deception. They regard themselves as rather "flexible and adaptive people who tailor their social behavior shrewdly and pragmatically to fit appropriate conditions."[101] Soon after meeting another person, the high self-monitor takes an active and controlling role in the conversation. In doing so, however, he communicates very little about his private attitudes, feelings, and dispositions. He tends to be very private and only releases that information which is instrumental in helping him get what he wants. High self-monitors often include trial lawyers, politicians, and actors. However, a high self-monitor who appears to be "too slick" or "too smooth" can suffer a loss of credibility. The attorney who is too glib and arrogant diminishes the probability that he will be liked. Principle 10 tells us that people are more easily influenced by people they like. "Obvious" high self-monitors run the danger of losing likability and ap-

[100] M. Snyder, *Self-Monitoring Processes* in 12 ADVANCES IN EXPERIMENTAL SOCIAL PSYCHOLOGY 85–128 (Academic Press, L. Berkowitz ed. 1979).

[101] *See* Snyder, *supra* note 98. *See also* Brandt, Miller & Hocking, *Effects of Self-Monitoring and Familiarity on Deception Detection*, 28 COMM. Q. 1–10 (1980); Snyder & Manson, *Persons Situations and the Control of Social Behavior*, 32 J. PERSONALITY & SOC. PSYCHOLOGY 637–644 (1975); Tardy & Hosman, *Self-Monitoring and Self-Disclosure Flexibility: A Research Note*, 46 W.J. SPEECH COMM. 92–97 (1982); Geizer, Rarick & Soldow, *Deception in Judgement Accuracy: A Study in Person Perception*, 3 PERSONALITY & SOC. PSYCHOLOGICAL BULL. 446–449 (1977); L. MALANDRO, THE PSYCHOLOGY OF A TRIAL 32–35 (Malandro Communication Inc., 1982).

proachability. The key for the high self-monitoring individual is to develop all the traits and skills of self-awareness and sensitivity to the highest level possible while displaying low self-monitoring traits.

Now let's switch our focus to the low self-monitoring individual. Low self-monitoring individuals have a lesser concern with adapting their behaviors and self-presentation in a situation. The low self-monitor is in control of his personal communication, but tends to use his values and attitudes as a basis for his behaviors rather than the external demands of the situation in which he finds himself. In other words, the low self-monitoring individual is less concerned with social and interpersonal specifications of behavioral appropriateness. "What you see is what you get" is the motto of the low self-monitor. Basically it can be said that the low self-monitor tends to accept the behavior of others at face value. He generally does not attempt to understand their psychological motivation. The low self-monitor is perceived as believable and approachable, and hence, more likable. He values and strives for a congruence between "who he is" and "what he does." A low self-monitor's actions are faithful reflections of how he feels and thinks.[102]

Understanding the characteristics of both high and low self-monitors has important implications in the courtroom. The high self-monitor, in the courtroom, is the chameleon, constantly adapting to changing stimuli. This ability to pace is extremely valued for a person engaged in the art of persuasion. The high self-monitor must constantly assess his external behaviors to make sure they do not appear to be "too flexible" or "too unbelievable." The low self-monitor, by contrast, is very believable and likable. People find the low self-monitor to be trustworthy primarily because his behaviors are a reflection of who he is. There are no guessing games about the low self-monitor—he presents himself as who he is. To increase his effectiveness as a persuader, the low self-monitoring individual needs to increase his sensitivity and awareness of people, situations, and environments. Specifically, he needs to develop the ability to read and adapt behaviors. (Part II of this chapter on pacing is of particular importance to the low self-monitor). Table 2–4 offers a summary of the primary characteristics of low and high self-monitors.[103]

---

[102] *See supra* note 101.

[103] L. Malandro, The Psychology of a Trial 86 (Malandro Communication Inc., 1982).

Table 2–4
Characteristics of High and Low Self-Monitors

Low self-monitors tend to be:

—introverted

—sincere and believable

—expressive about who they are

—willing to disclose information about themselves

—unaware (or have a low awareness) of nonverbal cues

—less concerned with behavioral appropriateness of their actions

—in supportive positions and do not actively seek leadership positions

—consistent in displaying actions which are a reflection of how they think and feel

High self-monitors tend to be:

—extroverted

—persuasive

—leaders

—unexpressive about who they are

—unwilling to disclose information about themselves

—flexible and adaptive

—good at reading others

—highly aware of nonverbal cues

—very concerned with the behavioral appropriateness of their actions

—controlled and do not usually display actions which are a reflection of how they think and feel

§ 2.67 —Influence of nonverbal cues on opinion change

A communicator's nonverbal behaviors have a definite impact on his persuasiveness. Nonverbal cues are interpreted as indicators of the speaker's credibility. For example, if the speaker is fidgeting, nervous, and avoiding eye contact, he can be perceived as lacking credibility. In fact, his nervous mannerisms will most likely be interpreted as attempted deceit or that he is communicating half-truths. Equally important is the factor that receivers tend to place confidence in their abilities to judge accurately the nonverbal cues they see. In a study by Hocking, Miller, and Fontes observers indicated a 58% confidence level in the evaluations they made of a stranger's nonverbal cues.[104]

What are the nonverbal behaviors that enhance a speaker's persuasiveness and thus his opportunity to produce opinion change? Generally, speakers who are more fluent, confident, outgoing, and self-assured are seen as more credible and thus as more persuasive. Using a simulated courtroom, psychologists Hemsley and Doob examined the impact of gaze aversion and gaze maintenance on the credibility of a witness's testimony.[105] The results verified the importance of eye contact. A witness who maintained eye contact with the target of his communication was perceived as more credible. The study concluded that "witnesses who averted their gaze were perceived to be less credible and, ultimately, the defendant for whom they testified was judged as more likely to be guilty."[106]

Communication researchers Sereno and Hawkins determined that nonfluencies influenced the perceptions of credibility in a negative manner.[107] Nonfluencies (such as "ah," the superfluous repetition of a word, and stuttering) related to a decrease in the perception of the speaker's competency and dynamism and thus his credibility.

The nonverbal area of voice tone has also been found to affect persuasion. Vocal characteristics that tend to be persuasive include a more expressive, more natural, more pleasant, and more warm sounding voice.[108] Other experiments that have been conducted have found that the more persuasive speaker was the person who had more eye contact with his audience, more vocal variety and inflection, more volume, a faster rate of delivery, more gestures, and appeared confident and more relaxed.[109]

---

[104] Hocking, Miller & Fontes, *Videotape in the Courtroom: Witness Deception*, 14 TRIAL 52–55 (1978).

[105] Hemsley & Doob, *The Effect of Looking Behavior on Perceptions of a Communicator's Credibility*, 8 J. APP. SOC. PSYCHOLOGY 136–144 (1978).

[106] *Id*. at 136.

[107] Sereno & Hawkins, *The Effects of Variations in Speakers' Nonfluency Upon Audience Ratings of Attitude Toward the Speech Topic and Speakers' Credibility*, 34 SPEECH MONOGRAPHS 58–64 (1967).

[108] Hall, *Voice Tone and Persuasion*, 38 J. PERSONALITY & SOC. PSYCHOLOGY 924–934 (1980).

[109] Mehrabian & Williams, *Nonverbal Concomitants of Perceived and Intended Persua-*

Table 2–5 summarizes the persuasive nonverbal behaviors which increase credibility.[110] Communication researchers Miller and Burgoon compiled this table of the nonverbal cues affecting the assessment of witness credibility in the courtroom. Their table outlines (1) nonverbal cues that are encoded by the speaker as persuasive or deceptive when sent to the receiver and (2) nonverbal cues that are decoded as either persuasive or deceptive when received by the listener. The terms "encoding" and "decoding" refer to the individual's perception of the behaviors. Encoding is a function of the speaker's perception while decoding reflects the listener's perception and interpretation. For example, Table 2–5 indicates that if a speaker uses continuous eye contact he may "encode" it or perceive it to be more persuasive. The interpretation of this behavior or the "decoding" process occurs within the listener. The listener will decode or perceive "more eye contact" to be persuasive. On the other hand, "less eye contact" would be decoded as deceptive.

What does all this mean to the attorney? Basically, people are more easily influenced by people they like (Principle 10) and, therefore, nonverbal cues which increase the perception of liking are the key to persuasion. The attorney would do well to relate to the following concept of immediacy expressed as: "People are drawn toward persons and things they like, evaluate highly, and prefer; and they avoid or move away from things they dislike, evaluate negatively, or do not prefer."[111]

Liking is promoted by behaviors that increase the closeness of people; avoidance is precipitated by behaviors that inhibit closeness. For example, we stand closer to people we know and like. We have direct eye contact with those we like. The more immediate behaviors that are used by the attorney, the more positive influence he will have on the jury. The more positive influence, the more persuasive he is. People buy people, and more importantly, people want to feel special. The following list of behaviors are referred to as "person" behaviors. An individual receiving

---

siveness, 13 J. PERSONALITY & SOC. PSYCHOLOGY 37–58 (1969); Zuckerman, DeFrank, Hall, Larrance & Rosenthal, *Facial and Vocal Cues of Deception and Honesty*, 15 J. EXPERIM. SOC. PSYCHOLOGY 378–396 (1979).

[110] G. Miller & J. Burgoon, *Factors Affecting Assessments of Witness Credibility* in THE PSYCHOLOGY OF THE COURTROOM 176–177 (Academic Press, Kerr & Bray eds. 1982). Reprinted with permission.

[111] L. MALANDRO, THE PSYCHOLOGY OF A TRIAL 86 (Malandro Communication Inc., 1982); *See also* A. MEHRABIAN, SILENT MESSAGES 118 (Wadsworth Publishing Co., 1971).

this type of nonverbal attention tends to feel more valued. These behaviors include:

(1) Using good eye contact

(2) Using animated facial expressions

(3) Keeping normal to close distance

(4) Using expressive vocal cues

(5) Displaying a sincere interest in others[112]

COMMENT: Nonverbal cues have a definite impact on jurors' perceptions. These perceptions in turn influence how effective the attorney will be in promoting persuasion and opinion change in the courtroom.

---

[112] MALANDRO, *supra* note 111, at 85.

Table 2–5
Encoding and Decoding of Nonverbal Cues

Nonverbal Code	Cues encoded as: Persuasive/credible	Cues encoded as: Deceptive	Cues decoded as: Persuasive/credible	Cues decoded as: Deceptive
Kinesics	More or continuous eye contact	Reduced eye contact (fewer, briefer glances)	More eye contact	Less eye contact
	More affirmative head nods	Fewer head nods		
	More facial activity	Less smiling; less happiness; displeased mouth movements; micromomentary expressions; but more pleasant faces by highly anxious	More facial activity	Less serious; less empathy; more smiling
	More gestures by women; more rhythmic, forceful gestures	Fewer gestures; fewer illustrators; more hand shrugs	More gestures; more illustrators	Excessive gestures

Nonverbal Code	Cues encoded as: Persuasive/credible	Cues encoded as: Deceptive	Cues decoded as: Persuasive/credible	Cues decoded as: Deceptive
	Moderate levels of postural relaxation; less trunk swivel by women	Frequent shifts in leg/body position; tense leg and foot positions; less leg and foot movement; leg crossing by males; body blocks; abortive, restless flight movements	Moderate relaxation	More tension and anxiety; more postural shifts
		Physiological indicators: blushing, blinking, shaking, perspiring, dilated or instable pupils		
Proxemics		Body less directly facing audience	Body less directly facing audience for males	
	Smaller reclining angle	Less forward lean		
		Greater distances	Closer distances	

Nonverbal Code	Cues encoded as		Cues decoded as	
	Persuasive/ credible	Deceptive	Persuasive/ credible	Deceptive
Haptics	Fewer adaptor behaviors and self-manipulations with receptive audience	More self-, face-play and object adaptors; longer adaptors	Less self manipulations and adaptors	Less self-grooming
Vocalics	Higher volume		Higher volume	
	Faster speaking rate	Slower or faster rate than normal	Moderate to slightly faster speaking rate	
	More fluency	More nonfluencies	More fluency	More nonfluencies
	More intonation		More intonation and pitch variety	
		Higher pitch	Lower pitch	
			More vocal involvement	
			Conversational delivery style	
		More pauses or probe openings		

Nonverbal Code	Cues encoded as		Cues decoded as	
	Persuasive/ credible	Deceptive	Persuasive/ credible	Deceptive
		More response latency		
		Shorter word duration; shorter speaking time		
			Use of General American Dialect	
Overall		Contradictions or inconsistencies among nonverbal cues	Positive violations of expectations (e.g., dressing unappealingly but conveying effective verbal message)	
		More information from hands and feet than face		Greater reliance on voice than face and on face than body

Chapter 3

SOURCE CREDIBILITY IN THE COURTROOM

III. Communication Techniques

KLUWER LITIGATION LIBRARY REFERENCES

JEANS, LITIGATION: Chapter 2, *Mind Set of the Advocate*; Chapter 5, *Trial Preparation*; Chapter 6, *Voir Dire*; Chapter 7, *Opening Presentation*; Chapter 8, *Direct Examination*; Chapter 13, *Cross-Examination*; Chapter 16, *Summation*.

PREISER & PREISER, HANDLING SOFT TISSUE INJURY CASES: Chapter 10, *Psychology of the Trial*.

I. Communication Principles

§ 3.01 Introduction to Communication Principles of credibility

There are many principles which could be discussed in the area of credibility. However, for the purpose of this work we have identified four primary principles that influence credibility or enhance credibility. The four principles are as follows:

Principle 13: People are more easily influenced by those they perceive as credible.

Principle 14: The perception of credibility is based on three factors: (1) competence/expertness; and (2) trustworthiness; and (3) dynamism.

Principle 15: People are influenced by the way the message is structured and delivered.

Principle 16: The perception of credibility is influenced by personal attributes.

The perception of credibility in a trial has a considerable bearing on whether or not jurors will believe the message which is being presented. The credibility of the attorney hence becomes one of the most important and predominant areas of consideration throughout the course of the trial. Any way an attorney can make himself more credible, whether it is through the use of personal appearance factors, vocal characteristics, the way in which he behaves in the courtroom, or the way in which a message is structured and delivered is important.

§ 3.02 —Principle 13: People are more easily influenced by those they perceive as credible

This is such a basic principle that it requires little explanation. The perception of credibility affects the persuasiveness of any message. The most important aspect to remember about credibility is that it exists in the minds of the jurors. It is not an actual physical attribute, affective attribute, or intellectual attribute. It is simply a receiver decision. In other words, it is the judgment made by the receiver. When we speak about credibility we are referring strictly to the "perception" of credibility. A person may be credible by all standards of society, but once he walks in the courtroom, it is going to be up to the jurors to determine whether or not they perceive this person to be credible in terms of specifics of the courtroom setting and the case.

We know that jurors are much more receptive to arguments from a source that they consider credible. This applies equally across the board to attorneys as well as witnesses. To jurors, credibility means that they can trust the words that are being said and, hence, they will listen longer and will give greater weight to the message presented by this individual.

Credibility factors are affected on several dimensions. One dimension is personal appearance. Certain personal appearance factors, can affect the perceptions of both credibility and approachability. A second factor that can affect the perception of credibility is behavioral patterns. The "act as if" technique for projecting confidence, for example, is another factor that tells us that behavior impacts on the credibility ascribed by the jurors to both attorneys and witnesses. A third factor is the use of powerful speech and special language techniques such as repetition, metaphors, similes, analogies, and rhetorical questions. The perception of credibility of attorneys is closely related to expectations that counsel knows where he is headed, knows how to present information, is understandable, is quick, and has a moderate to fast rate of speaking. All of these factors together help to add to the perception of credibility. It is important to remember, however, that the perception of credibility is an individual judgment which will not always remain the same across the board with different sources.

§ 3.03 —Principle 14: The perception of credibility is based on three factors: (1) competence/expertness, (2) trustworthiness, and (3) dynamism

The three factors which make up the general perception of credibility are competence/expertness, trustworthiness, and dynamism. Expertness and competence refers to the skill and knowledge of the individual. Trustworthiness refers to the fact that the individual presents information without bias—that the person is fair, ethical, and just. Finally, the concept of dynamism is measured by how forceful, bold, or active the person appears to be. Similar to the general concept of credibility, the perception of each of these factors is what matters. This is another receiver-oriented judgment. If the receiver perceives a source to be expert, trustworthy, or dynamic, the overall perception of credibility will be increased. Keep in mind that jurors act like detectives throughout every part of the trial and assembling this information is part of their detective-like process. They will collect clues to determine whether or not the attorney or witnesses will actually make the grade in each of these categories.

One of the most important factors for an attorney to determine in terms of his own credibility is to know how he is perceived by others. In order to understand credibility you must understand how others perceive you in varied settings. If you understand how you are perceived, then you will be able to identify how to project particular impressions in order to maximize the impact that you will have. Some of the ways in which you can obtain this feedback is to attend a professional speaking course or use videotape with an expert in communication. This way you not only receive a professional evaluation on how you project credibility, but you can also observe your own behavioral patterns. Any means by which you can learn more about yourself—how you respond, how you behave, and how you are perceived by others—will help you not only increase the perception of credibility, but will assist you in controlling and directing the perceptions others have of you. The extent to which an individual understands himself and his own personal power is directly related to how forceful he can be in the courtroom.

The perception of competence/expertness includes juror judgments of: (1) the experience of the individual; (2) "floating competence"; and (3) intelligence. We generally assume that greater experience equates with a higher degree of expertness. We use "experience" and "time" as indicators of a person's expert status. "Floating competence" simply means that if we see an individual as very competent in one area we tend to ascribe competence to that person in other areas regardless of whether he has the skills or background in the second area. The fact that he is already perceived as being competent gives him a type of "floating competence" which results in a continued perception of credibility in other, often unrelated fields. The third factor, intelligence, simply means that we will respond positively to those people who can control a situation, are quick to respond, and display other characteristics of intelligence. These three factors provide a composite picture of the criteria by which we judge an expert.

The element of trustworthiness is very important because the characteristic of trustworthiness allows a jury to build empathy with an attorney and his client. In addition, it is impossible to transfer a mood to a jury unless they trust you. If they do not trust you as being authentic and true, they will regard all information and all attempts at mood transference to be fake and insincere. In order to have the jurors trust you, one of the most important things you must do is to first trust the jurors. You must trust them to be able to make good and intelligent decisions. Your belief about the jurors will be communicated at both the conscious and unconscious levels. The first stage in the area of trustworthiness is to make sure you are, in fact, a trusting individual. The second factor of preparing for trustworthiness is to make sure that the attorney presents information in an ethical, fair, and unbiased way. Ask yourself whether or not you are the type of individual that somebody should, in fact, trust. Trustworthiness also includes the perception of sincerity and honesty. When people are sincere, we tend to give them more leeway. People are much less defensive with sincere people. As a result, they offer more information and the attorney obtains more information. We allow trustworthy people to have a greater influence over our decision-making processes.

The final element in the determination of source credibility is the dynamism of the individual. Dynamism refers to how forceful, empathic, bold, or active the individual is or appears to be. If the individual appears to be preoccupied or if he appears to lack competence through his vocal cues, he is perceived as having a low level of dynamism. Dynamic qualities refer to the ability of the speaker to communicate actual emotions or feelings. Dynamism portrays the attorney as having a sensitivity to issues that are being presented. Dynamism means a direct association with overall feelings about the case. It does not mean an insincere attempt at recreating feelings. When an individual is truly dynamic there is no question that a mood transference among the receivers or listeners will take place because the person is speaking from an actual feeling which they are experiencing at the moment.

The behavior we are talking about does not include acting or drama in the traditional sense. The traditional framework for acting and drama is that it is an attempt to "act like something or someone," or to "put on an act." In other words, acting is an insincere attempt at creating a message. But the best actors and actresses do not act at all. They actually relive the event and become the person so that they are no longer acting—they have actually achieved a state of high association. It is true that good actors, once they have created a part or character, do not need to method act night after night. They have learned the appropriate nonverbal behavior and vocal cues associated with the verbal content of the part they are playing so as to create a mood transference by actually feeling the emotion. In hypnosis this is called a light state of trance.

When one is really conveying a particular feeling, there is no separation between the person and the feeling he is conveying at that moment. If you are trying to convey a particular feeling, you cannot at the same time objectively watch yourself convey the feeling. When you are associated with a particular state or feeling, you should see, hear, and feel nothing other than that experience. When counsel is disassociated with a state it cannot be transferred to the jurors. If he tries, his actions will be perceived as insincere. This then becomes a critical difference between those people that have true dynamism and those people who attempt to emulate dynamic qualities. Only true dynamism works in the courtroom.

§ 3.04 —Principle 15: People are influenced by the way the message is structured and delivered

The way in which a message is structured and delivered definitely affects the perception of credibility. Two factors that enter into the jurors' mind will be: (1) is the attorney well prepared? (2) is the attorney thorough? These basic considerations are single pieces of evidence which tell the jurors whether or not they should listen to the information, and whether the information itself should hold any particular weight throughout the course of the trial.

A more important consideration to jurors is the way in which the information is structured and delivered. Is the message consistent, easily remembered, and well delivered? Jurors are more likely to perceive the source as credible when the way in which the message is presented allows jurors to feel both competent and intelligent. If the elements are confusing or are too numerous, jurors will discredit the information rather than discredit their own capability to understand the information. Therefore, counsel should not present information which is too complicated. Jurors will not perceive the attorney as being more intelligent because of the complexity of the message. It is more likely they will perceive an attorney as less intelligent and incapable of communicating a clear and simple message. Jurors will see themselves as doing the best they can with complex information, but if in their mind, the message is not properly structured and prepared, the speaker's credibility will be reduced. It is unlikely and very unusual for a receiver of a message to reduce his own credibility. Jurors will first look at the attorney (the source) to find out what is wrong with the information presented. The communication techniques part of this chapter will focus on various methods to structure and deliver a message which will increase high impact in the courtroom.

§ 3.05 —Principle 16: The perception of credibility is influenced by personal attributes

There is no question that the perception of credibility is a result of the perception of many personal characteristics. These characteristics include such elements as delivery, physical appearance, likability, and use of humor. In addition, another factor of "instant credibility" also affects the perception that jurors will form.

The speaker's delivery style has been discussed previously in terms of powerful and powerless speech. We know that communicators who are fluent and have a good delivery style will be perceived as more credible. Likewise, the communicator's physical appearance will affect the perception of credibility. A person who is obese, for example, will have less credibility than one who appears to be in good health. Likability is directly related to credibility. This underscores our principle of homophyly which says that we like those people that we perceive to be similar to ourselves. If we perceive a person as being similar to ourselves, we give him a sense of automatic credibility. The humor expressed by an individual is also an interesting factor that affects credibility. We assume that people who have a sense of humor and can participate in a humorous process can understand better what is going on and have a better handle on what it is they are presenting.

The concept of instant credibility refers to four primary factors. When an individual has instant credibility he either has: (1) prior reputation before entering the trial; (2) there is prior knowledge on the part of the jurors about special characteristics or background of the individual; (3) there is a positive endorsement coming from the outside regarding that individual before trial; or (4) there is exposure of the attorney through the media or perhaps through writing and publication of articles. Attorneys with credibility have an advantage because jurors will automatically see them as being credible and will not require them to demonstrate other factors bearing on their credibility. The principle of primacy is also in effect here as well. This means that information presented first by an individual with instant credibility in the courtroom will be believed. Even if contradictory information is presented subsequently throughout the trial, in most cases it will not damage the initial instant credibility. The fact that instant credibility existed during the primacy period of the trial will cause the original perception of credibility to be maintained.

§ 3.06 Introduction to source credibility

One text on communication, in discussing source credibility, states:

> Probably the clearest conclusion from the hundreds and hundreds of research studies investigating the process of influence in communication is that the credibility of the source of a message has a major impact on the degree to which that message influences the receiver.[1]

Credibility is the receiver's perception of the speaker's expertness trustworthiness, and dynamism. It is important that the attorney understand from the outset that credibility is a judgment made by the receiver; it may or may not be a correct judgment. Credibility is a function of the *receiver's* perceptions of the speaker. Once again, we are reminded of our first Communication Principle: Communication is based on perception. Even if an attorney is credible and knowledgeable, it will make little difference if he is not perceived in this manner. The critical link between an actual characteristic such as credibility and the jurors interpretation is how those characteristics are presented. In the courtroom, an attorney's credibility is subject to the perceptions of the juror. One authoritative text states that:

> A lawyer's credibility exists in the minds of the jurors. An attorney may have an outstanding reputation with his colleagues, he may be president of the local bar association, a patron of the arts, on the board of directors for several philanthropic organizations, and still not be perceived by those very important persons in the jury box as an individual who is intelligent, knowledgeable, and worthy of their trust.[2]

Communication scholars have generally defined speaker credibility as

---

[1] J. McCroskey & L. Wheeless, Introduction to Human Communication 350 (Allyn & Bacon, Inc., 1976).

[2] K. Taylor, R. Buchanan & D. Strawn, Communication Strategies for Trial Attorneys 42 (Scott, Foresman and Co., 1984). Copyright © 1984 by Scott, Foresman and Company. Reprinted by permission.

the receiver's attitude toward a source (speaker) at a given point in time.[3] It is important to understand that a speaker's credibility rests with the *audience's perception* of him. "Credibility and like terms do not represent attributes of communicators; they represent judgments by the listeners. . . ."[4] The attorney may be the most upstanding member of his community but if the jury in a particular case perceives him as untrustworthy or deceptive, he will, for them, be a person whose word is questionable.

The importance of credibility cannot be overstated. In the *Proceedings of the 1980 Conference of the Institute for Study of the Trial*, the importance of credibility of the attorney was underscored. "The credibility of a source is possibly the most important determinant of persuasiveness."[5]

Jurors tend to be more receptive to arguments of attorneys who they perceive as highly credible. Jurors are less likely to be persuaded by low credibility sources. This introduces Communication Principle 13: People are more easily influenced by those they perceive as credible.

§ 3.07 —Roots of source credibility

The roots of our modern day concept of source credibility can be traced back to the philosopher Aristotle. Aristotle's works, written over 2,000 years ago, are considered by some as the seminal treatises and the groundwork upon which much of communication theory is based.

In his book, *Rhetoric*, Aristotle discussed what it was that made some speakers more believed and trusted by their audience than others. He called the speaker's believability and trustworthiness with their audience "ethos":

> Persuasion is achieved by the speaker's personal character when the speech is so spoken as to make us think him credible. We believe good men more fully and more readily than others; this is true generally whatever the question is, and absolutely true where exact certainty is impossible and opinions are divided.
>
> There are three things which inspire confidence in the orator's

---

[3] J.C. McCroskey, An Introduction to Rhetorical Communication (Prentice-Hall, 1972).

[4] C. Sherif, M. Sherif & R. Nebergall, Attitude and Attitude Change: The Social Judgment-Involvement Approach (W.B. Saunders Co., 1965).

[5] Proceedings of the 1980 Conference of the Institute for Study of the Trial 26 (K. Taylor ed.) (Orlando, Florida, March 21–22, 1980).

> own character—the three, namely, that induce us to believe a thing apart from any proof of it: good sense, good moral character, and good will.[6]

The concept of source credibility has remained basically the same throughout the years. "Interestingly, much of the research since the late 1940's on source credibility has listed Aristotle's original hypotheses about ethos."[7]

§ 3.08 —Components of credibility

Credibility is a multi-dimensional concept. Researchers discuss credibility as consisting of three dimensions: (1) competence/expertness; (2) trustworthiness; and (3) dynamism.[8] Expertise (or competence) is the skill, knowledge, and judgment of the communicator on a given issue.[9] A source rated high in expertise would be considered qualified, skilled, informed, authoritative, able, and intelligent.[10] Trustworthiness is the "motivation to communication without bias."[11] An individual rated high in trustworthiness is regarded as, among other things, just, fair and ethical.[12] Audiences judge a person's dynamism by factors such as how forceful, emphatic, bold, or active he is during the communication.[13]

Other researchers have expanded on these three basic elements of credibility, but these three dimensions remain representative of the analysis of the components of credibility. Source credibility has traditionally been measured using the semantic differential scales as set forth below.[14]

The semantic differential scales were originally developed by Osgood

---

[6] THE RHETORIC AND THE POETICS OF ARISTOTLE 25 (The Modern Library, F. Solmsen ed. 1964).

[7] S. LITTLEJOHN, THEORIES OF HUMAN COMMUNICATION 134 (Wadsworth Publishing Co., 2d ed. 1983).

[8] Berlo, Lemertz & Mertz, *Dimensions for Evaluating the Acceptability of Message Sources*, 33 PUB. OPIN. Q. 563–576 (1967).

[9] P. ZIMBARDO, E. EBBESEN & C. MASLACH, INFLUENCING ATTITUDES AND CHANGING BEHAVIOR 98 (Addison-Wesley Publishing Co., 2d ed. 1977).

[10] E. BETTINGHAUS, PERSUASIVE COMMUNICATION 106 (Holt, Rinehart and Winston, 1968).

[11] ZIMBARDO, *supra* note 9, at 106.

[12] BETTINGHAUS, *supra* note 10, at 106.

[13] *Id.* at 107.

[14] *See, e.g.*, K. Andersen, An Experimental Study of the Interaction of Artistic and Non-Artistic Ethos in Persuasion (Wisconsin, 1961) (unpublished doctoral dissertation).

as a way to measure meaning. "Since the basic function of ordinary language was assumed to be the communication of meaning, ordinary language could be used to differentiate between concepts and measures of their meaning. The semantic differential technique is based on this premise."[15] A semantic differential scale is a 7-point scale separating bipolar adjectives. For example:

hard __ __ __ __ __ __ __ soft
good __ __ __ __ __ __ __ bad
fast __ __ __ __ __ __ __ slow
sour __ __ __ __ __ __ __ sweet

COMMENT: Principle 14 states: The perception of credibility is based on the three factors of (1) competence/expertness, (2) trustworthiness, and (3) dynamism. An attorney who is perceived to have these three characteristics will also be perceived to be more credible. Likewise, clients and witnesses are subject to the same analysis by jurors. Each of these characteristics will be examined individually in the sections that follow.

---

§ 3.09 Jury's view of attorney's credibility

> The credibility that you are perceived to possess is a function of your reputation (or what the audience knows of you prior to your actual public speech) and what you do during the actual speech situation.[16]

During a trial, jurors seek out clues to the attorney's credibility from a variety of sources. The process of credibility impression formation follows the same patterns as general impression formation. Jurors begin collecting and assembling the clues into a meaningful picture of the attorney from the very moment the attorney enters the courtroom. The role of the juror as detective emerges and attorneys, clients, and witnesses are carefully scrutinized for additional information.

---

[15] M. Fishbein & I. Ajzen, Belief, Attitude, Intention and Behavior 73 (Addison-Wesley Publishing Co., 1975).

[16] J. DeVito, Communicology 428 (Harper & Row, 2d ed. 1982).

Voir dire, therefore, is extremely important from the standpoint of impression formation relating to credibility. One specialist in communication comments:

> The most important part of the jury selection process may not be the actual selection itself, but the impression that the advocate makes on the jurors . . . since the jury will usually first be introduced to the attorneys during this process, that jury will get some impression of them during voir dire.[17]

Generally, the more credible the source the more persuasive his appeals are to the receiver (Principle 13). It is important for the attorney to realize that all communication, verbal, vocal, and nonverbal, is self-reflective. All communication indicates something about the speaker to the receiver. Therefore, the attorney should examine the components of source credibility so that he can understand the implications of the impression his communication behaviors convey.

One communication scholar noted: "It is important to recognize not only that others have some impressions concerning your credibility but also to understand what these impressions are. Only by understanding these impressions and evaluations will we be in a position to change them in the direction we wish."[18]

Attorneys often receive feedback from peers regarding how they are perceived. This feedback, although interesting, does not adequately provide the attorney with an understanding of how he would be viewed by the general public. It is invaluable to receive feedback from a mock jury or the actual jury following the trial. This is the first step towards increasing his persuasiveness as a speaker. The speaker must first know how he is perceived. Once he has this information, he can adjust or modify his behavior to produce a resultant change in the perception. For example, if an attorney identifies that he is perceived as intimidating to the jurors, he can then examine his behavior to determine what specifically is projecting this image. Characteristics which are often perceived as intimidating include: an overly loud voice, harshly formal attire, invading the space of the jurors, abrupt speech patterns, pointing at jurors or others in the courtroom, a large body structure (height and/or weight), and excessive eye contact (staring). To alter the perception of

---

[17] R. McGaffey, *Communication Strategies and Research Needs in Selecting Juries* in COMMUNICATION STRATEGIES IN THE PRACTICE OF LAWYERING, 1983 CONFERENCE PROCEEDINGS 265 (Speech Communication Ass'n, R. Matlon & R. Crawford eds. 1983).

[18] DEVITO, *supra* note 16, at 428.

intimidation, the attorney can begin by changing specific behavior patterns to determine if they produce an overall change in the jury's perception of him.

COMMENT: It cannot be stressed enough that understanding yourself and how others perceive you is the key to becoming a persuasive speaker. Any method from videotape feedback to group seminars which will provide a higher awareness of oneself is very beneficial. Only through conscious understanding of skills and behaviors can one change, alter, or improve.

One particular experiment was illustrative of the area of communicator credibility.[19] Subjects read one of four messages in which the source of the message was variously attributed to Robert Oppenheimer, a high credibility source, or *Pravda*, a low credibility source. (The credibility of these sources was determined on a pretest questionnaire). The high credibility source was responsible for a net opinion change of 23%. The low credibility source produced only a 6.6% net opinion change.

Other researchers discovered that a highly credible source produced more opinion change (specifically, a change in attitude toward a more lenient treatment of juvenile delinquents) than a low credibility source.[20]

§ 3.10 —Expertness

Expertness (expertise) is an important component of source credibility. Traditionally, an expert has been defined as a person who is the source of valid assertions,[21] or has been regarded as someone who knows the correct stand on an issue.[22] Expertness enhances the attorney's persuasive

[19] Hovland & Weiss, *The Influence of Source Credibility on Communication Effectiveness*, 15 PUB. OPIN. Q. 635–650 (1951).

[20] Kelman & Hovland, *"Restatement" of the Communicator in Delayed Measurement of Opinion Change*, 48 J. ABNORM. & SOC. PSYCHOLOGY 327–385 (1953).

[21] *See, e.g.,* C. HOVLAND, I. JANIS & H. KELLY, COMMUNICATION AND PERSUASION (Yale University Press, 1953).

[22] W. McGuire, *The Nature of Attitudes and Attitude Change* in 3 THE HANDBOOK OF SOCIAL PSYCHOLOGY (Addison-Wesley Publishing Co., G. Unczey & E. Aronson eds. 1969).

impact. It has been theorized that:

> To the extent that counsel is able to develop perceived expertise in the eyes of the venireman (specifically through a demeanor of confidence, efficiency, and moderate display of knowledge) his persuasive impact will be enhanced; however, emphasis on recondite points of law or a pedantic display of legal expertise may alienate the venireman by a loss of perceived similarity.[23]

Three elements enter into the perception of expertness: (1) experience, (2) "floating competence", and (3) intelligence. The higher the perception of experience, the greater the attribution of expertness. We associate experience with knowledge although this is not always a correct assumption. "Floating competence" refers to the assumption that if a person is competent in one area, he will also be competent in other areas as well. Intelligence, our third element, is also a necessary component in the perception of expertness.

The jury must perceive the attorney as knowing his case and representing the interests of his client in a competent and intelligent manner. For this reason, more senior attorneys may have a built-in advantage in credibility impression formation with the juror. Since the senior attorney or the partner in the large law firm is thought to have had more experience, the perception conveyed to the jury is one of more expertise than the junior or younger attorney. The important consideration is that we are still talking about perception. Therefore, the inexperienced attorney need only alter his communication behavior pattern to increase the perception of credibility.

The senior attorney may, because of his higher credibility rating with the jury, have more influence over the jury. His analysis and method of case presentation may be seen as more highly credible by virtue of the fact that his longer experience in the courtroom setting has given him more knowledge of how things should be done. The jury may be inclined to be more receptive to the more experienced attorney's approach. A sound element with regard to expertness is what we are referring to as "floating competence."

While the attorney may well appreciate the fact that competence in one area does not equate with competence in another area, the fact of the

---

[23] R. Bluck & B. Sales, *Persuasion During Voir Dire* in PSYCHOLOGY IN THE LEGAL PROCESS 47–51 (Halstead Press, B. Sales ed. 1977).

matter is that juries are not so discriminating. As one communication scholar states:

> " . . . people often do not make the distinction between areas of competence. Thus, a person who is thought competent in politics will often be thought competent in general and will thus be perceived when talking on health or physical education."[24]

The same pheonomenon exists in the legal setting. A juror may automatically assume that an attorney who is particularly successful in handling one type of case will also be expert in other types of cases.

Perceived intelligence, our third element, also adds to the attorney's credibility rating with the juror. "The more intelligent and knowledgeable a speaker is thought to be, the more the speaker will be perceived as credible, and the more likely it is that he will be believed."[25]

§ 3.11 —Homophyly

Another element of the attorney's credibility with the jurors is the judgment that the jurors make of the attorney in terms of perceived homophyly. Homophyly, or perceived similarity with the communicator, is an essential element of source credibility.

The degree to which the receiver can identify with the source, see the source as he sees himself, the more likely it is that the receiver will reach a positive evaluation of the communicator. Communication Principle 9: People are more easily influenced by others they perceive as similar to themselves, is the essence of homophyly. In the criminal trial setting, perceived similarity of attitudes was examined by researchers.[26] The results of the study indicated that the more dissimilar the attitudes of the defendant and the juror, the more likely the defendant was to be found guilty and the longer his prison sentence tended to be. In addition, a dissimilar defendant was found to be less attractive to the juror than a defendant with attitudes similar to those of the juror.

---

[24] DEVITO, *supra* note 16, at 430.

[25] *Id*.

[26] Griffin & Jackson, *Simulated Jury Decisions: The Influence of Jury-Defendant Attitude Similarity-Dissimilarity*, 1 SOC. BEHAV. & PERSONALITY 1–7 (1973); *See also* DEVITO, *supra* note 16, at 430.

§ 3.12 —Prestige

Prestige is related to status considerations such as socioeconomic position and occupation and can influence the receiver's perception of the source's credibility. For example, a person's socioeconomic level is generally regarded as an achieved status.[27] The higher the socioeconomic level, the more status and prestige is conferred on the individual. This is significant as some research has shown that a high socioeconomic status individual may be perceived as less blameworthy than a lower socioeconomic status person in a criminal trial.

Socioeconomic status (prestige) is an important consideration in jury verdicts. The bias which appears to be the most important single extralegal factor associated with jury deliberation is that of socioeconomic levels. One researcher investigated the effect of socioeconomic status in an analysis of court records from Montgomery County, Pennsylvania (for the time period January 1965 through May 1967).[28] The research "matched" 50 not guilty verdicts with 50 guilty verdicts. The cases were matched according to age, sex, race, and offense of the defendants. Each defendant was then scored on the NORC Prestige Scale for occupational status to determine a social prestige rating. The results reinforce the importance of understanding socioeconomic status in the trial situation. In 41 of the 50 sets, or 82% of the matches, the jury that voted to convict the defendant had a larger prestige difference with the defendant than jurors who had voted to acquit. The disparity between the socioeconomic status of jurors and defendants was a significant factor. Regardless of whether the defendant's socioeconomic status rating was high or low, jurors who shared the same socioeconomic status rating with him were more likely to vote for acquittal. Jurors who had a different socioeconomic status than the defendant were more likely to vote to convict.

Certain occupations also carry with them more status and prestige. The jurors' perception of the attorney's client or the attorney's witness can be affected by the prestige of the client's (or witness') occupation.

---

[27] Gleason & Harris, *Group Discussion and Defendant's Socioeconomic Status as Determinants of Judgments by Simulated Jurors*, 6 J. App. Soc. Psychology 186–191 (1976).

[28] Adler, *Socioeconomic Factors Affecting Jury Verdicts*, 3 N.Y.U. Rev. L. & Soc. Change 1–10 (1973).

§ 3.13 —Trustworthiness

The importance of having the jury trust the attorney is obvious. If the jury does not perceive the attorney as trustworthy, everything the attorney says during the trial, all the evidence he presents, and the testimony of his witnesses, will be suspect.[29]

One nationally-known trial attorney wrote of the importance of trust when he described his dealings with the jury who would decide the fate of a law enforcement officer accused of killing a fellow officer. He felt that the jury believed that his client was guilty.

> The jury trusted me, I thought. They were open, willing to discuss their feelings; we were talking as if we were a group of friends, now, unashamed of our frankness in this public place about private things, but trust creates the responsibility to be trustworthy, and should I betray them after they had trusted, they would mob me in horrible unison, me and Cantrell. I had not practiced law very long before I had learned the first truth of a courtroom—never lie to a jury. They are by far brighter with their twelve lives than I with my one lifetime's experiences. There is a composite wisdom in a jury that can be trusted if lawyers could only learn to tell the truth.
>
> . . . Perhaps my acceptance of people prejudiced against my client, my being open with them and, consequently, them with me, had provided Cantrell with the presumption of innocence after all. There can be no more important function of voir dire in a free society.[30]

Early studies in communication credibility at Yale in the 1950's substantiated the importance of trust for a communicator. In one seminal study, subjects were presented with communications on four different topics: (1) the advisability of selling antihistamines without a prescription; (2) whether the steel industry was responsible for the 1950's steel shortage; (3) how television affected movie theatres; and (4) how practical it was to build atomic-powered submarines.

Subjects were then presented with either a high credibility source for the communication (such as the *New England Journal of Biology and Medicine* for the antihistamine topic) or a low-credibility source (such as a monthly pictorial magazine). The communications attributed to highly

---

[29] Proceedings of the 1980 Conference of the Institute for Study of the Trial 26 (K. Taylor ed.) (Orlando, Florida, March 21–22, 1980).

[30] G. Spence & A. Polk, Gunning for Justice 403 (Doubleday, 1982).

credible sources were more persuasive. Subjects were more likely to change their views when the communication was attributed to a trustworthy source and less likely to change their views when it came from an untrustworthy source.

In this study, subjects were also given a factual quiz after the communication.[31] Interestingly, subjects did not remember any more information from the untrustworthy source than from the trustworthy sources. It would seem then that perceived trustworthiness affects the acceptance of the communicator's conclusions but does not influence the actual recall of the specific information or arguments.

This conclusion has special application in the courtroom. In jury deliberations, the jurors may be unable to recall arguments and details of the case, but they will be more inclined to *accept the conclusions* of the attorney whom they perceive as trustworthy. Thus, the attorney must be careful that he, in all aspects of his presentation, be perceived as trustworthy. The conclusions of the 1980 Conference of the Institute for Study of the Trial noted:

> In a legal proceeding, it is important that an advocate be concerned not only with his/her own credibility but with that of all the sources on which he/she may draw. If any source's trustworthiness appears to be suspect, that source can do much to damage a case even if he/she speaks the truth.[32]

Unfortunately, lawyers as a group are perceived as not as trustworthy as individuals in other occupations. One study researched this area and found as follows:

> A survey was taken several years ago to determine how persons in certain occupations and professions were perceived. Respondents were asked to rank the occupational categories on truthfulness and competence. Lawyers scored higher in competence than in truthfulness. They were ranked third on competence behind physicians and dentists. But they fell to ninth in truthfulness, lower than psychiatrists and college professors but just above policemen.[33]

It is very important that the attorney does what he tells the jury he plans to do and proves what he tells them he will prove. Consistency

---

[31] Hovland & Weiss, *The Influence of Source Credibility on Communication Effectiveness*, 15 Pub. Opin. Q. 635–650 (1951).

[32] *See supra* note 29, at 26.

[33] K. Taylor, R. Buchanan & D. Strawn, *supra* note 2, at 43.

becomes a key factor in being perceived as trustworthy. Trustworthy people are predictable people. As one communication scholar indicated:

> Public opinion polls have often indicated that Americans don't really trust lawyers. They expect "dirty tricks." I think that if the lawyer says something will happen and it doesn't happen, something will be proved and it is not, or the law will be explained one way and it is explained by the judge in a different way, the jurors' belief in the trustworthiness of the advocate will be damaged. That is why it makes strategic sense to bring out as soon as possible any weaknesses in your case, especially if they are inevitable, so that the jury will not only be prepared, but will not lose trust when those weaknesses appear.[34]

§ 3.14 —Objectivity and fairness

Two prominent criminal attorneys, F. Lee Bailey and Henry Rothblatt, recognized the importance of a positive perception of the attorney's fairness, when they wrote:

> Impress the jurors with your sincerity and fairness. Project yourself into the mind of each of them. Would you react favorably to a person who did not demonstrate complete fairness? If you, as defense counsel, do not appear sincere and fair from the very start a jury may never trust you.[35]

Sincerity and honesty are two of the most important and admired traits that people look for in another individual.[36] It is of great importance that the attorney be perceived as honest and fair in the eyes of the jury.

In addition to fairness, the attorney should be conscious of the impact of his perceived objectivity during the case. In discussing the role of persuasion during voir dire, two researchers commented on the implications of objectivity during this stage of the trial:

> To the extent that they view the attorney as being objective and un-

---

[34] R. McGaffey, *Communication Strategies and Research Needs in Selecting Juries* in COMMUNICATION STRATEGIES IN THE PRACTICE OF LAWYERING 269 (Speech Communication Ass'n., R. Matlon & R. Crawford eds. 1983).

[35] F. BAILEY & H. ROTHBLATT, FUNDAMENTALS OF CRIMINAL ADVOCACY 83 (Lawyer's Co-operative Publishing Co., 1974).

[36] Anderson, *Ratings of Likeableness, Meaningfulness, and Likeableness Variances for 555 Common Personality Traits Arranged in Order of Decreasing Likeableness*, 9 J. PERSONALITY & SOC. PSYCHOLOGY 272–279 (1968).

> biased, the veniremen should be more receptive to his persuasion. Therefore, counsel must be cautious in any persuasive attempt during voir dire since juror awareness of such an intent could damage his valence: arguments should be couched in terms of "clear evidence will show that . . ." or "The prosecution must prove beyond a reasonable doubt . . . Evidence that falls short of that dictates that the defendant must be acquitted . . ." The Constitution of the United States of our American system of justice demands this result.[37]

If a juror feels the attorney has an ulterior motive or is "up to something," he is less likely to be believed than the attorney who presents himself honestly. One authority concludes:

> An individual's motives or intentions are particularly important in determining credibility. The salesperson who says all the right things about a product is often doubted because his or her intentions are perceived as selfish; credibility is therefore low. The salesperson is less believable than a consumer advocate who evaluates a product with no motives of personal gain.[38]

An interesting application of objectivity in the courtroom was discovered in a study conducted by several psychologists.[39] The study concluded that if an individual admits to the receiver that he has a bias, the admission may actually enhance his credibility with that receiver. If a waiter, for example, discloses to a customer that the red snapper is not very good that evening, his credibility and trustworthiness will increase. In this instance he has admitted a weakness willingly and has demonstrated that he is not trying to hide anything.[40] One communications scholar, noted that this idea should apply to the attorney as well. The perception of an honest bias toward one's client should help the juror's perception of the attorney. Some attorneys try to make it very obvious that they like their client, believing that the jury's affection for them may be transferred to their client.[41]

---

[37] R. Blunk & B. Sales, *Persuasion During Voir Dire* in PSYCHOLOGY IN THE LEGAL PROCESS 47–51 (Halstead Press, B. Sales ed. 1977).

[38] DEVITO, *supra* note 16, at 430.

[39] Mills & Aronson, *Opinion Change as a Function of the Communicator's Attractiveness and Desire to Influence*, 173 J. PERSONALITY & SOC. PSYCHOLOGY 1 (1965).

[40] R. CIALDINI, INFLUENCE: HOW AND WHY PEOPLE AGREE TO THINGS (William Morrow & Co., 1984).

[41] MCGAFFEY, *supra* note 34.

§ 3.15 —Dynamism

The final element in the determination of the source's credibility with the receiver is the speaker's dynamism. As we stated earlier, dynamism represents the degree to which the speaker is forceful, emphatic, bold, or active during the communication event.[42]

We have all listened to speakers whose delivery was captivating and whose style was energetic and lively. We have also listened to speakers whose presentation style was listless, boring, and unenthusiastic. In general, a receiver forms a much more positive impression of the energetic and lively speaker. The lively speaker's dynamic style adds to his perception of credibility with the audience. History records a long list of dynamic speakers—Winston Churchill, John Kennedy, Ronald Reagan, and Martin Luther King, to name a few. The quality of energy both captivates and motivates an audience to respond in a favorable manner. Shy, introverted, and soft-spoken individuals are perceived as less persuasive than an extroverted and forceful individual. Generally, the more dynamic a speaker, the more credible he is perceived to be.[43] The extroverted and energetic speaker is perceived to be more open and honest.

Attorneys who exhibit obvious discomfort during these presentations tend to have less credibility with the jury. When we are asked to defend a position that is not consistent with our own beliefs, our delivery and approach to the communication may be of a less positive nature. Our lack of belief in the subject may cause the speaker to be less fluent, and be prone to vocalized pauses ("uh" and "um"), all of which tends to convey a less confident and skillful presentation. Jurors will interpret this halting, stumbling delivery as a negative factor. The simple translation is that the person does not know what he is talking about.

One group of researchers conducted an experiment where a subject was given information known to be counter to his beliefs.[44] The subject was then asked to write a response supporting the information. The subjects who wrote supporting articles known to be counter to their beliefs took longer to compose the articles and made more grammatical errors

---

[42] E. Bettinghaus, Persuasion Communication 107 (Holt, Rinehart and Winston, 1968).

[43] DeVito, *supra* note 16, at 431.

[44] Greenberg & Tannenbaum, *Communicator Performance Under Cognitive Stress*, 39 Journalism Q. 169–178 (1962).

than subjects who were asked to support positions that were consistent with their own beliefs.

This is consistent with Communication Principle 15. People are influenced by the way the message is structured and delivered. Word choice, main points, the order in which ideas are presented, rhetorical questions, and many other factors influence the perception of credibility. The structure and delivery of a message represent to the jurors an extension of the person. The attorney is additionally assessed based on his ability to "package" his thoughts in a manner that is most persuasive for the jurors.

§ 3.16 Checklist: Credibility considerations

As the preceding sections have indicated, the three dimensions of source credibility—expertise, trustworthiness, and dynamism—are important aspects in impression formation. The individual juror will, based on his perceptions of the attorney (or witness or client), come to a determination of the lawyer's credibility. It is of obvious importance that the perception of credibility reached by the juror be a positive perception since people are more easily influenced by those they perceive as credible (Principle 13).

The attorney should familiarize himself with the various elements of source credibility. He should then examine his own credibility by asking himself questions from the juror's point of view such as:

___1. Are you competent to speak on the issue? How do we know you are competent? What evidence is there attesting to your knowledge and intelligence?

___2. Are you honest and of good character? Can you be trusted to present the evidence and argument fairly and fully? What evidence is there for concluding that you are fair, honest, and of good character?

___3. Are your intentions selfish or are they to help the audience? Do you have ulterior motives for arguing the position you are advocating? If so, how does this influence what you are saying and what you want the audience to do? What evidence is there for your good intentions?

___4. Are you personable? Are you optimistic? Do you seem to have yourself together? What evidence is there for us to conclude that you are in fact together?

__5. Are you dynamic? Are you assertive and emphatic? Or are you withdrawn, hesitant, and nonassertive? What evidence is there for your dynamism?[45]

Table 3–1 which follows identifies factors which affect communicator credibility where a student is attempting to persuade others not to use drugs.[46] The table lists power, competence, trustworthiness, good will, idealism, similarity, and dynamism as important persuasive factors. Most importantly, in their column labeled "How to do it" they identify what the student will have to do in order to "link" to his audience. The attorney can follow the same process in developing an opening statement or closing argument. The critical questions center around how does one display power and competence in such a way that the jurors will form an accurate perception of the projected characteristics.

---

[45] DeVito, *supra* note 16, at 432. From Communicology: An Introduction to the Study of Communication, 2d edition, by Joseph A. DeVito. Copyright © 1982 by Joseph A. DeVito. Reprinted with permission from Harper & Row.

[46] Adapted from R. Hart, G. Friedrich & W. Brooks, Public Communication (Harper & Row, 1975), as appeared in P. Zimbardo, E. Ebbesen & C. Maslach, Influencing Attitudes and Changing Behavior 60–61 (Addison-Wesley Publishing Co., 2d ed. 1977). Excerpt on page 95 from Public Communication by R. Hart, G. Friedrich and W. Brooks, Copyright © 1975 by R. Hart, G. Friedrich and W. Brooks. Reprinted with permission from Harper & Row.

Table 3–1
Factors Affecting Communicator Credibility: A Specific Example of a Student Attempting to Persuade Others Not to Use Drugs

Conceptual Factors	Examples of Assets	Examples of Liabilities	How to Do It
Power	Not much. I might be able to show them that my speech could save lives.	They see me as just another person in class with no special power to reward and punish.	Dramatize the horrors of drug addiction; back it up with plenty of painful examples.
Competence	They know from Bob's comment in class that I made the dean's list last semester.	I've never told them about my interest in drug addiction. Could be starting from scratch with most of them.	Mention early in speech about my work with the Crisis Center. Get that *Time* article.
Trustworthiness	Some of them know I really followed through on the group assignment. They shouldn't feel that I'd trick them.	This will be a new topic for me. Most unlike my last speech on the campus election scandal.	Don't have much to worry about here. Might remind them that I stuck with them when the professor tried to spring a quiz on us!
Good will	My strong suit. By now the group knows that I'm majoring in social work—who could hate a social worker?	No problem as long as I stay with hard drugs. Can't come down hard on pot.	Many of them smoke, so I'd better steer clear of the marijuana issue or they'll see me as caring more about preaching than about them.

Conceptual Factors	Examples of Assets	Examples of Liabilities	How to Do It
Idealism	They know that I'm always up in the clouds and generally aspire to the same things they do.	Got to be careful not to get too carried away with the moral stuff. Stick to the "fully functioning human being" idea.	Should probably stress our common goals early in the speech before I mention drugs.
Similarity	I've been in class with them all semester. They know I dress and talk like most of them.	Could be a problem if I come on like Ms. Know-it-All. Have to steer clear of my religious views on the subject with these heathens!	Better tie this in with Claire's speech on legalizing pot. This should build more common ground between me and them.
Dynamism	My biggie! They know that they can't shut me up when I get committed to a topic.	No Problem! (As long as I remember not to talk too fast!)	Pace yourself, baby, pace yourself.

§ 3.17 Demonstrated credibility

Demonstrated credibility is the credibility the attorney "earns" during his encounters with others. For communicators who do not possess a strong "instant credibility" (or prior image) with their receivers, the extent of credibility earned becomes very important.[47]

For example, the speaker's delivery and speaking style can affect the receiver's perception of the communicator's credibility.[48] As we stated

[47] *See infra* § 3.18, *Instant credibility*.

[48] *See, e.g.*, Miller & Hewgill, *The Effect of Variations in Nonfluency on Audience Ratings of Source Credibility*, 50 Q. J. SPEECH 36–44 (1964); Serenko & Hawkins, *The Ef-*

earlier, a stumbling, and awkward presentation can leave the receiver viewing the speaker as less than competent and, therefore, less credible. The effect on a source's image of powerful speech over powerless speech has also been demonstrated.[49]

Physical appearance also affects a speaker's demonstrated credibility. A landmark study was conducted on the effect of attractiveness on source credibility.[50] A young woman was dressed attractively for one presentation and dressed to look unattractive for a second presentation. In the situation where she was dressed attractively, she was judged more positively and was rated more persuasive than when she was not dressed attractively.

One communication scholar offered the following observations concerning the process of earning credibility with the receiver.

> Generally, we perceive as credible or believable speakers we like rather than speakers we do not like. And, it seems, we like speakers who have what we commonly refer to as a "pleasing personality." We believe speakers who are friendly and pleasant rather than speakers who are unfriendly and unpleasant. Positive and forward-looking speakers are seen as more credible than negative and backward-looking speakers. Perhaps we reason that they have gotten themselves together and so are in a better position to know what is right and what is wrong. We would be leery of accepting marital advice from an unhappily married couple, perhaps for a similar reason. If they cannot solve their own problems, we reasonably doubt their ability to help us.[51]

Although the attorney can earn or demonstrate a positive image to the jury, he must also keep in mind that any prior reputation he has with the jury (his "instant" credibility) will interact with his demonstrated credibility to create a total picture in the juror's mind.

---

fects of Variations in Speakers' Nonfluency Upon Audience Ratings of Attitude Toward the Speech Topic and Speaker's Credibility, 34 SPEECH MONOGRAPHS 63 (1967).

[49] *See infra* § 3.20, *Establishing credibility through speaking style*.

[50] Mills & Aronson, *Opinion Change as a Function of the Communicator's Attractiveness and Desire to Influence*, 1 J. PERSONALITY & SOC. PSYCHOLOGY 73–77 (1965). *See also* Widgery & Webster, *The Effects of Physical Attractiveness Upon Perceived Initial Credibility*, 4 MICH. SPEECH J. 4–15 (1969).

[51] DEVITO, *supra* note 16, at 431.

§ 3.18 "Instant" credibility

Some communicators have "instant" credibility with their audience just as some attorneys have instant credibility with their jurors. Receivers frequently form images of a speaker without ever having met the speaker.[52] Instant credibility can, of course, be either positive or negative depending on the public image of the attorney.

A noted communication scholar has described instant credibility, or prior ethos, as including "prior reputation of the source, the endorsements and introduction he receives, his behavior and appearance up to the time of the inception of the message."[53] In other words, a juror can form an impression of the attorney's credibility without ever having had direct prior experience with the attorney. "The image that exists in advance of a given communication is based upon judgments about the source derived from 'experience' *associated* with the source."[54]

This scholar theorized that a receiver bases his perceptions of a communicator's image prior to the communication event on four factors.[55] First, how much direct or vicarious experience has the receiver had with the source? The receiver may actually know the source and have had first-hand experiences with him. But, knowledge of the source's activities (vicarious experiences) also allows a receiver to form impressions about the source's credibility.

Secondly, the communicator's image prior to the communication is affected by how much information is known about the source's referential class memberships, such as education, age, and group memberships. As a noted expert pointed out:

> The knowledge that a speaker is liberal, an Elk, a labor union leader, black, and happily married with three children certainly creates a different expectation than conservative, a Rotarian, president of a small, privately owned company, white, thrice married with no children.[56]

Third, a positive endorsement from a respected source can positively affect a speaker's image with the audience.

---

[52] Annis & Meier, *The Induction of Opinion Through Suggestion by Means of "Planted Content",* 5 J. Speech Psychology 65–81 (1934).

[53] K. Andersen, Persuasion 220 (Allyn & Bacon, Inc., 1971).

[54] Andersen, *supra* note 53, at 224.

[55] *Id.*

[56] Andersen, *supra* note 53, at 225.

Fourth, having received exposure from the print or electronic media will add to the source's perceived credibility by lending legitimacy to the speaker and his position on the topic.

The effect of a favorable prior image helps to enhance the persuasiveness of the communicator's position in many speaking situations.[57] Thus, the attorney who has positive "instant" credibility with his jurors is a step ahead in the trial persuasion process.

§ 3.19 Nonverbal aspects of credibility

An attorney's nonverbal behavior can have a definite impact on how persuasive he is with the jurors. This follows Communication Principle 16: The perception of credibility is influenced by personal attributes. Nonverbal cues are interpreted as indicators of the attorney's credibility. If the attorney is fidgeting, nervous, and avoids eye contact, for example, he will not be seen as highly credible. In fact, his nervous mannerisms will most likely be interpreted by the jury as meaning the attorney is trying to hide something or that he is not being totally honest.

Important, too, is the factor that jurors tend to place confidence in their abilities to judge the nonverbal cues they observe accurately. In one study, observers indicated that they had 58% confidence in the evaluations they had made of a stranger's nonverbal cues.[58]

There are particular types of nonverbal behavior that tend to enhance an attorney's credibility with his jurors. Generally, attorneys who are more fluent, confident, outgoing, and seem more self-assured are regarded by observers as more credible and thus more believable.

Using a simulated courtroom, one study examined the impact of gaze aversion and gaze maintenance on the credibility of a witness who was testifying.[59] The results verified the importance of eye contact. A witness who maintained eye contact with the target of his communication was perceived as more credible. Also important was the finding that "witnesses who averted their [the juror's] gaze were perceived to be less credible and, ultimately, the defendant for whom they testified was

[57] Andersen & Clevenger, *A Summary of Experimental Research in Ethos*, 30 Speech Monographs 59–78 (1963).

[58] Hocking, Miller & Fontes, *Videotape in the Courtroom: Witness Deception*, 14 Trial 52–55 (1978).

[59] Hemsley & Doob, *The Effect of Looking Behavior on Perceptions of a Communicator's Credibility*, 8 J. App. Soc. Psychology 136–144 (1978).

judged as more likely to be guilty."[60]

Other researchers found that the more persuasive speaker was the one who had more eye contact with his audience, more vocal variety and inflection, more volume, a faster rate of delivery, more expressions, and seemed confident and more relaxed.[61] The attorney should be aware of these findings and the resultant impact on his credibility with the jury.

Table 3–2 identifies nonverbal cues which are perceived as credible or persuasive behavior when decoded by the receiver.[62] It also lists which nonverbal cues are seen as deceptive cues when decoded by the receiver. When reading this table, the attorney should consider these cues as being decoded by the jurors in a trial situation.

COMMENT: General guidelines for appropriate nonverbal behaviors include:

(1) Use good eye contact;
(2) Use animated facial gestures;
(3) Display sincere interest in others;
(4) Keep normal to close distance;
(5) Use excessive vocal cues;
(6) Appear relaxed and confident.[63]

---

[60] HEMSLEY & DOOB, *supra* note 59, at 136.

[61] Mehrabian & Williams, *Nonverbal Concomitant of Perceived and Intended Persuasiveness*, 13 J. PERSONALITY & SOC. PSYCHOLOGY 37–58 (1969). *See also* Zuckerman, DeFrank, Hall, Larrance & Rosenthal, *Facial and Vocal Cues of Deception and Honesty*, 16 J. EXPERIM. SOC. PSYCHOLOGY 378–396 (1979).

[62] Miller & Burgoon, *Factors Affecting Assessments of Witness Credibility*, in THE PSYCHOLOGY OF THE COURTROOM 176–177 (Academic Press, Kerr and Bray eds. 1982). Reprinted with permission.

[63] L. MALANDRO, THE PSYCHOLOGY OF A TRIAL 86 (Malandro Communication Inc., 1982).

Table 3–2
Nonverbal Cues Perceived as Persuasive/Credible or Deceptive

Nonverbal Code	Cues Decoded as: Persuasive/Credible	Cues Decoded as: Deceptive
Kinesics	More eye contact	Less eye contact
(Body movement; gestures; postural orientation)	More facial activity; more involvement	Less seriousness; less empathy, more smiling
	More gestures; more illustrators	Excessive gestures
	Moderate relaxation	More tension and anxiety; more postural shifts
Proxemics (Space and territory)	Body less directly facing audience for males	
Haptics (Use of touch)	Closer distances; less self-manipulations and adaptors	Less self-grooming
Vocalics (Voice characteristics)	High volume; moderate to slightly faster speaking rate; more fluency; more intonation and pitch variety; lower pitch; more vocal involvement; conversational delivery style	More nonfluencies
Overall	Use of General American Dialect; positive violations of expectations (e.g., dressing unappealingly but conveying effective verbal message)	Greater reliance on voice than face and on face than body

§ 3.20 Establishing credibility through speaking style

The way in which an idea is presented to a jury is an important determinant of the attorney's credibility with the jury. Vocal cues and speaking styles play a major role in how the jury will react to the information being presented throughout the trial.

Competent information is conveyed primarily by the vocal characteristics of the speaker.[64] Credibility is thus directly related to vocal cues.

Nonfluencies or lack of fluency in speaking style have also been found to be related to the credibility of the speaker. Communication researchers have determined that nonfluencies such as "ah," superfluous repetition of a word, and stuttering influenced the perceptions of credibility in a negative manner.[65] Judgments of the speaker's competence and dynamism decreased when nonfluencies were prevalent. Thus, the credibility of the speaker was negatively affected.

The nonverbal area of voice tone has also been found to affect credibility. In one study subjects attempted to relate the vocal cues that senders use when trying to be more persuasive.[66] Vocal characteristics that tended to be more persuasive and credible were found to include a more expressive, more natural, more pleasant, and more warm sounding voice.

Credibility is also affected by the speech style used by the speaker. "Powerful speech," for example, has an effect on the impressions that are formed of a witness in a trial.[67] Perceptions of a witness's competence, intelligence, likability, and believability are the result of the vocal cues of powerful or powerless speech.[68]

The speed of delivery used by the attorney in the courtroom has an impact on the impression he makes with the jury.[69] One attorney once

---

[64] Hart & Brown, *Interpersonal Information Conveyed by the Content and Vocal Aspects of Speech*, 41 SPEECH MONOGRAPHS 371–380 (1971).

[65] Sereno & Hawkins, *The Effects of Variations in Speakers' Nonfluency Upon Audience Ratings of Attitude Toward the Speech Topic and Speakers' Credibility*, 34 SPEECH MONOGRAPHS 58 *et seq.* (1967).

[66] Hall, *Voice Tone and Persuasion*, 38 J. PERSONALITY & SOC. PSYCHOLOGY 924–934 (1980).

[67] Conley, O'Barr & Lind, *The Power of Language: Presentational Style in the Courtroom*, 6 DUKE L.J. 1375–1399 (1978).

[68] Goodman & Loftus, *Social Science Looks at Witness Examination*, 20 TRIAL 56 (1984). *See also supra* § 1.85.

[69] *See* O'Barr & Conley, *When a Juror Watches a Lawyer*, 3 BARRISTER 8-11, 33 (1976).

noted that "the faster talker is generally more favorably regarded by his listener. In addition, the listener tends to learn from the fast talker."[70] A speaker with a faster rate of delivery is more persuasive and is also seen as more intelligent, knowledgeable, and objective.[71] This does not mean that the attorney should rush through his presentation, going as quickly as he possibly can. What it does mean is that given the listener's ability to comprehend about 200 words per minute (the average speaking rate is between 125 and 190 words per minute), a faster rate of delivery will enhance the attorney's credibility with the jury.[72] A brisker, faster delivery leaves the juror with the impression of the attorney as confident, in control, and capable. Research has found that the combination of rate, pitch, and vocal quality lead to a perception of greater credibility for the speaker.[73] On the other hand, speaking at too rapid a rate could cause jurors to lose track of the argument or just quit listening.

A communication specialist attempted to verify the results of this laboratory research by examining transcripts from thirty-eight criminal trials. The results of his analysis indicated that successful prosecutors used language differently than prosecutors who lost cases:

> . . . prosecution attorneys who secured convictions spoke longer, asked more questions referring directly to the witness, and made more indicative statements than did their less successful counterparts. Prosecution attorneys who failed to secure convictions used more polite forms, more hyper-correct grammar, and more conditional statements than did those who succeeded in securing convictions.[74]

In addition, successful defense attorneys used more abstract language (perhaps in an effort to distance the accused from the crime), more legal jargon, and more ambiguous language.

Thus, speaking style does have an impact on the jurors' perception of

---

[70] Peskin, *Nonverbal Communication in the Courtroom. Part 3: Chronemics*, 3 TRIAL DIPL. J. 4 (1980).

[71] Miller, Maruyana, Beaver & Valore, *Speed of Speech and Persuasion*, 34 J. PERSONALITY & SOC. PSYCHOLOGY 615–624 (1976).

[72] M. KNAPP, ESSENTIALS OF NONVERBAL COMMUNICATION 218 (Holt, Rinehart and Winston, 1980). *See* also Andrews, *Exhibit A: Language*, 18 PSYCHOLOGY TODAY 30 (February 1984).

[73] Addington, *The Relationship of Selected Vocal Characteristics to Personality Perception*, 35 SPEECH MONOGRAPHS 492–503 (1968).

[74] Parkinson, *Verbal Behaviors and Courtroom Success*, 29 COM. EDUC. 29 (1981).

the attorney's credibility. It is important for the attorney to understand the various implications of speaking style on credibility.

II. Developing a Courtroom Image

§ 3.21 Attorney credibility in the courtroom

From the moment that the attorney first walks into the courtroom, the jurors are studying him, looking for clues upon which to base their assessment of the attorney's credibility. Since the jury usually first meets the attorney during the voir dire, the impression of the attorney begins during the process of jury selection.

> The voir dire is the first event, and this is the time when the first impression is made. The voir dire, of course, cannot be a substitute for the opening statement, but when the trial lawyer has completed the voir dire examination, the jurors have already developed their first-impression beliefs, and if the examination was successful they should firmly believe that counsel is an honest, sincere man who is frank and candid and talks straight from the shoulder.[75]

According to a noted psychologist, jurors wanted to know four things about the attorney in order to form an impression of him. First, they will ask "Do I like him?" Second, "Can I *trust* him to tell me the truth?" Third, they want to determine if the attorney is efficient and competent. Lastly, they will seek information about how confident and certain the attorney appears to be about his case.[76]

"Do I like him?" is an important question for jurors to answer in the affirmative. When we like someone, we tend to lean toward his positions, seeing ourselves as essentially similar to him. Liking an individual exerts a subtle but powerful influence on us. Thus, "If they like you, they unconsciously want you to win and will find it difficult to vote against you."[77] In fact, in a poll of actual jurors, the likability and skill of the attorney were judged the most important factors in the jurors' perception of the attorney.[78]

---

[75] A. Blunk & B. Sales, *Persuasion During Voir Dire*, in PSYCHOLOGY IN THE LEGAL PROCESS 42 (Halstead Press, B. Sales ed. 1977), quoting Wolfstone.

[76] Sannito, *Psychological Courtroom Strategies*, 4 TRIAL DIPL. J. 32–33 (1981).

[77] *Id.*, at 32.

[78] Sannito & Arnolds, *Jury Study Results: The Factors at Work*, 5 TRIAL DIPL. J. 8 (1982).

"Can I *trust* him to tell me the truth?" is another important issue for jurors to resolve. If jurors feel the attorney is being honest with them, their evaluation of his credibility is enhanced. According to research, sincerity and honesty are two personality traits most highly regarded in another person.[79]

If the attorney presents his case in an efficient and competent manner, his credibility is enhanced with the jury. Not only does the juror feel that the presentation is thorough and well-researched (and that they therefore know the essential elements of the case), but they also feel the client is receiving the best possible representation and protection of his interests.

Confidence is an important element to convey to the jurors. When the attorney conveys the impression that he is confident about his case, the jury also will tend to see the case as a stronger one. The attorney also leaves the jurors with a feeling that he is in control of his case and he is certain of his information. A hesitating, shaky presentation casts doubt on the attorney, his client, and his case as well.

In an interview with over 1,100 civil and criminal jurors who had served on juries in Maryland, one researcher found that the attributes listed *infra* § 3.32 were the elements most often related to a lawyer being perceived as credible.[80]

In addition, the lawyer should be aware of other cues that help the juror form impressions of his credibility. Loudness, for example, is related positively to perceived credibility.[81]

COMMENT: A word of caution is in order here: effective loudness is not akin to screaming and shouting at the maximum decibel level. Volume that conveys the impression that the attorney is in control, is confident, and knows what he is doing will increase the perceived credibility for the lawyer. The attorney should also keep in mind that researchers

---

[79] Anderson, *Ratings of Likeableness, Meaningfulness, and Likeableness Variances for 555 Common Personality Traits Arranged in Order of Decreasing Likeableness*, 9 J. Personality & Soc. Psychology 272–279 (1968).

[80] Cramer, *A View from the Jury Box*, 6 Litigation 3–4, 65–66 (1979), as presented in K. Taylor, R. Buchanan & D. Strawn, Communication Strategies for Trial Attorneys (Scott, Foresman and Co., 1984).

[81] Sannito, *Nonverbal Communication in the Courtroom*, 6 Trial Dipl. J. 28 (1983).

have found that both anger and contempt are expressed through increased vocal volume.[82]

Eye contact is also important to perceived credibility. Louis Nizer, offered the following advice to his fellow attorneys:

> It is an early opportunity to look each juror in the eye and by sincerity and earnestness make contact with him. It is interesting to observe the bland look on a juror's face when you begin, perhaps even a cynical smile, and how he is caught up in the drama of your recital, his face responding properly with varying emotions of sympathy or resentment as the arguments make inroads upon him. Finally, when you walk up and back, and his eyes follow and are riveted upon you, the persuasive effort has begun successfully.[83]

§ 3.22 Checklist: Jury evaluation of lawyers as credible communicators

As indicated in § 3.21, more than eleven hundred Maryland jurors were interviewed after their service in civil and criminal cases. These jurors gave high marks to lawyers who are professional, well-prepared, dynamic, and thorough.

- ____Professional
  - ____Careful preparation of evidence
  - ____Don't waste time
  - ____Have good command of case
- ____Well-prepared
  - ____Meticulous
  - ____Incisive
  - ____Enthusiastic about case
  - ____Concentrate on case
  - ____Mark documents as exhibits and introduce into evidence
- ____Dynamic
  - ____Have respect for and believe in client
  - ____Don't be too friendly with opposing counsel

---

[82] Costanzo, Mackel & Costanzo, *Voice Quality Profile and Perceived Emotion*, 16 J. Counseling Psychology 267–270 (1969).

[83] L. Nizer, My Life in Court 42 (Pyramid, 1961).

____Use language appropriate for courtroom
____Avoid slang, jargon and extreme informality

____Thorough
____Object vigorously
____Prepare clear and detailed opening statement
____Integrate evidence and jury instructions into closing argument

§ 3.23 Client credibility and its effect on verdict

Verdicts rendered by juries are a function of many different perceptions. Jurors always form judgments of the client during the trial. The more credible the client appears to the juror, the more likely the defendant is to receive a verdict favorable to him. Client credibility is a function of attributes of the client such as his attractiveness, similarity with jurors, and honesty and sincerity as judged through verbal, vocal, and nonverbal cues.

In one study, judges who had presided over actual criminal cases were asked whether they would have rendered the same decision their juries had reached.[84] The results of the survey indicated that in those cases where the judge and jury disagreed on the verdict, 11–14% of those disagreements could be attributed to the impression made by the defendant based upon his appearance.

Another study on the effect of attractiveness investigated the effect on the character of the parties on the jury's verdict.[85] The researchers reasoned that a socially successful (and thus attractive) person would be viewed more favorably by a juror than a person described to the jury as less successful (and therefore less attractive). The subjects in the study were presented with a negligent automobile homicide in which the defendant was described as either an attractive or an unattractive person in terms of his social characteristics.[86]

In another study, researchers attempted to determine the effect of attractiveness in terms of personal likability and not as a function of sympathy. Research indicated that a loving and warm defendant received a prison sentence almost three years shorter (6.52) years than a cold and

[84] H. KALVEN & H. ZEISEL, THE AMERICAN JURY (Little, Brown, 1966).

[85] Landy & Aronson, *The Influence of the Character of the Criminal and His Victim on Simulated Jurors*, 5 J. EXPERIM. SOC. PSYCHOLOGY 146 (1969).

[86] *See supra* § 1.72.

unapproachable defendant (9.22 years).[87]

One study was conducted concerning socially desirable characteristics and the effects of those characteristics on sentencing of defendants by mock juries.[88] Male and female mock jurors sentenced a defendant in a purse snatching case. The defendant was described as having only taken the victim's purse or as having beaten the victim as well as having taken the purse. In the process of attempting to escape from the police, the defendant was said to have suffered either no harm, moderate harm, or excessive harm. Not surprisingly, results indicated that the defendant who beat his victim was punished more severely than the defendant who only snatched the purse. In addition, the more severely hurt the defendant was in the escape attempt, the less severe was his sentence. These results point out the importance of social attractiveness in terms of the ultimate verdict or sentence.

Researchers investigated the effect of high status (attractiveness) and low status (unattractiveness) of defendants.[89] Jurors were individually asked to sentence the attractive and unattractive defendant. Individual jurors gave longer sentences to low status defendants but when the jurors met as a group (four to six jurors), the sentences rendered by the group were less severe for the low status individual (the discussion phase did not affect the sentence of the high status individual).

Credibility of the defendant appears to be enhanced when jurors perceived a similarity of attitudes between themselves and the defendant. One study presented mock jurors with different attitudinal orientations of a defendant. The versions are presented below.[90]

> *Version A:* He is described by the psychologist as a person with a firm belief in God, a strong allegiance to the American way of life, and as a person who feels that men cope with stress and financial matters better than do women. Further, the social worker characterizes him as a person who enjoys sports, dancing, and involvement

---

[87] Sigall & Landy, *Effects of the Defendant's Character and Suffering on Juridic Judgment*, 88 J. Soc. Psychology 149–150 (1972).

[88] W. Austin, E. Walster & E. Utne, *Equity and the Law: The Effect of a Harmdoer's "suffering in the act" on Liking and Assigned Punishment*, in Advances in Experimental Social Psychology (Academic Press, L. Berkowitz & E. Walster eds. 1976).

[89] Izzett & Leginski, *Group Discussion and the Influence of Defendant Characteristics in a Simulated Jury Setting*, 93 J. Soc. Psychology 271–279 (1974).

[90] Griffin & Jackson, *Simulated Jury Decisions: The Influence of Jury-Defendant Attitude Similarity-Dissimilarity*, 1 Soc. Behav. & Personality 3 (1973).

> in current social problems such as promoting the cause of public school racial integration. It was ascertained that he has no previous criminal record with the exception of one minor traffic violation.
>
> *Version B:* He is described by the psychologist as a person with a firm belief that there is no God, a negative opinion concerning the American way of life, and as a person convinced of the superiority of women in adjusting to stress and handling financial matters. Further, the social worker characterizes him as a person who does not enjoy such activities as dancing and sports, but is involved in current social problems such as a campaign to prevent public school racial integration. It was ascertained that he has no previous criminal record with the exception of one minor traffic violation.

Similar to the other studies on this subject, the more dissimilar the attitudes of the defendant and the juror, the more likely the defendant was to be found guilty and the longer his prison sentence. In addition, the defendant was found to be less attractive to the juror than a defendant with attitudes similar to those of the juror.

Using a female defendant as a subject, researchers hypothesized that "an attractive defendant would receive more lenient treatment than an unattractive defendant when the offense was unrelated to attractiveness; when the crime was related to attractiveness, the attractive defendant would receive relatively harsh treatment."[91]

When the crime was burglary (unrelated to the physical attractiveness of the defendant), jurors would impose more lenient sentences on the attractive defendant. When the crime was a swindle, however, it was viewed as related to attractiveness, and the defendant was perceived as having used her attractiveness to help perpetrate the crime. In that situation, jurors imposed harsher sentences on the attractive defendant. It appears that generally attractive people are viewed as "better" than unattractive people. When an attractive individual, however, deliberately takes advantage of her attractiveness, she is especially disliked.

One study demonstrated the impact of physical attractiveness through an experiment concerning cheating on a university examination.[92] Physi-

---

[91] Sigall & Ostrove, *Beautiful but Dangerous: Effects of Offender Attractiveness and Nature of Crime on Juridic Judgment*, 31 J. PERSONALITY & SOC. PSYCHOLOGY 410–414 (1975).

[92] Efran, *The Effect of Physical Appearance on the Judgment of Guilt, Interpersonal Attraction, and Severity of Recommended Punishment in a Simulated Jury Task*, 8 J. RESEARCH IN PERSONALITY 45–54 (1974).

cally unattractive cheaters were judged guilty more than the attractive cheaters and they were also given harsher punishments than attractive cheaters.

Vocal characteristics of the defendant also influence the jurors' perception of the defendant's credibility during a trial proceeding. For example, research has shown that defendants who spoke in grammatically correct English and complete sentences were acquitted more frequently than defendants who did not have a proper command of the English language.[93]

One researcher examined the testimony of defendants through trial transcripts. He reached the following conclusion:

> . . . defendants who used more markers of courtesy or deference, spoke in more grammatically complete sentences, and used more polite forms were most often acquitted. Unsuccessful defendants, those who were convicted, made more references to themselves in their testimony.[94]

§ 3.24 Witness credibility in the courtroom

The jury also forms perceptions of the credibility of the witness in the course of the trial. How much of an impact the witness' testimony will have with the jury often rests with how credible the witness appeared to the jury.

So important is the credibility of the witness that two researchers offered the following observation:

> In sum, when preparing for trial, attorneys should do more than simply rehearse the content of the testimony. Just as many attorneys might advise their clients to dress neatly for court appearances, they might also advise them to clean up their speech. The manner in which the witness imparts the testimony has a tremendous impact on the jurors. Enhanced credibility can be achieved by encouraging the witness to observe a few stylistic guidelines while testifying. Witnesses should be coached to speak in straight-forward, grammatically correct sentences. They should use a powerful, not a powerless speech style.[95]

---

[93] Parkinson, *Verbal Behavior and Courtroom Success*, 29 Com. Educ. 22–32 (1981).

[94] *Id.* at 31.

[95] Goodman & Loftus, *Social Science Looks at Witness Examination*, 20 Trial 57 (1984). *See also supra* § 1.85.

Pitch patterns are helpful to the attorney in spotting a person who is probably vulnerable to pressure. This pitch identification is useful both in voir dire and in the cross-examination of witnesses.

When cross-examining a witness with a high-pitched voice, the attorney should "turn up the heat." By keeping the pressure on, the witness is more likely to become increasingly uncomfortable with a resultant drop in his credibility in the eyes of the jury. The lawyer should also make sure his own witnesses have an appropriate pitch level so as to avoid damaging his own credibility with a "high, questioning voice."

A rising pitch also tends to indicate uncertainty. When answering a question, a witness ending his sentences with a rising pitch conveys a lack of confidence and certainty in his response.

COMMENT: To evaluate how sure a witness or potential juror is in what they tell you, listen to their vocal pitch as they complete their answer. Those who finish with a *rising pitch*, as if asking a question, are uncertain of the statement they are making. When we finish an answer with a rising intonation, we are wondering if our reply is acceptable, which means we don't know! . . . People who are confident, signal their certainty by punctuating their sentences with a lowered pitch. How they end any one statement will determine how much weighting to give their answer.[96]

In addition, witnesses who speak with an accent may be perceived as less credible than witnesses who do not have an accent. In a study of this area, individuals who spoke with an accent were found to be perceived as having lower social status.[97] Studies of witness credibility in the courtroom have found the same results: an accent or regional dialect or nonstandard English usage resulted in the decreased credibility of the witness.[98]

---

[96] Sannito, *Nonverbal Communication in the Courtroom*, 6 TRIAL DIPL. J. 27–28 (1983).

[97] Mulac, Hanley & Prigge, *Effects of Phonological Speech Foreignness Upon Three Dimensions of Attitude of Selected American Listeners*, 60 Q.J. SPEECH 411–420 (1974).

[98] *See, e.g.*, H. GILES & P. POWESLAND, SPEECH STYLE AND EVALUATION (London

Powerful as opposed to powerless speech has a significant impact on the perceived credibility of the witness' testimony. "Powerful speech" conveys perceptions of the witness' competence, intelligence, likability, and believability. The witness should be encouraged to use powerful speech in his testimony.

The impact of credibility impression formation of the witness is seen in the following excerpt in which the opposing attorney is urged to capitalize on nonverbal cues that indicate uncertainty and a wavering credibility with the jury.

> The evasive witness is the most vulnerable in cross-examination. He hesitates to give a responsive answer when he knows the answer is harmful. He will do this on even relatively minor concessions that should be made to the cross-examiner. Because of his lack of experience in the courtroom, he is not aware that he emphasizes the very things that he attempts to play down. For example:
>
> > Q. At the time you repaired the brakes on this automobile, how long had you been working in the brake department of the Acme Auto Service Company?
> >
> > A. I had been with the Acme Auto Service Company for 12 years.
>
> [The examiner should again ask the identical question very slowly to emphasize it.]
>
> > Q. At the time you repaired the brakes on this automobile, how long had you been working in the brake department of the Acme Auto Service Company?
> >
> > A. Two days.
>
> Another method of accomplishing the same objective is to ask the court reporter to read the question back. This is a change of pace, as the question is read back in a different voice; this further emphasizes the question that was asked. When the witness realizes that you are insisting on an answer to the question and sheepishly gives it, his lack of forthrightness is most apparent. Strangely enough, this type of witness will quite often continue to play into the cross-examiner's hands by supplying more of these opportunities. Often-

---

Academic Press, 7 European Monographs in Social Psychology, 1975). *See also* Conley, O'Barr & Lind, *The Power of Language: Presentational Style in the Courtroom*, 6 DUKE L.J. 1375–1399 (1978).

> times he will deliberately testify in variance to his deposition wherein he is committed to a contrary position. Then, of course, his value is practically destroyed by showing not only that he is not straightforward, but that he is actually lying to the jury.[99]

The credibility of the witness in the eyes of the jury has a direct bearing on the impact his testimony will have with the jury.

> If the direct examination is properly and skillfully conducted, the impression made by an honest witness is more lasting than any argument of counsel. The vivid story of a single witness told in a winning way will leave a first impression upon a juror's mind that no eloquence can efface.[100]

III. Communication Techniques

§ 3.25 Increasing the perception of credibility through the proper structuring and delivery of messages

We know that credibility is made up of the perception of three basic factors: (1) competence/expertness, (2) trustworthiness, and (3) dynamism. These three qualities combined provide an increased perception of credibility on the parts of jurors. Principle 15 sets forth one of the strongest concepts regarding credibility: People are influenced by the way the message is structured and delivered. In other words, credibility is a function of how people put together their messages and how they attempt to persuade others to their point of view. Increasing the perception of credibility through adept structuring and delivery of messages in questioning during voir dire, opening statement, cross-examination of witnesses, and closing argument becomes extremely important to counsel.

There are specific techniques which can be used to increase credibility of a message through both structure and delivery. Throughout Part III of this chapter, we will be discussing several techniques which can accomplish this goal. The first technique involves the development of a high-impact message. Specifically, we will look at the elements of simplification, repetition, and consistency in developing a message that will

---

[99] TRIAL DIPL. J. at 63 (1978), as cited in TRIAL DIPL. J., at 29 (1969). Reprinted with permission.

[100] Costopoulos, *Persuasion in the Courtroom*, 10 DUQ. L. REV. 398 (1972) quoting F. WELLMAN, DAY IN COURT 142 (1931).

have a long-lasting effect in terms of retention and will simultaneously increase the perception of credibility. The second technique that we will examine is the use of special language patterns to create high impact. These language techniques include such methods as repetition, metaphors, simile, analogy, and the use of rhetorical questions. Next, we will examine how to structure a message for high impact through the use of an 8-part formula for opening statement and closing argument. Finally, we will examine the delivery of a message. Once again, we will be focusing on the concept of how to create high impact. Specifically, we will consider how to increase the perception of (1) competence/expertness, (2) trustworthiness, and (3) dynamism. The means of reducing anxiety while speaking resulting in an increased perception of credibility and control will also be reviewed.

§ 3.26 Developing a high impact message

Messages which have high impact are remembered. With all the competing stimuli and information being presented in the courtroom your primary job is to get jurors to remember critical points. There are several elements which add to the impact of a message. These include simplifying the message, using the rule of three, selecting powerful words, creating mental images with storytelling, repeating the message, presenting a consistent message, juror-proofing the message, and focusing your message.

§ 3.27 —Simplifying the message

Simple is better. One way to do this is to use no more than 150 syllables for every 100 words. This rule of thumb will help keep your message clear. An example of the need to simplify messages can be found with Xerox in its design and development of the PSSII program known as Professional Selling Skills II. The program was used to teach salespeople to use two types of probes: direct and indirect. After years of market research they found that the salespeople did not distinguish well between direct and indirect probes. The problem was the terminology. They changed the words "direct probes" to "open probes" and "indirect probes" to "closed probes" and had much greater success with comprehension. The words "open" and "closed" are easy to understand. Although the words "direct" and "indirect" do not appear to be too complicated, they are unnecessary. If something can be explained in a simpler fashion, do it. The courtroom is not a place for the display of intellectual talents and sophisticated skills of logic; it is a place for good persuasive speakers.

The best professional speakers avoid jargon at all costs. If they do use jargon, they define their words at the precise moment they use them. Their messages are simple, strong, and remembered. The model professional speaker offers another example of the theory of "simple is better." Consider the books which are on the bestseller list at any given time. It is useful to read the bestsellers because they offer clues and information as to what the general public is responding. If you analyze the books that reach the top in sales in the general market you will see that they contain simple, down-to-earth language and predictable story lines. Review the television shows that have great commercial success. They will show you what appeals to the general public. Your role as an attorney is to select the communication channels and messages that have the best chance of getting through to the jurors. To do this you must understand how the jurors, as representatives of the general public, think. By studying professional speakers, books, television shows, and magazines you will be able to pace jurors more effectively by presenting information in the way they are used to hearing it. At all times, focus on maximizing the similarities between you, your client, and the jurors (Principle 9: People are more easily influenced by others they perceive as similar to themselves.).

Table 3–3 offers examples of legal jargon to be avoided in the courtroom. The best rule of thumb is to use words that are frequently heard in everyday conversation.

Table 3–3
Translating Legal Jargon into Plain English

Avoid	*Use*
Constitute	Make up
Prior to	Before
Implement	Carry out
Subsequent	After, following
Necessitate	Require
Aforementioned	Previously mentioned
In the event that	If
But for	Except
Accord	Give
Heretofore	Earlier
Concur	Agree
By reason of	Because
Cease	Stop
In lieu of	Instead
On or before	On
Said	The
Solely	Only

§ 3.28 —Simplifying the case theme

Counsel should be able to state a case theme in one sentence of no more than ten words. The retention value is higher and the theme can be easily repeated. A theme statement that is too long or cumbersome will not stick in the jurors' minds. Further, there should be a single case theme under which all other points are assumed. Multiple case themes do not work for the same reason—too much information, too much to retain. The clearest, most concise statement of your theme is the one which will work best.

An analogy that offers a better understanding of why a short case theme works best comes from the field of advertising. Slogans which are used for products are very simple and generally utilize anywhere from three words up to a maximum of seven words. Many advertising themes are built on the rule of three: three words have greater power, impact, and retention value.[101] Consider the following slogans which use only three words: "Parts is parts" (Wendy's); "The Real Thing" (Coca-Cola);

[101] *See infra* § 3.29, *The rule of three*.

"The Pepsi Generation" (Pepsi); "We try harder" (Avis). There are some advertising slogans which use a few more words. Once again, however, they keep the number of words to a minimum, usually ten or under. For example, Clairol claims that "Blondes have more fun;" or United Airlines says, "Fly the Friendly Skies of United." In all these examples we hear very short, concise statements of what the product is supposed to mean to the consumer. When you develop a case theme, it should follow this same formula. In addition, your ability to deliver a theme statement with high impact depends, to a great extent, on the simplicity of that statement.

For example, consider the medical negligence case involving an industrial doctor who never took an X-ray of a worker's infected foot but kept noting in the record that he thought the patient was better and sent him back to work. The worker eventually lost his foot and the case was brought to trial. The plaintiff's counsel decided that the theme for the case would focus on the doctor's mechanical and insensitive response of simply writing on each visit the words, "He's better." The theme became, "Better. Back to work." Four simple words repeated over and over again throughout the trial. Four words which cost a man his foot. You can well imagine the drama with which these words were delivered. This is an excellent example of simplifying the case theme. (For a detailed discussion, *see infra* § 7.08.)

Developing a case theme is not an easy task. Coca-Cola came up with their slogan, "The Real Thing," after years of brainstorming on what slogan would work. At a conference meeting, one of the participants in the brainstorming session finally threw up his arms and said, "What can we say about Coke, except it's the real thing." And so the slogan, "Coca-Cola—The Real Thing," was born.

COMMENT: Themes are critical to a case. They should not be treated lightly and they should not be thrown in as, "Well, this is it." Your first couple of drafts of a case theme should be just that—drafts. It should never go into the courtroom. Keep working on the theme, simplifying it and breaking it down until you come up with something catchy. Consider and review advertising slogans. Keep in mind that the general public is exposed to this type of persuasive message on a daily basis. Not only are they exposed to countless product slogans, but millions of dollars are spent on these slogans for one simple reason: they work. The public hears, sees, and feels the effects of advertising messages through television, print media, movies, and radio. Pace what the public is used to hearing by matching this same type of communication when you develop your theme. By doing this you will be linking to the jurors way of thinking.

---

§ 3.29 —The rule of three

Research findings indicate that messages that are presented in forms of three elements have a greater likelihood for retention. People easily remember three things. They can, however, remember up to seven elements as evidenced by zip codes and telephone numbers. When the number of elements to be remembered is greater than seven it takes more repetition, concentration, and effort to recall this information. Jurors are already expending a great deal of energy in attempting to understand the case; they will not expend extra effort on retaining the information. Therefore, it is up to counsel to present the information in the most effective form possible.

A second reason why the rule of three works effectively is that it creates a rhythmic pattern. Read the next sentence out loud and see how it sounds. I want you to remember three things: *A*, *B*, and *C*. The sentence structure allows enough variation for the voice to change on the "and" and it creates a rhythmic pattern. An example of this usage in the courtroom is illustrated by the following three statements: Read each one out loud and see which one has the most impact.

> Sentence 1: My client has suffered physical and emotional trauma.
>
> Sentence 2: My client has suffered physical, emotional, and financial trauma.
>
> Sentence 3: My client has suffered physical, emotional, financial, and personal trauma.

When read properly with effective voice tone and emphasis, sentence 2 will have the most impact and, therefore, the greatest likelihood of retention by the jurors. Sentence 1 is acceptable because it is simple. It is difficult, however, to establish a vocal cadence which has a dramatic impact with only two elements. Sentence 3 is the least effective. Sentences which contain four or more elements resulted in a long series of words which are eventually discounted in the minds of jurors. After the fourth element, most people begin to selectively listen by paying attention to only certain words and phrases. Retention is not only too difficult with too many elements; it is boring. The quickest way to lose rapport in the courtroom is to bore the jurors.

The rule of three applies not only to phrases and sentences; it also applies to the major statements or issues presented in the case. The case theme provides the overall statement for your case, your direction, the belief system from which you are operating. Your major points should be developed from the case theme and, of course, should support the case theme. It is best to develop three major points—no more, no less. If you have more than three points which you want to cover, simply broaden your three major categories and place the points within each category. It is also best not to have more than three points within any subcategory.

Using the rule of three will force you to simplify your message. It takes more effort to simplify and reduce a message than it does to build a complicated message with a multiple and extended sub-outline structure. By the conclusion of your opening statement, jurors should be able to outline your presentation. If it cannot be outlined easily, it will not be understood easily.

§ 3.30 —Selecting words

Three factors enter into word choice: (1) the use of parallel construction, (2) the use of a rhythmic pattern with syllables and combinations, and (3) the use of words which create visual images.

Parallel construction refers to maintaining a consistency in the types of words that are used. For example, the statement "My client has suffered physical, emotional, and family problems" is an example of poor construction. The word "family" does not parallel the words "physical" and "emotional." Both physical and emotional end in "al." This interrupts the cadence and rhythm. In addition, it is easier to remember words that are parallel. The three major points in your case should have parallel construction.

Below is an example of three major points which do not have parallel construction. Read them out loud and listen to how they sound.

Example 1

Major Point 1: Joe had a fervor for education.

Major Point 2: Joe wanted the best for his family.

Major Point 3: In the community, Joe was well-known.

It would be difficult to repeat these verbatim. The format is different in each question. Using the same three points, the following is an example parallel construction.

Example 2

Major Point 1: Joe had a strong commitment to education.

Major Point 2: Joe had a strong commitment to his family.

Major Point 3: Joe had a strong commitment to his community.

This example indicates that there are really only three words to remember—education, family, and community. We also have a second benefit from this example because of the repetition—"Joe had a strong commitment to. . . ." Some of the strongest messages we have heard have been presented with the element of repetition. Recall Dr. Martin Luther King's famous oration and the phrase he used over and over again: "I have a dream." That phrase was used countless times throughout the speech. By the end, everyone would remember that one phrase, "I have a dream." The same thing happened when Jesse Jackson presented his speech at the Democratic Convention in 1984. The phrase he used repetitively was "Our time has come." After that speech was given people would remember that phrase and the power with which it was delivered.

The example, "Joe had a strong commitment . . ." offers a message which when used repetitively will embed in the minds of the jurors that Joe was a committed man. All they have to remember are the three things to which he was committed. Once again, we are trying to simplify the statements and use repetition to lock them into the unconscious mind. The art of persuasive communication rests with engaging the conscious mind while communicating with the unconscious mind. Repetition is one method of locking messages into the unconscious mind. Advertising has done this for years. What do blondes have more of? "Fun," says Clairol, and millions of Americans will agree. We have heard this theme for years.

Attorneys commonly make a mistake in the courtroom because they don't use enough repetition. Therefore, the main points do not stay in the minds of the jurors. There is too much information being presented. The information that is presented in the most simple, concise manner and which is repeated enough will be retained by the jurors. Therefore, in Example 2, we have three strengths working for us: (1) the message is simple, (2) the message is repetitious, and (3) the message is parallel in construction. Not all messages can use parallel construction, but when appropriate, it will increase the effectiveness and impact of a message.

The second goal in determining word choice is the creation of cadence and rhythmic patterns. Research shows that powerful speakers mesmerize their audiences. Mesmerization is comparable to a light trance state in hypnosis in which the listeners are not only fully attentive to the message, but are compelled to listen to it. Top trial attorneys, oftentimes without realizing it, put jurors in a light trance state. The soothing quality of a voice, the rhythm of the words, and the repetition all serve to draw people to listen to the message. With enough repetition, the message will be embedded in the listeners' minds on an unconscious level. Information which is stored in the unconscious mind is often recalled later as actual "fact." Reading poetry out loud is very useful in learning how to develop a cadence and rhythm in your own voice. Whenever possible, listen to and study professional speakers and orators.

The third goal in word selection is to use those words which create strong visual images. Many people form visual images in their mind as you are describing an event or situation. The more words you can use that will help their perception of the image, the greater the value. Image building and visual words include: picture, image, perceive, look at it this way, bright, brilliant, focus.

§ 3.31 —Creating mental images with storytelling

Creating an image in a person's mind, involves the use of detailed descriptions so a person can actually "picture" what you are describing. For example, we can describe a curtain as the "red curtain." The only adjective used is "red." There is quite a difference if you call it the "soft, shimmering red curtain that fell to the floor." In that instance you get a much more complete and vivid description of the curtain. One of the common problems with storytelling in the courtroom is that the stories frequently lack description and imagery. They are missing critical details; they leave too much for the mind to fill in. Stories lose their drama and high impact when they are not properly developed. When we talk about someone whose leg has gone through extreme trauma, we could describe the leg as thin and gaunt, or we could use a strong metaphor to create an image by saying, "The leg looked like a broomstick." Immediately an image will come to mind, a comparison.

Whenever you are creating an image, there are three things you must remember, the words must be (1) descriptive, (2) concise, and (3) should use every form of sensory stimulation possible in describing all the events. When describing an event, describe how it looks, how it feels, and how it sounds. To get a good understanding of storytelling, it is worthwhile for the trial attorney to read fairy tales. Fairy tales are one of the most compelling types of stories that people hear or read because they completely engage the mind of the reader for two reasons: (1) they weave a story with great detail and use extensive visual images, and (2) they all have a moral. So should every story in a trial.

Read the following paragraph and see what type of mental imagery it creates for you.

Paragraph 1

"The princess was always alone in her room looking out of a window. One day she saw a man walking in the forest. He happened to look up and noticed the princess at the window. He smiled at her. She saw the man also and smiled at him. For an hour, they smiled at one another because they were too far apart to communicate in any other way."

This is an example of using very limited descriptive language. Now read Paragraph 2 which describes the same event with far more descriptive images.

"On the contrary, always alone in that room, with ladies in waiting who didn't so much as look at her, the princess spent her days wistfully at the window. She sat there leaning on the windowsill, and had she not thought to put a pillow under them, she would have got calluses on her elbows. The window looked out on the forest, and all day long the princess saw nothing but treetops, clouds, and down below the hunter's trail. Over that trail one day came the son of a king in pursuit of a wild boar. Nearing the castle known to have been unoccupied for no telling how many years, he was amazed to see washing spread out on the battlement, smoke rising from the chimneys, and open casements. As he looked about him, he noticed a beautiful maiden at one of the upper windows and he smiled at her. The maiden saw the prince, too, dressed in yellow, with hunter's leggings and gun, and smiling at her, so she smiled back at him. For a whole hour, they smiled, bowed, and courtsied, being too far apart to communicate in any other way."[102]

The second paragraph offers a much fuller description of the events. Here the author has involved us in a full use of our senses—we can "feel" the pillow the maiden uses, we can "see" the treetops and clouds, we can "hear" the prince in pursuit of the wild boar. The story uses words to create a strong visual image. We can "see" the prince smiling at the princess.

When you compare these two paragraphs, you will see by removing the descriptive language, as in Paragraph 1, you no longer create the same visual image. We have lost the mood, the intensity of the story. To use words effectively, you want to build the image and recreate the entire scene. One of the best exercises for doing this is to read stories and descriptive paragraphs that do just this. Take your models out of literature and fairy tales. The one thing that can gain anyone's attention is a story. More than anything else, people literally "sit up" and "listen" when they hear a story. It takes us back to our early childhood. Stories have morals and messages brought to us in an entertaining way. Popular books often are based on metaphors and stories, such as *Jonathan Livingston Seagull* by Richard Bach or *The One-Minute Manager* by Kenneth Blanchard and Spencer Johnson. Stories need to have visual descriptions so that the listener can create the image in his own mind.

§ 3.32 —Repeating the message

Repetition is the key to retention and memory. The study of psycho-cybernetics (the process of programming information into the unconscious mind) claims that it takes twenty-one repetitions for a message to be established, altered, or dismissed.[103] You can try an experiment by

---

[102] I. Calvino, Italian Folklores 53 (Pantheon Books, 1956).

[103] For the interested reader in the area of psycho-cybernetics, the following recommendations are offered:

M. Maltz, M.D., *Psycho-Cybernetics and Self-Fulfillment* (Bantam Books, 1970).

M. Maltz, Thoughts to Live By (Pocket Books, 1975).

M. Maltz, The Magic Power of Self-Image Psychology (Prentice-Hall, 1964).

M. Maltz, Psycho-Cybernetics (Prentice-Hall, 1960).

M. Maltz, Doctor Psycho-Cybernetics (Wilshire Book Co., 1953).

B. Smith, Self-Cybernetics (Littlefield, Adams, and Co., 1974).

moving the wastebasket in your office to a new location. See how long it takes you before you are able to throw the paper in the right location. If you have to think twice, you have not had enough repetitions. When the process of throwing the paper into the relocated wastebasket becomes mechanical (without conscious thought) you have had enough repetitions to lock the new behavior into the unconscious mind. Messages that are most strongly remembered are repeated over and over again so the unconscious mind (without conscious effort in thinking) can retrieve the information easily.

The strongest example of the effectiveness of repetition comes from the advertising market. Many hours, months, and years are being spent on creating a single advertising slogan. The ones that work all have something in common: they are simple, they are consistent, and they are repeated frequently. Read the following list and see if you can identify the company or product being sold.

Slogan

1. Blondes have more fun.
2. We try harder.
3. We're the high priced brand.
4. The Real Thing.
5. The taste you hate, twice a day.
6. We're ________________, doing what we do best.
7. Have it your way.
8. We're the other guys.
9. Fly the friendly skies of ________________.
10. The ________________ Generation.

If you can associate six of the ten slogans with the product or the company, you have just validated consumer research. Each of these companies has spent millions of dollars repeating the same message over and over again so that consumers would associate the message with their product and remember it on an unconscious level. The answers to the ten slogans are: 1-Clairol, 2-Avis, 3-Chivas Regal, 4-Coca Cola, 5-Listerine, 6-American Airlines, 7-Burger King, 8-B.F. Goodrich, and 9-United Airlines, 10-Pepsi.

C. Schreiber & M. Maltz, Live and Be Free Through Psycho-Cybernetics (O'Sullivan Woodwide and Co., 1975).

In the courtroom, your theme and three major points should be repeated during opening, closing, witness testimony, on graphs, and during cross-examination. The most effective repetition involves the use of the same words or key phrases. Remember that Coca-Cola has been "the real thing" for a long time. Coin your words and use them over and over again.

§ 3.33 —Presenting a consistent message

Communication Principle 2 provides that jurors actively try to make sense out of their environment. To take advantage of this, your message should stay consistent throughout the trial. If you change your theme during the trial you create confusion and uncertainty among the jurors. You and your case are no longer predictable. When predictability drops, so does comfort. When comfort drops, so do your chances for a successful verdict.

If you have new information or a new idea that has been uncovered in the trial, place it within the context of your existing structure. You should not create a new major point. Present the information as an important part of an existing major point.

One way to make sure that you continually present a consistent message in the courtroom is by reviewing your basic theme. Each theme should contain three major points. Psychological preparation helps to lock the basic theme and message into your mind and to focus your thinking. It is very easy for an attorney in the courtroom or a speaker in a classroom to get off on a tangent because he did not review his own structure and pattern frequently enough. When you develop your theme and three major points, have it typed or printed on a page with nothing else; just the theme and your three major points. As you go through the trial, keep looking at that one page. It will remind you of the message you are trying to get across to the jurors. Your effectiveness during the trial depends a great deal on your own psychological preparation. When you leave the trial at the end of the day, repeat the theme and the three major points over and over again. The more you have this embedded in your unconscious mind (rather than conscious mind) the greater the likelihood that you will communicate these messages to the judge and jurors. Psychologically preparing yourself will help your case by increasing your focus and concentration. You cannot expect jurors to focus on your message if you do not. To keep the message consistent, maintain a tight focus throughout every aspect of the trial.

§ 3.34 —Juror-proofing your message

The courtroom should not be used as a place for testing the impact of your message. Would any major advertiser spend money on a new slogan or ad campaign without first testing it?

A simple way to juror-proof your theme and message is to assemble a group of mock jurors and/or enlist the help of an outside consultant who has a more objective view of the case. This external feedback is important. Once you have become immersed in the case, your perspective necessarily narrows and focuses. It takes outside help to tie your case to the actual perceptions that will exist in the minds of the jurors.

A simple way in which to assemble mock jurors is to establish a profile of the types of jurors you will most likely have on the panel. Consider demographic characteristics such as marital status, financial status, and professional status. Give this information to an employment agency and ask them to select the people for you. For reliability and accuracy, use a minimum of six people.

Once the mock jury is assembled, inform them they they are working on a research project. It is most effective at this point to have the consultants conduct the mock jury research since they will be more removed from the case. A mock jury is useful in testing the impact of your theme, opening statement, arguments, and general perception of counsel, client, and witnesses.

It is important to test the impact of your theme statement. Most important of all, you want jurors to remember your theme. Several possible methods exist for testing your case theme as well as certain major points:

1. Read a series of theme statements out loud and ask the mock jurors to write down their interpretation of each statement. This allows you to compare their perception of your theme to your intended interpretation of the theme.

2. Read three to seven themes out loud in random order. Read this list three times, changing the order each time. Ask participants to write down every theme they remember. This allows you to see which themes are more easily remembered than others.

3. Present an opening statement which introduces your theme plus the three major points. Ask participants to write down the theme and to identify your major points. Do not tell them to identify the "three" major points. Allow them to recall them in the form and order in

which they remember them. This will tell you whether you have enough repetition, correct wording, and simplicity.

Many attorneys try this process on other attorneys. This does not produce reliable data. Attorneys are accustomed to collecting, sorting, and storing information. Therefore, their response will be more consistent with the response for which you are looking. In other words, attorneys are trained to think in a particular way and this thinking is not necessarily representative of how jurors think. A group of attorneys can usually identify the major themes even if they have insufficient repetition. Your best data collection will come from a group of people who most resemble the types of jurors who will be impaneled.

§ 3.35 —Focusing your message

Perceptions of credibility increase when the listener feels that the speaker is in control and knows where he is headed. For this reason, and to reduce uncertainty among jurors, it is important to focus your message at all times.

Several phrases can be used to communicate to the jurors that you are clearly focused and directed. These include: "Now this relates to," "What this means," "This ties in with our earlier discussion," "This is where we are headed," "I will be focusing on," "The third and final point I want you to consider is." These phrases serve the purpose of orienting the jurors to where you have been, where you are, and where you are headed. Although it may be obvious to you, it is not always obvious to a listener. You should continue to think of your listeners as constantly outlining what you are saying and help them in every way possible to build a correct and coherent outline.

To maintain your focal point, you must remember not to try and be all things to all people. In the publishing field, this principle is referred to as a "book for everyone is a book for no one." Jurors will listen to a message they feel is directed and targeted toward their specific understanding of the case and issues. To do this, a focusing statement and a simple outline are necessary.

§ 3.36 Using special language techniques to create high impact

Rhetorical devices have been used throughout history by powerful speakers to create a high-impact message. A rhetorical device specifically gives speakers much greater control over audience response. Rhetorical devices consist of specially designed words in a distinctive pattern in order to illicit a particular response. The following sections will discuss five specific language techniques which can be used in the courtroom: repetition, metaphor, simile, analogies, and rhetorical questions. Because stimulus variability is very important in the courtroom, these techniques also serve a function in keeping the interest level at a high peak. It also helps those people who have a mundane or monologue-type approach to speaking to increase interest and arousal levels so that jurors will continually listen to the message that is given.

In Chapter 4, particularly, you will note the influence of the use of language techniques in communicating to the unconscious mind. The use of these techniques or linguistic considerations with phraseology also helps to increase the perception of credibility by maintaining a high level of dynamism. Communication Principle 15 provides that people are influenced by the way the message is structured and delivered. Delivery with rhetorical devices provides an effective approach for counsel to stimulate both the jurors' interest and retention of information.

§ 3.37 —Repetition

Researchers have discovered that repetition is extremely important for retention. Specifically, it takes twenty-one repetitions of a particular message to ensure that it is incorporated into the unconscious mind of the listener. Repetition of critical phrases over and over again is probably the most popular and versatile of all rhetorical devices. Repetition of phrases can be used for creating an emotional effect at the beginning, middle, or end of a sentence.

Repetition can be used for several other purposes as well: (1) to focus attention, (2) to form a rhythmic pattern, (3) to stir emotions, (4) to forcefully drive a message home, and (5) to reinforce the speaker's beliefs. The following example came from a speech by John F. Kennedy in 1963: "I look forward to an America which commands respect throughout the world. I look forward to a world that will be safe." This is an example of taking the phrase, "I look forward to . . . " and using the repetition element to build impact. Repetition in that instance helped to increase the probability of retention by planting the idea into the subconscious mind. The phrase should be repeated as frequently as possible during the presentation in order to maximize the effectiveness.

There are two types of repetition which can be used throughout the trial. The first involves the repetition of a main message or case theme which the attorney should use throughout the trial. The other is the repetition that occurs within a short sentence structure such as Kennedy's phrase, "I look forward to an America. . . ." This is a very effective type of repetition because it builds momentum quickly and because it brings your listener back in and keeps them focused on the specific message that you are giving.

§ 3.38 —Metaphor

A metaphor can be described as a phrase which makes an implied comparison. A metaphor can be presented in the form of a story or an example. We find that jurors will listen very carefully to metaphors because it reminds us of childhood stories and fairy tales. The story *Green Eggs and Ham* by Dr. Seuss is a classical metaphor. The whole story is about a creature who hates green eggs and ham and refuses to even try them. The message behind it is that when you resist and avoid something, you never know if you will like it. Nowhere in the story is the word "resisting" used. The implicit moral throughout is to "try new and different things." This moral is never stated explicitly, rather it is developed expertly throughout the story until, finally, Dr. Seuss's character tries the green eggs and ham . . . and likes them.

A metaphor and analogy are similar in that they offer either an explicit or implicit comparison. One major difference is that the metaphor generally involves a story that has a point of conflict which is dramatized, then resolved. The way in which the conflict is resolved in the metaphor conditions the listeners to seek a similar resolution to their problem. By contrast, an analogy is a simple comparison and is often expressed in a statement rather than a story. Metaphors are extremely powerful when they are well selected and executed in the courtroom.

In the courtroom, a metaphor can be used effectively to diminish the defensiveness of listeners. Metaphors communicate to the unconscious mind because they are about an event that does not put the listener at risk. The event is removed from the trial itself and, therefore, jurors can relax and listen to the story. The unconscious mind, on the other hand, listens to the commands in the metaphor and transfers them to the current situation. The metaphor creates an opening to get through to the unconscious mind.

§ 3.39 —Simile

Simile is a rhetorical device that uses the words "like" or "as." By suggesting images in the listener's mind, the simile makes speaking more vivid and conveys the message more clearly. The simile becomes important because it activates many sensory associations such as hearing, seeing, and feeling. The more that you can use the multiple channels and encourage jurors to associate and experience a particular emotional event, the more likely that they will respond and remember it. Some common examples of similes include:

tough as nails

dull as a doorknob

wise as an owl

sweet as sugar

sharp as a tack

hard as a whip

In the courtroom, similes can be used very powerfully to describe physical injury to a client. For example, "Bob is only eighteen-years-old and for the rest of his life he will have a severe limp. He now walks like a man of seventy." The comparison, of course, is to the seventy-year-old man. The mind will do two things when it processes this information: (1) make a comparison between eighteen-year-old Bob and a seventy-year-old man, and (2) form a picture of Bob with the limp of a seventy-year-old. The simile helps to create word pictures and, therefore, can serve the purpose of dramatizing an event.

§ 3.40 —Analogy

Analogy is a form of comparison. It seeks to make something clear by comparing it to another element and bringing out an idea that is difficult to express. Analogies help the listener because they use a comparative form. Analogies can be used in many different ways. You might compare man to a machine or a swimmer to a fish.

COMMENT: It is valuable to understand your natural and instinctive uses of metaphors, analogies, and similes. Observe yourself during conversations or while reviewing your statements to discover whether you use these comparative forms of speech. If you already use them you can expand on more sophisticated metaphors. If, on the other hand, you find that your language patterns are devoid of these elements you can begin by consciously using them during everyday conversation. By practice and repetition you will eventually employ these techniques on an unconscious level.

---

§ 3.41 —Rhetorical question

A rhetorical question is a question that assumes its own answer. Although it is asked of an audience, you do not expect an actual response. What you do expect is for the unconscious mind to respond and that is even more powerful. A rhetorical question stimulates the audience because it reaches out and grabs their attention and focuses the message. Rhetorical questions are more effective when they are placed in the body of the speech because they are thought provoking and they cause the speaker to search for the answer in his own mind. When you ask the question, "How many of you have ever been in this situation before," the mind will automatically sort information for the answer to that question. You might ask, "How many people understand how important your role is in the courtroom?" The properly worded rhetorical question more often than not will also guide the unconscious mind to the answer you want.

One of the most important aspects of using a rhetorical question effectively is to pause for a moment after you ask the question to allow the listener's mind to search for an answer. Rhetorical questions are effective because they allow the speaker to (1) direct the unconscious minds of the jurors, (2) provide jurors with an opportunity to search for the information to respond to the question, and (3) involves the juror directly in the process. A rhetorical question can cause the juror to associate and identify more with what you are describing.

§ 3.42 Structuring a message for high impact

There is no question that an attorney's message must be structured so that it results in high impact. In that regard, Communication Principle 2 provides that people actively try to make sense out of their environment. Structure and consistency help jurors to "make sense" of the trial.

Messages that are put together randomly, haphazardly, or in typical outline form will lack the powerful effect of a message that is well structured by utilizing specific communication strategies. Sections 3.43 through 3.49 will examine a very specific strategy—the 8-part formula—which can be used during opening statement and closing argument.[104]

§ 3.43 Using the eight-part formula for opening and closing arguments

The eight-part formula is a specific technique designed by one of the authors and tested through years of observing top speakers' specific strategies used in delivering talks and testing their persuasive speaking techniques in many different settings. Through years of research and observation of this technique, it was discovered that powerful speakers who are very effective in motivating an audience to perform in a particular manner use the 8-part formula. There are eight steps which when used in a particular order, continue to engage the audience and focus their attention. The 8-part formula provides a logical structure so that the audience members do not have to work hard at listening to the organization of the speech. Once the need for organization and structure is satisfied, the jurors can relax and assimilate the information more readily. More importantly, once this need is satisfied, an opening to the unconscious mind is created, resistance is lowered, and the critical messages can be embedded.

Jurors have a need for structure and consistency. Once again, Communication Principle 15 provides that people are influenced by the way the message is structured and delivered. We can say more specifically that people are influenced when their thoughts are given a logical and unifying structure. If you do not offer them a solid structure, the jurors will attempt to build structure. The 8-part formula identifies the specific parts of a persuasive message:

---

[104] The 8-Part Formula, developed by Dr. L.A. Malandro, is a strategy for persuasive speaking.

Open

Focus

Connect

1–2–3 (Three major points)

Summarize

Close

These steps can be used during both opening statement and closing argument. Sections 3.44 through 3.49 will examine each part of the formula.

§ 3.44 —Open (the case to the jury)

Most speakers do not have an opening for their presentations. In the courtroom, an "opening" for the opening statement consists of the first few lines which are spoken to the jurors. Many attorneys start their opening statements with, "What I'm going to talk about today is . . . " or "the theme we want to discuss is . . ." or "we want to focus on. . . ." These are not good openings. This is the most critical time you have with your audience. You need to engage an audience (or jurors) within the first four minutes of your presentation. In the first four minutes you need to pace the jurors, and connect with them, so they will allow your message into their unconscious mind.

The purpose of the opening is to get the attention of your audience and to allow time for their minds to shift to what you are going to say and allow them to become familiar with your personality and style. When you begin a presentation without an effective opening, you stand to lose one to three minutes of listening time of your audience as well as the potential for establishing vital rapport with the jury.

An attorney's opening lines do not have to relate directly to the topic. It could consist of a few preliminary statements. Most importantly, the opening must contain what are called examples of pacing statements. You must pace the jurors and make statements which are factual, descriptive, and true. If you can make initial statements that describe an ongoing event which is true and factual, you will find that the jurors will automatically begin to assume that many of the statements you make from that point on are true and factual. A good example of a beginning for an opening statement would be as follows:

> "Ladies and gentlemen, you and I are here along with Judge Marcus and opposing counsel to hear about a personal injury case and to see

> that justice is done. We are all in this together. We are all alike. I am sure you are aware of how important your role is in the courtroom."

This becomes a strong opening because it says several things. The first statement that is made is a true and factual statement: "Ladies and gentlemen, you and I are here along with Judge Marcus and opposing counsel to hear about a personal injury case and to see that justice is done." The jurors identify that as a fact. The moment you begin with a factual statement and then follow it with a second piece of information, that second piece of information begins to take on the appearance of being true simply because it has been preceded by "observable" facts. The next lines are: "We are all in this together. We are all alike." Now you are programming that there is very little difference between the jurors and yourself and your client. You are maximizing the similarities. The next statement in which we say, "I am sure you are aware of how important your role is in the courtroom," is another pacing statement. You are reinforcing the role of the jurors and programming them to consider their importance. Further, you are demonstrating your respect for their role in the courtroom. You should stay away from starting an opening statement by immediately telling the jurors what you are going to do. Jurors, like any other audience, need to be paced to link them to you. The opening should be very well thought out and very well rehearsed. It should not require any conscious thought by counsel. It is critically important that the opening be very well executed. The perception of counsel's credibility rests primarily with the rapport which is built with jurors during the first four minutes of the opening statement. How you begin this conversation with the jurors establishes their receptivity for the information which you will present next.

§ 3.45 —Focus

Most attorneys begin with a focus statement when they present their opening statement or closing argument. In other words, they tell the jurors what they are going to tell them. This is fine, except it should come after the opening. The purpose of the focus statement is to direct the attention of the jurors to your theme. The focus statement might be, "There are three critical factors that we are going to look at in this case today."

If you start your opening statement with your case theme or a statement of the critical factors, you will find that you have not properly paced the jurors. Remember that pacing is one of the most important skills to maximize similarity and to move the jurors to receptivity and agreement with you. You want to start the very subtle process of getting jurors to agree with you, understand you, and see themselves as being like you and your client in the first four minutes of your opening statement. When you do this, you begin to communicate to the jurors immediately on an unconscious level. It is the engagement of the unconscious mind that allows for full and complete persuasion. The focus statement, following the opening, helps to give the conscious mind structure and relief from having to organize and sort the information which you will be presenting.

§ 3.46 —Connect

Never "speak" to the jurors, rather, speak "with" them. The only way in which you can truly speak with jurors is to connect to the way in which they think. An effective trial attorney should be highly flexible and adaptive. This means avoiding any planned or memorized presentation because it does not allow you to adjust to the changing "temperature" of the jurors. Each jury is different. The best way to organize a presentation is to learn extemporaneous speaking techniques. The 8-part formula is an extemporaneous speaking technique which maintains structure while allowing for flexibility within the structure.

You can connect to the jurors by referring to their intent, speaking their language, and responding to their spontaneous reactions as you speak. The best way to connect to the jury is to become like one of them in your thinking and actions. You have to remember that the way in which jurors think and act has to be part of what you assimilate. You have to keep identifying closely with them so that you can see yourself as very similar to the jurors. This needs to be underscored. If you walk in the courtroom and there is a barrier between you and the jurors and you do not identify with them and you see them as different, it will be very hard to persuade them. You need to do a great deal of preliminary psychological work to prepare your mind for understanding how you are exactly like those jurors in the way they think and feel. The more you become like them, the more they will perceive you as being like themselves and the greater the chance for persuasion.

"Connecting" to an audience can be done in a very short statement which in essence says, "What this means to you is . . ." or "This is important to you because. . . ." A connecting statement brings the jurors into direct involvement with what you are going to say.

§ 3.47 —Three major points

Every persuasive presentation should have three major points. Why three? People can remember three well-worded messages. When a juror can repeat the main points of your talk, they feel as if they have walked away with something tangible and that they have understood your message. In fact, they have. Even more significantly, jurors tend to like attorneys who can give the experience of being both intelligent and competent. Presenting more than three main points both confuses and diffuses the potential impact of your message.

Any presentation can be set up with three major points. If you have seven or eight points you want to make, simply broaden your presentation to three major categories and place your seven or eight points under this structure. You have to keep it simple and powerful. Refer often to your three major points. You can always refer to them as point 1, or "the first thing I want to talk about", or "the second thing", and finally "what I want to say is this. . . ." You do not want the conscious mind of the jurors working in the courtroom. If you make their minds work, they are going to be working on structuring the information when what you want them to do is to be receptive to the information which you are presenting on both a conscious and unconscious level.

§ 3.48 —Summarize

It is important to remind the jurors of what they have heard and what they should remember from what you have just told them. The summary is your opportunity to bring together the information so you tell them specifically what you want them to focus on. If you allow jurors to summarize for themselves, they will, and you may not be happy with the results. Control and direct the thinking of the jurors to the three main points you want them to remember. A summary should offer a factual, but brief, overview of the theme and three major points.

§ 3.49 —Close

Most inexperienced trial attorneys end their talks with a summary. They just simply summarize their three major points and they let it go at that. The best professional speakers will never end a talk with a summary. The most important thing to remember is that you always end a persuasive speech with a "close." Similar to the opening, the close is a critical factor in the 8-part formula. It must have high impact. To be done correctly, it must have high drama such as using a metaphor, story, analogy, or anything that can have the potential of bringing the jurors to the emotional state in which you want to leave them. One of the most important things you are trying to do in the close is to leave the jurors with a particular feeling. The close will refocus the jurors' minds from the cognitive message (rational, logical thought) to an affective message (emotional, intuitive). People remember what they feel.

§ 3.50 Delivering a message with high impact

The delivery of a message will significantly affect how it will be perceived by the jurors as well as the perception of credibility they will attribute to the speaker. There are four areas which need to be considered when delivering a message. One is the area of reducing speaker anxiety. Is the attorney anxious, exhibiting characteristics of being inexperienced, or portraying a lack of confidence in front of the jurors? Jurors take their cues from the attorneys. The other main areas include how to increase the perception of (1) dynamism, (2) competence/expertness, and (3) trustworthiness. All these factors become extremely important in the delivery of the message.

§ 3.51 —Fear of public speaking

One of the most common fears among all people is the fear of public speaking. The more practice and experience you have speaking, generally, the less anxiety you will experience. Most professional speakers recognize that some level of anxiety not only exists but is important for creating dynamism or excitement. People who are fearful of speaking in the courtroom often experience a sense of dread or impending doom when faced with the prospect of speaking before jurors. Basically, it is because they are uncertain about their abilities to perform effectively in the situation; they are anxious to begin and they imagine this situation as a threat to themselves.

One way to reduce anxiety is to practice your opening statement and closing argument on videotape and study your improvement. Relaxation and breathing is very important in reducing speaking anxiety. Before you speak, slow your breathing pattern and relax. Begin to picture yourself speaking in front of the jurors. Forget that you are "on" and remember that your main purpose is to connect with the jurors, to talk with them as people. If you focus in this way, you will begin to understand that you are not speaking in a vacuum, but you are trying to have an important conversation with the jurors. This will start to reduce the anxiety, or at the very least, transform it into useable energy to create a dynamic delivery. The following speaking anxiety test developed by Dr. Michael Scott and presented in Table 3–4 can help you identify whether or not you have any particular speaking anxiety.[105]

Table 3–4
How's Your "Speaking Anxiety?" Here's a Test

The following is a self-report measure of public speaking anxiety. Respond to each statement honestly and work quickly. Indicate the extent to which you agree or disagree and score yourself as follows: Strongly Agree = 1, Agree = 2, Undecided = 3, Disagree = 4, or Strongly Disagree = 5.

1. While preparing for giving a speech I feel tense and nervous.
2. I feel tense when I see the words "speech" and "public speech" on a course outline when studying.
3. My thoughts become confused and jumbled when I am giving a speech.
4. Right after giving a speech I feel that I have had a pleasant experience.
5. I get anxious when I think about a speech coming up.
6. I have no fear of giving a speech.
7. Although I am nervous just before starting a speech, I soon settle down after starting and feel calm and comfortable.
8. I look forward to giving a speech.
9. When the instructor announces a speaking assignment in class I can feel myself getting tense.
10. My hands tremble when I am giving a speech.
11. I feel relaxed while giving a speech.
12. I enjoy preparing for a speech.
13. I am in constant fear of forgetting what I prepared to say.

---

[105] Reprinted with permission from M. Scott, Malandro Communique (Malandro Communication Inc., June 1984).

14. I get anxious if someone asks me something about my topic that I do not know.
15. I face the prospect of giving a speech with confidence.
16. I feel that I am in complete possession of myself while giving a speech.
17. My mind is clear when giving a speech.
18. I do not dread giving a speech.
19. I perspire just before starting a speech.
20. My heart beats very fast just as I start a speech.
21. I experience considerable anxiety while sitting in the room just before my speech starts.
22. Certain parts of my body feel very tense and rigid while giving a speech.
23. Realizing that only a little time remains in a speech makes me very tense and anxious.
24. While giving a speech I know I can control my feelings of tension and stress.
25. I breathe faster just before starting a speech.
26. I feel comfortable and relaxed in the hour or so just before giving a speech.
27. I do poorer on speeches because I am anxious.
28. I feel anxious when the teacher announces the date of a speaking assignment.
29. When I make a mistake while giving a speech, I find it hard to concentrate on the parts that follow.
30. During an important speech I experience a feeling of helplessness building up inside me.
31. I have trouble falling asleep the night before a speech.
32. My heart beats very fast while I present a speech.
33. I feel anxious while waiting to give my speech.
34. While giving a speech I get so nervous I forget facts I really know.

To determine your score, first total the numbers you gave yourself for statements 1, 2, 3, 5, 9, 10, 13, 14, 19, 20, 21, 22, 23, 25, 27, 28, 29, 30, 31, 32, 33, and 34. Now subtract this total from 132 and add the difference to your total score on statements 4, 6, 7, 8, 11, 12, 15, 16, 17, 18, 24, and 26. Your score should be no higher than 180 and no lower than 34. If your score is higher than 100, you are moderately to highly fearful of public speaking. A score between 80 and 100 means moderate fear of and anything less than 80 means minimal fear.

§ 3.52 —Increasing the perception of dynamism

Increasing the perception of dynamism requires animation on the part of the speaker which means varied gestures, voice, and movement patterns. Dynamism involves activity and motion. In order to be effective, a speaker has to learn how to use these qualities. Most speakers do not allow their full personality to come out during a presentation. They always hold back. You can see this in the courtroom. Successful trial attorneys do not hold back and that is part of what makes them so dynamic. It is no longer an "act"; their delivery and words come straight from the "heart" and they present that information forcefully because it is a part of who they are. That is a very important quality. The more information you present that is truly embedded in your own belief system and structure, the more dynamic you can be. One of the first questions you want to ask is "Do you believe the information which you are presenting? Do you feel it; are you associated with it; is it something that really makes a difference to you; can you understand how important it is?" If you treat the information as logical, rational, and cognitive and you do not become emotionally involved with that information, it is very hard to present a dynamic quality. You should begin to feel and identify with the information that you are presenting. Make sure that it is important information for you and that you have a passion for justice in this case. If you genuinely feel these emotions, they will be naturally manifested in your presentation.

Keep in mind that people who are dynamic are people who are not only exciting but are excited about what they do. They have a strong sense of stimulus arousal which makes it very easy to transfer this mood to jurors. That is why when you hear the best trial attorneys in the courtroom, the arousal level gets communicated immediately. It really is not an acting level. We are talking about a complete association with the state in which they are feeling. It is such a highly associated state that it is easily transferred to jurors.

§ 3.53 —Increasing the perception of competence and expertness

Chapter 1 focused on many of the personal appearance factors used to increase the perception of competence and expertness.[106] Another way of doing this is by use of the 8-part formula. It provides a structured and organized format and it demonstrates to the jurors that there is thinking and logic behind what they are hearing. This increases the perception of competence. One of the major considerations in increasing the perception of competence and expertness is to ask yourself, "Do you feel competent and expert?" Experiencing yourself as competent and as an expert will dramatically increase your ability to project these qualities to the jurors.

§ 3.54 —Increasing the perception of trustworthiness

In order to be perceived as being trustworthy, one must be trustworthy. You must have those characteristics. This really goes back to yourself. Once again, you must trust yourself and have integrity about the information you are presenting and how you are presenting it. When you first have the psychological characteristics of being trustworthy, it becomes much easier to communicate this to jurors. It has been our experience that it is difficult, if not impossible, to communicate particular states in which the individual does not already feel that state and has not already identified with feeling what you are attempting to project. Trustworthiness is earned by honest attempts to clarify information, resolve problems, be part of a team, and to help others.

---

[106] *See supra* §§ 1.16–1.32.

Chapter 4

DECISION-MAKING PROCESS OF JURORS

KLUWER LITIGATION LIBRARY REFERENCES

JEANS, LITIGATION: Chapter 2, *Mind Set of the Advocate*; Chapter 6, *Voir Dire*; Chapter 7, *Opening Presentation*; Chapter 16, *Summation*.

I. Communication Principles

§ 4.01 Introduction to chapter

There is limited information available on how jurors make decisions. We know that groups make decisions differently from individuals which offers us a wide area of research and theory to examine how group decision-making occurs. In addition, we will discuss the actual postjury research that has been conducted in this area. Specifically, we know that jurors operate under unique sets of implicit rules about how they should behave and how they should render decisions in the courtroom. Before a case presentation is structured or an opening statement is written, the attorney must understand the decision-making process that the jurors will follow.

One of the most important concepts that arises in jury decision making is that the group makes different types of decisions than individuals. Groups influence individuals to such an extent that this phenomenon is called a "group mind." Specifically, we will be discussing the concept of synergism as it is created by groups. This is easily defined as the concept of one plus one equals three where the total sum is greater than the contribution of each individual. In the decision-making process of groups, a group decision will override an individual decision and, in many cases, cause an individual to be swayed by the movement of the entire group.

Another aspect of decision making that will be explored in this chapter is leadership in small groups. How are leaders selected, and specifically, in the case of the jury, how is a foreperson selected? Not surprisingly, we find that a foreperson is not selected through a deliberate, rational, and thorough decision-making process, but that the decision is based on very limited information and data. Hence, it will be much easier to identify who those forepersons could be and also to recognize that it is not a long decision-making process that takes place.

We will also be discussing the actual decision-making process of juries. This will focus on the stages that takes place in the jury's decision-making process and also how juries integrate information. We will find that jurors integrate and selectively filter the information that enters into their perceptual field. In addition, we will examine how equity theory (belief in a just and fair world) influences decision-making among jurors. Most jurors have a belief in what is called a "just world" concept. The belief in the "just world" system can basically be summarized in the statement "people get what they deserve." How jurors decide who deserves what and the critical difference that the structure of the opening argument makes as well as the importance of appealing to the idea of equity will be discussed.

Finally, we will be discussing the implications of the size of the jury, and its effect on decision-making and the ultimate verdicts which juries render.

§ 4.02 Introduction to Communication Principles and decision making

We have identified five basic principles that summarize the process of decision making by juries. These principles represent five fundamental principles in decision making and are not meant to be representative of all the research in the area of small group processes. The area of group decision making is complex and is itself a specialized field of study. Each principle we have identified will hopefully assist the attorney in understanding the decisionmaking process in terms of the communication and psychological processes which occur.

The following principles represent the communication principles for Chapter 4.

Principle 17: Jurors choose leaders rapidly and on limited information.

Principle 18: Jurors use information other than evidence in making decisions.

Principle 19: People make decisions by emotion (unconscious mind) and validate them with logic (conscious mind).

Principle 20: People more easily retain information which is anchored.

Principle 21: Jurors seek to render a verdict which they perceive as equitable.

Each of these principles will be discussed in the sections to follow. Part II of this chapter will focus on specific techniques to utilize the power behind each communication principle.

§ 4.03 —Summary of Communication Principles

The following will summarize the five principles identified in the area of the decision-making process of jurors. Each summary will identify some of the research that has been conducted in this area and will serve as a brief description of the principles in order to establish the groundwork for the techniques presented in Part II of this chapter.

§ 4.04 —Principle 17: Jurors choose leaders rapidly and on limited information

It is not surprising to find that the choice of a foreperson or leader by jurors is a very quick decision and is based on limited data. The first thing we know about leadership choice is that there are two types of status: ascribed or achieved. By ascribed leadership status we mean by prior reputation and prestige a person is given automatic leadership functions. Generally, in the case of the jury, you do not have somebody like this unless it is an individual who has already served on a jury and this is known to other jury members. In this case, the individual will have some immediately ascribed status and it would not be surprising to find that person as the head or the leader of the jury. Achieved status in a jury situation would be status that is based upon the merits of one's own accomplishments. As we have discovered with jurors, the merits of one's own accomplishments or achieved status may simply be evidenced by the individual who takes the initiative in the very beginning of the jury deliberations. This initiative to "talk first" often provides the person with a type of automatic or achieved status.

Another factor that becomes very important in the choice of leaders by jurors is that higher status persons tend to control communication interaction and, in fact, their comments will carry more weight. If there is a person of higher status on a jury and this is known to the jurors, the automatic response on their part is deference, thereby elevating the person to a more influential position tantamount to leadership.

Emergence of the jury foreperson generally occurs very quickly. Much of the available information and research suggests that the first person to speak has a significantly higher probability of becoming the foreperson. This suggests that the selection of a foreperson is more by "happenstance" rather than a strategic and deliberate attempt to select the most qualified person. The basic questions raised casually is, "Well, who wants to be leader?" The assumption is that if that person is bold enough to take the initiative to raise the question, then he is the most obvious choice as foreperson.

COMMENT: Choosing a foreperson is not done by means of listing qualifications and leadership skills, but instead by a very quick and practical process to select someone for the leadership position who will control and direct the deliberations. Basically, juries look for dominant or aggressive individuals; someone who will take the initiative.

The leader chosen by the jurors, regardless of the fact that he was chosen rapidly and on limited information, will exert considerable influence on the decision rendered. Leaders direct the course of a conversation. Hence, they can focus a group on particular information and cause them to bypass and avoid the examination of other information. The foreperson directs and controls what the other jurors see, hear, and feel. We know that the perceptual bias of the person in charge will, in essence, carry greater weight than the bias of other people during the course of juror deliberations. Basically, leaders direct the group's thinking in the critical evaluation of ideas during the decision-making process.

§ 4.05 —Principle 18: Jurors use information other than evidence in making decisions

When jurors makes decisions, they go through what is identified as a sequential decision-making process. This process includes four stages: (1) orientation, (2) conflict, (3) emergence, and (4) reinforcement. Through these four stages, jurors deliberate and then render their decision. What is most important to understand is that through the course of the four stages from orientation to reinforcement, information other than evidence or what we would refer to as testimonial information is used in making decisions.

Much of the information that is acquired will be based upon the jurors' perception of what is going on in the courtroom. Hence, the belief system of the jurors comes into play here. When attorneys present information in such a way as to integrate it into the jurors' existing belief system rather than forcing the jurors to develop new beliefs, there is a much greater chance that it will be understood and will influence each juror. It would be unreasonable to expect that jurors would change their own belief system to match what they hear from the attorneys. Instead they will change what they have heard from the attorneys to match their belief system.

COMMENT: Once again, attorneys who are very skilled in the courtroom will match their arguments to the existing belief systems of the jurors. Stated aptly, "It is always easier to ride the horse in the direction in which it is going."

The attention span of most adults is a maximum of eighteen minutes. This is the period of prime and focused attention. After that there is a definite need for stimulus variability. Since jurors use information other than evidence in making their decisions, it becomes important to use communication strategies and techniques to support the evidence. It is important to recognize that the evidence upon which jurors make decisions is not simply the factual information presented in the courtroom, but it is predominantly other vocal and nonverbal factors.

§ 4.06 —Principle 19: People make decisions by emotion (unconscious mind) and validate them with logic (conscious mind)

Hopefully, it has become clear in the discussion throughout the chapters that the purpose of an effective trial attorney is to engage the conscious mind while communicating to the unconscious mind. This being the case, the intent of this book is to bring these strategies to the conscious level so that they can be understood and used in a productive and influential fashion. One of the things we know about decision making is that decisions are made by emotions on an unconscious level, but they are validated with logic which comes through the conscious mind. People feel better if they can support a decision consciously by explaining how the decision took place and why they made the decision. However, they are still making those decisions based on some gut-level instinct.

One of the most important points to recognize is that the actual techniques for communicating in the courtroom have very little to do with conscious mind input, but have more to do with persuading the unconscious mind by embedding commands, anchoring information, pacing the jurors, and projecting the appropriate image with a witness. The unconscious mind has overwhelming power when it comes to rendering a decision. The conscious mind cannot operate without the consistency and support of the unconscious mind. An appropriate example of this would be an individual who wants to lose weight and consciously says over and over again that he wants to lose weight. He makes it a public commitment and claim, but for whatever reason, he cannot lose weight. At this point, it is clearly identified that there is a breakdown in communication between the conscious and unconscious mind. The conscious mind wants to lose weight; the unconscious mind, for some reason, does not. The unconscious mind may feel that losing weight is going to cause too much attention, that he is going to lose something that he doesn't want to get rid of, or that maybe his weight is part of his personality. The unconscious mind is what blocks people from getting what they want and can block people from being successful. You can consciously say you want to be successful or you want to lose weight, but unless you have the support of the unconscious mind it will not take place. The same principle applies in decision making. Unless the unconscious mind is supportive of the conscious decision, it will not allow that decision to take place. Jurors are like any other human beings in that they are persuaded on the unconscious level.

§ 4.07 —Principle 20: People more easily retain information which is anchored

Anchoring is a technique that can be most closely likened to classical conditioning where an identified stimulus will illicit a particular response. What is most significant about anchoring is that it occurs all the time in the courtroom. It is not surprising to find that attorneys use anchoring unconsciously. For example, when an individual takes off his glasses to make a particular point, it is a form of anchoring. However, if this same individual takes off his glasses later on in the trial because his eyes are tired, the anchoring process does not work. To be effective, anchoring must be consistent, repetitious, and use the identical methods for eliciting a particular response pattern.

Collapsing an anchor is an important skill for attorneys. If you see your opposing counsel building particularly strong and salient points in the minds of the jurors you need to identify whether he is doing this with voice tone, body position, movements, and/or the manipulation of space. You can collapse that anchor by using different voice tones and methods in the same location to create a conflict of information. In many cases, it is as important to collapse anchors as it is to build them.

The process of using anchoring in the courtroom is complicated. It may sound like a simple process, but it requires a complete understanding of it. Part II of this chapter will provide some basic ways in which anchoring is used in the courtroom and how you can use anchoring to achieve higher message impact.

§ 4.08 —Principle 21: Jurors seek to render a verdict which they perceive as equitable

Implicit in our society is the fact that we have a social contract to ensure justice. Most people believe that their role is either part of insuring justice for other people or helping to relieve injustice in the world. People who find themselves in an inequitable position often do many things to make sure that equity can be achieved. One thing we know is that equity is based upon several interlocking propositions. To review, we will list the propositions that form the basis and understanding of equity. The importance of this, of course, is understanding that equity becomes a primary consideration of jurors throughout the trial.

Proposition I: Individuals will try to maximize their outcomes (where outcomes equal rewards minus costs).

Proposition IIA: Groups can maximize collective rewards by evolving an accepted system for equitably apportioning rewards in costs among members. Thus, groups will evolve such systems of equity and will attempt to induce members to the system.

Proposition IIB: Groups will generally reward members who treat others equitably and generally punish (increase the cost for) members who treat others inequitably.

Proposition III: When individuals find themselves participating in inequitable relationships, they become distressed. The more inequitable the relationship, the more distressed individuals feel.

Proposition IV: Individuals who discover that they are in an inequitable relationship attempt to eliminate their distress by restoring equity. The greater the existing inequity, the more distressed they feel and the harder they try to restore equity.

These four propositions provide an understanding of equity and describe how people tend to behave when they find themselves in inequitable positions or are in the position of judging others where equity is a major issue. There is no question that in the courtroom, equity becomes a major issue. During the trial, jurors are trying to right "wrongs" that have been created so that equity can be restored.

There are several factors which will influence juries in making decisions that relate to equity. These factors include: (1) the defendant's attitude; (2) "defendant outcomes"; and (3) victim inputs. Defendant attitude refers to how the defendant appears to the jurors. For example, if the defendant appears to be more similar to the jurors, there will more likely be better results and more leniency in the sentencing that will occur. In terms of "defendant outcomes", if the defendant has already suffered during the perpetration of the act, jurors will take his suffering into account when they render verdicts. Therefore, what they will try to do is to restore the equity that needs to be restored. Victim inputs refer to the attributes of the victim. If the victim has positive attributes as opposed to someone with negative attributes, jurors will impose a longer prison sentence upon the defendant. For example, if the victim is a leader of a gang as opposed to a ten-year-old girl, he will receive less consideration in terms of equity because he (the victim) will be perceived as having negative attributes.

Generally, jurors who have a strong belief in a "just world" impose harsher sentences. That is not surprising to find. When you assemble a group of jurors and you can identify that they believe in a "just world" concept, you know that they will be more likely to impose harsher sentences or more substantial awards favorable to plaintiffs and prosecuting attorneys.

II. Communication Techniques

§ 4.09 Communicating with the conscious and unconscious mind

The art and science of persuasion in the courtroom rests with the attorney's ability to perform one single communication act: to engage the conscious mind of jury members while communicating to their unconscious mind. Effective persuasion encompasses the conscious mind by providing it with substantive, factual information while speaking to the unconscious mind with more subjective and experiential information. Both minds work together to determine an individual's decision-making process, but the way in which the right and left parts of the brain function together in a decision-making strategy is illustrated in Communication Principle 19 which states: People make decisions by emotion (unconscious mind) and validate them with logic (conscious mind). This principle clearly provides that the decisions in the final stage of the decision-making process are made on the basis of emotion (i.e., subjective and sensory experiences), but they are presented as objective and logical decisions in an attempt to provide the conscious mind with validation.

Understanding how the conscious and unconscious mind works is particularly important to the trial attorney in order to be able to persuade jurors. As jurors integrate new information, the content (i.e., facts and testimony) is filtered through their subjective and emotional experiences in the courtroom. The most effective trial attorneys will take the jurors through actual emotional experiences so that when they do make the decisions they have memories of powerful phrases, powerful moments, or a powerful experience the attorney has described. In other words, whatever the individual is experiencing at the moment will affect how he interprets the factual information. If a person is angry, for example, and while in that state of mind goes to a new restaurant for dinner, a response pattern will be established; primarily on an unconscious level. The restaurant will be associated with angry feelings even though those feelings have nothing at all to do with the restaurant. The purpose of the effective advocate is to influence the jurors' emotional pipeline by creating and directing the types of subjective experiences they want jurors to have.

It is important to keep in mind that the final step in the decision-making process for most people is a kinesthetic right-wrong or good-bad feeling that they experience. That is what we call a gut-level or instinctive feeling. This gut-level feeling utilizes subjective experiences stored in the unconscious mind. Thus, final decision-making strategies are made in terms of what "feels" right.

A good example of how this works concerns people who are excellent spellers and how they determine whether a word is spelled correctly or not. One of the most commonly used strategies of top-notch spellers is that when they see a word that is not correct, it actually bothers them to read it. They get a physical feeling that something is wrong. This alerts them to the fact that the word is incorrect. Very simply, excellent spellers know that a word is wrong because they feel badly. That is their way of validating that the word needs to be corrected and changed. This is an example of using the kinesthetic system as a final verification step in order to determine whether or not a decision is the correct decision. When a decision is made by jurors, we need to be concerned with how they feel, because that is going to be the basis for their final decision-making strategy.

It becomes increasingly important to understand how impression formation, persuasion, and credibility factors which have been discussed previously, establish the context for how the final decision will be made. Therefore, the attorney must control and direct the perceptions of himself and the witnesses, because all of these perceptions enter into the emotional pipeline. It can be summarized that the feelings jurors have about the attorney, the witnesses, the client, and the dynamics of the courtroom arena, will not only enter the decision-making process, but will predominate in that process.

In order to understand how to influence jurors by engaging the conscious mind while communicating to the unconscious mind, it is very important to understand both how the conscious mind and unconscious mind operates. By understanding the differences in how each mind processes information, the attorney can then direct his efforts toward appealing to both the conscious and unconscious mind. Throughout the trial, one should not trying to eliminate the use of the conscious mind. Rather, the most effective strategy is to maximize the use of both minds understanding that they both will enter into the final decision-making process.

§ 4.10 —How the conscious mind operates

The most understandable distinction between the conscious and unconscious mind is that the conscious mind primarily deals with content or factual information while the unconscious mind deals with experience. In working with both minds in the courtroom, it is very important to present the content and factual information to the conscious mind while helping to recreate an experience for the unconscious mind. This is critical because the unconscious mind must relate to an experience in order to make a decision, especially if that decision has some emotional aspect to it. Whether you represent a plaintiff or a defendant, there are emotional aspects of the case and it is a matter of directing the jurors to experience the emotions that you want them to have.

The conscious mind tries to control the individual's thoughts as if it alone can be trusted. For this reason we know that the conscious mind is very good at deciding goals and outcomes, in other words, unemotional decisions. The conscious mind recognizes itself as the only mind. It uses logic and reason for everything. That is why whenever we validate decisions, we usually go straight to the conscious mind to explain why we are doing something, how it works, and how it is the logical thing to do. Legal training clearly develops the use of the conscious mind (i.e., straight, logical, linear patterns of thinking). We know that while the conscious mind is logical, the unconscious mind uses nonlogical (not illogical) methods. What we need to understand here is that both minds are highly rational and both are capable of reasoning, but they reason with different types of information. The conscious mind reasons and deals with content, while the unconscious mind deals with experience.

Another important distinction between the conscious and unconscious mind, is that the conscious mind is severely limited in terms of the number and amount of information with which it can deal. We know that the conscious mind overloads with about five to nine pieces of information. That is why in the 8-part formula we use only three major points. We know that three main pieces of information are acceptable for the conscious mind and that it will not only keep the conscious mind engaged, but it will provide the logic and structure necessary to enable the conscious mind to make its decisions. When you start overloading the conscious mind, it will eventually short-circuit in an effort to reduce uncertainty, anxiety, and impulsive decisions. Unlike the conscious mind, the unconscious mind can handle much more information.

It is necessary and important to appeal to the conscious mind in the courtroom. The 8-part formula is very instructive and useful in this context because the structure is specifically designed to engage the conscious mind.[1] In other words, it gives the conscious mind direction, organization, and structure for what is going to take place next. At no point should the jurors feel like they are floundering or that they do not know what is happening next because this creates anxiety and loss of attention. Once structure is provided and uncertainty is reduced, then the unconscious mind can come into play.

COMMENT: Remember, the 8-part formula provides a structure for the conscious mind to sort logically and rationally while the unconscious mind will attend to the subjective experience. The subjective experience will include the dramatization of an event, perceptions of the attorney, voice tone changes, and behavioral changes. In short, anything that elicits or creates a sensory experience, actually feeling, seeing, or hearing about something.

If the plaintiff's attorney successfully recreates the experience about how his client's husband became brain damaged, he will elicit sensations, visual images, and sounds in the minds of the jurors. This is quite different from factual information which does not create an experience. Remember that factual information, unless presented experientially, will be processed solely by the conscious mind.

§ 4.11 —How the unconscious mind operates

The unconscious mind deals primarily with experience and uses a nonlogical method for processing that information . In other words, the unconscious mind can deal with a great deal of information and can piece it together in many different ways. It pays attention to little nuances and subjective communications. That is why personal appearance factors, for instance, as superficial as they seem to be the conscious mind, are very influential when perceived and processed by the unconscious mind. Because we know the unconscious mind will pick up nuances and little bits of information in the courtroom, these types of considerations, particu-

[1] *See supra* § 3.43, *Using the 8-part formula for opening and closing arguments*.

larly the factors presented previously, are significant.[2] In fact, they become quite significant when it comes down to the final decision-making process.

The unconscious mind is far more capable of processing large amounts of information than the conscious mind. It has no limitation on the number of variables that it can process. Like a computer with a million megabyte brain, the unconscious mind can process information simultaneously while the conscious mind will overload with only five to nine pieces of information and will sort only one piece of information at a time. The jurors act as detectives in an attempt to assemble both information and experience to assist them in the final decision-making process. Every juror, by the time he walks out of that courtroom, will have undergone a particular emotional experience. He will have liked this attorney or not liked that one. He will have favorable feelings about a witness and not so favorable impressions regarding another witness. He will have positive feelings about the courtroom or he might not have enjoyed the environment and so on. Each one of those emotional experiences will be processed by the unconscious mind and will have a significant influence during final deliberations.

There is a long history of reported use of the unconscious mind by performers and creative people. We can take this a step further and say that successful trial attorneys use the unconscious mind whether or not he realizes it. Einstein discovered the theory of relativity by imagining what it would be like to arrive at the end of a light meter. Until he had done that, he could not imagine how to even begin his formulations. He then spent five years backing up that experience with mathematical formulas.

The unconscious mind assimilates information as a whole. It does not try to think in linear steps as does the conscious mind. The conscious mind says that *A* produces *B* and together they produce *C*. Therefore, the conscious mind is very useful for assembling information in terms of relationships. The unconscious mind does not demand this, and therefore, can put information together in many different ways. It is very interesting to note that the conscious mind can be easily seduced when you give it structure and organization. This simply means that the more structure and organization you give to the conscious mind, which is the format and the framework in which it likes to deal with information, the

[2] *See generally supra* Chapter 1, *Impression Formation in the Courtroom*.

more apt you are to create a "window" in order to appeal to the unconscious mind.

Another important consideration about the unconscious mind is that it does not deal with negatives such as "not", "never", "no one". In other words, when you say to the unconscious mind, "do not think of a pink elephant", the mind will automatically think of a pink elephant. The reason for this is very simple. When you say the word "pink elephant," the mind will immediately go into a search pattern to "search" and "sort" for whatever image or reference it has to a pink elephant. The unconscious mind simply deletes the word "not" or "no" or "never". It does not respond to the absence of something. Therefore, when you tell the unconscious mind something and you put the word "not" in it, you may get the opposite response than that which you are requesting. A parent, for example, might yell to a child, "Don't drop that glass!" At the very moment the parent yells "Don't drop that glass," Johnny drops the glass on the floor, primarily because the command statement really said, "Drop that glass." The "don't" is deleted by the unconscious mind, and it follows the command exactly as it is stated from that point on.

This is a technique that can be used inside the courtroom. If you want the jury to feel a particular emotional state and yet you do not want to be seen as someone who is perpetrating or suggesting that they feel this emotional state, you can tell them the opposite. For an example, you might say to the jurors, "I would not want you to feel frightened by my client's experience." The statement actually is processed by the unconscious mind as, "Feel frightened by my client's experience." Because the word "frightened" is said, the jurors will automatically search and sort for their experience of the word "frighten." Regardless of whether you say "don't be frightened," you have now accessed their experience of the word "frightened." The most important thing to recognize is that whenever you use a word such as "frightened" that what it will do is to access the memory of what it feels like to be frightened. As a result, the jurors will immediately experience the emotion of "frightening" forgetting the fact that you said "Don't be frightened."

It is very important to appeal to the unconscious mind during the trial since it processes kinesthetic (feeling) or the experiential information necessary for deliberating and making a decision. This explains why so much of the technique sections are focused on unconscious mind communication. Successful trial attorneys already use many of these techniques, but they simply use them by intuition rather than by understanding how they elicit a particular response.

§ 4.12 Focusing jurors' perceptions

It is very important to focus jurors' perceptions in the courtroom. If the attorney does not take the lead role in focusing the perceptions of the jurors, they will simply begin to assemble their own perceptions and lead themselves in directions in which they wish to go. When this happens, the attorney has little control over how the jurors perceive the trial process. Most of the time, this is exactly what happens during the course of the trial. Without a basic strategy and full understanding of how the conscious and unconscious minds work, attorneys use random, nonintegrated communication techniques which do not produce predictable results. As a result, a little "knowledge" may be worse than no knowledge at all. These techniques are quite sophisticated and the serious student is advised to obtain formal training to develop these skills. It is important to remember three things when focusing on the perceptions of jurors. First, jurors' perceptions can be directed. Second, what you demand of the jury is exactly what you are going to get from them and, third, you need to focus both the conscious and unconscious mind on the information you want to be remembered and retained.

Successful trial lawyers are constantly directing the jurors' perceptions in the courtroom. Any good speaker has the ability to direct and focus the attention of the audience. That is why we recommend that attorneys attend speaking seminars in order to improve their ability to move and direct audiences. In addition, it is very important to study people who are already persuasive speakers, be they dramatists, professional platform speakers, or politicians. It is also important to note that these techniques offer knowledge and information. The actual effectiveness of this information will be determined by its use. It takes a great deal of skill and repetition to learn to use these techniques so that they are internalized and become a natural extension of your personality.

A second consideration in focusing jurors' perceptions is to recognize that what you ask the jurors to think about is exactly how their minds will begin to search and sort information. That is a very important element to understand in terms of language patterns. That is, if you suggest a particular word to someone, whether you want them to think of that word or not, they will automatically sort and search through their experiences to determine whether or not that word makes sense to them. Further, they will actually elicit any emotion with which that word is associated. So if we say the word "arrogant," you will automatically find that your mind will search and sort for either the experience of what is arrogant behavior or for a person who is arrogant. In a study conducted at universities, researchers embedded a particular word in the minds of students by repeatedly stating throughout the course of the semester (approximately twenty-five times) that the instructor was arrogant. By the end of the semester, the students filled out the class evaluation forms and over 90% of the forms had the word "arrogant" on it with reference to the instructor's personal characteristics. The following semester, using the same instructor with a new class, they embedded the word "friendly," using the same number of repetitions. By the end of the semester, not surprisingly, approximately 88% of the respondents wrote down that the instructor was friendly. Assuming that the instructor did not vary his personality traits by behaving differently from one semester to another, you should recognize the power of word association when it is placed in the minds of an audience.

The third element to remember is that you want to focus the jurors' perceptions on both the conscious and unconscious levels. It would be ineffective to communicate only to the unconscious mind because a decision made on the basis of subjective experience will still be validated by the logic of the conscious mind.

§ 4.13 —Asking jurors for what you want

To control the way jurors think, you must first establish an emotional climate, and you do this by suggesting to them the emotion that you want to go through their minds. Most attorneys use words and phrases which state the exact opposite of what they want the jurors to think. For example, a voir dire question might be structured to ask the following information by the plaintiff's lawyer in a wrongful death suit: "Do you have any quarrel with the burden of proof applied?" This question causes the mind to do several things on an automatic basis. First, it will force the mind to search for the feelings related to the word "quarrel." Quarrel is an emotion, and the very word will evoke a remembrance of that emotional state, so unless you want the jurors to feel "quarrel," or quarrelsome do not use the word. Further, and more significantly, the word "quarrel" is being equated with "burden of proof." The unconscious mind will automatically attach these two words and hence will make it more difficult for the plaintiff's attorney. Even when you say,

"We don't want you to quarrel with the burden of proof," you are still connecting "quarrel" and "burden of proof."

A more effective way in which to word this voir dire question is: "Are you in agreement with the burden of proof applied in this case?" In this structure, you identify what you want, which is agreement, and you focus the jurors on this emotional feeling. Program and use the words and phrases you want and not what you do not want. This will cause the jurors to search for the information in the direction that you want to lead them.

In the example, "Do you have any quarrel with the burden of proof applied to this case?" we have done several things by changing the verbal structure. The first thing we have done is focused on the word "agreement." What we are doing here is trying to create the emotional climate that we want jurors to have. The one thing we want them to experience is agreement with counsel. The second thing we have done is put the jurors in a position to agree with us. Rather than asking them to quarrel with us, we have asked them to agree with us. This will start the pattern of many minor agreements in order to lead to a major agreement—the verdict. The third level is that "agreement" (which is a positive state) is now connected with the "burden of proof." In other words, whenever the jurors think of agreement or burden of proof, they will associate the two together. The final factor that has occurred with the change and structure of this question is that we are now connecting "agreement" with the attorney. Therefore, the plaintiff's attorney has used the word "agreement" and the association is going to be "agreement" with this attorney.

Table 4–1, *Changing The Structure of Voir Dire Questions to Direct Jurors' Emotional Experience*, illustrates the differences between ineffective wording of a question and effective wording. What you will notice most predominately is, in every instance, the ineffective use of wording is programming information or an emotion that you do not want jurors to think about, but nevertheless that is what is being asked in the question. You will notice that in Table 4–1, the areas that are italicized will signify the information that is being programmed into the minds of the jurors.

For example, question 1 of the table provides: "Isn't there a chance that this will make my job of persuading you harder than the job of my opponent, the defense lawyer?" Right away we can see that the underlying statement is "Make my job of persuading you harder." So actually the command to the unconscious mind becomes "Make my job of persuading you harder." Moreover, we have linked it back to the lawyer. The better and more effective wording is "Can you be sure you will be as easily and fully persuaded to decide for the plaintiff as for the defendant, depending only on the facts of this case?" We have now used a phrase which represents the emotional state we want to create with the jurors of being "easily and fully persuaded." With proper rewording, we are able to plant this message into their minds. Question 4 in our table asks, "Does anyone disagree that each of these other areas also deserves to be considered separately for each person who suffered this loss?" More effective wording of this question would be, "Do you agree that each of these other areas also deserves to be considered separately for each person who suffered this loss?" Generally, questions should be stated positively and not negatively.

Another example is offered in question 10: "Does anyone feel it improper and unreasonable for these factors to be considered?" The more effective wording is: "Do you feel it is proper and reasonable for these factors to be considered?" Once again we place the focus on the emotional state we want the jurors to experience and/or we direct their thinking in a particular manner. In question 10, we want jurors to feel "proper and reasonable." When you word voir dire questions, make sure that you identify how you want jurors to think and that you select the appropriate words to focus their minds in the direction you want them to go.

Table 4–1
Changing the Structure of Voir Dire Questions to Direct Jurors' Emotional Experience*
(Plaintiff's lawyer in wrongful death suit)

Ineffective	*Effective*
1. Isn't there a chance that this will *make my job of persuading you harder* than the job of my opponent, the defense lawyer?	1. Can you be sure *you will be as easily and fully persuaded* to decide for the plaintiff as for the defendant, depending only on the facts of this case?

*Developed by Lanny Landteigen, President, Performance Excellence, 1985, Tempe, Arizona: Performance Excellence, Inc.

Ineffective	*Effective*
2. Has your reading of any of those articles *caused you in any way to be reluctant to render a fair and substantial verdict* if the facts justify it in this case?	2. Does your reading of any of those articles *leave you free to render a fair and substantial verdict* if the facts justify it in this case?
3. Do any of you *feel it is in any way improper* for these factors to be considered?	3. Do you *feel it is in every way proper* for these factors to be considered?
4. Does anyone *disagree that each of those other areas also deserves to be considered separately* for each person who has suffered this loss?	4. Do you *agree that each of those other areas also deserves to be considered separately* for each person who has suffered this loss?
5. If those factors fairly suggest an amount of five million dollars for the losses suffered by the plaintiffs in this case, would there be anything about your feelings or backgrounds that would *give you any hesitancy* at all about returning a verdict in the amount of five million dollars?	5. If those factors fairly suggest an amount in the excess of five million dollars for the losses suffered by the plaintiffs in this case, would your feelings and backgrounds *leave you sure* to return a verdict in the amount of five million dollars?
6. Is there anyone who has *any preconceived ideas* as to how much money would be fair for the loss of a life?	6. *Who has an idea* about how much money would be fair for the loss of a life?
7. Do you have *any problem with making a fair, just, and adequate award* to a person who has been injured through the wrongful conduct of another?	7. Are you *in favor of making a fair, just, and adequate award* to a person who has been injured through the wrongful conduct of another?

	Ineffective		Effective
8.	In this case we believe that the judge will instruct you that recovery is permitted for grief. Does it *seem unreasonable to you* that that is a loss which should be considered individually for each person who has suffered grief?	8.	In this case we believe that the judge will instruct you that recovery is permitted for grief. Does it *seem reasonable to you* that that is a loss which should be considered individually for each person who has suffered grief?
9.	The law also permits recovery for love, sorrow, companionship, comfort, guidance, pain, and suffering. Does anyone *have a problem with* allowing each of these losses to be considered individually for each person who suffered their loss?	9.	In addition to grief and sorrow, the law permits recovery for the loss of love . . . the loss of comfort . . . the loss of companionship . . . and asks us to consider the losses from mental suffering . . . from shock . . . and from pain. Do *you agree that each* of these losses can and should be considered individually for each person who suffered their loss?
10.	Does anyone *feel it improper or unreasonable* for these factors to be considered?	10.	Do you *feel it is proper and reasonable* for these factors to be considered?
11.	Is there anyone who *has any reluctance or hesitance* about returning a verdict for exemplary damages if there were aggravating factors which caused Jane Smith's death?	11.	If the facts show there were aggravating factors which caused Jane Smith's death, would you *feel right about returning* a verdict for exemplary damages?
12.	If this were your trial as a plaintiff, would there be any reasons you would *not want eight jurors like yourself*?	12.	Would you, if this were your trial as plaintiff, *be satisfied to have eight jurors* deciding your case who have the same frame of mind as you now possess?

§ 4.14 —Identifying how you want jurors to think

It is very important to consider exactly how you want jurors to think about the case and particularly the emotional feelings you want them to experience throughout the trial. One of the most significant areas which will begin this process is the structure and wording of questions during voir dire. This underscores our early principle about primacy (Principle 6) which says that people attempt to maintain their original perceptions regardless of contradictory information. Voir dire is the most important time to set up and establish exactly how you want jurors to think.

The first step in structuring questions for voir dire is to identify how you want jurors to think. The words you use and the specific linguistic patterns which you select will establish how jurors will sort and process information. Important questions to consider include, "Do you want jurors to feel a particular emotion, see a certain picture, retain particular key phrases?" Think of the mind as a computer which responds to the information with which it is programmed. Specific word choices and phraseology used during voir dire will not only start jurors thinking in a particular way, it will also program their thoughts so that you can elicit these particular thoughts and experiences at a later time.

The lawyer must decide not only what facts he wants jurors to know, but he has to decide how he wants them to mentally and emotionally receive these facts. On the explicit level, the attorney wants the jury to think that his client is innocent or the opposing side wants the jury to think the client is guilty. On the implicit level, jurors will perceive everything through an emotional pipeline, in other words, information will be processed through whatever they are experiencing at that time. For example, if a person is angry when you shake his hand, even if you have nothing to do with the anger that they have, it will become transferred to you. Consequently, when you shake his hand on another occasion, it will tend to elicit that same angry response. That is why it is critical to consider what emotional state the person is in before presenting information. Attorneys have a tremendous ability to influence the emotional pipeline of jurors by understanding how to communicate to the unconscious mind.

For example, if the jury is upset, because they think the judge gave them too little time for lunch and they come in impatient, this is not the time to tell them the most detailed or complicated facts about the case. You will find that their impatience or anger will prevent them from actually understanding what is going on. Later, during the deliberations they will only remember that they were angry at the information. They will not understand that it was incidental; that they were impatient and the information was presented at the same time. This tells us about a simple, classical conditioning process which provides that information presented simultaneously with an ongoing emotional experience will be associated together. Therefore, the emotional experience a person has at the time the information is being presented will determine how that information will be interpreted at some later point in time.

Another example of this association factor is found in the stories of Don Juan. When Don Juan would talk to a woman, he would get her to describe in detail her emotional experience during a very deep love relationship. By describing this experience in detail the woman would actually recreate the feelings that she had and would begin to experience them in present time. When she was fully associated and experiencing this state of being "in love", Don Juan would touch her and look deeply into her eyes. Without knowing it, the woman would associate being "in love" with Don Juan. At another time, all Don Juan would have to do is touch her in the same place and look into her eyes in the same way and he would elicit her emotional experience of being "in love". This is an example of using an anchoring technique.[3]

Specific word choices and phraseology will not only start jurors thinking in a particular way, it will also program their thoughts and emotions so that you can recall them at a later time.

§ 4.15 Using embedded commands

An embedded command is a technique for engaging the conscious mind while communicating to the unconscious mind. Specifically, the embedded command identifies a specific action message which it gives to the unconscious mind. Keep in mind that the unconscious mind is very much like a computer. It acts on commands and when it hears a particular action, the conscious mind allows the action request to come through. The key to this process is to be able to break through the conscious mind, to break through the logical and rationale decision-making process.

An embedded command will actually command the person to perform, think, or feel in a particular way. The unconscious mind is not selective. It will hear the command, and it will respond impartially. A simple example of an embedded command might be a sentence which says, "I'm wondering whether you know that you are beautiful." The first part of that sentence is, "I'm wondering whether" and it serves as a preface for the conscious mind. The next part of the sentence which says, "you are beautiful" goes straight to the unconscious mind.

Before we can identify this as a true embedded command, two things

[3]*See infra* §§ 4.34–4.37, for extensive discussions concerning anchoring techniques.

must be present. First, there must be a preface for the conscious mind such as "I'm wondering whether." This allows the conscious mind to relax because the preface only asks for awareness and not action. It also does not tell the conscious mind what to do. When the conscious mind receives an order it either stops or begins preparing defenses. The command or order, "you are beautiful," is slipped into the unconscious mind. The second requirement to make this an embedded command is the need for a pause and then a voice change beginning with the word "you." The first part of the statement should be said casually as if a person is truly just wondering or curious. On the command part of the statement, the voice tone should become lower and stronger as it would in giving any command. These shifts in voice tone and the pause pattern serve to cue the unconscious mind that the following information is for it. Remember that the unconscious mind picks up on nuances and behavioral changes. That is why this form of cueing is so effective.

In structuring a command, there are three steps which you want to perform. First, decide on the command with which you want compliance. Secondly, preface the command with a tentative or permissive phrase and, thirdly, use a pause and shift in voice tone when going to the command.

There are several types of prefaces which can be used to create a window to the unconscious mind. They include the following:

I'm curious to know if

I'm wondering whether

What if you could tell me exactly what

What if you could remember

Is it possible to

I knew a man once who

I know you're wondering if

I was thinking about whether you are aware of that

Do you realize

The important thing to note about the preface statement is that it asks for a capability rather than action. The conscious mind will tend to respond to your question with a "yes" if you say, "I wonder if you know?" The reason why the conscious mind will repond with a "yes" is because the preface asks only if they knew or could do something. It does not tell them to do something. As we have discussed, the conscious mind reacts very strongly to being told what to do. That is why you use a tentative or prefacing phrase. In the courtroom, you might say something like, "Mr. Jones, is it possible to remember exactly what happened that evening?" The conscious mind automatically responds by saying, "Yes, it's possible" and the unconscious mind takes the command which is "remember exactly what happened that evening."

The embedded command really goes right to the unconscious mind. Therefore, what we are trying to do is to pacify the conscious mind to allow information into the unconscious mind. Embedded commands are particularly useful with children and you can understand why. A child does not like to be told what to do, but if you preface the statement with an innocent phrase statement such as, "I'm wondering if you could tell me exactly what two plus three is" then you can get the child to tell you the answer. The first part of the sentence is permissive. Always structure a command with a permissive sentence, then the actual command will have a much better chance of getting through to the unconscious mind. The following sections will identify specific ways in which you can (1) get a request through to the unconscious mind, (2) engage the unconscious mind, (3) mark the command so that it has high impact, and (4) use the embedded command during voir dire.

§ 4.16 —Getting a request through to the unconscious mind

Once you understand how the conscious mind works, it is not difficult to get a request through to the unconscious mind. You must first, however, satisfy some of the needs of the conscious mind. Remember, that the conscious mind does not like being told what to do. It will automatically have a polarity response which simply means it will rebel to an explicit command statement. So if you say, "Don't touch that," you will find that the most common reaction to that type of statement is to perform the very action which is not desired. We do not like to be told what to do. This is a response that people develop very early in childhood, so consequently, we can understand how it comes into play in the courtroom.

It is important to understand also that the unconscious mind will not accept a command that is against the best interest of the person. The unconscious mind is specifically set up to protect itself. That is why even in hypnosis you will find that if the person feels that what they are being asked to do is either nonsupportive of them or has a potentially harmful effect, they will not, in fact, perform the action.

To get requests through to the unconscious mind several things must take place. First, the request must be preceded by permissive language, or a preliminary phrase. Secondly, the requests needs to be marked with a pause prior to the request to indicate that a shift is taking place to the unconscious mind, and third, the request needs to be marked with a vocal tone change or even eye or facial changes. This also marks the command and directs it to the unconscious mind. Keep in mind that the unconscious mind will process information on an experiential level and needs this kind of marking in order to get the information through. What you are doing in this process is pushing the conscious mind out of the way by eliminating the potential for defensiveness or any need to protect itself against what it might consider harmful requests.

§ 4.17 —Engaging the conscious mind

The basic way to get through to the unconscious mind is to engage the conscious mind. This is very important to do in the courtroom because the conscious mind is going to be assembling the logical and factual information into an objective order. One means of engaging the conscious mind is to elicit curiosity. If the conscious mind is curious, it quits trying to defend. Curiosity is a positive emotional state, while creating apprehension is not. So what you want to do is try to arouse the curiosity of the conscious mind so that you can then provide it with new information. An example of arousing curiosity would be a phrase such as this: "You may find out some very interesting things other than what the other attorney wants you to know by the end of the trial." This type of statement will arouse the curiosity of the jurors to think about what is following in the trial. By doing this, both the conscious and unconscious minds will start working together to collect the information.

Another point to remember when we engage the conscious mind is that it can be easily overloaded with too much information. When this occurs, anxiety is created and the result is usually an impulsive decision-making strategy in order to quickly reduce the uncertainty. That is why, once again, you can engage the conscious mind with very simple, logical cause and effect information. Hence we recommend the three major points in the 8-part formula and a short theme statement. We want to give the conscious mind structure and organization without overloading it.

In addition, the conscious mind is easily seduced by words. The unconscious mind will take the words and translate them into experiences.

The unconscious mind needs words, therefore, that are as descriptive of an experience as possible. When you are talking to the unconscious mind, use the multiple language systems of visual, kinesthetic, and auditory predicates, because this will provide a full sensory experience for the person. The conscious mind does not need direct sensory words in order to understand something. Words represent a person's experience. Therefore, the unconscious mind needs statements about experience and action, while the conscious mind needs facts and objective considerations.

Engaging the conscious mind is a preliminary step to the effective use of embedded commands. If you're able to engage the conscious mind, you can then plant the commands into the unconscious mind and have both minds of the jurors directed and focused on the information which you would like them to consider.

§ 4.18 —Marking the command

An embedded command, as we have explained, is a directive to do something or to perform a specific action. It is not a request. The embedded command is a telling statement; it does not ask for something. Since most people do not like to be told what to do, we need to engage the conscious mind. Jurors are told that they are decision makers. Therefore, they definitely will not like being told what to do, except perhaps by the judge. What we want to be able to do then is to give the jurors a directive about how we want them to think, but we want to bury it so that it is hidden from the conscious mind. When the command is "buried," the conscious mind will not block or defend against submission of further information to the unconscious mind. The way in which we can do this is by marking the command so the unconscious mind actually receives the message. Marking of a command means that through the use of changes in voice tone, pauses, and other forms of behavior such as gestures and eye and facial movement, the command is directed to the unconscious mind. Curiously enough, the unconscious mind will pick up a change and shift of tone in voice, because it pertains to all subjective experience.

The process by which we can mark a command will occur in the following order: First, we want to decide what the directive is, in other words, identify what particular emotional state we want jurors to experience, what we want them to feel, or what words we want them to think about. Keep in mind that any word that we give to the juror is going to elicit a corresponding emotional state. So if we use the word, "quarrel" we're going to have them thinking about what it was like to quarrel. If we use the word, "hot" we're going to have them thinking about everything that is associated with hot. The second step in this process is to precede the command with a permissive statement. The purpose of the permissive statement such as "I'm wondering if" will simply draw attention to the subject and it engages the conscious mind, and that's what we want to do in order to get the command through to the unconscious mind. The third step then is to mark the command so that the words that are part of the command statement are set apart from other words.

If the command is, "I'm wondering if you could finish this report right now," we first recognize that the permissive statement is, "I'm wondering if you could." It is permissive, it allows the mind to make a choice, and it is simply asking for capability. The conscious mind says, "Yes, of course, I've got the capability of doing that." At this point, there must be a pause and the voice tone has to change so that the final part of that sentence becomes a statement or a directive, which is "finish that report right now." If you separate the phrases in this manner, the embedded command will go to the unconscious mind and you have received permission to send this message. To mark an embedded command, you can use a pause. Use a pause right before the command statement appears, and then change your voice level. When you give the embedded command, the voice level can become much more directed as if that were a statement telling a person what you want them to do. It will not sound as if you told them what you want them to do, because the first part of the sentence, which is the permissive clause, is not only a permissive statement, but it is said in such a way that it allows jurors to casually process that information and to allow the information in.

Marking can also be achieved by a change in tone and tempo of the voice. You can also mark a command by changing eye contact. For example, you may be looking off and the moment you want to give the command, look to the person and give them direct eye contact. If the command is, "What if you could remember everything that took place that night," the first part of that statement is "What if you could" which is permissive, and the command becomes, "remember everything that took place that night." Here we have the direct command that takes place. When you go to the command, "remember everything that took place that night," that is the time to mark it, to shift your eye contact to the person that you want to remember this. So you can use eye contact to mark a command. The most important thing to keep in mind is that you're marking out the commands so it just makes enough of a shift that the unconscious mind picks up and begins to assimilate this information.

§ 4.19 —Using embedded commands during voir dire

For the purposes of using embedded commands, there are four specific voir dire functions that occur during: (1) jury education, (2) jury selection, (3) jury rapport, and (4) jury preparation. Jury education is a very important process of voir dire, because during this point, you are educating the jury as to the type of information you want them to consider, how you want them to think, and what their roles are going to be in the courtroom. You are setting the stage for everything that is going to follow.

Jury selection is the explicit function of the voir dire process—selecting those jurors which will be fair and impartial to your client. The third aspect of voir dire is jury rapport. To create rapport we want to maximize the similarities between counsel and the jurors to increase the chances that they will like you. We want jurors not only to like the attorney, but also to agree with him.

The fourth stage is a very important stage in voir dire—jury preparation. What we are trying to do is prepare the jurors for how we want them to think and listen. We want to gear their minds to what is important. That is why the types of words we choose and the phraseology that is used in the beginning of the trial becomes very important.

The use of embedded commands early on in voir dire can help you get your message across more easily throughout the course of the trial. If you say to the jurors, "Are you aware of how important it is to be completely honest with every answer to each question for the next two hours?" you have presented an embedded command. You have asked, "Are you aware?" That is a question that has a permissive quality to which the conscious mind responds, "Of course, I've got the capability of being aware. I am in fact aware." Then the next command is, "How important it is to be completely honest with every answer to each question." So the command begins with the words, "be completely honest with every answer to each question for the next two hours." We know that information set up in this format will tend to slide past the conscious mind and will have greater impact.

If, on the other hand, you simply tell the jurors, "I think it is most important that you be fair and impartial throughout the trial," what the jurors will understand from this is that is what you want. It has not been an experience for them. In other words, you have not activated their experience of the words "fair and impartial." Herein lies a very important point to the embedded command. When you use an embedded command that says, "Are you aware of how important it is to be completely honest with every answer to each question for the next two hours," the jurors will begin to assess what is meant by the words, "honest and fair" because you have asked them to consider this. When you tell them it is what you want them to consider, they do not have to search and sort for that experience because it is your experience. From postjury research, we know that when juries receive instructions from another person, they will actually give themselves permission to ignore the instructions, even if they represent the law. Because it was not something that they experienced themselves, they made exception to it. What you want to do is make sure that you communicate messages in such a way that the jurors have to sort and search for the words that are used to create an experience for them.

The importance of embedded commands during voir dire is they will actually engage jurors in experience, and it is no longer outside of them. What we are trying to do throughout the trial is to get jurors to associate with the actual experience that took place. This means we want them to place themselves inside an experience, rather than to be an observer of an experience. Once a juror actually "feels" what the client feels, rather than observing what the client feels, the likelihood of being persuaded to make a favorable determination is that much greater.

§ 4.20 Creating a high impact emotional message

There are several specific techniques which can be used to create a high impact emotional message. We often think that if you describe an emotional event, jurors will automatically have sympathy for your client and, therefore, they will empathize with the client. Just describing an event, regardless of how great the tragedy or how dramatic the experience, will not automatically produce empathy. The verbal patterns and structure will determine whether a true linking or empathy takes place between the jurors and client.

To create a high impact emotional message, several things must be considered—the first of which is that there should be no difference between real as opposed to imagined events as they are described. The next consideration is that there should be a way to increase the jurors' association with the emotional messages. Specifically, what we are trying to do is to have jurors not only hear the emotional message, but actually to go through the experience that the other individual had. This is called association. The next factor is that we want to be able to move jurors across time and space lines. Whenever we are describing an event in the courtroom, we are describing an event that took place in the past. If we describe that event as it took place in the past, the jurors simply look at it as an event from which they are distanced and to which they have no immediate reaction. What we have to be able to do is to use verbal techniques to move jurors across time and space lines and move them back in time to the particular event.

When creating a high impact emotional message we must also be able to both associate and disassociate with the emotional message. This is going to become very important to the attorney. In order to be effective in persuading the jury, counsel must know how to associate with the message. In other words, they must know how to experience the event in order to convey its essence to jurors. Likewise, they have to know the techniques for disassociating and stepping out of it, so that they can go back to the more objective, logical appeal. Finally, we want to look at how to avoid or, in the alternative, create emotional distance with language. The plaintiff's attorneys want to limit any emotional distance with language, while a defendant's attorney will want to use language that creates a distancing factor, so that they can reduce the drama and emotional impact of an event.

§ 4.21 —Real versus imagined events

The unconscious mind cannot distinguish between a real event or an imagined event. We need to qualify this remark by saying that when the unconscious mind recreates an experience that took place and that picture is fully described in terms of sensory stimulation from hearing, seeing, and feeling, the unconscious mind will treat that as an actual experience. Therefore, if you can create an image in the mind, it actually becomes the real event and the full experience is created. This is a technique that has been used by many sports performers. A champion golfer, for example, will actually replay a shot that he already performed to watch it again and to feel what happened. As he is replaying the shot, he is tensing and changing his body position, and he is feeling the swing as it actually took place. This same technique of practicing events in the mind is used by many athletes. They will actually see the event in their mind and their body will go through the entire emotional and physical experience as if they were actually performing the behavior. If you are observing an individual recreating this experience in his mind you might notice a tension in the neck area, muscles start to change, an entire series of micromuscle movements occurring, along with eye lid movement.

When you create an explicit video in the mind, it becomes a real event. Once a person has an experience, whether it is real or imagined, it now remains in his memory and then it becomes indistinguishable between a real and an imagined experience. This explains, in part, why people who are very convincing liars can tell a lie and actually believe that they have not told a lie at all. What they have really done is to create the experience in their minds and they have created it so fully, that, to them, it has actually become a real experience. When they tell you about what has taken place, they simply return to that videotape in their mind which is an event of something they have seen themselves doing, (not only seeing themselves doing but felt themselves doing) and, therefore, they are telling you from their direct experience, and not from a "made-up" event in their heads. To them, it is real.

It is very important to recreate the experience of your client for the jurors because once that experience is recreated, there is no difference between the real and the imagined experience. When you are telling a story about a plaintiff who suffered a serious, lifetime injury, you need to recreate the event so that the jurors can actually "feel" the accident, "hear" the sounds, and "see" the event fully in their minds. The most skillful trial attorneys do just this. They are able to create the full experience so that the jurors actually relive the event. When you are creating the experience for the jurors you are not trying to tell a story. Rather you are trying to get the jurors to experience the actual feelings that took place at that time.

§ 4.22 —Increasing jurors' association with emotional messages

Since emotion is the result of perception (Principle 1: Communication is based on perception), what we are trying to do is direct the jurors' perception so that they can feel and experience an emotion. There are several ways in which this can be done. One method to increase association is to move the jurors across, time and space lines. We want to move them to the actual time of that event. Another method for increasing jurors' association with emotional messages is to make sure that we give them a full and complete description using auditory, kinesthetic, and visual predicates. The more emotional reaction that you want, the more fully you have to recreate the experience for the jurors.

Association is often likened to using drama and acting, but as we said earlier, what we are talking about is not acting at all. The very finest of actors and actresses put themselves in the event and become that person, so there is no longer any acting involved. They completely identify with the character they are portraying. The attorney in his case must become the client. He must sit in the client's seat and see the world through his eyes and allow himself to actually feel the pain. That is why attorneys cannot distance themselves from the event. By the very nature of courtroom work and the volume of cases with which attorneys have to deal, there is going to be a certain distancing factor that takes place just to protect themselves, but the successful trial attorney, before he goes into the courtroom, knows he has to go through the actual experience. He has to relive the trauma of somebody going through a car accident and losing his arms and legs. If he can associate with an event, then a mood can be transferred. Jurors have a collective consciousness and will pick up whether or not the attorney is associated. The very act of association is extremely persuasive and powerful in the courtroom.

§ 4.23 —Moving jurors across time and space lines

Any intuitive speaker understands that moving the listener in time helps us to experience something to a greater or lesser degree. One example is when we have a painful experience that we do not want to relive, simply think of it as happening in another time. We put it in the past tense. In the courtroom, the plaintiff's attorney definitely wants the jurors to experience the event fully so that they can identify with his client. The only way this can be done is to allow the jurors to move back in time to the past, and what we are trying to do then is to take the jurors through the actual experience.

Since most cases appear in court three to six years after an event has actually taken place, there are several considerations which we cannot forget with regard to the client. The client most likely has distanced the event from himself, so that he does not have to feel the pain everyday, especially if the pain is very severe, such as in a wrongful death case of a loved one or a plaintiff who has become a paraplegic. Whatever the case may be, they have to do this in order to survive emotionally. The first thing that happens is that he attempts to distance himself emotionally from the event. The trial, however, will become a very painful experience for the plaintiff, because the attorney will have to help the plaintiff reassociate with that event so that by the time he gets to the courtroom, he is retelling the event as if it happened just that very day. If you cannot get your client to reassociate with the event, it will be very difficult to convince the jurors and bring them through that event also. You do have to caution your client, however, that he is going to have to go through and relive the pain again.

When we move people across time and space lines, we have to keep in mind what we are asking them to do. For example, you might tell a child, "Someday you will thank me for this." The child does not understand, because we are now asking him to move ahead in time and imagine what that would be like. A child cannot jump into the future from his framework because his full time framework has not yet been developed.

Language controls how thoughts are processed and what experience they elicit. This becomes very critical. An example of making a simple shift when telling a story about an individual is to change tense. The statement reads: "She drove down the expressway thinking about what she might buy for her husband." You can see that that sentence is in the past tense. You can change that to: "She is driving down the expressway thinking about what she might buy for her husband." The very act of changing it to an i-n-g, active present tense verb, puts it into the present tense and the person begins to see the event taking place. If you use a past tense verb such as "she drove," the mind will not create the experience as vividly as if you ask the jury to participate in it. When you use "i-n-g" verb forms you are asking the person to step inside that experience and see it as you are recreating it.

§ 4.24 —Disassociating with an emotional event

Disassociation for the attorney is a very important skill to consider. Once the attorney has told the story, and has become very associated with it (in an associated state the attorney will actually feel pain or other emotions), he must learn how to be able to step out of that experience so that he can go back and talk to the jurors and regain present time. One way to do this is to reorient yourself to the present. If you do this, the emotional intensity will not exist in this time frame. The way to do this is to simply remind yourself of the present state or real time orientation and step back as an observer of the event. Then, you will see the event happening, and you will see the pain as separate from yourself. Most attorneys tell the story in the courtroom as an observer. They see the event happening, and then they tell the story. There is a major difference between telling a story of a traumatic, emotional event which you heard about and telling a story from the position of having been in the event. Actually having been there and associated with the event is much more powerful. The critical skill is for the attorney to actually associate with the event and feelings rather than to tell the story as an outside observer. When you tell the story as an observer, drama techniques and acting skills are not going to help to convey that message, because it is not a real, actual, and genuine feeling. Jurors are as perceptive as any audience is and will pick up the difference.

§ 4.25 —Avoiding or creating emotional distance with language

In the plaintiff's position, one wants to decrease or remove any distance which the jurors might experience from the event, the emotion, or the client. In the defendant's position, the exact opposite is true. The defendant's counsel wants to increase the distance factor so the jurors do not associate an emotional event with the client. There are specific ways to obtain distance through use of language. In fact, language can either create distance for a person or bring him very close to the event.

§ 4.26 —Nominalizations to create distance

One of the language techniques that can create distance is the use of nominalizations. This is a term in which we take words and we put them in a noun form, which serves to increase the distance or puts us at an emotional arm's length from the event. For example, if an individual says, "My divorce was painful," the word "painful" is a nominalization. In other words, it is a word that is treated as a noun, and it becomes a "thing". Little emotional content is conveyed. "Painful" will not elicit the feeling or the experience of pain. It is a different statement if somebody says, "My divorce caused me pain." That is a more associated statement, and it will elicit the response of pain. If you use nominalizations, the thing that will happen is that the jurors will not feel that the event was real. It becomes a distance factor from there. It "was painful" as opposed to it "caused me pain."

§ 4.27 —Verb forms to eliminate distance

Let us take a question that might be used during voir dire. The question is, "If the loss that each person has suffered individually as a result of the defendant causing the death of Jane Smith, will you consider each loss for each person?" Now the phrase that we are most concerned about is the "death of Jane Smith." "Death" is being used as a nominalization.

It has become a thing. It creates a distance in the question. Now, if the plaintiff's attorney is asking this question, we do not want to create a distance between Jane Smith and the death, so we need to change it to an actual verb. It would read as follows, "If the loss that each person has suffered individually as a result of the defendant causing Jane Smith *to die*, will you consider each loss for each person?" When we change it to "to die," we have a closer language link and we have changed it to an action verb. You will find that it will actually cause a different type of association with the feelings that it will elicit from a person. If you just read the sentences out loud, you will hear a difference between "causing the death of Jane Smith" and "causing Jane Smith to die." The first is a nominalization, the second is changing it into verb form.

COMMENT: A simple rule of thumb is that a plaintiff's attorney should avoid using any nominalizations or any language that distances the jurors from the actual event. They should try to use action words that are in the present tense to get as close to recreating that event in the present time as possible. Defense attorneys want to do the exact opposite. Because they want to increase distance they will want to use nominalizations, treat events as things, and put events into past tense to create a distance between the jurors and the actual event that took place.

---

§ 4.28 Using verbal techniques

Words are a direct representation of all the experiences that we have in life. They allow us to represent or recreate a particular experience. There are various techniques that can increase the power and impact of certain phrases that you want jurors to remember. In the following sections, we will be discussing the importance of (1) sequencing phrases and words, (2) increasing the power of questions and statements by linking them together, (3) creating a movie in the jurors' minds, and (4) creating photographic stills in their minds.

The use of techniques is very important in the courtroom, because words are the method by which we implant the commands and requests into the unconscious mind.

§ 4.29 —Sequencing phrases and words

The basic rule to understand with regard to sequencing phrases and words is that when people do not know what they are supposed to do, they will not process the information being given to them. For example, in the statement "If you were thirty-one-years-old, instead of fifty-one, single and no children, in good health, would you take skydiving lessons?" What will happen in the first part of that sentence is the person will automatically reserve judgment until you present all the information necessary in order to make an informed decision. In that sequence you have put the conscious mind into a very tentative state, and the mind will not proceed with any decision until you give them the final piece of information which is, ". . . would you take skydiving lessons?" We can examine this process and see that it sets up four particular roadblocks to the conscious mind. First, the person's reaction will be held in abeyance until the entire question is asked. Secondly, he will start to set up the scenario, which will be meaningless because it is taken out of context. Third, the way the sentence is sequenced will reduce the amount of impact the question has. Fourth, it immediately signals suspicion and defensiveness on the part of the conscious mind, because the conscious mind will ask, "What are they trying to get me to agree to?"

The rule of primacy is involved here, because we are demonstrating the importance of sequencing critical information first in the structure of a sentence (Primacy is embodied in Principle 3: Perceptions are organized and structured within a brief period of time). The critical information has to be presented first in the sentence because we do not want the mind to wait for additional information. A question that might be asked in voir dire could be something like this, "Would you fail to consider them, even if the law permits them?" Now, we can dissect this question and see what is happening. The first phrase, "Would you fail to consider them," forces the mind to wait for the end of the question. This is a very weak construction, because it does not establish a strong cause and effect relationship. The person will have to wait until the end of the sentence to understand the full context. A better construction would be, "If the law permits them, will you consider them?" The reason why this becomes a stronger construction is we are now putting "if the law permits them" first so the jurors know what is being asked. By using this sentence construction, counsel now need only demonstrate that the law will, in fact, permit them. The third factor that has just occurred by changing the sequence is we have now obtained a public commitment to a cause and effect relationship which says "if the law permits them, then the juror will consider them."

We can make this link even stronger. We can change the sentence structure to read as follows: "If the law permits them, will you permit them?" We have removed the choice of the word "consider" and it forces the stronger link. Counsel will merely have to demonstrate that the law permits them and then the juror will feel compelled to permit them, because they have already answered that question. Remember Communication Principle 8 which states: People have a need to be consistent. Once a public commitment is made, there is an automatic need to maintain that consistency throughout the trial.

§ 4.30 —Increasing the power of questions and statements by linking

Linking increases the power of questions by placing the factual information first (i.e., that information which is accepted as fact by the jurors) and linking it to new information which they want the jurors to see as factual. This very linking and association will direct the mind to consider both pieces of information as causally related and as factual information. A second function that linking provides is that it engages the conscious mind and allows the unconscious mind to receive more information. If you talk to salespeople, you will recognize that effective salespeople will automatically link factual information, followed next by information which is not as yet accepted as fact. This linking process is very effective in opening statements, especially when you are building a "picture for jurors."

A very powerful yet simple rule that applies to increasing the power of questions by linking is as follows: When you make a true statement (one that is accepted as true by the listener) and link it in the same sentence to another statement, this increases the likelihood that the second clause will be perceived as accurate also. For example, an insurance salesman might say, "You're twenty-seven-years-old and we feel you need at least $50,000 coverage in life insurance." The first part of the statement is true, the client is in fact twenty-seven-years-old. Now that we link it with the word "and" and we follow it with "and we feel you need at least $50,000 coverage in life insurance." There is an automatic reaction to accept the second part of the statement as being true as well when it's linked in the same sentence. This is far more effective than the inverted statement, "You need at least $50,000 in coverage, and this is based on the fact that you're twenty-seven-years-old."

There are many different types of linking words that you can use. "And" is a very common link, it simply links two sentence structures together. Make sure to state the factual information first and then follow it with the information you want accepted as fact. Another linking clause is "since/then." For example, "*Since* you are coming to the party tonight, *then* would you be able to stay later?" Another one is "as/will" as in the following example. "*As* you are sitting here listening, *will* you try to remember what happened last night?" These are ways of linking together various clauses of a sentence.

Linking statements help to remove periods and definite stops in the language pattern. When you can remove the periods from a language pattern what you will have is a much more fluent flowing language rhythm that tends to mesmerize listeners and communicates more fully with the unconscious mind. Some of your most effective speakers never speak with periods, until they get to the dramatic points.[4]

One of the reasons that linking is so effective is that it employs a force of logic for the conscious mind. You are telling the conscious mind since this is true, then that must be true. Automatically a connection will take place. The mind is directed to make this connection and it will seek the connection because the language has directed the mind to move in a particular pattern.

§ 4.31 —Creating a movie in the mind

Trial attorneys are quite familiar with how to recreate an event and to tell a story in the courtroom. What becomes very important in the story telling is that there are very explicit rules which must be followed if you really want the jurors to experience the event that you are trying to recreate for them. The first thing to recognize is that a movie is a memory of an actual event. In order to recreate this memory, it must be reviewed in chronological order. It begins to lose its impact if you start in the middle of a movie and go backwards. Thus, if you are talking about the fact that a man lost his foot, and then you go back to the time when he lost his foot, you have not followed chronological order. When you do not follow chronological order, you lose curiosity and suspense. In addition, since events in real life occur chronologically, by placing it out of

---

[4] *See infra* § 4.31, for a disussion of the importance of fluid language patterns.

order, it becomes a "surreal" event. The result is that it will be difficult, if not impossible, to get jurors to associate with the event itself. It is, therefore, a mistake to give the "punchline" and then build to it. It will no longer be a movie and it will, in fact, lose its impact.

To create an actual experience for a person (e.g., to get them to associate with an event), the movie will have to feel real. If it is in jumbled chronological order, it will not become a real experience, because real experiences in life do not occur in a jumbled order. To do this, there are several factors that you have to keep in mind. The first thing is to use "i-n-g" verbs and present tense. When you present something in the present tense, you will get the client to experience it as it is happening at that moment. The second thing to do is to make sure you use conjunctions or linking words such as "and," "as," "while," "since," and "then." A third factor to consider in creating movies in the mind is to use longer sentences. Use longer sentences with a flowing rhythm and which do not end abruptly. Finally, whenever possible, talk without "periods" by using only commas. Keep everything moving very quickly as one sentence leads automatically into another. By doing this, you mesmerize the jurors and are able to enter into their unconscious minds.

There is only one place to use abrupt, short types of sentence structures and that is when you get to the critical point of the story. Then you will see a clear difference between creating a movie in the mind and using photographic stills in the mind to create high drama and suspense.

§ 4.32 —Creating photographic stills in the mind

As discussed previously, an event must be presented in a flowing, fluent manner and in chronological order to create a movie in the minds of jurors. This serves a very important purpose of engaging the mind, and also of mesmerizing the jurors and bringing them along to the areas to which you want to direct their attention. When you build to a highly dramatic point, you want to shift from creating a fluid, chronological movie to using photographic stills. A photographic still is used to increase drama and impact, very similar to a horror movie where everything is smooth until you begin approaching the terrifying moment. At that point, it will change to short photos or short clips which start to build the suspense. This same technique can be used during an opening statement.

To create a photographic still, you must use shorter sentences with periods, instead of long drawn out sentences. At this point, you want to use disjointed, abrupt sentences to create impact and excitement. In addition, try to use clipped and articulated words. To create maximum impact, build the movie with long and conjunctively connected phrases and then suddenly start using short, abrupt sentences. An example of using photographic stills would be as follows: "There is a sudden blur of image. Something much larger than your vehicle is coming at you from the side. You feel the impact. Your mind begins to dim and go black. Your steering wheel hits your chest. Your leg is locked underneath you."

This example gives you a series of short slides. You will notice that every sentence is like switching a slide and you see a new picture that takes place.

§ 4.33 —Using verbal techniques in opening statement

In this section, we will take an example of a partial opening statement and will restructure it line by line to show you the use of embedded commands, developing movies in the mind, switching from past tense to present tense to minimize distance, critical word selection, sequencing sentences, deleting powerful phrases for opposing counsel, and using photographic stills to create impact. In the following, you will read an example of the partial opening statement as it exists now. Then, you will have an analysis of verbal structuring of the partial opening statement where we will present the original sentence, the restructured sentence, and then an analysis explaining what changes were made and why. Finally, we will offer you another reading of the restructured opening statement so that you can compare the two.

It is very useful to tape-record the original opening statement and then tape the restructured statement. Play it back and notice the differences that you experience as you listen to both readings. See if listening to one or the other causes you to associate with the event more fully. You can also conduct this experiment on another person. Read each opening statement and ask him his feelings and responses to the statement. To conduct a true experiment, have one group listen to the original opening statement and another to the restructured opening statement. Then ask questions about how they felt about Eddie. The following analysis is quite detailed and will provide you with an understanding of the use of talking to the conscious mind while engaging the unconscious mind.

Example of Partial Opening Statement

(1) "December 15, 1982, was like any other day for Eddie Jones. (2) At least that was what he thought that evening. (3) He had finished work early, but stayed in his blue jeans and blue denim work shirt. (4) As was his custom, he and a couple of his fellow construction workers went across the street to Harold's Bar for a couple of beers after work. (5) They had gotten off at 5:00 in the evening. (6) By the time they got to the barroom, it was already dark. (7) Eddie was sitting in there with his two friends, Harold James and Larry Brown, and he had no idea what was happening down the street. (8) The first thing he knew of the commotion in the front of the dark in the barroom. (9) He heard a male voice asking: 'You're sure this is the place you saw him run into?' (10) A female voice answered in a hysterical high pitched tone, 'I'm sure! I'm sure! I'm sure!' (11) Eddie Jones did not pay much attention. (12) He felt that whatever was going on did not concern him. (13) He turned back to Larry Brown to continue his conversation about the lousy season the New Orleans football team was having. (14) It was the usual type of conversation two men would have in a bar. (15) Suddenly, he felt himself jerked off of the bar stool from behind. (16) He did not know what was happening. (17) He was thrown face down on the ground and was being roughly and brutally beaten. (18) He started cursing, as anyone would. (19) Suddenly, he felt his arms being pinned behind him and heard the noise of the clasp as the handcuffs were being clamped on him. (20) He kept screaming, 'What's this about!? What's this about!? G__ D__, what's happening,' he protested. (21) Someone kicked him in the mouth. (22) All he saw was a black shoe. (23) Momentarily, he was rolled over and a flashlight was in his face. (24) Two policemen were looking down at him and asking the woman, 'You're sure this is the man?' (25) She was crying and hysterical and kept mumbling the word, 'Yes! Yes! Yes!' (26) Then as he lay there, Eddie knew that she could not be right, he had done nothing wrong. (27) He later found out that a man had come up from behind her and snatched her purse. (28) As he ran past her, she only saw him from behind on the dark street. (29) He happened to be wearing blue jeans and a blue denim shirt, similar to that of Eddie Jones'. (30) He would later also learn that the lady was not really sure where she saw the man run into. (31) She thought she saw him heading into the barroom. (32) Importantly, the evidence will show that no one

found the purse. (33) The police looked for it all over the barroom. (34) They even searched the patrons in the barroom. (35) But the evidence will show that there was no purse in the barroom. (36) The evidence will clearly show ground for a reasonable doubt regarding this alleged identification of Eddie Jones. (37) The evidence will show that the whole case rests on the testimony of the victim who saw her assailant only from the back as he ran past her after snatching her purse. (38) Her only grounds for identifying him is that he is of similar build and was wearing similar clothing."

Verbal Restructuring of Partial Opening Statement

SENTENCE (1)

ORIGINAL: December 15, 1982, was like any other day for Eddie Jones.

RESTRUCTURED: No change necessary.

ANALYSIS: None.

SENTENCE (2)

ORIGINAL: At least that was what he thought that evening.

RESTRUCTURED: At least that was what he *was thinking* that evening.

ANALYSIS: The first change which needs to be made in this opening statement is to move the sentence into the present tense by using "ing" words. The phrase "was thinking" begins this process. This allows us to increase association and moves jurors across the time lines to make this a present event. The goal is to begin the association process with the jurors so that they can "see" themselves involved in the actual event. Past tense verb forms will distance the event and the emotional response of the jurors. We want to maximize the emotional response of the jurors in any way possible.

SENTENCE (3)

ORIGINAL: He had finished work early, but stayed in his blue jeans and blue denim work shirt.

RESTRUCTURED: He had finished work and had stayed in his blue jeans and blue denim work shirt.

ANALYSIS: In the restructuring of the original sentence we have deleted the word "early." because there is a later reference in sentence number 5 that says "getting off at 5 o'clock". This is incongruent with what most people consider to be "early", with regard to getting off work. We do not want to set up any type of dissonance in the minds of the jurors. If they have a question about the facts and whether they make sense, they will either place the information in abeyance or they will begin to discredit other events as being true. Rather than take a risk that information will be perceived as contradictory or incongruent, it is better to be very explicit and remove information which may result in confusion.

We have also deleted the phrase "but stayed in his blue jeans" and changed it to "and stayed in his blue jeans" to indicate that it is a common behavior for somebody to stay in the clothes that they had on at work.

SENTENCE (4)

ORIGINAL: As was his custom, he and a couple of his fellow construction workers went across the street to Harold's Bar for a couple of beers after work.

RESTRUCTURED: No change necessary.

ANALYSIS: None.

SENTENCE (5, 6)

ORIGINAL: They had gotten off at 5:00 in the evening. By the time they got to the barroom it was already dark.

RESTRUCTURED: They had gotten off at 5:00 in the evening, and at this time of the year, it was already dark.

ANALYSIS: At this point, we want to begin the linking process to make the sentence structure more fluid and smoother so that we can create a movie picture. In order to do this we need to use conjunctions such as "and", "since", or "as" to tie sentences together. The purpose is to create the impression of continuous motion as one would see in an actual movie frame. The original sentence structure has two abrupt sentences. In the restructured sentence, we have combined them and made one sentence.

We have also deleted the phrase "by the time they got to the barroom." This phrase is not congruent with information presented later that says that the bar is just across the street. It is very important when structuring an opening statement that you check for any nuances that may cause the jurors to question the information. Once the information is being questioned, even if it is on only one minor point, that questioning attitude will be carried across to all other points. It does not make sense that by the time they walked across the street it was already dark because one would assume that this distance is covered in a matter of minutes. The mind, at this point, will hold these inconsistencies in abeyance and will halt the movement of the movie we are trying to create.

SENTENCE (7)

ORIGINAL: Eddie was sitting in there with his two friends, Harold James and Larry Brown, and he had no idea what was happening down the street.

RESTRUCTURED: Eddie is sitting in there with his two friends, Harold James and Larry Brown, and he *has* no idea what was happening down the street.

ANALYSIS: In this analysis, a change to present tense has been made to keep the jurors more closely associated with the event.

SENTENCE (8)

ORIGINAL: The first thing he knew of the commotion in the front of the dark in the barroom.

RESTRUCTURED: The first thing he *knows* of any commotion *came from* the front of the dark barroom.

ANALYSIS: This is an interesting combination of using both present tense and past tense combination in order to create two very explicit states. Present tense is used when we say "the first thing he knows of any commotion" because we want the jurors associated with the situation. We want them to be right beside Eddie as he is going through this experience. However, the second part of the restructured sentence reads: "came from the front of the dark barroom". The reason we use the phrase "came from" here is that we are switching over to past tense because now we want to distance Eddie from the actual event that took place.

This is a verbal pattern that will allow the jurors to participate in Eddie's experience and also notice the fact that he is separated from the event that took place. This is a way of removing the actor from the acted upon. It removes Eddie from the commotion that took place in the barroom. It also creates a separating state and simply moves him farther away. Throughout the opening statement, the intent is to maintain association with Eddie, but continually distance the event from him so that he is perceived as a victim and not a participant. The only way this can be done is through the careful selection and sequencing of words and phrases. Anything that is said in the opening statement sets the pattern from that point on.

SENTENCE (9)

ORIGINAL: He heard a male voice asking, "You're sure this is the place you saw him run into?"

RESTRUCTURED: He *hears* a male voice asking, "You're sure this is the place you saw him run into?"

ANALYSIS: A change is made to present tense to maintain an associated state with the jurors.

SENTENCE (10)

ORIGINAL: A female voice answered in a hysterical high-pitched tone, "I'm sure! I'm sure! I'm sure!"

RESTRUCTURED: A female voice *answers* in a hysterical, high-pitched voice, "I'm sure! I'm sure! I'm sure!"

ANALYSIS: Once again we are using the present tense to continue the motion picture movement.

SENTENCE (11, 12)

ORIGINAL: Eddie Jones did not pay much attention. He felt that whatever was going on did not concern him.

RESTRUCTURED: Since it is no business of his, Eddie *ignores* it.

ANALYSIS: This restructuring illustrates a very important point. In the original sentence structure, the jurors are asked to believe that Eddie did not pay attention to what was going on in the bar. The original sentence reads: "Eddie Jones did not pay much attention." The phrase "did not pay much attention" suggests that he had to pay some attention. In fact, what that particular phrase suggests to us on the conscious and unconscious level is that he had to pay enough attention to actually determine that what was going on did not concern him. The very word choice will access the thought of Eddie paying attention. We need to be careful of what words we access, so the words "pay attention" have been deleted. A much stronger sequencing pattern is to begin with the word "since". The word "since" sets up the acceptance of the second clause. Even though this is not a logical connection, the perception will exist that these two statements are cause and effect oriented because it starts with "since" which implied a link or connection. We also have deleted the phrase "did not pay attention to" to avoid accessing the thought that Eddie was paying attention. Finally, we have used the phrase "Eddie ignores it" after we have established a reason for this. This sequencing will allow the jurors to accept this as factual, rather than narrative information.

SENTENCE (13, 14)

ORIGINAL: He turned back to Larry Brown to continue his conversation about the lousy season the New Orleans football team was having. It was the usual type of conversation two men would have in a bar.

RESTRUCTURED: He *turns* back to Larry Brown to continue his conversation about the lousy season the New Orleans football team *is* having, and any listener would recognize it was just the typical conversation two men would have in a bar.

ANALYSIS: The first change is to use the present tense to help the jurors associate with the event. The second change is to link with the word "and" to keep the movement of the movie image. The third change involves the use of the word "just" because this is a strong word which indicates nothing out of the ordinary. The fourth change is the use of the word "typical" which suggests it is a normal everyday occurrence. Typical is a more powerful word than "usual" in creating the perception of a normal occurrence.

SENTENCE (15)

ORIGINAL: Suddenly, he felt himself jerked off of the bar stool from behind.

RESTRUCTURED: Suddenly, he *feels* himself jerked off of the bar stool from behind.

ANALYSIS: At this point a change to photographic stills will help to increase the intensity and drama. In order to do this, we need to use shorter sentences and more clipped patterns of speech. This will build the pattern of short photographic stills similar to what you would see at the dramatic points of a horror movie.

SENTENCE (16)

ORIGINAL: He did not know what was happening.

RESTRUCTURED: He can't imagine who *is doing* it or why it *is happening* to him.

ANALYSIS: The original sentence structure begins with the phrase "he did not know". This phrase immediately accesses the concept of "knowing". Remember that the unconscious mind deletes the word "not", so in the phrase "he did not know" the actual message is "he did know". This will cause the jurors to think about what he did know and what he did not know. We want the perception to be that Eddie was in a complete state of unawareness about the events around him. We do not want to use the word "know" because it suggests that "knowing" could be a possibility. A second change is to the present tense with the phrase "is doing". The third element that we have altered is the phrase "is happening to him". The original structure of this said "what was happening". The restructured version utilizes passive victim language indicating that it was happening to him and that Eddie was the victim in the event and not a participant. We want to structure it so that we are making a clear distinction between victim and participant. Counsel needs to create a picture of Eddie as a victim who was unaware of what took place throughout the entire scenario.

SENTENCE (17)

ORIGINAL: He was thrown face down on the ground and was being roughly and brutally beaten.

RESTRUCTURED: He only knows he *is being* thrown face down on the ground and being roughly and brutally beaten.

ANALYSIS: The strength of the original sentence has been increased by adding the phrase "he only knows he is being." This moves us to the present tense and suggests that Eddie knows nothing else; it also maintains the victim state.

SENTENCE (18)

ORIGINAL: He started cursing, as anyone would.

RESTRUCTURED: He *cursed* as anyone might.

ANALYSIS: Several things have been changed in this sentence. The first change is the use of past tense. Up to this point, we have been using the present tense to increase the association with jurors. The original phrase "he started cursing", however, is a phrase for which we do not want juror association. Counsel wants to tell the jurors that his client cursed before the opposing party brings out this information. This will reduce the shock value to the jurors. In so doing, however, it is important to position this phrase as a distant factor. This can be accomplished through the use of past tense, "he cursed". The implication is now that he cursed in a moment of surprise. Most people can accept cursing that occurs on one occasion, but continuous cursing is an entirely different story. The change to past tense creates a distance to imply a one time event. The second change has been made in the second clause of this sentence. The original phrase was "as anyone would". This original phrase requires that the jurors agree that "anyone would" curse in a similar situation. This is not a true statement and it could be very offensive to some jurors who would say "there's no way under any situation that I would start to curse". The original language structure requires the jurors to associate and identify with a phrase to which they may or may not agree. If, in fact, they do not agree with that phrase, two things might occur: (1) they will discount additional information, or (2) perceive themselves and the attorney to be dissimilar because they do not agree. At all costs, avoid placing jurors in any situation where they are asked to accept a statement that is not acceptable within their belief system. The phrase is changed to "anyone might". This allows choice; it allows the jurors to make the decision as to whether or not a person might perform this action in a similar situation. We have not challenged their belief system or interrupted the flow of the movie by creating dissonance in their mind. This is an excellent example of how the selection of a single word phrase will direct the experience and the perceptions the jurors will form.

SENTENCE (19)

ORIGINAL: Suddenly, he felt his arms being pinned behind him and heard the noise of the clasp as the handcuffs were being clamped on him.

RESTRUCTURED: His arms are pinned behind him and clamped there with something that makes a metallic sound.

ANALYSIS: In this sentence we want to make sure that we are establishing the victim situation. Therefore, the original phrase, "suddenly he felt his arms being pinned" has been changed to "his arms are being pinned behind him". We are back to the movie scene, and we are describing the event as it took place in chronological order. Further, we are letting the jurors know that Eddie Jones was not a participant in this situation, rather he was a victim. The word "he felt his arms being pinned" places Eddie into a participative act. The phrase "his arms are being pinned behind him" sets up a narration of this movie and positions Eddie as an innocent, unsuspecting victim. The next change in this sentence is very significant. The original sentence reads: "He heard the noise of the clasp as the handcuffs were being clamped on him." Because the original sentence specifically and explicitly refers to the term "handcuffs", we know that Eddie is aware of the fact that he is now having handcuffs put on him. We can go a step further and assume he is aware that the "police" are putting the handcuffs on him. This suggests a state of "knowing", and "participation." We do not want Eddie to be perceived as highly aware as to what is occurring. Eddie hears sounds, feels his arms being pinned, even realizes exactly what is happening. We want the jurors to experience the same surprise that Eddie experienced. We can do this only if we keep Eddie in the victim state. Therefore, our goal is to set up a scenario that describes that "something is happening" but that Eddie is still fuzzy at this point as to what exactly is going on. The language must reflect this. The new phrase reads: "It clamped there with something that makes a metallic sound." The key word in this sentence is "something." It implies that he is unaware and that he is not even able to make a determination as to what exactly is being clamped on him. The word "something" when delivered, needs to be marked verbally to separate it from other words.

SENTENCE (20)

ORIGINAL: He kept screaming, "What's this about; what's this about; God Damn, what's happening," he protested.

RESTRUCTURED: He *keeps* screaming, "What's this about; what's this about; Damn it, what's happening?"

ANALYSIS: In this instance, we return to present tense because we want to keep the movie going. In the original statement we have "God Damn, what's happening". Because there is shock value with language, particularly the phrase "God Damn", we want to avoid any alienation if possible. In the second restructured sentence the word "God" has been eliminated and "damn" remains. This still lets the jurors know that Eddie did swear. The way in which this phrase is delivered will be critical. The emphasis needs to be placed on the second phrase in the restructured sentence which is "what's happening", so that the phrase "damn it" is quickly passed over vocally.

SENTENCE (21)

ORIGINAL: Someone kicked him in the mouth.

RESTRUCTURED: Someone *is kicking* him in the mouth.

ANALYSIS: The change made in this restructured sentence is to "kicking him in the mouth". It again puts Eddie in the situation of being the victim and the receiver of the act rather than a participant in the act. Present time usage is also maintained.

SENTENCE (22)

ORIGINAL: All he saw was a black shoe.

RESTRUCTURED: All he *can see* is a black shoe.

ANALYSIS: Once again we use the present tense.

SENTENCE (23)

ORIGINAL: Momentarily, he was rolled over and a flashlight was in his face.

RESTRUCTURED: He's *being* rolled over and a flashlight *is* in his face.

ANALYSIS: We are following the same pattern using present tense as well as positioning Eddie as the victim. "He's being rolled over and a flashlight is in his face," becomes a narrative and descriptive event. The phrase "momentarily" in the original sentence weakens the effect, therefore it has been deleted. We do not want to suggest that there is something "momentarily" happening. We want to suggest that it is happening as an ongoing event.

SENTENCE (24)

ORIGINAL: Two policemen were looking down at him and asking the woman, "You're sure this is the man?"

RESTRUCTURED: Two policemen *are* looking down at him and asking the lady, "You're sure this is the man?"

ANALYSIS: Once again in the restructured sentence we are using the present tense. "Two policemen are looking down at him" helps to create the picture of Eddie being looked down on. The word woman has been changed to lady, because "lady" creates a distance and reduces credibility somewhat.

SENTENCE (25)

ORIGINAL: She was crying and hysterical and kept mumbling the word, "Yes! Yes! Yes!"

RESTRUCTURED: She *is* crying hysterically and *keeps* mumbling the word, "Yes!"

ANALYSIS: A change is made to effectuate the present time and to place the emphasis on the words "hysterical" and "mumbling." When this sentence is read vocally it should stress that the woman was out of control. The vocal emphasis must be put on the words "hysterical" and "mumbling".

SENTENCE (26)

ORIGINAL: Then as he layed there, Eddie knew that she could not be right, he had done nothing wrong.

RESTRUCTURED: Lying there *bleeding*, Eddie *knows* that she *was* wrong, that somehow she *had* identified the wrong man.

ANALYSIS: The original sentence structure begins with the phrase "then as he layed there." We need to bring this back into the present tense and create the picture so the phrase has been restructured to read: "lying there bleeding." We then have a much more descriptive phrase about what is going on. In the second clause, the phrase "Eddie knows" is used. We are asserting the present tense because we want to be clear that Eddie knows and is very aware that the woman is wrong in her identification of him. Here is another good combination of using both present and past tense in the same sentence. In the second clause, we say, "Eddie knows that she was wrong." We do not say "she is wrong." The reason is that when we use the phrase "she was wrong," it sets this statement in concrete. It makes it a historical sentence; history cannot be debated. It is what has happened. This is a slick transition from present to past tense. "Eddie knows" meaning he knows, even at this moment in the courtroom, that "she *was* wrong," and she identified the wrong man. Now we have created a distance. We have set up a historical statement that cannot be challenged as easily as if we had stated in present tense that "she is wrong."

SENTENCE (27)

ORIGINAL: He later found out that a man had come up from behind her and snatched her purse.

RESTRUCTURED: He later *finds* out that a man had come up from behind her and snatched her purse.

ANALYSIS: Present tense is used by changing the word "found" to "finds".

SENTENCE (28)

ORIGINAL As he ran past her, she only saw him from behind on the dark street.

RESTRUCTURED: As he ran past her, she only saw him from behind on the dark street and noticed his clothing.

ANALYSIS: A clause has been added to the original sentence. The clause that has been added is: "and noticed his clothing." We want to make it clear that that is all she was able to notice. We have selected the word "notice" very carefully. Notice is different from "observed" and "saw" because it implies that this "noticing" happened very casually and very quickly. We want to start embedding that into the minds of the jurors.

SENTENCE (29)

ORIGINAL: He happened to be wearing blue jeans and a blue denim shirt, similar to that of Eddie Jones'.

RESTRUCTURED: He happened to be wearing blue jeans and a blue denim shirt. The reason Eddie was identified and beaten and handcuffed and humiliated in front of friends was because he chose blue jeans and a blue denim shirt to wear that day.

ANALYSIS: The original sentence accesses certain thoughts in the mind that we want to avoid. In the original sentence, it says, "He happened to be wearing blue jeans and a blue denim shirt, similar to that of Eddie Jones." The phrase that we have to be careful about is "similar to that of Eddie Jones." When the word "similar" is used, this will force jurors to access the concept of a similarity between Eddie Jones and the "criminal." In no way do we want to suggest that there is any similarity between these two. The word "similar" must be completely eliminated. The phrase, "he happened to be wearing blue jeans and a blue denim shirt" has been added. Now we are going to explain to the jurors the reason why Eddie was selected by this woman—the reason why Eddie was "identified, beaten, handcuffed, and humiliated;" here we have four words that we will set up as a rhythmic pattern. Because impact and power increases with three words, they need to be read as "identified" as the first word, "beaten" as the second word, and "handcuffed and humiliated" should be read as the third word, rather than vocally separated as two words. This creates a rhythm of three and allows the drama (e.g., anger) to build.

SENTENCE (30)

ORIGINAL: He would later also learn that the lady was not really sure where she saw the man run into.

RESTRUCTURED: Eddie would learn later that the lady was not even sure where she saw the man run.

ANALYSIS: Several critical changes have been made. The first one is that we have put the word "Eddie" into the sentence. We want to keep Eddie associated and personalized with the jurors. The word "really" has been changed to the word "even." In the original sentence it says, "not really sure." The change reads: "not even sure." This is a major difference. When we say "she is not really sure," this means there is some doubt taking place. When we say "she is not even sure," this suggests that there is not only doubt with regard to this event, but implies she is also incorrect or confused in other areas. In the second clause of the sentence, another important change has been made. The original phrase reads: "she was not really sure where she saw the man run into." In the restructured sentence, this has been changed to: "where she saw the man run." We do not want to suggest that she saw the man run *into* anything. We only suggest that she saw him "run". The moment we suggest that he ran *into* anything, we have already connected with the fact that Eddie is in a bar which sets up a logical pattern that he ran "into" something, which, in this case, is the bar. A great deal of care needs to be exercised in choosing words so that they will not support opposing counsel's position by creating visual images in the minds of the jurors that weaken your position.

SENTENCE (31)

ORIGINAL: She thought she saw him heading into the barroom.

RESTRUCTURED: No change necessary.

ANALYSIS: None.

SENTENCE (32)

ORIGINAL: Importantly, the evidence will show that no one found the purse.

RESTRUCTURED: No change necessary.

ANALYSIS: None.

Sentence (33)

Original: The police looked for it all over the barroom.

Restructured: No change necessary.

Analysis: None.

Sentence (34)

Original: They even searched the patrons in the barroom.

Restructured: No change necessary.

Analysis: None.

Sentence (35)

Original: But the evidence will show that there was no purse in the barroom.

Restructured: But the evidence will show there was no purse in the barroom. What they did find was blue jeans and a blue denim shirt; items to be found, of course, in most any barroom.

Analysis: No change has been made in the original sentence, but an additional sentence has been added. We want to create a contrast to show the absurdity of what they did *not* find in the barroom and what they *did*, in fact, find. This is a contrast factor. In the restructured sentence, we say, "but the evidence will show there was no purse in the barroom," the second sentence has to show what they did find. "What they did find was blue jeans and a blue denim shirt, items to be found, of course, in most any barroom." Notice that the phrase "items to be found, of course" implies that there is no question that you would find this attire somewhere else. The phrase "in most any barroom" is used because we do not ever want to leave the jurors with anything they could argue with or fight with. We are using tentative language where it is appropriate to allow the jurors choice and allow them to stay with us in this associated picture.

Sentence (36)

Original: The evidence will clearly show ground for a reasonable doubt regarding this alleged identification of Eddie Jones.

RESTRUCTURED: The evidence will show clear grounds for you to find reasonable doubt regarding this alleged identification of Eddie Jones.

ANALYSIS: The phrase, "the evidence will clearly show ground for a reasonable doubt" has been changed to "the evidence will show clear grounds." This is more active and helps to create involvement. We use the word "you" to speak directly to the jurors. The next phrase, "to find reasonable doubt" is our embedded command. The entire embedded command is "for you to find reasonable doubt." In order to make this an effective command statement you will need to mark this with a voice transition and a pause. Prior to the word "you," pause and change your voice tone to give a more authoritative tone. This will mark out that phrase of the sentence and you will also make the jurors access the experience of what it is like to "find reasonable doubt."

SENTENCE (37)

ORIGINAL: The evidence will show that the whole case rests on the testimony of the victim who saw her assailant only from the back as he ran past her after snatching her purse.

RESTRUCTURED: The evidence will show that the whole case rests on whether you doubt that testimony of a person, upset, who saw her assailant only from the back as he ran past her with her purse.

ANALYSIS: Another embedded command has been added. We have changed the original sentence to "The evidence will show that the whole case rests on *whether you doubt that testimony of a person*, upset." This is a very important change because we now have an embedded command which says: "doubt that testimony of a person, upset." The embedded command starts right before the word "doubt" and should be preceded by a pause and change of voice pattern.

In the latter part of the sentence, we have added the word "only": "who saw her assailant *only* from the back." "Only" is a very strong word and it shows that that is clearly all she saw. The next change is to eliminate the word "snatching." "Snatching" is a word that creates a picture of the criminal act that has taken place. It builds the image and accesses the experience of having something "snatched." This is a word that the prosecutor should use.

You should avoid using words or phrases that opposing counsel can build on. The word "snatching" has too much power to it. Even though it is being said that it is somebody *else* who snatched her purse, we are talking about Eddie in this entire situation so the association is going to be between *Eddie* and snatching the purse. We want to be very careful not to help opposing counsel with powerful imagery words.

SENTENCE (38)

ORIGINAL: Her only grounds for identifying him is that he is of similar build and was wearing similar clothing.

RESTRUCTURED: Her only basis of identification was that the assailant was of similar build and was also wearing typical working clothes: blue jeans and a blue denim shirt.

ANALYSIS: The phrase, "her only grounds for" has been altered because it is much too powerful. It accesses the concept of "having grounds" or a "solid base." It has been changed to "her only basis of identification." This phrase does not have nearly the impact and power as the original phrase and will not access the picture of a solid "base" or "ground".

Example of Restructured Opening Statement

(1) December 15, 1982, was like any other day for Eddie Jones. (2) At least that was what he *was thinking* that evening. (3) He had finished work *and* had stayed in his blue jeans and blue denim work shirt. (4) As was his custom, he and a couple of his fellow construction workers went across the street to Harold's Bar for a couple of beers after work. (5, 6) They had gotten off at 5:00 in the evening,

and at this time of year, it was already dark. (7) Eddie was sitting in there with his two friends, Harold James and Larry Brown, and he *has* no idea what was happening down the street. (8) The first thing he *knows* of any commotion *came from* the front of the dark barroom. (9) He *hears* a male voice asking, "You're sure this is the place you saw him run into?" (10) A female voice *answers* in a hysterical, high-pitched voice: "I'm sure! I'm sure! I'm sure!" (11, 12) *Since it is no business of his*, Eddie *ignores* it. (13, 14) He *turns* back to Larry Brown to continue his conversation about the lousy season the New Orleans football team *is* having, *and* any listener would recognize it was *just* the *typical* conversation two men would have in a bar. (15) Suddenly, he *feels* himself jerked off the bar stool from behind. (16) He can't imagine who *is doing* it or why it *is happening* to him. (17) He *only knows he is being* thrown face down on the ground and being roughly and brutally beaten. (18) He *cursed*, as anyone *might*. (19) *His arms are pinned behind* him and *clamped* there with *something* that makes a metallic sound. (20) He *keeps* screaming, "What's this about; what's this about; *Damn* it, what's happening?" (21) Someone *is kicking* him in the mouth. (22) All he *can see* is a black shoe. (23) He's *being* rolled over and a flashlight *is* in his face. (24) Two policemen *are* looking down at him and asking the lady, "You're sure this is the man?" (25) She *is* crying hysterically and *keeps* mumbling the word, "Yes!" (26) Lying there *bleeding*, Eddie *knows* that she *was* wrong, that somehow she *had* identified the wrong man. (27) He later *finds* out that a man had come up from behind her and snatched her purse. (28) As he ran past her, she only saw him from behind on the dark street and *noticed his clothing*. (29) He happened to be wearing blue jeans and a blue denim shirt. The reason Eddie was *identified* and *beaten* and *handcuffed and humiliated* in front of friends was because he chose blue jeans and a blue denim shirt to wear that day. (30) *Eddie* would learn later that the lady was not *even* sure where she saw the man *run*. (31) She thought she saw him heading into the barroom. (32) Importantly, the evidence will show that no one found the purse. (33) The police looked for it all over the barroom. (34) They even searched the patrons in the barroom. (35) But the evidence will show there was no purse in the barroom. *What they did find* was blue jeans and a blue denim shirt; *items to be found, of course*, in most any barroom. (36) The evidence will show *clear grounds* for *you* to *find reasonable doubt* regarding this alleged identification of

Eddie Jones. (37) The evidence will show that the whole case rests on *whether you doubt that testimony of a person, upset*, who saw her assailant only from the back as he ran past her *with* her purse. (38) Her only basis of identification was that the assailant was of similar build and was also wearing typical working clothes: blue jeans and a blue denim shirt.

§ 4.34 Using anchoring techniques

Anchoring techniques are a means of locking in a particular experience, event, or a major point for jurors. The principle behind this comes out of neurophysiological connections which simply says that any element of any experience, when repeated, brings back all elements of the experience. For example, remember "your song" with a particular lover. Even though the relationship may have occurred over twenty years ago, when you hear the song, you will find that it will bring back the full original experience. That tells us that any associational method which triggers events in the mind, will bring up the whole experience.

In the courtroom, what you want to do is illicit the emotional state that you want the jurors to have and then the moment they begin to feel that state (which you can identify or validate through facial expressions, skin color changes, breathing patterns, eye-movement changes), then you want to anchor that state so that you will be able to call it up at a later time. For example, let us assume that you are now using photographic stills in your opening statement which you are using to build to a peak. What you want to do at this point is build it to a high peak and when you see the jurors sitting on the edge of their chairs, leaning forward, and listening very carefully, anchor that event, maybe by moving to a particular spot in the courtroom and standing there while they are in that heightened emotional state.

This form of anchoring sets up a conditioning pattern. What you are now doing is conditioning that spot which becomes a stimulus or trigger later to elicit the same emotional state or experience that they had at that moment. This anchor will only be effective if you use the exact same location. You have to be precise each time that you use the anchor in order to elicit the emotional state. After you have anchored a spot to a particular emotional experience and later you return to the same spot, it will trigger a recreation of the emotional experience without the spoken word.

What this does is allow the jurors to go back and feel a particular emotion without your having to take them through the entire process again. This is very useful in closing argument when you want to trigger jurors' emotions on various points. If you set your anchors up throughout the course of the trial, you will be able to use them effectively in closing to create a very strong emotional impact.

§ 4.35 —How to anchor

Anchoring can be accomplished by various methods. Several of the common methods of anchoring involve the use of different types of marking systems. For example, you can anchor with space, anchor with vocal marking, anchor with eye movement and facial behavior, or anchor with gestures.

To anchor with spacial marking, select a particular area that you are going to use as a sensitive spot. If you are limited to the podium in the courtroom, all you have to do is move to the side of the podium. This anchor will work if you move to the side of the podium only to present the critical information and when you have the jurors in a particular emotional state. Keep in mind what you are trying to do is to condition the jurors to a certain emotional response. As the individual begins to fully experience the emotion as evidenced by nonverbal behavioral changes, move into your anchor position, (e.g., move to the left of the podium) and deliver your information. Then move back out of the anchor position until you want to elicit that state again.

You can do this same type of marking with eye-movement and facial behavior. As you are giving critical information, you can use eye contact to mark it. In other words, you can anchor by looking at the jurors in a certain way or by using a particular facial expression. In addition, you can use gestures. For example, if you are going to bring your hand up in the air at a particular point, use a particular gesture, but only use it repeatedly and consistently with the same type of information.

§ 4.36 —When to anchor

You should anchor any emotional experience that you want jurors to have. For example, if you're the plaintiff's attorney and you can work the jurors to a highly emotional state, you want to anchor that state. You can also anchor your critical points or your case theme, because this is information that you want the jurors to remember, but you have to do it when you create a particular emotional state. Because you are trying to anchor an emotional state, what you want to do then is to get the jurors to experience a particular emotion which supports your client.

If you are the defendant's attorney, you may want to anchor a very matter-of-fact, objective, distancing state so the jurors stay unattached to what is going on. For example, the defendant's attorney might want to place the jurors in a highly objective state, or into a factual state which can be anchored. You can anchor specific emotional states that you want the jurors to feel and experience at a later time. You can also anchor critical information or major points in the same manner.

§ 4.37 —Collapsing anchors

Collapsing anchors actually involves the strategy of neutralizing an anchor that has been set up by opposing counsel. For example, let us assume that opposing counsel has built an anchor with a particular sensitive spot in the courtroom. The way you can collapse this anchor is to change the feeling the jury will experience when you go to that spot. If your adversary has used a particular spot for a highly dramatic point when the jurors are experiencing fear, for example, what you want to do is get the jurors to experience a new emotion, such as relief or relaxation and anchor that in with a cough or another behavior. After you have anchored in this state, move into that same sensitive space that your adversary used after you have gotten the jurors to experience the new emotion. This will collapse the existing anchor. Now the jurors will experience the new emotional state while you're standing in that same sensitive spot.

III. Overview of Decision-Making Process of Jurors

§ 4.38 Introduction to small group persuasion

Small groups are pervasive to our society. We all belong to a number of groups, whether it is the family group, business associations, social groups, professional organizations, athletic teams or any of a vast number of small groups. One researcher estimated that there are anywhere from four to five million groups in existence at any one time in our society.[5]

Not only do we belong to a great number of small groups, we also

---

[5] James, *A Preliminary Study of the Size Determinant in Small Group Interaction*, 46 AMER. SOC. REV. 474–477 (1951).

spend much of our time interacting in the group setting. One study of an individual's interactions with others, concluded that 52% of the person's interactions were with two or more people.[6] They found that a person spends approximately 19% of his time interacting with two other people, 11% of this time with three people, and 22% of his time is spent interacting with four or more people.

Small groups have been defined by a variety of researchers. The definitions tend to emphasize the particular area of the small group that is of interest to the scholar. Three general definitions of a small group are offered here in order to provide a framework for the discussion which follows.

A widely-read scholar of small groups developed a definition of the small group that has been accepted by a great number of small group scholars.

> A small group is defined as any number of persons engaged in interaction with one another in a single face-to-face meeting or series of such meetings, in which each member receives some impression or perception of each other member distinct enough so that he can, either at the time or in later questioning, give some reaction to each of the others as an individual person, even though it be only to recall that the other was present.[7]

Another definition is as follows:

> . . . the small discussion group consists of 3–25 people who perceive each other as participants in a common activity, who interact with each other dynamically in a face-to-face setting, and who share information and attitudes through verbal and nonverbal systems of codification.[8]

Still another social psychologist defines the small group as "two or more persons who are interacting with one another in such a manner that each person influences and is influenced by each other person."[9]

From these three definitions of the small group, it should be apparent

---

[6] Wheeler & Nezlek, *Six Differences in Social Participation*, 35 J. Personality & Soc. Psychology 742–754 (1977).

[7] R. Bales, Interaction Process Analysis: A Method for the Study of Small Groups 33 (Addison-Wesley Publishing Co., 1950).

[8] S. Jones, D. Barnlund & F. Haiman, The Dynamics of Discussion 24 (Harper & Row, 1980).

[9] M. Shaw, Group Dynamics 8 (McGraw-Hill, 3rd ed. 1981).

that the jury falls within the definition of a small group. Because the jury is a small group, we can examine the jury by applying the principles of small group communication. ". . . [T]he fact that the jury is a small group operating with a distinctive task and a set of instructions allows us to speculate about its processes by applying small group theory."[10]

It is of the utmost importance, however, to keep in mind throughout this discussion that the jury operates in a different context than the ordinary small group.

> The jurors know their decision counts. They are actors in a drama which has significance beyond their solution of a dispute in a given case. As the jurors are community representatives, the resolution of the dispute defines and reaffirms the community's standards. Since all are expected to accept the decision, the drama enhances the community's integration and solidarity. Although these contextual factors make the jury a special case of a small group, still, the jury is a small task-oriented group working to achieve a consensual decision.[11]

Juries also operate under a set of rules that tend to be unique. These rules have an impact on the jury's deliberation process by setting the guidelines and expectations for the jury's decision-making process. There are six rules of jury deliberations.

1. The jury as finder of fact and the judge as "law giver."
2. Consider only the evidence presented in court ("evidence rule").
3. Arrive at a unanimous decision (or near unanimous decision in civil proceedings).
4. No time limits on the length of deliberation.
5. Vote your conscience.
6. Deliberate or debate the evidence.[12]

---

[10] M. Levine, M. Farrell & P. Perota, *The Impact of Rules of Jury Deliberation on Group Developmental Processes* in THE TRIAL PROCESS 266 (Plenum Press, B. Sales ed. 1981).

[11] *Id.*

[12] *Id.* at 267.

§ 4.39 —Individual versus group persuasion

The collection of individuals known as the small group has been studied in terms of its performance as compared to an individual's performance. The most often studied area of group versus individual performance has been in the area of judgment. Does the group make better judgments than an individual acting alone? A commentator articulates the two areas of inquiry as:

> 1. Does the quality of group judgment exceed that of the average individual performance of group members?
> 2. Does the quality of group performance exceed that of the most proficient member of the group?[13]

Results have generally supported the first area of inquiry, that is, group judgments are usually as good as and often superior to individual judgments. In studies conducted by various small group researchers, the increased quality of the group decision is explained by the increased number of judgments expressed (each group member), the increased number of evaluations of those judgments, and the wider range of information and knowledge available to the group judgment because of the composition of its membership.[14] However, the group decision is not usually of a higher quality than that of the most capable individual member who operates alone.[15]

Social benefits also arise from the small group process. Group members generally feel more confident, satisfied, and more accurate in the judgments of the group than do the individuals who are working alone.[16]

Groups are usually able to conduct the problem-solving process in a manner superior to individual problem-solving. One researcher concludes that "the evidence thus strongly supports the conclusion that groups produce more and better solutions to problems than do individuals . . ."[17] It should be noted that groups generally take more time to reach their solutions than do individuals working alone for the obvious reason that it takes three or more people more time to process all the

---

[13] SHAW, *supra* note 9, at 57.

[14] *See, e.g.*, the review of literature in SHAW, *supra* note 9, at 57–59.

[15] SHAW, *supra* note 9, at 60.

[16] *Id.*

[17] SHAW, *supra* note 9, at 63.

individual ideas and comments than it takes a person working alone to process his own individual viewpoint.

The following conclusions are offered concerning individual versus small group performance:

> Groups are more effective than individuals on tasks which require a variety of information, which can be solved by adding individual contributions, and which require a number of steps that must be correctly completed in a definite order; individuals are better on tasks that call for centralized organization of parts. Groups perform better than individuals when the process is learning or problem solving, but not necessarily when the process investigated is judgment.[18]

Studies have been conducted which investigated the influence that a groups' discussion has on the ultimate decision that the group makes. One communication scholar, for example, concludes that discussion of the case by the jury tends to enhance the initial position of the majority.

> In one simulation of cases involving traffic violations, defendants were made to appear either low or high in apparent guilt. In the low guilt condition, jurors after discussion were more definite in their judgments of innocence than they had been when they entered the room. After discussion cases where the defendant clearly appeared guilty, the jurors returned verdicts are recommended punishments even more severe than their initial inclination.[19]

Psychology researchers note that the literature in this area supports the view that jury deliberation tends to reinforce the position of the predeliberation majority.

> In studies of both real and experimentally created juries, deliberation clearly has an effect on jurors' verdict and the pattern of effect appears quite stable. The data show that postdeliberation votes of individual jurors shift to greater extremes in the direction of the predeliberation majority. If one considers only a discrete conviction/acquittal vote, the final verdict of real juries almost invariably shifts toward the initial majority. . . .[20]

---

[18] SHAW, *supra* note 9, at 67–68.

[19] K. TAYLOR, R. BUCHANAN & D. STRAWN, COMMUNICATION STRATEGIES FOR TRIAL LAWYERS 106 (Scott, Foresman & Co., 1984).

[20] M. Kaplan & C. Schersching, *Juror Deliberation: An Information Integration Analysis* in THE TRIAL PROCESS 239 (Plenum Press, B. Sales ed. 1981).

The group also tends to influence the individual group members in a number of ways.[21]

§ 4.40 —The group mind

Small groups possess an identity beyond that of any of the individual members. This concept is referred to as synergism or 1 + 1 = 3. Translated it means that the sum of the whole is greater than the sum of each individual part. A group is more than a collection of individuals; it develops its own identity and personality beyond those of the individuals in the group. We need only think of the small groups to which we belong to know that certain characteristics are associated with certain groups. Groups cannot think or feel independently of their members.[22] However, the very fact that group members share the group's values, tasks, or goals give the members much in common. At times, groups can exert a great deal of pressure on individual members to conform to the group's standards and norms.

When an individual stands alone in a judgment (or belief) against the unanimous majority, it is extremely difficult for that single member to hold out against the majority's view. In one experiment, individuals would, even if they believed the group's judgment to be incorrect, conform to the majority opinion. The possible effect of the jury group on the lone dissenting juror is apparent.[23]

The influence of the group on individual members can take an interesting turn. In highly cohesive groups, pressure toward uniformity can result in ineffective group decision making labeled by one theorist as "group think."[24]

The existence of group think is characterized by the following symptoms:

1. the illusion that the group is invulnerable, which in turn creates an unwarranted feeling of optimism;
2. the group engages in collective efforts to rationalize the

---

[21] P. Zimbardo, E. Ebbeson & C. Maslach, Influencing Attitudes and Changing Behavior (Addison-Wesley Publishing Co., 2nd ed. 1977).

[22] F. Allport, The Group Fallacy (Sociological Press, 1927).

[23] Asch, *Effects of Group Pressure Upon the Modification and Distortion of Judgments* in Groups, Leadership and Men 171–190 (Carnegie, H. Guetzkow ed. 1951). *See also* Asch, *Opinions and Social Pressure*, 193 Sci. Am. 31–55 (1955).

[24] I. Janis, Groupthink: Psychological Studies of Policy Decisions and Fiascoes (Houghton Mifflin, 1982).

course of action decided on and to discount negative information;

3. a tendency to believe, without question, the group's inherent morality, leading to an inadequate consideration of the group's moral and ethical consequences;
4. leaders of other groups are stereotyped as weak, stupid, evil;
5. direct pressure is applied to group members not to express opinions counter to the group view;
6. dissent is not allowed, thus creating a group self-censorship of deviations;
7. a shared illusion of group unanimity;
8. the emergence of "mindguards" who take it upon themselves to keep the group from negative opinion.[25]

Obviously, an effective group decision is not possible when group think occurs.

In order to help insure effective small group decision making, some noted scholars advocated vigilant group decision making, which will help guard against inappropriate group-induced pressure to conform. Vigilance refers to the sensitivity displayed by groups for a careful and intensive analysis of the decisions they are considering. A decision-maker is vigilant when he:

1. thoroughly canvasses a wide range of alternative courses of action;
2. surveys the full range of objectives to be fulfilled and the values implicated by the choice;
3. carefully weighs whatever he knows about the costs and risks of negative consequences, as well as the positive consequences, that could flow from each alternative;
4. intensively searches for new information relevant to further evaluation of the alternatives;
5. correctly assimilates and takes account of any new information or expert judgment to which he is exposed, even

[25] *Id.* Adapted from GROUPTHINK: PSYCHOLOGICAL STUDIES OF POLICY DECISIONS AND FIASCOES, by Irving L. Janis. Copyright © 1982 by Houghton Mifflin Company.

when the information or judgment does not support the course of action he initially prefers;

6. reexamines the positive and negative consequences of all known alternatives, including those originally regarded as unacceptable, before making a final choice;
7. makes detailed provision for implementing or executing the chosen course of action, with special attention to contingency plans that might be required if various known risks were to materialize.[26]

§ 4.41 —Models of small group persuasion

The manner in which small groups make decisions, that is, the manner in which small groups persuade their members that a particular action is appropriate in a particular problem situation, has been the subject of considerable research in a variety of disciplines. Small groups are found throughout society, and one small group in particular, the jury, is asked to decide issues of the utmost importance both to the individuals involved and often to society as a whole.

The following models proposed to describe and explain the process of small group persuasion provide a representative picture of the process small groups go through to make their decisions.

§ 4.42 —Model of small group decision making

A noted communication scholar, analyzed the interactions that take place in small groups. He hypothesized that most of the communication in a task-oriented small group was related to the development of a decision. By classifying speech acts according to their content, he outlined how a decision is made in a small group.

The four stages of Fisher's Decision Making Model are: Orientation, Conflict, Emergence, and Reinforcement.[27] Each stage will be described briefly and a sample interaction will be given to illustrate the stage. The interaction excerpts are from a six person mock jury deliberation in which the jurors evaluated an auto-pedestrian accident.

---

[26] I. Janis & L. Mann, Decision-Making: A Psychological Analysis of Conflict, Choice, and Commitment 11 (The Free Press, 1977). Reprinted with permission of The Free Press, a division of Macmillan Publishing Co., Inc. Copyright © 1977 by The Free Press.

[27] B. Fisher, Small Group Decision Making 140–145 (McGraw-Hill, 1974). Copyright © 1974, McGraw-Hill Book Company. Reprinted with permission.

The first stage through which the group moves is the Orientation Stage. Here the group attempts to get acquainted and establish their place in the group. This stage is characterized by clarification of proposals and ambiguously worded statements. Members offer tentative positions, being careful not to introduce tension. A high level of agreement among members takes place in this stage. Members also tend to move from one idea to another, tentatively agreeing with each other.[28]

The interaction excerpt below illustrates the Orientation Stage. (Roger Adams was the driver of the car that struck Alfred Derby. Derby is the plainiff, seeking damages.)

A. First of all, we decide whether it's a case of liability or negligence.

D. Yeah . . . negligence.

A. It's the same thing. In other words, you all feel that Roger Adams alone was negligent without the contributory negligence of Derby—or was it Derby's fault as much as Adam's fault—or was it either's fault—or was it just a plain accident.

C. Guilty or not guilty.

A. It's not just those two choices, though. We've got three choices.

D. What else can there be, though? I mean . . .

A. It's not a criminal action like whether he robbed a store. It's just whether he is negligent, both of them are negligent, or whether . . .

D. Yeah, I see. But there are still only two verdicts. Do we give the plaintiff any money or not.

A. First of all, how many people here feel that just Roger Adams alone was negligent and that Alfred Derby, the person who was hit, in no way contributed to this negligence and therefore should receive compensation?[29]

The second phase of decision emergence is the Conflict Stage. Tensions begin to surface in this phase and disputes and dissension occur. Group members begin to solidify their positions, arguing and attempting to persuade other members to their position. The group also becomes polarized on the proposals, forming subgroups with those who agree with them.[30] The Conflict stage can be seen in this section from the transcript:

[28] *Id.* at 140–141.

[29] *Id.* at 212.

[30] *Id.* at 121–142.

A. The thing to decide is was Roger Adams in a hurry. And did he act in such a manner that a reasonable, adult, mature person would.

C. You have to consider him a reasonable, prudent person. He was waved on by another person who was going to make the turn, irregardless [sic] of whether he was in a hurry or not.

A. I would say that if he is reasonable, he wouldn't take another person's word for it.

C. Oh, come one now! There is only one car on the street.

A. I certainly wouldn't do it.

C. Do you consider yourself reasonable?

A. I'm not reasonable. I'll admit it, too. But what does that have to do with it? I wouldn't want to use myself as an example. That doesn't say that he wasn't reasonable.

B. Then we're not going to get any place. You have to give some criteria. You can't just say he wasn't reasonable and let it go at that.[31]

Emergence is the third stage and is characterized by dissipating conflict. Cooperation begins to prevail following polarization and members begin to soften their positions. Again, ambiguity appears and this time represents a "mellowing." The direction in which the group is leaning becomes clearer and members begin to shift in that direction.[32]

A. Let me ask one more question. Do you think Derby (the plaintiff) was in the crosswalk?

D. I don't think so.

C. No, I don't. I don't think that has too much to do with it, though.

D. I agree.

C. I know there are some statutes about the crosswalk, but I mean the fact that he was in . . . I don't know. That might be kind of important.

D. He was on the roadway is really the issue.

C. I don't think it really happened exactly the way the defendant described it. I think he embellished it a little toward his side. I think it happened close enough to it, though.

---

[31] *Id.* at 214.

[32] *Id.* at 142–143.

F. As far as that goes, Derby may have his own story, too. I mean each would be looking out for himself. That's only natural.

D. Of course you are going to get this in any situation.

F. That's just it. Both of them. You can't use the two prime subjects. You have to try and go on the witnesses. Of course they are witnesses, too, and you have to consider them. And they are important, too, but . . .[33]

Reinforcement is the last phase of the decision-emergence process. Although group members have pretty much arrived at a decision in the Emergence Stage, the Reinforcement Stage serves as a means by which the decision is solidified. Members support, reinforce, and unify behind the group's decision. Ambiguity declines and statements in favor of the proposal increase.[34] The following excerpt illustrates these points.

E. Everybody saw the car coming.

B. Besides that, he said his lights were on.

C. His turn signal was on. It was obvious that he was coming. That would make it all the more easier [*sic*] to see the car coming.

D. Practically everybody saw that car coming. His lights turning.

E. That guy that was on the sidewalk. . . . He saw all this traffic, and he also saw Adams coming. That's why he didn't go. Why did Derby go? He has to be at some fault.

C. I feel sorry for him, and I'd like to help him out, but I just don't think I can.

D. I agree.

B. You can't base it on an emotion . . .

D. Of course not.

C. I don't think we should take into any account what they told us at the beginning, either—about Adams being a drunkard and that.

B. No. Don't even mention that.

F. No. Don't worry about it.

C. No.[35]

---

[33] *Id.* at 217.

[34] *Id.* at 143–144.

[35] *Id.* at 220.

The movement of the group through these stages is a gradual movement and may not be as easily discernable as the transcript examples.[36] His four phases are a viable model to explain how groups make decisions.

§ 4.43 —"Reach-Test" model of group decision making

According to other theorists, group decision making can be explained as the result of the cumulative development of concensus decisions.[37] Each decision provides the starting point for the next group decision. "Groups achieve consensus on decisions through interaction patterns which modify, reject, accept, or combine previously introduced decision proposals.[38]

Linear models had been proposed previously by scholars to explain group decision making. Groups were thought to proceed through a series of steps, moving from one step to another only after the previous step had been accomplished. If the group were to deviate from the prescribed order of steps or perhaps skip a step, the group would be described as inefficient or dysfunctional.

Two theorists, Scheidel and Crowell, proposed the "reach-test model" of group decision making, proposing in the process that group decisions follow a spiral rather than a linear path.

According to this theory, when a group member proposes an idea, the other members react to that proposal. They may agree, disagree, revise, or otherwise respond. If, after discussion, the group agrees with the proposal, that proposal becomes the new anchor point for the interactions to follow. Another new idea is then presented, the group's reactions are sought, making sure that all members understand the idea ("reach") before the group evaluates and criticizes the idea ("test"). If the group agrees with the new idea, it will be their new anchor point and the decision-making process will continue. If the group rejects the idea, the group will return to the previously established anchor position and proceed from there, soliciting other new ideas. Groups thus develop ideas cumulatively rather than linearly. Feedback is an important element in this model.[39]

---

[36] *Id.* at 222–223.

[37] Scheidel & Crowell, *Idea Development in Small Discussion Groups*, 50 Q. J. Speech 140–145 (1964).

[38] Fisher, *supra* note 27, at 145.

[39] *Supra* note 37. *See also* Scheidel & Crowell, *Feedback in Small Group Communication*, 52 Q. J. Speech 273–278 (1966).

A communication theorist and scholar offers the analogy of the children's toy, the "Slinky," as an explanation of the reach-test model.

> As you stretch the Slinky, you will notice that the spirals can be compressed at one end with relatively wide spaces between spirals at the other end and in the middle. But the spirals are all interconnected in a single continuous band of spring steel. In this way the spirals of reach-tested ideas are compressed during the final period as consensus decisions become increasingly obvious to the group members. But those decisions are possible only because of the previously anchored positions of agreement developed in earlier phases. The process is cumulative rather than linear.[40]

§ 4.44 —The "forming, storming, norming, and performing" schema

Another way to look at small group persuasion is to examine both how the group manages the interpersonal relations of its members and how it accomplishes its task.

After a review of the literature in which he examined the models proposed by a number of small group scholars, a noted scholar devised his own model of small group decision making. Building on similarities he found among the various models, he proposed a four phase schema. He labeled his phases (1) forming, (2) storming, (3) norming, and (4) performing.[41] In a later article he added a fifth phase, adjourning.[42]

This theory recognized that small groups simultaneously deal with two types of problems throughout their decision making. First, it was noted that groups deal with group structure problems, that is, how do the members relate with each other. Secondly, the group must deal with task achievement problems, that is, how does the group go about accomplishing its goal. Thus, for each phase of the model, both the group structure (social) problems and the task problems that a group might encounter were noted.[43]

The first stage of his model, the forming stage, is characterized by a

---

[40] FISHER, *supra* note 27, at 138-189.

[41] Tuckman, *Developmental Sequences in Small Groups*, 63 PSYCHOLOGICAL BULL. 384–399 (1965).

[42] Tuckman & Jensen, *Stages of Small Group Development Revised*, 2 GROUP ORG. STUD. 419–427 (1977).

[43] Tuckman, *supra* note 41.

concern of the group members with orientation. Both the relationship among members and the task of the group are addressed in this stage.[44]

Storming, the second stage, is marked by conflict and polarization. Interpersonal relations (social problems) are in conflict here. Storming is also reflected in the task behaviors of group members as well.[45]

The third stage, norming, is when the group begins to resolve its conflicts. New standards are set, the roles of the various group members are established, group cohesiveness begins to appear, and the group begins to develop a good feeling for itself.[46]

Performing is when the group, in the fourth stage, begins to achieve its task. Solutions are emerging and the interpersonal relations among the group members have come together so that the members are working toward the achievement of the group's task.[47]

Adjourning, the last stage, is when the group members begin to express the positive aspects of the group experience, what they have learned from each other, and a feeling that the group had been an entity that some will miss. This stage can be thought of as the group's "termination review."[48]

§ 4.45 Leadership in small groups generally

Leadership is an extremely important role within the small group. The degree to which the group can function effectively is largely dependent on how well-coordinated the group members are.[49] One professor of psychology, explained group leadership as "a special case of social influence, namely, the exercise of power by an occupant of a particular position in the group structure."[50] As we review the area of leadership in small group communication, Communication Principle 17 will become operable: Jurors choose leaders rapidly and on limited information.

In a comprehensive review of the literature on small group leadership, it was noted that there were eleven basically different views of the leader-

---

[44] *Id.*

[45] *Id.*

[46] *Id.*

[47] *Id.*

[48] Tuckman & Jensen, *supra* note 42.

[49] *See supra* §§ 4.38–4.44 for a discussion of group dynamics.

[50] SHAW, *supra* note 9, at 316.

ship process.[51] For the purposes of this text, however, leadership will be viewed as an influence process in an attempt to reach a goal. In the particular application of this perspective to the courtroom, the foreperson of the jury is in the position to influence his fellow jurors to reach a verdict.

By examining the status of the jurors, the emergence of the foreperson, the characteristics of group leaders, and the influence group leaders can exert over members, the attorney should gain a better understanding of the process of leadership in the small group setting, the jury.

§ 4.46 —Ascribed and achieved status

Status, defined as "one's position or rank relative to others in a group,"[52] is an important consideration to understand in the trial process. Those individuals who are seen as high status persons are perceived as more able to control their situation and more likely to have intended to perform a particular behavior. A lower-status person, on the other hand, is more likely to be seen as being controlled by events and pressures outside his own control. A lower-status person is perceived more as the type of person to be a follower than an initiator.[53]

Leadership of the group is linked to the status of the participants. Usually, the higher the status of the individual, the more likely he is to emerge as the leader or to be chosen by the members as the group's leader.

Status can be thought of as either (1) ascribed status or (2) achieved status.[54] Ascribed status is considered to be "the prestige that goes to a person by virtue of some characteristic such as his family wealth, good looks, or age."[55] Achieved status, on the other hand, is status that an individual has earned based on the merits of his own accomplishments.

Socioeconomic status is generally regarded as an achieved status. Socioeconomic status has a decided effect on leadership of the jury. Studies conducted with mock jurors have demonstrated that the foreperson of

---

[51] R.M. Stodgill, Handbook of Leadership (The Free Press, 1974).

[52] S. L. Tubbs, A Systems Approach to Small Group Interaction 122 (Addison-Wesley Publishing Co., 1978).

[53] Thibaut & Riechen, *Same Determinants and Consequences of the Perception of Social Causality*, 24 J. Personality 113–133 (1955).

[54] *See, e.g.*, Davis, *The Child and the Social Structure*, 14 J. Educ. Soc. 217–229 (1940).

[55] Tubbs, *supra* note 52, 122.

the jury is more likely to be a person of higher socioeconomic status. In addition, high socioeconomic status members tend to participate more in jury deliberations.[56]

Individuals of higher status have more communication acts directed toward them and these communication statements tend to be more positive than statements directed to lower-status members. Thus, high status persons have an inordinate ability to control the flow of the group's interaction.[57]

Not only is it possible for the higher status person to control the communication interaction, but the higher status person's comments and remarks are treated deferentially. Lower status individuals tend to be less critical of statements made by higher status persons.[58] Group members also tend to defer to the higher status individual, addressing the higher status person in a more formal way while talking to lower status individuals often on a first name basis.[59]

Some occupations carry more status than others. A person's occupation is thought to be related to his abilities and personality traits. A jury composed primarily of blue-collar workers will probably afford a doctor in their midst high status. Foremen of juries tend to be from certain higher status occupations such as professional or proprietor positions.

Research also tends to indicate that a high status individual's comments and ideas carry more weight and are less carefully evaluated and criticized than contributions made by other group members.[60] The inclination toward less critical evaluation (or deference) of a high status person's remarks may make the group less accurate in its decision-making process in the event that the higher status person's remarks were in error.

§ 4.47 —Predicting the emergence of the jury foreperson

In their study of actual jurors who had participated in jury deliberations, several communication scholars were able to profile the typical

---

[56] Strodtbeck, James & Hawkins, *Social Status in Jury Deliberations*, 22 AM. SOC. REV. 713–719 (1957).

[57] Kelly, *Communication in Experimentally Created Hierarchies*, 4 HUM. REL. 39–56 (1951).

[58] D. GOURAN, MAKING DECISIONS IN GROUPS 135 (Scott, Foresman, and Co., 1982).

[59] Thibaut, *An Experimental Study of the Cohesiveness of Underprivileged Groups*, 3 HUM. REL. 251–278 (1950).

[60] Torrance, *Some Consequences of Power Difference on Decision-Making and Permanent and Temporary 3-Man Groups*, 22 WASH. ST. C. RESEARCH STUD. 251–278 (1954).

leader of the jury, the foreperson. The most common trait of the juror usually elected foreperson was that he was exceptionally talkative.[61]

Not only were forepersons perceived as talkative, they were usually among the first to speak when the jury began deliberations. The study notes that, "36 percent of the jurors indicated that the foreperson was the very *first* person to speak, and 50 percent of the forepersons themselves thought they spoke first."[62] A typical verbal exchange in the initial deliberations might be: "Well, who should we pick as foreman?" "Why don't you be foreman?"

This phenomenon has been explained as perhaps the effort of jurors to find "someone willing to take the 'heat' for his decision, and the person bold enough to speak first may seem like the obvious choice."[63]

Another finding was that forepersons were also seen as confident individuals as well as warm persons. "Psychologically, it seems that this individual takes pressure off fellow jurors by initiating discussion, eases their tension by his sanguinity, and reduces their uncertainty with his confidence."[64]

In 1982, there was another reported survey of jurors to determine what individual traits helped to predict the emergence of a foreperson.[65] Although the study was unable to establish any one trait as a statistically reliable predictor, it was determined that the foreperson tended to be talkative as well as friendly and bold.

Talkativeness in jury deliberations was also reported by other researchers. A mock jury's deliberations were tape-recorded and then juror statements were classified into categories such as (1) positive reactions (statements such as "That's a good idea."); (2) attempted answers (statements such as "Why don't we . . ."); (3) questions (statements such as "What can we do about . . ."); and (4) negative reactions (statements such as "That's a stupid thing to say.")[66] The following con-

---

[61] Sannito & Arnolds, *Jury Study Results: The Factors at Work*, 5 TRIAL DIPL. J. 7 (1982).

[62] *Id.*

[63] *Id.*

[64] *Id.* at 8.

[65] Jorasky, *Jury Study*, 4 TRIAL DIPL. J. (1982).

[66] B. EAKINS & R. EAKINS, SEX DIFFERENCES IN HUMAN COMMUNICATION 33 (Houghton-Mifflin Co., 1978). The authors report the results of a study by Phillip Goldberg, *Are Women Prejudiced Against Women?* in TOWARD A SOCIOLOGY OF WOMEN 10–12 (Xerox College Publishing, C. Safilios-Rothschild ed. 1972).

clusions from the study are of interest to the attorney:

> Females scored significantly higher than males in positive reactions. Males scored higher than females in the more aggressive category of attempted answers. Overall, men originated significantly more speech acts than women. The investigators conclude from this that men "pro-act." They direct "long bursts of acts" aimed at solving the problem. Women "react" to the contributions of others, agreeing, understanding, and supporting. Further, less than one-half as much of the women's talk as the men's showed antagonism or tended to lower another's status.[67]

Of interest as well is the finding from this study that men dominated the discussion. Sixty-seven percent of the 127 jurors were men, but they accounted for almost four-fifths of the conversation during deliberations.[68] Therefore, it would appear that men are most likely to be chosen the foreperson of the jury.

There is additional data indicating that it is likely that men will be elected as foreperson of the jury over women jury members. For example, women are much less likely to be chosen foreperson in civil trials (3% of the time, even when women composed 36% of the civil juries). Women have been chosen even less often as the foreperson in criminal trials.[69] The foreperson will most likely be a male (seven out of ten times) and white (95% of the time).[70]

In mock jury studies, the effect of socioeconomic status on foreperson selection has been demonstrated. The foreperson of the jury is more likely to be a person of high socioeconomic status. In addition, jurors of high socioeconomic status are more likely to participate actively in jury deliberations.[71]

The physical location of a juror around a rectangular jury table has been found to influence the probability of a juror's selection as the foreperson of the jury. Those jurors who sit at the end of the table (at the head or foot) are much more likely to be selected as the foreperson. The location at the table influences the juror's visibility with other jurors, his

---

[67] *Id.*

[68] *Id.*

[69] R. Simon, The Jury: Its Role in American Society 44 (Lexington Books, 1980).

[70] Sannito & Arnolds, *supra* note 61, at 8.

[71] Strodtbeck, James & Hawkins, *supra* note 56.

opportunity to enter the discussion and yield to other jurors, his opportunity to enter the flow of the discussion, and his ability to yield the floor to another.[72] If people sitting around a jury table behaved and were treated equally, each would have the same likelihood of being selected foreperson, receive the same number of sociometric (group preference) votes, and make the same number of communicative acts. We can see in the data, however, that seat position about the table is systematically related to these variables. End seats average much more than their expected share; other positions average at or less than that expected under an equality hypothesis.[73]

§ 4.48 —Leadership characteristics

Who becomes the leader of the small group is the function of a number of interrelated variables. As has already been discussed, the physical position that a member has in the group can influence whether he is perceived as exhibiting leadership.[74]

In addition, the most vocal members of a group are also more likely to be chosen as leader.[75] The more verbal contributions that a participant makes to the discussion, the increased likelihood that he will be perceived as possessing leadership abilities.[76] How much is said (quantity, or amount of contribution) appears to be more important to the perception of leadership than what is said (verbal content, or quality of contribution). Outside observers have been able to identify leaders in a small group by the amount of participation they exhibit.[77]

In a study of nonverbal aspects of leadership, one communication researcher discovered that nonverbal activity was also related to the perceptions of leadership.[78] He found that the more gestures and other

---

[72] Strodtbeck & Hook, *The Social Dimensions of a Twelve-Man Jury Table*, 24 SOCIOMETRY 397–415 (1961).

[73] M. SAKS, & R. HASTIE, SOCIAL PSYCHOLOGY IN COURT 73 (Van Nostrand Reinhold Co., 1978). This chart is adapted from the study by Strodtbeck & Hook, *The Social Dimensions of a Twelve-Man Jury Table*, 24 SOCIOMETRY 397–415 (1961).

[74] *See supra* § 4.47, *Predicting the emergence of the jury foreperson*.

[75] *Id.*

[76] Sorrentino & Boutiller, *The Effect of Quantity and Quality of Verbal Interaction on Ratings of Leadership Ability*, 11 J. EXPERIM. SOC. PSYCHOLOGY 403–11 (1975).

[77] Stein, *Identifying Emergent Leaders from Verbal and Nonverbal Communications*, 32 J. PERSONALITY & SOC. PSYCHOLOGY 352–361 (1975).

[78] Baird, *Some Nonverbal Elements of Leadership Emergence*, 42 S. SPEECH COM. J. 253–261 (1977).

nonverbal movements exhibited by a group member, the more likely it was that the group would perceive that member as displaying leadership qualities. Another study concluded that people who are perceived as influential, gesture more often than people who are perceived as less influential.[79]

§ 4.49 —Influence of leaders

Leaders of small groups can exert considerable influence over the group. Group leadership has been defined as a type of social influence where the leader exercises power in the group structure, can direct the group's thinking, critical evaluation of ideas, and decision-making process.[80]

Research on emergent leaders is appropriate to this discussion because the jury foreman emerges from the group deliberations and is chosen by the other jury members to serve as their leader.[81] Research conducted found that emergent leaders tend to behave in a more authoritarian manner.[82] Emergent leaders tended to be highly motivated leaders.[83]

A leader is effective as long as the members support and follow him. Group members have indicated that they are more influenced by an elected leader than by an appointed one. In addition, members are more willing to accept selfish actions from their leader when the leader was elected rather than appointed.[84]

Groups also tend to perform better with a leader they select themselves than one that has been appointed for them. In a study of judicial tribunals (composed of 3–9 judges)[85] who were deciding matters in a court of last resort, the following observation was made:

---

[79] O'Connor, *The Relationship of Kinesic and Verbal Communication to Leadership Perception in Small Group Discussion*, 32 DISSERTATION ABSTR. INT'L 6589 (1972).

[80] *See supra* § 4.45, *Leadership in small groups generally*.

[81] *See supra* § 4.47, *Predicting the emergence of the jury foreperson*.

[82] Carter, Haythorn, Shriver & Lanzetta, *The Behavior of Leaders and Other Group Members*, 46 J. ABNORM. & SOC. PSYCHOLOGY 589–595 (1951).

[83] Crockett, *Emergent Leadership in Small Decision-Making Groups*, 51 J. ABNORM. & SOC. PSYCHOLOGY 378–383 (1955).

[84] E. Hollander, J. Julian, & F. Perry, *Leader Style, Competence, and Source of Authority as Determinants of Actual and Perceived Influence*, Technical Report No. 5, DNR Contract 4679, SUNY at Buffalo, 1966), cited in M.E. SHAW, GROUP DYNAMICS 321 (McGraw-Hill, 3rd ed. 1981).

[85] Walker, *Leader Selection and Behavior in Small Political Groups*, 7 SMALL GROUP BEHAV. 363–368 (1976).

> Some of these groups employed an arbitrary method of selecting the formally designed leader (known as the *chief justice*) and others employed systems of selection that involved merit. Performance was measured by level of dissent on the cases that came before the tribunals. The mean index of dissent for groups with merit leaders was 8.18 as compared with 14.13 for those groups with arbitrarily selected leaders. If level of dissent is indeed an index of performance, merit leaders performed better than arbitrary leaders.[86]

Leaders can exert influence in a number of ways, depending upon the functions a particular group requires.[87]

§ 4.50 Juror roles in deliberation

> A verdict does not come from 12 individuals but from a group whose interactions are critical to the outcome of the trial. People's attitudes and behavior are influenced by those around them: shut in a room together, feeling the weight of the decision ahead and the confusion of the instructions, most jurors turn to one another for help in making up their minds or for reassurance that their initial reactions are right. Members of a jury begin to form relationships during the trial. They begin to know which of the other jurors they like and respect. As jurors' interactions begin to solidify, so does the verdict. Thus, accurate predictions about who will exercise leadership and in what direction, as well as who will be receptive to that leadership, are key components in jury selections.[88]

It is important for the legal professional to understand how the individual juror will most likely function as a member of the jury group. We need to look not only at the characteristics of the juror as a unique individual, but also the characteristics of the juror that will help us understand how he will function in a group. We must understand the following group roles: leader, follower, filler, negotiator, and holdout as well as the formation of subgroups.[89] We will briefly examine the implication of each role on the decision-making process.

It is also important to identify those jurors who will emerge as leaders in jury deliberations because leaders exert a strong and often subtle

---

[86] SHAW, *supra* note 9, at 323.

[87] JONES, BARNLUND & HAIMAN, *supra* note 8, at 206–213.

[88] JURYWORK: SYSTEMATIC TECHNIQUES 206 (National Jury Project, B. Bonora & E. Krauss eds. 1979).

[89] *Id.*

power in the jury's final verdict.[90] We should be aware of indications of leadership such as (1) high status and authority, (2) high intellectual abilities, exemplified by strong, calm, articulate answers to difficult questions, (3) decisiveness and strong will, exemplified by self-confidence and strength of conviction, and (4) past leadership training or experience.[91]

Another role a jury member may assume in deliberations is that of a follower. A follower may know how he wants to vote, but does not want to assume a leadership role. He will, therefore, support a leader who articulates his position. Another type of follower may take on the proposed solution presented by a leader who is perceived favorably by the follower. Followers are generally less assertive and aggressive, have lower social status, and are somewhat more intimidated by the courtroom setting.[92]

A filler is described as a person who, for whatever reason, is unable to make a decision. These jurors usually go along with the majority during jury deliberations. A filler may be identified by his uncertainty in responding to voir dire questions ("I'm not sure"), his lack of self-confidence, and/or his difficulty in understanding the implications or details of the case.[93]

Negotiators help a jury reach a compromise decision. When tensions are high and the deliberations are becoming polarized, the negotiator will help work things out usually by emphasizing the logical aspects of the case. A person who sees himself as "even-tempered" or who prides himself on being able to understand both sides of an issue is a likely candidate for the negotiator role.[94]

Holdouts are those persons who are able to maintain their positions in spite of the majority decision and pressures that the majority may bring to bear on that person. An individual who does not appear ruffled by the differences of opinion or tensions in voir dire may turn out to be a holdout juror. Jurors who are nonconformist, stubborn, and unintimidated by authority figures may also be likely holdouts.[95]

It is more difficult for an individual to continue to resist the pressures

---

[90] *See supra* §§ 4.45–4.49.

[91] Bonora & Krauss, *supra* note 88, at 206–208.

[92] *Id.* at 208.

[93] *Id.* at 208.

[94] *Id.* at 208–209.

[95] *Id.* at 209.

of the group than it is for a subgroup to resist. Subgroups can draw strength and reassurance from the other members who see the verdict as they do. The similarity principle (Communication Principle 5) operates in a subgroup formation and the alert attorney can observe possible subgroup alliances during jury selection. Those jurors who have similar backgrounds, interests, attitudes, and experiences are more likely to affiliate with each other as a subgroup during jury deliberations.[96]

§ 4.51 The decision-making process generally

Juries are small groups theoretically composed of a microcosm of society at large. Members of the jury must evaluate the evidence and testimony in order to reach a group decision, their verdict. They must be able to articulate their individual viewpoints and then integrate as many of those positions into a decision that the group as a whole agrees to and supports. The most fundamental information we have about jurors is reflected in Communication Principle 18: Jurors use information other than evidence in making decisions.

Small groups have been studied and found to go through particular functions in the process of making their decisions. Actual juries have been found to go through the same functions as other types of decision-making groups.

§ 4.52 —Stages in a jury's decision-making process

> If we know the form that the jury's deliberation will assume, then, to a certain extent, we can arrange the content of argument and the presentation of witnesses in a manner that will facilitate this deliberation, and will supply the jury with a set of proposals appropriate to its needs.[97]

Research indicates that jurors tend to make their decisions in a case, that is, reach their verdicts, through a sequential decision-making process.

Various studies have found that juries move through four stages in their decision-making process: (1) Orientation, (2) Conflict, (3) Emergence, and (4) Reinforcement.[98]

---

[96] *Id.* at 209.

[97] Anthony & Bodaken, *Jury Communication: Phases in the Deliberation Process*, 5 TRIAL DIPL. J. 25 (1982). Reprinted with permission of Trial Diplomacy Journal.

[98] *See supra* §§ 4.41–4.44. *See also* Anthony & Bodaken, *supra* note 97, at 23, and B.

The Orientation Stage is exemplified by ambiguous communications among the jurors. Uncertainty about the setting and the task is great as is the tension the jurors feel in this, their first deliberating effort as a group. Jurors spend their time becoming better acquainted with one another, settling into the appropriate styles necessary to analyze the trial proceedings. The jurors usually elect their foreman at this point, probably because that task was assigned to them by the court.

> For a period of anywhere from thirty to sixty minutes, communication is clearly characterized by a norm of agreement in which jurors ask questions of each other, take special care to be deferential, and generally attempt to get along. The selection of a foreman, introductory attempts at knowing more about each other, and telling case-relevant stories are further illustrations of orientation phase messages.[99]

The Conflict Stage is the phase of deliberation during which the jury begins to focus on the issues of the case, set criteria for their forthcoming verdict, and argue, disagree, or debate with one another.

> In one simulation, as we prepared for a complicated product liability case involving many exhibits like charts and graphs, our jury was discussing general issues and exchanging personal experiences about a product from the defendant company. As the jurors began discussing exhibits, they started to make decisions about which of them were most central to the case. Now there were different opinions. As these opinions about the exhibits were strengthened, disagreement clearly emerged. The tone or quality of tentativeness gave way to certainty, a characteristic of the conflict period of deliberation.[100]

In the Emergence Stage, the decision toward which the jury is leaning becomes apparent. Research indicates that ambiguous messages reappear during this stage, but this time ambiguous messages provide jurors with time to change their positions to reflect the majority view, a means to save face.

> Recently, in a simulation relevant to an air safety case, a juror who had argued forcefully for the plaintiff's claim was presented with some new and incontrovertible data refuting his position. His state-

---

Fisher, *Decision Emergence: Phases in Group Decision Making*, 37 SPEECH MONOGRAPHS 53–66 (1970).

[99] Anthony & Bodaken, *supra* note 98, at 24.

[100] *Id.* at 24.

> ment during the emergence phase that 'these kinds of things happen all the time' was seen as a qualification of his earlier position, in which he supported the plaintiff's claim. . . . His later vote for a defense verdict was not unexpected.[101]

The jury tends to focus on proposals that reflect the verdict to which they are leaning. Proposals inconsistent with the jury's probable decision do not receive support during this stage (as they probably would have in the Conflict Stage).

The Reinforcement Phase finds the jury solidifying the reasons for its decision and reiterating the appropriateness of it. The jury is unified at this stage. "Names and addresses may be exchanged, jokes will be made about the deliberations, and various forms of reinforcing behavior will be exhibited, all evincing the absence of disagreement and dissent."[102]

§ 4.53 —Information integration process of jurors

A juror must integrate multiple pieces of often conflicting information into a unified whole in order to make a decision. Information integration theory attempts to explain the processes that an individual, a juror, goes through in the evaluation of evidence and testimony in order to determine what the verdict should be. "Information integration theory . . . is a model of human judgment that may conceptually unite the various elements involved in the juror's evaluation, weighing, and combining of evidential and nonevidential information. . . ."[103]

A juror is asked to make many judgments during the course of a trial. An example of a judgment that a juror is asked to make is the evaluation of a defendant's innocence or guilt. This judgment will be made on the basis of various beliefs that the juror holds about the defendant's motives and capabilities.[104]

During a trial, a juror must sift through many beliefs. These beliefs will be of differing importance and relevance to the final decision. "All beliefs do not contribute equally to judgment."[105] The juror will deter-

---

[101] *Id.* at 25.

[102] *Id.* at 26.

[103] M. Kaplan, *Cognitive Processes in the Individual Juror*, in THE PSYCHOLOGY OF THE COURTROOM 198 (Academic Press, N. Kerr & R. Bray eds. 1982).

[104] *Id.* at 199.

[105] *Id.*

mine, based on the principles of perception discussed previously, which beliefs will be weighed more heavily in his final judgment.[106]

Weighted beliefs are then integrated into a total view of the trial from the juror's standpoint, or perception. Such integration of information was placed into a formula by one theorist who articulated the information integration theory. In its most general form, the theory is expressed:

$$J = \frac{EWkSk}{EWk}$$

where J is the judgment, S is the scale value for k, pieces of information evaluated by the juror, and W is the weight (importance, relevance, or credibility) placed on that item of information by the juror.[107]

The processes of judgment utilized by the juror are based on the person perception principles articulated previously. As with person perception, for example, the initial impression is very important. Moreover, the juror's needs and wants influence the judgments he makes during trial, just as an individual's needs and wants influence the person perception process. Past experiences of the juror also enter into and influence the juror's judgments.

The process of judgment formation was summarized as follows:

> The person apprehends knowledge or information about the object in the form of beliefs about events. These beliefs are each evaluated with reference to the necessary judgment (scale value assignment) and are compared for relative importance for that judgment (weighting). The separate evaluations are then averaged, each weighted by its importance, into a unitary judgment, which also includes an initial impression value with some degree of importance.[108]

It must be noted here that the juror brings particular biases to the judgment process. These biases can and do influence the judgment process. These juror biases have been termed "extralegal" because they represent influences beyond the evidence presented in the courtroom itself.[109]

---

[106] *See supra* Chapter 1, *Impression Formation in the Courtroom*.

[107] Anderson, *Cognitive Algebra: Integration Theory Applied to Social Attribution*, in ADVANCES IN EXPERIMENTAL SOCIAL PSYCHOLOGY 7 (Academic Press, L. Berkowitz ed. 1974).

[108] Kaplan, *supra* note 103, at 200.

[109] *Id.* at 201.

These biases include: (1) personal biases, (2) biases introduced by trial conditions, (3) biases introduced prior to the trial (i.e., pretrial publicity), (4) effects of inadmissible evidence, and (5) biases due to defendant characteristics.[110]

In complex cases, there are special considerations and the advocate's role is to simplify and clarify the issues so that lay jurors can understand and remember the points which support the advocate's position.

The incredible complexity of some cases is illustrated by Philadelphia's National Union Electric Corporation (and later joined by Zenith) suit filed over ten years ago against Japanese electronics firms which allegedly sold products below their market prices to force U.S. firms out of business. The case came to trial in 1979, complete with more than a million documents and over 100,000 pages of testimony.[111]

The length of trial, the number of issues (both factual and legal), the number of witnesses and the vast volume of documents all require effective information management techniques in order to gain and hold the jury's attention.

The attorney for MCI Communications in its antitrust suit against AT&T emphasized the attorney's responsibility to make the case understandable to the jury. "It's incumbent upon lawyers to simplify, clarify, and teach the jury."[112] In the MCI case, the attorney recognized the importance of educating the jury about the issues involved:

> We have a teaching function, and our case against AT&T is a good case in point. We used demonstrative evidence for the jury—movies, graphs, expert witnesses. And we wanted to make sure our witnesses spoke *English*.[113]

> **COMMENT:** The attorney should repeat important points so that the jury will remember them, being careful not to patronize the jury or repeat so often that the jury becomes bored or irritated with the repetitions. Summaries are an important technique. The attorney should also highlight key

[110] *Id.*

[111] Jenkins, *Is the Jury Out?*, April 1981 TWA AMBASSADOR 67.

[112] *Id.* at 67.

[113] *Id.*

documents, making sure that the jury understands the impact of the document.

The attention span of the juror is, on the average, about eighteen minutes, even among those jurors who are intensely interested in the proceedings.[114] One communication scholar also noted that the juror is at the optimum attention state during the beginning of the trial:

> When the opening statement begins, the jury is already interested because of the dramatic nature of the proceedings. They are probably more attentive at this time than in later portions of the trial. They know there is a story to be told: their natural curiosity is aroused, and they are especially susceptible to what you say. In fact, you can count on their being influenced one way or the other. You have their initial attention, not by your magnetic power, but rather by the power of the drama inherent in any trial.[115]

The maximum number of arguments or issues that can command the attention of the average juror ranges from a low of six to a high of eleven.[116] For most people, the maximum number of objects that can be adequately processed in a fifty minute period is fifteen.

The human mind is capable of processing information five times faster than man can speak.[117] At other times, individuals allow their minds to wander, tuning out the message at hand. It is important that the attorney know when the juror is not paying attention and try to recapture his attention.

The attorney should also keep in mind that the juror's attention span is shortened when the juror is tired, hungry, feeling ill, or is simply not interested in trial proceedings. By using short, simple vivid language, some repetition, and variation in intonation, volume and pacing, the attorney can maximize the chances that the jurors will continue to pay attention to the case he is presenting.

Courts have held that the inattentiveness of jurors is not a cause for a

---

[114] Vinson, *Juries: Perception and the Decision-Making Process*, 18 TRIAL 52 (1982).

[115] TAYLOR, BUCHANAN & STRAWN, *supra* note 19, at 70.

[116] Vinson, *supra* note 114, at 53.

[117] R. ADLER & N. TOWNE, LOOKING OUT/LOOKING IN, at 218 (Holt, Rinehart and Winston, 3rd ed. 1981).

new trial. In *Hasson v. Ford Motor Company*,[118] Ford Motor Company appealed the jury's decision claiming that jurors had not paid attention during the course of the trial and that this inattentiveness (reading books and doing crossword puzzles) constituted misconduct. The Supreme Court of California refused to overturn the jury's decision.

The way in which jurors integrate information is most significantly displayed in Communication Principle 19: People make decisions by emotion (unconscious mind) and validate them with logic (conscious mind). This is one of the most significant principles because it underscores one of the most important aspects of persuasion which is to engage the conscious mind while communicating to the unconscious mind. It is most commonly known that the unconscious mind deals with information in a very impartial way. The unconscious mind takes information in through an emotion pipeline and, ultimately, most decisions are rendered based upon the emotional gut-level response that people have. The way in which it is validated is through conscious mind control. The conscious mind must have logical information and make reasonable attempts at sorting out what makes sense. Therefore, the conscious mind structures a rationale for why decisions are made. This becomes very important in the courtroom, especially for those attorneys who prefer to use logical, rational arguments. There is nothing wrong with these types of arguments so long as the attorney understands that he must also have a second strategy for engaging the unconscious mind. Effective trial attorneys do this without even knowing about it. They automatically engage the unconscious mind by changing their voice tones, by moving and anchoring positions, and by pacing jurors.

The reason it is so important to communicate with the unconscious mind is the fact that it is that level of understanding that really makes the decision. The unconscious mind impartially selects information and operates based upon the information that it receives. Thus, Communication Principle 19 becomes very important in the overall understanding of persuasion.

Anchoring is another important factor which determines whether or not jurors retain the information disseminated at the trial. Communication Principle 20 provides: People more easily retain information which is anchored. Anchoring is a form of classical conditioning which sets a pattern for a specific behavior to elicit a specific event or vice versa. For

---

[118] 32 Cal. 3d 388, 650 P.2d 1171, 185 Cal. Rptr. 654 (1982), *cert. denied*, 459 U.S. 1190, 103 S. Ct. 1167, 75 L. Ed. 2d 422 (1983).

example, if you put on a song from the 1960's, it will evoke feelings and thoughts about a particular time or person. It only takes a small stimulus to bring up a whole series of feelings and thoughts. A song can transport us into another world and can anchor for you particular feelings depending on what emotional state you were in when you first heard the song. The process of anchoring occurs in the courtroom, often unconsciously. If you use a certain spot in the courtroom to anchor a theme statement and you only use that spot when you talk about your theme statement you will find that you have anchored or sensitized that spot so that statements made from that spot will elicit a particular behavior pattern.

§ 4.54 Equity theory and its influence on decision making

Members of society continually make judgments as to what is fair or unfair, just or unjust. "That's just not fair!" "It will catch up with you someday!" Even advertisers use appeal to equity with slogans such as "It's a square meal, square deal."

Equity theory is a general model for understanding interpersonal relationships. The theory posits that an equitable relationship exists when the "outcomes" that an individual receives are equal to the "inputs" he has invested in the situation. Equity theory can be thought of as a type of implicit social contract to ensure interpersonal justice. Individuals tend to attempt to maximize their own rewards in a given transaction; the basic idea that man is selfish is central to the equity theory analysis. Society attempts to temper this strain of individual self-interest in order to allocate more appropriately the resources and rewards of society at large.

The importance of understanding the equity theory for the trial attorney is expressed in Communication Principle 21: Jurors seek to render a verdict which they perceive as equitable. Given this predisposition, the perception of fairness will enter into the final decision-making process.

Of course, rewards are not always allocated equitably. Some individuals manage to obtain much more than their fair share and other members of society suffer from an inadequate allocation.

Psychologists note that the equity theory can help "predict which individuals will perceive that they are justly treated and how they will react when they find themselves enmeshed in unjust relationships."[119] As one researcher states, "equity norms require allocating greater resources to those whose inputs in a relationship are greater relative to others; equity therefore ensures that order, cohesion, and justice will prevail."[120]

§ 4.55 —Equity theory definitions and propositions

The major terms used in equity theory analysis include: scrutineer, inputs, outcomes, net gains, and relative gains.[121]

Scrutineer is the person or group who is observing and examining the exchange relationship. The scrutineer, who may be a participant in the exchange or an outside observer, will determine if the exchange has been a fair or unfair one. "In the judicial setting, the scrutineer is responsible not only for judging the equitableness of an exchange between the victim and the defendant, but in the case of an inequitable relationship, the scrutineer is empowered to restore equity by alerting the outcomes of one or more of the participants."[122]

The contributions that the participants make to the exchange are called the *inputs*. An individual's inputs in turn entitle him to rewards. If an individual's inputs are insufficient ones, or liabilities (such as cruelty), he may have to suffer costs (punishments). "Once a scrutineer senses what participants have put *into* their relationship he can gauge whether or not they are getting the outcomes they deserve from the relationship."[123]

Outcomes are considered to be "the positive *and* negative consequences that a scrutineer perceives a participant has received in the course of his relationship with another."[124] Outcomes can either be positive ones (rewards) or negative ones (costs or punishments). When eval-

---

[119] Walster, Berscheid & Walster, *New Directions in Equity Research*, 25 J. PERSONALITY & SOC. PSYCHOLOGY 151 (1973).

[120] Sampson, *On Justice as Equality*, 31 J. SOC. ISSUES 46 (1975).

[121] Aristotle, *Ethica Nicomachea*, cited in E. WALSTER, G. WALSTER & E. BERSCHEID, EQUITY: THEORY AND RESEARCH 209 (Allyn and Bacon, 1978). Copyright © 1978 by Allyn and Bacon, Inc. Reprinted with permission.

[122] J.K. Toomb, *Equity Theory and the Law: An Experimental Study to Assess the Effects of Belief in a Just World on the Sentencing of Mock Jurors* 5 (Ph.D. dissertation, Florida State University, 1981).

[123] WALSTER, WALSTER & BERSCHEID, *supra* note 121, at 12.

[124] *Id.*

uating the participant's outcomes in equity theory, the outcomes are equal to the value of the rewards minus the costs.

Equity theory makes a calculation of how "profitable" a particular exchange has been to the participants. The *net gain* of participants is to be "simply their outcomes from the relationships minus their inputs to the relationship."[125]

Relative gains, on the other hand, are considered to be the net gain relative to the participant's inputs. "It is the equality or inequality in relative gains that determines whether or not a relationship is equitable."[126]

Two other terms, compensation and justification, should be explained at this point. If the scrutineer determines that inequity has occurred, equity may be restored either through compensation or justification. "*Compensation* occurs when the individual attempts to restore actual equity by actively altering the actual outcomes experienced or inputs contributed to the exchange."[127] For example, a person may resort to the courts in order to obtain payment or to have the other party punished. Compensation can be thought of as the ways we attempt to increase the wronged person's outputs.[128]

"*Justification* occurs when the individual misperceives the outcomes experienced or inputs contributed to the exchange and thereby restores psychological equity."[129] The process of restoring psychological equity involves a distortion of reality using justification techniques such as blaming the victim, minimizing the victim's suffering, and denying responsibility for the suffering of the victim.[130]

The study determined that "an equitable relationship exists when a person scrutinizing the relationship concludes that all participants are receiving equal relative gains from the relationship."[131]

---

[125] *Id.*

[126] *Id.* at 14.

[127] Izzett & Sales, *Person Perception and Juror's Reactions to Defendants* in THE TRIAL PROCESS 213 (Plenum Press, B. Sales ed. 1981).

[128] *Id.*

[129] WALSTER, WALSTER & BERSCHEID, *supra* note 121.

[130] *Id.* at 10.

[131] *Id.*

Equity theory is based on the following four interlocking propositions:[132]

PROPOSITION I: Individuals will try to maximize their outcomes (where outcomes equal rewards minus costs).[133]

This proposition articulates the basic premise of equity theory, which is that man is selfish. In any given social exchange situation, members can be expected to attempt to achieve as much as they possibly can for themselves. Left unrestrained, this tendency of individuals would play havoc with social order. Individuals have thus agreed to a social compromise, which allows them to maximize a collective reward while lessening the chances of societal upheaval. Proposition IIA is that compromise.[134]

PROPOSITION IIA: Groups can maximize collective reward by evolving accepted systems for equitably apportioning rewards and costs among members. Thus, groups will evolve such systems of equity and will attempt to induce members and adhere to these systems.[135]

This proposition assumes that members are able to identify the inputs and outcomes in a particular situation and that the members are able to evaluate the relative merits between these items. In addition, this proposition is an incentive for society's members to be equitable in their dealings with each other. "Proposition IIA proposes that groups will insure the profitability of equitable behavior by rewarding members who treat others equitably and by punishing those who do not."[136] Thus, only equitable relationships are tolerated and then rewarded.

Proposition IIA is also related to the Just World Hypothesis. This hypothesis states that "Individuals have a need to believe that they live in a world where people generally get what they deserve."[137] In other words, where an individual's inputs were of lesser value, other members believed in the fairness of the system so that his reward would not be as great as the reward to a person who had contributed much more.

---

[132] *Id.*

[133] *Id.* at 6.

[134] *Id.* at 8–9.

[135] *Id.* at 6.

[136] *Id.* at 9.

[137] Lerner & Miller, *Just World Research and the Attribution Process: Looking Back and Ahead*, 85 PSYCHOLOGICAL BULL. 1030 (1978).

The belief in the Just World Hypothesis may help encourage society's members to engage in long-term commitments to society. The belief that a greater input (long, formal education such as required for law school or medical school) will result in a greater outcome (higher earning power, more social prestige) is one such example of the application of a Just World belief.[138]

> PROPOSITION IIB: Groups will generally reward members who treat others equitably and generally punish (increase the costs for) members who treat others inequitably.)[139]

This particular proposition has a direct relationship to the court system. Situations often occur where the participants disagree on how the rules under which they are governed are to be applied in a particular situation. At times, individuals also deliberately violate the rules. A method must be set up by society to handle the evaluation of these situations. One authority noted that:

> The courts decide whether an inequitable relationship exists and determines the extent of the inequity. If the relationship is judged inequitable the costs of the defendant are increased in order to restore equity. In civil cases these costs may take the form of a financial award to the victim. In effect, this restores equity by lowering the outcomes of the defendant and increasing the outcomes of the victim. In criminal cases the victim's outcomes rarely are changed. Instead, the defendant's outcomes are lowered by increasing his costs through imprisonment.[140]

> PROPOSITION III: When individuals find themselves participating in inequitable relationships, they become distressed. The more inequitable the relationship, the more distress individuals feel.[141]

Research relating to this proposition indicates that whether an individual is overcompensated or undercompensated (a beneficiary or victim), he still feels distress over the outcome. Research has demonstrated this result through an experiment in which subjects were told they were to be paid $2 an hour for participation in a proofreading exercise. When students received their pay, they were either overpaid, equitably paid, or

---

[138] *Id.*

[139] WALSTER, WALSTER & BERSCHEID, *supra* note 121, at 6.

[140] Toomb, *supra* note 122, at 14.

[141] WALSTER, WALSTER & BERSCHEID, *supra* note 121, at 6.

underpaid. Students in both the overpaid and underpaid situations were less satisfied than the equitably paid students. It would also appear that the greater the inequity, the greater the distress.[142]

PROPOSITION IV: Individuals who discover that they are in an inequitable relationship attempt to eliminate their distress by restoring equity. The greater the inequity that exists, the more distress they feel, and the harder they try to restore equity.[143]

This proposition affirms the need that individuals have to obtain an equitable solution. They may feel the need to restore equity in one of two situations: (1) restore actual equity or (2) restore psychological equity.

For example, a worker who discovers that his contractor has been paying him less than minimum wage may restore actual equity in the following ways:

(1) he can lower his own inputs (e.g., he can start to "fool around" on the job);

(2) he can raise his own outcomes (e.g., he can start to steal equipment from the company);

(3) he can raise his employer's inputs (e.g., he can make mistakes so that the contractor will have to work far into the night undoing what he has done); or

(4) he can lower his employer's outcome (e.g., he can damage company equipment).[144]

If the worker felt overworked and underpaid and also realized that there was nothing he could do to rectify the situation, he could attempt to persuade himself that the situation is actually an equitable one. He could try to restore psychological equity in the following ways:

(1) he can minimize his inputs ("After all, I don't have very much social polish, education, or get-up-and-go.");

(2) he can exaggerate his outcomes ("This kind of work gives me a chance to see my family, and in the end that is what really matters.")

---

[142] Austin & Walster, *Reactions to Confirmations and Disconfirmations of Expectancies of Equity and Inequity*, 30 J. PERSONALITY & SOC. PSYCHOLOGY 208–216 (1974).

[143] WALSTER, WALSTER & BERSCHEID, *supra* note 121, at 6.

[144] *Id.* at 18.

(3) he can exaggerate his employer's inputs ("Without my boss's know-how, the company would fall apart and I would have no job."); or

(4) he can minimize his employer's outcomes ("The tension on his job is probably giving him an ulcer.")[145]

§ 4.56 —Application of equity theory to the courtroom

One commentator has stated the following:

> The jury and the judge have the formal equity **decisionmaking** power in the American judicial system. They decide whether an inequitable relationship exists between the victim and the defendant, and what change in the defendant's outcomes would restore equity to the relationship. Ideally their decisions are based on the relative merits of the evidence presented in the case.[146]

The decisions jurors make have been studied primarily through mock jury research. In the mock jury situation, subjects are asked to decide cases as they would if they were actual jurors in the case. Most mock jury research has studied the various aspects of either the defendant (such as the defendant's personality traits, attitudes, and physical attractiveness) or the victim (such as the victim's positive attributes and character). By then analyzing the jury's decision, the researcher has been able to focus on the variables that have relevance to a juror's decision-making process. In equity theory terms, the inputs would be the aspects of the plaintiff (or victim) and the outputs would be the verdict rendered by the jury. Thus, equity can be studied by examining the inputs and outputs and assessing whether an equitable relationship has prevailed.

Various defendant inputs have been studied by mock jury researchers. A landmark study examined the effects of personality traits and social attributes on the juror's judgment.[147] The researchers reasoned that a socially successful (and thus attractive) person would be viewed more favorably by the jury than a person described to the jury as less successful (and therefore less attractive). The subjects in the study were presented with a negligent automobile homocide in which the defendant

---

[145] *Id.* at 18–19.

[146] Toomb, *supra* note 122, at 14-15.

[147] Landy & Aronson, *The Influence of the Character of the Criminal and His Victim on the Decisions of Simulated Jurors*, 5 J. EXPERIM. SOC. PSYCHOLOGY 141–152 (1969).

was described as either an attractive or an unattractive person in terms of his social characteristics.

For example, in the attractive defendant situation, the defendant, Sander, was described as a hard-working and friendly 64-year-old widower who was suffering from cancer. During the course of the auto accident, he reinjured an old and painful wound. In the unattractive defendant situation, Sander was described as a twice-divorced 33-year-old janitor who had two misdemeanors on his record for breaking and entering and a drug violation. When Sander was described as having attractive characteristics, jurors assessed a shorter prison term (nine years) than when Sander was described in the negative situation (twelve years).

One study attempted to determine the effect of attractiveness in terms of personal likability and not as a function of sympathy for the defendant because of the injury he had suffered.[148] The defendant was described as "loving and warm" (attractive) versus "cold and unapproachable" (unattractive). The loving and warm defendant received a prison sentence almost three years shorter (6.52 years) than the cold and unapproachable defendant (9.22 years).

In describing the defendant in a simulated automobile negligent-homicide case, one study varied trait characteristics.[149] The negatively described defendant was found to have the most guilt and was given the harshest sentence while the positively described defendant was treated less severely in his sentencing.

The effects of attractiveness and race of the defendant on jury verdicts were studied by other researchers. The sentence imposed was found to be a function of the attractiveness of the defendant and the characteristics of the jurors. Here again, attractiveness of the defendant affected his sentence with the more attractive defendant receiving a lesser punishment. Attractiveness in this experiment meant "a likeable, middle-class, upstanding citizen with no criminal record" while unattractiveness re-

---

[148] Sigall & Landy, *Effects of the Defendant's Character and Suffering on Juridic Judgment*, 88 J. Soc. Psychology 140–150 (1972).

[149] Kaplan & Kimmerick, *Juror Judgment as Information Integration: Combining Evidential and Nonevidential Information*, 30 J. Personality & Soc. Psychology 492–499 (1974).

ferred to a "working class citizen who has had marital difficulties and has a criminal record."[150]

An equity theory explanation for the above results would be that the more negative the personality traits, or inputs, the greater the need for the jury to adversely affect the outcome in order to insure equity. A negative outcome in these cases would be considered to be a "punishment" through the verdict rendered by the juror.

The defendant's attitudes can also have an influence on juries. The idea that we are most positively attracted to those we see as similar to ourselves has been demonstrated through mock jury research.

For example, one experiment presented a mock juror with four different attitudinal orientations of the defendant.[151] The result was that the more dissimilar the attitudes of the defendant and the juror, the more likely the defendant was to be found guilty and the longer his prison sentence was likely to be. In addition, the defendant was found to be less attractive to the juror than a defendant with attitudes similar to those of the juror.

Physical attractiveness has also been studied and found to exert an influence on juror's perceptions. One study demonstrated the impact of physical attractiveness through an experiment concerning cheating on a university examination.[152] Physically unattractive cheaters were judged guilty more often than attractive cheaters and they were also given harsher punishments than attractive cheaters. Researchers explain this result as follows: "From an equity perspective, the subject-jurors will have less of a need to adversely affect the outcomes (sentence) experienced by the physically attractive defendant than the unattractive one."[153]

Defendant outcomes have also been studied by jury researchers. Results have shown that when the defendant (harmdoer) has suffered during the perpetration of the act, juries have taken the suffering (outcome) into account when rendering their verdicts. This study determined that

---

[150] Nemeth & Sosis, *A Simulated Jury Study: Characteristics of the Defendant and the Jurors*, 90 J. Soc. Psychology 221–229 (1973).

[151] Griffin & Jackson, *Simulated Jury Decisions: The Influence of Jury-Defendant Attitude Similarity-Dissimilarity*, 1 Soc. Behav. & Personality 1–7 (1973).

[152] Efran, *The Effect of Physical Appearance on the Judgment of Guilt, Interpersonal Attraction, and Severity of Recommended Punishment in a Simulated Jury Task*, 8 J. Research in Personality 45–54 (1974).

[153] Izzett & Sales, *Person Perception and Jurors' Reactions to Defendants*, in The Trial Process 218 (Plenum Press, B. Sales ed. 1981).

mock jurors take a criminal's suffering (or nonsuffering) into account when they are attempting to fix their verdict.[154]

For example, mock jurors were asked to sentence a defendant in a purse snatching case. The defendant was described as having only taken the victim's purse or as having beaten the victim as well as having taken the purse. In the process of attempting to escape the police, the defendant was said to have suffered either no harm, moderate harm, or excessive harm. Results show that the defendant who beat his victim was punished more severely than the defendant who only snatched the purse.

When the defendant was described as having suffered great injury and pain during the perpetration of the crime, he was said to have suffered already and was given a lesser prison sentence. This was termed the "Suffering in the Act" hypothesis. Mock jurors were determined to be more lenient in their sentencing of a defendant who was said to have suffered during the course of the act.[155]

The above results are compatible with an equity theory explanation. "From an equity standpoint, knowledge of the past suffering of a defendant (a defendant outcome in the equity formulation) produces a juror reaction which reduces the need to adversely affect further defendant outcomes."[156]

The severity of the sentence as a defendant outcome was examined by one commentator.[157] Subjects read a murder trial transcript in which there was conflicting evidence. In an attempt to determine if subjects would take into account the consequences of the verdict they rendered concerning this case, the author varied the decision alternatives available to the mock jurors. He discovered that subjects were less likely to find the defendant guilty when their alternatives were restricted (when they were instructed to find him guilty of first degree murder or not guilty) than when their alternatives were less restricted (for example, when manslaughter was an alternative). If mock jurors chose the not guilty verdict, it was found that they tended to justify that decision by saying the defendant was not such a bad person or that he was really a likable person,

---

[154] W. Austin, E. Walster & E. Utne, Equity and the Law: *The Effect of a Harmdoer's "Suffering in the Act" on Liking and Assigned Punishment*, in ADVANCES IN EXPERIMENTAL SOCIAL PSYCHOLOGY (Academic Press, L. Berkowitz & E. Walster eds. 1976).

[155] Shaw & McMartin, *Effects of Who Suffers in an Automobile Accident on Judgmental Strictness*, 1 AM. PSYCHOLOGICAL ASS'N PROC. 239–40 (8th Annual Convention, 1973).

[156] Izzett & Sales, *supra* note 153 at 221.

[157] Vidmar, *Effects of Decision Alternatives on the Verdicts and Social Perceptions of Simulated Jurors*, 22 J. PERSONALITY & SOC. PSYCHOLOGY 211–218 (1972).

and so on. Again, these results were explained within the equity theory interpretation:

> Subject-jurors, if uncertain of the severity of the crime committed by the defendant, and if concerned with the equitableness of the outcomes dispensed to the defendant, should be more prone to find him not guilty than find him guilty of a charge which produces too severe an outcome. Even if the defendant is guilty of at least some offense (manslaughter), subjects appeared to favor letting a defendant go rather than subjecting him to an "unfair" penalty.[158]

Victim inputs also have been found to have an impact on the verdicts rendered by jurors. A landmark study also varied the attributes of the victim (the victim's input in equity theory terms). When the victim was described as possessing positive attributes, the defendant received a longer prison sentence than in the situations where the victim was described as having negative attributes.[159]

In another study investigating the effect of victim input, the researchers told subjects that the murder victim was either a ten-year-old girl (who was shot seven times at point blank range on a playground) or the leader of a rival gang.[160] Not surprisingly, the defendant accused of shooting the ten-year-old was more likely to receive a harsh punishment from the jury. An equity theory interpretation posits that a "greater sense of distress or inequity should then heighten the subject's motivation to restore an equitable balance for the victim (or society) by adversely affecting the outcomes experienced by the defendant and seeing to it he got his 'just desserts.' "[161]

An area of perception that falls directly under the concept of equity theory and the law involves the perceiver's (juror's) need to believe in a just world. Recall from the explanation of the principles of equity theory, Proposition IIA states that society sets up and enforces a system in which a person's inputs entitle him to a fair outcome. The Just World Hypothesis has been found to be a relevant characteristic of jurors.[162]

---

[158] Izzett & Sales, *supra* note 153, at 221–222.

[159] Landy & Aronson, *supra* note 147.

[160] Hester & Smith, *Effects of a Mandatory Death Penalty on the Decisions of Simulated Jurors as a Function of Heinousness of the Crime*, 1 J. CRIM. JUST. 319–326 (1973).

[161] Izzett & Sales, *supra* note 153, at 222.

[162] Lerner & Miller, *Just World Research and the Attribution Process: Looking Back and Ahead*, 85 PSYCHOLOGICAL BULL. 1030–1051 (1978).

Individuals have been found to vary in their belief in the Just World Hypothesis. A scale to measure a person's belief in a just world, the Just World Scale, was developed. It consists of a series of belief statements which, when scored, help quantify the subject's belief in this area.[163]

§ 4.57 Implications of the size of the jury

The traditional American jury, composed of twelve men who were to represent the conscience and voice of the community, has been redefined through a series of court decisions since 1970. In 1970, in *Williams v. Florida*,[164] the United States Supreme Court held that a jury of six people was "functionally equivalent" for some criminal offenses to juries of twelve and thus did not violate Constitutional guarantees, even in cases of serious criminal charges. The assumption of the Court was that there would be no difference in the behavior of smaller juries. *Johnson v. Louisiana*[165] and *Apodaca v. Oregon*[166] held that jury verdicts need not be unanimous. *Colgrove v. Battin*[167] established that a six-person jury was also acceptable in federal civil litigation.

Numerous studies have been conducted concerning the impact of the reduction in jury size. Generally, results have shown that the quality of the jury group's discussion is higher in larger groups than in smaller groups. Minority viewpoints have a better chance of being voiced and considered in larger groups. Smaller groups tend to be dominated by a few vocal individuals, inhibiting even a persistent minority juror. Trial scholars note the implications of this situation:

> Nevertheless, for one or two jurors to hold out to the end, it would appear necessary that they had companionship at the beginning of the deliberations. The juror psychology recalls a famous series of experiments by the psychologist Asch and others which showed that in an ambiguous situation a member of a group will doubt, and finally disbelieve, his own correct observation if all other members of the group claim that he must have been mistaken. To maintain his original position, not only before others, but before himself, it is nec-

---

[163] Rubin & Peplau, *Belief in a Just World and Reactions to Another's Lot: A Study of Participants in the National Draft Lottery*, 29 J. Soc. Issues 73–93 (1973).

[164] 399 U.S. 78, 90 S. Ct. 1893, 26 L. Ed. 2d 446 (1970).

[165] 406 U.S. 356, 92 S. Ct. 1620, 32 L. Ed. 2d 152 (1972).

[166] 406 U.S. 404, 92 S. Ct. 1628, 32 L. Ed. 2d 184 (1972).

[167] 413 U.S. 149, 93 S. Ct. 2448, 37 L. Ed. 2d 522 (1973).

essary for him to have at least one ally.[168]

The Defense Research Institute lists the following tentative conclusions which have been drawn from the studies done on the impact of jury size:

—The six person jury tends to work to the disadvantage of the defense in criminal cases. Less reliable data is available for civil cases.[169]

And generally,

—Small jury panels lead to less comprehensive fact-finding and less productivity.

—Small jury panel verdicts are less consistent.

—There are fewer 'hung juries' with small jury panels.

—Small jury panels reduce the representativeness of minority groups in the community.

—Small jury panels return quicker verdicts.

—The 'influence' of the foreman decreases in small jury panels.

—Small jury panels bring in more verdicts for plaintiffs but more conservative compensatory and punitive damage awards.[170]

---

[168] H. KALVEN & H. ZEISEL, THE AMERICAN JURY (Little, Brown, 1966).

[169] Defense Research Institute, Inc., Toxic Torts Defense Tactics and Techniques Coursebook, at H-7 (Scottsdale, Arizona)(January 6-8, 1983). Copyright © 1983, The Defense Research Institute, Inc. Reprinted with permission. All rights reserved.

[170] *Id.*

Chapter 5

PREPARING FOR EFFECTIVE COURTROOM COMMUNICATION

I. Initial Client Interview

II. Controlling Evidence Development Through Aggressive Discovery Techniques

KLUWER LITIGATION LIBRARY REFERENCES

JEANS, LITIGATION: Chapter 1, *The Relationship of Advocate and Client*; Chapter 2, *Mind Set of the Advocate*; Chapter 4, *Discovery*; Chapter 5, *Trial Preparation*.

JOYE & LOVETT, DRUNK DRIVING: THE TRIAL WORKBOOK, THE TRIAL SOURCEBOOK, THE TRIAL NOTEBOOK: Chapter 102, *Outline: Preparation for Trial*; Chapter 111, *Client*.

PREISER & PREISER, HANDLING SOFT TISSUE INJURY CASES: Chapter 1, *Interviewing the Client and Preparing for Investigation of the Case*; Chapter 2, *Investigating the Case*; Chapter 3, *Overlooked Witnesses and Evidence*; Chapter 4, *The Most Overlooked Element of Damages: Reduced Capacity to Earn*; Chapter 5, *Use of Discovery*; Chapter 11, *Selecting the Jury*; Chapter 12, *Opening Statements*.

I. Initial Client Interview

§ 5.01 Establishing rapport

The application of the principles of communication presented in the previous chapters begins with the initial contact with the client. Good attorneys are effective communicators; effective attorney-client communication yields a mutually beneficial relationship. It is essential for the attorney to establish rapport, build trust, and gain control of the client from the beginning.

The initial client interview presents the opportunity to establish rapport by pacing the client through matching. The purpose of pacing is to increase the perception of similarity between the attorney and the client.

Matching occurs on three levels, the verbal, the vocal, and the nonverbal levels. Pacing occurring on the verbal level entails the matching of words and phrases which the client uses during the interview. Select their key words and use their structure. Pacing on a vocal level means matching the rhythm at which they speak. For example, if the client speaks very slowly, it is important to slow down your pace. If, on the other hand, your client talks quickly and tends to get to the bottom line issues, it is important for the attorney to match those issues in the same way. Nonverbal pacing is the pacing of physical positioning, body movements, gestures, and eye contact. Complementary pacing entails doing the opposite: for example, if you have a client who is restless while sitting in his chair, complement his behavior by slowing down the cues and sitting back in the chair. For pacing to be effective it must be covered on all three levels. The attorney's effort to establish rapport by pacing the client through matching culminates in a subconscious level communication to the client that we like him and therefore that he likes us.

§ 5.02 Building trust

In addition to presenting the opportunity to establish rapport with the client, the initial client interview provides the opportunity for the establishment of the trust relationship through listening. At the beginning of the interview it is essential to obtain the client's initial impression of what happened in a manner that is not influenced by our leading questions. Allow the client to talk a while before asking specific questions and obtaining specific details. The use of open-ended questions when requesting information regarding the incident allows the client to give a narrative description of what happened and also allows the attorney to obtain the client's initial version of the facts. Later on during the interview, the attorney can use leading questions to refresh the client's memory or improve the client's phraseology. Our listening to and our pacing the client takes place simultaneously. Properly performed, the initial interview is the cornerstone of the trust relationship between the client and the attorney.[1]

§ 5.03 Gaining control of the client

Pacing is a process which continues throughout the client interview. As you are listening to the client, asking direct questions, or even leading an interview, continue to match and complement the behavior of the cli-

[1] *See infra* § 5.06, *Phrasing the questions*.

ent. If the client begins to talk while you are talking, begin the pacing behavior. Stop talking, allow him to start talking, go into a listening mode, and avoid interrupting at this time. You are continually staying in sync with the rhythm of the client. By matching his rhythm, you increase his level of comfort and this relates very specifically to Communication Principle 2, that is, people actively try to make sense out of their environment. That principle is based upon the concept of uncertainty reduction; the more you can reduce uncertainty during the client interview, the more you increase the client's level of comfort. Successfully done, this becomes a basis of controlling the client.

Prior to meeting with the attorney, the client should have filled out a questionnaire regarding essential information such as name, address, phone number, nearest relatives, phone contacts, details regarding the nature of the incident, and the reason for consulting an attorney.[2] Prior to meeting with the client, the attorney should review this questionnaire and prepare psychologically to deal with the client. Try to imagine what this client looks like, anticipate the gamut of the client's possible anxieties, ask yourself what prejudices this client could have and what you can do to counter them. For example, if this client is of a different ethnic background or race, try to picture the fears he may have of coming to you. In essence, put yourself in a state of mind which is receptive to the client and understand his needs. One must first establish the proper mood to build rapport and gain control.

As the client is ushered into the office, the attorney should always stand up, come forward and greet the client from a standing position. After greeting the client, sit in a chair directly across from him. If possible, do not have your desk blocking your view of the client as access to his body cues is essential. During this interview, you are also evaluating the client as to what impact the client will have on a judge and jury. Such an evaluation should provide insight into whether this is the type of client whose case should be tried before a jury or, if he is not appealing "jury material," should be tried to a judge. You can better make these assessments if you are sitting across a low, coffee-type table talking to the client, rather than behind a desk.

Again, it is strongly recommended that during the initial interview the attorney sit directly across from the client in the same type of chair, and without any physical barriers separating the two. This will allow you to

---

[2] *See generally* S. PREISER & M. PREISER, HANDLING SOFT TISSUE INJURY CASES Chapter 1 (Kluwer Law Book Publishers, 1985).

establish better rapport with the client by (a) interpreting his body movements and body cues and (b) by his being able to react with a relaxed stance. Your body cues should exude warmth and friendliness.

Remember Communication Principle 3 relating to primacy: "Perceptions are organized and structured within a brief period of time." The initial impression the client gets of the lawyer within the first three or four minutes is most probably a lasting one. Therefore, the initial impression the client has of the lawyer will strongly influence the entire relationship between the lawyer and client over the next several years. It is essential that the lawyer build rapport and gain the confidence of the client in the first few minutes.

§ 5.04 Interpreting nonverbal cues

One aspect of the initial client interview that is fraught with particular difficulty is the successful interpretation of the client's nonverbal cues, body movements, behavior, and positioning. Is the client exhibiting nervousness? Is this behavior attributable to an anticipated degree of apprehension regarding an interview with an attorney, or is the degree excessive even for a person in such a situation? Could this nervousness be a result of the trauma of the injury? All of these questions can be answered by properly analyzing and interpreting the cues given by the client.

Most clients do exhibit some degree of anxiety during the interview by the lawyer. The essential question raised is whether the client's increased anxiety is due to deception or simple nervousness.

Basic behavioral patterns must be noted prior to observing deceptive cues. To establish normal (baseline) behavior, ask questions that would produce comfort; for example: where are you from?, where do you live?, what have you been doing? Situational anxiety occurs when a person is confronted with issues that tend to increase his anxiety level. Watch for a deviation away from the norm towards behavior more closely associated with situational anxiety. For example, a client during his normal behavioral patterns is very comfortable, very quiet, and exhibits very little body movement; but during the situational anxiety period, he exhibits increased body movement. This client's deviation from his normal behavior would be an indicator of a change of direction and, possibly, a change into the area of deception. On the other hand, if his normal behavior is very fidgety, then during the context of situational anxiety he may become very still and quiet. For this latter client, such a change in behavior may indicate an increase in deception, or at least a tendency towards deception. Remember, no single behavioral pattern is a predicator of deception; it is unique to the individual, and accuracy in interpretation depends upon observing his normal behavior. The attorney must always carefully observe differences in response patterns.

Behaviors commonly associated with deception, taken by themselves, are rarely accurate indicators of the truthfulness of the subject. For example, a 1974 study by Knapp, Hart, and Dennis,[3] reports only two significant variables regarding nonverbal cues: duration of adaptor cues and eye contact. Deceivers and nondeceivers did not differ significantly in speech errors, word and phrase repetitions, pauses, total words, leg movements, gestures, duration of gestures, and the frequency of establishing eye contact. According to this study, an attorney may not rely on the majority of nonverbal cues as valid indicators of the veracity of the client's statements.

In fact, the only way to determine truthfulness may be by subsequent investigation of the facts. From the interview alone, with respect to nonverbal cues, the interviewing attorney, attempting to interpret the client's truthfulness probably can only rely on the duration of adaptor cues, such as fidgeting, or excessive movements over a long period of time, and the inability of the client to maintain prolonged eye contact with the attorney. Other stereotypical behavior associated with lying, such as hesitancy, uncertainty, generalized nervous fidgeting from time to time, withdrawal of eye contact, and inaudible speech, have not proven to be accurate indicators of veracity.[4] There is also a study indicating that visual cues may actually detract from the accuracy of the observer in determining whether or not the subject is being truthful.[5]

A 1980 study succeeds in defining a major reason for the difficulty in determining truthfulness during the initial interview: deceivers are able to control their nonverbal behavior and thus lie more convincingly when there is little or no chance of punishment for lying.[6] When there is an

---

[3] Knapp, Hart & Dennis, *An Exploration of Deception as a Communication Construct*, 1 HUM. COM. RESEARCH 15–29 (1974).

[4] Miller, Bauchner, Hocking, Fontes, Kaminski & Brandt, " . . . *And Nothing But the Truth*", in THE TRIAL PROCESS 145–179 (Plenum Press, B. Sales ed. 1981).

[5] Maier & Thurber, *Accuracy of Judgments on Deception When an Interview is Watched, Heard, and Read*, 25 PERSONNEL PSYCHOLOGY 23-30 (1968).

[6] Hocking & Leathers, *Nonverbal Indicators of Deception: A New Theoretical Perspective*, 7 COM. MONOGRAPHS (June 1980).

increased chance of punishment for the lying, there is an increased chance of detecting deceit because, at the moment of deception, there will be greater nonverbal cues which can be more readily interpreted as being part of a deceptive statement. The study also indicates that conscious control by the deceiver of such things as facial expression, fidgeting, and so forth is likely, but that the deceiver is less likely to be able to control vocal cues. They state in an article from *Communication Monographs*:

> "It is the susceptibility to conscious control that mostly differentiates such kinesic cues as gestures and facial expressions from vocal cues, however, recent research suggests that vocalic cues are extremely difficult to control consciously for at least two reasons. First, the heightened anxiety which is experienced at the time of deception is reflected persistently and continuously in increased vocal nervousness and a number of nonfluencies seem to defy conscious effort to control or suppress them. Second, the changes in 'microtremors' of the voice, which have been detected by machine at the moment of deception, are not thought to be controllable by the central nervous system. . . . Deceiving subjects did not sustain contact with the interrogator as long as the truthful subjects, but they did not look away from the interrogator as often as truthful subjects."[7]

An important aspect of the initial interview is the attorney's evaluation of the client's truthfulness. This can most accurately be ascertained by relying on the normal behavioral patterns exhibited by this client and the deviations therefrom. Adaptor cues such as fidgeting, abnormal body movements, and brushing the hair, are accurate cues of deception only if they are considered within the context of baseline (normal) behavior patterns.

§ 5.05 Obtaining the facts

The attorney has established rapport with the client, built his trust, evaluated his veracity, and made a good initial impact. Simultaneously, the attorney has been evaluated by the client. It is now time to obtain the facts. During the initial portion of the interview a general description of the incident was obtained when the client offered his version of the incident in response to open-ended questioning. Now specific, follow-up questions are asked so as to determine particular facts that apply to the pertinent legal issues. At this point the attorney is considering potential

[7] *Id.*

causes of action. Is this merely an auto collision case? Is there a second impact case? Is there a products liability case? The attorney might be considering whether this is merely a medical malpractice case or whether it also involves a products liability action for the failure of a medical device or the failure of the drug company to adequately warn regarding an adverse reaction to a particular drug. The attorney should obtain all the relevant factual information and develop all possible theories of recovery. Then a file memo should be dictated in front of the client, first telling the client that he is to correct the attorney if anything dictated in the file memo is factually incorrect. In addition to their check on your accuracy, such action impresses the client with the amount of work you are already doing on his case. Thus, the file should contain more than just the handwritten notes of the lawyer. Often others are going to be reviewing the file. At the very least, a typed file memo is easier to interpret than the handwritten notes taken by the attorney during the initial interview.

§ 5.06 Phrasing the questions

Questions, during the initial interview, for the reasons previously stated, should be phrased in an open manner. These types of questions will encourage a narrative response by the client and this will help establish rapport. They should be followed with questions such as: "what else happened?" or "what happened next?" It is important for the attorney to use congruent nonverbal and verbal cues at the same time. It is appropriate to use "encouragers," such things as a head nod, leaning forward, pausing when appropriate, not interrupting, showing interest and enthusiasm in the voice. By doing this, the response to the question and the likelihood of obtaining self-disclosed information is greatly increased.

After this questioning has evoked a narrative response, specific factual questions should be asked. Specific questions should be more leading in nature, for example: "Do you or do you not know whether the drug taken was DES?" or "Were you told simply that it was a white pill?" or "Do you remember the color of the pill?" or "If we show you pictures of pills could you identify it?" This type of detailed follow-up questioning develops the necessary information to complete the factual picture and dictate an accurate file memo. Finally, it may become necessary to commit the client to a particular crucial fact during the interview. This can be accomplished with a truly leading question, for example, state the following: "So it is true, and you know of your own knowledge that. . . ." This type of phraseology will cause the client to commit to the answer and cause the client's story to remain consistent on essential facts (Principle 8: People have a need to be consistent).

§ 5.07 Analysis of answers

A good interviewer is, of course, also a good listener. The attorney should "listen with a third ear"; that is, listen for not only what the client is saying but how the client is saying it. Listen carefully for any deletions or something missing from the client's responses. The obviously deleted step may itself be what actually did occur. Continually evaluate the answers of the client. Are the answers truthful and, even if truthful, do the answers appear to be deceitful? Do the client's nonverbal cues indicate the stereotype of a person who is deceitful? In your analysis, remember that the information offered by the client about the incident is based upon his memory.

A word about memory. Everything that our mind is exposed to is recorded in one's memory, but the ability to recall these memories is the crucial issue. It is sometimes true that the client is not able to recall the facts accurately. In one case, the plaintiff swore that he was run off the road by a car coming toward him in his lane. Despite the testimony by the client, plaintiff's counsel was able to establish through physical evidence and a psychologist's testimony that the client had fallen asleep at the wheel. He was then able to successfully contend that the incident was the fault of the plaintiff's employer for overworking the client.

The attorney needs to be aware that the client's ability to recall may be impeded by the client's emotions regarding the incident. Memory may also be impeded by retrograde amnesia, inherent bias, and prejudice. It may even contradict actual physical evidence. For example, in the case where the plaintiff fell asleep at the wheel, the client fully believed that a car coming toward him on the wrong side of the road had pulled into his lane and forced him off the road. This is what the client stated during the initial interview and this is what the client testified to at deposition despite advice that this couldn't have happened. The physical evidence supported the fact that the client had fallen asleep at the wheel. The client had simply failed to make a turn and had run directly off the road. This was the testimony of both the investigating police officer and accident reconstruction expert. Further, the testimony of a psychologist indicated that drivers who fall asleep at the wheel often remember it differently because psychologically they do not admit to themselves that they fell asleep; they are not aware in their conscious mind that they had reached a state of sleep. They then envision a version of the accident which indicates that they were not at fault, i.e., that they were forced off the road. Thus, it can be seen that by analysis of a client's answer, by comparing the answers to actual physical evidence, and by using common sense, the client's own version of an incident may be proven inaccurate. The lawyer should always be listening with the "third ear."

§ 5.08 Follow-up questions

As described in the section on phrasing, follow-up questions are essential.[8] By follow-up questions we mean that certain facts form the basis to elicit subsequent facts. This is particularly true in the areas of complex litigation such as products liability or medical malpractice. Follow-up questioning of the client is necessary after the initial information is analyzed. For example, a client has narrated her version of a possible medical malpractice situation involving a traumatic labor and delivery. Often crucial details are missing from the narrative. Was the mother on a pitocin drip? Was a fetal monitor in use? The mother may or may not have this information. She may or may not know what medication, if any, was administered to her intravenously. This information may be established by follow-up questions or subsequent investigation.

Medical textbooks and basic reference books should be consulted during the initial interview. Checking on drugs or other information during the initial interview impresses the client and builds an image of the lawyer's credibility in the client's mind. The client, to whom the case is crucial, doesn't mind sitting there while the attorney looks up a particular drug in the reference book or verifies an impression in a medical textbook. The information contained in these books will often lead to subsequent follow-up questions. The attorney must be prepared to ask follow-up questions at the initial interview to develop the case as much as possible.

§ 5.09 Necessity for taking the complete medical history

It is essential that a complete medical history of the client be taken by the attorney. Often preexisting conditions, familial predispositions, drug usage, drug interaction, and so forth are considered and used by defendants as potential defenses. Unless a complete medical history of the client and of his family members is taken, there may be an opening for

---

[8] *See supra* § 5.06, *Phrasing the questions*.

defense counsel to use the client's unfavorable medical history as a defense.

§ 5.10 —Past medical history

As stated previously, the attorney must obtain a complete medical history. He should specifically learn whether the client had the usual childhood illnesses and whether there were any particular incidents of significance during childhood in terms of injury, whether anything unusual occurred during the birth process of the client, i.e., was the client a premature baby? Was the client full-term? Was the client's mother a user or abuser of drugs or of alcohol? These types of detail questions regarding medical history must be asked. Every aspect of every symptom, every medical condition, and every hospitalization must be discussed, developed, and carefully analyzed.

§ 5.11 —Present illness in detail

After determining the medical history, the present injury or illness needs to be described by the client in detail. If one is dealing with a rear-end collision, the attorney must ask the client specific details as to the time of the onset of the pain, the nature of the pain, the changes in symptoms, if any, since the accident occurred. For example, the client needs to be specifically questioned about any pains in the arms, legs, hands, feet, and so forth. The client may feel that these symptoms are not related and, therefore, may fail to report them to the treating physician. The attorney's questions regarding specific symptoms should be designed to provide him as well as the treating physician with essential information concerning the client's condition. For example, in a rear-end collision, one needs to ask whether the client has experienced any dizziness, blurring of vision, sensations of coldness, or effects on memory. The attorney may want to examine the client's memory in terms of short-term and long-term logic, and the ability of the client to comprehend abstract concepts or ideas. These questions, while not leading to a direct diagnosis, may be indicative of actual or potential brain damage. Often, minimal brain damage is missed by attorneys because they do not ask the necessary questions in sufficient detail regarding the present illness.

An example of the importance of detailed questioning occurred in the case of a young girl who was injured while riding on a bicycle. The girl crashed her bicycle into a parked car while looking back at a vicious dog that was in rapid pursuit. She was catapulted off the seat of the bicycle onto the roof of the car and, as a result, suffered severe facial injuries requiring not only plastic surgery but the wiring of her jaws until the mandibular fractures healed. Fortunately, the owner of the dog had liability insurance. After a month of hospitalization and two surgical procedures, she was released with only residual facial scarring. However, she continued to complain of back pain which the treating physicians attributed to prolonged bed rest and inactivity. However, during a detailed client interview, the attorney determined that the area of pain specified was very low, indeed below the sacrum. The attorney had the young girl examined for a fractured coccyx. The examination and X-rays revealed that the girl did indeed have an undiagnosed fractured coccyx.

§ 5.12 —Eliciting and preserving signs and symptoms

It is, of course, essential to elicit all of the signs and symptoms of the injury suffered by the client. This can be accomplished by taking the detailed medical history. In addition to a narrative history, it is a good practice to have the client list his symptoms. Then the attorney should list symptoms that are associated with the particular problem involved. For instance, the following are symptoms associated with a neck injury: (1) spasm; (2) tenderness; (3) limitation of motion; (4) dizziness; (5) ringing in the ears; (6) blurred vision; (7) radicular pain in the arms; (8) loss of sensation; (9) positive neurologic signs; (10) effects on memory; (11) effects on personality. To develop a complete picture of the client's physical complaint, it is necessary to develop a list of the signs and symptoms of a particular medical entity from the medical literature. It is also essential to make the client aware of the signs and symptoms he may develop.

It is not enough merely that the client describe all the signs and symptoms, it is essential to preserve them. If there are bruises, cuts, scrapes, or other visible signs of injury, they should be photographed. Generally, it is better to photograph these with 35mm film rather than with a Polaroid so that they may be enlarged for trial purposes. You may either use a professional photographer or have someone on your staff do the photography.

Some signs of disease or injury are better preserved on videotape. For example, severe limitation of motion should be videotaped. To lay the basis for the admissibility of such a film or videotape, it is best to have the videotaping done at the physician's office. The physician can then testify that he was putting the patient through the range of active and passive motions while the videotape was taken. Thus, the physician lays a foundation at trial that the videotape accurately portrays the client's limitation of motion found on that particular day. Use of this technique should be for those cases where the lawyer on initial interview has attempted to both actively and passively put the patient's neck or back through a range of motion and found it to be severely limited. Severe limitation of motion on videotape can make dramatic evidence at trial and in many cases can lead to early settlement of the lawsuit.

§ 5.13 Taking the complete liability history

Counsel should develop the complete facts regarding liability. Again, the nature and phrasing of the questions is essential.[9] Frequently, there are alternate theories of liability that can be used by the skillful practitioner. In considering each one, the attorney must take a complete history regarding the incident as well as a history of prior similar incidents which might constitute notice to the defendant. Detailed questioning regarding all the facts is essential, regardless of the relevance of the facts at the moment.

§ 5.14 —List all potential defendants

Counsel should get into the habit of making a list of potential defendants during the taking of the history. For example, in a malpractice case, everyone whose name appears in the medical record is a potential defendant. This includes the hospital, every nurses' aide, every R.N., the surgeon, the referring physicians, the various laboratories, the anesthesiologist who supervised the C.R.N.A. who administered the anesthesia, the C.R.N.A. or anesthesiologist who did the preanesthetic work on the patient, the X-ray technicians, and anyone else who came in contact with the patient in any way. From this list you can then decide who to name and who not to name as defendants on an intelligent basis.

§ 5.15 —List all factors contributing to the injury

In addition, counsel should likewise list all possible factors which contributed to the plaintiff's injuries and which may relate to the negligence or potential strict liability of the defendant[s]. Counsel should also list factors which may have contributed to any secondary injury; this serves as a checklist in analyzing potential defendants.

---

[9] *See supra* § 5.06, *Phrasing the questions* and § 5.07, *Analysis of answers*.

§ 5.16 —Analyzing contributing factors as related to potential defendants

After a list of all the contributing factors has been compiled, counsel should analyze what each potential defendant did to contribute to the conditions which caused the injury. For example, in the analysis of an industrial plant explosion, counsel may determine that safety regulations were violated in the original design plans. These may be attributed to the general architect, to the original contractor, or to subsequent subcontractors. Similarly, actions of supervisors or coemployees may have contributed to the condition. Anyone whose actions may have contributed to the injury is a potential defendant provided that counsel is not prohibited from naming such defendants by a workmen's compensation statute.

There are numerous complex fact patterns which illustrate the analysis of contributing factors. For example, in one instance, the patient was a seventeen-year-old girl with hyperthyroidism who was being treated by an endocrinologist with propylthiouracil (PTU) for the past three or four years. While on the drug, she developed swelling in the joints for which the endocrinologist referred her to a rheumatologist. The rheumatologist made a diagnosis of juvenile rheumatoid arthritis and treated her with aspirin. She continued on the aspirin for several months and then developed a rash. She went to a separate clinic and was seen by a dermatologist where she admitted to having taken her sister's penicillin. He told the patient that she is allergic to penicillin and instructed her to take no drugs that contained penicillin. The rash did not subside. The dermatologist then referred the child to his partner, an endocrinologist. He obtained her case history and noted that she was being treated by the other endocrinologist for hyperthyroidism and that she had been on the drug propylthiouracil for several years. He took over the treatment of the child, treating her swollen joints and rash as allergic reactions. He instructed her to avoid aspirins and drugs with codeine, in addition to penicillin, but all to no avail. Finally, the patient scratched the rash and a primary infection set in. The second endocrinologist treated the infected rash with the drug prostaphillin. Forty-eight hours later there was a fulminating effect in the skin of the lower half of the body resulting in a vascular necrosis which killed the skin on the lower half of her body. Like a burn victim, she became so ill she was considered terminal. She was admitted to a major medical center, where she was treated intensively for six months. The physician at that particular hospital realized that the drug PTU can cause a rash and swelling in the joints; he diagnosed a reaction to PTU, withdrew the drug, the patient's rash cleared and her joint swelling subsided. However, she was severely injured from the adverse reaction to propylthiouracil. A list of all potential defendants would include all physicians who had seen her, including the original endocrinologist, the rheumatologist, the dermatologist, and his partner, the second endocrinologist. Their partners in the various clinics are also potential defendants, but more importantly, the manufacturer of each and every drug that she ingested is a potential defendant.

After a careful analysis of the literature, the attorney concluded that a contributing factor in her care was a hypersensitivity to the drug which was reflected by her development of a rash and swelling in the joints. The literature discusses rash combined with swollen joints as an absolute indication to cease further administration of the drug PTU. A further analysis of the facts revealed that the defendants were going to take the position that there was insufficient notice for them to know that the causative agent was PTU. In such a situation, counsel must sue all four physicians involved and the manufacturers of PTU. Counsel should allege that the drug was defective because its insert and the literature published by the manufacturer contained inadequate warnings of the danger. With both the physicians and manufacturer as defendants you have codefendants pointing fingers at one another. If an attorney sues only the manufacturer or only the physicians, the named defendants have the opportunity to try "an empty chair."

It is the detailed analysis of contributing factors and potential defendants that leads the attorney to name all viable partners. In all situations, every potential defendant whose conduct in any way contributed to the situation should be sued initially.

§ 5.17 Preserving the evidence

The need to preserve evidence for trial is essential to proper case preparation. For example, in most cases medical records are essential, but many attorneys do not obtain complete copies of medical records and make no effort to have the originals preserved. If they are not preserved either by agreement or court order, health care providers will routinely, and sometimes conveniently, destroy the original records. The attorney is then left with unreadable microfilm copies. Of course, any other visible evidence needs to be preserved photographically as soon as possible. In addition, in cases involving a death where an autopsy has been performed, make sure that the pathologist keeps paraffin blocks of the tissues and the actual pathological slide that are used to make a diagnosis. Often these can be lost or destroyed. The best thing to do is to order a duplicate set of slides made from the existing paraffin blocks. Lost X-rays are a common experience of many trial lawyers. It is essential to subpoena the X-rays early on in the case and to either order copies or obtain a court order sealing the original X-rays in the court record. In a products liability case, any physical evidence that may be present relating to the product itself needs to be preserved. In cases where there has been an explosion or a fire, the attorney needs to have an investigator sifting through the ruins while they are still smoking to make a proper determination of the cause of the fire. If your client is seriously disabled, for example, if he is a quadriplegic, it is essential to have a "day in the life" film made soon after the injury. This film should demonstrate the client's ability to communicate with relatives only by blinking the eyes and other graphic horrors of the injury. Remember that these seriously injured plaintiffs may die unexpectedly, making these visual records essential.

In a criminal case, counsel needs to engage in proper discovery to determine the physical evidence the police took from the scene of the crime. The trial attorney should visit the scene of the crime and develop his own physical evidence. The attorney must remember that an essential part of preparation for trial is preserving the physical evidence.

§ 5.18 —Use of personal diaries

In addition to preserving physical evidence, other types of information regarding the incident in question may need preservation. A prime method of preserving information is to have the client transcribe, while it is fresh in his mind, both the details of the incident and the continuous nature of the pain and suffering and the treatment. To do this, it is advisable to have the client purchase a diary. It should be a cheap paper covered diary from a local stationary store, because it must not be perceived by the jury as having been manufactured by the attorney. (Principle 1: Communication is based on perception.) Inform the client that the diary may be used at trial. Ask the client to keep a daily record of any additional thoughts regarding the incident involved, the nature of the ongoing pain and suffering, and to the degree possible, an itemization of expenses and losses connected with the injury. These diaries make excellent tools to prepare the witness' testimony prior to the client taking the stand. While the client usually does not read from the diary on the stand, the mere existence of a diary often makes a wonderful retort by the client during cross-examination. Often, the client who has certified to his pain and suffering over several years, will be cross-examined on his memory. The tenor of the cross-examination frequently involves a degree of skepticism regarding the client's ability to remember details a year or two after the incident. This line of cross-examination quickly ceases when the client mentions the diary and it is ultimately produced as a valid refreshment of the client's recollection.

§ 5.19 —Developing photographic evidence

As previously stated, it is better to have any necessary photographs taken with a 35mm camera. It is also preferable to have independent professional photographers take the photographs. In smaller cases, it is acceptable to have the client take his own photographs. Regarding admissibility, in almost every jurisdiction, such photographs have been held admissible if the client can testify that they accurately reflect what he saw at the time, that the camera was in no way tampered with, nor the film in any way improperly exposed. Although a professional photographer is not required in order for the photographs to be admissible, the psychological effect of the photographs can be heightened if the professional photographer testifies as to their accuracy, the date taken, and the objectivity of the photographs.

Often, photographs must depict distance. On smaller objects this can be done with a ruler or a yardstick. Where long distances are involved it may be essential to mark off the area and to place markers showing the distances from the intersection. In addition, aerial photographs may be essential in certain cases. Standard photos can frequently be purchased from the local governing body or the state government. This is particularly true of interstate highways; all interstate highways have been surveyed by aerial photography. It may be necessary to hire a plane or helicopter and have a professional photographer experienced in aerial photographs develop an overview of the area.

§ 5.20 —Videotapes as evidence

In addition to the use of videotape evidence of physical examinations,[10] the plaintiff undergoing physical therapy or any other type of rehabilitation may be videotaped. Obviously, "day in the life" videotapes of a seriously injured quadriplegic client or a paralyzed client may be very dramatic as well as essential to your case. It is better to have professional

---

[10] *See supra* § 5.12, *Eliciting and preserving signs and symptoms*.

help in the production and development of the documentary videotape than to do it yourself.

A new area of videotaped evidence is in reconstruction of the accident. Working with engineering and/or accident reconstruction experts and possibly with computers, videotaped evidence can be developed which will show a vehicle coming down a roadway at the specific speeds at issue or it may also show vehicles entering an intersection from specific distances at given speeds. Such videotaped evidence can dramatically heighten and/or undercut verbal eyewitness accounts. Of course, a foundation is necessary to establish the accuracy of the reconstruction based upon the times and speeds testified to at trial. The combination of videotape and computer analysis of a fact situation leaves counsel limited only by imagination in terms of developing evidence to the fullest.

§ 5.21 —Statements of witnesses

The statements of witnesses are not generally admissible at trial. Counsel may then ask, why take them? One takes witness statements to preserve their position and to insure their integrity. It is important to obtain a statement from any witness whose identity is known.

There are various techniques for taking the statements of witnesses. The witness may write out the statement. This technique has its advantages and disadvantages. The advantage, of course, is that it is very difficult for the witness to repudiate a statement he wrote. On the other hand, this is cumbersome and often the witness may not know how to phrase the statement and may be unwilling to accept detailed, word by word assistance regarding the phrasing of the statement.

The second way to take a statement is for either you or your investigator to write out the statement, then have the witness initial any change or errors and to have him sign each page. In that event, the statement must be sequentially numbered and should indicate the total number of pages as well. In other words, page 1 of a statement would read at the bottom—"page 1 of 6 pages." The advantage of this type of statement is that a comprehensive development of the facts can be fully expressed in better detail.

A third form of statement is a tape-recorded statement. The major advantage of taped statements is the ease of recording over the telephone with the consent of the witness.

Whatever the method chosen, it is essential that every witness, or potential witness, who is not a defendant or potential defendant give a statement. These statements, placed in the file, will preserve witness integrity from future outside pressures. Even a witness who states: "I know nothing," should be asked to give a statement, because he may still show up on the stand with his memory remarkably refreshed. Under such a circumstance it is a distinct advantage to have a statement wherein he admitted knowing nothing.

Remember that there are certain psychological factors associated with the initial contact with a potential witness (Principle 6: People attempt to maintain their original perceptions regardless of contradictory information). The rule of primacy governs the initial contact with the potential witness. His lasting impression of you as well as his willingness to cooperate in giving a favorable statement may well be controlled by his initial impression of you. This initial impression in a face-to-face meeting occurs within the first four minutes. Therefore, it is essential that the attorney have a planned approach to the witness before contact is made. The attorney should analyze on a conscious level whatever information is available regarding the personality type of this witness. Is race a factor to be considered? Are you dealing with inherent biases or prejudices? Is he of the same or different ethnic background? What stereotypes will he apply to your client and what generalizations does he have about people who make claims and/or people who are charged with a crime? Be prepared before ever contacting the witness to deal with his stereotype and to link to his existing belief system. This will enable the attorney or investigator to establish the early rapport that is crucial in the concept of primacy.

The proper technique for interviewing a potential witness is the use of pacing and leading to establish rapport. If the witness is a blue-collar worker, when you approach the witness at least undo your tie and take off your coat. (Principle 5: People tend to see others as similar to themselves.) Attempt to appear visually like your potential witness. Match his vocal and nonverbal cues during the interview. After talking to the witness about the generalities of the situation and introducing yourself, begin matching his movements and gestures. After you have established rapport, begin to lead, that is, change some of your gestures and note if he will match. If this occurs you are now successfully leading the witness and you can begin taking a very favorable statement from a cooperative witness.

At this point, recall the necessity of interpreting the witness' nonverbal cues. Does he appear nervous or agitated? Is he able to maintain eye contact with you for any significant duration? Is he fidgeting or shuffling his feet? Are his facial expressions consistent with the verbal statements? If he is exhibiting any negative cues, is the reason simple anxiety or does this witness have a reason for bias or prejudices to deliberately mislead you? Does the witness have a self-interest, such as a relationship with a party, be it plaintiff or defendant, which would tend to color his memory more favorably to one side than the other? If you are leading the witness can you, by assisting the witness reconstruct his memory, obtain admissions that are favorable to your side?

§ 5.22 Closing the initial interview

Another important part of the initial interview is the close. At this point the client signs the retainer agreement, or in a criminal case the client agrees to pay your fee. You should have the client relaxed before discussing the financial cost of your services in detail. It is essential to bring this matter into the first interview so that the client will understand the arrangement. Fee agreements should always be in writing so that future disputes can be avoided. Fee disputes lead to a rapid deterioration of your ability to adequately represent the client. This should be avoided at all cost.

When discussing fees it is important not to change your behavioral pattern. If you are sitting in a chair, relaxed, and talking in a low voice tone, discuss fees in the same matter of fact mood, as this encourages the client to respond in a consistent manner. Most of the problems that occur when discussing fees is that the attorney's cues shift; he changes his pace and his movement pattern and this cues the client to be wary of whatever is coming next. Further, the vocal characteristics when discussing fees are extremely critical. For example, if the attorney feels that a fee is too high, his vocal characteristic pattern will make that feeling all too evident. Have confidence in what you are proposing, know that it is appropriate and that, in fact, you are rendering the value of that fee.

§ 5.23 —Explaining the lawyer's function

It is important to explain the function of the attorney and his role as an advocate. The role of the attorney is often a mystery to laymen. They simply do not understand what lawyers do. The client needs to appreciate that the attorney, unlike the physician, does not require the physical presence of his client to do work on the case. He must understand that the attorney has other cases and that his case will be processed in a reasonable and orderly fashion. It is important to explain that the attorney can neither control the court dockets nor how quickly the case is going to come to trial. It is reasonable, however, to give a realistic estimate as to when the case might be brought to trial.

The steps of the litigation process should be explained in detail. The client further needs to understand that during the initial investigation there will be contacts with an insurance adjuster and that at some later point there may be consultation with the lawyer to discuss the possibility of settling the case, and that this discussion may be over the phone or in person. Explain to the client that it will be his option whether to accept or reject any offer. After the attorney attains authority he can negotiate with the adjuster. Often, there are differences of opinion as to the value of the case; if the adjuster offers only a few thousand dollars less, it may be better to settle the claim rather than waiting to go to trial several years later. Early settlements will inevitably bring the attorney future clients from satisfied former clients.

In addition to explaining in detail the function of the attorney, it is essential that the lawyer explain the function of his staff. An investigator, secretary, or paralegal who is working with the attorney on the file should be introduced to the client at the initial interview. The client needs to be told that the attorney may not be available for consultation on the telephone. The client must understand that questions can and will be answered by the lawyer but often this has to be done through the intermediary—the paralegal, the secretary, or even an associate lawyer—where applicable. The way in which this is told to the client is more important than the actual content. In other words, the entire office support staff, secretary, paralegal, and associate attorneys must say this in such a way that it neither puts the attorney in a formidable position, nor in an arrogant position, nor on a pedestal; that in fact the entire group is working for the client in the way that is most efficient and effective for the client's case.

§ 5.24 —Explaining the duties of the client

After the client understands the duties of the attorney and his staff, he needs to be made aware of his own responsibilities, especially the importance of following up on the previously discussed assistance in developing evidence. If the client is to keep a diary he needs to be reminded again. Most importantly, the client needs to be instructed not to discuss this matter with people outside his own family or with anyone other than the attorney or his staff. The client must understand that you are the attorney, that you are the one that will now have contact with the insurance adjuster and with anyone wanting to ask questions about the situation. Any problem regarding his case, the nature of his injuries, and the nature and progress of his treatments must come to your attention. It is critical for the client to understand that he is not to go to another physician simply because his current physician makes a referral. Often, it is essential to have the client referred to a physician who is familiar with court procedures and comprehends the necessity of an accurate and intelligent report. For example, if the client is being treated by a general practitioner but the injuries demand treatment by an orthopedist or neurosurgeon, the attorney should recommend which physician should be consulted. It is, of course, better for the treating physician to refer to the orthopedist or neurosurgeon where this can be accomplished.

All of this needs to be discussed with the client at the close of the interview. It must be emphasized to the client that he is not to be referred to other physicians without checking with you, nor is he to sign anything, nor is he to give any tape-recorded statements to anyone.

§ 5.25 —Explaining the initial medical problems

Finally, when closing the initial interview, it is beneficial to explain to the client the nature of the injuries involved in both medical and nonmedical terms. This impresses the client, enhances your image, and builds your relationship. However, the primary purpose is to make the client understand the nature of the injuries as well as the potential for future symptoms. Often, clients develop future symptoms which though related are not reported to the attorney or the treating physician. The client simply does not feel that the new symptom is significant. For example, a patient with a cervical strain injury develops a tingling in the hands. This may indicate that in addition to a cervical strain the patient is suffering from radiculapathy, and may have a potential ruptured disc. If the patient is not informed about the symptomatology associated with cervical injury, he may consider this important symptom to be insignificant and not report it to either the attorney or the physician.

Hopefully, the necessity of discussing the medical problems the patient may encounter is obvious. Physicians do not take the time to do this and often, because of the nature of their busy practice, they do not adequately question the injured party to develop this material. It is therefore essential in closing the interview that where applicable, the client be given a full description of the medical aspects of his injury. The client should be shown charts of the anatomy and physiology involved. He will most likely understand the information if it is presented in three ways: visually so he can see it, orally so he can hear it, and then the culmination of the two so he can feel what the information actually means regarding his own injury and the potential for future problems (Principle 15: People are influenced by the way the message is structured and delivered).

II. Controlling Evidence Development Through Aggressive Discovery Techniques

§ 5.26 Psychological considerations and discovery

As with every communication process, there are psychological factors to be considered regarding your relationship with the defense counsel, or the adjuster, or the prosecuting attorney.

§ 5.27 —Pacing the defendant

The initial consideration in dealing with an adversary, as with witnesses and others, is the establishment of rapport. This can be effectively accomplished through verbal and vocal pacing over the telephone and through using other pacing techniques during face to face contact. Sometimes your pacing with an adversary may not necessarily be a matching pace experience. Complementary pacing requires that you "fill in a need" of the other person. Your pacing does not necessarily match this person's actions, but rather complements those actions. If the subject is one who needs a strong personality to lead him to a conclusion, then the attorney may use complementary pacing to fill that need. If the person is a strong willed, bombastic person, one may want to complementarily pace the person by appearing to be the submissive type, but simultaneously lead his bombastic personality to a favorable conclusion.

§ 5.28 —Gaining control of the case

It is important that you, as an advocate, gain control of the case. It is essential that you take an aggressive lead in initiating the discovery process, developing your own theories of liability, developing your own medical theories, and moving forward to prove these theories. Sometimes the attorney needs to develop red herrings which will send the opposing counsel chasing in the wrong direction. It is important that you move the file forward aggressively; it is also important for the plaintiff in a civil case to schedule the first round of depositions and issue the first series of interrogatories. This action alone will help establish your leadership since such early aggressiveness will psychologically prepare your adversary to consider you as a competent attorney and to seriously consider settling the matter.

§ 5.29 —Anchoring techniques as applied to opposing counsel

Anchoring refers to classical conditioning, that is, obtaining a specific response. One particular anchoring technique for use on an adversary is to call him at precisely the same time on certain days of the week to discuss the case. When your call comes, he knows it's you and he knows you want to discuss the case. Even if you don't make contact with him he begins to expect the call and responds to set stimuli. Another anchoring technique applicable to every conversation with opposing counsel is to open and close with the same phrases. The phraseology need not be related to the case, this is simply an attempt to set up a conditioned stimuli, a red flag to say you are there and that you are in control of the situation.

§ 5.30 —Verbal and vocal considerations in discussions with opposing counsel

When discussing matters with defense counsel, we want to use powerful, positive language. Never tell opposing counsel that "'we allege" or "we contend" or "I submit to you." Such phraseology indicates some disbelief regarding whatever incident you are claiming is an absolute fact. Whatever you are submitting to opposing counsel should be put in terms of concrete facts with positive language! Always talk about your side of the case with positive language: "the fact is Mr. Defense Counsel that your client ran the red light; the fact is Mr. Prosecutor you simply can't prove the case against my client and you know it." Your statement should reflect the conclusion as a proven fact.

In addition to verbal considerations and the use of powerful speech as opposed to powerless speech, vocal cues are used to indicate that you are a forceful and dynamic person. To the degree compatible with your personality, your vocal cues show that you are in control of the situation. The proper use of pauses, voice inflection, voice volume and rate of speech all tend to create a feeling of dynamism. Remember that, within reason, the faster you speak the more credible you appear. Therefore, your speech with opposing counsel needs to sound self-assured and rapid, with proper pauses for emphasis. An increased inflection in the voice, in a controlled manner, is used where appropriate to emphasize a point.

Volume should be intentionally rich and full to avoid a sound of weakness and timidity. These are vocal cues which you may control and which are significant in projecting an image to the defense counsel. Remember that during the discussions with you, opposing counsel is evaluating you as a potential adversary in the courtroom. His reports on you, the trial attorney, are sent to the insurance company, or to the prosecutor's office or district attorney's office; these evaluations all play a role in whether or not your client achieves an acceptable plea bargain or settlement.

§ 5.31 —The operation of primacy in discovery

The principle of primacy operates even in the discovery process. Put your strongest facts and arguments first. Primacy operates even when you begin to make a presentation to opposing counsel over the telephone. If you have one strong fact in your favor always start off by discussing that fact. It may be the horrible injuries to your client, as opposed to liability. If liability is your strongest suit, approach opposing counsel with those facts or arguments initially. These facts can form an anchor of sorts in that they become the first words that you greet your adversary with in any discussion. Primacy is a powerful weapon and one should always use it effectively on an adversary (Principle 3: Perceptions are organized and structured within a brief period of time).

There are certain instances when you desire not to establish rapport with opposing counsel. If the liability is overwhelmingly clear, the damages are great, and the insurer is one known for unreasonable offers, then you may not be interested in having rapport with opposing counsel. In such a situation, you may want to deliberately mismatch with your adversary. By mismatching we mean deliberate pacing in opposition to his pace. If he speaks rapidly, you speak slowly and vice versa. The same would apply to all the areas of matching, except you mismatch him in all areas. This causes dissonance between yourself and your adversary; he will not like you or even want to talk to you. You probably will not get an offer to settle until or unless there is pressure from the judge or someone else. But these tactics, in the appropriate situation, can work to your advantage. In essence, use the adversary's own hostility as a tool against him; keeping him off balance interferes with his ability to think clearly about the case itself. Hostility can keep opposing counsel chasing bogus issues and engaging in irrelevant discovery as he is chasing red herrings while you build the case for trial. This type of case is settled only after opposing counsel is forced to realize that he is in deep trouble usually by the third day of trial. If you had established rapport rather than a mismatching, you would have probably tipped him as to the seriousness of the case and some issues that he ought to be investigating and researching. It is impossible not to "telegraph" some information to a person with whom you have rapport. Thus, mismatching your adversary can work to your advantage. A word of caution, however, before you start mismatching, make sure that you have a solid case on liability issues and clearly provable serious injuries.

§ 5.32 The importance of developing a case theory

The initial interview is the ideal time to develop a case theory even though it may take further investigation, such as visiting the scene or interviewing other witnesses, to develop additional facts. Develop the case theory early; it is to your advantage to know exactly where you are going, especially if you represent the plaintiff in a civil action and have the burden of proof.

In some situations, i.e., where a car ran a red light, the case theory is obvious. In many situations, however, the theory of liability and the reasons supporting causation are not necessarily obvious. Nonetheless, the theory of the case must be developed before any discovery begins. You can adequately control discovery only if you know where you are going. It is advantageous to shield the case theory from the opponents for as long as possible, but make sure that before you conduct discovery you have a battle plan. If you simply open the file and let it sit there, eventually the other side will develop a battle plan. They will gain control of the case and control discovery. They will develop the theory of defense and begin to build on it. This is what you absolutely must not allow and the only way to avoid it is to develop your own case theory early.

§ 5.33 —Nature of the liability

To develop a case theory, look at the nature of the liability question. Analyze both the strong and weak points of the liability issues in a civil case. In a routine automobile case, analyzing the nature of your liability problem is relatively easy, i.e., you know whether you have adequate witnesses on the color of the light. However, as you progress to more technical matters, such as medical malpractice and products liability cases, it is essential that you understand not only the nature of the liability, but the inherent problems as well. If the case is a medical malpractice case, you must know specifically what the medical standards are, where they are published, and how they were violated. For example, when dealing with a case with an infant with cerebral palsy resulting from defendant's failure to perform a C-section, understanding the nature of the liability includes knowing exactly what the standards are as to when a physician should perform a C-section. An infant with cerebral palsy is not in and of itself proof of negligence. The defendant's conduct must be checked against the standards set out in medical textbooks. For example, has the woman delivered several babies prior to this one? Did she receive an oxytocic intravenously? Does the fetal monitor strip show vigorous labor for many hours? If so, there may be liability. Did the defendants adequately monitor the mother receiving pitocin? The monitoring standards are set out by, among others, the American College of Obstetrics and Gynecology, commonly referred to as the ACOG standards and may be obtained from this association for a minimal fee.

Dealing with a products liability case also demands knowledge of the nature of the liability. Establish what the design standards were for the particular product. Some of these design standards are published by the American Standards Association.

It cannot be said too often: before discovery begins, one must know the nature of the liability problem. If you know where you are going, as well as the nature of your liability problems in detail, you can often shape the discovery process to your advantage. Do not volunteer any information to the opposing counsel to make evident your knowledge; instead, use your knowledge to control the discovery process.

§ 5.34 —Consideration of causation problems

The development of liability is important, but potential problems on causation cannot be overlooked. Often, defendants can successfully defend a case where they have been negligent by raising a causation question. Causation questions can run a wide gamut. For example, the defendants may admit that a product did not meet general design requirements, but they will insist that the product was misused; thus, this misuse, not the design defect, was the cause of the injury. Moreover, a defendant is really defending on lack of causation when he attempts to shift the liability, e.g., to the manufacturer of a component part. Because of this tactic, it is essential to develop a list of all potential defendants before the applicable statute of limitations runs. It is simple for a defendant to defend causation where he can point the finger of guilt at someone not named by you. In complex litigation the experts must be retained and computer research of the literature is essential before suit is filed; otherwise, through plaintiff's neglect, the defendant can build yet another defense.

Let us digress to the PTU case discussed earlier,[11] in which the patient developed a severe reaction to the drug. The primary defense in that case was that she had experienced an autoimmune response of unknown etiology. Earlier the opposing counsel, perhaps in a mistaken attempt to make evident his knowledge, let it be known that the anticipated defense was Systemic Lupus Erythematosis. Early analysis of the literature by plaintiff's counsel forced the defense experts to admit that this type of reaction did not fit the clinical picture of SLE. Because the defendants could not call the adverse reaction Systemic Lupus Erythematosis, they were forced to defend on another basis. They had to claim that the adverse reaction was an extremely rare autoimmune response, not yet in the literature and of unknown etiology. Plaintiff's counsel was able then to successfully label this defense as the "African Tsetse Fly Disease." If the causation problem had not been adequately developed and studied prior to beginning discovery, the defendants would have been able to successfully defend this allergic reaction as being Systemic Lupus Erythematosis.

A defense on causation must always be anticipated. Only by such anticipation can the necessary research be accomplished prior to the beginning of discovery. In some cases, one may have a causation problem due to a lack of proof. In those situations, counsel may try to assert the legal doctrine of res ipsa loquitur. But one cannot rely on this doctrine without analyzing the nature of the causation problem in detail before discovery begins. This was evident in the following case. A forty-seven-year-old woman underwent open heart surgery, one of the first such surgeries at this particular hospital and one of the first such bypass surgeries in the United States. However, after the patient was discharged from the recovery room, she began to complain of pain in her left arm which became progressively more severe and disabling over the next several days. Eventually, she developed causaglia (severe pain coupled with exquisite sensitivity to touch) and a clawing of the ring and little finger of the hand termed by some physicians as a Pope's sign. Several operations to relieve the pain only worsened the condition and she became totally disabled from a severe nerve injury. The medical records gave no indication as to what happened to her arm. The only way to win this case was to rely on the doctrine of res ipsa loquitur. If the specific fact situation provides

[11] *See supra* § 5.16.

counsel the opportunity to use this doctrine, the burden shifts to the defendants to prove that they were not negligent. In essence, causation is assumed.

With regard to this case, the literature theorized that once the sternum is split in half and the ribs spread apart, the first rib would rotate back against the clavicle, thereby crushing the brachial plexus (a group of nerves in the shoulder). The article presented the details of six or seven cases where this had occurred, and experiments performed on cadavers reproduced this mechanism. However, the literature also showed that in all cases these were generally temporary injuries and that the mechanics of crushing the brachial plexus would cause symptoms in all three nerves of the arm—the median, radial, and ulnar. Consultation with plaintiff's neurologist and neuropathologist, and a reading of the medical reports, clearly indicated that this client had suffered injury only to the ulnar nerve. A defendant neurologist examined the plaintiff and agreed with this finding. Therefore the anticipated defense could not be founded on fact because of lack of injury to the median and radial nerves.

Because plaintiff's counsel had developed his theory of causation early, he planned his discovery and correctly anticipated the defense. Plaintiff's counsel questioned the surgeon who performed the bypass surgery on the plaintiff as to what caused the injury. The surgeon proudly stated that there was an article in the literature which showed that this plaintiff's injury was a risk of this kind of surgery; he did not have the article available, but stated that he had read it and clearly, this was a complication of this surgery. He also stated that this type of surgery was just recently developed and he did not know this injury could occur.

Much to his chagrin, shock, and dismay, plaintiff's counsel produced this article. The surgeon was taken through the article, one step at a time, and forced to agree that the article clearly indicated that these brachial plexus injuries caused symptoms in all three nerves of the arm. He also agreed with the medical reports and the expert testimony that it was clear the plaintiff had only an ulnar injury and that, therefore, it could not have been his operation that caused the injury. The plaintiff ultimately received a substantial award based on the doctrine of res ipsa loquitur. However, plaintiff would not have succeeded if the defendant had been able to foster upon counsel and the court an incorrect theory of causation indicating that the injury was a risk of the operation.

§ 5.35 —Nature of the injury

In addition to developing an understanding of any causation problem, it is essential to understand in detail the nature of the plaintiff's injury. This knowledge allows plaintiff's counsel to adequately defend a causation problem and to avoid many pitfalls. If the nature of the plaintiff's injury is, for example, the activation of a preexisting asymptomatic condition, e.g., osteoarthritis, then you must understand the nature of osteoarthritis as well as the nature of the injury. Osteoarthritis (bone build-up) in and of itself does not necessarily cause pain. This is a condition that can remain asymptomatic for many years, but be put into a symptomatic state by trauma. On the other hand, one may be dealing with traumatic osteoarthritis. This is a completely different condition wherein osteoarthritis is actually seen to rapidly increase on the X-ray. It is extra bone build-up which irritates nerves into a permanently symptomatic condition. It must be understood before discovery begins whether one is dealing with asymptomatic osteoarthritis, made symptomatic by the trauma or traumatic osteoarthritis.

§ 5.36 —Effects of the injury

The attorney must understand both the short-term and long-term effects of the injury. For example, in a cervical sprain injury, defense counsel will attempt to negate a serious long-term effect by stressing the absence of any muscle spasm during several exams by the defendant's physician. Counsel must be aware that a cervical sprain injury usually results in muscle spasms, but only during the acute phase of the injury. Thereafter, muscle spasms occur only intermittently. If muscle spasms were found to be present during every examination over a six or eight month period, it could be assumed that the plaintiff was doing something prior to the examination to worsen the injury. Therefore, the fact that defendant's physician examined the plaintiff and did not find muscle spasms is no proof that there was no injury; neither does it negate the possibility of a long-term effect. Thus, it is imperative that counsel understand the effects of the injury in order to deny the defendant an opportunity to stress an illegitimate issue.

Such knowledge is also essential in criminal cases. If the state is trying to prove its case through the pattern of blood stains on a pillow or wall, understanding the trajectory that a bullet can take through a victim and its effects on the body is crucial in the defense. To appreciate the potential complexity of this type of injury, one need only look at the volumes of information written subsequent to the assassination of President Kennedy. It will always be a hotly contested issue as to whether or not a single bullet pierced President Kennedy's neck and went on through John Connally's shoulder and had sufficient force remaining to fracture his wrist.

COMMENT: Thus, the effects of the injury in both criminal and civil cases can be crucial. The potential effects of the injury must be understood before beginning discovery. This knowledge is significantly determinative of the legal and medical issues at stake. Advance knowledge of what is in the literature on these issues is essential for proper preparation.

---

§ 5.37 —The permanence of disability

The permanence of the disability is an issue in every plaintiff's case. Although frequently the severity and permanence of the disability cannot be determined early in the case, an awareness of the potential for permanent disability is important so that plaintiff's counsel can avoid an inadequate settlement of the case. Often, in cervical sprains and low back injuries there is an attempt by the defense to conclude the matter after a couple of months. At least six months should lapse, if not longer, after the resolution of all symptoms before settling these cases. In a study of patients who has settled their claims,[12] a Tennessee physician wrote:

> Of 100 patients with whiplash type injuries who were interviewed subsequent to settlement of legal claims for damage, 88% have recovered, 54% with no residual, and 34% with minor symptoms not requiring therapy. *12% continued to have severe symptoms but only 6% of these were under medical treatment*. Surgery was necessary in only two cases and was beneficial in both. (emphasis added)

Research into the effects of the injury is essential as you begin the case. For example, what starts off as a simple whiplash injury may develop into a full-blown ruptured disc requiring subsequent surgery. The client has to be put on notice to look for potential future symptoms. This is

[12] Gotten, M.D., *Whiplash Injuries*, 162 (No. 9), J. A.M.A. 865, 867 (October 1965).

true not only in cases involving simple injuries, but in more complex matters as well. For example, in cases involving negligence during labor or in the birth process, the baby may suffer short term anoxia (lack of oxygen to the brain). When you are faced with these facts, it is imperative to delay settlement of that case until the child is seven- or eight-years-old. It is only when the child is attempting to function at school age that the full extent and nature of the brain damage can be determined. These children may appear neurologically normal, have normal encephalograms and test within the normal range during their first two or three years. The only symptom of the impending problems may be hyperactivity. One also has to realize that neurological testing not only may have a high degree of morbidity and mortality, but may totally miss some neuropathological conditions. A neuropsyschological team administering tests based on the Halstead Reitan neuropsychological battery is the only way to prove the existence or nonexistence of generalized brain damage due to anoxia. Angiography (putting dye in the brain) and pneumoencephalography (putting air in the brain) cannot prove generlized brain damage; these tests can find only specific localized lesions. This is also true of the CAT scan.

Diagnostic validity of neuropsychological testing has been supported in the medical literature. The validity of the Halstead Impairment Index was substantiated in a 1974 article by Matarazzo, et al., wherein they state:

> "No matter whether one is dealing with individuals who by all the relevant clinical findings are finally judged to be normal functionally, psychiatrically disabled, or brain damaged, including any of the many well known variants of these global clinical designations, clinical neuropsychology has developed so rapidly in the past decade that the validity for a practitioner's individual judgments from the Halstead Impairment Index (especially of 'normal') is no longer a hope but an increasingly more probable and supportable conclusion."[13]

It is clear that early in the case, the potential for severity and permanence of the disability must be understood. If necessary, consult with experts and research the medical literature to become completely informed as to the possible effects of the injury.

A word of caution regarding disability ratings is appropriate at this

---

[13] Matarazzo, *Psychometric and Clinical Index in a Sample of Healthy, Young Normal Men*, 158 J. Nervous & Mental Health Disease 37 (1974).

point. Often orthopedists and other physicians rate a disability in terms of the degree of impairment. For example, following successful lumbar disc surgery and fusion, a medical report by an orthopedist or neurosurgeon may state that the patient has a permanent disability rating of 10% of the back. This is merely a rating of the functional limitation of movement of the spine and that impairment rating may have nothing to do with the actual disability. If your client is a desk worker, a 10% disability of the spine may not be very significant. But if your client does manual labor for a living, a 10% disability impairment of the spine can be totally disabling.

Understanding the permanence and nature of the client's disability is based either on experience in previous cases, or consultation with experts, or current research of the literature. Clearly, if the injury is one that trial counsel has not handled before, it is essential that he go through the literature and study the subject matter.

§ 5.38 —Medical malpractice considerations

Often, counsel may be dealing with a situation where the original injury does not appear severe, yet a serious result ensues. A simple shoulder injury may result in the plaintiff's death because of intervening medical malpractice. In a situation of that type, a decision must be made early on concerning whether or not to sue the potentially liable intervening tort-feasor, the medical health care provider. Most jurisdictions hold that the original tort-feasor is liable for the resulting death or increased disability, even though the original injury was minor. For example, a defective bike pedal, with saw-like teeth, reversed direction and severed a young boy's achilles tendon. Properly treated, this injury should not result in a permanent disability. However, in this particular case the emergency room physician failed to notice the severed tendon. He sutured the patient's heel without reattaching the tendon. The result was a recoiling of the tendon which created the need for extensive reconstructive surgery, six months in a cast, and significant permanent impairment of the foot. The rule of law in most jurisdictions is that, given those circumstances, the original defendant in the products liability case may be held liable for all the negligence, even though most of the plaintiff's problems were caused by medical malpractice.

Therefore, it may not be necessary to name the health care provider as a defendant if the original case is one of strong liability with a financially responsible defendant. In fact, in such a situation there may be no need for plaintiff to raise the medical malpractice issue at all. However, if it is anticipated that the named original defendant is going to raise that issue, then the negligent health care provider should be named as well. The plaintiff can then allow the two defendants to fight it out among themselves as to which one should ultimately be held liable.

On the other hand, if the original liability issue is weak or the defendant is not financially responsible, it may be necessary to sue on a medical malpractice theory. In such a situation, early medical research is essential. If, for example, you are handling an anesthesia case, read all applicable literature. Every specialty has its accepted texts which set out many of the standards. In addition to certain minimum standards published by Medicare and Medicaid and the Joint Commission on Accreditation of Hospitals, various professional associations publish their own standards. All of this material must be researched at the very beginning of a medical malpractice case.

After you have become completely familiar with the applicable medical standards, consult with the injured plaintiff's treating physician. You may find that although he agrees with your theory of malpractice, he will not testify. Indeed, too often the treating physician will not even talk to you. In that case, a consultation with a friend in the medical profession will further add to your knowledge. However, if he is not familiar with medical malpractice claims, he may commit one of two fatal errors: he may tell you there is no malpractice when, in fact, there is or he may say there is malpractice when in fact there is none.

After researching the medical literature and discussing the case with either the treating physician or a friend, consult with an expert in the same specialty as the defendant. This is often easier said than done because finding such an expert is almost always a problem. Generally, he cannot be found in the same medical community. There are certain services which provide experts, but one of the best sources for finding a medical expert is a nearby major medical school. Generally, these specialists do not rely on the rest of the medical community for referrals; therefore they are more willing to become involved in medical malpractice cases. In addition, a very fine source of medical experts is the group of physicians who have written the principles involved in the literature. They are generally from out of town and more willing to testify. They make good witnesses because the principles they have stated in the literature are less subject to attack than those espoused by an unpublished expert. If an expert has published an article stating that physicians should perform a medical procedure using a certain method, his testimony cannot be attacked as being for the purpose of litigation. He published for the purpose of teaching other physicians and, therefore, he is not a hired gun but is simply testifying to what he has already written.

COMMENT: Obviously, any type of medical malpractice case covers very complex subject matter. It is not our purpose here to discuss that subject matter in detail, indeed, that would require a textbook. When faced with this complex matter, it is essential for inexperienced counsel to seek the advice of experienced attorneys specializing in this area of litigation.

This litigation is frought with all kinds of psychological considerations. Medical malpractice cases have become emotional battles. Physicians who believe they are infallible cannot accept the fact that they have made a mistake. Their cases are defended vociferously on all fronts and all types of excuses and claims are raised in defense. They are seldom settled early in the case. Medical malpractice claims are the most complex forms of litigation and they are rampant with all types of psychological considerations. They demand the most exquisite understanding of human nature and trial advocacy if counsel is to handle them successfully.

§ 5.39 Interrogatories as a discovery tool—phrasing of interrogatories

Interrogatories are simply written questions sent to the opposing counsel. They are usually answered in an offhanded manner and generally the answers are evasive. If one is to properly enforce this type of discovery, properly phrased interrogatories are essential.

The key to effective phrasing of interrogatories is specificity. The interrogatory must state clearly what is being requested, yet at the same time must be broad enough to encompass all the information sought. Opponents may allege that a question is irrelevant to the subject matter of the action and is not reasonably calculated to lead to the discovery of admissible evidence, or is burdensome or oppressive. If counsel is to properly enforce discovery through interrogatories, then proper verbal consideration is essential.

Interrogatories are most effective in obtaining general background information, and some specific information such as insurance coverage. As a general rule, questions asking for opinions or opinions mixed with facts should be avoided. An interrogatory that asks for an opinion, as well as a fact, invades the realm of the expert witness. In some states, such an interrogatory would be stricken because expert opinions are not considered discoverable.[14] However, in most jurisdictions, inquiries regarding opinions and contentions of experts are either discoverable outright or are discoverable within the discretionary power of the judge.[15]

Courts also have the discretion to allow or disallow entire sets of interrogatories which the court deems too burdensome. Consideration of the extent and nature of the information sought, the effort the party requesting the information will have to expend to obtain the information sought, and its relevancy is necessary to avoid using interrogatories which will be held as too burdensome for the answering party. Courts generally will now allow interrogatories to be "used to sap the opposing party of its will to fight, as much as to gain information essential to case preparation."[16] To guard against oppressive interrogatories while insuring that each party contributes to the development of necessary information, the courts have developed standards governing what is a permissible burden. Each case is assessed as to its peculiar characteristics, and the need for the information will be balanced against the time, expense, and personnel which the responding party must use to provide an appropriate answer.

COMMENT: The well-drafted interrogatory avoids the pitfall of the opposing counsel's motion for a protective order. Again, the key to good phrasing of interrogatories is specificity. The interrogatory must state clearly what information

[14] TREADWELL, NEW FEDERAL CIVIL DISCOVERY RULES SOURCEBOOK 107 (1972).

[15] *The Advisory Committee's Notes to the Federal Rules of Civil Procedure*, 48 F.R.D. 524 (1970).

[16] UNDERWOOD, 1983 SUPPLEMENT TO A GUIDE TO FEDERAL DISCOVERY RULES 99 (1983).

counsel is requesting, yet at the same time, must be broad enough to encompass all the information sought.

---

§ 5.40 —Other psychological considerations

Interrogatories are less intimidating than other forms of discovery. Depositions put the responding party on the spot by demanding spontaneous answers which often leads to further inquiries concerning discomforting issues. Since interrogatories are in written form, it is impossible to introduce a new line of inquiry opened up by an answer. Further, opposing counsel is provided with additional time to fortify his position by the time new interrogatories are drafted. Lawyers also have control over drafting responses which limits their utility in eliciting answers. Interrogatories do remain an effective way to gain specific, relatively uncontroversial information. Moreover, by presenting a party with the time and the opportunity to have his own counsel assist him in preparing answers to uncontroversial and potentially complicated issues, counsel can create a less intimidating atmosphere at a deposition.[17]

COMMENT: Counsel should use interrogatories to learn the general nature of the opponent's position and the names and addresses of any witnesses he intends to call at trial. After this, depositions are the tool of choice to discover specific detailed facts and opinions from individual witnesses. Note, however, that interrogatories may be used as a follow-up to a deposition to discover facts and opinions regarding newly obtained material.

---

§ 5.41 —Types of information sought in interrogatories

Fundamental facts about an opposing party and his case can be learned through use of interrogatories in order to prepare for a deposition. Interrogatories can be most useful in obtaining lists of all persons known by the party to have information relevant to the incident under

[17] *Id*. at 113.

litigation, business statistics, lists of relevant documents, and information concerning the structure of a corporation or other organization.

Detailed technical information of an uncontroversial nature might best be sought through interrogatories, thereby expediting a deposition by giving counsel more time beforehand to prepare precise questions. However, interrogatories presented prior to a deposition may ruin the frequently desirable element of surprise.[18]

Interrogatories might serve as an aid to resolving disputed issues important to a motion for preliminary injunction. In some situations preliminary interrogatories may be essential, particularly if the litigation involves complex issues. For example, in a design copyright case where the actual design is different than, but substantially similar to, the copyright design, interrogatories which are not too lengthy are appropriate to discover how the non-copyrighted design was created.[19]

§ 5.42 —Defendant's background; corporate structures

Deposition rules permit service of notice to take a deposition on the corporate party, while at the same time requiring the party to indicate the person within the organization with knowledge of the subject in question. Interrogatories may be used strategically to expedite this process by requesting a specific response as to the person's identity or relevant records. Discovering the identity of such individuals through interrogatories puts the requesting party in a better position to choose the order of his deponents. He may also be better armed with relevant documents prior to conducting the deposition.

When submitting interrogatories to corporations, plan not only the types of interrogatories to be asked, but also the most advantageous time to submit them. At the outset of pretrial discovery, the plaintiff's attorney should avoid exasperating defense counsel with an exhaustive set of questions, many of which might later be useless. Counsel should limit himself to identifying witnesses and documents, and depending on the case, significant points of admission.[20]

---

[18] *Id*. at 112–113.

[19] TREADWELL, *supra* note 14, at 107.

[20] *Id*. at 107–108.

§ 5.43 —Insurance coverage

Carefully drafted questions should provide access to all relevant documents, including, in most jurisdictions, a defendant's insurance policies. This information may be essential to plaintiff's counsel in evaluating his strategy. For example, the extent of the coverage mandates early settlement without incurring substantial litigation expense if insurance coverage is limited. The converse would, of course, also be true.

The Federal Rules of Civil Procedure permit discovery of the existence and contents of any insurance agreement under which an insurance company may be liable to satisfy part or all of a judgment, or to indemnify or reimburse for payments made.[21]

COMMENT: Interrogatories are a useful discovery tool for the plaintiff in ascertaining a defendant's insurance policies, including the existence of excess insurance.

---

§ 5.44 —Witnesses and statements

Interrogatories are essential in identifying witnesses, especially experts. The Federal Rules require disclosure of the identities of persons to be called as expert witnesses at trial, the subject matter on which experts are expected to testify, and facts and opinions to which these experts are expected to testify as well as a summary of the grounds for these opinions.[22]

If an expert is retained in anticipation of litigation but is not expected to be called as a witness at trial, the parties seeking discovery of facts known or opinions held must show either "exceptional circumstances" or that the expert is an examining physician under Federal Rule 35(b). In one case, *In re Burch*,[23] the court refused to excuse the plaintiff from discovery rules requiring disclosure of the plaintiff's handwriting expert who was to testify as a rebuttal witness. The plaintiff had limited her initial response to an interrogatory relating to the name and address of

[21] FED. R. CIV. P. 26(b)(2).

[22] FED. R. CIV. P. 26(b)(4)(A)(i).

[23] 33 Bankr. 1015 (D. Md. 1983).

her expert because she only intended to call him as a rebuttal witness. The judge observed that effective discovery would be frustrated if the parties were permitted to assert that the identity or opinion of their witnesses is irrelevant because these experts were only intended to be called for rebuttal purposes.

There is a split of authority as to whether identity of nontestifying expert witnesses is discoverable. In one case, the court held that exceptional circumstances need not be shown to obtain discovery of the identity of a nontestifying expert who is specially retained but who is not expected to be called at trial.[24] Conversely, in *Perry v. W.S. Darley & Co.*,[25] the court denied, for two reasons, the defendant's interrogatories requesting disclosure of experts who had examined the truck *after* the accident. First, the defendant failed to show that these witnesses would be called at trial, and second, because these experts were not "actors or viewers with respect to . . . transactions or occurrences that [were] part of the subject matter of the lawsuit."[26] The court, influenced by the "rigorous standard" imposed by Rule 26(b)(4),[27] held that the identity of nontestifying witnesses is not discoverable absent "exceptional circumstances."

An interrogatory may call for an answer in the form of an opinion or a contention as to fact. For instance, if a party sues for the reasonable value of services rendered and the opposing party wants to discover the basis for the value of these services, one court might strike the interrogatory as requiring an opinion, while another might uphold the question. Many courts regard such questions as sharpening the issues and thus allow such interrogatories. Such cases illustrate the discretion allowed courts regarding the use of interrogatories.

§ 5.45 —Sample interrogatories

Rules 26 through 37 of the Federal Rules have been interpreted liberally to permit maximum discovery. The scope of discoverable issues through the use of interrogatories is broad where the court perceives the

---

[24] Sea Colony, Inc. v. Continental Insurance Co., 63 F.R.D. 113 (D. Del. 1974). *See also* Guilloz v. Falmouth Hospital Ass'n, 21 Fed. R. Serv. 2d 1367 (D. Mass. 1976).

[25] 54 F.R.D. 278 (E.D. Wis. 1971).

[26] *Id*. at 280.

[27] *Id*.

relevant subject matter as potentially leading to other admissible evidence.[28]

For example, in *Buffington v. Gillette Co.*, the court considered an action to recover actual and punitive damages for personal injuries and property damage allegedly sustained by plaintiffs in a fire caused by a defective butane cigarette lighter.[29] Plaintiff objected to defendant's interrogatories claiming they were either clearly irrelevant or would not lead to admissible evidence. The court considered the following interrogatories:

INTERROGATORY NO. 1:

Please state by brand name each drug received by plaintiff, Ann Buffington, during the period from January 1, 1975, to December 31, 1975.

ANSWER NO. 1:

Objection. The information sought is not relevant evidence, does not appear reasonably calculated to lead to the discovery of admissible evidence, is privileged, is unreasonably burdensome to compile, and, arguendo, if relevant its probative value is substantially outweighed by the danger of unfair prejudice, the confusion of issues, is misleading to the jury and is a waste of time.

INTERROGATORY NO. 2:

For each drug identified in your answer to Interrogatory No. 1, please state the following:

(a) the daily dosage or quantity of each drug received (approximate if necessary), and;

(b) the period of time each drug was received (approximate if necessary);

(c) the name[s] and address[es] of each person prescribing and/or furnishing the above drugs to Plaintiff Ann Buffington;

(d) the name[s] of each person who administered injectionable drugs to Plaintiff Ann Buffington.

ANSWER NO. 2:

Objection. See objection in Answer No. 1.

---

[28] Weddington v. Consolidated Rail Corp., 101 F.R.D. 71 (N.D. Ind. 1984), involving an accident at a railroad crossing.

[29] Buffington v. Gillette Co., 101 F.R.D. 400 (W.D. Okla. 1980).

INTERROGATORY NO. 3:

State the full name[s] and address[es] of any physician[s] or other person[s] who prescribed and/or furnished any drug[s] to the Plaintiff Ann Buffington during the period January 1, 1975 to December 31, 1975.

ANSWER NO. 3:

Objection. See objection in Answer No. 1.

Similarly, Defendants' Interrogatories Nos. 15, 16, and 17 and Plaintiffs' responses thereto read as follows:

INTERROGATORY NO. 15:

State the name[s] and address[es] of each hospital, whether publicly or privately owned, where Plaintiff Ann Buffington was admitted, treated, diagnosed, or examined for any reason, during the period January 1, 1975 to December 31, 1975.

ANSWER NO. 15:

Objection. The information sought is not relevant evidence, does not appear reasonably calculated to lead to the discovery of admissible evidence, is privileged, is unreasonably burdensome to compile, and, arguendo, if relevant its probative value is substantially outweighed by the danger of unfair prejudice, the confusion of issues, is misleading to the jury and is a waste of time.

INTERROGATORY NO. 16:

State the date[s] of admission and the date[s] of discharge (approximate if necessary) for each such treatment[s], diagnosis[es], admission[s] or examination[s] set forth in your answer to Interrogatory No. 15.

ANSWER NO. 16:

Objection. See objection to Answer No. 15.

INTERROGATORY NO. 17:

State the full name[s] and address[es] of each physician who examined, treated, or rendered any professional service to Plaintiff Ann Buffington during the hospitalizations in the answer to Interrogatory No. 15 above.

ANSWER NO. 17:

Objection. See objection to Answer No. 15.

> The court was not persuaded that the requested discovery was clearly irrelevant to the subject matter of the action and ruled that plaintiff's objections to the interrogatories on the basis of relevancy were without merit.[30]

The foregoing is intended to give the reader some example of the types of interrogatories that are asked in civil litigation. Interrogatories are generally not available to defense counsel in criminal matters.

§ 5.46 Requests for admissions

Requests for admissions are not used primarily to obtain information as are interrogatories and depositions, but rather to narrow issues for trial. The major function of requests for admissions is to resolve as many conflicts as possible prior to actual litigation. Admissions help to minimize the expenses of investigation prior to trial. Serving opposing counsel with detailed requests for admissions will cause him to carefully consider the litigation and create greater opportunities for settlement. Furthermore, if an admission is denied and later proven to be true at trial, the opposing party will be assessed for all costs incidental to proving that fact. Moreover, obtaining admissions at an early stage enhances the possibility of a motion for summary judgment.[31]

Each issue sought to be admitted must be set forth separately in the request for admission. Federal Rule 36(a) requires service of copies of documents, the genuineness of which is sought to be admitted, along with the request for admissions, unless the documents have been otherwise furnished or made available for inspection and copying.[32]

Requests for admissions are extremely useful in authenticating documents before trial and are favored for this purpose.[33] The procedure usually involves submitting allegations to the opposing party which are supported by records and documents and which focus directly on the opposing party's own evidence. This procedure therefore advances the pretrial process by forcing parties to reveal how their own evidence relates to their specific allegations. The effectiveness of admissions in expediting trial was demonstrated in *Donovan v. Carls Drug Company, Inc.* [34]

---

[30] *Id. See also* United States v. American Tel. and Tel. Co., 83 F.R.D. 323 (D.D.C. 1979).

[31] Donovan v. Carls Drug Co., 703 F.2d 650, 651 (2d Cir. 1983).

[32] Brown v. Arlen Management Corp., 663 F.2d 575 (5th Cir. 1981).

[33] Caparelli v. Proceeds of Freight, Inc., 390 F. Supp. 1351 (S.D.N.Y. 1974).

[34] 703 F.2d 650, 651 (2d Cir. 1983).

The court noted that admissions could be used for a motion for summary judgment under Rule 55. The court stated that its confidence in the district court's decision to rely on admissions was reinforced by an examination of the employer's work records. These records suggested that the employer "would not have improved its presentation of the merits of the action had it been released from its admissions."[35]

Any matter admitted is conclusively established and may only be amended or withdrawn by permission of the court. Since 1970, admissions in the Federal courts have had a conclusive binding effect rather than operating exclusively as evidentiary admissions. This means that admissions are not later rebuttable by the party making them, the reasoning behind this practice being that "unless the parties securing an admission can depend on its binding effect, the party cannot safely avoid the expense of preparing to prove the matters on which he or she has secured the admission and the purpose of Rule 36 is frustrated."[36]

However, in *Wilson v. Johns-Manville Sales Corp.*, the court noted that admissions made by a party are not necessarily irrebuttable.[37] In the absence of an adversary's justified reliance in preparation for trial, a party may withdraw even formal admissions. This emphasizes the importance of having the action resolved on the merits.

§ 5.47 —Proper phrasing

The scope of discovery is broad, but it is not unlimited. The basic question is one of relevance, which includes the possibility that the requested information will lead to other admissible evidence. Beyond considerations of relevance, the statement of fact set out in a request for admission should be cast in simple and concise terms, simple sentences, and numbered separately, so that admission or denial occurs with an absolute minimum of explanation or qualification. Counsel should phrase the request in such a manner that the response must be in the affirmative, forcing the opponent to either answer in the affirmative or state that he does not know the information sought, or by an explanation that the party served cannot answer. The requesting party should not state "half truths" which force the responding party to qualify his answers. Requests for admissions should not be phrased so as to be purely rhetorical

---

[35] *Id*. at 652.

[36] Baise v. Alewet's Inc., 99 F.R.D. 95 (W.D. Mo. 1983).

[37] 221 U.S. App. D.C. 337, 684 F.2d 111 (1982).

or to set semantic traps. Such requests are improper and in such a situation the court will not order the recipient to respond.

A party's request for admission should not extend further than the inquiry into literature of which the opposing party is aware. The court in one case noted that requests for admissions must be limited to matters within the knowledge of the parties and agents.[38] In that case, the plaintiff sought to recover damages for injuries allegedly sustained when the plaintiff ate artificial sausage casing. The defendant requested admissions relating to plaintiff's knowledge of literature suggesting whether artificial sausage casings were hazardous if ingested. The court held that such requests were beyond the scope of the plaintiff's knowledge.

§ 5.48 —Requests regarding liability

Requests for admissions may be used to establish issues relating to a party's liability. For instance, requests have been used to establish knowledge of a dangerous condition which can be a key element in a tort case.[39]

In addition, requests for admission may be accompanied by written documents and photographs which can be extremely effective in obtaining an admission of liability. For instance, in one slip-and-fall case, requests were admitted as a matter of law by the magistrate and read to the jury. The court characterized the admissions establishing knowledge of a dangerous condition as critical to the case.[40] This relieved the plaintiffs of having to prove negligence at trial in order to sustain their overall burden of proof.

However, requests for admission may seek the admission of facts only, not opinions or legal conclusion. Thus, a defendant in a civil action may not be requested to admit or deny his own negligence as this calls for an opinion and legal conclusion.

§ 5.49 —Used to prove wage loss information

A plaintiff might successfully seek admissions by an employer to prove loss of wages. In *Donovan v. Carls Drug Co.*,[41] the Secretary of Labor brought an action against the employer drug company alleging violations

[38] Baise v. Alewet's, Inc., 99 F.R.D. 95 (W.D. Mo. 1983).

[39] Brown v. Arlen Management Corp., 663 F.2d 575 (5th Cir. 1981).

[40] *Id.*

[41] 703 F.2d 650, 652 (2d Cir. 1983).

of the Fair Labor Standards Act. The action involved the employer's overtime pay policies for its pharmacist employees. The employer admitted it was subject to the FLSA and that it failed to pay its pharmacists overtime pay clearly owed to them. The appellate court examined the defendant's work records and expressed its belief that the district court had properly relied on the employer's admissions in granting plaintiff employees' motion for summary judgment. This case clearly demonstrates how a request for an admission accompanied by documentary evidence from an employer results in an admission as to specific wage loss information.

§ 5.50 —Used to prove employment relationship

Whether or not an employee was within the course and scope of his employment at the time of the negligent act is a crucial issue in a respondeat superior situation. Answers to interrogatories tend to be evasive on this point; therefore, before taking depositions which may require extensive travel and other costs, counsel should serve the employer with a request for admission asking him to admit that (name of employee) was acting within the course and scope of his employment at the time. When confronted with a request for admission, the employer is forced to squarely face the issue, being cognizant of the consequences. If the employer denies the truth of the submitted admission, and the plaintiff successfully proves it at trial, the court will assess all costs of proving this fact, including attorneys fees, against the employer.

§ 5.51 —Sample requests for admissions

Properly phrased requests for admissions expedite the trial process because of the court's willingness to accept these requests and responses as conclusive. In one case, plaintiff slipped and fell on the sidewalk outside a store in an area covered by a metal porch.[42] In this case, wherein plaintiffs made out a prima facie case of negligence, the requests for admissions were as follows:

> 28. That no corrective repairs were made in the area being pointed to by the person in the photos marked No. 1 or No. 2 in Exhibit A hereto.
>
> 29. That the channel iron roof support pointed to in an upwards direction by the person in the photos marked No. 1 or No. 2 in Exhibit A herein . . . had corrosion noticeable by a person standing

[42] Brown v. Arlen Management Corp., 663 F.2d 575 (5th Cir. 1981).

in the position of the person shown in the two photos marked No. 1 or No. 2 in Exhibit A on September 18, 1975 [the date of the injury].

30. Prior to September 18, 1975, one or more of the defendants were aware or had noticed that there was a slippery area in the porch area pointed to in a downward direction by the person in the photos marked Nos. 3, 4, 6, and 7 in Exhibit A hereto, following a rain after other areas of the porch had dried from the rain.

31. Prior to September 18, 1975, one or more of the defendants were aware or had noticed that there was a wet area in the porch area pointed to in a downward direction by the person in the photos marked Nos. 3, 4, 5, 6, and 7 in Exhibit A hereto, following a rain after other areas of the porch had dried from the rain.

A request for admission must be phrased to elicit specific details. This is but one example of the judicious use of the request for admission.

§ 5.52 Independent medical examinations

In personal injury cases, a defendant may request that the injured plaintiff be examined by a physician of the defendant's choosing. These independent medical examinations generally are requested in mild and moderate injury cases. Requests for independent examinations of severely brain damaged children, quadriplegics, and burn victims are generally not necessary because the defendants know from the hospital records and medical reports that these are objective serious injuries and the so-called "independent" medical examination is going to do them no good.

§ 5.53 —Psychological considerations

The first psychological consideration involves terminology. Counsel for the plaintiff should *never, never, never* refer to the examination requested by defense counsel as an "independent medical examination." Defense counsel generally selects the physician, has used the physician before, and the physician is known within the medical community for his arch conservative position. There is nothing independent about the medical examination, therefore, it should be labeled for what it is—an examination of plaintiff at the request of the defendant.

Further consideration should be given to the psychological effects of such examination on your client. Often, these examinations are used as part of the psychological warfare of litigation. They can be made to be embarrassing, humiliating and intimidating so as to put pressure on the client to accept an inadequate settlement. It is traumatizing for anyone, but particularly a female client, to be required to go to a physician, disrobe and submit to a medical examination conducted by a person the client knows to be an adversary. This physician is not trying to help, he is someone who is waiting anxiously for the client to say or do something that can be used in court to weaken or destroy the client's case. Professional defendants' witnesses, and that's what they are, use all kinds of tricks to create a negative impression of the client's injury. They usually attack the honesty and integrity of the client by implying that the client is malingering, although generally the use of the word itself is avoided.

These defendants' experts frequently use boilerplate language which is repeated over and over in all of their medical reports. One orthopedist who regularly examined individuals for insurance purposes always indicated that in order for the examination to commence the patient was required to disrobe completely. When the patient was properly draped, the examination began. In the case of male clients, he would routinely comment on how gingerly and quickly they jumped out of their clothes, implying there was no injury to their back. In one case, through clerical error, such a comment was inadvertently included in a report on a young, attractive female patient. He was, of course, embarrassed at trial when pressed with the fact that his medical report indicated that he had watched the young lady disrobing.

The defendant's medical examination may be used to the plaintiff's advantage, but early preparation is required. This preparation begins with the first request for a so-called "independent medical examination."

§ 5.54 —Preparing the client

Reaching mutual agreement on the physician who will perform the independent medical examination is easier said than done. The ideal defendant's physician from the plaintiff's point of view, is one known as extremely fair, objective, but simply conservative. However, the defendant's first choice should always be rejected as a matter of principle. Remember, that this selection is part of the adversary process. You should always be concerned with projecting your personality over that of the defense counsel. It is a question of making the defendant back down on one more issue or at least causing him to rethink his position. Generally, one does not go to court over which physician is to examine the plaintiff. If you know, or can prove, that the physician chosen by the defendant is extremely prejudiced, has testified regularly for that defendant in the past, or has engaged in some conduct which would impugn his integrity, you can successfully defend a request for a court order to have your client examined. The first psychological consideration therefore, is to force the defense counsel into picking a reasonable defense physician.

After the parties have agreed on the physician, the client must be notified. The best way to do this is to write to the client, citing the particular statute of law which requires submission to an "independent medical examination." Inform the client of the date, time, and physician's name and address, and then set up a conference with yourself or your paralegal a few days ahead of time. In the letter tell the client that you and he will meet to prepare him for this examination. At the conference the client needs to be told that this examination is part of the adversary process. The client needs to understand that this is not like going to see a friendly doctor whose purpose is to treat an injury. Rather, this physician's purpose is to find discrepancies which will be used to impeach the client's credibility. The client should then be informed as to his rights. The examination should not be done in a manner which is extremely painful, should be limited to taking a history, physical examination and X-rays, and nothing further. The examination should not be embarrassing and at no time should a client be completely disrobed for the examination, whether that client be male or female. The client is not to tolerate anything which he feels is tantamount to intimidation and he has the right to walk out if he thinks this is taking place. Further, the client must not discuss the facts regarding liability with the physician. Tell the client that you are sending these facts to the physician and give the client a copy of the summary of the facts. Tell the client to refer the physician to that summary and to explain to the physician that since this matter is in litigation he is not at liberty to discuss the facts regarding liability. This denies the physician the opportunity to misconstrue or misstate crucial facts on liability in his medical history at trial.

§ 5.55 —Scope of examination

The client must be told specifically what is and what is not allowable during the examination. Sometimes this is negotiated with the opposing counsel prior to the examination. Certain types of painful procedures, e.g., biopsies, are generally not allowable, but this will depend upon the nature of the injury. Plaintiff's counsel may need to ask the court to rule on the scope of the examination if mutual agreement cannot be reached.

§ 5.56 —Nature of examination

Frequently the examination to be performed is a general orthopedic and neurological examination of the spine or one of the extremities. In such a case the client needs to be aware of the nature of the examination, what the physician is looking for, and what is going to be done. The client needs to understand the straight-leg raising test and the various "tricks" that the physician could use to verify the test. For example, the straight-leg raising test is performed while the patient is lying on his back on the examining table. The knee is kept extended and the leg raised. This puts stress on the sciatic nerve and is said to be positive if the raising of the leg to a 90 degree angle causes pain in the back, particularly pain shooting down the extremity being tested. However, insurance oriented physicians will often report a slightly positive straight leg raising test but then impeach it by saying they did the same test with the plaintiff in the sitting position on the examining table. That is, they straightened out the knee and pretended to be examining the ankle and, thus, put the same stress on the sciatic nerve. If the patient doesn't complain of the pain at this point in time, they will claim that there is a so-called "inconsistency in the exam." What actually happens is the plaintiff avoids the pain by leaning back and, therefore, does not complain. If the plaintiff is not made aware of this fact prior to a basic orthopedic and neurological exam involving a low back injury, he can be trapped into giving what appears to be inconsistent statements when the findings really are consistent. Likewise, if the client has complained of radicular pains in any extremity, the physician will test for loss of sensation to pin prick. The client needs to be made aware of the pattern of this examination, "stocking type hypothesia." That is, loss of sensation over the entire extremity can be viewed as hysteria or faking. The client has to be aware that there are fixed patterns of sensation, called "dermatomes" for each nerve and that loss of sensation will fit a particular pattern. The client should not be told, ethically, the exact dermatome patterns but simply that it dermatome patterns exist and that he should not try to impress the physician by stating that the entire leg is numb.

§ 5.57 —Providing written history to defendant's physician

As mentioned previously, it is essential that a written history be forwarded to the defendant's physician. This history should be as complete and detailed as necessary to establish the mechanics of the injury. The cover letter to the physician should state that you do not want your client interviewed about liability issues, therefore, you are rendering that unnecessary by sending this history. If the physician questions your client regarding liability anyway, then you have great leeway to show his hostility and uncooperative nature at trial. In addition to sending a written history, counsel should send the treating physician's medical reports and reports of any examining physicians and hospital records and copies of articles in the medical literature. Most of the time the defendant physician will not read these materials, claiming that he wants his opinion to be unbiased. Often, at trial you can show that what he really achieved was an uneducated and biased opinion.

§ 5.58 —Controlling the defendant's physician's attitude

Psychological considerations also apply to controlling the defendant's physician's attitude. If the defendant's physician is totally biased then nothing can be done to control his attitude. He is embittered, embattled, and hardened by years of testifying for defendants and nothing will change this attitude. Assuming the physician is somewhat objective you may psychologically effect the outcome. Your written history and cover letter show expertise in the medical subject matter; it is all part of the psychological warfare. If he perceives you as being somewhat like himself, i.e., having an understanding of medicine, he will begin to like you (Principle 9: People are more easily influenced by others they perceive as similar to themselves, and Principle 10: People are more easily influenced by people they like). After the medical literature has been sent to the defendant's physician, call him on the telephone to see if he received it. Sometimes you may even send a medical textbook on the subject matter. You would be surprised how much goodwill a $20 or $30 textbook will create. Remember, Principle 3 provides that first impressions count and first impressions over the telephone are made during the first thirty seconds or so. Therefore, you should immediately attempt to establish rapport with the physician by verbal and vocal matching over the telephone. As you begin to pace the physician, notice his use of medical terminology and match him by using the same medical terminology. Indicate your understanding of the terminology by defining the medical terms as you use them. This shows the physician that you understand the basic medical terminology and that you are not afraid to use it. This not only matches him, but in some cases intimidates him. He begins to realize he is dealing with an attorney who will not be intimidated or mislead by medical terminology. He begins to see you more and more like himself and considers you an equal. Close the conversation by asking him to send a copy of his medical report directly to you.

Over the years, a plaintiff's attorney can establish a rapport with an honest defendant's physician wherein that physician respects counsel's medical knowledge. With this type of support, the attorney can obtain reasonable answers to medical questions on cross-examination of the defendant's physician. The defendant's physician will no longer be the complete advocate. By proper pacing he can be controlled and neutralized. Instead of an advocate he becomes a medical examiner who simply gives a conservative, but basically honest, opinion. It is far better to have your client's "independent examination" performed by this type of physician. An effective cross-examination at trial is accomplished by creating agreement based on honest medical principles. This is far better than attacking a physician's credibility. It is always dangerous to attack a physician on the witness stand unless you can totally destroy his credibility. In the eyes of the jury you have attacked a very well-respected stereotype. It is often wiser not to run the unnecessary risk of unsuccessfully attacking a physician. A more effective and less risky cross-examination can be conducted by having the "independent medical examiner" simply admit to a series of good medical principles. All of this can be accomplished if you have first properly prepared your client and then controlled the defendant's physician's attitude prior to his so-called "independent medical examination."

§ 5.59 Depositions as a discovery tool

The most versatile, accurate tool of discovery in modern civil litigation is the oral deposition under oath. Depositions are used extensively and it may be argued that they are overused. It is certainly true that the extensive use of depositions frequently tends to educate the other side as to your evidence and your theories of the case. It also educates opposing experts as to your style of cross-examination. Properly planned and prepared depositions, however, can be a very valuable discovery tool.

§ 5.60 —Psychology of timing

Timing is essential in the taking of depositions, and since the plaintiff has the burden of proof in civil litigation, it is essential that he engage in aggressive discovery. The plaintiff should depose the defendant, his factual witnesses, and ultimately his experts in rather rapid succession. The plaintiff should be able to accomplish this because he has developed the theory of the case, he understands the medicine, the liability problems, the causation problems, and what defenses he will have to overcome. Often, the busy defense counsel handling a larger number of files than plaintiff's counsel is not as well prepared early in the proceedings. If the plaintiff loses this aggressive edge, this psychology of timing, he loses a valuable opportunity. This opportunity properly used allows counsel to catch the defendant off-guard and not nearly as well prepared as he will be later on. If plaintiff's counsel delays a significant advantage will have been lost. The major disadvantage to the plaintiff is that the defendant will be able to discover the plaintiff's position and theory of the case first. Defendant's counsel will then prepare his theory of defense and be in a much better position to prepare his witnesses for the taking of their depositions. Timing is therefore part of the essence of effective deposition taking. Remember as a general rule whoever first serves notice to take a deposition is entitled to depose first. For this reason it is wise to serve notices of deposition of the defendant and key fact witnesses when commencing the lawsuit. This puts timing on the plaintiff's side from the very beginning; it eliminates any chance of the defense counsel noticing the plaintiff and his witnesses' depositions first.

§ 5.61 —Psychology of territoriality

By the psychology of territoriality we mean the advantages and disadvantages of the specific locale of deposition. Usually, the plaintiff wants to take the deposition of an opposing party in plaintiff's offices because the opposing party will feel extra pressure and be off-guard. This may or may not apply to defendant's experts. If the expert is hostile, as in a medical malpractice case where the expert is the defendant's friend or associate, you want it taken at your office. On the other hand, where the defendant's expert is a conservative but honest physician, engineer, safety expert, or so forth, take that expert's deposition at his office. The advantage of this concession is an attempt to build rapport with the honest expert. You have done him a favor and he will feel obliged to reciprocate (Principle 7: People feel obligated to repay others regardless of whether they like the gift or the giver).[43] Reciprocity can be a powerful and effective tool, and the degree of reciprocity is not controlled by the size of the original favor. Furthermore, while at his office the expert will be working on other cases, other patients, and will be distracted from concentrating on preparation for the deposition. He will be on his own territory and be more relaxed. It will be easier to build on verbal, vocal, and non-

---

[43] *See generally supra* § 2.03, for a discussion of this principle.

verbal cues. As always, these cues can help establish rapport by pacing the expert. The more rapport one builds with the expert, the more likely it is that he will make key admissions and give an honest deposition.

§ 5.62 —Seating arrangement at depositions

The seating plan at a deposition does make a difference. In one case, day long negotiations were necessary before an agreement regarding the seating plan was reached. The attorneys representing a brain damaged seventeen-year-old boy wanted certain seats at the table while counsel for the defendants wanted the same seats. This actually happened and illustrates counsel's perceptions of the importance of seating at the tables during a deposition.[44]

The strategy of seating is heightened in importance and intensity when the number of parties increase. In cases with multiple parties represented by six or more lawyers, it is essential to arrive early so that you may obtain an appropriate place at the table. Otherwise counsel may sit down at the end of the table away from the witness and may then have difficulty hearing the testimony. Even where there are only two or three lawyers and a witness involved, psychological considerations regarding seating remain paramount.

Basically, when we are seated directly opposite, face-to-face, we confront people. When people are at our side, psychologically they are with us. When a person turns their back to us, that is a form of rejection. These are but a few of the significant factors associated with seating.

Obviously, counsel should attempt to sit across from his adversary. To project an image of power and control you should sit at the head of the table. This puts you in a position of authority and dominance psychologically. If the witness is an opposing expert or someone you know to be adverse, seat him so that you are confronting the witness during questioning. Counsel should attempt to place his associates or paralegals on either side of the witness. If at all possible, you should have two other people with you at the deposition so that you have friendly people on either side of you handing you pieces of paper with questions, giving you assistance, handing you literature, quotes, and so on. Such a situation can be a psychologically effective method of controlling the witness through intimidation. The witness sees your dominance, your importance, your authority. The witness tends to be more respectful of your

---

[44] *See supra* § 1.78, *Perceptions of spatial arrangements and seating behavior.*

questions and to perhaps become even a little apprehensive. Of course, this set up, with you at the head of the table and the witness at the other end, with you surrounded by friends on both sides, is the ideal. But the bottom line is you must insist that an adverse party or an adverse witness sit across from you when you are taking his deposition. It is a time for facing the person, it is a time to make him face the truth, it is a time for confrontation. This can only be done effectively with a frontal attack.

§ 5.63 —Pacing at depositions

Do not forget about the power of pacing. At the very beginning of the deposition remember to begin pacing the witness. Be conscious of the witness, assess how he is dressed, assess his gestures, take note of his facial expressions, his eye movements, his blinking rate. Assess and take note of his posture, his leg movements, and use of his arms. All of this is essential information necessary to pace the witness and to assess verbal and nonverbal cues.

§ 5.64 Matching or mismatching at depositions

Pacing the witness entails either matching the witness or mismatching the witness. In matching, we attempt to track the witness' vocal, verbal, and nonverbal cues. We match his gestures, facial expressions, eye movements, breathing and so on. At the start of the deposition try to establish all aspects of interactional pacing. The matching may also be what is called complementary matching, i.e., feeling a need of the witness and matching by complementing the witness' actions rather than matching directly. Matching builds rapport. It causes the witness to open up. As the rapport builds he wants to give us all he knows about the case. In one case at the conclusion of a deposition, after an adverse witness was matched for two hours, he proceeded to follow the deposing attorney out of the room volunteering all sorts of additional information. This behavior was a direct result of the witness having been properly paced. On the other hand mismatching is disquieting, it disrupts rapport, and it builds a dissidence. It causes agitation and nervousness. Mismatching results in vocal difficulties; in other words, the witness begins to hesitate and this results in lost credibility.

COMMENT: During the course of a discovery deposition counsel may want to use both matching and mismatching at different times. Both of these are effective methods for pacing the witness, even though they accomplish opposite goals.

---

§ 5.65 —When to match or mismatch

In most cases we want to pace the witness at the beginning of the deposition by matching him. Generally, it is a good idea to offer the witness a cup of coffee, or a soft drink, or a glass of water before the deposition begins. He is expecting you to be an ogre, and he is caught off-guard when you are nice and friendly, always remembering the power of reciprocation (Principle 7: People feel obligated to repay others regardless of whether they like the gift or the giver). The cup of coffee is a favor that always goes a long way. The process of matching starts during the opening moments of your contact with the witness. The witness' first impression of the opposing attorney ought to be one to help build rapport. People who have a rapport with the attorney who will depose them tend to give more information, tend to open up, tend to be honest (Principle 7). You want to match a witness who you believe is basically honest and at least half-way fair, including an expert witness. By matching him, you are able to gain a great deal more information than if you begin by mismatching. Furthermore, once you have mismatched, it is very difficult to go back to matching.

Begin the deposition by matching the witness. Then chronologically examine all of the events surrounding the subject of the litigation. Ask open-ended questions, questions which encourage the witness to talk. The witness, speaking in a narrative form, begins to volunteer information, which can often be very helpful even if unrequested. The matching period, if it is a complex case, may last several hours or several days. Whatever length of time it takes, you want to continue to match the witness so long as you are seeking information.

You should seek to commit the witness to his testimony after you have completely discussed all aspects of the case and covered chronologically every event involved. At this point you gradually drift out of matching the witness and begin to mismatch. Now you want to create dissidence. You want to use the authoritarian position set up by the seating to advantage. You want to bring now your power to its full effect. The questions become more rapid and are definitely leading. They cry out for a commitment in the form of a yes or no answer. Now you are mismatching the witness. Now the witness is nervous. There is a conflict between his initial impression of you and what he now sees. He tends to try and hold on to the more comfortable feelings created by his first impression. He wonders what he said to make you angry. He wants to be cooperative, but now he is nervous. While he is in this psychological state is an ideal time to gain positive admissions. Now you are going back through the notes of his narrative answer committing the witness to his admission. This is when you should force the witness to agree with your theory of the case. Now you are using hypothetical questions. Now you are demanding answers—not asking for them.

§ 5.66 —Interpreting behavioral cues

While you are pacing the witness as described previously,[45] you are also simultaneously interpreting his verbal, vocal, and nonverbal cues. Generally, you should not rely on the witness' facial cues. These are generally easy to control. On the other hand, there will frequently be cues obtained from body movements of the witness. These are not as easily controlled.[46] Note if the witness begins speaking at an increased pitch, and at a more rapid rate with fewer illustrations and analogies, this may be indicative that the witness is not being truthful.[47] The witness also may make a greater number of errors in speech.[48] Some of the cues may not be directly related to deceit. They may be related to anxiety or nervousness, particularly during the phase of the deposition where you are mismatching the witness. One would expect increased anxiety cues that could be misinterpreted by the laymen as indicating deceit during the dissidence resulting from a mismatch. Studies of the trial process have concluded that some of the same cues that may be misinterpreted as signs of lying or deceit, may actually be cues that indicate anxiety or a high degree of motivation. One study indicates that the only reliable indications of deceit on a nonverbal level deal with two variables. These

---

[45] See supra § 5.63, *Pacing at depositions* and § 5.64, *Matching or mismatching at depositions).*

[46] Littlepage & Pineault, *Detection of Deceptive Factual Statements From the Body and the Face*, 5 PERSONALITY & SOC. PSYCHOLOGY BULL. 325–328 (1979).

[47] Ekman, Friesen & Scherer, *Body Movement and Voice Pitch in Deceptive Interaction*, 16 SEMIOTICA 23–27 (1976).

[48] Mehrabian, *Non-Verbal Betrayal of Feelings*, 5 J. EXPERIM. RESEARCH IN PERSONALITY 64–75 (1971).

two variables are adaptation and eye contact duration.[49] Adaptation refers to the length of time during which the hands are used to manipulate foreign objects, clothing, or parts of the body. Eye contact duration deals with the length of time that the subject is able to maintain eye contact. Remember that it is not the frequency of eye contact, nor is it the number of times a reciprocal gaze is initiated by either party, that determines truthfulness. Rather it is duration of eye contact, the length of time a reciprocal gaze is sustained. Eye contact duration may vary depending on whether the subject matter of the questioning involves the witness' personal response or opinions regarding a situation, or whether the questions refer to only factual content.

The attorney, during the taking of the deposition, must not only be asking questions, but must be doing more. He cannot become so wrapped up in his questions, following his checklist and notes, that he is not listening to the answers. In addition to evaluating the witness' nonverbal cues he must also listen to the content of the answers, as this may lead to other areas of questioning. In addition to listening to the content, counsel must picture in his mind how that content is being phrased and how it will appear in the written deposition. Often, what is said has a certain meaning to everyone at the table. This is because it is being communicated on three levels: verbal, vocal, and nonverbal. However, when it is typed by the court reporter it is only transmitted visually. It may lose a lot of its meaning. Therefore we must develop a knack, as attorneys, for picturing what the answer is going to look like when typed. If the meaning of the answer is not going to be clear on paper, then additional questions need to be asked to make the meaning clear. You may even tell the witness at that point in the deposition that you would like him to "explain an answer further, so it will be clear on the record." Perhaps even point out to him that an answer such as "not necessarily" is not a direct answer to the question. You try then to rephrase the question and ask the witness to answer the question with a yes or no response and then to explain the answer. This way the answer will be clear and meaningful on the record. Explain that this is necessary because even though everyone in the room knows and understands what he is saying, that it may not necessarily convey the same meaning on the record. You may want to describe for him that he is communicating right now on

[49] Knapp, Hart & Dennis, *An Exploration of Deception as a Communication Construct*, 1 HUM. COM. RESEARCH 15–29 (1974).

three levels and that his message is clear, but that the answer is being recorded on only one level, the verbal level.

§ 5.67 —Questioning techniques

Your goal in a deposition is not merely to obtain information. The purpose of taking a deposition is to obtain that information in such a fashion that it is usable at trial. The admissions and information contained in the deposition are not usable at trial if, when the witness is confronted with the deposition during cross-examination, he is able to say effectively, "I didn't say that," or "I didn't mean it," or "What I really meant to say was . . . ," or "The court reporter made a mistake," and so on. In general, the only way to avoid a witness squirming out of an admission at deposition is to have that admission in the deposition more than one time. Many lawyers will argue that if a witness makes a crucial mistake and gives you an admission against interest, you should leave it alone and not give him a chance to "slip off the hook" in the deposition. This may be true in rare instances where the witness has clearly made a startling and unequivocable admission. Experienced trial lawyers know, however, that this happens more rarely than most people think. Often, the associate returns and informs the senior partner that the witness made a tremendous admission during the deposition and he therefore questioned the witness no further on the subject matter. However, when that admission is typed up, it is often weakly worded and the witness is in no way pinned down to the answer. At the very least, when such admissions occur they need to be followed with questions designed to pin the witness down.

What do we mean by "pinning" questions? We mean a question that forces the witness to commit to the answer he has just given. It pins the witness down on paper, that the answer is intended. The question can start with a phrase such as: "so, Mr. 'Witness' what you are saying is. . . ." Pinning questions are questions that summarize the previous response and cry out for a yes or no answer. Pinning questions are leading questions. They may also start with the classical starting phrases of leading questions such as: "the truth is," "the facts are," "you would agree would you not," and so on.

Once the witness is sufficiently pinned to an answer, you have established a strong ally. (That ally is embodied in Principle 8.) If the witness gives an answer you really want him to stick with, point it out to him. Make sure he understands that he is on the record. As described previously,[50] once a person is committed to an idea, that person's self-image changes to remain consistent with that commitment. Once committed we tend to follow-up on our commitments. Rarely will a witness realize his mistake. Once a witness is clearly committed to an answer, it is a good idea to approach the same subject matter from another direction an hour or so later. Usually this comes up in the natural flow of conversation when he is testifying in the same or a similar area. You then pin him further and say: " . . . when you told us a while ago . . ." or " . . . what you really meant was . . . ". Usually you can accomplish this two or three times during the deposition.

The importance of emphasizing the admission can be crucial. One example occurs when a witness has made an admission during the deposition and is now being cross-examined at trial. Unless he was pinned successfully three or four times during the deposition, he will find all kinds of ways to effectively "get off the hook." He can reverse his ground. He can say that his memory was faulty then and is not faulty now and give reasons. He can close his eyes and give very dramatic testimony as to why what he said then was incorrect. He can doubt the accuracy of the court reporter or simply say: "when I put it that way I was mistaken . . . ", and so on. The only way to effectively cross-examine such a witness is to point out that on page "20" of the deposition, he then made a mistake when he said: " . . . ". Then point out that he was asked the same thing on page "160", that was a mistake also. Finally, ask if he made another mistake on page "340". After you do the same thing on page "420" and page "425", you have made the point that the witness could not have made that many mistakes, rather that he is not telling the truth now. But if you had not effectively pinned him several times during deposition, you could not effectively cross-examine him at trial.

Another technique to be used in a deposition is "boxing" questions. This is an attempt to make sure that you have gotten all of the details that there are on a particular point. It establishes that there is nothing else that will refresh the witness' memory. In essence you are "boxing him in." For instance, when you are reading through a medical record with a physician, particularly a long and complex record, after each date or series of events you may ask as follows: "Doctor, now, is that everything that took place on that particular day?"; "Is there anything else that you want to tell us?"; "Is there anything written or unwritten that

[50] *See supra* § 2.04.

would refresh your memory regarding the events we have discussed?"; "I want to be sure doctor, that I will not be surprised at trial, and that you have told us everything that you can remember that went on during this particular date and time, event, and so forth." By using such boxing questions you are assuring yourself of obtaining complete and full details of the event in question. You are saying to the witness: "I do not want you to come up with anything further and say that you did not think of it now. Take your time, but think of it now." After asking a boxing question you may even note that you are going to pause your questioning and give the witness time to think about his answer. This forces the witness not to hold anything back. This makes it clear to him that if he does hold back, he is going to have a hard time explaining why he can remember this detail several years later at trial, a time much further removed from the event in question. Boxing questions assure you of complete and full details.

To make sure your deposition is complete, you must prepare for it. You prepare for the deposition by going over your records, going over your theory of liability, your problems of causation, and in general, thinking about the case. You then make a checklist, not of specific questions, but of areas that require further inquiry. You use this checklist to make sure that you have covered every area that needs to be covered. If you are dealing with more than one set of medical records, the checklist should cover all of these. It should contain a listing of all the key dates and contacts the witness had with your client or the product or whatever is involved in the litigation. It should have a complete list of all the details available on the witnesses' backgrounds. The checklist should also include coverage of prior similar incidents where this witness may have been involved, such as prior accidents, prior difficulties with a particular product, prior claims made against him, and so forth. Without such a predeposition checklist you cannot be assured of taking a complete full deposition.

Another form of questioning used effectively in the discovery deposition is generally used with expert witnesses. Often an expert witness giving an opinion will leave out a salient fact, or misstate the conclusion of another expert, or take some tact that you feel is contrary to the evidence, or you may have some salient facts at your disposal through good predeposition work-up that the other side does not have available. These facts may be contained in areas of the medical records that the expert physician has not reviewed. Whatever the situation you will find yourself obtaining a negative answer to a question which should be positive if the witness was confronted with certain salient facts. Sometimes that witness may even deny such facts when confronted with them. In this situation, use the hypothetical question. A hypothetical question should contain a complete chronology of all the salient facts. It must be accurate if you intend to use the answer to it at trial. If your hypothetical question is reasonably supported by the evidence it can become an effective weapon. It is particularly effective because the witness may be willing to give you admissions while believing the facts are not proven, either because he does not know of the evidence supporting it, or because he steadfastly refuses in his own mind to believe that such facts could be true.

An example of the effective use of hypothetical questioning can occur in the simplest of cases. Assume that you are dealing with a case where the client has preexisting osteoarthritis. It was asymptomatic and this will be supported by the testimony of the family physician and family friends. A rear-end collision occurred and a cervical injury was superimposed on the preexisting osteoarthritis. The client has been sent to the defense doctor who states that it is his opinion that the preexisting osteoarthritis was so severe that it had to be causing pain prior to the collision and that the present pain is secondary to the preexisting osteoarthritis and not the rear-end collision.

Under that set of facts you are now taking the deposition of the doctor examining for the defendant. At the deposition he insists that the man was having pain prior to the incident. You know that this is not correct. You might confront him with the fact that the family physician and lay witnesses will testify that the client's osteoarthritis was asymptomatic. The probability is that he will deny that they know what they are talking about, and that he will still stick to his story. On the other hand, you might consider using the hypothetical question. Force the witness to assume the man was having no pain prior to the collision. Once he makes this assumption you can then force an honest physician to admit that the cervical trauma is the cause of the man's pain and not the osteoarthritis. You can do this because he was pinned during his deposition to the fact that this is not traumatic osteoarthritis, that is, a rapid increase in osteoarthritis. Once the witness accepts the hypothetical that the plaintiff was not having pain before, counsel can force him on a medical basis to admit that the osteoarthritis is not the cause of the problem. This leaves the only explanation being the trauma the client received in the rear-end collision.

§ 5.68 —Adversary's acknowledgment of case theory

If you are the plaintiff in a civil action, now is the time to have the defendant, or his expert, acknowledge your case theory. If you have followed the other principles, that is, you have engaged in aggressive discovery and you have timed your depositions correctly, you have a tremendous advantage. The advantage is that you have developed a case theory early in the proceedings. You know what you want to do and where you are going, and because you have prepared your case properly you are taking the defendants depositions first. The defense has not had time to engage in discovery. Therefore, the defense does not know where you are going with the questions and this is a decided advantage. The defendant may be guessing wrong, he may have been prepared on the wrong points. Hopefully you have thrown out a red herring to defendant's counsel so he is not quite sure about your case theory. This is the advantage that wins lawsuits. This is the advantage of surprise. It is the advantage that works magic!

Every magic trick which appears to be an illusion is really simple. The essence of every magic trick is surprise. You do not know how to figure what the magician is doing because you do not know what is going to happen next. If you did, the trick would seem simple. That is why magicians "never repeat a trick." It becomes too easy to anticipate what happens next.

With the element of surprise, you can gain crucial admissions at deposition. They need not be in any logical order. Carefully woven into your scenario are questions which search out admissions either through the use of pinning questions, boxing questions, or hypothetical questions as discussed previously.[51] Slowly, but surely, you should be able to have the witness agree, at least hypothetically, with your theory of the case. Such agreement is easier to obtain now than at trial. Witnesses are not as hardened in their positions at deposition nor are they as psychologically prepared now as they will be on the stand. So whatever your case theory, whether it be a failure to warn in a products liability case, or a failure to adequately inspect in a slip-and-fall situation, or a failure to obtain an informed consent in a medical malpractice action, you are sure to gain more favorable admissions in a properly prepared deposition.

---

[51] See supra § 5.67, *Questioning techniques*.

§ 5.69 —Adversary's acknowledgment of medical theory

Your medical theory should be acknowledged in the deposition also. We previously presented an example of the use of hypothetical questions to force a defense expert to agree with your medical theory of the case. Now, let us discuss a possible medical theory for a young person who has complained of pain for several years following a rather average rear end collision. The medical theory of the case might be that the client suffered a sufficient hyperextension-flexion injury so as to have ripped the muscles in the neck. These muscles have healed with scar tissue which, of course, is permanent and is now causing chronic pain, particularly when the weather changes. You further hypothesize, based on the medical literature, that your client falls within the 12% who statistically do not recover from this type of injury even after settlement.

If that is your medical theory, then those are the points you want to have the defense orthopedist admit on cross-examination. You want to have him admit, if you can, that the literature substantiates that these injuries can cause tearing of muscles. Taking him one step at a time, you then have him admit that torn muscles when they heal can heal with scar tissue. You have him acknowledge that there have been studies indicating this fact. Once these admissions are pinned, it is an easy step to have the defendant admit that there are cites to the literature which indicate that 12% of the people who suffer whiplash injuries, even after settlement, do not recover. He will have to admit that it is at least hypothetically possible that your client suffered a hyperextension-flexion injury which tore muscles and which resulted in permanent scar tissue, and which explains why the client may fall within the 12% who do not get better. This is having the defense agree with your medical theory of the case.

§ 5.70 —Use of authoritative material at depositions

Remember that we generally do not want to educate a defendant or an opposing expert at their depositions. We want to gain information without "tipping our hand." This being our goal, you do not want to use your authoritative materials at deposition. Generally, you want to save the use of the materials for trial, but it is mandatory that you understand those materials when taking the deposition of the key defendant and/or his experts. If you are relying on a violation of an OSHA standard, know the standard by heart at deposition. You may not want to confront the expert with that standard, but certainly do phrase your questions using the language found in the standard. For example, a situation wherein an item fell off of scaffolding is covered by an OSHA standard which requires a "toe board" to surround the platform. In this case, the defendant did not place the required toe board around the scaffold platform which resulted in a direct violation of the OSHA standard. You should certainly know the standard and know what is required before you take the deposition. Do not, however, necessarily pull out the OSHA standard to impeach the witness at the deposition, rather you should save it for use at trial. Likewise, when dealing with medical experts, you generally do not want to confront them with medical treatises, texts, or even the *Physician's Desk Reference* during the deposition, but do understand the material and use the terminology.

There is a valid purpose to questioning the defendant or his expert at deposition about published authoritative material. You want to have the expert list all of the materials that he relies on regularly in his business, as well as everything he considers to be authoritative. Often you will have a difficult time at trial having him admit what is authoritative, but this generally will not occur at deposition. At deposition, after you have established rapport, you will generally have an easier time having him tell you what books he generally uses as authoritative sources.

Note that you may not necessarily want to use the word "authoritative" when questioning a witness as to what source he relies on since this word has been overused so frequently by attorneys, particularly in state court cases, that the word "authoritative" is a red flag. However, an expert would not regularly rely on a book that is not "authoritative." Therefore, an admission by the expert that he regularly relies on a certain book should be sufficient to have him admit its authoritativeness at trial.

There is an instance when you may want to use your authoritative materials at the deposition. If there is a serious question about liability, you may want to use the materials to encourage settlement. However, once you have used a direct quote from the material at deposition, counter-materials will miraculously appear at trial which can explain why your particular source is not authoritative. Again, remember that one of the most effective weapons at trial is the element of surprise. Save some of your strongest evidence for the trial. Keep the "smoking gun" if you can, so you can use it effectively at trial.

III. Videotape Depositions

§ 5.71 Judicial considerations

The use of videotape technology to present the testimony of absent witnesses is becoming a more frequently used method and has been increasingly accepted by the courts over the last ten years. This procedure started in the early 1970's in most states. Videotaped depositions have a distinct advantage over counsel's reading the deposition to the jury. In reading a deposition to the jury, the party presenting the testimony usually has the opportunity to choose an individual to read the witness' responses and most judges grant wide latitude in this regard. However, the person reading the deposition is critical to the interpretation of the content through nonverbal behavior and cues, and can often influence the jury's assessment of the credibility or veracity of the absent witness. Videotape is a definite advantage, in terms of fairness, because of its ability to preserve the nonverbal and vocal behavior of an absent witness.

In 1970, the Federal Rules of Civil Procedure were revised to allow the use of electronically recorded depositions. Federal Rule of Civil Procedure 30(b)(4) provides as follows:

> "The court may upon motion order that the testimony at a deposition be recorded by other than stenographic means, in which event the order shall designate the manner of recording, preserving, and filing a deposition, and may include provisions to assure that the recorded testimony will be accurate and trustworthy."

Further, besides the change in the Federal Rule, between 1970 and 1980 almost every state court, either by statute or judicial decision, determined that videotaped depositions were permissible. In 1975, a comprehensive study of the subject was performed by the National Center for State Courts. The committee concluded that more extensive studies were needed to determine the impact of the video medium upon the jury's perception and decision-making process when compared to the live trial.

Operating under this rule, in some instances, the courts have allowed depositions to be taken of a party at the place where the negligent incident occurred.[52] It is now widely accepted that the finder of fact will often gain greater insight by viewing a videotaped deposition because he or they can see the manner in which the answer was delivered. Further,

---

[52] Carson v. Burlington Northern, Inc., 52 F.R.D. 492 (D. Neb. 1971).

the videotape should avoid the tedium produced when counsel reads a lengthy deposition into evidence at trial.

As can be seen from the foregoing, the advantages of videotaped depositions include avoiding the tedium of reading the deposition, providing the jury with vocal and nonverbal cues of the witness, and increasing the interest level of the jurors in the testimony. However, these goals have been circumvented particularly in the federal courts, by federal district judges, either individually or through local court rules, requiring that the deposition be taken with only one camera and that the camera remain on the witness. As can be seen from the previously quoted Federal Rule, a federal judge has the discretion to enter an order to protect the "accuracy and trustworthiness of the testimony." The main reason for the one camera rule is that the judges, through ignorance, fear that the party taking the deposition may heighten the significance of a particular point and thereby unfairly motivate the jury. However, what their attitude fails to recognize is that unless those operating the equipment know all the nuances of the case, they can hardly be expected to know what is an important point, or specifically how to emphasize important parts of the testimony. On the other hand, a static shot on the witness' face, or a "talking head" deposition, is so boring as to be worthless. In one case, the first case in which Louisiana state courts allowed the use of a videotaped deposition, the tape only showed the "talking head" of the expert witness. The three hours of a "black and white talking head" proved so straining, tedious, and boring that after a short time, many members of the jury actually fell asleep. Counsel found themselves yawning and the judge shaking his head. The videotape presentation was stopped and, much to the relief of everyone, it was determined by stipulation of both counsel and by order of the court, that counsel return to the old method of reading the deposition. There is no way to effectively present testimony with one camera from one angle, showing one shot continuously.

COMMENT: Thus, it is suggested that when trial counsel is considering the use of a videotaped deposition for use at trial, he should negotiate the use of two cameras with the opposing counsel. The deposition must have a visual quality that approaches the jurors' expectations. If counsel must obtain an order from a federal court judge to use two cameras, it is suggested that a brief be done on the technical literature which indicates that changing shots will not substantially affect the credibility of the witness and that the failure to do so may make the deposition worthless. Conservative traditional attitudes toward the techniques of taking a videotape deposition need to be changed.

---

§ 5.72 Use of cameras

Whenever possible the use of a single camera should be avoided. Moreover, at no time should one camera with a one angle lense be used so that the jury continuously views the witness at the table. This is called a continuous long-shot and technical research has established that the continuous long-shot destroys a witness' credibility.[53]

§ 5.73 —Mixing shots

A mixer allows the director or person making the videotape to edit the shots from the two cameras onto one tape as the deposition is progressing. There is a solution to the objection that the use of two cameras results in the witness not being seen by the jury at times. That solution is that one camera be a wide shot that includes the attorney and the jury, and that the second camera be used for varying shots of the witness. That is, that the wide shot be used to change the shots of the witness. In other words, at some points in the deposition one would want a head shot of the witness or a close-up. At other times a medium-shot, which would be upper body and head, and at other times a full shot. With one camera, however, it is impossible to change the shots of the witness without going out of focus and creating a distraction. Therefore, the long-shot is used essentially to break the monotony and to cover the change back to the witness from a close-shot to a medium-shot and so forth. Such mixing shots during a video deposition are essential. They give the deposition the type of quality that will maintain the interest of the jury and enhance witness credibility. Jurors are used to seeing professionally edited TV shows. These TV shows change shots every thirty seconds to maintain visual interest. The deposition to be credible must, in the jurors' minds, fit the stereotype of what is an acceptable television presentation. Therefore, the deposition must change shots and be of sufficient

---

[53] G. Millerson, The Technique of Television Production 27 (Hastings House, 1961).

quality so as not to destroy the credibility of the witness and/or the lawyer presenting it.

§ 5.74 Use of demonstrative aids during the videotaped deposition

Another solution to the visual integrity of a videotaped deposition is the planned use of as many demonstrative aids as possible. If X-rays are important to the case, use them! Similarly, the use of anatomical models, photographs, and charts aid in the production of a visually effective deposition. In fact, the extensive use of demonstrative aids is the only solution for a videotaped deposition when one is forced to use one camera. Put the witness, standing up, in front of a blackboard and allow him to draw an explanation of anything pertinent.

COMMENT: If you are forced to use one camera, then use demonstrative aids throughout the deposition.

The witness should definitely know in advance that the deposition is going to be videotaped and the reason for the use of so many visual aids. Generally the witness needs to be reassured that these aids are not an aggravation, but will make him more effective on television. Often one will find, if a witness is properly handled, that even the most aggressive and hostile expert witness will respond favorably when he finds out that you, the attorney, are going to make him a "television star." Thus, the use of two cameras,[54] the mixing of shots,[55] as well as the use of demonstrative aids, should all be combined to make for the most effective deposition.

§ 5.75 Technical research regarding video techniques

There has been considerable technical research on the value of varying TV shots, and on the effects of videotaped presentation of testimony at trial as opposed to live testimony. In order to better understand the use of videotaped depositions and to intelligently discuss the subject matter with judges and even to properly instruct the person taking the video-

[54] *See supra* § 5.72, *Use of cameras*.

[55] See supra § 5.73, *Mixing shots*.

taped deposition, the attorney needs to understand what the research reveals regarding the effects of various video techniques. Thus, we will attempt to summarize some of the findings of the current research in both the broadcast field and in those studies directed toward the use of videotapes at trial.

A good bit of the research performed by those in the broadcasting industry indicates that: "A dynamic style of editing a television program is superior to a static style in terms of information gain."[56] One author in the broadcast medium has stated that without the proper mixing of shots those viewing the videotape will be "watching instead of looking, or hearing instead of listening." The same author went on to state that "certainly, more shots in live television outstay their welcome than understay it."[57]

The opponents of mixing shots recognize the fact that in modern television it is the "stock and trade of the director to constantly vary the picture from close-ups to long-shots."[58] This study seems to indicate that varying shots have no effect upon the viewer's interest.[59] It was shown that while the static medium shot was just as effective in terms of achieving a high interest level, the interest level may be related to the dynamic presenter.[60] The same author in a 1968 publication, after further research, went on to conclude the following:

> The results [of Williams' second study] may be summarized as follows:
>
> 1)—The three basic film shots do have measurably different effects upon interest.
>
> 2)—A close-up does not significantly increase interest levels of a film presentation.
>
> 3)—A loose shot does significantly decrease interest levels of a film presentation.
>
> 4)—If the relative tightness of shots is selected on the basis of the amount of interest inherent in the subject matter at any given time,

---

56 MILLERSON, *supra* note 53, at 312.

57 *Id*.

58 Williams, *The Value of Varying TV Shots*, 9 J. BROADCASTING 33 (1965).

59 *Id*. at 42.

60 *Id*. at 43.

an increase in interest may be achieved in medium interest subject matters, but a loss in low rated portions may be expected.

5)—If the relative tightness of the shot is in opposition to the interest inherent in the subject matter, there will be a decrease in interest.[61]

The broadcasting industry literature has established some relationship between camera angle and communication credibility. A study by Robert K. Tiemens of Wayne State University, published in 1970, indicated that there was some relationship, but that further study was needed.[62] A more recent study by McCain, Chilberg, and Wakshlag, using both a single camera and double camera concluded that: "High angle shots appear to raise a televised figure's credibility on a number of dimensions."[63]

These authors went on to state:

> "The authors suggest from the findings of the studies reported here, that televised personalities and newscasters would enhance their credibility and task attractiveness if the predominant shot is higher than its corresponding reference shot. We would also recommend that low angle shots may increase credibility and attraction, but only when they are used sparingly."[64]

What the attorney can learn from referring to the broadcast literature is that mixing of shots is necessary to avoid visual tedium and a resulting loss of the witness' credibility. Further, the more professional looking the video appears to be to the jury, i.e., the more the videotape deposition resembles a professionally produced TV show, the higher the attorney's credibility. Secondly, when close-up shots are used, they do not necessarily, from the broadcast point of view, heighten interest and they should be selected on the basis of showing detail. In essence, interest has to be inherent in the material presented and the tightness of the shot must be relative to and correspond with the inherent interest in the subject matter, otherwise the viewer will lose interest and credibility.

---

[61] Williams, *Film Shots and Expressed Interest Levels*, 35 Speech Monographs 166–169 (1968).

[62] Tiemens, *Some Relationships of Camera Angle to Communicative Credibility*, 14 J. Broadcasting 483–490 (1970).

[63] McCain, Chilberg & Wakshlag, *The Effects of Camera Angles on Source Credibility and Attraction*, 21 J. Broadcasting 35, 46 (1977).

[64] *Id*. at 44.

§ 5.76 Studies regarding various modes of communication

In addition to research done in the general broadcast field, specific research has been published regarding videotaped witness testimony. One early study concluded that if inherent interest in the subject matter was strong, viewers of testimony tended to remember the last portion of the message better than the first; if there was little interest in the subject matter, viewers tended to remember the first part of the message and forget the last.[65] In 1973, a pilot study at the Arizona State University Law School compared live testimony to black and white videotape, audiotape, and transcripts read aloud. Their limited study found that a black and white videotape presentation generally produces fewer positive ratings from experimental witnesses than did the live testimony of witnesses.[66] After viewing a videotaped trial, student jurors were interviewed regarding the attribution of negligence, the dollar award, perception of attorney credibility, retention of information, and motivation or interest. The research concluded that the videotaped medium had no dilatorius effects on trials and that black and white was superior to color videotape for evidence presentation. This research does indicate that there are differences between camera and live presentations and jurors react differently to live presentations as opposed to videotaped presentations of evidence.

In 1973, a study was conducted in an actual criminal trial in California of entered videotaped testimony; it concluded that video presentation was felt by the jurors to be impersonal.[67] Further, another study in 1969 concluded that the presentation of the emotional content of the testimony at trial may be affected by electronic transmission of the testimony.[68] A more detailed study in 1973 also indicated a relationship between emotional content of testimony and the method of presenta-

---

[65] Miller & Campbell, *Recency and Primacy in Persuasion as a Function of the Timing of Speeches and Measurement*, 59 J. ABNORM. & SOC. PSYCHOLOGY 1–9 (1959).

[66] Butler, The Use of Videotape in the Courtroom to Convey Demeanor Evidence (May 1973) (unpublished report on file at Brigham Young University Law School). This study was a student project at Arizona State University Law School.

[67] Bermant, Chappell & McGuire, Liggans vs. Hanisko, Juror Reactions to Videotaped Trial Testimony in California, 1973 (unpublished manuscript, Battelle Memorial Institute, Seattle, Washington).

[68] Jorgenson & Howell, *Judging Unposed Emotional Behavior*, in PSYCHOTHERAPY: THEORY, RESEARCH & PRACTICE 161 (1969).

tion.[69] The study concluded that emotional content is received by jurors through various communication channels depending upon their mood. Since the electronic medium would eliminate certain channels of communication, jurors in certain moods would be affected differently.

Since this early research into the field of videotape presentations, Brigham Young University Law School conducted two extensive studies in the field of videotaped presentation of testimony. The first study, published in the Brigham Young University Law Review, used an extremely complex variance analysis of comments by jurors on live testimony, read transcript, black and white and color videotape presentations. Professor Williams rated the juror response according to twenty-nine bipolar adjective scales. The primary conclusion of Williams' first study was that the reading of a transcript as opposed to electronic communication of the testimony, interfered with the ability of jurors to evaluate the competency of the witness.

COMMENT: Thus, if one has a weak witness who is neither competent nor dynamic, his testimony ought to be preserved with a written deposition and not videotaped.

The study went on to conclude: "all three electronic methods of presentation (audiotape, black and white videotape, and color videotape) were superior to the read transcript method in their ability to approximate jurors' perception of live testimony. Each of the methods demonstrated unique advantages and disadvantages compared to the other two."[70] Interestingly, this study concluded that while the live presentation had the most emotional impact on the jurors the audiotaped presentation resulted in more emotional involvement than did either the black or white color videotape. This is an important finding of the study and emphasizes the importance of the verbal communication. The reason the audiotape was more effective emotionally than the videotape relates to

[69] Burns & Beier, *Significance of Vocal and Visual Channels in the Decoding of Emotional Meaning*, 23 J. Com. 118 (1973).

[70] Williams, Farmer, Lee, Cundick, Howell & Rooker, *Juror Perceptions of Trial Testimony as a Function of the Method of Presentation. A Comparison Live, Color Video, Black-and-White Video, Audio, and Transcript Presentations*, 1975 B.Y.U. Law Rev. 408 (1975).

the differences in the effects upon audiences between radio and television. When you listen to a radio show you have to use your own imagination, and generally visualize in your own mind, what is taking place. What we conceive in our own minds can be much more frightening than anything which can be shown to us visually. Thus, radio, (audio presentation only) has a greater impact upon emotion than a TV presentation. The significance of this finding is that if the primary purpose of presenting your witness is to persuade through emotional content, then that witness really needs to be presented live not in videotape. Further, the first Williams study concluded that black and white videotape presentations caused emotional distancing; ratings on friendliness of the witnesses and attorneys dropped significantly. The study went on to conclude that "of the four media tested, color videotape was rated closest to the live trial in appearance aspects and its ability to reproduce the live jurors' responses to the preferential choice with regard to friendship and preferred counsel questions."[71]

In 1978, Dr. Gerald R. Miller, a widely recognized communications expert, published a report prepared for the National Science Foundation on the effects of videotaped materials on juror response.[72] The study contrasted live testimony as opposed to videotaped testimony. This rather lengthy study reached some interesting conclusions. For example, if opinion or emotional testimony was involved, judgments regarding the witness' veracity were more favorable where only body shots were shown of the witness on videotape as compared to head and body or head only. Determinations regarding factual deceit were spotted more easily in a medium head and body shot rather than a body only shot. Videotape color was more helpful to the jury in determining veracity than black and white videotape. Further, attorney credibility was increased by improved video techniques such as the use of the split screen approach and presumably the mixing of shots, and so forth.

In contrast to what is found in broadcast industry journals, witness credibility was not affected by the type of shot, i.e., close-up or long-shots. The study also indicated that when a plaintiff's expert was presented on videotape as opposed to the defendant's expert's live testimony, there was a statistically significant higher amount awarded to the

[71] *Id*. at 410.

[72] Miller & Fontes, *Real Versus Reel: What's the Verdict? The Effects of Videotaped Court Materials on Juror Response*, Final Report, Department of Communication, Michigan State University, 1978 (NSF–RANN Grant APR 75–15815).

plaintiff. This may indicate that jurors have increased the credibility of the plaintiff's expert by subconsciously conferring on him a higher status, similar to that given by the general public to those who appear on television. It should be noted, however, that the status conferral effect on individual jurors may not statistically affect the final outcome of the group interaction of all the jurors.

Further, as would be expected, strong witnesses were perceived as more credible and competent with more of their information retained than that of weak witnesses. The important finding was that strong witnesses were perceived as significantly more qualified in the close-up shot. However, when the long-shot was used, jurors retained more information presented by the weak witness than by the strong witness. This finding may be due to the fact that the weak witness' fidgeting and other bad nonverbal cues which are distracting are not visible during the long-shot of the weak witness. Dr. Miller concluded that the camera shots overall did not have the significant effects that would have been expected. However, even though he did not study the interactions of mixed shots, he did emphasize that:

> "The effects (of camera shots) may very well have been different, if different shots were employed contiguously" and "a close-up shot may consistently provide dramatic emphasis only when preceded by the longer shot. Moreover, the emphasis may increase if the preceding shot is a long-shot rather than a medium-shot. . . . Also it is important to know that the findings do not generalize to the numerous combinations of shots that could be employed."

Dr. Miller in his general conclusions went on to state that:

> When videotape is considered alone, no single shot or camera strategy will be uniformly most effective. Instead some attorneys and witnesses will exert the greatest impact on the jury in the live setting, whereas others will be more effective on videotape. In a similar vein some attorneys and witnesses will enhance their effectiveness by being close-up while others will profit from the reduction in detail resulting from a longer shot.

Another study concurred with the prior one that strong witnesses were more authoritative in a close-up shot, and that jurors retained more information of weak witnesses shown in a long-shot.[73] However, interest-

---

[73] Kaminski & Miller, *How Jurors Respond to Videotaped Witnesses*, Section 679, Conclusions regarding videotaped depositions, Winter 1984 J. COM. 88, 100.

ingly, the weak witness appeared more composed in the close-up shot. This recent study also indicated camera angles may make a difference. This study went on to conclude: (a) a decision to use one camera shot over another should take into account the type of witness to be videotaped; (b) if a strong witness is being videotaped, and there is concern for his perceived authority, then a close-up shot should be employed; (c) if a weak witness is being videotaped, and there is concern for his perceived composure, then a close-up shot is recommended; (d) if, however, there is a greater concern for the amount of information retained by the jurors, then the long-shot is recommended.

COMMENT: Obviously, in some instances the attorney may be unable to call a witness in person at trial. He is then left with the decision whether to have that witness' testimony read from a deposition or whether a videotaped deposition should be taken. In making this decision the following six rules should be considered:

First and foremost, one needs to evaluate the witness before the decision is made. If a lawyer does not know the doctor, expert or other witness to be videotaped, he needs to meet him and analyze the witness before making that decision. If he is a dynamic, strong witness then he should be videotaped. If the witness is a weak one, the lawyer may fare better by reading the deposition to the jury. If the lawyer has doubts about the witness' credibility, then certainly, reading the deposition is preferable. Second, consider whether the information being presented is purely factual or whether there is an emotional element, which includes in some instances, opinion testimony. If an emotional element is to be conveyed to the jury then clearly live testimony is far better. In one demonstration, a good trial lawyer giving a summation with emotional content, through nonverbal communication, brought an audience of three hundred and fifty attorneys to tears. When the same summation was played back on videotape, however, it did not have the same emotional impact. Videotape cannot possibly have the emotional impact of live testimony, but if the witness is not available, and a lawyer has no choice, then clearly color videotape is far better for the presentation of the witness with an emotional message or opinion testimony. Third, organization of the testimony on videotape may be affected by the nature of the witness. If a strong witness is involved then the important message that you want to put across to the jury should be last. On the other hand, if the witness is weak, then the important message should be conveyed first. Fourth, the attorney has to take into consideration that his overall credibility with the jury is essential to his persuading them in final argument to make a favorable determination. Therefore he has to do all in his power to maintain that credibility. The better the production, the more credible the attorney. This being true, for the sake of attorney credibility, it is important that the attorney do all within his power to produce a videotaped deposition that lives up to jurors' expectation of the medium. Fifth, presentation of a videotape, in some instances, has the ability to confer status. This being true, if a witness makes a particularly good impression, is attractive, looks like a TV star, is dynamic, and can make a strong on-camera impression, it may be better to go ahead and videotape that witness. Use his videotape and take advantage of the status conferral effect, particularly when counsel is dealing with an expert witness. Finally, if one is videotaping a strong witness then close-up shots should be maintained longer and used more often than other shots. On the other hand, if counsel is dealing with a weak witness, then the long shots should predominate. However, if a weak witness' composure and credibility are poor, then more close-up shots are called for.

IV. Psychological Factors in Structuring the Case for Trial

§ 5.77 Climax and anticlimax considerations

In structuring your case for trial, consider a psychological principle that debaters have long used for structuring arguments for debates. When structuring arguments, you should not argue "anticlimax climax," that is, you do not put the weakest argument first with the hope of building a crescendo. Rather, you put your strongest argument first, followed by weaker arguments in order of strength. The reason for this psychologically is a solid one. If you present your weakest arguments first and those subject to your persuasive abilities are not convinced, your credibility is damaged. That decreases receptiveness to your persuasiveness in presenting the next argument. By the time you reach your strongest argument, i.e., the one they clearly ought to believe, they will reject that one too. The losing pattern you have set will prevail. Therefore, you should always put your strongest arguments first.

Likewise, in structuring the order of witnesses for trial, try to call one of the strong witnesses first. Never start the case with a weak witness. The first two or three witnesses should be relatively strong, but this does not mean that you do not need a strong closing witness for your case. Usually if you have a plaintiff who is testifying in a personal injury case, he will be your closing witness. The same principle would apply to criminal trials. For example, if your defense in a criminal trial is insanity, then your very first witness should be the psychiatrist who has examined your client and can clearly and unequivocally testify that there was no way your client could have distinguished right from wrong at the moment of the crime. Counsel should be aware when structuring a case, that generally trials, like good plays, good books, or good shows have three parts. They have a beginning, a "muddle," and an end. And what do we mean by "muddle"? Jurors tend to remember some of the testimony presented at the beginning of the case, and more of the testimony presented at the end; but, what was presented during the time frame constituting the middle of the case is generally a blur, unless something striking or extremely important occurred. Recognizing this, if one has a weak witness who is essential to the case, call this witness during the middle of the case.

COMMENT: Remember, your case must have a strong opening to get the jury's attention, and a strong close, preferably a witness who presents a great deal of emotion-packed testimony.

There are other considerations an attorney should review when structuring his case. Generally, schedule as few witnesses as possible to testify. This leads to simplicity and reduces the chances of surprising twists or turns in testimony. If you can prove pain and suffering with one or two good lay witnesses, do it. Do not put on repetitious testimony. On the other hand, where there are neutral witnesses who do not necessarily help, but who will probably be called by the defense if you do fail to call them, by all means call these witnesses and leave the defense with nothing to put on, but the defendant himself. In the eyes of the jury, in a psychological sense, they will consider all of these witnesses yours and make a mental assumption that they were favorable to you. For this same reason when a defendant is pressed by his expert to allow him to testify out of turn, never object! Let him put his expert on the stand during the middle of your case. However, it is crucial that your expert has already testified before the defense expert and the principle of primacy is working. Make sure all of your favorable testimony has been presented before any defense witness is called. The most fundamental principle favoring the plaintiff in a civil case is primacy; use it to full advantage. The first impression of the evidence is very significant. Make sure that the first impression left by the opening witness is significant. Be sure that when you say "plaintiff rests," you have proven your case in a strong and positive manner and have ended on a high note.

§ 5.78 Developing your case theme

Every case should have a case theme. A case theme is the thread that runs through the entire case. It should be cemented in such a fashion that it becomes a psychological anchor. That is, when you present the case theme, the words ought to be said the same way with the same tone of voice, from the same spot, and with the same gestures everytime. This anchor or theme should run throughout your case.

What is a theme? A theme is a series of words said together, hopefully ten or fewer words, that changes why your client should win and win big.[74] Possible case themes should be contemplated from the time you start handling the file. Put a pocket in the file and deposit theme ideas there. Start thinking of the case by beginning with the phrase, "This is a case of . . . ". If you think of your case as "This is the case of . . . ", you will usually arrive at one or two or three words that set the tone of the case. This then becomes a case theme.

In addition, case themes need to be psychologically acceptable to the jurors. They should tie into Communication Principle 4 (People use ste-

[74] *See supra* § 1.47.

reotypes to organize their perceptions). For example, your case theme might encompass the idea that human life is valuable, a very acceptable value. Or, it might encompass the idea that just debts ought to be paid. Most everyone accepts this theme as a fact of life.

Two examples of case themes are appropriate to illustrate the point. In one case, a 1½-year-old child was partially blinded and brain damaged as a result of the osteopathic anestheseologist failing to promptly treat a laryngeal spasm. The evidence indicated that whether or not he failed to notice the onset of the laryngeal spasm, during the resuscitation attempt he had thrown instruments across the recovery room. Various themes were contemplated. One finally was chosen and worked very well, "This is the case of a professional who panicked." This phrase: "the professional panicked" was used throughout the trial very effectively. It was used as the case theme. It was the thread that held the case together. Every time it was used it was anchored. Another example is the case of a plant built by a large well-known construction company. The plant blew up and seriously burned one man and killed another. The evidence showed that in constructing the plant the defendant construction company had installed 132 valves backwards and violated known safety standards. They had installed valves which bleed volatile hydrocarbons directly into the atmosphere. The explosion occurred during an attempt to correct a bleed into the atmosphere. In that case, the theme was: "Instead of building an oil refinery they built a bomb." Throughout the case, the jury heard about the contractor who contracted to build a plant and instead built a bomb.

The knack for developing a case theme, like swimming or riding a bicycle, comes with practice. In some instances, such as a rear-end collision where the defendant admits liability, your theme may simply be a stock trade theme like the value of human life, or it may focus on the injury. For instance, if the case involves a man who had asymptomatic osteoarthritis made symptomatic by trauma, perhaps the theme should be: "This is the case of the man with the egg-like neck." But whatever themes you develop, each case should have a theme, it should be as short as possible, and it should sum up your case and your major proposition as to why your client should prevail.

§ 5.79 Use of impact words and phrases

In addition to using a case theme, be aware of impact words and phrases. The need to use them in presenting and structuring a case is overwhelming. For example, never tell the jury that the client was in an "accident." The word "accident" has a psychological connotation that indicates no one was at fault. Substitute the word "incident" instead. An advocate's choice of language should denote impact and strength. Your client was not "struck from the rear." Instead your client was "sitting at the red light when suddenly there was a horrendous crash. His neck was violently snapped backwards. It recoiled forward ripping and tearing the muscles and fibers of the neck. There was hemorrhage and bleeding. Ultimately this ripped and torn neck healed with scar tissue." Note the impact words and phrases and how they paint word pictures. Your client did not suffer whiplash; your client became a "neck cripple."

Of course, impact words and phrases can be applied to situations other than rear-end collision cases. If you are trying a flammable garment case, you might talk about the garment being made out of "magician's flash paper." If you are trying a DES case, you might talk about the drug "slinging the seeds of cancer in the system of an unborn baby." All of these impact words and phrases paint word pictures.

§ 5.80 Use of powerful language

While nonverbal considerations control better than 50% of the persuasiveness of the verbal message, you should not, when structuring your case, ignore verbal considerations.[75] Never talk about the case with "weak language." Weak language is language which denotes doubt about the speaker's position; that is why counsel should never use the phrases: "we allege," or "I submit," when discussing his position in a case. Never use phrases which indicate the statement to be your opinion rather than fact. Never say for example: "we think . . . " or "we believe . . .", and so on. It is not what you or the client believe that is significant; rather, it is what the evidence proves that is decisive. So, linguistically, discuss your case as though it is proven. Talk about it in terms of "the facts are . . . " and state your case in a positive manner.

When you are discussing the case linguistically, paint word pictures; the jury ought to be able to picture in their "mind's eye" what occurred. People tend to sort information through three primary channels: kinesthetic, auditory, and visual. If the case involves the death of a child who was struck by a truck, describe it in such a fashion that the child and the incident can be pictured. You want to talk about the weather, the time of day, what the child was doing before the incident, what the child

[75] *See supra* §§ 3.15 & 3.30.

looked like, what the child was wearing, and any other relevant information that will help the jury form a picture in their "minds' eye" of how the incident occurred. It is much easier for the jury to recall the details of an incident they have "seen" in their minds' eye. Remember, in painting a word picture that the more unique or vivid the impression, the more easily it will be recalled.

V. Simplifying the Case

§ 5.81 The psychological necessity for simplification

Psychological studies show that jurors really decide a case on one or two issues, three at the most. They simply ignore most of the remaining issues.[76]

If you are a plaintiff in a civil case having the burden of proof you should follow the salesman's rule of "KISS"; that is, "Keep It Simple Stupid." Most people are already overtaxed, uncertain, and groping for security. Too much information, too many issues, and too much complexity confuses them further. Creating more uncertainty will work against the plaintiff. Ultimately, if you fail to keep it simple, a confused jury will decide that in a case as complex as this one, you could not possibly have proven all the elements of each issue.

On the other hand, it is advantageous to take the opposite tact in a criminal case where the state has the burden of proving the defendant's guilt beyond a reasonable doubt. In defending the accused, make the case complex, raise as many issues as possible, confuse and confound the jury. Jurors are in an uncomfortable position; capitalize on the natural uncertainty of the situation. Psychologically, creating confusion can ultimately lead to a conclusion that the state failed to carry its burden.

Keeping it simple means avoiding unnecessary defendants. For example, in one very complex malpractice trial, plaintiff's attorney included as a defendant a hospital clearly not liable, and against whom he produced no evidence. After a powerful summation by plaintiff's counsel, the hospital's attorney simply stood before the jury, scratched his head and said, "I don't know why the plaintiff sued my client. Plaintiff's counsel has not even presented any evidence against my client." Obviously, plaintiff's counsel failed to keep it simple.

On the other hand, failing to include anyone who may have potentially

[76] *See generally* §§ 1.48–1.56.

contributed to the negligence creates an opportunity for the defendants to blame the "empty chair." Empty chair defenses can be extremely dangerous, particularly in a comparative negligence situation. Often, inexperienced counsel makes the mistake of not suing all potential defendants. For example, if counsel sues the physician for an adverse drug reaction, the physician will claim a failure to adequately warn on the part of the drug manufacturer. The physician may do this successfully unless the drug manufacturer is a named defendant. So while keeping it simple means suing as few defendants as possible and raising as few issues as possible, this consideration has to be counterbalanced by the "empty chair" defense. This is a difficult area and does require some fine judgment calls. Each case has its own unique facts, and must be analyzed individually. The attorney must ask himself whether this action is simplifying the case or whether this action is creating an "empty chair" defense. If it creates even the possibility of an "empty chair" defense, then by all means, name that defendant. You create a bargaining position by suing them now with the prospect of reaching some agreement later regarding realignment of the parties. This is often the wisest strategy in multidefendant litigation, especially in those situations where the facts are clear cut. Naming all potential defendants not only denies them the opportunity to point to the "empty chair," it also forces all parties to discuss the liability of the primary defendant.

§ 5.82 Issues selection

Issues selection is a process that is vital in both the civil and criminal case. If you are plaintiff in the civil case, you have the advantage of primacy. Because you go first, you can select the issues. Obviously, select issues on which you can win. Making the other side play in your ball park creates a home field advantage. If both the law and evidence are clearly in your favor, issues selection is simple: "did the defendant run a red light?" or "was the product unreasonably dangerous?" In such a situation, the defense will attempt to create collateral issues and try those issues as an integral part of your case. For example, "what color coat was plaintiff wearing when he was hit by the car?" or "what was the industry standard for the product?" or "how was the standard incorporated in government regulations?" Do not allow the defense to emphasize those types of collateral issues in the case.

COMMENT: Beware of collateral issues; the defense can win the case by creating confusion and doubt in the minds of the jurors. Be aware of the issue picking game and make sure the case is tried on the issues you have selected.

On the other hand, if you are defending a criminal case, the issue is always a simple one: "did the state bear their burden of proof?" The issue is not the guilt or innocence of the defendant. If you let the prosecution try the case on the issue of guilt or innocence you will inevitably lose as most jurors will presume the defendant guilty because he has already been indicted or charged by the D.A. Thus if you are defending a criminal case, you must establish the D.A.'s burden of proof as the issue, underline it, reinforce it, anchor it, and use every psychological technique possible to stress that issue.

Issue selection is an important part of the adversary process. Issues need to be verbally tied to the forthcoming jury charges; that is, frame your issues verbally so as to mirror the words which the judge will use in his charge to the jury.

Further, it is tremendously beneficial to tie case themes to issues. As with wording the case theme, wording the issue in terms more psychologically acceptable is important, i.e., tie in a preexisting belief system, stereotypes, and personalized generalizations. For example, in a products liabilty case, the theme should deal with the image of "the defendant who values money more than people," while the issue is: "did the defendant put safety ahead of profits?" Psychologically, everyone believes that safety should precede profits, that human life ought to have a higher worth than money.

§ 5.83 Discovery used to limit issues

As discussed previously, if you are defending a criminal case, multiple collateral issues may be a benefit. This is particularly true when you are defending a criminal case where the evidence indicates your client is guilty. The client may have admitted guilt to the police, then your best defense may be through the use of multiple collateral issues, to raise doubts and create confusion. This can be successful only because the prosecution has the burden of proof, a stiffer burden of proof than in a civil case. On the other hand, a plaintiff in a civil case seeks to limit the issues to avoid confusion and doubt in the minds of the jurors.

A major goal of the discovery process is limiting the issues. Depositions are taken; interrogatories are filed; and requests for admissions are sent to discover where the other side stands and what they will or will not admit. An excellent tool not previously discussed, to limit the issues on discovery, is the motion for summary judgment. Often, a motion for summary judgment will smoke out information that routine use of interrogatories, requests for admissions, and depositions will not. A plaintiff's motion for summary judgment puts the burden on the defendant to prove that there is an issue of fact inherent in the case. The defense must come forward with affidavits or other proof to substantiate the existence of a factual issue. If there is no fact at issue, summary judgment will be granted. Therefore, motions for summary judgment can be used as a discovery tool to eliminate issues.

All discovery techniques should aim toward the goal of eliminating issues. The fewer the number of issues, the fewer the problems that can suddenly arise, thus making it easier to try the case. Plaintiff's attorney should keep in mind that the goal is issue elimination. Ask questions designed to eliminate issues and to bring out the defendant's position and collateral issues.

§ 5.84 —Use of stipulations to eliminate proof of issues

Stipulations are used to eliminate the necessity of proving issues, thereby further limiting the number of issues to be decided by the jury at trial. For example, it is always to the plaintiff's advantage if the amount of the medical bills can be stipulated and these should be submitted to the defense early in the case. This is also true of loss of wages, salary at the time of the injury, and if possible, the total amount of past lost wages. Thorough discovery early in the case should provide sufficient evidence to convince the opposing counsel to stipulate to this as fact. Another potential issue ripe for stipulation is course and scope of employment, frequently confirmed through the use of a request for admission. Through proper discovery this type of issue should be eliminated.

Prior to trial, it is advantageous to check the list of facts to be proven at trial in the hope of obtaining a stipulation from opposing counsel. Stipulations are an advantage to both sides.

§ 5.85 —Use of summary judgment

As mentioned previously, summary judgment is another excellent tool that can be used to simplify a civil case. Summary judgments, of course, are not available in criminal cases. Under the Federal Rules, partial summary judgments are available. In addition, partial summary judgments either by statute or by judicial decision have become available in most state courts in civil proceedings. A summary judgment may be obtained not only as to general areas such as liability, but also concerning specific areas. Summary judgments can be used with regard to such specific issues as course and scope of employment, seaman status, and other such issues in most jurisdictions.

VI. The Trial as a Unit

§ 5.86 Setting goals generally

As the trial attorney contemplates litigation, he sets a goal for every action he will take, as well as specific goals for each individual aspect of the process, including voir dire, opening statement, direct and cross-examinations, and summation.

§ 5.87 —Voir dire

The primary goal in voir dire is to select an unbiased jury; that is, to select a jury where you at least have a chance to win. There are other goals in voir dire, such as establishing rapport, obtaining information, using the information in exercising peremptory challenges, gaining commitments, obtaining a pattern of agreement, and educating the jury.[77]

§ 5.88 —Opening statement

The purpose of an opening statement is to take full advantage of the principle of primacy. This is the jury's first impression of the case. The opening statement should create an impression that you are right, that you ought to win, and you ought to win big (Principle 3: Perceptions are organized and structured within a brief period of time). If you can successfully accomplish this goal you have enlisted a powerful psychological aid because you have placed primacy on your side.

---

[77] *See generally* Chapter 6, *Selecting the Jury: A Two-Way Communication Process*.

§ 5.89 —Direct examination

Your goal in direct examination is to present your evidence in such a manner that the jury will remember it. This includes decisions regarding the order of witnesses and the order of proof as discussed earlier. The goal in direct examination is only achieved by the presentation of evidence with impact.

§ 5.90 —Cross-examination

The goal in cross-examination is to create the impression that the other party's witnesses have not hurt your case.[78] Generally, only on television is it possible to completely devastate the witness and totally discredit his testimony. Your goal during the cross-examination is to state your case, by preventing the other side from creating such an unfavorable impression that you lose the winning edge previously established through achieving your goals in voir dire, opening, and direct examination.

§ 5.91 —Summation

Summation is your chance to paint word pictures and to integrate the evidence with impact. It is where you bring together the evidence, the law, and the emotional elements of your case. The bottom line goal of summation is to motivate the jury to take the action required by your client's interest, to return a verdict in your favor.

§ 5.92 The integration of goals; the whole trial concept

It should be obvious that each of the goals described previously[79] must be well integrated, because each one is dependent upon the success of the others and the failure of one could lead to the demise of the whole.

What we are really talking about is the concept of the "whole trial." If you attend enough continuing legal education seminars, you will hear the same speaker discussing different phases of the trial. On one occasion the speaker may tell you that summation is the most important part of the trial while on another occasion the same speaker will tell a different audience that the opening statement is the most important part of the trial. These statements are not inconsistent. When that individual phase of the

---

[78] *See generally* Chapter 9, *Cross-Examination: Controlling the Case*.

[79] *See supra* § 5.87, *Voir Dire*, § 5.88, *Opening Statement*, § 5.89, *Direct Examination*, § 5.90, *Cross-Examination*, and § 5.91, *Summation*.

trial is taking place, that phase, at that moment, is the most important part of the trial.

A chain is only as strong as its weakest link. So too, are your goals during the trial. Your failure to achieve any one of the essential goals can cause you to lose the case. The trial attorney may give a brilliant explanation in opening statement of why his client ought to prevail. He might follow that with a superb presentation of the evidence, a devastating cross-examination, and a tremendously motivating summation. However, if the goal of voir dire was not achieved, that is, you failed to pick a jury which is at least going to give you a chance to win, the whole trial will be lost. The same is true regarding each goal in the trial. Pick a fair jury, but fail to motivate them at opening statement, or fail to take full advantage of primacy and you will probably lose.

VII. Creating a Presence

§ 5.93 Visual impact

Jurors form their initial impressions during the first four minutes. Their assessment is based primarily on their visual perceptions. They tend to accept the visual and nonverbal cues while rejecting the verbal cues. Thus, based on the first two communication principles, that communication is based on perception and people actively try to make sense out of their environment, a trial lawyer must be aware of visual and nonverbal cues which will be perceived by the jurors in the courtroom environment. This includes dress, gestures, facial expressions and all forms of nonverbal behavior. Remember that the perceptual process incorporates verbal, vocal, and nonverbal variables in reaching an initial perceptual judgment.

Initially the jurors will try to organize and structure the perceptual cues they perceive (Principle 4: People use stereotypes to organize their perceptions). Visual impact is important and is something that must be considered. Visual impact regarding the attorney in the courtroom goes beyond his dress, although dress is very significant. Counsel should match customs of the area in which the case is being tried. This means taking into account the personalized generalizations and stereotypes that are probably existing in the minds of the jurors. In most jurisdictions, the male attorney is expected to dress conservatively in a pin-striped suit. Females are expected to fulfill a similar stereotype by wearing a tailored suit. If he or she dresses conservatively and looks like a successful attorney and matches the jurors perception of a successful attorney, they will perceive that he or she is a successful attorney. Successful attorneys, jurors assume, only handle winning cases. Remember also Principle 5: People tend to see others as similar to themselves, and Principle 9: People are more easily influenced by others they perceive as similar to themselves. Dressing "to be liked" includes some degree of identification with the jurors. Many jurors may come to the courtroom in sport and casual clothes. Generally, it would be inappropriate for the attorney to wear sport clothes. What the attorney may do, if the attorney knows the jury will consist predominantly of blue-collar workers, is to change his style of dress ever so slightly so that he is more easily identified with the working class. All this, of course, varies from region to region. The more the jurors perceive the attorney and the client as being like themselves, the more they will like the attorney and the client and the easier it is going to be to persuade them of the veracity of the attorney's point of view.

Visual impact is concerned not only with what the attorney wears, but with everything about the attorney that can be perceived visually. This includes his facial expressions, his gestures, his touching of the client, his mannerisms. You need to be aware of this and be in control of your nonverbal behavior in order to live up to and fit the model or expectations of the jurors of what a successful attorney ought to look and act like. All of this has to do with creating visual perception.

§ 5.94 —Jury observance of the trial lawyer

Jurors attempt to make sense of their environment and reduce uncertainty (Principle 2: People actively try to make sense out of their environment). The attorney should do everything in his power to aid the jurors in achieving their goals. It is very disconcerting to jurors, and the attorney can suffer a lack of personal credibility, if he is seen having an altercation with members of his staff. Similarly, the jurors are closely watching his relationship with the opposing counsel. Unlike lawyers, laymen do not understand that advocacy is a process we engage in, that it is not a way of life. Jurors do not understand that we really do not necessarily dislike the other side or their attorney because of the position they have taken. Jurors do not understand how the two attorneys after battling in the courtroom all day can go to dinner together or have a drink together and discuss settlement of the case that same night. The attorney should never be seen conferring with or appearing friendly to the opposing counsel in front of the jurors. To do so would be conduct which fails to fulfill the jurors' existing belief system. It creates dissidence in the jurors' minds and can become a bit of extraneous information to which they can attach all types of unwarranted inferences. Therefore, no matter what the out of court personal relationship with the opposing attorney might be, do not appear friendly with him or interact with him in front of the jury. Do not take the chance that such gestures can be misinterpreted. This is particularly true if you are defense counsel in a criminal case or plaintiff's counsel in a civil case. In both instances jurors consider counsel as an outsider going up against the establishment. To a degree you are perceived as Don Quixote and your case is right and just. In most instances, you are going to ask the jurors to return a verdict against the establishment, to refuse to send an innocent man to jail, to find that a product was indeed unsafe, to find that a drug was harmful instead of beneficial, and so forth.

On the other hand, if you are either the prosecutor or counsel for the insurance company, you may want to appear more friendly with the opposing counsel. You may want to put your hand on his shoulder, and in essence bring him back into society. The prosecutor or insurance counsel is telling the jury in a nonverbal manner and on an unconscious level, that it is okay for this attorney to take on the state or the large corporations. The implication is that "we really are friends, and he really doesn't mean what he is saying." In essence, it is a very subtle way to attack opposing counsel's credibility with the jury.

In response to such a tactic, defense counsel in a criminal case, or plaintiff's counsel in a civil case, must verbally, or at least visually, emphatically reject any friendly advances from the adversary in front of the jury. You must not allow him to deprive you of your image as Don Quixote taking on the corporation, the image that you sincerely believe the state is wrong in prosecuting your client, or that this corporation built automobiles that explode when they are tapped from the rear.

§ 5.95 —Jury observance of counsel's relationship with judge

Most jurors are authoritarians, indeed there is a little bit of authoritarianism in all of us. We have been taught by school teachers and parents to respect authority. The judge, to most jurors, symbolizes authority in the courtroom. He is at the head of the judicial family. He is colloquially speaking the father of the judicial family and he has the last word.

Therefore, whenever possible, you as a trial attorney should attempt to link to the judge's authority as this will increase your credibility with the jurors (Principle 11: The perception of credibility increases with the perception of authority). The highest authority in the courtroom is the judge. The jurors' perception of you as an authority is greatly increased if it appears the judge is favorable to you. Many jurors are actually looking for cues from the judge as to how he wants the case decided.

Always be courteous to the judge. Any arguments with the judge on technical matters should take place outside of both the sight and hearing of the jury. Never indicate in front of the jury that you are in disagreement with the judge. Even if you feel the judge has been ridiculously improper, you should take advantage of his authority. Always compliment him in opening and closing statements as to what a good judge he is and how right he is in his instructions on the law. No matter how he rules during the course of the trial, never appear in any way hurt or disgruntled by his rulings, rather, appear to agree with his ruling. Most jurors are not cognizant of the significance between an objection that is "sustained" and an objection that is "overruled." No matter what the ruling and what you think of the ruling always smile and say: "Thank you, your honor," and the jury will perceive that the judge agreed with you. That is all that counts! Your relationship with the judge must appear to the jury to be friendly at all times.

Experienced trial lawyers have all faced situations, sometimes in other jurisdictions, where the judge has decided in advance to attack the trial lawyer in front of the jury. Faced with that difficult situation, it may be impossible to link to the judge and the only hope is to become, in the eyes of the jury, the "underdog." Attempt in every possible way to let the jury know that you are trying to be fair, that you are attempting to try your case, that you are trying to present your evidence, and the judge is being unfair and cutting you off. This is called the "wounded fawn" approach. It may not be much, but it is all you have to work with when the judge is unfair to your cause.

§ 5.96 —Jury observance of attorney's relationship with client

Not only are the jurors observing your relationship with the judge and opposing counsel, they are also observing your relationship with your client. This observation takes place while the trial is in process, in the elevators, in the hallways, and even outside of the courthouse. You certainly want the jury to like your client. Based on Principle 9: (People are more easily influenced by others they perceive as similar to themselves), remember that people decide what is appropriate behavior based on what they see others do in a similar situation. A classic example of this principle is the man standing on a street corner looking up. Soon, others are standing nearby, also looking up. We do what others do and what we see others doing. This theory of social proof encompasses the concept that we see an action as more appropriate when we see others doing it. Therefore, jurors will tend to like your client, if they see other people who like your client. It is important that they see your client surrounded with affectionate family members and it is certainly important that you appear at all times to like your client. This includes talking to your client, putting your hand on his shoulder, and generally showing in any way, both visually and nonverbally, that you really care about the client.

If the attorney feels that he cannot convince the jury that this relationship is real and sincere, he ought to consider not trying this client's case. Unfortunately, the attorney's dislike of the client is, after all, also perceivable by the jury. Be aware that you have to communicate your likability of the client in a nonverbal manner to the jury.

Chapter 6

SELECTING THE JURY: A TWO-WAY COMMUNICATION PROCESS

III. Obtaining Information

KLUWER LITIGATION LIBRARY REFERENCES

JEANS, LITIGATION: Chapter 6, *Voir Dire*.

JOYE & LOVETT, DRUNK DRIVING: THE TRIAL WORKBOOK, THE TRIAL SOURCEBOOK, THE TRIAL NOTEBOOK: Chapter 105, *Juror Questionnaire*; Chapter 106, *Voir Dire*.

PREISER & PREISER, HANDLING SOFT TISSUE INJURY CASES: Chapter 7, *How to Handle Problem Situations*; Chapter 10, *Psychology of the Trial*; Chapter 11, *Selecting the Jury*.

I. Goals

§ 6.01 Goals in voir dire; picking an unbiased jury

There is one overall goal in voir dire; that is to pick an unbiased jury so that you have a chance of winning your case.[1] It is a goal that is statutorily mandated and one that is recognized by the courts. If bias is obvious, you may have a juror eliminated for cause. If the bias is not obvious, you may have to use a peremptory challenge to eliminate the juror. Although there can be no doubt that your overall goal is to pick an unbiased jury, there are several additional important goals that need to be accomplished in voir dire.

§ 6.02 —Establishing rapport

Voir dire is the only time during the trial when the attorney speaks to the jurors and the jurors have the opportunity to respond. This unique time is one of the most vital parts of the trial. It is the time to establish an initial rapport with each individual juror.

That goal, establishing rapport with the jurors, is an essential goal, if not the most essential goal, that you wish to accomplish during the voir dire. The purpose of communication with the jury is to engage the conscious mind while communicating to the unconscious mind. Chapter 1 established the basis for the fact that the unconscious mind accumulates all sorts of information. Chapter 4 established the basis for the fact that information accumulated by the unconscious mind is also used in the decision-making process. It is for these reasons that during voir dire, although the conscious mind is engaged by a series of questions, it is your communication to the unconscious mind that makes the difference. It is your tone of voice, the nature of your eye contact, how you move, how you ask the question, and particularly how you listen to the response that communicate to the juror.

§ 6.03 —Obtaining information

A secondary goal during voir dire is obtaining information about the jurors and their attitude toward your client, the case, and other general issues. It must be obtained not only to form the basis for challenges for cause, but for the intelligent use of your peremptory challenges. This goal can be accomplished if the proper vocal and nonverbal cues are

[1] *See generally supra* § 5.87, *Voir dire*.

given to the jurors. How to obtain information from jurors, how to get them to open up, how to get them to talk, and how to get them to give information in narrative form will form part of the techniques described in this chapter.

§ 6.04 —Using information

Not only must you obtain information from the juror, but you must use that information intelligently. To use the information effectively, first establish the profile of an ideal juror, including the community stereotypes and belief systems that are going to be in the minds of the jurors. This profile can be established by the attorney himself or in conjunction with a social scientist. The scientist offers a different perspective for he looks for behavioral cues based upon research that suggests how jurors will make decisions. This type of assistance in a trial, particularly a major trial, is extremely beneficial because it offers a more objective point of view and is based upon validated principles and research from the literature. This process needs to be organized so that it can be used effectively during voir dire.

It is recommended that during voir dire, even in the more minor cases, you have someone from your office sitting at the table taking down individual information on each juror in some particular format. It is only possible for the trial attorney to establish a rapport with the jurors, to relate to them, to listen to their answers, to ask intelligent questions, and to make judgments about them while information is being gathered so that it can be intelligently used. The key facts regarding each juror, such as occupation and general impressions, can be kept in a box-like grid drawn on a sheet of paper and corresponding to the juror's seating arrangement in the jury box. In addition, one ought to work up a profile indicating the variables on which each juror will be rated. The rating system can be based on personality variables, occupational variables, geographic variables, and verbal, vocal, and nonverbal variables. These six variables can constitute, if you desire, a ten point scoring system, so that each juror can be rated on the basis of one to ten as to that juror's desirability.[2]

Prior to the voir dire, you should establish guidelines for the selection or elimination of jurors. They can be drawn up by a professional or someone on your staff with extensive experience in jury selection so that

---

[2] *See infra* § 6.49, *Using a systematic selection process.*

you will feel confident with the guidelines if you do not draw them up yourself.

§ 6.05 —Obtaining commitment

People have a strong need to be consistent (Communication Principle 8). In 1968, Knox and Inkster[3] performed a study regarding the placing of bets at a racetrack on two separate occasions. The results were the same on both occasions. Just after placing the bet, people were much more confident of their horse's chance of winning than they were immediately before laying down the bet even though nothing had actually changed with regard to the horse's chance of winning. It is just that once the people had placed the bet, they needed to be consistent with the action that they had taken. In essence the bet was a commitment, and once we have made a commitment we tend to behave in a manner consistent with that commitment.

Once people have made a public commitment in writing, the need to be consistent with that commitment is even greater.[4] Let's examine the success experienced by the communist Chinese captors of American prisoners of war during the Korean conflict. They attained much of their success by getting American prisoners to make a written commitment, of any nature, stating something that was even partially favorable to communism. Two prominent social psychologists, Martin Deutsch and Harold Gerard,[5] conducted an experiment with groups of college students. In one experiment, the college students were asked to estimate the length of lines they were shown. The first group committed themselves publicly to their answers, the second wrote their answers on a "magic" erasing pad—the type that erases itself, and the third committed themselves privately. The results indicated that those who committed themselves privately gave up their incorrect estimates easily, while those committed publicly and those committed in writing that was erased later were much more dogged in maintaining their estimates despite contradictory information. Thus it can be seen that the need to be consistent with commitments, particularly if those commitments are in writing, can be a very persuasive psychological motivation.

---

[3] Knox & Inkster, *Post Decisional Dissonance at Post Time*, 8 J. PERSONALITY & SOC. PSYCHOLOGY 319 (1968).

[4] *See supra* Chapter 2, *Persuasive Strategies in the Courtroom*.

[5] Deutsch & Gerard, *A Study of Normative and Informational Social Influences Upon Individual Judgment*, 5 J. ABNORMAL & SOC. PSYCHOLOGY 629 (1955).

It is apparent that on any crucial issue it is necessary to get commitments from the jury during voir dire. These commitments should relate to what are called "red flag issues," those which are crucial to your case and to which a juror's commitment is essential. For example, if the law and the evidence are clearly in your favor, get a commitment from the jurors that they will follow the law and the evidence. Sometimes the peculiar facts of the case require more specific commitments. If you are dealing with a situation where you have a rear end collision causing serious injury, even though there was not a great deal of contact between the two vehicles, you need a commitment from the jurors that if the evidence shows that a light impact can cause a serious injury that they will accept that fact. Whatever the special issue in your case, you need to obtain a commitment from the jurors that they will follow the law regarding that issue and that if the evidence supports you, they are committed to decide in your favor.

§ 6.06 —Obtaining a pattern of positive answers

At the close of the voir dire you should have established a series of "yes" answers, in other words, questions asked of the jurors to which the answer is obviously "yes." For instance, will they follow the law as given to them by the judge? Will they follow the evidence from the stand and decide the case only on that evidence? Do they believe in the jury system as a fair way of settling disputes? Do they believe in the sanctity of the rule of law? Can they pay attention to the evidence as presented in bits and pieces? Can they be equally fair to both parties in the lawsuit? This is a series of questions to which almost any juror will automatically answer "yes". These "yes" answers establish a pattern of agreement. This communicates on the unconscious level that he, the juror, is in agreement with you. This positive pattern should then be anchored in the minds of the jury. It is valuable to anchor a "yes" response given by a juror by using one consistent nonverbal regulating cue. Such a cue might be nodding your head, smiling, clearing your throat, or any verbal response in a tone of voice that says thank you. These anchoring cues are positive rewarding nonverbal cues. When you anchor a "yes" response by rewarding the juror with some behavior, you are classically conditioning that "yes" response to be a repeated pattern. Let him know that he is telling you exactly what you want to know. If you have already established rapport by using proper pacing and getting the juror to like you, he will want to give you this "yes" response even more. If the juror does not give you this "yes" response at this point, it may be that you have not yet established sufficient rapport.

§ 6.07 —Educating the jurors

In addition to communicating with the jurors on the unconscious level, you must, of course, communicate with the jurors on a conscious level. You should communicate to the jurors the entire nature of your case—the points against your case as well as its positive side. Some years ago, when the Association of Trial Lawyers of America held its midwinter convention in London, a number of English barristers attended a series of lectures on voir dire examination. The panel of barristers was then asked to comment on the differences between voir dire in America and voir dire in criminal trials in England. (In England, jury trials are now reserved predominantly for criminal and libel cases.) The statement made by the senior barrister succinctly addressed the importance of effective communication during voir dire. He answered: "In England, when we have completed voir dire, the case has just begun; but in America when you fellows have completed voir dire the case is all over." By the close of the voir dire, you should have brought out every salient point about the nature of the case, who is going to testify, and what the evidence will show; any weak points that you know of will be best presented by you rather than your opponent. In other words, the jury needs to be educated completely about the case.

§ 6.08 Education as it relates to primacy

The reason for the need to accomplish this goal in voir dire lies in Communication Principle 3 (Perceptions are organized and structured within a brief period of time). Remember that first impressions are formed within the first three to four minutes and that under the principle of primacy, first impressions count. Once the juror has a first impression of the case in his mind he will tend to refer to that impression and reject information presented to the contrary (Principle 6: People attempt to maintain their original perceptions regardless of contradictory information). As the plaintiff in a civil case, you present your arguments first and, therefore, have primacy on your side. Primacy is on your side during the voir dire because the defendant has not yet had an opportunity to say a word to the jury. Therefore, you need to educate the jury about the case, its nature, the issues, and the reasons why you should be awarded damages before the defendant has a chance to diffuse, in any way, the impact of your presentation.

II. The Means of Accomplishing the Goals of Voir Dire

§ 6.09 Establishing rapport: pacing prospective jurors

Remember Principle 5: "People tend to see others as similar to themselves," Principle 9: "People are more easily influenced by others they perceive as similar to themselves," and Principle 10: "People are more easily influenced by people they like." Knowing this, if we can appear like the jurors, to any degree possible, and if we get them to like us, it is reasonable to assume that they will like our clients. In addition, if on a nonverbal level (through mood transference), we actually like the jurors and can transmit that feeling to them, they will reciprocate. That is the essence of establishing rapport. It is important to know that the feeling of genuinely liking the jurors and establishing a sincere rapport with them is actually a prerequisite to pacing. It is impossible to pace someone on an artificial or manipulative level. In other words, pacing is a direct result of your having empathy with the jurors. It is seeing the world through their eyes or stepping into their shoes. It cannot work unless it is genuine. Anyone who reads about the concept of pacing and then attempts it purely as a technique will discover that it does not work. The ability to feel the mood and have genuine empathy for the jurors is a very important part of working and making pacing effective.

Rapport is a similarity of feelings, rhythm, and style, and it occurs predominantly on an unconscious level. The question is: "How during voir dire do you establish this rapport?"[6] It is by the use of the technique of pacing that, on an unconscious level, we cause the jurors to perceive us as being like them. This technique must be applied to each juror individually as he is being questioned. Pacing is a very powerful technique and works effectively because it takes advantage of the propensity of people to see other people as being like themselves. In other words, while you are communicating with the conscious mind through the verbal content of your questions, you should also be communicating on an unconscious level through the technique of pacing. You can then check your pacing to see whether it has been established by leading the jurors. If you are able to lead the jurors in their nonverbal behavior, then you know you have jurors with whom you have established rapport.

---

[6] *See supra* §§ 2.19–2.52, for a detailed discussion of the technique of pacing.

§ 6.10 —Using their words

Verbal pacing is one of the key elements in the technique of pacing. By this we mean that you listen to their words and phrases, and then use them in the same way as they use the words. For example, if a juror says, "Now, the bottom line is . . ."; the attorney says: "OK, so what I understand the bottom line to be is . . . ." The attorney will hear key words used by the juror (e.g., "higher up" may be used to define something). Rather than change the phrase (e.g., "it seems to be the highest piece . . ."), the attorney ought to use "higher up." Verbal pacing can also be accomplished by using the same "class" of words. A juror who is visually-oriented and uses the word "focus" can be paced by responding with "let's look at this." Both "look" and "focus" represent visual predicates.

§ 6.11 —Imitating their body movements

In addition to verbally pacing the jurors, pace their gestures as well. This a crucial part of the pacing process. Make eye contact with the jurors; match their body movements and their facial expressions. If they are sitting with their arms folded, fold your arms. If a juror is sitting there with his hand on his chin, in an unobtrusive manner put your hand on your chin. If the juror pushes his hair back, perform a similar action. It is important to know that when you subtly and sincerely pace or match the behavior of a juror it will not be picked up on the conscious level. In fact, you will find that as you observe people, they very unconsciously mimic and match each other's movements when they have a rapport with each other. Indeed, the entire basis of pacing the juror is that pacing is a common result when people have good rapport; it is not subject to manipulative behavior.

§ 6.12 —Copying voice levels and patterns of jurors

Each individual has a different voice level and pattern of speaking. While we do not want to sound like a mimic (therefore do not copy it exactly), we should attempt to match a juror's voice level to some degree. In other words, we should modulate our voice tones to blend in with those of the jurors. If the juror has a deep voice, counsel should talk in a deeper voice than normal; if the juror has a high-pitched voice, we should raise our vocal level slightly without sounding artificial.

One of the most important aspects is to attempt to match the particular rhythm pattern of a particular voice. If someone is a slow speaker, he will be much more comfortable if your pace or your rhythm of voice slows down. If you happen to be speaking quickly you may find that not only do you make him uncomfortable, but you may produce an increase in his level of anxiety. Conversely, if a juror talks at a fast rate and you tend to ask questions slowly, he may be telling you that he would like to move more quickly toward the bottom line. You should, of course, quicken your pace. As you are questioning each juror, matching the voice rhythm probably is a more important ability than matching tone of voice.

In addition to voice levels, everyone has a pattern of speaking, that is, a certain way of taking a breath and having words follow that breath during exhalation. We all have a certain pattern of pausing and with practice you can learn to identify patterns of speech and patterns of pauses. Stop and identify the juror with whom you are speaking in terms of his speech patterns and pauses. Then, as with the other areas like verbal and nonverbal matching, match his vocal cues. Vocal matching will help complete the pacing of the juror.

§ 6.13 Leading the jurors

After you have established rapport with the jurors through pacing, you need to check the extent of that rapport. You check rapport by leading the juror.[7] You will find that after you have paced someone successfully, you can make a gesture and they will unconsciously follow that gesture. Take, for example, the story about the professor who had food in his beard. He was successfully paced and then led until he unconsciously stroked his chin and knocked the food from his beard. This is what is meant by leading. Check the success of your pacing by implementing a new behavior to see if jurors follow your lead. All of this is encompassed in the feeling of rapport that should be continuously building between you and each juror as the questioning process is taking place.

§ 6.14 —Confirming rapport with jurors

We confirm juror rapport, as described above, by leading. Only if we can effectively lead a juror do we have rapport. In addition, there is a certain feeling that takes place between two people; it is a feeling in the pit of the stomach, a sixth sense. But it is there and you should use it. The need to confirm rapport with jurors is one reason why you, the trial lawyer and no one else, should make the final decision on picking jurors.

---

[7] *See supra* § 2.40.

You alone know whether or not you really have rapport with that juror. He may be, on paper, the perfect juror. He may fit the profile made up by the sociologist, psychologist, or communication expert sitting at your table. That expert may be telling you to take that juror, but if you have not established rapport with him and do not have a good feeling about him, do not select him.

§ 6.15 —Interpreting images of jurors

This is what has been referred to by some attorneys as the "hound dog" approach. The "hound dog" approach is basically very simple but effective. If you ever see two hound dogs that do not know one another meet on the street, observe what happens. First, there is prolonged staring at one another until one dog finally makes the first move. If they do not like one another, the hair stands up on the back of their necks and they growl at each other. It is an instinctive reaction. The same thing happens with human beings. If you have a feeling that you do not like a person, even if you have no real reason for that feeling, then by all means do not select that juror.

"Reading the jurors," as any trial lawyer will tell you, is always difficult. Numerous books have been written on body language. You are told to excuse a juror if he is folding his arms. However, he may be folding his arms because it is cold, because he is more comfortable like that, or for any other number of reasons, none of which have anything to do with whether he likes or dislikes you or your client. Much of the research that has been done in the area of nonverbal communication tells us that although there may be general patterns, there are idiosyncratic differences. Therefore, when we talk about somebody folding his arms, it should not be interpreted as any particular cue. The best use of nonverbal communication is the observation of what is considered normal behavior and those types of behavior that deviate from the norm.

It should be kept in mind that there are some subculture variations whereby people of different ethnic groups and subcultures have been trained from birth to avoid eye contact as a means of showing deference and respect to an individual. Thus, what is normal for one group may not be normal for another.

Remember that jurors are continuously assessing information in the courtroom. While forming impressions, they are assessing information on all levels. The attorney is doing the same thing. We are jointly forming impressions. The question here is: "Is the impression that you, the trial lawyer, are forming of the juror an accurate one?" Theories of personality suggest that all jurors function similarly, but that each juror's assessment is individualized with respect to linking together traits, stereotypes, and belief systems. In essence, we each have "a private theory" of what people are like, and jurors are confident of their ability as "amateur psychologists." They engage in detective work, assembling all types of information, and then, through "free association," expand their information about us while we are doing the very same thing about them. Remember, in checking the accuracy of our impressions of jurors, there are two major considerations.

First, we must take into account that we are judging a person who is in a very strange situation. He is experiencing situational anxiety and has a great need to reduce uncertainty. This can affect his choice of words, speech pattern, facial expressions, and indeed all other cues we are receiving. Second, we must consider the sociological makeup of the juror. For this we can look at his ethnic background, his occupation, and other factors determining what we think he would be like. Thus we are looking at the juror and assessing him through our own value system, our own belief system, our own conscious stereotypes, and free associations.

It is crucial that the trial lawyer see others accurately and assess different stimuli and translate those into a meaningful picture in a very short period of time. This can only occur by understanding the process of impression formation,[8] then applying that information to increase your accuracy in forming impressions of others. Remember, too, that the behavior of others, for many reasons, can be neatly designed to deceive us. In selecting a juror we must accurately perceive his various traits, sometimes based on occupation and other demographic information alone.

§ 6.16 —Meaning of overt actions by jurors

In the early 1970's, a major malpractice case was tried over a period of six weeks by the attorney-author in New Orleans, Louisiana. During voir dire, panelist John Doe smiled at plaintiff's counsel and, looking him in the eye, gave all the right answers. During direct and cross-examination, plaintiff's counsel looked over at the jury to check the effect of his questioning and juror John Doe was nodding his head in agreement. If there ever was a juror that appeared to be in the plaintiff's corner, it was John Doe. After six weeks of trial, a substantial verdict was ren-

[8] *See supra* Chapter 1, *Impression Formation in the Courtroom*.

dered in favor of the plaintiff. Fortunately, a nine to three verdict was sufficient to carry the day, for John Doe was the ringleader for the defense.

About a year later, following an automobile accident, John Doe sought out this same plaintiff's counsel to represent him. Mr. Doe indicated he thought counsel was the most competent attorney he had ever seen, that being the reason he sought his representation now. He explained his vote in favor of the defendant a year earlier simply by saying he felt people should not sue doctors and certainly should not bring in "hired guns" (the term for out-of-towners) to testify. Further questioning indicated that Mr. Doe wanted to get on the jury so as to be in a position to protect the physician. He had formed the impression from the very beginning, based on his own belief system and stereotyping, that doctors could do no wrong.

We need to be very careful of any juror who breaks the social mask with counsel regularly. If a juror appears to overtly favor you, beware. Even gregarious people in the strange setting of a courtroom tend to be reserved. Generally, because of the formal setting, they do not establish an open, warm relationship; they do not telegraph their feelings openly. When this does occur it very well may be a conscious effort on their part to influence you and, under most conceivable circumstances, the reason for this conscious effort is to influence you incorrectly.

Discussions with numerous lawyers who have tried many cases over the years bring forth many instances of a juror who broke the social mask, who was overtly friendly only to cast his vote later in opposition to that particular counsel and his client.

Trial lawyers need to develop the skills necessary to accurately assess their impression formation abilities. Like the development of any skill, this skill is best developed by learning the problems inherent in the process and being aware of the pitfalls. We need to practice developing these skills constantly in order to check our accuracy.

COMMENT: Counsel should be aware that jurors frequently experience situational anxiety in the courtroom and therefore they may not behave normally. This knowledge will help us evaluate more accurately the verbal cues the juror is giving. By learning to analyze what they are like apart from the courtroom environment, we become more accurate in our impression formation of potential jurors.

Finally, we must realize that we are viewing jurors through our own rose-colored glasses of prejudice. Our belief system, stereotypes, and trade associations play a role in the evaluation process. Being aware of this fact and understanding that we can and will make errors in accurately assessing jurors helps us to increase our level of proficiency. No one will be accurate all of the time in assessing jurors. However, if we are aware of the principle discussed here, we can substantially increase our accuracy. We will become like the marksman who, when he started learning to shoot, could hardly hit the target. While we still will not hit a bull's-eye every time, we can certainly, with study and practice, substantially increase our accuracy and hit the bull's-eye more often.

§ 6.17 Evaluating eye and body movement patterns

In evaluating jurors during voir dire, keep in mind that they are assessing information through the three basic areas: they are simultaneously assessing information at the vocal, visual, and nonverbal levels. Realizing this, we know that we cannot accurately interpret a juror's reaction to us while singling out any one trait such as body position, body movement, or eye contact. We, as trial lawyers, assess the information that is available to discover if, in addition to communicating with the juror's conscious mind, we are reaching his unconscious mind through the kinesthetic, visual, and auditory channels.[9]

More important than eye movements, the trial lawyer needs to interpret eye contact. Obviously, if a juror refuses to make eye contact with the lawyer for any length of time, this juror may not be able to relate to that particular lawyer. There is clearly dissonance between two people if one cannot look the other in the face.[10]

At various times during the questioning of the jurors, counsel should try to make eye contact with them. The significance of making eye contact is that the potential juror becomes classified as one whom you relate to. However, the number of times eye contact is made is not important.

---

[9] *See supra* Chapter 4, *Decision-Making Process of Jurors*, for a discussion of eye movement patterns.

[10] *Id.*

The question is whether eye contact can be maintained for a significant period of time.[11] Thus, it is the duration of the eye contact that is of the utmost importance.

COMMENT: An example of the duration of eye contact as an indicator of the degree of rapport can be seen by watching a couple in love. They seem to stare at one another for endless periods of time. They have almost 100% rapport. They are in love. They signify this by the duration of their eye contact.

As we are interpreting eye contact, eye duration, eye movements, and body movements, we are still in the process of pacing the jurors. If we feel we have established rapport with the juror and have successfully paced the juror, then we may attempt to lead him to see if he will follow our gestures as we stand there questioning him.

§ 6.18 —Confirming jury rapport through use of chosen phrases

As we proceed with the voir dire, we begin the process of educating the jurors about our case, the law relating to it, and our arguments and positions regarding our client. It is important to see if the juror understands our position regarding these facts and principles of law and whether he can accept them. Generally a juror will agree that he can accept them, but we need to be sure that he also understands them. In essence, we need to confirm not only that we have established some rapport with this juror, but that we are able to communicate with him.

One way to accomplish this is to choose specific phrases regarding your description of the case. These phrases should not be technical legal language, but rather language that a layman can understand. For example, in a products liability case we should not talk about the principle of law being that of "strict liability for a defective product"; instead, we should talk about it as a "product that is dangerous because it can easily cause injury to its users." We would then attempt to have the jurors understand that if a product is dangerous (i.e., can easily cause injury to

[11] *See supra* Chapter 5, *Preparing for Effective Courtroom Communication.*

its users), the person or company manufacturing the product and obtaining the profit is liable for the injury even if he was careful in making the product. Put another way, the juror is asked to understand that there is no way to carefully make a dangerous product. That is the type of phraseology that communicates the principle of strict liability in lay language.

After communicating that principle to the jurors, while still pacing them, see if they pick up the language you have used in their own answers. Ask each one if he understands this principle, and he will simply say yes. Then ask each one to describe how he feels about this principle regarding dangerous products and listen to their answers. See if the jurors are picking up the phrasing that you used, such as: "dangerous products," "products that easily injure," and manufacturers who are liable even though they "carefully made the product."

COMMENT: To reiterate, the careful choice of language regarding your case during voir dire is essential. Using this conscious phrasing for the explicit purpose of offering it to the jurors to see if they will use it is part of the process of pacing and leading. Remember that it must be language that you would expect the jurors to use, not technical language. Those jurors who begin to use that language in their narrative answers are confirming their rapport with you. This is a clear indication that you have successfully paced a particular juror and that you have the ability to lead him; the ability to lead is a strong indication of good rapport.

---

§ 6.19 Questioning techniques: open-ended versus leading questions

All questions, with respect to their phrasing, fall within limits ranging from the totally open-ended question to the obvious leading question. An open-ended question is one that can only be answered in a narrative fashion. It is a question which it is impossible to intelligently answer with a yes or no. For example, "What do you think of that?", is obviously not a question that can be answered yes or no; it demands a totally narrative response. On the other hand, the leading question, by definition, demands a yes or a no response. For example, the question "You agree, do you not, that the light was red?" not only demands a yes or no answer, it also tells the person being questioned that he is expected to state that the light *was* red. It telegraphs the answer. Of course, there can be a combination which falls somewhere in between the perfectly open-ended question and the leading question. For instance, you can have a question that telegraphs what the answer ought to be without it crying out for a yes or a no answer. Example: "What, if anything, do you know about the light being red?" This question is leading to a degree (it gives an indication of what the answer ought to be), but does not require a yes or no answer. There are, therefore, only three basic techniques that apply to the asking of all questions: a question may be open-ended, leading, or a combination of both.

In addition to the primary goal of not selecting biased jurors, we also have other major goals during voir dire. Two of these goals are best served by the use of open-ended questions which require a narrative answer. These are the goals of obtaining information and establishing rapport. We cannot accomplish either of these goals with leading questions. On the other hand, the two other goals of obtaining commitments and establishing a pattern of positive responses can only be accomplished through the use of the leading question.

The final goal relating to questioning technique is education. This goal is best established through questions which combine open-ended and leading questions. In other words, questions that telegraph certain amounts of information but, on the other hand, require more than a yes or no answer. If phrased as leading questions, they would be objectionable not only as being argumentative, but also as not being questions. Therefore, if you attempt to educate the jurors about your case, put the facts and the law in the form of a question. For example, to educate jurors about the fact that your client was drunk, that he was asleep on the railroad tracks when the train ran over him, and that you are depending on the doctrine of "last clear chance" to win your case, you might question the jurors as follows:

Q. What, if any, feelings do you have about people who drink too much and pass out? (Explore all positive answers.)

Q. What if the evidence showed in this case that my client was drunk and passed out on the railroad track? Would you decide this case against him on these facts alone or would you be able to wait and listen to His Honor's charge on the law before deciding this case?

Q. How do you feel about a law that says: "A railroad cannot run over drunks asleep on the track if they should have seen them and been able to stop the train?"

Q. If His Honor charges you that this is the law, i.e. that the railroad does not have the right to run over drunks sleeping on the tracks, will you be able to accept that law and follow it?

This is done not only for the purpose of obtaining their commitment regarding the subject matter, but also to educate them as to the weakness of your case on the facts and the favorable law in regard thereto. As a plaintiff in a civil case, this is the type of information that the jury should hear coming from you. As a trial lawyer, you will always want to be the first to bring out the weak points of your case. This takes the sting out of these weaknesses and may even avoid serious damage to your case by your opponent. Thus if you are a plaintiff in a civil case, you have a distinct advantage in going first during the voir dire questioning. Take advantage of primacy during the voir dire. Make sure that you explore all of the weak points so that they are not exploited first by the defendant. You can accomplish that effectively by educating the jurors through the use of a questioning technique which combines leading and open-ended questions.

Recall that once you have established rapport and have successfully paced the jury you can then begin to lead them. Therefore, begin to ask leading questions to establish a pattern of affirmative responses after you have sufficiently paced either a single juror or the jury as a whole. Always ask the question so that it demands a positive rather than a negative answer. People tend to like and associate with those they perceive as having a positive image. If you have successfully anchored a series of positive answers, you are successfully leading the jury and helping to build rapport. Leading questions aimed at establishing a pattern of affirmative answers might be phrased as follows:

—Do you believe that the jury system is a fair method for resolving disputes?

—Do you feel that an injured person has a right to recover for pain and suffering?

—Do you think that it is all right for injured people to seek money damages?

—Do you think you will be able to follow the law as the judge gives it to you?

—If you see the evidence as supporting the plaintiff, can you follow that evidence and give the plaintiff a verdict?

—If you hear evidence from the plaintiff's expert that the plaintiff has suffered a serious injury can you return a commensurate dollar award?

—Can you be fair to both lawyers and both parties in deciding this case?

Note that these questions are phrased to run the gamut in terms of whether they are appealing to a person who is predominantly kinesthetic, auditory, or visual in his mode of assessing information. We are assuming that this series of questions will be asked to the jury as a whole rather than to individual jurors. When attempting to obtain a pattern of positive answers from an individual juror, you might want to frame your questions to parallel his predominant channel.

The leading question technique can also be used during voir dire in an attempt to disqualify a juror who has given behavioral cues of bias or prejudice. In framing and asking these questions, remember that people tend to adhere to belief systems and stereotypes despite the presentation of contrary information. If a juror has indicated a potential bias or prejudice, either vocally or nonverbally, you may want to develop that bias in terms of a challenge for cause. If so, recognize the bias or stereotype as existing in the community as a whole and as being acceptable. After you have recognized it and have identified with it in some fashion, attempt to obtain the admission that this bias, stereotype, or prejudice may, in some way, color that juror's view of the evidence. In developing the line of questioning to challenge for cause, do not focus on forcing the juror to admit prejudice or bias. Rather, attempt to show that one side or the other would not start off even or that the particular bias under discussion would influence or color this juror's view of the evidence. Most reasonable judges would find this testimony sufficient to establish a challenge for cause and the judge should not require you to have the juror state that the bias under discussion would so influence him that he would be prejudiced. Almost no one will admit to being "prejudiced."

For example, assume you are representing a black plaintiff who has been severely injured in an automobile accident. The jury in this southern town is predominantly white. Your follow-up questioning of any particular juror might be patterned as follows:

Q. I take it from the way you answered the last question that you do have some feelings regarding blacks?

Q. You understand that most people who belong to one ethnic group have certain negative feelings about other ethnic groups?

Q. Most whites raised in the South, as you were Mr. Doe, were raised during a time when people had negative feelings regarding blacks. In fact, we can all remember a time when the laws of the South recognized negative feelings regarding blacks. My client Larry Jones, myself, and all of us in this room know that most of us continue to harbor these feelings about blacks and can you recognize, Mr. Doe, and accept the fact that a lot of Caucasians have negative feelings about blacks?

You have now recognized a stereotype and linked to it.

Q. Tell us, Mr. Doe, how do you feel about/how do you see (phrasing will depend upon his predominant channel for assessing information) blacks?

If he is fair, you will get a narrative answer.

Q. Then, from what you feel (or have heard or seen, etc.), you do feel (use his own language here) about blacks?

You have now acknowledged the general stereotype about blacks, linked up with it, and had a particular juror acknowledge that he shares that stereotype. Now use leading questions. Commit the juror to the particular bias in such a manner that the judge or opposing counsel will not be able to rehabilitate him.

Q. So, feeling as you do, Mr. Doe, you would certainly agree, would you not, that when it comes to evaluating the evidence in this case that my client, Larry Jones, who is black and the defendant driver, Mr. Smith, who is white, would not start off perfectly even; there would be some difference?

Q. You would agree, would you not, that the difference (using language that he has just used) would have some influence on the way you would feel or see the evidence in this case?

Q. So you would agree that when you begin to discuss the evidence in the jury room, to at least a degree, your view of the evidence would possibly be influenced by the way you feel about or see blacks?

Use open-ended, then leading questions, to establish prejudice or bias and to disqualify the juror. During the questioning, whenever the opportunity arises, refer to your client by his first name and the defendant as Mr. Smith. This is an effort to personalize your client and depersonalize the opposing side. It is easier for jurors to return a verdict in favor of one side and against the other side if the other side has been depersonalized in their eyes. This is why the armed forces depersonalizes the enemy. It is easier to kill a "commie" than a fellow human being. It is easier to return a verdict against a depersonalized defendant.

§ 6.20 Questioning techniques used to position the lawyer

Determining jurors' preconceived expectations and positioning the lawyer in the jurors' minds so that he meets those expectations is another concern of counsel during voir dire. The attorney must create an image. In most cases, the predominant jurors tend to be authoritarian; therefore the lawyer should be dressed in a conservative suit and fit the visual image of a lawyer.[12] The essence of the image the attorney wants to project during voir dire is that of being a warm, open person. This image is created and projected not only by personal appearance, but by gestures as well. During voir dire, the attorney wants to establish an open body style where his gestures are expansive and his hands and arms are moving in large circles rather than small, tight ones. Since the attorney wants to establish rapport, he must be open and accessible to the jurors. He should unbutton his coat, stand with his legs slightly apart, and avoid the use of blocking gestures, such as folding his arms during the questioning. This increases the perception of immediacy (openness).

Of course, in addition to dress and movement in the courtroom, an attorney wants to project a verbal image which will increase his trustworthiness, competence, and dynamism. These are projected by his behavior, his confident style of speech, the rapidity with which he speaks, and the authority he projects. If the attorney has not received formal training in public and/or professional speaking, it is desirable to attend an intensive seminar limited to a small number of people that will allow the attorney to practice on video. The ability to be persuasive and really natural in the courtroom is part of developing professional speaking skills. If there is one form of behavior that can be studied, learned, and practiced, it is the art of persuasive speaking.

There is an effective technique to project an image of fairness while simultaneously obtaining information from the jurors. Even more important, this technique denies opposing counsel an opportunity to build his own relationship with the jurors. Assuming you are plaintiff's counsel in a civil suit, ask both sides of every question. Never simply ask the

[12] *See supra* Chapter 1, *Impression Formation in the Courtroom*.

juror if he has been a defendant in a civil action; rather, ask if he has ever been a plaintiff or a defendant in a civil action. If you do not ask it, you can be sure the opposing counsel will during his voir dire.

Do not ask the jurors whether they have ever been sued, but ask whether they have ever filed suit or been defendants in a lawsuit. Ask whether or not they can be fair to both the plaintiff who was injured and to the large corporate defendant. Ask whether they can decide the case in favor of the defendant corporation if the evidence presented so indicates, even if they feel sorry for the plaintiff. Ask questions that the defense counsel would be asking and show that all you are trying to do is to select jurors who are objective and will be fair to both sides.

This approach to questioning the jurors accomplishes two goals. First, it makes you appear to be eminently fair in their eyes. You are not looking for jurors prejudiced in your favor but simply for fair jurors. This makes you appear trustworthy and increases your credibility. Second, by asking both sides of every question before defense counsel has the opportunity to do so, you deny him the opportunity to talk with the jury and project his personality. If you ask all the possible questions regarding the case, you leave the defense counsel with little time to build rapport and project his personality to the jury.

COMMENT: Remember, at this point an important principle working in favor of the plaintiff's counsel is primacy. Take full advantage of it. You are questioning the jurors first, so make a good impression in the first four to six minutes; it will probably last throughout the trial.

If you have succeeded with this technique during voir dire, defense counsel will be left with almost nothing to ask. If he repeats the same questions, the jurors will react with boredom at hearing it all over again. Thus, phrasing the questions to cover both sides of an issue is an excellent technique that accomplishes several goals.

Another technique that projects a desirable image is to tell the jurors that it is okay to talk about personal prejudices and feelings. Generally such a personal disclosure will increase your image of fairness. The increased likability leads to warmth and to the further establishment of rapport (Communication Principle 10: People are more easily influenced by people they like). Find a reason to tell the jurors something about your personal background. The disclosure, of course, must tie in to the particular subject being discussed during voir dire at that moment. If it is to be effective, it cannot be made up. It must be something real and personal. Offering a real piece of information about yourself insures that the jury will not read the action as phony. Your facial expressions and behavior will come across much more persuasively if the disclosure is real.

§ 6.21 —Body movements of the lawyer

The lawyer's body movements during voir dire are important.[13] Whenever possible, the lawyer should stand and address the jury rather than sit at a table. If the judge will permit it, the lawyer should avoid standing behind a podium while asking his questions during voir dire. He should stand in front of the jury box and face it as he addresses the jurors. He should not pace up and down when he asks questions and he should make strong eye contact. The best way to establish rapport and open two-way communication is to look someone in the eye and address him face to face.

The jury box itself constitutes the jurors' "space." You must try to be close enough to the jury box to establish rapport and build a feeling of openness and friendliness. On the other hand, invading the jurors' space will cause resentment. Therefore, it is recommended that you stand facing the jury box and discuss the voir dire questions with them while remaining a few feet back from the jury railing.

COMMENT: Once again, your body movements, particularly the movements of your hands and arms, need to be full, round, and open. Do not exhibit blocking gestures with your body, such as crossed arms or legs. Further, your gestures must be appropriate to the questions being asked. Gesturing is something that can become more effective with practice. Stand in front of a mirror and practice it; with some

---

[13] *See supra* § 6.11.

work, it will become natural. Use only those gestures that feel natural.

---

§ 6.22 Evaluating vocal and nonverbal cues during questioning

In addition to interpreting verbal cues, the trial lawyer, during voir dire, should be evaluating the vocal and nonverbal cues of the juror. When questioning a juror about an area of possible bias, the interpretation of behavioral cues is important. Does the juror's answer have long pauses and is his voice squeaky? If it is squeaky, is this a normal voice for this juror? Does the discussion of this area indicate a potential bias, thereby making the juror apprehensive? If not, why is the juror apprehensive?

This is what the trial lawyer should be asking himself as he is evaluating the nonverbal cues of a juror during voir dire. Most jurors will not directly admit bias to the other jurors, counsel, or judge. If they feel biased or prejudiced and you have established rapport, however, they will usually intimate the bias in some form if encouraged. Assume, for example, that you are defending a Hispanic client in a criminal trial in southern California. You are questioning an Anglo-Saxon juror. He will not say that he does not like Hispanics, but he may verbally admit that he dislikes attending a social function at which a very large proportion of the guests are of Spanish descent. You would, of course, then follow this admission up with an attempt to have the juror admit his bias or prejudice in some overt form so that you could have the judge excuse this particular juror for cause.[14]

Sometimes the juror's prejudice will not surface in his actual testimony. In the criminal case in southern California, the juror may be too embarrassed to communicate verbally to others his inner feeling of dislike for Hispanics. This may only surface in his behavior, as in the nature of his answer. If, while the juror is saying that he would not mind attending a party with a large number of Hispanics and that he thought he could enjoy himself, the voice may be in a raised pitch, there may be pauses, there may be "ums" and "uhs", clearing of the throat, and other nonverbal cues which clearly indicate that the juror is uncomfortable with that answer. The trial lawyer, of course, must attribute some signif-

---

[14] *See supra* § 6.19 for a discussion concerning the specific questioning techniques.

icance to such behavioral cues. In some instances, the juror may be giving off these nonverbal cues because of situational anxiety or the cues may be related to the answer. One way of determining whether the cues are related to situational anxiety or the truthfulness of the specific answer being given is to establish a mental norm of the vocal pattern of each juror as you begin talking to him. Consciously note the level of each juror's voice, his rhythm of speech, his choice of words, the nature of his pauses, and the rapidity with which he speaks. Keep this information stored so that when you notice significant nonverbal behavior, you can determine whether this behavior is occurring throughout his answers or whether these nonverbal cues are occurring solely in conjunction with certain answers.

§ 6.23 —Open-ended questions to whole panel versus obtaining individual answers

The ideal voir dire would provide the attorney with the opportunity to ask individual questions of each individual juror and to obtain individual responses to every question. As a practical matter, judges generally will not allow this as it will cause the voir dire to become tedious, boring, and intolerably long. Therefore, a mixture of specific questions to individual jurors and open-ended questions is needed. The open-ended questions may be used when the area being discussed is not critical and when you are simply attempting to establish rapport with the entire jury, or perhaps, you are attempting to get the entire jury to enter into a pattern of positive responses. Certain questions seeking individual background information, of course, have to be asked of each individual juror. Vary your pattern and rhythm so that you ask some open-ended questions, but work in as many individual questions as possible. Individual questions are necessary regarding key issues.

§ 6.24 Use of "red flag" questioning

When planning the voir dire, plan your "red flag" questions to meet your "red flag" issues. Analyze your case and decide which issues are crucial to the case. For example, if you are dealing with a case where the crucial issue is aggravation of a preexisting condition, then the law on preexisting conditions is a "red flag" question. If the case is a medical malpractice case and you are using an out-of-state expert, a "red flag" question may be whether or not the juror can give equal weight to the opinion offered by your out-of-state expert. They are questions on which you want a definite commitment from each individual juror. Remember, once a commitment is obtained, people change their viewpoint in order to think consistently with that commitment (Principle 8: People have a need to be consistent). If the commitment is in writing and is made public, it is far more binding and has greater influence than a privately made commitment.

It is suggested that the following technique be used to emphasize commitments made in regard to one or two key "red flag" questions. Once the commitment is made and each juror has clearly committed to the principle, then you need to emphasize that this is a public commitment and that it is in writing. Obviously, this is not the type of question to address to the whole panel; rather, "red flag" questions are asked of each individual juror. Seek a commitment in some form from each individual juror. If the juror simply nods his head yes in agreement with the principle stated in the "red flag" question, indicate *for the record* that the juror has nodded his head affirmatively in answer to your question.

§ 6.25 —Importance of public commitments

Once you succeed in gaining a juror's acknowledgment you have a commitment, but the commitment is similar to that made by placing a bet at the racetrack. It is a private commitment and not the public commitment that you sought. It is a public commitment that makes such groups as Weight Watchers and Alcoholics Anonymous effective. It is the fact that the overeater or the alcoholic stands up in public and commits to do something about the problem that forces him to be consistent with the public commitment.

Recall the study by Deutsch and Gerard[15] wherein college students were asked to estimate the length of lines they were shown.[16] Remember that the students who committed their estimates to writing on a "magic writing pad" and then erased the estimates were much more inclined to stick to their initial judgments when presented with the true length of the lines. It is clear that putting a commitment in writing can have startling effects. This is particularly true if that writing is then made public. This is why the Chinese who captured our American soldiers during the Korean War were so startingly effective in obtaining cooperation and encouraging defections to communism. They held an essay contest in which the prisoners were given a small reward, perhaps a bowl of rice, if

[15] Deutsch & Gerard, *A Study of Normative and Informational Social Influences Upon Individual Judgment*, 5 J. ABNORM. & SOC. PSYCHOLOGY 629 (1955).

[16] *See supra* § 6.05.

they wrote an essay containing an approving comment regarding Chinese communism. It did not matter that the essay emphasized democracy. One small procommunist comment was enough. The prisoner would then find copies of his essay posted around the camp. It had been made public and the prisoners were psychologically forced to act consistently with their written public commitment. We do not have to look to the Chinese communists, however, to realize the importance of obtaining some small written commitment and its effectiveness in influencing a person. Consider American cereal companies who are constantly running essay contests giving large prizes for the best essay which says in twenty-five words or less: "I like ABCD cereal because. . . ." The advantage to the company is that thousands upon thousands of people write an essay that says something favorable about their product. These people are then committed in writing to liking this product.

A further point needs to be made here. Commitments, when made public, can produce a long-term commitment if based on a valid inner motivation. A 1966 study conducted by social psychologist Dr. Jonathan Freedman sampled the reaction of two groups of young boys.[17] Each group was put into a room with five toys, one of which was a very expensive and attractive robot. The first group was told not to touch the robot after the doctor left the room simply because it was wrong to do so. The second group was also told not to touch the robot after the doctor left the room; in addition, they were told that touching the robot would make the doctor angry and that he would be forced to do something. A significantly higher number of boys from the second group, the one given the threat, played with the robot. The boys in the first group, those given a reason which allowed them to accept inner responsibility for their actions, were much less likely to play with the robot.

The question is, how can we, as trial lawyers, apply these principles during voir dire? We know that we must try to obtain a commitment to the "red flag" issue that is the key to our case. Even if we cannot obtain this type of commitment, however, we can certainly obtain a general commitment to follow the law.

§ 6.26 —How to obtain a public commitment

How do we use the knowledge that a commitment made in public and in writing, with a valid inner reason for it, is long lasting and influences

[17] Freedman, *Long-Term Behavioral Effects of Cognitive Dissonance*, 4 J. EXPERIM. & SOC. PSYCHOLOGY 195 (1966).

the person to be consistent with the commitment? Certainly the court would not allow us to ask the jurors to put their commitments in writing or to write an essay about why they should follow the law and the evidence in the case. How then can we obtain a public commitment from each juror that he will follow the law and the evidence in the civil case or acquit a criminal defendant if the state fails to bear the burden of proof even though the juror may feel the defendant is guilty?

Obtain even the most minute specific commitment to either a general or specific "red flag" question from each juror. If the juror does not verbally answer yes to the question, encourage him to do so. If you are unable to obtain a verbal response in agreement, at least attempt to get him to nod his head up and down in an affirmative manner.

COMMENT: Never accept general silence from all twelve jurors as an answer to a "red flag" question. If the best commitment you can obtain is a positive nod of the head, then certainly indicate to the court reporter (specifically referring to the juror by name) that "Mr. Doe has nodded his head affirmatively. Please show such in the record."

Even though the juror has not written down the commitment himself, it has been "written down" in the court record by the court reporter. Ask the reporter to transcribe that portion of the voir dire for you. Make it clear and obvious what you are doing; that is, since the jurors cannot write it themselves, you are having it put in writing for them. Now they have made a commitment in open court and it has been pointed out to them that it is in writing. They are now in a position similar to that of the students that committed to the length of the lines on the magic writing pad once their commitments had been put in writing.

After you have obtained a public commitment and pointed out that you have put it in writing, you still need to make the commitment long-lasting. You do that by giving the jurors a valid reason which allows them to accept inner responsibility for their actions. Like the children with the toys, tell the jurors that it would be wrong for them not to follow the law and that you know they want to be fair to all parties and follow the law and the evidence or tell them that it would be wrong for them not to follow the specific principle of law encompassed in your specific "red flag" questions. It would be wrong because it would indicate they were not being fair to one of the parties and you know they want to be fair to both parties. Thus you are giving them a valid reason for their written commitment and they can now justify the commitment internally.

Commitments obtained during voir dire, if properly handled, become powerful tools in influencing the jurors to your side of the case. You, of course, will use the phrasing of a particular commitment in both opening statement and summation. When the time for summation arrives, drive home the commitment by showing the jury the transcript of their commitment on an overhead, blown up and projected onto a big screen. It will appear larger than life to them; it is the closest thing to having the jurors read it in their own handwriting. Their written commitment which was given for a good reason is there for all to see. They should, according to every indication of social psychological research, make every attempt to be consistent with that commitment.

III. Obtaining Information

§ 6.27 Reasons for obtaining information

As stated previously, a primary goal during voir dire, in addition to establishing rapport and obtaining commitments, is to obtain information about individual jurors.[18] Some courts provide lawyers with access to background information on each juror, such as place of employment, age, sex, and marital status. Some courts publish lists of the jurors a month or two in advance to allow investigation of the whole panel by an attorney. But no jurisdiction allows lawyers to interview individuals who are potential jurors or even to contact them directly. The attorney may, in most jurisdictions, contact the person's neighbor to obtain some background information. Of course, especially in a major case, the attorney should work with a communication-social science team in obtaining background information on the type of jurors involved, their stereotypes, and belief systems, even though they will not be able to obtain specific information about specific jurors.

Therefore, the only opportunity for the trial attorney to obtain specific and relevant information on the background of these jurors occurs dur-

---

[18] *See supra* § 6.03.

ing direct questioning in voir dire. Obtaining this information forms the basis not only for challenges for cause, but for the intelligent use of your peremptory challenges. The trial attorney is not limited to obtaining information directly related to issues constituting recognized challenges for cause. The law gives trial counsel the use of peremptory challenges and inherent in that right is the right to obtain sufficient information about the jurors' background to use those challenges intelligently. Therefore, information which may show some type of inherent bias that might affect your client or your cause in any way is relevant and may be probed during voir dire. Many lawyers fail to realize this and are effectively cut off in their voir dire by opposing counsel making objections about relevancy that are sustained by the judge. Do not fall into that trap; research the law in your state and be prepared to support your right to use your peremptory challenges for cause intelligently by obtaining information you feel is important to your decision-making process.

§ 6.28 Work history

Counsel will want to know how long the juror has worked at his particular job. This information is an indicator of the juror's stability. It may indicate whether he is easily influenced by authority figures or has problems coping with authority. Often, just the nature of the employment tells very little about the juror himself. The juror who tells you that "I work for the local XYZ Hotel" may tell you about his place of employment and he may even tell you that he does or does not hold an executive position there, but this does not tell you specifically what he does. Each juror should be asked to describe his daily duties and what they include.

For example, it is important in a civil case and perhaps even when defending a criminal case, to know whether or not the duties of the juror's employment include making judgments regarding other employees. An employee who handles claims for on-the-job injuries may not be a desirable plaintiff's juror in a civil case. Determining the details of their duties aids in assessing their degree of respect for authority and independence. It is also important to know whether they benefit from a reward system based on individual effort. Generally, salespeople are considered good plaintiff's jurors. They usually think in big money terms and are not the type who have to dot "i's" and cross "t's" all day long. They are more creative and more of the egalitarian type.

Knowledge of the work history of the individual juror alone is not sufficient. Counsel should also determine the work history of the juror's spouse. In the vast majority of households today, the spouse is also employed. In most civil cases and in some criminal cases, the jurors are not sequestered. They go home at night and despite admonitions not to discuss the case with their spouses, many do and are influenced by their spouses' views. Therefore, it is essential to know the spouse's occupation and, in addition, the occupations of anyone else living in the household.

It is important to have a complete picture on the juror's work background so, unless he has held his current position for ten or fifteen years or more, ask about previous employment. Did he start at the bottom and fight his way up or was he given the job because of connections or influence? This type of valuable information will only be obtained when one does a careful and detailed questioning of each juror regarding his work history.

§ 6.29 Education and training

In addition to specific employment history, find out about the education and training of each juror. Often people have received education and training that they are not using in their current job and may not have used in any previous job if they are working in a totally unrelated area. Such background information can give us important clues about the personality of the juror. For example, if a juror has training in the health care field and then chose to go into sales, this may indicate that the juror did not want to make an economic sacrifice to "take care of people." Depending upon the demographics of your particular plaintiff, this type of person may or may not be a good juror for you. On the other hand, if that juror has been in sales for a long time, he may still make an excellent plaintiff's juror.

As with work history, the educational and training background of other household members is important. It is important, for example, in a medical malpractice case to know if the wife is working as a nurse. Obviously, a juror whose wife is a nurse, even though he is an ideal plaintiff's juror on paper, may be so influenced and intimidated by his wife's nursing position that he may be unable to find against a hospital or physician. Moreover, the juror may have an only child who is a medical student for whom he has made sacrifices to enable that child to attend medical school. In that case, your potential juror would obviously be a very poor choice as a plaintiff's juror in a medical malpractice case. The relationship may not be direct, but it is still significant. The examples are endless, but the point to be made is that the education and training of your potential juror and all his family members are essential pieces of information to have on every juror in every case.

§ 6.30 Family experience

Remember that you are attempting to obtain detailed information on each juror's background for the intelligent use of peremptory challenges. Therefore, while a juror's family background may not be relevant to challenges for cause it can give us valuable clues as to the juror's thought patterns and belief systems. For example, a male juror who has been divorced three or four times may not make a good plaintiff's juror if the plaintiff is female. It may be that this particular juror just does not relate well to women. In today's mobile society, to begin to understand the background of a juror, we need to know where he was born, where he was raised, and whether the original family held together or his parents divorced. These are obviously very personal questions and they have to be handled delicately. The jurors need to be told that it is important for you to know a little bit about them so you can represent your client effectively. You may even want to start such a line of questioning by asking the jurors if they understand that your duty during voir dire is to ask questions. Obtain a specific promise from them that asking these background questions will not be held against you or your client. To encourage the disclosure of such personal information you might consider disclosing some personal background information about yourself, where you grew up as a child, what your family experience was like, and so forth. Remember that while all this is going on you are also pacing the jurors and attempting to build rapport. Family experience is important and is an area that needs to be explored to some extent in every case.

§ 6.31 Opinions regarding lawyers

Recall that one of the goals during voir dire is to build rapport with each individual juror. This is really the key to successfully picking the jury. Every juror comes into the courtroom with a certain stereotypical image of an attorney. That image may match the general attitude of the local community or it may be a generalization based on prior personal exposure. Whatever the juror's attitude is, you need to find out about it. Always ask him, therefore, whether there are any lawyers in his family? How does he feel about lawyers? Has he ever been represented by a lawyer or seen a lawyer for any reason? Ask also whether he has ever been sued by a lawyer. These questions will tend to bring out his general opinion regarding lawyers. Remember that this is a person with whom you are trying to build rapport. If he has had a negative experience with lawyers, it may be impossible to build rapport with him. He may just not trust lawyers.

§ 6.32 Opinions regarding the type of litigation

Many jurors may not have had personal contact or experience with lawyers or claims. Nevertheless, they have been "exposed" to courtrooms and litigation through television and the press. They may have had a conversation with a family doctor about the "medical malpractice" crisis or they may have been exposed to the "products liability" crisis either through TV or the newspapers. Alternatively, they may have been influenced by programs espousing the view that crime is rampant in America and that we have been too easy on criminals. Potential jurors can have very fixed opinions about any particular type of litigation. An open-ended question must be asked to elicit their feelings about the type of litigation at issue. If your case is a medical malpractice case, you want a narrative discussion from each potential juror as to how they feel (see, think, etc.) about this type of litigation. The same would be true of a products case, a rear-end collision case, a slip-and-fall case, and so on.

§ 6.33 Opinions regarding physicians

Remember that one of the key judgments we are attempting to make regarding each juror is to assess to what degree that juror is respectful of authority as opposed to an independent type of individual. Generally, though not in all cases, those with a deep respect for authority tend to be defense jurors in civil cases and prosecution jurors in criminal cases. Respect for the medical profession is a good indicator of the degree to which a person has an authority-oriented personality. The type of person who will do absolutely anything the physician instructs and would never question the judgment of a physician is one who is overpowered by and very respectful of authority.

Further, in many criminal and civil cases, medical testimony is going to be presented by both sides. If the medical testimony is strongly in your favor, then you may want someone who reveres the medical profession. On the other hand, if medical causation in your case is weak, you may want to stay away from people who revere the medical profession. Rather, select people who tend to follow their own common sense as opposed to the "opinions of doctors."

COMMENT: As with any other piece of information, the opinion of jurors toward physicians is not controlling. It is but one piece of the puzzle that will enable you to put together a composite picture of each individual juror.

---

§ 6.34 Exploring preconceived notions or ideas of jurors

All of us have stereotypes which we use as shortcuts in making judgments. They are used to process information quickly so we can easily reduce uncertainty.[19] Stereotypes are often believed despite the presentation of contradictory evidence (Principle 6: People attempt to maintain their original perceptions regardless of contradictory information). A stereotype is the composite picture resulting from a general belief that most people from a given community share regarding a particular place or socioeconomic group. It is impossible to know the exact stereotypes in each juror's mind unless you discuss the subject matter with them, whether it is stereotyping of ethnic and racial groups, professions, or traditions and mores.

This type of subject matter needs to be tailored to your individual case. You may be representing a Hispanic in the Southwest, a Puerto Rican in New York, or a black in the South. You may be representing a plaintiff in a medical malpractice case in which your only concern may be the possible stereotyping of a defendant doctor as perfect. Or you may be up against the belief in a products case that a manufacturer would not knowingly make a dangerous product. All of these are examples of stereotypes that need to be explored.

The way to explore these stereotypes is not by a direct attack. Rather, during voir dire these stereotypes need to be brought to the surface and recognized.

Identify the stereotype problem involved in your particular case, link up with it, and then distinguish it. Certainly the first two steps, recognizing the stereotype and linking up with it, should be accomplished in voir dire. In most cases, you may also begin to make the distinction that will

[19] *See supra* § 1.54, *The use of stereotypes and personal generalizations.*

separate your client from any stereotype a particular juror may have of him.

§ 6.35 Exploring racial and other biases

One of the strongest stereotypes involves racial biases. It is deeply seeded throughout the country although the particular subject group varies from locale to locale. A failure to deal with racial biases, either against your client or in favor of the opposing side, could be disastrous.

Explore the bias even if it is in your favor, ultimately committing the juror to being fair. This maneuver may deny your opponent the opportunity to eliminate this juror by using a challenge for cause. On the other hand, if a juror feels committed to the fact that his inherent bias or prejudice should not play a role, he may even bend over backwards in order to appear fair. If your gut reaction is that the bias or prejudice will tend to sway this juror then he should be eliminated for cause or with the use of a peremptory challenge.

An effective technique used to explore biases is to subtly provide the juror with the opportunity to discuss the prejudice in a narrative fashion. Once he has done that, the trial lawyer can explore how deep the bias runs and make an informed judgment based on the information obtained as to how to handle that juror. Several sample questions which can be used to entice jurors to open up and discuss racial bias follow.

Q. Can you tell me what the word "racism" means to you?

Q. Have you yourself ever had any experience with discrimination, for example, seeing it, hearing it, or feeling it?

Q. Do you think that [blacks, Hispanics, Orientals, etc.] have been treated fairly in this community?

Q. Have you or members of your family ever felt racial tension in any situation?

Q. Can you tell us with what frequency and on what occasions you or members of your family have had contact with [minority group]?

Q. What are your feelings [or other wording depending on juror's primary mode of accessing information] regarding interracial marriage?

Armed with these types of questions and with the determination that this subject must be tackled, you can do an adequate job in handling racial bias and other prejudices. Remember that the secret is to recognize the existing bias, to link up with it, and then to distinguish your client from the bias on some rational basis.

§ 6.36 Previous jury experience

Another vital area of concern in terms of obtaining background information from jurors relates to their previous jury experience. In most states and in most district courts, the judge will allow you to discuss any previous jury experiences with prospective jurors. However, many judges will not allow you to ask specifically about what went on during the previous jury process or its outcome. Your jurisdiction may even allow you to research, in advance, each particular juror's previous experience, although again, you generally will not be able to discover the outcome.

A key question for the plaintiff in a civil case is whether the prior jury experience was civil or criminal. The answer to this question could provide you with the opportunity to accomplish another goal (i.e., educating the other jurors regarding the different burdens of proof). If you are fortunate enough to obtain the answer from one of the jurors that he has had previous jury service on a criminal jury, then you can ask that juror whether he feels he can distinguish between the criminal burden of proof (where the state has to prove its case beyond a reasonable doubt) and the civil burden of proof (where a preponderance of the evidence allows the juror to decide in the plaintiff's favor even though he still may have many doubts). Proper use of this question will educate not only the juror who answered positively regarding criminal jury experience, but also the other jurors.

§ 6.37 Jurors' hobbies explored

Another area to be explored with each juror concerns hobbies and leisure time activities. Knowledge of hobbies gives us insight into that juror's feelings on a subconscious level.

For example, if a juror's hobby is carpentry work, ask what type of carpentry work. If it is building boats and framing houses for sheer pleasure, he may make an excellent plaintiff's juror. On the other hand, if the juror's hobby is cabinet making and he produces fine detail work where everything must fit perfectly, he may not be able to deal with the plaintiff's burden of proof in a civil case. The juror may want your case to fit together as precisely as his cabinets.

Another example of a hobby that tells us something about a person is hunting and fishing. Particularly with the hunter, look for a person who may be insensitive to the pain and suffering of others. He does not seem to be concerned with bleeding and suffering, at least in the case of animals. Thus, while it is certainly not true in all cases, the stereotype of a hunter is one of a tough person, one who can tolerate the pain of others. In a case where your main element of damage is conscious pain and suffering, the hunter may not be a good plaintiff's juror despite other favorable background information. Again, this is just *one* of the factors that go into the overall picture. On the other hand, a person who's main hobby is golf or tennis may make an excellent plaintiff's juror. People with these types of hobbies are used to wide margins of error and to human mistakes. They relate well to others and tend to be "people's" people. If the golfer or tennis player is a member of the local country club, however, his "easy come, easy go" type of personality may not be of much help at all. In fact, he may not relate well to your laborer plaintiff. Hobbies often give us the key to valuable information about prospective jurors.

§ 6.38 Jurors' knowledge of law and medicine

Often you will find that individual jurors have some rudimentary knowledge of law or medicine. Ask whether or not any juror has had any training or experience that would give him any medical knowledge. The juror may have been a corpsman in the army. He is the type of person who may enter the jury room and ignore the medical evidence presented in your case. He may start talking to other jurors about the fact that "he" was a corpsman during World War II and he knows about (whatever the medical problem is), and then go on to use that leverage to persuade the other jurors to decide the case against you.

The same thing is true for people who have been exposed to, or for some other reason have a knowledge of, the law. If they have worked in any law office position, taken any business law courses, or become involved with anything of that nature, they may consider themselves amateur lawyers. Be very careful of these people. Unless you are sure that this juror is on your side, he, like the juror who was a corpsman in the army, can use that knowledge to establish his leadership role among the other jurors. If he can convincingly talk about a law course he took wherein the professor said ". . .", he may successfully contradict the judge's charge on the law and certainly could overwhelm your interpretations of the law during argument. Remember, as trial attorneys, we should present our cases in such a way as to do away with uncertainty regarding the anticipated outcome. Do you recall the example of the lawyer who wanted to wear a ring on his pinkie. He was told, "you can't afford to take that kind of chance."

COMMENT: As a general rule, if a juror has some knowledge of law or medicine, the answer is the same. Unless you are overwhelmingly convinced that you have great rapport with that juror and that he is on your side, you cannot afford to take a chance with such a juror.

---

§ 6.39 Pretrial publicity

This is another area that needs to be probed in detail with the individual juror. This is obviously true in a criminal case which has gained attention in the press. All of the techniques we have described previously for handling bias and prejudice and questioning jurors apply to handling this subject matter. There are, however, more subtle types of pretrial publicity which can affect the outcome of your case and are more difficult to handle. This is the pretrial publicity about the particular subject matter of your case. If your case is a products liability case, the jurors may have been exposed to press or media coverage regarding the problems with products liability lawsuits and insurance rates. The same is true regarding medical malpractice cases. Even if it is an ordinary automobile case, the jurors may have been exposed to the fact that their insurance rates may be affected by their verdict. This is a difficult problem and deserves some attention.

In most instances, trial publicity regarding the medical malpractice or products liability case can be raised directly. In those situations, you can ask the jurors if they have read anything in the newspapers, seen anything on television, or heard anything on the radio (make sure to cover directly all three in lay terms) about the case.

Voir dire on pretrial publicity may provide an opportunity to discuss insurance. In some states such as Florida, Louisiana, and Wisconsin, under most circumstances, the insurance company is sued directly and is a defendant. Therefore, you can mention the word "insurance" and discuss the publicity that the jurors have been exposed to regarding the so-called crisis and its effects on insurance rates. Of course, all the jurors have been exposed to some publicity about insurance rates going up, including their own, because of automobile losses. This is an area of pretrial publicity that needs to be examined in every injury case. Obviously, if you are allowed to mention insurance, obtain a "red flag" type of commitment from the jurors that they will not be influenced by the fact that this verdict may affect their own automobile insurance rates. The theme running through this type of questioning is that they may not be influenced by anything but the law and the evidence and they should reject any argument brought up in the jury room about any subject matter that is not covered by the evidence or not charged in the law by the judge.

The more difficult problem arises when an attorney is not permitted to mention the word insurance or discuss it in any way. In that case, you have to emphasize to the jurors that they may not be influenced by any outside publicity, especially anything they may have heard about cases involving claims for injury. The following is a series of questions that can be utilized to defeat an objection that you are discussing insurance:

Q. Do you understand that you may not decide this case on the basis of sympathy for the plaintiff?

Q. Do you understand that sympathy is a form of charity, that it is demeaning to my client who has been seriously injured, that he has been demeaned enough by the injury, and that he does not need to be demeaned by your charity?

Q. Do you understand, therefore, ladies and gentlemen, that you may not be concerned about whether or not my client needs the money?

Q. Do you understand that you may not be concerned with what my client is going to do with any money you may award him?

Q. Do you understand that you may only be concerned with whether the law and the evidence show the defendant is responsible and what is an adequate award under the evidence?

Q. Do you understand that just as you should not be concerned with what the plaintiff will do with the money if you award it, so too you may not be concerned with how the defendant is going to pay any judgment in this case?

Q. Do you understand that you may not be concerned with where the money will be coming from, as this is an extraneous matter and should not be considered by you?

Q. Do each of you promise me now that you will not consider where the money is coming from, how the defendant is going to pay the award if you return a verdict for the plaintiff, or what the plaintiff will do once the funds are received?

Q. Do you understand that these matters are not covered by the evidence or the judge's charge on the law and that you must be governed only by the law and the evidence?

Always call the issue you are attacking the so-called or alleged crisis regarding medical malpractice or products liability claims. If you obtain a positive answer, ask that juror to discuss what he has heard. If you feel that this juror may mention prejudicial information, then request that the juror be questioned out of the hearing of the other jurors. Again, the strategies of "red flag" questions and commitment apply.[20]

§ 6.40 Contact with witnesses

Another area that is sometimes overlooked is prior contact with witnesses in the case and/or parties and their law firms. It is always a good idea to read to the jury a list of all the witnesses in the case and to be sure that the jurors have had no contact with any of them. This may be particularly true of physicians testifying for one side or the other. Potential jurors may presently be under that physician's treatment or may have previously been treated by that physician. Naturally they will give more weight to the opinion of the physician they know personally. The potential juror also may have had some contact with any one of the individual lawyers in the case or the firm. If you are the plaintiff in a civil case, it is always a good idea to read the three, four, or five names from your letterhead and then the names from the defense firm's letterhead which may number as much as twenty, thirty, or more. If your firm is smaller than the defense attorney's firm, the contrast will make yours appear smaller, weaker, and cast you in the role of the underdog. It will create a feeling of sympathy. The jurors will understand that you are challenging a monolith on behalf of the plaintiff.

§ 6.41 Acceptance of the jury system

Unlikely as it may sound, some prospective jurors just do not believe in the jury system. They simply do not accept it as a means of settling disputes. Certainly, these people are not in the majority, but they do exist. Therefore, this is an area that needs to be discussed.

---

[20] *See supra* §§ 6.05, 6.24–6.26.

Inquiry into this area can also be used to educate the jurors as to the importance of the jury system as well as the importance of their role as jurors. It is essential, if you are the plaintiff in a civil case or a defendant in a criminal case, to make the jury realize the significance of their power and the importance of their task. In a criminal case, unless the jury feels that their role is important and powerful, they will continue to adhere to the concept that the state would not be prosecuting someone unless he were indeed guilty. You might consider the following questions in attempting to educate all of the jurors as to the importance of the jury system:

Q. Do each of you realize that you, as jurors in this case, are performing a very important part of the function of government?

Q. Do each of you as jurors realize that in settling this dispute between two citizens you are acting as the oil in the machinery of justice?

Q. Do each of you as jurors realize that the jury method of settling disputes is over two hundred years old and that it is the only system that effectively eliminates individual bias and prejudice and insures equal justice for all the citizens of a society?

Q. Do each of you as jurors realize that in making your decision in this case you are representing the conscience of the community in which we live?

Q. Do each of you as jurors realize that your role is important because your decision in this case aids in setting safety standards for all of us to live by?

Q. Do each of you as jurors realize that you are saying which standards of conduct are acceptable and which are not in this community, as well as what is going to be tolerated and what is not going to be tolerated?

Q. Do each of you believe in the jury system as a fair and equitable means of settling disputes between parties?

§ 6.42 Feelings toward court and the law

Remember that one of our goals during voir dire is the development of our courtroom image through the projection of credibility.[21] One way to do this is to be identified with a source of authority. Obviously, the highest source of authority in the courtroom is the judge. He appears in

---

[21] *See supra* § 6.02.

black robes, he is sitting higher than anyone else, and the jurors already know that the judge has the ultimate word on all questions of law. He is the lawgiver and he is the authority figure. Your purpose in discussing the jury's feelings toward the court and the law is not to obtain information; you already know the jurors are going to express respect for the judge and will promise to follow the law as given by him. Your purpose in discussing the court and the law with the jurors is to link yourself, and thereby your client, with the source of authority in the courtroom. It is a method by which you can increase your image of credibility with the jury. Therefore, in discussing this matter you should show deference to the judge. The jurors have great respect for the judge and may even be a bit frightened of him. When you show deference to the judge, you appear to the jurors as being like them. (Communication Principle #5: People tend to see others as similar to themselves.) This aids in building rapport in addition to increasing credibility. Therefore, questions regarding their feelings about the court and the law, and whether they can accept the court and the law, are always to be prefaced with positive remarks about the judge—what a fine judge he is, what a good job he is doing, how well he knows the law, and how the jurors should follow the judge's directions regarding the law and ignore anything the attorneys may say about the law. Then close the discussion by simply asking the jurors if they can ignore any remarks you make about the law if the judge does not instruct the jury on that law. On the other hand, after the judge instructs the jury on the law to be followed, it is your job as counsel to comment on the law in closing argument; they need to be able to understand that and to be able to listen to your argument. Then they will decide if your argument is supported by the law as given by the judge.

When questioning jurors in this manner, you are identifying with authority figures showing proper deference for its source and, at the same time, leading the jurors to believe the law is in your favor. After all, no one would encourage the jurors to follow the law as given by the judge unless he knew that the law was going to be in his favor.

COMMENT: If, however, your case is very weak on the legal issues involved, it might be a tactical error to emphasize that part of your case.

---

§ 6.43 Feelings toward damage awards

Every court has rules limiting questions which pertain to damage awards. The following question may be asked in almost all jurisdictions, even though it would not be allowed by some district court judges:

Q. If through the evidence we are able to prove serious injury and serious permanent disability, would you be able to return a significant verdict in monetary damages commensurate with the injuries?

In some jurisdictions, further detailed questioning is permitted. In other jurisdictions, you do not have to phrase the questions as carefully and can actually discuss dollar amounts. In such a jurisdiction, the attorney would want to ask, if the evidence supports the plaintiff's allegations and the serious injury is proved, will the jury be able to return a verdict in the amount of the ad damnum or prayer in the petition or complaint, $500,000, $1 million, $2 million, or would they reject such an amount out of hand as being too large? We are obviously tying into the exact monetary amount to achieve a significant psychological effect. If you can get the jurors to commit to return that amount if the injury is serious, you have achieved a significant psychological advantage in terms of influencing them. This, of course, is the exact reason many courts have been very restrictive in terms of allowing questions regarding damage awards.

Another approach to the damage award amount is in terms of the various elements of damages that are permitted under the particular state law. Discuss whether or not the jury would reject the total amount simply because it is large or whether they would be able to follow the law.

Q. His Honor is going to instruct you that we are entitled to receive damages for several different elements in this case. Do each of you understand that you will receive that information? (Accept silence as an answer.)

Q. Do you understand that those elements include past and future loss of wages, past medical expenses, projected future medical expenses, pain and suffering, disability, and the impairment of the ability to enjoy life in the future, each of these are separate elements of damages? (Accept silence as an answer, being sure that your language tracks the judge's charge.)

Q. If that is what His Honor says *is* the law, will you be able to consider each of these elements in arriving at the total amount of damages in this case as required by the law? (Again, accept silence as an answer.)

Q. Should I take it by your silence, ladies and gentlemen, that each of you will consider each and every element of damages as charged by the judge and come up to a total amount to be awarded to the plaintiff and follow the law in that regard? (Now obtain a specific affirmative response from each juror.)

Q. His Honor is also going to charge you to consider the plaintiff's life expectancy, or the time he will live in the future, as an element in determining the award. Will each of you be able to follow the law on that? (Get specific answers from each juror.)

Q. When you sit down in the jury room and consider damages, and consider the law, and consider each element, and the length of time that Mr. Jones will live in the future, and try to decide on an adequate amount for each element of damage, considering all of these factors and the total of those all together, you may find yourselves with a very large sum of money. Do each of you think that that can happen? (Accept silence as an answer.) I take it by your silence that you do think this can happen?

Q. My question to you now, ladies and gentlemen, is that when you consider the amount to be awarded for each element and the life expectancy of Mr. Jones and when you put them all together, if you come up with a large sum of money, will you reject that sum of money out of hand simply because it is large and you do not believe in large awards; or will you be able to follow the law and give a large award where it is justified by the evidence in the case? (Obtain a specific answer from each juror on this question and if damages are the big issue in your case, this may be your "red flag.")

The element of damages that requires closed questioning is whether or not the jurors are willing to award money for pain and suffering. They are often willing, in a serious case, to compensate for medical expenses, future medical expenses, and past and future loss of wages. If the special damages add up to a large amount of money, they seem reluctant to award any additional money for pain and suffering. They have to be made to understand that the evidence is going to show that past and future medical expenses and lost wages come to "several hundred thousand dollars" (or words to that effect). The jurors then must realize that they need to award a sum in addition to that amount to compensate for pain and suffering. The questioning should be geared to assure that they believe that not only is it just to award a large sum of money for pain and suffering, but that this amount can be added to the already large sum given for medical expenses and lost wages.

§ 6.44 Feelings toward the burden of proof

You may not be fortunate enough to have a juror with previous criminal jury service to give you the perfect opportunity to discuss the burden of proof. This subject matter, however, should be approached in both the criminal and civil case—the basic reason being the necessity to educate the jurors as to this issue and to place that concept in their conscious minds in terms which are favorable to your particular position. In other words, burden of proof, when described by you, can be put in a favorable light and used effectively whether you are plaintiff's counsel in a civil case or defense counsel in a criminal case.

If you are plaintiff's counsel in a civil case, your questioning regarding the burden of proof should indicate that it is not a heavy one, that it simply requires a preponderance of the evidence. The questions should further indicate the burden does not require the elimination of doubt and that the jury may render a verdict for the plaintiff even though the evidence does not fit together perfectly and they still have doubts. Discuss the plaintiff's burden of proof in a civil case as a mere tipping of the scales of lady justice. There are analogies that apply and can be used in phrasing voir dire questions on burden of proof relating to such things as baseball scores being 2 to 1 and still being a win or the type of ordinary business judgments that go into selecting a car. The questions, of course, all stress the ease with which the plaintiff can meet his burden of proof. The attorney should attempt to obtain a commitment from the jury that they will not hold the plaintiff to a more stringent burden of proof than is required by law.

On the other hand, in a criminal case, defense counsel's questions should stress that the only issue in the case is satisfying the state's heavy burden of proof. One of the important aspects of the American system of justice is the fact that the state has to prove defense counsel's client guilty of the crime charged beyond a reasonable doubt. Stress that all reasonable doubt must be eliminated and the jurors must be convinced of each and every fact or element necessary to constitute the crime with which the defendant is charged. Stress that if the state does not prove its case as required by law—and it must prove each and every element of its case—then they, the jury, have to find a verdict of not guilty even if they believe it reasonably possible that the defendant is, in fact, guilty. Overall, the questioning in the criminal case stresses the fact that the issue involved is not guilt or innocence; that issue is not theirs to decide. The issue that the jury must decide is whether the state has met its heavy burden of proof.

§ 6.45 Feelings toward defendants in criminal cases

In the criminal case, another area of concern is that the jury will disregard the presumption of innocence that is guaranteed under the United States Constitution. Despite this presumption of innocence, many jurors, particularly those tending to believe strongly in authority, believe that a person would not be charged with a crime unless he were guilty. These jurors believe that the state would not prosecute an innocent person. Like other biases and prejudices, this belief needs to be probed extensively with each juror in the criminal case. Again, open-ended questions matching the primary mode by which the individual juror assesses information must be used to encourage the juror to discuss his feelings on the subject. The defense lawyer in the criminal case needs to assess the nature and extent of such a bias or prejudice and determine whether it is of sufficient degree to ask for a challenge for cause. If the juror is not going to be challenged, it is necessary to commit that juror to the promise that he will follow the law and presume the defendant innocent even if the defendant does not take the stand in his own defense. The "red flag" questioning technique is again appropriate for use in obtaining this commitment. If your client is not going to take the stand, this may be just the type of "red flag" question to pose to the criminal jury.[22] Then, have the court reporter reflect the jury's commitment in the record so that you can refer back to it during your summation.

§ 6.46 Determining leaders on the jury panel

Another matter deserving assessment during the voir dire is to determine which of the jurors you believe will assume a leadership role during the course of the trial. Leaders are obviously going to influence the other jurors and in group dynamics, one can see that leaders are crucial in determining how the group will react to the evidence and the law. Therefore, it is essential to identify the leaders so that it may be determined whether a particular leader is favorable to your position or whether this is a leader you want to eliminate from the jury.

COMMENT: If you are absolutely convinced by all the

[22] *See supra* §§ 6.24–6.26, for a complete discussion of "red flag" questioning.

available information and the use of rapport-building techniques, including your leading and his following, that the leader is on your side, then you certainly should keep him on your jury. He will be a powerful ally. On the other hand, if there is any doubt whatsoever about the leader's rapport with you or your client, for any reason, then *do not take the chance*.

The failure to eliminate an unsympathetic leader leaves you with a one-man trial instead of a jury trial. If you had wanted the prejudice of a one-man trial you could have waived the jury and had the case tried by a judge. Therefore, in the great majority of instances, eliminate the leaders of the jury by challenges for cause, if possible, or by peremptory challenges if necessary.

There are obvious ways to determine potential leaders. Leaders can be determined by their relationship with the rest of the group. Usually they are among the stronger personalities on the jury. Some people are clearly leaders because of their background. If a juror is a supervisor at work, has a position of leadership in his job, or has authority over other people, then he is a leader. Generally, he would not have been selected for his position otherwise. In addition to a juror's employment status, his socioeconomic status may rank him as a leader. Obviously, a bank president is a leader. Accountants, physicians, dentists, and so forth are usually leaders. Anyone who has attained a socioeconomic status far ahead of the other jurors is probably a leader. This type of leader can be particularly dangerous and particularly strong. Fortunately, these types of leaders, because of their job position or socioeconomic status, are easy to spot.

The other types of leaders have to be identified by their personality type. There is a simple method which can be used to indicate leaders. It is called the "Big I, Little I" Rule. It is employed early in the voir dire when you are developing the work history of each individual juror. Instead of asking, "where do you work?" or "what do you do for a living?", phrase the question exactly this way: "by whom are you employed?" That question is designed to elicit the place of employment of each juror. On responding, the juror will either simply give the name of the place where he is employed or he will place before his answer the word "I"; for example, "I work for the First National Bank." We can obtain an indication of leadership potential by how frequently and how strongly he uses "I". The bigger the "I", the stronger the leader. If the juror uses no "I" before giving his place of employment, he is probably not a leader. This is what is referred to as the "Big I, Little I" Rule.

§ 6.47 Determining personality types

In 1961, O. J. Harvey, David E. Hunt, and Harold M. Schroder developed four conceptual systems of personality organization.[23] Organizational system #1 is the classic authoritarian. This is the person who is humble and timid toward the judge and the attorney. He answers all the questions "yes, sir" or "no, sir" whether asked by the attorney or the judge. He is highly committed to the rule of law and to religion, and tends to see the world in terms of black and white. This personality type is responsive to people in power and believes that there is an absolute truth. He projects his own values onto others. The authoritarian is not a good juror for plaintiffs in a civil case and is most definitely not a good juror for defendants in a criminal case.

Organizational system #2 is represented by the clinical person, that is, someone who is still a bit of an authoritarian, but has a negative attitude toward the rule of law and does not follow tradition and authority although he does not always reject it. He is, on occasion, argumentative and sometimes opposes the system.

Organizational system #3 is similar to #2; however, this person, although he has a negative attitude toward rules and tradition, needs to emphasize harmony, agreement, and friendship. This personality type has a strong drive to help others and he is particularly interested in those people worse off than himself. Organizational system #3 jurors are good jurors for plaintiffs in a civil case, particularly if the plaintiff is a member of a minority group. The same thing would apply to jurors for defendants in a criminal case.

Organizational system #4 is the egalitarian or creative personality. This is an open-minded personality; he tends to think in the abstract. He solves problems with a general broad stroke of the brush. His attitude toward the rule of law is that if it works it is okay, but if the rule does not do justice, he is perfectly willing to bend it. This is the ideal juror for the plaintiff in a civil case and defendant in a criminal case.

---

[23] O.J. Harvey, D.E. Hunt & H.M. Schroder, Conceptual Systems and Personality Organization (John Wiley & Sons, 1961).

Questioning the juror during voir dire should allow you to determine whether the juror fits in System 1, 2, 3, or 4. Obviously, where you rate this juror's personality characteristics will help you determine whether or not to keep that juror.

§ 6.48 Using obtained information

Jurors respond well to an attorney who makes them feel confident about themselves. Jurors also respond well to attorneys who are well prepared. This applies even during voir dire; however, voir dire for the trial lawyer can be the most stressful part of the trial. He is asking questions and forming impressions about each individual juror. It is impossible to ask these questions, build rapport, gain commitments, and effectively examine the jury if the lawyer at the same time is trying to record the information on each individual juror. Even with all of the various systems devised for remembering jurors' names and faces, it would be impossible for anyone to record and accurately evaluate from memory all of the information on each of the prospective jurors.

Yet the trial attorney does not want to make the mistake of using his own stereotypes and other biases in selecting the jury. Nor does he want to base his decision to select or reject a juror on only one piece of information. As can be seen, accurate analysis of jurors and jury selection is a complex and learned art form. It is the successful integration of many bits of information. To rely on one piece of information is to invite the opportunity to make a critical mistake. In one case we know of, the trial attorney excused a potential juror after assessing her facial expression, duration of eye contact, and blocking movements of folding her arms and crossing her legs when questioned by counsel. After the trial began, the woman remained in the courtroom listening to the evidence. Finally, out of curiosity the attorney approached the woman and asked her why she had remained. She replied that she had realized the serious nature of the plaintiff's injuries as the voir dire developed. She remained to watch the trial because she was concerned about the plaintiff and wanted to see if the jury brought back an adequate award. The lawyer had obviously erroneously relied on only one small bit of information in that instance.

Techniques must be developed for the intelligent use of our peremptory challenges and for the use of the information we are obtaining during voir dire. Quite frankly, it is impossible for the trial lawyer to do this alone. It is essential during voir dire to have a secretary, an investigator, a paralegal, or another attorney at the counsel table charting the information given by each juror on his background and rating that juror. In a major case, this person ought to be a trial behavioral consultant trained in reading nonverbal cues. That person can better assess the jurors' conduct. In addition to the information on the individual jurors, the composite of the jury must be considered when contemplating the use of peremptory challenges. Certainly of great importance is a factor that can only be supplied by the trial attorney himself—i.e., the degree of rapport the trial lawyer feels he has established with a particular juror through his pacing and leading of the juror. It takes at least two people to adequately assess the potential jurors in the average civil or criminal case. In a major case, the team may well consist of several people.

When using a trial behavioral consultant in the courtroom, it is essential that his function is not known to the jury. If possible, that information need not be given to opposing counsel either. The consultant can simply be a new paralegal or an investigator from your office. It simply is not ethically required that you voluntarily disclose the methods you are using to evaluate the jurors and any information you are obtaining during voir dire. To allow his function to become public knowledge is to invite problems. Opposing counsel will immediately raise an objection on the basis that he has no such assistance. Uneducated judges, in some cases, have barred the trial consultant from the courtroom or, at the very least, have refused to let the trial consultant sit at the counsel table. In one case, the trial attorney was instructed by the judge not to even look at the trial consultant seated in the back of the courtroom. As absurd as this ruling sounds, it actually happened. Remember that judges tend to be very conservative and generally are not on the cutting edge of trial tactics.

§ 6.49 Using a systematic selection process

A pretrial investigation of the local community environment by a trial behavioral consultant is one method of systematic selection. The factors evaluated include, among others, personality, demography, attitude, and verbal and nonverbal variables. When working with a trial consultant, this complex form of evaluation yields more accurate information than is generally available. A trial behavioral consultant can also be used to rate systematically each potential juror giving five points for each of the four major variables and thereby rating the desirability of the jurors on a scale of 1 to 20. However, most lawyers cannot justify the use of a trial behavioral consultant in every case.

A system is needed whereby fellow attorneys and others can systematically rate jurors for the trial attorney, thereby assisting in the recall and assessment of information and as it relates to the particular client and the nature of his case. It is therefore suggested that an index card with the name and voir dire number be made out for each individual juror. It should also list the factors to be evaluated, with adequate space for the numerical assessment, using a scale from one to ten. The categories listed on the card should be as follows:

1—Occupation

2—Age and sex

3—Ethnic or racial background

4—Religion

5—Party biases

6—Education

7—Personality type

8—Body type

9—Evaluation of nonverbal cues

10—Expressed biases

Each juror's rating card would look something like this:

MATTHEWS, JOHN D.		Juror # 1234
INFORMATION OBTAINED:		RATING RELATIVE TO CASE:
1—	Carpenter	1—
2—	22, male	2—
3—	Hispanic	3—
4—	Catholic	4—
5—	Democrat	5—
6—	Vocational School	6—
7—	Authoritarian	7—
8—	....	8—
9—	....	9—
10—	....	10—
	Total	—

In addition to using a systematic selection process for each juror, it is essential that we rate and consider the group dynamics involved. It is essential that a master seating plan be set up on paper. Draw blocks on the sheet which correspond to the jury box seats. As jurors are selected or eliminated, the appropriate index cards are substituted on this master seating plan. This pooling of information on all twelve jurors gives us an idea of the picture of the total jury, the overall educational level, the gender makeup, and the overall socioeconomic level of the jury. This will give us an idea of the dynamics involved on a systematic basis. Information in the blocks will appear as follows:

Matthews	Smith	Jones	Garcia	Goldberg
Carpenter	Machinist	Banker	Paralegal	Medic
Male	Male	Female	Male	Female
Vocational	Twelfth grade	College	College	College

The foregoing technique is one systematic approach to the intelligent use of peremptory challenges. It is but one of many variations of this approach. Any system which facilitates the organization of information by someone else in such a manner that it permits the trial attorney to make efficient use of the mass of data is an effective system. Ideally the system also provides an area for displaying the known information about those jurors yet to be called. Some court rules permit the lawyer to know the order in which the jurors will be called, while others require each new juror to be selected at random. In other courts, jurors are put in the jury box and questioned simultaneously, then all the attorneys are required to use all their peremptory challenges to reduce the jury to twelve. In federal court you would, of course, be reducing to six.

In conclusion, recall that there is one overriding factor in the jury selection process—the trial attorney's instinct. You are going to try this case. Sometimes other people may rate a juror differently than you would. You, however, are the one who has engaged in the two-way communication process with those jurors. You are the one who has looked the juror in the eye, only you can rate the duration for which the eye contact was maintained, only you can assess the juror's nonverbal cues, only you can feel your "gut" reaction to that juror. In the final analysis, this is the ultimate rating. The trial lawyer always has veto power over the recommendations of an assistant or a trial behavioral consultant in selecting the jury. No matter what anyone says, if the lawyer feels that he cannot talk to the juror, then that juror should not be picked. After all, it is the trial attorney who has integrated the information gathered by himself and others. It is the trial attorney who has the opportunity to do what no one else is permitted to do, that is, to interact with the individual in a one-to-one relationship. In the final analysis, it is the responsibility of the attorney to internalize a myriad of information sources; therefore, it is his prerogative to decide how best to utilize his knowledge in the jury selection process.

Chapter 7

OPENING STATEMENT: GETTING THE JURY COMMITTED

KLUWER LITIGATION LIBRARY REFERENCES

JEANS, LITIGATION: Chapter 7, *Opening Presentation*.

JOYE & LOVETT, DRUNK DRIVING: THE TRIAL WORKBOOK, THE TRIAL SOURCEBOOK, THE TRIAL NOTEBOOK: Chapter 107, *Opening Statement*.

PREISER & PREISER, HANDLING SOFT TISSUE INJURY CASES: Chapter 7, *How to Handle Problem Situations*; Chapter 8, *Final Preparation for Trial*; Chapter 10, *Psychology of the Trial*; Chapter 12, *Opening Statements*.

I. Nonverbal Considerations

§ 7.01 Primacy: the first four minutes

Primacy is the weapon of the plaintiff in the civil action and the prosecution in the criminal case. (Principle 3: Perceptions are organized and structured within a brief period of time.) The first-impression stage of the trial process is considered to encompass voir dire, opening statement, and the first witness. These three areas form the basis of the jury's first impression of the case. The jury needs to be educated as to the issues of the case.[1] This education includes the disclosure of the weaknesses of the plaintiff's case. You should try to "innoculate" the jury from the "sting" of the opponent exposing the weak points of your case.

Primacy as a principle applies not only to the whole trial, it also applies to each stage of the trial. Primacy must be a consideration when structuring voir dire questions. For example, during voir dire the strong points should be presented before the weak ones. Also, in structuring the

[1] *See supra* Chapter 6, *Selecting the Jury: A Two-Way Communication Process.*

testimony of each witness for direct and cross-examination, present the strong aspects first. In preparing for closing arguments, the principle of primacy is of paramount importance.

The stage in which the principle of primacy is most effective and dramatic is opening statement. Primacy is the essence of opening statement. During the opening statement, the attorney is painting a verbal picture of the incident which enables the jury to understand why the plaintiff deserves an award. The plaintiff in the civil case who makes a strong first impression, particularly on issues of liability, has dealt the defendant a devastating blow. Once the jurors have internalized the impression that the plaintiff should prevail, there is a tremendous burden on the opposing counsel to explain away the impact made in your opening statement. In a criminal case, the same, of course, applies to the state.

Some years ago a study on jury trials was performed at the University of Chicago. For purposes of that study, opening statements in a civil case were performed before mock juries. The jurors were instructed by a judge to keep an open mind. Yet, later interviews indicated that 80% of the jurors made up their minds on liability at the close of the opening statement without even hearing the first witness. This study indicates the overwhelming effect of the principle of primacy.

The primacy principle applies to the structuring of the opening statement itself. In all probability, only at the beginning of opening statement will the attorney have the full attention of the entire jury. We know that in a face-to-face interaction, the primacy principle operates for the first four minutes.[2] It is during the crucial first four minutes of opening statement that the jury's attention is at its highest and the impression made in their minds is most likely to remain fixed. Do not waste those precious minutes. Use those four minutes to accomplish two things: first, build rapport with the jurors (pace them);[3] second, anchor your case theme psychologically.[4] The case theme *must* be developed *very* early during opening statement. Every time you mention the case theme, use the same gestures and the same tone of voice, stand in the same spot, use the same facial expressions, and perform some distinctive motion which indicates the existence of your case theme. Once your theme is anchored, you can communicate it to the subconscious minds of the jurors by

---

[2] *See supra* Chapter 1, *Impression Formation in the Courtroom.*

[3] *See supra* Chapter 6, *Selecting the Jury: A Two-Way Communication Process.*

[4] *Id.*

standing in the same spot and using only part of the gestures which originally formed the anchoring process.

Remember that when the jury's attention level is highest, you are most likely to persuade the majority of the jurors. These first four minutes are the time to pace the jurors, to maximize the use of salient facts, and to anchor it in the jury's mind. This is the time to prepare the jurors psychologically to accept you, your client, and your case. Avoid long explanations as to what constitutes an opening statement, what is the burden of proof, who you are, as well as the identity of the client. Such information can come later in the opening statement.

COMMENT: During those first four minutes, primacy is working in favor of the plaintiff; take full advantage of it. Make those the most effective four minutes of your opening statement.

---

§ 7.02 Persuasive delivery

Trial counsel are often told by conservative law professors that the opening statement is "not an argument," that it should simply inform the jury about the case and that it should not be persuasive. The goal of the opening statement, as at every stage of the trial, is to persuade those who will decide your case that you ought to win. Obviously, if an opening statement is not persuasive, it should not be given. While the opening statement cannot be a direct frontal attack, it must be "argued" as persuasively as possible. In fact, counsel should argue the opening statement as much as the judge will allow, keeping in mind that there are subtle differences between the opening statement and closing argument.

During opening statement the use of analogies, rhetorical questions, and other argument techniques is generally not permitted. Counsel is not free to make editorial comments or arguments per se during the opening statement. On the other hand, the opening statement can be used to tell the jury, with impact and emotion, what the evidence will show. With regard to liability issues, the opening statement is probably the most crucial phase of the trial, since most jurors will form their first impression based on your opening.

§ 7.03 Structuring the opening statement: climax and anticlimax

Certain tactics should be applied to structuring the opening statement. It must have a strong beginning and ending. The case theme, which should be presented early in the opening statement, must be anchored.[5] Thereafter, consider the presentation of your case in the "climax and anticlimax" order.[6] That is, the strongest arguments should be presented immediately after offering and anchoring the case theme. Only after this is done may one go on to amenities such as telling the jury what an opening statement is, perhaps discussing why the plaintiff presents his case first in a civil matter, and who has the burden of proof. When defending a criminal case, discuss why the state presents its case first and the tremendous burden that the state has with regard to "proving guilt beyond a reasonable doubt." The attorney should try to undo any advantage gained by the state through the principle of primacy. Counsel should further try to "collapse any anchors," thereby destroying the images that have been established in the minds of the jurors by counsel for the state. "Collapse the anchors" by discussing them and then explaining how they are misleading or false. Tie into the statements that have been anchored by opposing counsel, stand in the same spot used by the opposing counsel, link up with the statement, then knock it out as untrue and unrealistic. Only after this is accomplished should the opening statement cover questions of causation, liability, and damages. Close your opening statement on a high point with emotional impact, discussing the real issues in the case. For example, if the issue in a given case is the value of human life, stress that issue during your close. If the key issue is safety, you may want to play to the emotions of the jury by asking them if they feel safe while walking down the street or when using public transportation.

It is not always true that the attorney normally first discusses the facts involving liability in the opening statement. In some cases, the damages aspects of the case may be so overwhelming as to warrant, under the climax and anticlimax principle, being presented first. Thus counsel may wish to discuss the extent of the damages before explaining why the defendant ought to be held liable for those damages.

The following is an example of how to emphasize damages in an opening statement. As we similarly did in Chapter 4, the following opening

---

[5] *See supra* § 7.01, *Primacy: the first four minutes.*

[6] *See supra* § 5.77, *Climax and anticlimax considerations.*

statement shows you the original opening statement and then shows a restructured statement using the verbal patterns of creating movies, photographic stills, association and disassociation, and sequencing of phrases as well as embedded commands. This will give you a better idea of how to precisely structure an opening statement to maximize the impact for the jurors.

Original Opening Statement

(1) "Ladies and gentlemen, this is the case of [whatever your case theme is]. . . . (2) The evidence in this case will show that my client, Mary, as you see her sitting over there, works as a secretary every day behind a desk for the Green Textile Company. (3) Everyday she has a lunch hour at noon. (4) When noon comes, the other secretaries at the Green Textile Company get together and go to lunch at the restaurant across the street. (5) They talk about Christmas shopping; about their families; about their boyfriends. (6) Mary, unlike the other secretaries, does not go to lunch. (7) When she stops typing, she picks up her lunch in her brown bag from her desk drawer and goes down to the parking lot in front of the Green Textile Company. (8) As she leaves the building, she puts on her brown cotton overcoat. (9) She drives from the Green Textile Company, about one mile, in her grey 1970 Ford. (10) It has a knock in the engine and sputters along. (11) She drives to 111 West Hilldale Street, to a red and brick building. (12) There Mary parks her car during her lunch hour and walks everyday down the same green tile, sterile corridor, that has a green ceiling, green tile walls and a green tile floor. (13) At the end of the corridor, she comes to a brown wooden door. (14) The simple number 209 is over the door. (15) Mary goes into the dimly lit room where there is located a hospital bed; in the hospital bed is a man who Mary goes over to and kisses on the forehead. (16) He cannot feel the kiss, but she knows that he knows she is there because he blinks his eyes. (17) She takes out her handkerchief and dabs the tears away. (18) She pulls up a plain, wooden chair and sits next to the bed. (19) She takes her lunch out of the bag and begins to talk to the man in the bed. (20) From the conversation, you can tell that the man in the bed is her husband. (21) She tries to tell him about the kids, how they are doing in school, and what is going on in her life; as she talks more tears roll out of his eyes and she dabs them away. (22) Several times she has to look away from the bed so that she can regain her own

composure. (23) Finally, Mary notices that the time alloted out of her lunch hour has expired. (24) She puts the scraps of her lunch back in the brown paper bag and kisses her husband goodbye. (25) He cannot feel the kiss, he cannot respond, he cannot move. (26) He is conscious and communicates with her by blinking his eyes. (27) One blink for yes and two blinks for no. (28) But that is the only body function that he can control. (29) He is a quadriplegic. (30) John Brown, the man laying in the bed, was a healthy 27-year-old when he went into the hospital for a simple hemorrhoid operation. (31) He came out brain damaged and quadriplegic. (32) Let me tell you what caused that!"

Verbal Restructuring of Partial Opening Statement

SENTENCE (1, 2)

ORIGINAL: "Ladies and gentlemen, this is the case of [whatever your case theme is]. . . . The evidence in this case will show that my client, Mary, as you see her sitting over there, works as a secretary every day behind a desk for the Green Tile Company.

RESTRUCTURED: The evidence in this case will show that my client, Mary, as you see her sitting over there, works as a secretary everyday behind a desk for the Green Textile Company.

ANALYSIS: We have deleted the first sentence that says "Ladies and gentlemen, this is the case theme of." We deleted this phrase because it is not a strong opening. We do not want to start an opening statement by immediately going to the theme. [Refer back to Chapter 4 where we offered a sample opening.] Assume that this opening statement starts with a few lines to build rapport. Only after rapport has been established is it appropriate to discuss the actual content of the case. After opening remarks, we can then begin with "The evidence in this case will show. . . ."

SENTENCE (3)

ORIGINAL: Everyday she has a lunch hour at noon.

RESTRUCTURED: No change necessary.

ANALYSIS: None.

SENTENCE (4)

ORIGINAL: When noon comes, the other secretaries at the Green Textile Company get together and go to lunch at the restaurant across the street.

RESTRUCTURED: When noon comes, the other secretaries at the Green Textile Company can be seen getting together and going to lunch at the restaurant across the street.

ANALYSIS: We want to move to the present tense with the phrase, "can be seen getting together." We want the jurors to become engaged in the process of watching them doing this. We are going to put the jurors in the position of watching a movie and change to "ing" verbs to create that present tense association.

SENTENCE (5)

ORIGINAL: They talk about Christmas shopping, about their families, about their boyfriends.

RESTRUCTURED: They listen to each other talking and chatting about Christmas shopping, about their families, about their boyfriends.

ANALYSIS: The proper phrase should be "they listen to each other talking and chatting." The original sentence said "they talk about Christmas shopping." In the restructured sentence, we are more precise concerning what is happening and we are creating a full sensory experience of what is going on by narrating what is occurring as a present time event. This will allow the jurors to more fully associate with what is happening.

SENTENCE (6)

ORIGINAL: Mary, unlike the other secretaries, does not go to lunch.

RESTRUCTURED: No change necessary.

ANALYSIS: None.

SENTENCE (7)

ORIGINAL: When she stops typing, she picks up her lunch in her brown bag from her desk drawer and goes down to the parking lot in front of the Green Textile Company.

RESTRUCTURED: No change necessary (Active "ing" words are used).

ANALYSIS: None.

SENTENCE (8)

ORIGINAL: As she leaves the building, she puts on her brown cotton overcoat.

RESTRUCTURED: No change necessary.

ANALYSIS: None.

SENTENCE (9)

ORIGINAL: She drives from the Green Textile Company about one mile in her grey 1970 Ford.

RESTRUCTURED: No change necessary.

ANALYSIS: None.

SENTENCE (10)

ORIGINAL: It has a knock in the engine and sputters along.

RESTRUCTURED: She is used to hearing a knock in the engine and the sound of sputtering.

ANALYSIS: This change was made to put the sentence into the narrative form to allow the jurors to participate in the observation process.

SENTENCE (11)

ORIGINAL: She drives to 111 West Hildale Street, to a red and brick building.

RESTRUCTURED: No change necessary.

ANALYSIS: None

SENTENCE (12)

ORIGINAL: There Mary parks her car during her lunch hour and walks every day down the same green tile sterile corridor, that has a green ceiling, green tile walls and a green tile floor.

RESTRUCTURED: No change necessary.

ANALYSIS: None.

SENTENCE (13)

ORIGINAL: At the end of the corridor she comes to a brown wooden door.

RESTRUCTURED: No change necessary.

ANALYSIS: None.

SENTENCE (14)

ORIGINAL: The simple number 209 is over the door.

RESTRUCTURED: No change necessary.

ANALYSIS: None.

SENTENCE (15)

ORIGINAL: Mary goes into the dimly lit room where there is located a hospital bed; in the hospital bed is a man who Mary goes over to and kisses on the forehead.

RESTRUCTURED: No change necessary.

ANALYSIS: None.

SENTENCE (16)

ORIGINAL: He cannot feel the kiss, but she knows that he knows she is there because he blinks his eyes.

RESTRUCTURED: He cannot feel the kiss, but she knows that he knows she is there because she sees him blinking his eyes.

ANALYSIS: We have changed the phrase "she sees him blinking." The original phrase was "he blinks his eyes." We want to let the jurors know that she is there watching, observing, feeling, hearing, and listening to him. She is right there as a participant at the scene. In order to do that, we must keep Mary in the description. Further, we specifically want the jurors to feel what Mary is feeling. We can only accomplish this by creating a vivid description of her full sensory state, including what she sees, what she hears, and what she feels.

SENTENCE (17)

ORIGINAL: She takes out her handkerchief and dabs the tears away.

RESTRUCTURED: No change necessary.

ANALYSIS: None.

SENTENCE (18)

ORIGINAL: She pulls up a plain, wooden chair and sits next to the bed.

RESTRUCTURED: She pulls up a plain wooden chair and sits next to the bed, taking her lunch out of the bag.

ANALYSIS: We are linking two sentences together so that we can create the present tense pattern of taking her lunch out of the bag. We want to continue to create a fluid motion for the movie that we are establishing. Whenever we want to create a movie scene that maintains fluidity, we drop abrupt sentence structures and we try to link sentences with words such as "and" or commas so that they flow continually. Sentences which sound as if one flows into another have a very powerful mesmorizing effect on the listener. We are drawn into the story; there is no time to sit back and observe.

SENTENCE (19, 20)

ORIGINAL: She takes her lunch out of the bag and begins to talk to the man in the bed. From the conversation, you can tell that the man in the bed is her husband.

RESTRUCTURED: She begins talking to the man in the bed, and from what she's trying to say, you can tell that the man in bed is her husband.

ANALYSIS: Here we have gone to "ing" words and we have used the words "she begins talking" and the next phrase "she's trying." We are putting it into present tense, again creating the movie and fluidity. We have linked these two sentences with the word "and" to continue the flowing pattern of the story.

SENTENCE (21)

ORIGINAL: She tries to tell him about the kids, how they are doing in school, what is going on in her life; as she talks more tears roll out of his eyes and she dabs them away.

RESTRUCTURED: She is trying to tell him about the kids, how they are doing in school, what is going on in her life, and as she's talking, more tears roll out of his eyes and she's dabbing them away.

ANALYSIS: Again we go to the words "she is trying," "she's talking," and "she's dabbing." These three phrases put us back into the present tense, and the "ing" suffix makes it an actual event that is taking place. In addition, we have a fuller description and appreciation for what Mary is experiencing.

SENTENCE (22)

ORIGINAL: Several times she has to look away from the bed so that she can regain her own composure.

RESTRUCTURED: Several times you see her having to look away from the bed so that she can have a chance of regaining her composure.

ANALYSIS: We have changed the beginning phrase to, "several times you see her having to look away" because we want to use this as an embedded command ("see her having to look away."). In order to make this an effective embedded command, you must change and switch your voice tone right before the command. At this point, you now have the jurors' unconscious mind attuned to the command they are about to receive and a close association with Mary is created. The other change is "regaining her composure" because we want the jurors to feel her in the process of regaining her composure.

SENTENCE (23)

ORIGINAL: Finally, Mary notices that the time alloted out of her lunch hour has expired.

RESTRUCTURED: No change necessary.

ANALYSIS: None.

SENTENCE (24, 25)

ORIGINAL: She puts the scraps of her lunch back in the brown paper bag and kisses her husband goodbye. He cannot feel the kiss, he cannot respond, he cannot move.

RESTRUCTURED: She puts the scraps of her lunch back in the brown paper bag. She kisses her husband goodbye still knowing he cannot feel the kiss; he cannot respond; he cannot move.

ANALYSIS: We have put the phrase "still knowing he cannot feel" in because we want a strong, emotional build up. She still knows of his disability, she may try to forget it or push it aside, but she still knows he cannot feel. We have also used the element of three because we have three phrases that can be used together. Those three phrases are "he cannot feel the kiss; he cannot respond; he cannot move." With all of these phrases you want to build them to a crescendo. We have the element of three to create that type of strength.

SENTENCE (26)

ORIGINAL: He is conscious, and communicates with her by blinking his eyes.

RESTRUCTURED: He is conscious but must tell her all that's in his heart by only blinking his eyes.

ANALYSIS: We want to create some emotion here. The original structure says "he is conscious and communicates with her by blinking his eyes." The restructured sentence states that he is conscious and adds the change that, "but must tell her all that's in his heart" by only blinking his eyes. We are building the emotional pattern here and want to accent the word "heart" because we want the jurors to think about the sentimentalities and emotions of this. We want to keep them associated with the injured party in this situation.

SENTENCE (27)

ORIGINAL: One blink for yes and two blinks for no.

RESTRUCTURED: No change necessary.

ANALYSIS: None.

SENTENCE (28)

ORIGINAL: But that is the only body function that he can control.

RESTRUCTURED: But that is the only body function that is under his control.

ANALYSIS: We use the phrase "under his control" instead of the phrase "that he can control." This puts him into a victim position because it is no longer under his control. A true victim does not have the experience of control; a true victim experiences the result of circumstances beyond his control.

SENTENCE (29)

ORIGINAL: He is a quadriplegic.

RESTRUCTURED: No change necessary.

ANALYSIS: None.

SENTENCE (30, 31, 32)

ORIGINAL: John Brown, the man laying in the bed was a healthy 27-year old when he went into the hospital for a simple hemorrhoid operation. He came out brain damaged and quadriplegic. Let me tell you what caused that!

RESTRUCTURED: John Brown, the man laying in the bed, was a healthy 27-year-old going into the hospital for a simple hemorrhoid operation. They eliminated the hemorrhoids. They also eliminated his ability to do any of the things you and I are doing everyday. He cannot feel; he cannot talk; he cannot move. John, at 27-years-old, is now a quadriplegic. Let me tell you what caused that.

ANALYSIS: We are creating a photographic still because now we are building to the final event of disclosing exactly what happened to John Brown. Because this is the most important element in the opening statement, we want to make sure that the build-up is significant and long enough to create the impact that we want.[7] We keep the first sentence and the first change is the sentence, "They eliminated the hemorrhoids." We want to use repetition so we began the next phrase with "They also eliminated." This is where the drama comes in. They not only eliminated the hemorrhoids, but they also eliminated his ability to *do* any of the things "you and I are doing everyday" (pacing comment). Not you and I do everyday, but you and I *are doing*. (Present tense.) We also use the element of three. "He cannot feel; he cannot talk; he cannot move." At the end we say "John . . ." and we pick up repetition with the phrase "at 27-years-old" because we are trying to create the contrast between being 27 and what has happened to change his entire life, by dramatically stating: "is now a quadriplegic." We are using this restructured pattern to create more drama and more curiosity. We know that we can engage both the conscious and unconscious mind with curiosity. When we get to the point of using photographic stills, we want to use repetition to anchor critical points such as the word "eliminated" or "27-years-old." We have also used the element of three to build three impact statements so that the jurors can continue to associate with John.

COMMENT: You must put your strongest argument first; if you have a "strong damages case," you should emphasize the damages and take advantage of the climax and anticlimax principle. You should set a mood wherein if you show any negligence at all during the rest of the trial the jury is likely to decide in your favor.

---

[7] *See infra* § 7.22, *Closing the opening statement.*

§ 7.04 Anticipating defenses and using issues

Counsel for plaintiff must, for the reasons previously discussed, try to anticipate defenses.[8] If a defense of comparative or contributory negligence is possible, it is best discussed and neutralized in the opening statement. Similarly, if the major issue is one of causation, it is best covered in opening statement. The jurors must be innoculated against any defense that opposing counsel may attempt to inject. Give the jury a little preview in the opening statement, and take the sting out of your opponent's arguments. As with a smallpox or polio vaccination, by exposing the jurors to a small dose of the disease they can, in essence, become resistant to it. They will not accept the defense without serious thought because they have already heard it from you, and hopefully, you have effectively convinced them that the defense does not apply.

For example, if comparative or contributory negligence is a possible defense in an automobile case, discuss the alleged facts relating to the defense in your opening statement. If you are rebutting the defense of comparative or contributory negligence with the use of the doctrine of sudden emergency, discuss it in the opening. If the judge will not permit a discussion of principles of law in the opening statement, counsel should stress that the plaintiff was faced with a "sudden emergency," and that although it may be shown by the evidence that his choice was not the best choice, it certainly was a reasonable one. Plaintiff may have been better off crossing over to the other side of the road, but he did not know that there were no cars coming. Instead, he headed for the ditch, which caused his car to flip over and caused his injuries. The evidence will show, however, that he normally does not drive into ditches and that he was forced into the ditch by the defendant who was on the wrong side of the road coming at him head-on. The fact that plaintiff chose a more dangerous course of action under the circumstances is not negligence.

Similarly, if counsel has a causation problem and the defendant's negligence was one of several factors which brought about the total injury, present it during the opening statement. The jury needs to be told that the evidence will show that the defendant's negligence was one of the causes of the plaintiff's condition and that the plaintiff had preexisting conditions which also contributed. Then, stress that under the law the defendant is responsible as long as his action was a proximate cause and the evidence will show that had it not been for the defendant's actions,

---

[8] *See supra* Chapter 6, *Selecting the Jury: A Two-Way Communication Process.*

the other causation factors would not have been triggered. It should be stressed, in order to limit the impact of a causation defense, that the defendant's action does not have to be the only cause of the injury and resulting disability as long as it is a precipitating cause. Whatever defenses and issues are going to be raised have to be anticipated and they have to be covered in the opening statement. This is similar to "using the mosquito bite repellent rather than the mosquito bite lotion"; that is, it is better to avoid being bitten at all than to treat the sting of the defense raising these issues. The raising of issues can be used, of course, as a basis for bringing the opening statement closer to a closing argument.

The discussion of issues which the defense will probably raise can be appropriate in the opening statement and it can be an effective tool in making the opening statement that much more effective and persuasive. In a medical malpractice case where the plaintiff's two witnesses are both from out of state, counsel should tell the jury that the evidence will show that these very same witnesses could not testify in their own community because of the conspiracy of silence. While it is true that the plaintiff could not get a local doctor to testify, the evidence will show that this is not because defendants were not negligent. Rather, it is because local doctors cannot testify against other doctors from the same area. Indicate that you intend to introduce evidence on this point. It is crucial to introduce such evidence and to make such an argument in every medical malpractice case. In most instances, the plaintiff's expert, because of the local conspiracy of silence, is from out of town. The defense that the plaintiff's expert is not a local resident must be debunked in the opening statement.

These are some of the techniques that can be used in the opening statement in anticipation of the defenses and issues that will be raised by the defense counsel in his opening statement.

COMMENT: You must consider the potential issues and what your adversary might say and imply. If you handle these issues effectively in your opening statement, their impact in the hands of defense counsel will be limited. If the jury has heard these issues before the defendant's opening, they are going to assume that those issues are not significantly damaging. If the plaintiff brought up these issues, on a subconscious level the jury will believe that the issues do not damage the plaintiff. The potential to destroy your position with these witnesses has been eliminated or, at the very least, severely restricted.

---

§ 7.05 Handling objections: the "evidence will show" technique

There is one very effective technique to make the opening statement persuasive and to avoid the objection that the statement is argumentative. Plaintiff's counsel should use the phrase "the evidence will show," strategically but sparingly during the opening statement. After the case theme has been properly "anchored," explain to the jurors that what you are about to tell them is exactly what the evidence will show. When making this statement, gesture toward the witness stand with an open hand and make sure that all eyes look at it. This causes the witness stand to subconsciously become your ally. The jury should understand that you are going to prove your case from the witness stand and not by your words alone. State: "But, this is what the evidence will show!" Then, tell the story of how the incident occurred without further use of the phrase. As counsel finishes the opening statement, there should be an attempt to persuade the jury. The evidence in the case raises certain issues, yet most judges will hold that a discussion of issues is appropriate only during closing argument. An objection by opposing counsel can often be avoided by the use of the phrase "the evidence will show that the only issue in this case is . . .". Opposing counsel has learned and believes that opening statement is, in fact, "what the evidence will show." When he hears those magic words, he tends not to raise an objection; he tends to let it go. Even if he does object, frequently the judge will overrule the objection because you have told the jury only "what the evidence will show" and you stated that to the judge. Often these magic words work with His Honor, as well. Of course, if the objection is sustained, graciously thank the judge for his ruling and comment that this is what the evidence will show and go back into your opening statement.

§ 7.06 Projecting feeling through vocal and nonverbal cues

Verbal, vocal, and nonverbal considerations are important every time one talks about the case.[9] Of course, an opening statement should use

[9] *See supra* § 5.80, *Use of powerful language*.

positive words. One should not say "we allege", or "we think", or "we submit". This is weak language. In the opening statement the case must be put in terms of "the evidence will show" and then the facts stated as proven facts.

In addition, there are vocal considerations applied to opening statement. Your opening statement should not be bland or presented in a monotone. It should convey a certain amount of emotional dynamism which projects your intensity of belief in the case as well as its veracity and importance. This emotional content is communicated vocally, that is, through the use of voice and inflection.

This is accomplished by the proper use of vocal intonations at the appropriate times. For example, when discussing key issues, the voice should be raised; when discussing damages, the voice should be softened; when attacking an issue which will be raised by the defense, the voice should sound incredulous. Likewise, emotional content is communicated through nonverbal cues. Use of eye contact is important during the opening statement. Look intently at each juror and make eye contact of significant duration with each of them at some point during the opening statement. These are all techniques which apply to selling your case.

Changing pace is also important in any opening statement. The opening statement should not be presented at one constant vocal or emotional level. A constant monotone will not sell the guilt of the defendants, and/or the severe damages suffered by the plaintiff will not be well received by the jury. Pace has to be changed appropriately throughout the opening statement to maintain interest. Your anchoring of the case theme, which occurs early on in the opening statement, must, of course, be intense and dramatic. Then, the pace should be changed as appropriate to conform to the subject matter. Generally, the more inherent interest in the subject matter, the more intense the presentation needs to be. However, there are some matters which are important and which must be covered, but to which one does not attach emotional impact. For example, always advise the jury as to who has the burden of proof during the opening statement. Moreover, during the opening, identify the clients and offer some information which will personalize the client. This personal information should be stated in a much lower tone; counsel should act very calm and neutral.

COMMENT: Counsel should vary the intensity level in order to sustain the jury's interest. Doing so should also make counsel's argument more persuasive during a period of increased intensity. As one reaches the middle of the opening statement generally, the intensity level should be reduced, and as one covers damages and comes back to the key issues in the case, the intensity level should rise significantly.

Recall Principle 1: Communication is based on perception. Feelings of both counsel and client regarding the case need to be communicated to the jury during opening statement. These are communicated by effective use of vocal and nonverbal cues. Even though this is the "opening statement" and not the "opening argument," the effective use of vocal and nonverbal cues allows the communication to the jury of intense feelings regarding the client's cause and the righteousness of that cause.

II. Verbal Considerations

§ 7.07 Verbal considerations based on jury makeup

There are certain verbal considerations which apply to opening statement. In addition to stating the case in a positive manner,[10] there are certain verbal considerations which relate to and should be based upon jury makeup. For instance, the primary channel by which information is processed for some jurors may be auditory; they will have talked about the way they hear things. Or, the primary mode of processing information for other jurors may be visual; they will have talked about the way they see things. If they communicate primarily in the kinesthetic mode, they will talk about how they feel about things. The attorney must recognize what the primary channels of processing information are for both the jurors and their leaders. Counsel must then take this into consideration when determining the phraseology to be used during the opening statement, carefully matching the jurors' own phraseology at key points. This matching of language creates the image that counsel has a great kinship with the jurors. The more you are perceived as being like them verbally, the more they will tend to like you; jurors decide cases in favor of lawyers they like. (Communication Principle 9: People are more eas-

---

[10] *See supra* § 7.06, *Projecting feeling through vocal and nonverbal cues.*

ily influenced by others they perceive as similar to themselves; Principle 10: People are more easily influenced by people they like.)

COMMENT: Careful questioning and listening to the jurors during voir dire allows the attorney to ascertain the primary mode by which the jurors process information. This is particularly important for those jurors with leadership potential. Verbal considerations during opening statement can help build rapport and foster the jurors' affection for you.

Be sure that you or an associate take notes during voir dire and pay particular attention to the verbal patterns, phraseology and predominant processing channels of the jurors. This will help you in making a correct assessment of the jury's verbal patterns, which is a prerequisite to determining which verbal patterns you should use for your opening statement.

§ 7.08 Choosing a psychologically acceptable case theme

As discussed previously,[11] the case theme should be presented early during the opening statement and should state why plaintiff should win. In some cases, however, counsel can develop a case theme that not only sets out emphatically why the plaintiff should prevail, but also explains why the incident happened. If one can develop this type of case theme, it ought to be repeated on several occasions throughout the opening statement. In other words, if one can develop or choose a truly appropriate case theme, then that theme needs to be repeated and anchored throughout the opening statement.

Consider, for example, the following fact pattern from a recent case involving a sixty-year-old black male who had a 125-pound pump liner dropped on his foot at work. Three days after this accident, the plaintiff went to the company doctor who noted that the toe was infected. He did not take a culture of the open sore on the toe, he did not take an X-ray, nor did he even consider that the blister on the toe might be a fracture blister. Instead, he treated the man with antibiotics for three months without ever taking an X-ray of the toe. On ten different occasions, the doctor noted in the medical records that the toe was better. On two

[11] *See supra* § 7.03, *Structuring the opening statement: climax and anticlimax.*

occasions the company doctor sent the man back to work telling him that it would "get better with time if he worked on the toe." Finally, the man's employer sent him back to the company doctor stating that this employee should be admitted to the hospital so they could "find out what is wrong with his toe." Only then did the defendant company doctor take an X-ray and discover that the infection in the toe had spread into the bone including a good part of the foot. As a result, this man's entire foot was amputated at the ankle.

When searching for a case theme, consideration should be given to the motivation behind the defendant's acts and how and why the defendant's doctor failed to take an X-ray in a situation like this where a heavy object fell on plaintiff's toe. Looking at the office record encompassing three months of care, it was noted that the physician wrote the word "better" many times and on two occasions told the man to go back to work when the toe was obviously still infected. It was blatantly obvious that the toe in fact was not getting "better" internally, although the skin healed because of the antibiotic treatment. In fact, the lack of adequate medical care in the case was so obvious and heinous that there was some concern that the jury may not believe the facts on the face of the record without some plausible explanation for the doctor's conduct. In such a case, a psychologically acceptable case theme which explained not only why the plaintiff should be successful, but also why this tragedy occurred was therefore essential in this case. One plausible explanation for this doctor's conduct could be his philosophy in managing a routine industrial medical practice. He was not interested in the complaints of his patients, he was only interested in getting employees back to work and, unfortunately, in many areas of the country this is typical of the attitude of physicians working in industrial clinics. Their referral sources are usually employers and their insurers. Their practice does not usually include patients unrelated to the company. The employee is required to go to the company doctor and since the employer or his insurer is paying the bill and referring the next patient, the company doctor has an obvious inherent bias. Thus it was obvious that the only explanation of and motivation for the defendant physician's conduct in this case was the inherent bias typical of a company doctor.

Counsel had to determine the most effective method of delivery and the best way to sell this idea in the opening statement. Remember that most judges believe that the opening statement is not the proper time for argument but instead should be used to talk about the facts of the case. Direct discussion about inherent biases and prejudices clouding this physician's judgment may be classified an argument. A case theme was needed which could deliver this thought clearly and effectively, and yet in such a manner that it would not be subject to a sustainable objection from opposing counsel. The theme should also force each juror to visualize in his mind's eye the way this physician, this company doctor, practiced medicine. Ultimately, a case theme was developed describing a company doctor practicing medicine with a blindfold on and using a rubber stamp printed "Better, back to work".[12] The first sentences of the opening set the psychologically acceptable theme which could be easily "anchored". The opening statement began by counsel delivering the following message to the jury. We set forth the original opening statement and then present a restructured statement. This will give you a better idea of how to precisely structure an opening statement to maximize the impact for the jurors.

Original Opening Statement

> (1) "Ladies and gentlemen, we are all here concerned with how and why Leroy lost his foot. (2) The evidence will show Leroy lost his foot because Dr. Jones, the company doctor, practiced medicine with a blindfold on; the blindfold which is caused inherently by company doctors being more concerned with getting patients back to work and keeping the company happy, than with what is wrong with the patient. (3) The evidence will show that Dr. Jones, psychologically had a rubber stamp. (4) That rubber stamp said "better". (5) That with that attitude Dr. Jones kept stamping in his record the word "better" and on several occasions told Leroy to get back to work. (6) The evidence will show that Dr. Jones was more concerned that Leroy get "better and back to work" than with what was wrong with Leroy's foot.

Verbal Restructuring of Partial Opening Statement

SENTENCE (1, 2)

ORIGINAL: "Ladies and gentlemen, we are all here concerned with how and why Leroy lost his foot. The evidence will show Leroy lost his foot because Dr. Jones, the company doctor, practiced medicine with a blindfold on; the blindfold which is caused inherently by company doctors being more concerned with getting pa-

[12] *See supra* § 7.01, *Primacy: the first four minutes.*

tients back to work and keeping the company happy than with what is wrong with the patient.

RESTRUCTURED: The evidence will show that it is common for company doctors to be more concerned with getting patients back to work and keeping the company happy than with what is wrong with the patient. The evidence will also show that these same company practices often result in their doctors needing to perceive the patient as getting consistently better. The evidence will show that this particular company doctor, Dr. Jones, practiced medicine with a blindfold; the psychological blindfold was a result of his desire to get patients back to work quickly.

ANALYSIS: In this analysis, we have made many changes. The first and most significant change involved deleting the original first line which says "Ladies and gentlemen, we are all here concerned with how and why Leroy lost his foot." If we are going to create a dramatic scenario, we want to remember that an actual event in real life does not occur with the conclusion first. In order to build an event, we have to build it chronologically. We want to build to the conclusion. We deleted the original opening line because it is anticlimatic at this point. We want to begin in the present tense because we want the jurors to start feeling and understanding what took place here. The first phrase we use is "getting patients back to work and keeping the company happy." We want to embed this as the main concern of most company doctors. We are going to create a logical connection between most company doctors and Dr. Jones. We want the jurors to understand that this is a commonplace occurrence and although it is not acceptable, it has occurred before. We then use the phrase "what is wrong with the patient," because we want the jurors to assess in their minds what is wrong with Leroy. We want them to know that the doctor should have been concerned about what is wrong with Leroy. The next phrase says, "these same company practices." We want to establish why Dr. Jones would act this way and perceive Leroy this way. We have to explain to the jurors logically and chronologically why it is that Dr. Jones would act as a "rubber stamp" in this case. We use the phrase "needing to perceive." This becomes a critical phrase because we want the jurors to know that the doctor had a need to perceive the patient as getting consistently better. Everything about his practice and his role in the company puts him already in that framework of having to justify returning Leroy to work. "Dr. Jones practiced medicine with a blindfold." The blindfold is explained as his desire to get patients back to work quickly. Now we have set the scene to explain why and how this occurred, how this doctor's actions compare to other company doctors, and why this doctor operated with a blindfold. Now that we have set the stage we can move on and talk about this blindfold and start to build a case theme.

SENTENCE (3)

ORIGINAL: The evidence will show that Dr. Jones, psychologically had a rubber stamp.

RESTRUCTURED: Dr. Jones, psychologically actually had a rubber stamp saying "better".

ANALYSIS: We start with the phrase, "Dr. Jones psychologically actually had a rubber stamp saying 'better'." We use the word "actually" because "actually" brings it back to reality. It means he really had a rubber stamp. It makes it a sentence more closely associated with the jurors.

SENTENCE (4)

ORIGINAL: That rubber stamp said "better".

RESTRUCTURED: So he kept "stamping" in his record the word "better" and on several occasions he even told Leroy to get back to work.

ANALYSIS: We definitely want to move to present time because we want the jury to see Dr. Jones stamping. We start the phrase with, "he kept stamping." With this phrase, we want the jurors to see that it was a process repeated over and over again. We show that he kept stamping in his record book the word "better." The next phrases says, "on several occasions, he *even* told Leroy to go back to work." Now we are creating the entire scenario and it must be created chronologically as a movie would be.

SENTENCE (5)

ORIGINAL: That with that attitude Dr. Jones kept stamping in his record the word "better" and on several occasions told Leroy to get back to work.

RESTRUCTURED: The evidence will show that Dr. Jones was much more concerned that Leroy return to work, disregarding what was wrong with Leroy's foot. So he worked, following the doctor's orders, for the next three months because he *is* conscientious and believed in his doctor. He worked for three months in spite of the constant pain in his foot. Each return visit is duly noted in the doctor's chart. It shows "better, back to work" with rubber stamp authority.

ANALYSIS: We start with the first phrase "Dr. Jones was much more concerned that Leroy return to work," because we are staying in the present tense. We want to make it clear to the jurors that something was wrong with Leroy's foot and we have already explained why the doctor is continually overlooking this phenomenon. If you notice the phrases throughout this restructuring, we are staying with present tense except in this one situation. We say "So he worked, following the doctor's orders, for the next three months because he is conscientious." At this point, we are saying he *is* (rather than he *was*) conscientious because we want them to know that Leroy is a conscientious person. The next phrase we changed to past tense to say "believed in his doctor." The reason we changed to past tense is that we want the jurors to know that Leroy believed in his doctor at one time, but no longer believes in him. Obviously, because he no longer has his foot. The next sentence says "he worked for three months in spite of the constant pain in his foot." We want to say "in spite of" knowing that he had pain in his foot and he kept returning to the doctor. The final phrase states "better, back to work with rubber stamp authority." We want to keep reinforcing the element of the "rubber stamp" authority. Authority is a key word because it shows that it was not just anybody using a rubber stamp, it was a doctor with authority. It was such a convincing statement that Leroy, because he is conscientious and believed in his doctor, followed that command.

SENTENCE (6)

ORIGINAL: The evidence will show that Dr. Jones was more concerned that Leroy get "better and back to work" than with what was wrong with Leroy's foot.

RESTRUCTURED: Then it all ended: the pain, the doctor visits, the long nights. It ended because Leroy's foot had to be cut off. He wasn't really better and he'll never go back to work.

ANALYSIS: We have used a photographic still phrase "then it all ended" to build to the climax. You notice that we use a colon here because we want to pause. Now we have an element of three; the pain, the doctor visits, the long nights. That has to be said in such an emotional and dramatic way that it builds empathy and curiosity. The next sentence says "It ended because Leroy's foot had to be cut off." There is a difference. We could have said "because Leroy lost his foot," but if you say this you are using distancing language, it is no longer current time and the jurors no longer associate themselves with the incident. When you say it ended because Leroy's foot had to be cut off, the very phrase "cut off" creates the image of somebody cutting off a foot. That is what we want the jurors to think of. We do not want them to think of this as a surgical operation that took place but as a brutal event for a person to have to lose his foot. The final sentence emphasizes that he wasn't in fact better and he now will never go back to work.

This case theme was "anchored" by counsel standing in a particular spot and removing his glasses, which reinforced the concept of blindness. Every time the word "better" was mentioned counsel formed his right hand into a fist as though holding a rubber stamp, and "stamped" the word "better" with a downward motion of the hand. Thereafter, throughout the opening statement, every time counsel even mentioned the physician writing the word "better" and encouraging Leroy to go back to work, counsel stood in the same position, removed his glasses, and made a stamping motion with the right hand. The appropriate and effective words were "better, back to work." This psychologically acceptable case theme was visually anchored thereafter throughout the entire trial. On appropriate occasions, counsel would stand in the same spot and talk about Leroy getting better when he was not, he would use the same voice level, and he would remove his glasses and make a fist with the right hand. As the trial progressed, it became unnecessary to even say "better, back to work." Counsel simply stood in the same spot and removed his glasses and said nothing. This technique is very effective in communicating with the unconscious mind of the juror. It continually reinforced the case theme. This then is what is meant by choosing a psychologically acceptable case theme and properly anchoring it.

§ 7.09 Choosing impact words and phrases

When constructing a case theme do so with impact words and phrases. Use known literary techniques to improve the effectiveness of your statement. For example, one can use alliteration, that is, in the key phrase all words start with the same letter. In the preceding case the case theme took advantage of all the key words starting with the letter "b". The key words in that theme being: blindfold, better, and back to work.[13]

The case theme should contain action words, which should be both definitive and have impact. They should also be short and utilize as few words as possible. Never use weak words which indicate doubt. One does not "suspect" or "suppose" why Leroy's foot was amputated. Counsel must understand and should explain emphatically to the jury why the foot was amputated. The foot was lost because the physician, Dr. Jones, practiced medicine wearing a blindfold and also because this physician was concerned with "better, back to work."[14]

---

[13] *See supra* § 7.08, *Choosing a psychologically acceptable case theme.*

[14] *See supra* § 5.80, *Use of powerful language.*

§ 7.10 Painting word pictures

Word pictures have impact—the more vivid the picture, the more easily it is retained and recalled.[15] Therefore, counsel should attempt to paint a colorful word picture in his opening statement, so that each juror can see the incident involved happening in his "mind's eye."

COMMENT: The painting of a vivid word picture can help the jurors retain the images of the incident which caused plaintiff's injuries. Thus, in a case where a young child was struck and killed by a truck on the way home from school, counsel should describe that occurrence in vivid detail, filling in colors and other exacting details, so that each juror can see the event in his "mind's eye." Describe the little girl in her school uniform, giving a detailed description of her blonde hair, her pigtails, the color of her skirt, blouse, the time of day, the kind of weather, everything that would be necessary for them to have an accurate picture of exactly what happened. The opening statement should then describe this child moving along a given street, performing as most children do, with abandon. She would be carefree, happy, and thinking about the cartoon that she would soon see on TV. Counsel, in his opening, would then paint a picture of a careless truck driver and would describe what he looked like, with color and detail. The color of the truck, its size, would be set forth in graphic terms. Then build to an impact as the little girl is crushed and mangled beneath the wheels of this giant ponderous vehicle.

An accurately painted word picture can bring the juror's mind's eye back to the scene of the incident. If done effectively, counsel can feel the jury react as the little girl is struck by the truck, and he can see the look of horror on each juror's faces as he sees, in his "mind's eye," this little girl being rundown by this careless truck driver. This is effective word-picture painting in opening statement.

[15]*See supra* § 5.79, *Use of impact words and phrases.*

III. Structure of the Opening Statement

§ 7.11 The opening line

The importance of establishing the case theme early in the opening statement cannot be stressed enough.[16] In this regard, note that the opening line itself may start to build toward the case theme. The first line may also be a statement that sets a mood or tone in the courtroom. Psychologically it puts the jury in the frame of mind in which they will hear, for the first time, your side of the case. It is a time for seriousness, not laughter. It is a time during which the jurors individually and collectively must realize that you are dead serious about this case and about the fact that plaintiff deserves a favorable verdict. However, counsel's first words are not an appropriate occasion for apologies or amenities. The opening line must be carefully considered, structured, and rehearsed.

§ 7.12 Using amenities to further rapport

After the opening line sets the mood, the tone, and seriousness of the case, use amenities to further build rapport with the jurors. Now could be the time to reintroduce yourself and the client to the jury. Always talk about the client by using his first name. Counsel should strive to build rapport with the jury by humanizing the client and then destroy any possibility of jury rapport with the opposition by dehumanizing the defendants in as tactful a manner as possible. Other amenities that can be used to build rapport are promises to be brief, an explanation of the purpose of the opening statement, why the plaintiff goes first, and a little bit about the burden of proof.

All of these statements constitute amenities that help build rapport with the jury. Remember that the feeling of rapport is a two-way communication. You must feel warmth for the jury and you, the lawyer, must be genuinely concerned about their needs. This rapport had been initially established during voir dire when we recognized the feelings and concerns of the jurors and empathized with those concerns. Counsel must explain why they need not be concerned, and how easy he is going to make it for them to decide this case in his client's favor.

---

[16] *See supra* § 7.01, *Primacy: the first four minutes.*

§ 7.13 Telling the "story" of the case

Every case should be presented in a story format during the opening statement. The series of events leading up to the incident, the incident itself, and its sequelae should be presented chronologically. Avoid legal terminology whenever possible; also avoid the frequent reminder that this "story" will come in as evidence and that one witness will testify as to this fact while another witness will swear to the opposite. Deliver the opening statement as though you have invited the jury into your home, as you would any friend, and say to them: "Let me tell you what happened yesterday. . . ." Then simply tell it as if the "story" is occurring before their eyes. Remember that the story should be told in a narrative, without references, and without referring to specific witnesses and pieces of physical evidence.[17] It should be phrased in the present tense so the jury can actually visualize the event occurring.

§ 7.14 —Civil case

In the civil case, as counsel for the plaintiff, take advantage of primacy in telling your story. Include in your narration why plaintiff should be awarded damages, why the incident occurred, and in some cases, even how such gruesome injuries may be avoided in the future. The story should attempt to recognize and associate with the existing belief systems of the jurors.

On the other hand, the defendant in the civil case must work hard to overcome the effects of primacy. His opening statement should stress the fact that the jurors should not decide the case until they hear the defendant's side. He should drive home the fact that there are two sides to every story, stressing those pieces of evidence which are inconsistent with the "story" told by plaintiff's counsel. The defendant's opening statement in a civil case should attempt to take apart the "story" told by plaintiff's counsel in opening statement. If plaintiff's counsel has used a case theme and anchored it, defense counsel should attack the plaintiff's case theme. In the case of the man whose foot was amputated due to infection, the defense counsel attempted to limit the effectiveness of plaintiff's case theme of "better, back to work" by stressing in his opening statement that the evidence would indicate that the words "better"

[17] *See supra* § 7.08, *Choosing a psychologically acceptable case theme*; § 7.10, *Painting word pictures.*

and "back to work" were in fact handwritten in the record and not put there with a rubber stamp.

COMMENT: Thus, in the civil case, it is the defense counsel's goal to diffuse the advantage of primacy by encouraging the jurors to keep an open mind and then holding up to ridicule the "story" of the case as told by plaintiff's counsel.

The following plaintiff's "story" was set forth in a civil case involving a rear-end collision. The original opening statement is provided along with a restructured statement. This will give you a better idea of how to precisely structure an opening statement to maximize the impact for the jurors.

Original Opening Statement

(1) "December 15, 1982, was a typical New Orleans winter day. (2) It was cold and rainy; my client, Diane, whom you see sitting over there, had just finished working as a secretary for the Harold Green Insurance Agency. (3) It was 5:30 in the evening, and she was on the way to do some Christmas shopping. (4) She was heading down the Interstate highway in her 1976 blue Ford Torino. (5) She was proud of that car. (6) She kept it in good condition. (7) It was polished and regularly maintained. (8) It looked newer than it actually was. (9) She drove down the expressway thinking about what she might buy for her husband, Jim, at the shopping center. (10) They had only been married two years. (11) She thought perhaps a cashmere sweater, but she couldn't afford that. (12) As she turned off the Interstate onto the boulevard leading into the shopping center, the traffic was heavy. (13) In the cold rain she saw the red tail lights of the cars ahead of her coming on. (14) She had been going at a reasonable speed so she had no trouble braking her car to stop. (15) She did not know that at this instant her whole life was about to change. (16) Suddenly, Diane was jarred from her thoughts by a horrendous noise. (17) The first thing she heard was the sound of the crash. (18) The next thing she knew, she was being propelled forward from her dead stop at a rapid speed into the car ahead of her. (19) She had her foot on the brakes. (20) Her muscles tensed as she started forward, but it did not help. (21) She felt her head being ripped backwards, and the next

thing she knew she was looking at the ceiling. (22) She kept thinking, 'Oh, my God! Oh, my God! What happened?' (23) She heard the second crash; her head recoiled down on her chest, and she remembers it hitting the steering wheel. (24) For a few moments she was completely dazed. (25) Everything was spinning around. (26) Her first thought as she looked around was, 'Thank God, I had on my seatbelt.' (27) There was a man at the window suddenly, knocking on it. (28) It was Harold James, the defendant. (29) Diane looked up through the window and realized suddenly that his face was out of focus. (30) Then she realized she no longer had on her glasses. (31) She started fumbling for the knob to turn down the window. (32) For an instant she panicked because she could not find the knob. (33) She couldn't seem to make her hands work. (34) They were numb. (35) She finally was able to feel the knob and to start working it down. (36) That's when she first noticed it. (37) The terrific pain in her neck and the back of head. (38) Then she was finally able to get the window down, and the cold air rushed in and the windows in her car fogged up. (39) She heard the man's voice saying: 'Are you all right lady?' (40) She wanted to be alright so she responded, 'I think so.' (41) She said that even though her neck was hurting. (42) She did not, could not, accept the fact that maybe she was hurt. (43) She started looking for her glasses. (44) She felt on the seat and looked on the floor. (45) Much to her amazement she found them on the back seat. (46) Diane kept trying to compose herself and to think of what she should do and the pain in her neck was growing more severe, more intense."

Verbal Restructuring of Partial Opening Statement

SENTENCE (1)

ORIGINAL: December 15, 1982, was a typical New Orleans winter day.

RESTRUCTURED: December 15, 1982, was a typical New Orleans winter day, cold and rainy.

ANALYSIS: We have to understand that most people will not know what a typical New Orleans day is, so we need to provide more descriptive phrases for that, so we've added the phrase "cold and rainy". One of the things we want to do in any creation of a scene is to be as descriptive and precise as possible so that the jurors can associate and feel the actual event as it occurred. We also want to use commas, dashes, and any type of verbal pattern so that we can start linking sentences together to create a forward motion in the movie scene and a flowing, uninterrupted story line.

SENTENCE (2)

ORIGINAL: It was cold and rainy; my client, Diane, whom you see sitting over there, had just finished working as a secretary for the Harold Green Insurance Agency.

RESTRUCTURED: My client, Diane, whom you see sitting over there had just finished working as a secretary for the Harold Green Insurance Agency.

ANALYSIS: We have a phrase in both the original and restructured sentences which says, "my client, Diane, whom you see sitting over there." It is very important at this point that the attorney, while making this statement, turns and looks at his client, gestures towards her with a palm-open hand, holds that eye contact for just a moment, and shows a feeling of compassion and empathy for the client. This clearly shows to the jurors that there is an actual bonding that is taking place between the attorney and the client. It is very important that in the first association with the client when you say, "my client, whom you see sitting over there" that the nonverbal cues congruently and consistently show great respect, admiration, and empathy for the client. If this phrase is passed over too quickly and there is just a slight turn of the head to the client or no turn at all, it will be perceived as a negative connotation that the attorney, in fact, does not have any link to the client. The jurors may also perceive that the attorney does not like or respect the client and, if so, then why should they.

SENTENCE (3)

ORIGINAL: It was 5:30 in the evening, and she was on the way to do some Christmas shopping.

RESTRUCTURED: It was 5:30 in the evening and she is on the way to do some Christmas shopping. If you were watching Diane on this cold and rainy day, this is what you would be seeing.

ANALYSIS: We are moving quickly into the present time to create the association of the event, and we use the phrase "she is on the way". In the first phrase the word "and" is being used to link the sentences together so that we keep the picture of motion going. Now we have added the phrase, "if you were watching Diane on this cold and rainy day". We use the word "you" because we want to bring the jurors back into the picture; we've also used the phrase "on this cold and rainy day" again because we want to keep reinforcing in their mind what type of day it is. The more sensory stimulation we give the jurors, the more they can become involved with the picture and what is actually happening. The final phrase says "this is what you would be seeing". Once again we bring the jurors personally into it with "you" and "seeing", which is an active event. We are suggesting to them that we want them to see what is occurring on this particular day.

SENTENCE (4)

ORIGINAL: She was heading down the Interstate highway in her 1976 blue Ford Torino.

RESTRUCTURED: She is heading down the Interstate highway in her 1976 blue Ford Torino.

ANALYSIS: The change that has been made is to bring the event into the present time ("she is heading").

SENTENCE (5, 6)

ORIGINAL: She was proud of that car. She kept it in good condition.

RESTRUCTURED: She feels proud of that car and keeps it in good condition.

ANALYSIS: We establish present tense by saying "she feels proud". We also use the word "feel" because we want the jurors to start accessing the feelings that Diane is having as she is going through this event. We also added the word "and" because we wanted to use the conjunction.

SENTENCE (7, 8)

ORIGINAL: It was polished and regularly maintained. It looked newer than it actually was.

RESTRUCTURED: You can see it is highly polished and regularly maintained and even looks newer than it actually is.

ANALYSIS: We use the word "you" again in the phrase "you can see it", in order to keep the jurors involved.

SENTENCE (9, 10)

ORIGINAL: She drove down the expressway thinking about what she might buy for her husband, Jim, at the shopping center. They had only been married two years.

RESTRUCTURED: She is driving down the expressway thinking about what she might buy for her husband, Jim, at the shopping center, and remembers they have only been married two years.

ANALYSIS: Again, we are keeping present time association. The final change we made was using the conjunction "and" to tie the two sentences together.

SENTENCE (11, 12)

ORIGINAL: She thought perhaps a cashmere sweater, but she couldn't afford that. As she turned off the Interstate onto the boulevard leading into the shopping center, the traffic was heavy.

RESTRUCTURED: She thinks perhaps a cashmere sweater, if she can afford that, and with these pleasant thoughts, she turns off the Interstate onto the boulevard and into the heavy traffic leading into the shopping center.

ANALYSIS: We are doing exactly the same thing again, we are linking two sentences with the word "and" to keep it flowing.

SENTENCE (13, 14, 15)

ORIGINAL: In the cold rain, she saw the red tail lights of the cars ahead of her coming on. She had been going at a reasonable speed so she had no trouble braking her car to stop. She did not know that at this instant her whole life was about to change.

RESTRUCTURED: Through the cold rain she sees the red brake lights of the cars ahead of her coming on, and since she is driving at a reasonable speed she has no trouble braking her car to a stop; having no idea that at this instant her whole life is going to change.

ANALYSIS: We start with the phrase "through the cold rain" because we want the jurors to actually feel her going through the cold rain that she sees. We want to keep the scenario from a position of what Diane is seeing, feeling, and sensing because the jurors will have a much greater opportunity to understand what is going on if they can watch it through her eyes. We do not want to set up this scenario as one seen from the eyes of an observer. We want the jury to be right there with her. Now we go to the second change, which is the phrase "and since". By using this phrase, we are linking the two sentences and setting up a causal relationship. The clause "and since she is driving at a reasonable speed" must be put first before we can say the next clause which is "she has no trouble braking her car to a stop". The implication is that if you are driving at a reasonable speed, you should have no trouble bringing your car to a stop. Now the final clause says, "having no idea that at this instant her whole life is going to change" We have not made a verbal change here, but the most important change is going to be the pause. There must be a significant pause that occurs after the word "change". Allow the jurors' curiosity to set in, allow them to lean forward waiting for what is going to come next, because the next thing that is going to happen is that you are going to move into photographic stills as you describe the actual event.

SENTENCE (16)

ORIGINAL: Suddenly, Diane was jarred from her thoughts by a horrendous noise.

RESTRUCTURED: Without warning, Diane is jarred by a horrendous noise.

ANALYSIS: This is the beginning of the photographic stills. We want to start out with the phrase "without warning" because that tells us that she is not prepared for what is going to happen next. Then, we move to the shorter, more dramatic sentences and any time we can cut words down we do. We've cut out the words "from her thoughts" because we don't have to indicate that she was jarred from her thoughts, we've already implied that.

SENTENCE (17)

ORIGINAL: The first thing she heard was the sound of the crash.

RESTRUCTURED: The first thing she hears is a crashing sound.

ANALYSIS: We want to experience it from Diane's standpoint. We know that what she hears is a crashing sound. "Crashing" as a verb with "ing" keeps the action close to us, and is more powerful than using it as a noun.

SENTENCE (18)

ORIGINAL: The next thing she knew, she was being propelled forward from her dead stop at a rapid speed into the car ahead of her.

RESTRUCTURED: She feels herself being propelled into the car ahead of her.

ANALYSIS: We are relating to the jury what she is experiencing at that moment.

SENTENCE (19)

ORIGINAL: She had her foot on the brakes.

RESTRUCTURED: It makes no sense because she has her foot on the brakes.

ANALYSIS: The phrase that becomes very important in the beginning is "it makes no sense". We want to clearly indicate that she is in a state of confusion even though she has done everything possible and what is happening now is not consistent with all the precautions she has taken. This allows us and the jurors to see her as a victim. We also note that she has her foot on the brakes, again in the present tense.

SENTENCE (20)

ORIGINAL: Her muscles tensed as she started forward, but it did not help.

RESTRUCTURED: Her muscles tense as she is thrown forward. It does not help.

ANALYSIS: The first sentence has been restructured in order to get into the present tense. We use a period, rather than conjunctions, because we are now into photographic stills. We want to break the original sentence into two sentences. They must be abrupt, and short with the appropriate pausing in between letting the jurors know what is happening.

SENTENCE (21)

ORIGINAL: She felt her hand being ripped backwards, and the next thing she knew, she was looking at the ceiling.

RESTRUCTURED: She feels her head being ripped backwards. She is looking at the ceiling.

ANALYSIS: Once again we are in the present time. Also, we break the sentence and get rid of the conjunctive word "and".

SENTENCE (22)

ORIGINAL: She kept thinking: "Oh, my God! Oh, my God! What happened?"

RESTRUCTURED: She can only think, "What's happening? What's happening to me?"

ANALYSIS: "She can only think". Remember, that the word "only" is a very powerful word and it tells us that nothing else could possibly enter her mind at that time. We've changed the phrase "Oh my God, Oh my God" to "what's happening, what's happening to me" because there may be a set of jurors who dislike the word "God". In this way, we try to minimize any negative perception.

SENTENCE (23)

ORIGINAL: She heard the second crash, her head recoiled down on her chest, and she remembers it hitting the steering wheel.

RESTRUCTURED: She hears a second crash making her head recoil back down upon her chest. Her head is hitting the steering wheel.

ANALYSIS: "She hears a second crash making her head recoil". Again, we are now in the present time. Also, we break up the sentence into two sentences. We start the final sentence with "Her head is hitting" because we want the jurors to see her head hitting the steering wheel.

SENTENCE (24)

ORIGINAL: For a few moments she was completely dazed.

RESTRUCTURED: She is completely dazed.

ANALYSIS: We dropped the phrase "for a few moments," because this weakens the construction. What we are trying to get across is that right now she is completely dazed. We don't need the qualifying phrase, because it reduces the power of the impact that has taken place.

SENTENCE (25)

ORIGINAL: Everything was spinning around.

RESTRUCTURED: Everything is spinning around.

ANALYSIS: We go to the present time to create the association.

SENTENCE (26)

ORIGINAL: Her first thought as she looked around was, "Thank God, I had on my seatbelt."

RESTRUCTURED: Her first reaction is being grateful that she had her seatbelt on.

ANALYSIS: What we have is a terrific contrast between a woman who is involved in a crash, total confusion and panic abound, yet all she can be grateful for at this moment is that she had her seatbelt on. That is very little to be grateful for, so we are creating a paradoxical setup at this point.

SENTENCE (27)

ORIGINAL: There was a man at the window suddenly, knocking on it.

RESTRUCTURED: Suddenly, she sees a strange man looming in her window.

ANALYSIS: We start with the word "suddenly" because at this point we are going to pull her back to another state of consciousness. We specifically use the words "she sees a strange man looming in her window", because that is an appropriate description of what Diane is seeing. What we want to do is create the association of the two words—strange and looming—with the defendant.

SENTENCE (28)

ORIGINAL: It was Harold James, the defendant.

RESTRUCTURED: That man is Harold James, the defendant.

ANALYSIS: "That man" is a distancing phrase. Utilizing the word "that" pushes the defendant away and makes him more impersonable and not real. At this point it is appropriate that the attorney turns to "that man", and makes sure that he uses a pointed finger to point at him or at least gesture toward him with the palm down. This gesture should only be used when referring to the defendant. Remember that in the previous sentence we already established the association that that defendant was a strange and looming man in Diane's eyes. So we've started the distancing pattern here.

SENTENCE (29)

ORIGINAL: Diane looked up through the window and realized suddenly that his face was out of focus.

RESTRUCTURED: Diane cannot see him clearly because her eyes cannot focus.

ANALYSIS: We use the word "because" since it suggests a cause and effect relationship occurring here. It also links it to the present and establishes what type of state she is in.

SENTENCE (30)

ORIGINAL:	Then she realized she no longer had on her glasses.
RESTRUCTURED:	Delete
ANALYSIS:	We've simply deleted the sentence because it was low impact. We will pick this information up later.

SENTENCE (31, 32)

ORIGINAL:	She started fumbling for the knob to turn down the window. For an instant she panicked because she could not find the knob.
RESTRUCTURED:	She starts fumbling for the knob to open the window and panics because she cannot find the knob.
ANALYSIS:	We are using the word "and" because we want to create the connection. We've deleted the phrase "for an instant" because, like the phrase "for a few moments," it decreases the impact of the statement.

SENTENCE (33)

ORIGINAL:	She couldn't seem to make her hands work.
RESTRUCTURED:	She can't even seem to make her hands work.
ANALYSIS:	"Even" is a very strong word because it tells us that that is all she can do at that moment in time.

SENTENCE (34)

ORIGINAL:	They were numb.
RESTRUCTURED:	She cannot feel them.
ANALYSIS:	This is a very important change that has taken place. Everybody has felt "numbness" before—it is a distant feeling. We've all had numb hands, numb feelings, numb fingers. But to say that "she cannot feel them" is much more present and intense, and it's much more frightening to know that you cannot feel your own hands. It conveys the actual frightening experience that we want the jurors to understand that she is having.

SENTENCE (35)

ORIGINAL: She finally was able to feel the knob and to start working it down.

RESTRUCTURED: She fights the fear and panic, and finally, she is able to start working the window down.

ANALYSIS: "She fights the fear" conveys the present time. The word "finally" shows how she has tried, what she has gone through, and what she has to fight to at last just be able to roll down the window.

SENTENCE (36)

ORIGINAL: That's when she first noticed it.

RESTRUCTURED: That's when she first notices it.

ANALYSIS: We are now in the present.

SENTENCE (37)

ORIGINAL: The terrific pain in her neck and the back of her head.

RESTRUCTURED: She is aware now of the terrific pain in her neck and the back of her head.

ANALYSIS: We have added the clause "She is aware now". The most important word is the word "now" because we are trying to show that her awareness is now coming back. It also suggests that the pain has always been there, but because of the fear and fright she has experienced the awareness is just coming back to her right now.

SENTENCE (38, 39)

ORIGINAL: Then she was finally able to get the window down, and the cold air rushed in and the windows in her car fogged up. She heard the man's voice saying, "Are you all right lady?"

RESTRUCTURED: She finally gets the window down and hears the man's voice saying, "Are you all right lady?"

ANALYSIS: We tightened up the sentence to "she finally gets the window down" to emphasize the word "finally", and then the immediate question is "Are you all right lady?" This is important because "lady" is very impersonal and it shows that the defendant is not recognizing and linking to the emotional state that Diane is in.

SENTENCE (40)

ORIGINAL: She wanted to be alright so she responded, "I think so."

RESTRUCTURED: She wants to be alright so she tells him, "I think so."

ANALYSIS: We are now in the present. "Tells him" is much more direct than "she responded." "Responds" is a distance word: "tells" is exactly what you would hear or see in a narration. We have to remove all formal language barriers to keep creating the association.

SENTENCE (41)

ORIGINAL: She said that even though her neck was hurting.

RESTRUCTURED: She says that though the pain in her neck is almost overwhelming.

ANALYSIS: "She says that though the pain" brings us back into present time. We've also changed the phrase in this analysis to "the pain in her neck is almost overwhelming". It has much more power than "was hurting", and also has a long rhythmic pattern so it can be drawn out with the voice.

SENTENCE (42)

ORIGINAL: She did not, could not, accept the fact that maybe she was hurt.

RESTRUCTURED: She does not, cannot, accept the fact that maybe she is really hurting.

ANALYSIS: "She does not, cannot, accept the fact." This is a present tense phrase, a two-part phrase which can be built up in terms of the vocal qualities. We also changed the final phrase which was originally "she was hurt" to "she is really hurting" not only because it moves us into the present, but because we want to associate with the feelings that Diane is having.

SENTENCE (43, 44, 45)

ORIGINAL: She started looking for her glasses. She felt on the seat and looked on the floor. Much to her amazement she found them on the back seat.

RESTRUCTURED: She starts looking for her glasses and much to her amazement finds them hurled on the back seat.

ANALYSIS: "She starts looking" brings us into the present tense. We use "and" as a conjunction to tie the sentences together. The word "hurled" suggests that it took a powerful motion to toss those glasses all the way to the back seat.

SENTENCE (46)

ORIGINAL: Diane kept trying to compose herself and to think of what she should do and the pain in her neck was growing more severe, more intense.

RESTRUCTURED: Diane keeps trying to compose herself, trying to think of what she could do, but the pain in her neck is growing . . . more severe, more intense.

ANALYSIS: "Diane keeps trying". Here the phrase conveys that she is still actively pulling herself together. She's "trying to think of," "the pain in her neck is growing," once again conveys present time. We have a scenario of three words in the clause "the pain in her neck is growing . . . more severe, more intense"; the three words we are going to emphasize as a pattern are "growing," "severe", and "intense".

§ 7.15 —Criminal case

In the criminal case, the prosecution should strive to take advantage of the theory of primacy. The prosecution's opening statement should be restructured in a manner similar to that described for civil cases. The prosecution should be telling a horror "story," but, unlike the civil case, the prosecution in the criminal case should stress the physical evidence and the inferences derived from it that will prove the case "beyond a reasonable doubt." The prosecution has a very difficult burden of proof, and the prosecutor needs to deal with the phraseology "beyond a reasonable doubt," for surely the defense will stress and exaggerate this burden. He should acknowledge that the state has the burden of proving the defendant guilty beyond a reasonable doubt and then indicate that the burden will be met. In emphatic terms, using impact words and phrases and painting word pictures along the way, the prosecutor should illustrate precisely why the evidence carries this burden of proof.

On the other hand, defense counsel in the criminal case should always "tell a different story," saying that "you just heard this story from the prosecution, now let me tell you what really happened." Defense counsel should then tell his story in a narrative fashion frequently stressing that he does not have the burden of proof. His opening statement should stress that as long as there is doubt, even if the jury tends to feel the defendant is guilty, they must acquit him. He should discuss how the evidence does not prove anything conclusively and how, under the evidence the state will present, there is great doubt as to the effectiveness of their proof. The position of defense counsel in the criminal case is, of course, greatly controlled by the nature of the proof he knows the state will present. Unimpeachable eyewitness identification, or a videotape of the defendant making the payoff, is the type of evidence which must be discussed in the defendant's opening statement. It must be shown to be invalid or not applicable. In some cases, it may be tactically beneficial for the defense counsel to admit all of the facts save one, for example, the sanity of the defendant at the moment of the commission of the crime.

§ 7.16 Introducing the medical theory of the case

Where medical testimony is essential to the case and will be forthcoming, presentation of the medical theory of the case appropriately follows that part of the opening statement wherein counsel has told the case "story."[18] Tell the jury in vivid detail just what happened to this person medically. The medical issues may be simple or very complex, depending upon the case.

For example, the following opening statement excerpt might be used to present the medical theory of a routine rear-end collision:

> Mary did not know it then, but when her car was suddenly rammed from the rear without warning and knocked into the car ahead of it, the muscles in her neck were ripped and torn. They bled and hemorrhaged; that is why shortly afterward she began to feel severe pains in her neck. When the muscles hemorrhaged, the neck swelled up and went into spasm. It became stiff and immobile.

---

[18] *See supra* § 7.13, *Telling the "story" of the case*; § 7.14, *Civil case*; § 7.15, *Criminal case*.

Over the next few days, the healing process took place. The tissues healed with fiberblast. They thickened and they scarred. The evidence will show that Mary has permanent scar tissue in her neck and that while the acute symptoms of severe pain have gone away, she will have problems with her neck and limitations on her lifestyle for the rest of her life. She no longer has a normal neck. She has scar tissue, and it is permanent. In essence, Mary, because of the admitted negligence of the defendant in rear-ending her vehicle, has become a "neck cripple."

§ 7.17 Handling damages: the psychological aspects

As a general rule, the jury is not really ready to probe into damages during the opening statement. In most cases, the issue that needs to be covered in detail during opening statement is liability. The opening statement is better suited for conditioning the jury as to why plaintiff should be awarded damages rather than the specifics of the damages award itself. Clearly, however, where liability has been admitted, damages are the only subject that can be covered in opening statement. Similarly, if damages are so devastating as to be overwhelming, under the rule of primacy as well as the climax and anticlimax rule, damages should be emphasized in the opening statement.[19]

This does not mean that the subject of damages should not be discussed at all during the opening. There must be some discussion of the nature of the injury, the resulting disabilities, and the reasons why this is a serious and important case during the opening statement. The jury must know, from the very beginning, that this is a serious case with serious injuries. With respect to how much time is allocated to damages, the manner in which the damages are stressed, and whether or not monetary figures should be presented is a question of judgment in each individual case. In most instances, this question of judgment revolves around the strength of plaintiff's position regarding liability. The weaker the case for the plaintiff (i.e., the tougher it is going to be to prove liability), the less should be said about damages. The stronger the liability issue, the more the jury is psychologically prepared to consider damages.

§ 7.18 —The major impairment

In every case during opening statement, plaintiff's counsel should at least discuss the nature of the most serious impairment suffered by this

[19] *See supra* § 5.77, *Climax and anticlimax considerations.*

plaintiff as a result of this incident. For example, it may be that when the weather changes, your client is going to suffer pain and disability. In such a case, the theme phrase "neck cripple" should be repeated over and over throughout the opening statement. As the disabilities and impairments become more significant, the more time should be spent in discussing the impairment.

Do not forget the necessity of discussing the difference between disability and impairment. One can have a functional disability with no impairment. When physicians discuss disability, they are talking about the simple inability to use some portion of the body. They usually rate this disability with a percentage factor. The jury must understand that the percentage of disability and what the physicians say about it is insignificant. Many of us, in fact almost all of us, have some disabilities, something in our bodies that does not function at 100% capacity. Most of us, however, do not have impairments. Impairments relate to how the disability affects the particular individual involved and his life-style. It is important to make this distinction in opening statement because in most cases the defense is going to talk about the impairment as though it was a simple physical disability. The defense will probably have a "defendant's" physician rate the disability at a very small percentage of that bodily function as a whole and try to make it seem insignificant. Therefore, the jury must understand fully the difference between disability and impairment. This discussion is also a nice lead-in to a discussion of the evidence that will be offered regarding the impairment. It is a way to emphasize the importance of the testimony regarding pain and suffering which will be forthcoming to prove the damages.

§ 7.19 —Discussing monetary losses

In most cases, some mention of monetary losses is necessary. For example, if there have been medical bills and loss of wages, the opening statement is the appropriate vehicle for informing the jury that these losses exist, but it is not necessarily the appropriate time for discussing the amount involved.

In some cases, there is an element of monetary damages which is being claimed, but which is not subject to exact proof, such as impairment of earning capacity. Impairment of earning capacity refers to a theory where the plaintiff is claiming damages for his injuries for dimunition of what he may be able to earn in the future. It is not, in fact, loss of present wages. It may also be possible, assuming that he continues to be employed, that the plaintiff may not lose wages in the future. However, should circumstances change making it necessary for him to reenter the job market, it is possible that he could not compete equally with other workers. If so, that too is considered impairment of earning capacity. Thus it is possible in most states to have a disability which impairs earning capacity and causes a potential economic loss, but which is not subject to exact proof.[20]

COMMENT: Therefore, when seeking monetary damages which are not subject to exact proof, but which are recoverable under the law, mention this fact to the jury during opening statement. Stress that there will be no exact proof in mathematical terms as to the amount of this economic or monetary loss; nonetheless, the injured party is entitled to be compensated for this loss. The same subject matter should have been covered during voir dire. The fact that monetary damages can be recoverable even though they are not subject to exact proof is a new concept to the layperson and must be repeated and reinforced with the jury throughout the trial.

---

§ 7.20 —Predicting pain and suffering

During opening statement discuss not only past pain and suffering but also pain and suffering which will be endured by the plaintiff in the future. It is important to emphasize to the jury that no one can know exactly what the future will bring, but that under the civil burden of proof, the plaintiff's future pain, suffering, and disability need not be proven with certainty. Attempt to take these factors out of the realm of speculation by discussing in detail the evidence which will be used to predict the probability of future pain and suffering and disability. This evidence, of course, is the medical evidence presented by the doctor coupled with the lay testimony as to past pain and suffering and disability. It should be emphasized to the jury during opening statement that it is part

---

[20] Jordan v. Travelers, 231 So. 2d 678 (La. Ct. App.), *cert. denied*, 256 La. 68, 235 So. 2d 96 (1970), *amended*, 257 La. 995, 245 So. 2d 151 (1971).

of their function not only to listen to the evidence being presented, but also to rely on their common sense to draw reasonable inferences from that evidence. Counsel should then describe why a reasonable inference can be made from evidence that the past pain and suffering which has continued for two or three years or longer is likely to continue into the future. You should also emphasize that while it is not possible to predict on what days, during what months, and how many times during each year these episodes of pain and suffering will occur, it is possible to show that these episodes will happen and that proving this is all that is required under the law to entitle the plaintiff to claim future pain and suffering. The jury, of course, should have been educated and conditioned as to these types of damages and claims during voir dire. Now it is necessary to reinforce the acceptance of these concepts in the jury's minds by repeating them during opening statement.

§ 7.21 —When to mention the amount of damages demanded

In every case involving personal injury, plaintiff's counsel should mention something about the nature of the impairment, the monetary losses incurred, and the future pain and suffering that are being claimed. It is questionable, however, as to whether specific monetary amounts should be mentioned for each item and particularly whether the total claim for damages should be mentioned. Mentioning of the ad damnum in the opening statement is subject to a great deal of debate among experienced trial lawyers. Most experienced trial lawyers who take the position that the ad damnum should not be mentioned during opening statement generally are of the opinion that the jury is not psychologically ready to talk about monetary damages or discuss large figures. Conversely, other equally experienced trial lawyers take the position that if the jury is conditioned in the very beginning of the case to these large figures, they are more likely to award these amounts at the conclusion of the trial.

A significant consideration in deciding whether to mention the ad damnum during opening statement is the difficulty in proving the liability issues. If liability is either admitted or is overwhelmingly clear, and particularly where there are punitive factors involved, the ad damnum should be mentioned and emphasized. If, on the other hand, the liability issue is a significantly difficult one, it is enough to have the jury simply accept liability during the opening statement and not be burdened with dealing with the ad damnum. After they have accepted proof of the liability issue, then mention the ad damnum. Therefore, whether to mention the total amount of the monetary award sought is a question of judgment in each individual case. Another reason to refrain from mentioning the total amount of monetary damages is to avoid committing the trial lawyer to a specific amount. If the evidence does not appear to be as convincing as anticipated, the lawyer may want to reduce the amount that he originally intended to seek. On the other hand, if the evidence on liability turns out to be more favorably received than anticipated, the attorney may well want to ask for a greater monetary award. Thus delaying the discussion of the ad damnum has additional advantages which ought to be considered.

§ 7.22 Closing the opening statement

As with every portion of the trial, the opening statement must have a good ending, with emotional impact. It is during the closing line of the opening statement that counsel may wish to revert to his bottom line argument. The techniques previously discussed are applicable; this is the time where counsel should use the phrase "the evidence will show . . ." before stating the closing line. In other words, the closing line should be a return to the case theme.

For example, in the ordinary rear-end collision case, a simple theme is that your client has a severely injured neck and requires a substantial award. Usually liability has been admitted. Consider the following closing lines:

> Ladies and gentlemen, the evidence in this case will show that the only issue before you is the value of human life in this community. There will be no question when the evidence is in, and we are talking about evidence from the witness stand [pointing to and looking at the witness stand], that my client has become a permanent "neck cripple." We do not know when she will suffer spasm and pain in the future. We cannot predict to you what day or what time of day, but, anytime the weather changes or she overuses her neck, she has trouble with it now. The physicians will tell you this is probably going to continue to occur the rest of her life, and you must deal with that. You must consider that she has 30.8 years to live. You must award damages in the future. This is her one and only day in court, and the one and only issue before you is the value of human life and what this pain and suffering is worth over that many years.

The opening statement should end on a high note and, of course, thank the jury for their attention and ask them to pay attention to the opposing counsel and see which side of the case is really supported by the evidence.

Psychologically, this request makes you appear fair to the jury and it returns to the building of rapport that began during voir dire.

IV. Communication Techniques Used During Opening Statement

§ 7.23 Developing case theory during opening statement

Every case has two theories. The liability theory is that part of the "story" dealing with what happened and why the opposing party is at fault. The damage theory tackles causation (i.e., that the plaintiff's injuries were proximately caused by the wrongful conduct of the defendant). The theories dealing with both liability and damages must be explained in detail during your opening statement.

Simplicity is a key concept in the construction of your case theories. As plaintiff's counsel in a civil suit, remember the salesman's rule of KISS (Keep it simple, stupid). Your case theory ought to be geared to "making the case easy for the jury." Plaintiff's counsel, having the burden of proof, should strive to eliminate extraneous issues and indeed to point out to the jury any so-called red herrings. A *red herring* is a collateral or side issue which is not determinative of liability or damages but is raised for either a judicial reason or as an intentional attempt to make the case appear more complex than it really is. For example, the color of the raincoat the man was wearing when he crossed the street on a sunny day has nothing to do with whether the light was red or green as he went into the intersection. It may imply that he may be a bit eccentric for wearing a raincoat on a sunny day, but it is not an issue in the case. Every case has red herrings. In your opening statement they ought to be labeled red herrings, side issues, collateral issues, something which the jury should ignore. This tends to eliminate extraneous issues and simplifies the case. Usually the case can be simplified to one or two major issues.

§ 7.24 —Determining case issues

The plaintiff's attorney has an advantage in that primacy allows him essentially to select the issues. He has the opportunity to delineate and underline the issues first. He is, in essence, obtaining the home-court advantage. Counsel should always attempt to capitalize on the plaintiff's home-court advantage of selecting the issues first.

To capitalize on that advantage, select those issues which can be won on the available evidence. Thus the plaintiff in the civil case ought to be able to carry his burden of proof; if not, the case should be settled or abandoned. Ultimately, the plaintiff's case will revolve around only one issue. If the jury will follow the law and the evidence, the case will give them no problem. This is why a promise from the jury during voir dire to follow the law and evidence is essential.

COMMENT: Stress at opening statement that the jury must simply follow the law and the evidence and the plaintiff must prevail. This not only simplifies the case, but underlines the fact that the law and the evidence are in the plaintiff's favor. It psychologically says to the jury that the plaintiff is confident, that he knows he ought to win, and that the law and the evidence are really in his favor.

The same principles that apply to the plaintiff in a civil case apply to the prosecution in a criminal case in terms of simplifying issues and making the case easy for the jury. The party with the burden of proof must always perform this function. On the other hand, defendants in both a criminal and civil case have a different goal. Their goal is to raise red herrings. Their goal is to make the issues complex. Their goal is to talk about technicalities. If they can achieve this goal, the jury will be out for many hours, will become confused discussing the complex and technical issues, and will, more often than not, reach the conclusion that the side with the burden of proof, the plaintiff in a civil case or the state in a criminal case, has not carried its burden. This factor more than any other is what results in defense verdicts in both civil and criminal cases. To avoid this problem it is essential that the plaintiff or the state, on opening statement, develop their case theory in simple terms, eliminate collateral issues, and make the case as simple and as easy as possible for the jury to understand.

§ 7.25 Conforming to the evidence; avoiding overreaching

One thing that all parties, both plaintiffs and defendants in civil cases, and the state and defense in criminal cases, must do is to conform their opening statement to the evidence. By this we mean that they must know what the evidence is going to show. If they are not sure, they must avoid that area like the plague in the opening statement.

COMMENT: It is critical that neither side overstate its position in opening statement. If you overreach in opening statement, if you make promises in opening statement which you cannot deliver, it can have disastrous effects upon your case.

One famous civil trial lawyer made a critical mistake by overreaching in his civil case opening statement when he told the jury that the defendant's conduct was of such a heinous nature that it was "almost criminal." As a result of this overreaching, the jury ultimately found for the defendant. They decided that the plaintiff indeed had proven that the defendant had told untruths about the plaintiff, but that this was not a case of criminal liability. They decided the plaintiff had not carried the burden of proof. They further based this decision on plaintiff's failure to prove, at least to their satisfaction, any sort of heinous criminal intent. Always be very careful to conform the opening statement to the evidence and never overreach as it can yield disastrous effects at the end of the trial.

§ 7.26 Use of visual aids during opening statement

Most conservative judges do not permit the use of visual aids during opening statement. However, it appears that more and more judges are willing to allow the very limited use of visual aids in complex cases to simplify issues and to help the jury understand the case.[21]

The use of visual aids allows you to communicate in a "third dimension."

---

[21] Massey-Ferguson, Inc. v. Laird, 435 So. 2d 1259 (Ala. 1983); Powell v. Sears, Roebuck & Co., 268 Ark. 1093, 598 S.W.2d 449 (Ct. App. 1980); Caley v. Manicke, 24 Ill. 2d 390, 182 N.E.2d 206 (1962); Mohler v. Blanchette, 106 Ill. App. 2d 545, 62 Ill. Dec. 189, 435 N.E.2d 1161 (1982); Levenson v. Lake-to-Lake Dairy Cooperative, 76 Ill. App. 3d 526, 32 Ill. Dec. 20, 394 N.E.2d 1359 (1979); Cartwright v. Atlas Chemical Industries, 593 P.2d 104 (Okla. Ct. App. 1978).

COMMENT: It is strongly recommended that some type of visual aid be used during the opening statement if permitted by the court. It should be kept simple and be used in such a way as to not impinge upon or sound like argument. Such a visual aid can be a blackboard upon which the attorney can simply write down and explain terminology in a complex case, or it could be a chart of the intersection where the automobile collision occurred. It can be used to demonstrate plaintiff's contentions regarding how the incident occurred.

In cases involving a lengthy series of events leading up to the incident at issue, the attorney may need to use a chart illustrating the chronology of the events which emphasizes the time factors in question. This is particularly true when time lapse is the essence of the plaintiff's allegation of negligence. In a recent case, plaintiff alleged that an infection in his foot developed because no X-ray or culture was taken for three months. A chart similar to the one set forth in Figure 7–1 was used during opening statement to illustrate this critical passage of time. The chart was designed to look like a calendar and psychologically emphasize the fact that months rather than days or hours passed during which time the physicians ignored the infection in the plaintiff's foot and failed to take X-rays.

As can be seen from Figure 7–1, visual aids can be extremely helpful during opening statement. They help us to communicate more effectively. Remember that jurors tend to retain 60–70% of the information they perceive through both sight and sound, but only 20–30% of the information perceived by sound alone. Therefore, they will remember the graph and the message it sends.

Choice of colors to be used in any chart or graph is also a significant consideration.

Figure 7–1

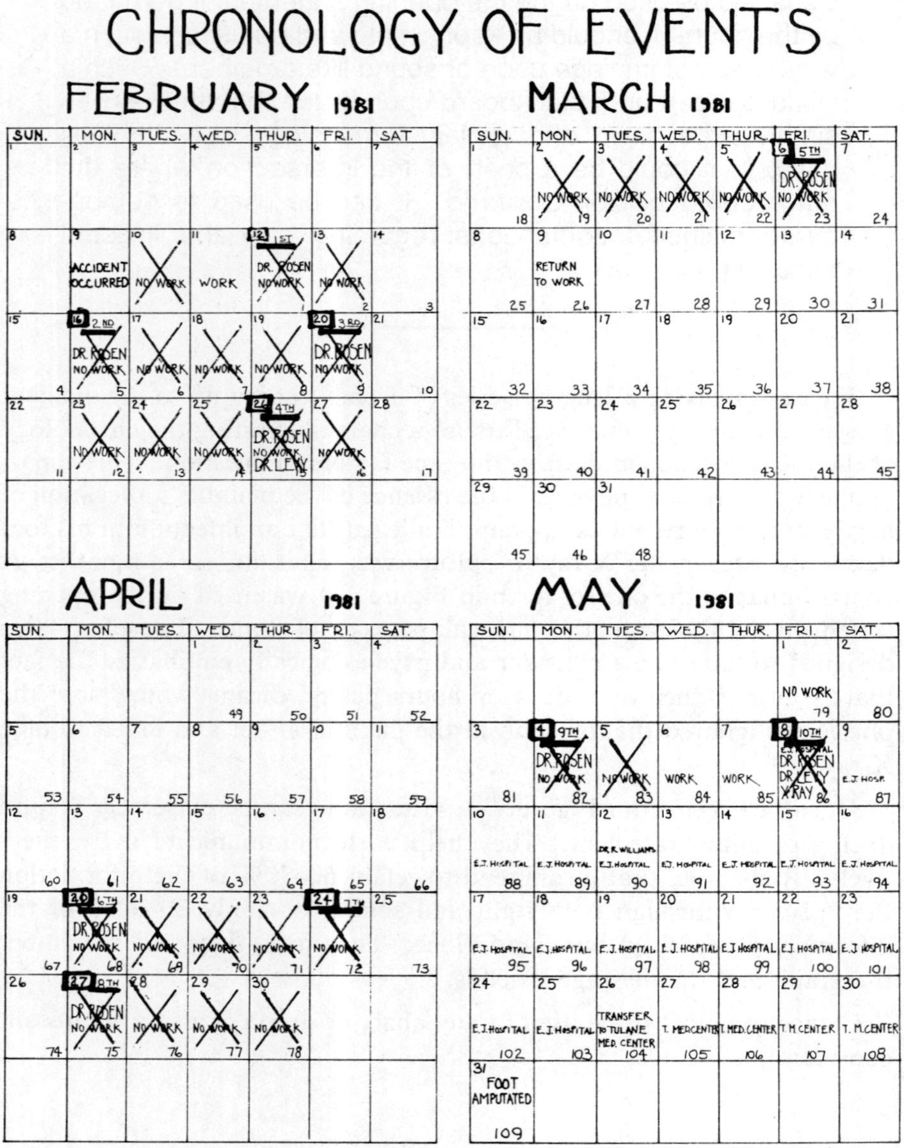
CHRONOLOGY OF EVENTS
FEBRUARY 1981
SUN. MON. TUES. WED. THUR. FRI. SAT.
ACCIDENT OCCURRED
NO WORK
WORK
1ST DR. ROSEN NO WORK
2 ND DR. ROSEN NO WORK
3 RD DR. ROSEN NO WORK
4TH DR. ROSEN NO WORK DR. LEVY
MARCH 1981
5TH DR. ROSEN NO WORK
RETURN TO WORK
APRIL 1981
6TH DR. ROSEN NO WORK
7TH NO WORK
8TH DR. ROSEN NO WORK
MAY 1981
NO WORK
9TH DR. ROSEN NO WORK
WORK
10TH E.J. HOSPITAL DR. ROSEN DR. LEVY X RAY
E.J. HOSP.
E.J. HOSPITAL
DR. R. WILLIAMS
TRANSFER TO TULANE MED. CENTER
T. MED. CENTER
31 FOOT AMPUTATED

§ 7.27 Style of delivery

The style of the delivery of the opening statement depends a great deal on the personality of the attorney. The delivery must fit his own style. If the attorney is soft-spoken and unemotional, depending primarily on the use of logic, he should not abandon his style. The style of delivery of the opening statement should come as close as possible to the style which will be used during closing argument.

COMMENT: Even though this is an opening statement and is not argument *per se*, it should be presented in a style which delivers some emotional impact. It should never be delivered in a monotone voice. Finally, it should be in the style of a "storyteller" and build in intensity as it reaches its close.

---

§ 7.28 Humanizing the client

During opening statement do not forget to humanize the client; never refer to him as the "client" or the "plaintiff." Rather, always refer to the plaintiff by his or her first name. It should be: "What happened next to 'Mary'," never "what happened next to 'the plaintiff'."

In addition, it is important to demonstrate affection for the client nonverbally. During opening statement, when referring to the client, look at him, stand by him, and be seen touching the client. You want the jury to like the client. Remember that if people see that we like our client they will tend to accept this fact and like our client as well.

On the other hand, if you are the defendant in a civil case, you should attempt to dehumanize the opposing party. You should try to make the plaintiff appear to be something other than a warm and loving human being. Similarly, if you are the prosecution in a criminal case you need to dehumanize the defendant, never calling the defendant by his name. Rather, point to the defendant, use abrupt movements, and call him "the defendant", saying it with a despising tone and look on your face (negative facial expressions). It is easy to deny recovery to the injured plaintiff and convict the defendant when he has been dehumanized.

The dehumanization of the opposing side is a concept that has been used frequently during wartime. During World War II, Americans did not kill people who were German or Japanese; they killed "Krauts" or "Japs." In Korea, it was "Commies" and in Vietnam, it was "Charlies." Labels tend to dehumanize the opposition and make killing them easier. Similarly, in the courtroom it is psychologically easier to reject a plaintiff than to reject Mary, who is a quadriplegic because of the alleged negligence of the defendant, or to convict John and send him to the electric chair if he is simply a defendant.

COMMENT: It is therefore essential for the plaintiff in a civil case and the defense in a criminal case to humanize their clients and for their opponents to dehumanize them.

---

§ 7.29 Motivating the jury

The opening statement is an attempt to motivate the jury. This is accomplished through the effective use of a theme, impact words and phrases through eye contact, and other aspects of verbal, vocal, and nonverbal communication. It is accomplished by linking to existing stereotypes and by the emotional content of the opening statement. Thus, with the proper use of the techniques discussed in this chapter the opening statement truly becomes an opening argument. It has sufficient impact to motivate the jury to your point of view, telling them why, in no uncertain terms, you ought to win. It should, through both the verbal and nonverbal levels, motivate them to decide in your favor.

The motivating factors delivered to the jury during the opening statement vary with the issues at hand. Thus, in the products liability case, the jury is motivated by your emphasis that a verdict for the plaintiff results in safe products for the public. You may do this by using a theme which states that the defendant put profits ahead of safety. In the medical malpractice case, motivate the jury by emphasizing that they, the jury, set the standards by which medicine is practiced in their community and that what the experts from both sides are going to give them is simply an opinion as to what the standards ought to be. The standards in fact are determined by the jury; they, the jury, say how medicine ought to be practiced. Do they want safe medicine as espoused by the plaintiff?

Or do they want sloppy statistical medicine which is what is practiced under the standards of the defense experts? It is the use of these types of techniques that motivates the jury, indeed this is all a part of the psychological effect of the opening statement.

COMMENT: Always be concerned that your opening statement contains proper motivational material. Every opening statement must show the jury the rational reason why your side must prevail.

Chapter 8

DIRECT EXAMINATION: PRESENTING THE EVIDENCE WITH IMPACT

KLUWER LITIGATION LIBRARY REFERENCES

JEANS, LITIGATION: Chapter 8, *Direct Examination*; Chapter 9, *Direct Examination of Expert Witnesses*; Chapter 10, *Nontestimonial Evidence*.

JOYE & LOVETT, DRUNK DRIVING: THE TRIAL WORKBOOK, THE TRIAL SOURCEBOOK, THE TRIAL NOTEBOOK: Chapter 112, *Defense Witnesses*.

PREISER & PREISER, HANDLING SOFT TISSUE INJURY CASES: Chapter 3, *Overlooked Witnesses and Evidence*; Chapter 4, *The Most Overlooked Element of Damages: Reduced Capacity to Earn*; Chapter 6, *Medical Preparation and Preparation of the Medical Witness*; Chapter 8, *Final Preparation for Trial*; Chapter 15, *Proving Amount of Economic Loss and Reduced Earning Capacity*.

§ 8.01 Reducing lay witness' anxiety and establishing rapport

In dealing with lay witnesses, especially those who have not testified previously, it is important that we first reduce their anxiety. The prospect of testifying in a court of law before the all powerful judge is terribly frightening. After all, the judge in his majestic black robes has the power, in the layman's mind, to send them to jail. Most laypeople are not able to attribute legal value to their statements, nor are they used to being on stage and being viewed in a spotlight. Most lay witnesses work for someone else; they are not "the boss." No one really listens to them, not even their spouses, and in most instances, not even their children. They are in an entirely new and frightening situation. They have a great deal of natural anxiety, and they approach the witness stand with great trepidation. The first job of the trial lawyer in preparing lay witnesses is to recognize and deal with this natural anxiety. By doing so, the trial lawyer will prepare himself as well as the witness. After all, the better the witness is prepared, the better the job the trial lawyer can do when conducting the direct examination of that witness.

COMMENT: Thorough preparation is the key to dealing with witness anxiety, to preparing the witness, to making the witness a better witness, and to conducting a better direct examination of that witness.

Dealing with the witness' natural situational anxiety effectively can be accomplished in one of several ways. First of all, the attorney himself needs to deal with the witness' anxiety by establishing rapport with this witness. Rapport is established by pacing the witness and as discussed previously, effective pacing must take place on all three levels: verbal, vocal, and nonverbal. Sometimes, the pacing is accomplished not only by matching but by complimentary pacing as well. Thus, if the witness is nervous or anxious, rather than matching the witness' nervous or anxious behaviors, you should compliment this behavior and be calm in response to it. This will cause the witness to calm down. In essence, the witness should have confidence in the attorney. You want to communicate to the witness that you are the witness' protector and that he can have confidence in you.

The process of instilling confidence is integral to establishing rapport. This confidence is built as you sit with the witness and prepare him for testifying. Tell the witness that it is your job to prepare him for this experience. First, you are going to ask him to tell you what he knows about the circumstances of the case and what he actually saw. After he has done that, tell him that you are then going to go over the questions you are now preparing. Listen to the answers and outline the testimony. The lay witness must clearly understand that it is your job and your responsibility to prepare him and yourself by assisting him to frame his answers. The attorney should stress that all he wants the witness to do is tell the truth, but that making an accurate statement is often not enough. Express that, in addition to the verbal communication itself, vocal and nonverbal levels of communication can be utilized effectively. Consider offering the following example to the witness: A parent asking his child the age-old question "Do you love me?" receives a "yes" response. Depending, however, on how the child says the word "yes", the response could mean "no," "I don't know," or "I love you very much." Mimic these different vocal intonations to the witness and explain that you are concerned not only with what he says, but how he says it. Discuss with the witness the importance of his testimony to your client. Explain why you are calling him, and how and why his specific testimony is going to help the case. Discuss words from part of the theme of your case and how his testimony can be more persuasive and therefore more effective if certain impact words and phrases are used. Do not demand that the witness use these impact words and phrases, but rather drop the suggestion and see if he cooperates. If he does, you will have successfully led the witness and this will confirm that your pacing has established rapport. Never demand that a witness use certain words and phrases. This will cause his testimony to be neither effective nor believable. On the other hand, if the witness is cooperative, he may pick up those key phrases and effectively use them to help you weave the case together. As you go through the actual questions you anticipate asking on direct examination, have the witness give his answers. As he answers, compile a checklist of his key words to use at trial as reminders of any forgotten answers.

Witnesses need to be aware of the "leading question." Tell the witness that you may not ask leading questions and that your questions may not suggest an answer. Then, inform him that you may need to direct his attention toward the deficiency of a particular answer and that your question may be interpreted as leading by the opposing counsel. Indeed, he may even object to the question as leading. Although you will then ask another question, the witness should be told that you are really trying to remind him of the deficiency of the answer in the prior question. Prepare the witness for objections and how to handle them, telling him not to answer the question until the judge has ruled on an objection. Explain to the lay witness that it is not important that he understand the legal technicalities of the ruling. Rather, he should wait for the ruling and then listen to the next question from the lawyer. He should not be concerned with the nature of the objection, and with who won or lost that particular battle. Instead, he should be concentrating on what his answer is going to be to the particular question which will follow the objection and the ruling.

§ 8.02 Preparing lay witness for cross-examination

In addition to preparing the witness' testimony by building rapport with him, soothing his anxiety, and then demonstrating that you and he are going to be well prepared, the attorney needs to prepare the lay witness for cross-examination. Remember that most laymen view cross-examination as almost a masterful, mystical power by which tricky lawyers can sweat the answers out of a witness, twisting and distorting those answers beyond recognition. Explain to the witness that this is not true, but that on the other hand, overall communication is based on perception and that sometimes lawyers can ask a series of questions which scream out for a "yes" or "no" answer. If the lay witness falls into that trap and gives a series of affirmative answers, particularly on irrelevant issues, then the lawyer may indeed create the impression that this witness "agrees with him." The lay witness needs to avoid answering a series of questions with either "yes" or "no" responses. If the witness feels the attorney is asking this type of question, the witness needs to stop the lawyer, so that he can explain his answers and break the rhythm of the cross-examination. It is then a good idea to demonstrate a cross-examination by actually conducting one on the witness. Demonstrate how a series of "yes" answers can create the impression that he is agreeing with the other side. After the questions and answers have been outlined, it may be a good idea to have an associate from your own office do the cross-examination after you have taken the witness through an actual direct examination.

§ 8.03 Videotaping mock examinations

This part of the pretrial preparation of lay witnesses can be significantly enhanced by videotaping mock direct and cross-examinations of the witness. Allow the witness to view himself answering the questions. Instruct him to look at his body positions. For instance, you might point out that if he is sitting with his head up very high, and consequently his nose in the air, the jury might interpret this nonverbal cue as arrogance which, of course, is not a desirable image to project. Further, leaning forward might be perceived as a display of aggressiveness. While we cannot change all the body movements, such a demonstration will make the witness more aware of his nonverbal behavior. When videotaping these mock examinations, start off with basic (baseline) questions, those which have no emotional content, such as, "Where are you from?", "Where do you live?", etc. Then, follow with aggressive questions about the case which do have an emotional element. When you replay the videotape, ask the lay witness to see if he can spot differences in his nonverbal behavior responses to the nonemotional basic questions as opposed to the more emotionally charged questions. As the witness sees the contrast on the videotape, explain that controlling his emotions on the stand by staying closer to the basic type of behavior projects a more confident and calm, and therefore more believable, image. It is important to explain that he should not express anger on the stand, indeed if anyone is to express anger about what has occurred in this case, it ought to be the lawyer. This is not the function of the witness because people are turned off by anger. The average person will cross the street to avoid seeing a fight in progress. The average person hates the boss when he loses his temper. We do not like anger; we do not identify with anger and neither do jurors. They are turned off by anger. They won't listen to or believe someone who expresses anger and therefore we must avoid having the emotion of anger in any way expressed during the testimony of a lay witness. This actually has been observed in the courtroom. In one case involving an automobile collision wherein the defendant's vehicle went into reverse gear and struck the plaintiff's car at 30 m.p.h., the plaintiff, despite coaching and preparation by his attorney became angry and hostile during cross-examination. Plaintiff was denied recovery on the basis of a slight degree of contributory negligence. If a lay witness is an expressive type of person, particularly if he is aggressive, he must be counseled so as to tone down his personality. Aggressiveness can be interpreted as a form of anger and hostility, and it is something that will turn most people off.

§ 8.04 Importance of witness' appearance

It is important to discuss Communication Principle 1 (Communication is based on perception) and Communication Principle 3 (Perceptions are organized and structured within a brief period of time) with the witness. Tell him that as a witness, he is observed by the jury visually from the time he enters the courtroom. They will form a perception based on what they see in a brief period of time, and this first impression is one to which they will tend to adhere. For this reason, the choice of clothing for his courtroom appearance is very important. Demonstrate to the witness how clothing or artifacts can change perceptions. Do this by putting on and taking off a pair of glasses, by picking up and laying down a pipe, by putting on and taking off your jacket. Discuss what clothing to wear in the courtroom, and if this is a very important witness, have him come back to your office on a different day wearing the actual clothing that he has selected. Go through the testimony and observe how he sits in the clothing. It is important that the total appearance and effectiveness of the witness be assessed by you before that witness enters the courtroom. Once he has entered the courtroom, the first impression is made, and you must live with it.

COMMENT: Remember that your overall goal is to make this witness effective in the courtroom. This is done primarily by preparing yourself and the witness regarding the questions to be asked and the answers to be given. Sometimes this preparation alone cannot help the witness overcome the situational anxiety of facing a judge and a jury in the stressful situation of the courtroom. Most lay witnesses have never been in a courtroom and have never testified. Therefore, whenever possible, but particularly if this witness is a key witness, take him to the actual courtroom where the trial will be conducted. Let him see what it looks like and stay there until you think the witness feels more comfortable. Spend some time sitting with the witness and talking with him in the courtroom. If possible, have the witness sit in the actual witness chair. All of this will help reduce the witness' situational anxiety. It is not desirable to have that witness walk into the courtroom for the first time on the day of trial at the very minute he is about to testify. This will create great situational anxiety which could have been avoided to a certain degree by bringing the witness to the courtroom ahead of time.

§ 8.05 Changing the witness' image

Changing the witness' image involves both internal image changes and external image changes. External image changes refer to changes in personal appearance, movement, and behavior.[1] Internal image changes are concerned with changing the attitudes and beliefs that the witness has previously internalized. Briefly, a lay witness should not dress out of his socioeconomic status. If that lay witness is a laborer, you should not put him into an expensive suit, because he will look and feel out of place. On the other hand, if you want a witness to evoke sympathy, he should present a soft appearance. If you want the witness to appear as a victim, as in the Patty Hearst case, dress the witness to look that way. On the other

[1] The importance of external appearances was previously discussed *infra* §§ 1.09–1.46.

hand, if you want the witness to appear authoritative, then dress him in a classical, conservative suit.

In addition to dealing with the external image of the witness, one has to consider the witness' own internal image regarding lawyers, your client, the courtroom, and any other preexisting attitudes and general belief systems. For example, a belief that all attorneys are "bad guys" who make too much money will alter the nature of his testimony and could make him an ineffective witness. Regardless of how much he tries to mask such feelings, they will come through in the courtroom particularly during cross-examination. Thus once you have established rapport with the witness, you need to discuss these feelings and the problems that they can create for the witness and your client in the courtroom.

Remember Communication Principle 6: People attempt to maintain their original perceptions regardless of contradictory information. Also remember that in order to change existing stereotypes and belief systems, one has to identify the belief system, link with it, and then give information as to why a particular belief system or stereotype should not be maintained.[2] The trial attorney needs to establish initial rapport with the witness to facilitate the disclosure of these very basic feelings regarding lawyers, the client, and the courtroom. Not only should the attorney express that it is appropriate to feel this way about courtrooms, lawyers, and judges, but that the attorney himself has reciprocal feelings regarding this belief. Remember one of the basic rules of communication is that self-disclosure is promoted by reciprocity. If the witness feels there is an equal exchange of personal information, he will be more likely to maintain rapport with the trial attorney and ultimately to change or alter this internal belief system. On the other hand, if the witness feels that at any point in time there is a significant imbalance in the exchange of information, he will feel that the attorney is not reciprocating and will probably start censoring the information he is giving to the attorney. Obviously, a serious problem arises if previously undisclosed information is presented in the courtroom. Therefore, it is always essential in the preparation of a lay witness to explore his preexisting belief systems and to exchange ideas regarding these beliefs. This not only helps the attorney to establish rapport, but it also allows him to gain an insight into the witness which is not otherwise possible. It is the exchange of information regarding the witness, what he is going to say, how he is going to say it, and the prob-

[2] *See supra* §§ 1.06–1.54, regarding the use of stereotypes in the courtroom.

able effect of his testimony that properly prepares both the lay witness and the attorney himself for an effective direct examination.

§ 8.06 Witness' body position on the stand

It is necessary that the witness understand the importance of his body position on the stand.[3] Body position is extremely important because, on a nonverbal level, it conveys all types of attitudes. In understanding the importance and function of body position, one has to make a distinction between what is perceived and what is intended. A juror may perceive a gesture (i.e., the witness has his arms folded) and attach a significant meaning to it even though that particular body position was not intended to communicate anything. Therefore, when we discuss position, we are not concerned with intention, but rather with perception. It is not important what the witness through his body position intends to communicate; it is important how one or more jurors may perceive that particular body position.

Engage the witness in the following exercise to make evident the significance of body position. Ask him to recall a feeling of anger and to assume a body position indicative of that feeling. Invariably, the witness will move forward in the chair and straighten his back. Then ask the witness to remember a time when he was depressed or sad. He will sit back in the chair and collapse his thoracic cavity as his shoulders move forward. Engaging in this exercise with the witness not only shows him the significance of body position, but it also makes him cognizant of the appropriate body position to assume so as to be congruent with the nature of his testimony.

Another consideration of body positioning that is important in the witness chair deals with the angle at which the head is held. This is probably one of the most significant means of nonverbal communication in that the potential for serious damage to the credibility of the witness and the client is great. Holding the head too high is considered a display of arrogance. If the chin is tilted up and eye contact is made by looking down, the witness will be perceived as "looking down his nose at us." It is certainly considered pompous. On the other hand, if the chin is down and the eyes are looking up, this is considered a display of submissiveness and kindness, which is desirable most of the time. There are also situations wherein a witness needs to appear soft and helpless. This is projected by tilting the head either to the right or the left and casting the

---

[3] *See supra* § 8.03, *Videotaping mock examinations.*

eyes downward. An endearing look is accomplished by changing the eye angles.

While some body positions may be appropriate for lay witnesses, the opposite body positions are appropriate for expert witnesses. The attorney wants the expert witness to look credible, authoritative, and therefore not submissive. His shoulders should be back in a more formal posture. While he should not be rigid, he should be more upright than the lay witness in terms of his back posture. This nonverbal posture on the stand will help him to be perceived as more credible.

Some experts and even some lay witnesses are exceptions to the rule. One exception is that of the "folksy" credible witness. Even as an expert witness, his position and posture should be casual and, using appropriate vocal and verbal cues, he will be perceived as having credibility. The "folksy" credible witness can be very effective because such a witness can establish rapport with the jury on an informal level and still sell the message.

§ 8.07 Verbal and vocal considerations

During witness preparation, in addition to nonverbal communication, witness image, and body positioning on the stand, you have to consider the witness' verbal and vocal cues.[4] Some witnesses naturally send appropriate and therefore believable verbal and vocal cues while other witnesses may not be consistent. Verbal cues refer to the witness' word selection and phraseology. Vocal cues deal with how the witness says the words, his tone of voice, his rate of speech, and so forth.

There are several principles that need to be kept in mind when considering vocal and verbal cues in the preparation of lay witnesses. For example, there is a perception of greater credibility if the voice is lowered. Generally higher voice tones are associated with a lack of honesty by most people. Tightening of the vocal cords causes a constricted type of voice pattern that is perceived as less credible. Jurors perceive people who have a constricted-sounding, high-pitched voice as nervous and anxious. This is interpreted as a sign of tension and therefore a sign that the witness may not be telling the truth. In addition, remember that the jury is not aware that this witness' usual voice tone is perhaps a high one. Indeed, this tone may not be a deviation from the normal speech pattern. If the witness has a naturally high-pitched voice, he needs to practice

[4] *See supra* §§ 1.36, 1.79–1.85, for a general discussion of verbal and vocal cues.

putting some resonance into his voice in order to change his speech pattern and increase his credibility.

It is also important to consider the lay witness' breathing pattern. People who become anxious breathe rapidly, in irregular patterns, and breathe shallowly. This can be interpreted as a sign of an anxious and nervous witness who perhaps is not truthful. Coach your witness to breathe deeply and evenly. This tends to even out the vocal tone and it helps the witness to control his own natural situational anxiety.

§ 8.08 —Choice of words and phraseology

In addition to coaching the witness on his vocal cues, the attorney must discuss choice of words and phrases with the witness. The attorney has to educate the witness as to the use of impact words and phrases, including how to use language to paint word pictures. The witness needs to know that he is not testifying about an "automobile accident"; rather, the incident has to be presented in terms of a "collision" which ripped and tore the cars to shreds. Whatever key words and phrases are planned for the trial should be incorporated into the witness' vocabulary. For example, the lay witness testifying as to the victim's pain and suffering as a result of the rear-end collision has to be instructed not to talk about that friend as having suffered a "whiplash" injury. The term "whiplash" injury has become synonymous in the mind of the general public with malingering or faking. Therefore, the witness should talk about his friend's neck injury and how the resulting pain and suffering have crippled this previously active man. In a cervical sprain case, it is important that all of the witnesses repeat and use often the word "neck." This has a positive psychological message in that laymen visualize and picture the neck as something that is very vulnerable and subject to injury. We learned as children that we shouldn't play rough because we could "break our necks," and we all know that if you really want to hurt someone, you hit them in the neck. If, in a neck injury case, your theme is that human life is valuable, then your lay witnesses, especially those talking about pain and suffering, ought to stress the value of human life. The witness ought to talk about the fact that he himself enjoys playing with his grandchildren, that he has seen your client, Joe, try to do this, that Joe cannot do it, and that he has seen how this inability upsets Joe because that was a "valuable" part of Joe's life.

Remember, however, that you must pace and lead your witness to use key phrases; never demand that he do so. Thus, when discussing choice of words with the witness, assure him that you are not trying to put words in his mouth and that he does not have to use the words you are suggesting. He should only use these words if he feels comfortable with them and if he feels they accurately describe his impressions. Tell him that it is perfectly proper for you to help him with word choice so that he can accurately paint a picture of what actually occurred and what he can now see in his mind's eye. Explain that he can only do this by using appropriate nonverbal behavior and adequate vocal cues, and by selecting the proper verbiage to describe what actually occurred. Thus, the properly prepared lay witness should be cued to use and repeat impact words and phrases which tie into your case theme.[5]

Having the witnesses use impact words and phrases that tie into your case theme applies not only to the lay witness but to the expert as well. In the medical malpractice case, for example, teach your expert not to use the phrase "guilty of malpractice" and "guilty of negligence." The word "guilty" psychologically connotes that someone is going to jail and that there is a criminal penalty involved. In the medical malpractice case, stress to the jury that the doctor would be required to pay civil damages, like anyone else would, for the wrong he has done. The proper term is "negligence" or "medical negligence." The term "malpractice" is interpreted by laymen as an act that is horrendously wrong and of a nature far greater than simple negligence. To the layman, the term "malpractice" implies almost an intent to do wrong. Although this is not the law, it is the psychological connotation that has been attached to the word "malpractice." As we all know, the doctor is liable for a simple, careless, but innocent negligent act. Our expert witness should be prepared to talk about the defendant's conduct in terms of "negligence." In addition to the conscious avoidance of negative terminology in the "medical negligence" case, the expert should use positive analogies and positive terminology. If you are going to describe the incident as occurring because the defendant "ran a medical red light," then your expert should talk in terms of this analogy. He should talk about the medical standards as being medical red lights and describe in detail how they were violated.

§ 8.09 Using trial consultants in preparing lay witness

Trial consultants usually have a behavioral or social science background. Fields of expertise and degrees generally involve communication, psychology, and sociology. When selecting a trial consultant, verify

[5] *See supra* § 1.85, regarding the use of powerful versus powerless speech.

his academic background and credentials. In addition, verify his training in the trial area and his past performances with other attorneys.

Trial consultants can be particularly effective in working with witnesses because witnesses are generally nervous when dealing with lawyers. Similarly, many attorneys are nervous about dealing with the witnesses. A third person observing the development of the relationship between the lawyer and the witness can apply behavioral and communication information to the setting. He can be particularly effective in helping develop the witness and the lawyer's techniques for questioning the witness.

In many instances a third party's objective point of view can be crucial in heightening the witness' or party's effectiveness in the courtroom. The trial consultant, like the attorney, must work originally at establishing rapport with the witness. He will assist the lawyer in explaining to the witness in layman's terms, why nonverbal, verbal, and vocal cues are important. Once the witness understands why this is important, the witness will generally be more willing to work to establish good nonverbal, verbal, and vocal cues. Further, the witness may be more willing to accept coaching from a trial behavioral consultant employed especially for that purpose than from the lawyer. When the witness understands that because this is a serious case, the lawyer and the client are spending substantial money to bring in this highly trained behavioral science expert, he is likely to be impressed. The more impressed he is, the more he is apt to listen to the person who is discussing these matters with him and to accept the coaching and to mold his testimony to achieve the desired results.

§ 8.10 —Other functions of trial consultants

The use of the trial consultant in preparing witnesses enables the attorney to handle the myriad of other pressing matters related to the trial. It also affords the attorney the opportunity to observe the scenario between the trial consultant and the witness. In so doing, the trial attorney will better understand the witness and how that witness can be effectively controlled and his testimony projected in the courtroom. Often, a trial consultant can prepare both the attorney and the witness so that the testimony and its effect will be consistent throughout the presentation as well as consistent with the goals of the trial. With this type of preparation, even a minor witness' testimony can have a major impact.

The use of a trial consultant is not limited to witness preparation. He can assist the attorney to establish a theme and to choose impact words and phrases which will have a significant behavioral perspective. He can prepare the attorney to repeat and develop the theme throughout the trial and show him how that theme can be anchored and used to reframe the jury's point of view.

Another area where the trial consultant is very effective is in jury selection.[6] A trial consultant often should be at the attorney's side during the jury selection process. He can make a more objective assessment of a prospective juror's response to the attorney than the attorney can himself. While the attorney is preparing the jury, the trial consultant is free to analyze the prospective juror's nonverbal information and to evaluate the extraneous information cues.

In a major case, a trial consultant can provide substantial benefits throughout the entire trial. He can establish a "shadow jury" as has been done in cases involving substantial amounts of money, such as plane crashes and antitrust litigation. The shadow jury is one that consists of jurors with demographic characteristics comparable to those of the actual jury that is seated in the courtroom. The shadow jurors, headed by a research assistant, are seated in the back of the courtroom. The shadow jurors absolutely do not know which side has employed them. They are simply interviewed at the end of each day regarding their perceptions and evaluations of what transpired in the case that day, how they viewed the attorneys, what they thought was effective, and what impressed them. A shadow jury can provide invaluable information on whether a witness has been perceived as credible or arrogant, and which characteristics made him less credible than was desired. A trial consultant can also use "mock juries." Mock juries are generally employed before trial. Depositions and other key testimony is read to the mock jury. Witnesses, either live or videotaped, are presented in addition to any visual aid projected for use at the real trial. The jurors then assess the witnesses and the information. Mock juries are not as effective in evaluating the trial process as are shadow juries. Shadow juries have a marked advantage because they are actually present in the courtroom on a day-to-day basis, and they see what is taking place and not what the trial consultant or lawyer thinks is going to take place.

---

[6] *See supra* § 6.49, regarding the use of trial consultants in the jury selection process.

§ 8.11 —Importance of trial consultants

The use of a trial consultant is particularly important if the attorney has been working on a case for many years and, because of this, no longer has an objective perspective. Unless an attorney spends his full time in the area of behavioral science, he cannot have the same type of perspective as someone trained in the behavioral science field. The field of the behavioral science (i.e., communication, psychology, and sociology) is so diverse and complex that it takes someone fully trained in that field to really understand it and to provide the proper direction for the application of the principles of the field to the trial process. Although many trial attorneys are very skilled in the behavioral sciences, many are misled by relying on isolated items of information which lead to misinterpreting cues given by jurors and witnesses. For instance, if an attorney has read material dealing only with body language but not with the overall interpretation of verbal, vocal, and nonverbal cues, he will often reject a good juror simply because the juror is engaged in a single nonverbal action, such as folding his arms. On the other hand, a good trial attorney can often correctly interpret the verbal, vocal, and nonverbal cues of witnesses and jurors on an unconscious level although he does not realize what he is doing. A good trial attorney already knows how to pace, how to mismatch, and how to anchor themes, but he simply is not aware that he is doing it and consequently does not use these techniques consistently or strategically. The trial consultant can help to bring these behavioral techniques to the conscious level. This allows the attorney to look at these behavioral techniques and to have more direct control over them and therefore to use them even more effectively.

§ 8.12 Preparing the expert witness

Many lawyers make a fatal mistake when they assume the expert witness can testify from his report and that he needs no preparation prior to trial. The error lies in believing that because he is an expert, he has testified before and knows what to do in this particular situation. In truth, many experts have testified for years and have never been confident communicators. Just because a man is an expert in a particular medical or scientific specialty does not make him a good witness. This is particularly true of witnesses who hold scientific degrees and law degrees.

COMMENT: Thus, as an almost absolute rule, all expert

witnesses, including those with whom you are intimately familiar, need some degree of preparation prior to trial.

Most experts do not understand their role in the adversary process, yet this understanding is essential to the testimony. A failure to understand his role allows an expert to give the case away on cross-examination and, in many cases, not even be effective on direct examination. He needs to understand that he must communicate his opinion forcefully and sell his ideas to the jury. Therefore, you should explain to the expert that you wanted him to be totally objective when you hired him, that you hired him to research "whatever subject matter is involved," to come to objective conclusions, to advise you of the weak and strong points of your case, and to verify the validity of his opinion. After he has formed an opinion, however, it is no longer his duty to be an objective, fair, and unbiased witness. You are calling him to testify regarding his favorable opinion. It is his job to communicate that opinion forcefully and to defend it because this is how the truth is searched out in the adversary process. He must understand that after he gives his opinion forcefully on the stand and defends it, the other side will produce an opposing expert who will give the opposite opinion just as forcefully. Truth is searched out by the two opinions clashing and the jury coming to a middle ground. The adversary process will not work if your expert weakens his opinion and moves toward the middle ground. To do that is to give the other side an unfair advantage. It's like going into a fight with one hand tied behind your back or giving an equally fast runner a head start in the race. There is no way you can win if your side gives the other side an unfair advantage.

It is essential that your expert understand this concept before you start to prepare him on the subject matter and his testimony. Additionally, you must educate the expert witness to the fact that the jury is not only listening to his technical verbal presentation, but observing him and picking up on his vocal cues and nonverbal behavior. The expert witness must understand that his testimony should be directed to the members of the jury and that when he answers any question, either yours or that of the adversary, he should look at the jury and make eye contact with as many individual jurors as possible. He must also be told that the jury will, at least initially, perceive him as an advocate. They will expect him to be overly favorable to the side for which he is testifying. You must then explain to him that you want him to win over the jury by becoming a teacher in their eyes. One of the techniques used to do this is to get the expert witness off the stand and in front of the jury with a blackboard, chart, or model. He then visually and psychologically takes on a new role. Most expert witnesses have taught and are good teachers. Tell the expert that you want him to start to teach the subject matter to the jury as if they were a freshmen class learning the basics. Explain to the expert why you are putting him into the pedagogical position. Once he understands this he is more willing to participate in the process and will really work at becoming a teacher and not just an expert "advocate" who is spouting a technical opinion from the witness stand.

COMMENT: In addition, each expert needs to be put in a teaching position for the reasons set out above. You must find something for him to explain to the jury that requires a drawing on the blackboard. If your expert is a treating physician in a "whiplash" case, have him explain the hyperflexion and hyperextension process by drawing it on the blackboard or using an anatomical chart on an easel placed in front of the jury. Have him demonstrate inertia by pulling a piece of paper from under a glass of water. All of this is effective testimony, because it not only explains a vital principle to the jury, but it also provides a visual effect and has a certain entertainment value.

---

§ 8.13 Pacing the expert

By pacing the expert, we mean that the expert needs to understand the role of his opinion and its effect on the total case. He must know why he is being called, what information he is giving, and how it relates to the other testimony. Explain to him the importance of a case theme and of key impact words and phrases. After you have explained your case theme and impact words and phrases to him, help him find a way to work the case theme and these phrases into his testimony.

As an example, if you were preparing a treating physician to talk about the plaintiff in a rear-end collision case, you would want that physician to talk abut this being a "neck injury" and to explain why this injury has had a “crippling” effect on the plaintiff’s life-style. He must also talk in terms of the reduction in the quality, and therefore the value, of the plaintiff’s life because of the impairments on his life-style. In essence, he must be paced so he uses the exact theme and words which you have covered in the opening statement and to which other witnesses will refer. It relaxes a jury and captures their attention. The properly paced expert can be a very effective witness, particularly if he talks directly to the jury and continues to maintain eye contact with them throughout his testimony.

§ 8.14 Leading the expert

In some jurisdictions, the attorney is allowed to lead the expert witness. However, a properly prepared expert witness does not need leading. A lawyer leading the expert witness around by the nose is obvious even to a lay jury. Certainly, the lawyer is perceived as the one who is testifying. The jury knows that the attorney is the advocate and would probably say almost anything to help his side of the case. Therefore, the “lawyer’s testimony” is given little weight and credibility by the jury. For this reason, avoid excessive leading of the expert. On the other hand, sometimes an expert can wander far afield or by his answers create certain impressions that need clarification. This is the only time when leading the expert is required and should be done. Outside of this limited use of leading, even where it is allowed, the expert witness should not be led.

§ 8.15 Educating and preparing the expert for cross-examination

Do not assume that the expert is familiar with all of the journal articles and technical material in his field. The trial attorney should be educated and thoroughly familiar with the technical subject matter and the materials contained in the standard textbooks and journals. Copies of all technical articles, standard materials, and other documentation that the lawyer anticipates using should be sent to the expert ahead of time. The lawyer should go over each of these documents with the expert and discuss these articles as either in harmony with, or in conflict with, his testimony. It is during this educational process that the expert witness needs to be effectively prepared for cross-examination.

Do not assume, moreover, that an expert witness knows how to handle cross-examination. He must understand that the jury really does not have a good grasp of these technical materials. Rather, they will decide the case based on overall impressions. Impressions are formed rather rapidly, and they are controlled to a great extent by vocal and nonverbal cues. This is clearly true when the jury is evaluating the expert witness under the pressures of cross-examination. The expert needs to know that fidgeting, eye blinking, or any other movement which could be interpreted as nervousness under cross-examination must be avoided at all costs. These nonverbal cues can be interpreted by some jury members as meaning that the expert is deceitful and will cause them to reject his testimony. Further, the expert witness should not become aggressive or hostile during cross-examination but rather should remain calm, listen to the cross-examiner's questions, and then turn, face the jury directly, and give the answer in a calm manner.

Finally, the expert witness needs to know about the trap of answering a series of questions, even though irrelevant, with positive responses. That is, opposing counsel can create a favorable impression in the jurors' minds by making the testimony appear as though this witness agrees with his side by the use of a series of questions answered with the simple word "yes". This is done by asking the expert witness a series of extremely simple questions collateral to the real issues in the case. If the witness falls into the trap of simply answering "yes" repeatedly, he will damage the jury's perception of him even though in fact his testimony is correct. Therefore, the expert must be coached that even when asked simple questions where a "yes" answer would be sufficient, he must break the rhythm of the cross-examiner's questions by saying "yes, but . . .". Generally, the attorney should work with the expert witness regarding this by demonstrating a series of such questions and then breaking the rhythm. As with the lay witness (and if the expert witness will do it), it is always a good practice to have yourself or someone from your office conduct a short cross-examination as part of the preparation process.

COMMENT: Despite impressions to the contrary, the expert, particularly the medical doctor, is impressed with a well-prepared, experienced trial lawyer who explains these matters to him in detail. If the attorney properly paces and handles the expert, he can establish great rapport with him while teaching him how to testify and how to defend himself on cross-examination. Once the expert realizes that the lawyer is confident, knows what he is talking about, and is in control of the situation, the expert will not only become a better witness, but he will feel more comfortable on the stand and have more confidence in you as a trial lawyer. This, in turn, will allow you to further develop more favorable answers from him during direct examination and to teach him how to defend his position effectively on cross-examination.

---

§ 8.16 Developing demonstrative aids in general

As has been emphasized throughout this text, the most basic principle of communication is Communication Principle 1: Communication is based on perception. Perception involves all of the factors affecting the witness' testimony. It involves the verbal and vocal channels (i.e., what the witness says and how he says it) and the nonverbal channel (e.g., facial expression and eye contact). It also involves visual cues, that is, what the jurors see. Whenever it is logical and possible, the information that the witness will present should be presented visually. The reason for this is that we tend to be more impressed by those things we see in print. Things we can see have higher credibility. Further, the things we see are better retained than information which is just heard. Thus, we can see it is essential that all crucial information presented by any witness should be reinforced and anchored by using a visual display.

The use of demonstrative aids by expert witnesses is clearly essential to the case. Most lay witnesses are presenting evidence which rarely lends itself to a visual presentation. On the other hand, the expert witness can use the visual aid to come off of the witness stand and to put himself in a teaching position and to communicate that posture subliminally to the jury.[7]

The expert witness should be consulted during the preparation phase regarding the kind of models, charts, or overheads he would like to use. Have those prepared well in advance of trial for use in the preparation of the expert. Do not allow the expert to protest that he doesn't need aids. Explain why the demonstrative aid is necessary and why he ought to be familiar with it and use it.

Each case has some facts which lend themselves to the development of a demonstrative aid. For example, in an intersectional collision case, de-

---

[7] *See supra* §§ 8.12–8.15.

monstrative aids can be developed to show that if certain testimony is considered hypothetically correct, then the cars approached the intersection at certain speeds and distances. This information can be projected visually with the use of acetate overlays showing the vehicles approaching one another at different angles at different times. A more effective way to present this information is by the use of computerized movie or videotape presentations. Computers can now be used to actually reconstruct the various distances and speeds and to give varying hypotheticals visual impact. Where external injuries are involved, demonstrative aids can be developed to show graphically the nature of the injury to the jury. In one case, a well-known trial lawyer needed to demonstrate a compound and open fracture of the arm. Based on the emergency room doctor's description of the fracture and the bone piercing through the skin, the lawyer had a medical artist depict the injury graphically during its acute phase. The physician was able to testify that the medical illustration was an accurate depiction of what he had seen. The demonstrative aid was admitted into evidence and a substantial verdict resulted.

A little imagination goes a long way in the development of demonstrative aids. With the use of imagination and understanding, effective demonstrative aids can be developed in every case. Indeed, not only can they be developed, they should be developed with consideration of the overall perspective of the case, the jurors' perspectives of the case, and what information needs to be emphasized. This crucial information needs to be presented using demonstrative aids so that it can be assessed visually as well as verbally.

§ 8.17 —Models

One of the more expensive but most effective demonstrative aids is the model. Models of railroad cars are commonly used in FELA cases. In admiralty cases, trial lawyers often use models of ships. In products liability cases, models have been developed demonstrating the details of all sorts of machinery. In a Ford Pinto case, one trial attorney effectively used a model to show the structure and dynamics of gas tanks in rear-end collisions.

Models, of course, take a great deal of time and effort to build and are expensive. Therefore, they should only be used in major litigation. There is a caveat with the use of models: if the models have working parts, the attorney must be sure that those parts work as they are supposed to work. One must be sure that the model or demonstration to be used in the courtroom can be used effectively. The model must be tested repeatedly so that its use can clearly and unequivocably demonstrate the purpose for which it was constructed. Nothing can be more devastating for an attorney than to have an expert use a demonstrative model and have that particular experiment backfire in the courtroom.

One example of this occurred several years ago in a medical malpractice case tried in New Orleans. In that case, the mother of an unborn child died because of the failure of the defendant doctor to diagnose eclampsia. During a critical examination on the day of her death, the doctor attempted to check the protein level of her urine by rubbing the "dipstick measure" across her wet pubic hair rather than dipping it into a sample of urine. It was plaintiff's contention that this was a grossly inadequate way to do urinalysis and that such a use of the "dipstick," because of contamination, yielded results that were invalid. The defense expert attempted to disprove this argument by the use of a demonstration. He had brought with him a syringe, an egg, and several dipsticks. He used the syringe to extract the egg's white portion, which is pure protein. He then placed the protein on his hairy arm and proceeded to rub the dipstick across it. His previously untested demonstration to show that the dipstick would accurately detect the presence of protein failed with each of several successive attempts. The defense witness' expertise and testimony was totally destroyed by the use of a demonstration which had not been tested ahead of time. He had taken the stand believing that the experiment would work, casually assuming that the dipstick would show up the pure albumin in the egg. In fact, the demonstration proved just the opposite and successfully supported the plaintiff's position.

On the other hand, demonstrative aids that have been properly tested have dramatic and powerful effect in the courtroom. A well-known Phoenix trial lawyer once obtained a substantial award in a slip-and-fall case by dramatically demonstrating what happens when a marble floor is improperly waxed. Two slabs of the exact marble used on the floor were placed at 45° angles. One was waxed properly, and one was waxed improperly. Weights were put into the actual shoes involved in the case so as to approximate the coefficient of friction of her shoes to the floor. When the expert put the shoes on the improperly waxed slab of floor material, the shoes slid right down. When placed on the properly waxed floor sample, the shoes dramatically hung on the 45° board as though magnetized there. This courtroom demonstration illustrates the effective use of a model to portray graphically the differences in the coefficients of friction.

§ 8.18 —Demonstrations

On other occasions, instead of using models, the actual object involved in the lawsuit can be introduced as evidence and used dramatically in the courtroom. For example, remember the medical malpractice case, discussed *supra* § 7.26, where the physician failed to take an X-ray of the toe of a working man who had sustained an injury when a 125-pound pump liner fell on his steel-toed work boots. The physician's position was that his examination didn't reveal any reason for an X-ray. Plaintiff's position was that a 125-pound object falling on the foot was sufficient reason in and of itself to take an X-ray. This company doctor treated the man's foot for three months before ordering an X-ray, at which time it was noted that the bones in the foot were eaten away with osteomyelitis and the foot required amputation.

At the trial, the actual pump liner, a large solid steel ring which was 3 feet in diameter was brought into the courtroom. The coemployee who actually handled the liner at the time it fell on the plaintiff's foot was called to testify. He identified the pump liner and then was asked to testify if he knew how high he was holding the pump liner when it slipped and fell. He testified that he had been back to the scene and measured the distance from the ground. He knew it was 1½ feet above the ground. He was then asked to step down from the witness stand and, standing in front of the jury box to hold the liner 1½ feet off the ground, just as he had on the day of the incident. The jury's attention was riveted on this small witness holding this very heavy pump liner right in front of the jury box. Beneath him was a 2-inch-thick piece of plywood which had been used to carry the liner into the courtroom. Counsel used a premeasured 1½-foot stick to measure the exact distance. In the meantime, defense counsel attempted to distract the jury's attention by placing himself between the jury and the demonstration. Having thus positioned himself very near the liner, he had the opportunity to jump backwards as he heard the witness say, "I dropped it like this." As the judge uttered the words "Don't drop that," the liner fell only 1½ feet causing a great clang and putting a gash 3 inches long and 2 inches deep into the solid plywood plank. Most fortunately, defense counsel was not injured. The witness appropriately apologized to the judge, saying that it slipped out of his hands before he could stop from dropping it just as it had on the day in question. This demonstration worked very effectively and made the jury aware that if a 125-pound pump liner falls on somebody's foot, an X-ray ought to be ordered and taken immediately.

COMMENT: Models and demonstrations can form very forceful pieces of demonstrative evidence. They can also be disastrous if not properly designed and tested before trial. The use of a little imagination and a little effort can result in very effective models and demonstrative aids being developed, which in most cases can be the most important form of visual evidence.

---

§ 8.19 —Overhead projections

Most modern litigation involves numerous printed and written exhibits, including medical reports, quotes from medical textbooks, and hospital charts. In most cases, the jury listens to testimony that is comprised of someone reading from these exhibits. Unfortunately, in most cases, enlargements of these exhibits would not only be too expensive, but also would be too cumbersome to handle. Fortunately, however, overhead projections can now be made on the office copying machine. Indeed, any document to which you may refer at trial ought to be reproduced on an overhead. Jurors who see the evidence and hear the testimony are more impressed. Not only do they retain the information better, but they also attach more credibility to it. Every trial attorney should own or have access to an overhead projector. In some cases, special projectors can be used to project opaque objects, but in most cases simple projectors with office-made overheads can be used effectively. The caveat is to use the original document or a dark and legible copy to produce the overhead.

In federal cases, the use of overhead projections of authoritative treatises is specifically authorized and can be very important and very effective. Under Federal Rule 805, authoritative treatises supporting expert testimony are admissible, and the witness can quote from the treatise; however, the text may not be introduced to the jury as an exhibit. Therefore, the only way to reinforce visually what the jury is hearing from the expert is to have the expert read from that article while it is projected on a screen. This is far more effective than having the expert hold the article in front of him on the witness stand and read it to the jury. In fact, the expert will be positioned in front of the jury, with the print blown up larger than life on the large white screen. He then carefully reads the words which support his position to the jury. This is probably the most effective means by which an expert can establish what the standard of care is in a medical negligence case. Usually the defense cannot support its contention that this kind of conduct meets a standard of care printed in a textbook.

§ 8.20 —Slides

Unlike other demonstrative aids, slides have a major weakness in that they are most effectively viewed in a totally darkened courtroom in which counsel cannot accurately observe the jury. Some jurors will find the totally dark courtroom an excellent time to doze off and grab a quick wink. For this reason, it is recommended that overhead projections rather than slides be used for medical texts and documents. If anatomy is to be described and illustrated, a blowup of that anatomical picture should be used rather than a slide projection. A further disadvantage of slides is their size; even if they do become exhibits, the jury cannot readily view the information in the jury room.

On the other hand, slides do have certain advantages. The concerned juror's attention is forced exclusively on the information projected. This is all the juror can see. And, in some instances, slides may be the best way to present certain types of demonstrative evidence, particularly if that evidence needs to be shown in full color. One area where slides are very effective is in the presentation of pathological findings originally viewed under a microscope. Various types of colored chemicals are used to stain the tissue specimens. The pathology diagnosis is made by interpreting various shades and hues of colors. Most pathologists are set up to take Kodachrome slides of their pathological findings though a camera attached directly to the microscope for this purpose. The use of color slides in the courtroom allows the pathologist to show the jury what he has actually seen under the microscope and its significance. If the pathologist is going to show a number of slides, a break every 15 or 20 minutes is essential to avoid having one of the jurors fall asleep during this crucial testimony. Darkness, particularly after lunch, is conducive to napping. If this problem may be avoided, pathological microscopic findings can be shown dramatically through the use of color slides in the courtroom.

§ 8.21 —Blowups

Various types of evidence are more dramatically presented when enlarged. In the courtroom, blowups have the advantage of being visible in the fully lit courtroom. They are also permanent exhibits which the jury can take into the jury room. In addition, they can be easily put on an easel to cross-examine the next witness. Their major disadvantage is that they are cumbersome to handle, and they cannot be easily handled in large numbers. Therefore, when dealing with a quantity of exhibits, overheads should generally be used except for three or four crucial exhibits which should be blown up so that they are permanent and easily available.

Photographic blowups can be extremely effective demonstrative aids, and they can be made of any document. They can zero in on a particular piece of handwriting or on a particular typewritten letter. They can be used to show anatomy, the scene of the accident, or the plaintiff's head encased in crutchfield tongs while recovering in the hospital from a broken neck. Blowups should be used in every case involving any type of serious damage to present key pieces of evidence to the jury. This even includes statements from medical textbooks which clearly set out the standard of care. Blowups of heavily damaged automobiles, roadways, and accident scenes can be very graphic demonstrative aids.

Sometimes blowups can be used as impeachment evidence. In one case, a blowup of one area of one page of a hospital chart was used to impeach a licensed practical nurse who had written over a critical time.[8]

§ 8.22 —Charts

Charts are an efficient means of displaying bits of information which have been summarized and organized in some graphic form. Charts are not admitted directly as evidence but can be used as exhibits once their authenticity has been verified. Charts, for example, can summarize the course of a hospital stay and/or the course of treatment by a particular physician over a period of several months. In one case involving a bone infection that was undiagnosed for over three months, a chart was used during opening statement and trial to summarize the dates on which the

[8] *See infra* § 9.10, for a detailed description of how the blowup of this write-over was used during cross-examination.

plaintiff saw the treating physician and when he worked and did not work.[9]

Another chart that needs to be used in most medical malpractice and/or products liability cases is one which summarizes the standards of care as well as what conduct violated the standards of care. In addition, the chart will cover what the design standards are and what aspects of the product violated the design standard, thereby making the product unreasonably dangerous. An example of such a chart in an obstetrical case is seen in Figure 8–1.

Figure 8–1

Failure of Baby to Descend the Birth Canal

Standards	*Dr. X's Actions*
1. Take complete history; do pelvic measurements, if indicated (pelvimetry).	1. Failed to find out about previous very large baby; did not do pelvimetry.
2. Monitor fetal heart tones every 5 minutes if mother is receiving Pitocin drip.	2. Ordered fetal heart tones monitored every thirty minutes.
3. Do cesarean section if no progress after two hours on Pitocin drip.	3. Failed to do cesarean section even though no progress was evident after twelve hours on Pitocin drip.

Similarly, a well-known Texas trial attorney trying an asbestosis case used charts to demonstrate the extensive cover-up by Johns Manville of letters and articles discussing asbestosis. The effective use of this type of chart, summarizing several decades of suppression of such information, resulted in a substantial punitive damage award.

Charts are traditionally used during closing argument to itemize special and general damages and to total up the amount of damages demanded. In the past, trial attorneys always used such charts; however, this may be overreaching in the moderate case in which less than

[9] *See supra* § 7.26, Figure 7–1.

$100,000.00 is realistically expected. The jury may feel that you are trying to impress them with the individual figures and may reject out-of-hand any suggestions you have. In such a moderate-size case, it may be better for the jury to determine a figure on their own after you make your simple and direct request for the total damages without itemizing the individual elements.

Charts and diagrams can be prepared for use in every case. Generally, it is wise to show the chart to opposing counsel and the judge prior to its use seeking a stipulation as to its accuracy. In most cases, an experienced trial judge realizes that an accurate chart can aid the jury substantially in understanding the case and will rule that it may be used as a demonstrative aid.

§ 8.23 —Blackboards

Another example of an effective demonstrative aid is a blackboard. The major advantage of a blackboard as opposed to charts, blowups, or overhead projectors is that the blackboard, on a subliminal level, is identified with the teacher figure. Therefore, when either you or the expert take the chalk in hand and use the blackboard, you are communicating to the unconscious mind of the juror that you are a teacher. Teachers they know can be trusted, therefore, the use of the blackboard may increase your level of credibility. This advantage is limited by the penmanship of the writer. A blackboard can be used effectively if the trial attorney or expert has good freehand style and is able to write legibly on the blackboard.

The ability of the opponent to erase the facts and figures, previously thought of as a weakness of the blackboard, can be used to your advantage. For example, in one case, a well-known trial lawyer itemized the damages on a blackboard during summation. Of course, the opposing counsel erased the figures, called them ridiculous, and wrote down much lower figures. In the rebuttal argument, the plaintiff's lawyer told the jury that he knew that the opposing counsel would take a cavalier attitude about the serious injury and about the figures, and predictably, would erase them. In fact, he was so positive that opposing counsel was going to take a hostile attitude that, as a precautionary measure, he had earlier taken a photograph of the blackboard, had it blown up, and taped onto the other side of the board. He then turned the blackboard around and reiterated his figures to the jury from the blowup that was taped to the wall side of the blackboard and which had gone unnoticed by the opposing counsel. This piece of advocacy was extremely effective and resulted in a substantial award for the plaintiff.

§ 8.24 —Color exhibits

The purpose of any exhibit is to provide information. The purpose of consciously choosing a color or colors for the presentation of that information is to make its delivery as favorable as possible. Classically, red is associated with blood and passion while black has a connotation of demise, doom, and death. Generally, a basic color is chosen for the exhibits to be presented, and it is used throughout the trial for all evidence that you consider positive. A dramatic change in color (i.e., to orange or even passionate red) should be used when you desire to either highlight a particular fact or impeach a fact presented by the opposition.

In addition to color coding the exhibits, it is important to establish a consistent grid or pattern. By pattern or grid, we mean that the exhibits should have a band of a particular color framing them. An example of such a grid is the red color framing the cover of *Time* magazine. The red grid has successfully anchored the cover of *Time* to the extent that, even without any lettering, the public recognizes the cover of *Time*. The use of such a grid establishes a consistent thread which should be applied not only to the blowups and charts, but also to the overheads as well. All of the exhibits in the case should have the same color for positive evidence, the same color for damaging evidence, and the same grid pattern. This ties them together and anchors them.

Special care has to be taken in criminal cases. As a general rule, the attorney representing the defendant in a criminal case should never use red because of its association with violence, crime, blood, and so forth. The defense in a criminal case would want to use soothing colors, such as a light blue or a pastel. Black is generally considered a little too harsh, but brown is more acceptable. Some colors should be avoided simply because they are hard to read. Yellow is one of the colors that should be avoided not only because it is hard to read, but because yellow is associated with caution or a penalty flag. It is a color that has negative connotations to it and should not be used on your charts.

The most important thing about coding and/or color coding the exhibits is to anchor them. Do not change the color pattern or the grid. If you anchor the visuals consistently, you will have established a thread which will psychologically increase predictability and reduce uncertainty, thereby making the jurors more comfortable with the exhibits. Once the jurors identify with the exhibits on the subconscious level, the credibility level of the exhibits will increase dramatically.

§ 8.25 Outlining witness testimony

When preparing witnesses, some attorneys write out the entire question and then the entire anticipated answer. This is not only cumbersome, but extremely time-consuming as well. A more efficient way to prepare direct examination is to outline the witness' testimony covering the major points. Phrasing questions during direct examination so as to avoid sounding like they are leading questions does take some experience. This is particularly true if the witness has inadvertently forgotten to mention an important time, date, or incident. The verbal crutch, "what, if anything," can be successfully employed to stir the witness' recollection of the importance of bringing forth this valuable knowledge. For example, a lay witness is asked about pain and suffering:

> Q. "You did hear Mr. Jones complain of pain on a number of occasions, did you not?"
>
> A. "Yes."

This is obviously a leading question which would warrant an objection that probably would be sustained. On the other hand, the use of this verbal crutch successfully reminds the witness of the important fact and avoids the objection, as follows:

> Q. "What, if anything, do you know about whether or not Mr. Jones complained of pain on some occasions?"
>
> A. "He complained of pain many times."

Mastering this technique will alleviate the necessity, unless one is dealing with a detailed hypothetical question, of asking questions verbatim. The witness will not answer the question verbatim. Further, a witness who has memorized answers will sound rehearsed and, lacking spontaneity, he will not project a credible image.

Therefore, when preparing a witness for his experience on the stand, discuss the subject matter and work out an outline which will serve as a checklist during trial. It is a checklist not only for your questions, but for all the information which the witness possesses as well. It gives you an index of the various matters which need to be covered with this witness. It is not something from which you are constantly reading; it is simply a guide.

A sample of such an outline of the expert testimony of a treating physician in a cervical sprain case is set forth in Figure 8–2. Obviously, the outlines vary greatly from witness to witness and subject matter to subject matter.

Figure 8–2

TESTIMONY OF DR. HAROLD JONES
CLINIC OF INDUSTRIAL MEDICINE

PATIENT: Mary Hyatt

DATES OF TREATMENT: July 1, 1984 through June 19, 1985
OUTLINE OF TESTIMONY:

I. *Qualifications*

(A) Practicing twenty-two years.

(B) Board-certified general surgery—Subspecialty: Traumatic surgery.

(C) Staff—Kruger Foundation Hospital.

(D) Chairman of Department of Traumatic Medicine.

(E) Associate Professor at Tulane Medical School.

(F) Practice limited to industrial and traumatic medicine—examines for defendants and insurance companies and for plaintiffs—50/50 proportion.

II. *Initial History*

(A) Saw plaintiff July 1, 1984—History: Rear-ended without warning—No symptoms for 24 hours—Then severe symptoms—Waited 4 days to go to doctor because thought it would get better.

(B) X-ray finds—Davis Series—Definitely flattened lundosis.

(1) Explain soft tissues not shown.

(2) Explain flattened lundosis.

(3) Show X-rays (side by side).

(4) Use overheads of outlines of vertebra from X-rays to show lack of movement.

III. *Physical Examination*

(A) Initial examination: limitation of motions, rotation at 80°, flexion and extension at 70°—palpated spasm—trapezius muscle—sternocleidomastoid muscle—bilateral spasms.

(1) Explain spasm v. tenderness.

(2) Describe whiplash mechanics.

(3) *Use anatomy chart—show affected muscles.*

(4) Explain nature of scar tissue.

(5) *Tell why damage is permanent.*

IV. *Initial Diagnosis*

(A) Cervical sprain.

V. *Treatment Recommended*

(A) Pain medications.

(B) Muscle relaxers.

(C) Physical therapy.

(D) Thomas Collar.

VI. *Follow-Up Visits*

(A) 07/01/84: Limitation of motion and spasm.

(B) 07/16/84: Spasm, motion limited.

(C) 08/20/84: Spasm, motion limited.

(D) 09/11/84: Spasm, motion better.

(E) 11/14/84: Spasm, motion OK.

(F) 01/08/85: Spasm, motion OK.

(G) 03/20/85: Spasm, motion OK.

(H) 05/22/85: No spasm, motion OK.

(I) 06/19/85: No spasm, motion OK.

VII. *Final Visit*

(A) Final diagnosis: Cervical sprain with myofesitis.

(B) Prognosis: Chronic bad weather and overuse symptoms permanent.

VIII. *Medical Expense*

(A) Introduce bills in evidence.

The detailed outline such as that in the hypothetical cervical sprain case in Figure 8–2 allows the attorney not only to ask the questions and carefully listen to the answers, but to monitor the jury responses as well. As discussed earlier, when the attorney stands by the jury box, he forces the witness to look at and talk to the jury. Using phraseology such as "would you tell us. . ." and "could you explain to us. . ." gives the trial attorney the opportunity to subliminally become the thirteenth juror. Use the checklist from voir dire and match the phraseology used by some of the jurors during voir dire. If a juror has exhibited a preference for assessing information primarily through the auditory channel, then ask the witness to discuss "what he heard about . . .". Similarly, if some of the jury members primarily assess information through the visual channel, use the phraseology "what did it look like to you?" By matching jurors' primary channels of information assessment with your phraseology, you will create harmony and identification with the jury members. You will be putting the questions in the very words that the jury would have used to ask the questions. Remember to keep the questions simple and in terms a layman can understand.

COMMENT: Direct examination has a rhythm. Avoid the use of all long questions with short answers as much as the use of all short questions requiring long answers. Rather, strive for a pleasant balance of the two considerations. As in music, very frequent repetition of the same notes in the same sequence produces monotony and boredom. A rhythm or mixed pattern of your questions causes the whole picture of your direct examination to be changing and shifting slightly. This helps to hold the interest and attention levels high.

---

§ 8.26 Psychological importance of the closing answer

The last question directed to a witness needs to be a strong one. It should be on a salient point and should be designed to end the examination on a high note. It should require an answer that sounds spontaneous. It ought to be one of the most important things that this witness has to say. Jurors tend to retain the very last thing they hear from a witness. It is the impression and impact created by this witness during that last question which will linger in each juror's memory.

The late great Moe Levine was a master of ending the testimony of witnesses with a strong closing response. In one case he was representing a man in his thirties who had lost both legs. Everyone expected him to belabor the everyday aspects of life with no legs. He had prepared the plaintiff for this testimony only by mentioning that a very personal question would be asked. He wanted the answer to be spontaneous. After a brief direct examination, he said:

Q. Son, would you tell us how you are when you are with your wife?

A. (Young man hangs his head.) I am so clumsy!

Q. No further questions.

This is the epitomy of a good closing answer. It says it all, and with impact. When a juror hears that answer, he really needs to hear no more. No matter what type of witness you are questioning, the testimony ought to be constructed and designed to build to a good closing answer, one that has emotional impact and strong psychological value.

Chapter 9

CROSS-EXAMINATION: CONTROLLING THE CASE

KLUWER LITIGATION LIBRARY REFERENCES

JEANS, LITIGATION: Chapter 13, *Cross-Examination*; Chapter 14, *Cross-Examination of Expert Witnesses*.

PREISER & PREISER, HANDLING SOFT TISSUE INJURY CASES: Chapter 15, *Proving Amount of Economic Loss and Reduced Earning Capacity*; Chapter 16, *Cross-Examination of the Defendant's Doctor*.

I. The Psychology of Control

§ 9.01 Cross-examination in general

Several of the communication principles discussed in Chapters 1 through 4 play a role in the art of effective cross-examination. When we truly understand Communication Principle 1, that "communication is based on perception," we understand why the communication process can be controlled. Since people form impressions based on their perceptions, what the witness actually says does not, alone, necessarily persuade the jury. Jurors may not even grasp the importance or significance of testimony although, in the minds of all the attorneys involved, this testimony was critical. Rather, the jurors form an opinion about the witness, his strengths and weaknesses, his honesty, and his degree of influence, based on the overall impression created by him. Their opinion is based on the witness' demeanor on direct examination and the impression the witness creates on cross-examination. Did the witness hold up under cross-examination? Or, did he agree with the other side and give the case away on cross-examination? Remember also, Communication Principle 6, that "people attempt to maintain their original perceptions regardless of contradictory information." In addition to their original perceptions and their rapidly structured original impression (*see* Communication Principle 3), jurors tend to maintain their impression of a witness, including any stereotypes which exist in their minds.

The trial attorney must at all times be aware of the impression that a witness makes and what can be done on cross-examination to affect that impression. Techniques and goals on cross-examination, therefore, are likely to shift depending upon the trial attorney's impression of the witness. Is this witness a strong witness? Is the witness actually telling the truth? Can the witness' credibility be effectively attacked? Is this a witness that you want on the stand for a long period of time because he is making good points for you as well as the other side? Is this a strong witness to whom you should address only a few questions and then get him off the stand before he further injures your position? As one can see from the nature of the questions posed, the choice of cross-examination techniques is influenced by the nature of the witness. If the witness is a weak witness who is slanting the truth and that can be shown, a certain approach to cross-examination is justified. On the other hand, if he is an unshakably strong fact witness who is telling the truth as he perceives it, a short cross-examination, or perhaps none at all, may be called for. Certain witnesses can be easily attacked for dishonesty, advocacy, or hostility. If the attorney believes such an attack can be successful, it should be made. Yet, certain stereotypical witnesses, such as physicians, receive a great deal of respect in a jury's mind so much so that it is usually folly to attack them directly. In some cases the witness may be considered akin to "the king" and we all know the often quoted statement: "Never attack the king unless you can kill him."

Thus, when considering the goals of cross-examination, always keep in mind that we are talking about taking actions which tend to create an overall specific impression in the jurors' minds. Communication from the witness, like everyone else, is based on how the jurors perceive the witness overall. Jurors decide lawsuits based on their impressions or, in essence, their "gut" feelings. When we understand this principle, we understand that the primary goal of cross-examination is to create an impression that the witness' testimony is at least partially favorable to your side of the case.[1]

This is accomplished by the use of leading questions that elicit a string of positive answers. It can also be accomplished by establishing a rhythm to the cross-examination and by structuring the cross-examination towards a strong close. If these techniques are properly used, the jury may understand that the witness is only favorable to the other side on collateral issues which do not affect the real merits of the case. As long as the cross-examination creates an overall impression that the wit-

---

[1] *See infra* §§ 9.11–9.18, for discussion of techniques for creating the impression that the witness was favorable to your position.

ness "agrees with us" to some degree, that cross-examination can be said to be effective because it fulfilled a primary goal.

The secondary goal of cross-examination is the obtaining of favorable admissions and the creating of an impression that the witness is to some degree dishonest, or that the witness is hostile or acting as an advocate rather than being objective. We obtain favorable admissions by knowing ahead of time what the witness has to offer. This information should have been obtained by the effective use of interrogatories and depositions.[2] Admissions properly obtained in deposition should be reinforced by having them admitted in several different ways and at several different times. These are admissions that need to be on our cross-examination checklist so that we can obtain them at trial. Occasionally a favorable admission can be obtained, even if it has not been anticipated, by listening to a witness' answer and judging whether that answer might lead us into an area to gain favorable admissions. In most cases, however, favorable admissions are something that the witness has given us in advance through proper discovery, and now it is our job to highlight those favorable admissions by emphasizing them during cross-examination.

The goal of creating an impression of dishonesty, hostility, or advocacy is accomplished by techniques discussed in later sections of this chapter.[3] Sometimes the witness can be directly impeached with a prior statement or testimony or an actual piece of physical evidence. However, when we do not have the so-called "smoking gun," we use positioning and mismatching to create the impression that the witness is not being completely honest. Sometimes the mismatching can create the appearance of anger and hostility in the witness which demonstrates to the jury that the witness lacks objectivity. In some instances when we mismatch, we lose control of the witness entirely because he never intends to answer our questions and always advocates his side of the case. At such times, it is advantageous to show that the witness is a total advocate, is not objective, and therefore his testimony lacks credibility.

§ 9.02 Obtaining admissions

Thorough discovery provides the attorney with the information necessary to gain admissions on cross-examination. A significant area to explore on cross-examination is any fact dealing with the witness' perception; that is, did this witness actually see or hear what he perceives

[2] *See supra* Chapter 5, *Preparing for Effective Courtroom Communication*.

[3] *See infra* §§ 9.03–9.10.

he saw or heard? Exploring the environmental factors can also yield admissions: was his view distorted by the angle from which he saw the scene; what were the lighting conditions; were there other significant noises in the area? If the attorney is accurate in obtaining this information, he can generally force the witness to admit, as he did during discovery, that the witness is not really 100% positive of the facts which he related so dutifully to the opposing counsel on direct examination. For example, in an intersectional collision case, a fact witness testified at deposition that he saw a traffic light change from "red then turn yellow and then turn green." The color sequence of traffic lights is red—green—yellow—red—green, and so forth. The light does not turn to yellow before turning green. A fact witness' lack of accuracy in part can be used to attack the credibility of his testimony in whole. This is even true of admissions concerning subjects not directly relevant to the issues of the case. Usually such admissions have been obtained earlier at depositions and they are simply reintroduced at the trial through cross-examination. In the example above, at trial, the witness may attempt to correct the testimony previously given regarding the traffic light color sequence by stating that he realized that the earlier testimony was an error. The witness' credibility is now impeachable to some degree, however, because the jury knows the witness has given two different statements under oath.

In addition to obtaining favorable admissions regarding fact testimony, the lawyer needs to obtain favorable admissions regarding opinions. Generally there are two means of impeaching opinion testimony. First, it can be impeached by showing that the facts or information upon which the expert based his testimony were not accurate. Second, it can be impeached by showing that the opinion was colored by his inherent biases and prejudices. For example, the plaintiff's physician testifies that the low back pain syndrome resulted directly and solely from the trauma suffered; the defense attorney successfully impeaches his testimony by presenting evidence of the existence of the syndrome in the plaintiff's medical history prior to the trauma at issue. On the other hand, if there is no presentable factual information to impeach the physician's testimony, an attack may be launched on his credibility. Such a strategy might show that this particular physician treats many patients for this attorney, that he habitually testifies for injured plaintiffs, and that he waits for the outcome of the litigation to be paid the balance on his bill.

Thorough discovery provides the attorney with the information necessary to gain admissions; a cross-examination checklist provides the necessary reminder of this information during trial. Such a list ought to be a routine part of the procedure in preparation for any trial. In many cases, the substance of the cross-examination is not as important as the impression it creates. During the process of cross-examination we may obtain a few admissions, but the primary goal is to create an impression that the witness is also favorable to our side.

Consider the case of a rear end collision for which the defendant admitted liability. The plaintiff was a 43-year-old housewife. It was the plaintiff's position that as a result of the hyperextension mechanics involved in a rear end collision, she had suffered damage to annulus fibrosis at the C5–C6 level causing a posterior, right lateral bulge in the disc wall which was irritating the C5–C6 nerve root on the right side. It was the defendant's position that the plaintiff did not have a ruptured disc and that she had suffered a simple cervical strain which should have cleared up long ago. While the defense did not say it directly, they implied that the continuous symptoms were inconsistent and that they were brought on by a concern for the litigation and a desire for increased compensation of the injury.

Plaintiff was initially seen by her family physician who had treated both herself and her mother for a number of years. He was a general practitioner. He treated her for a cervical sprain for six weeks at which time he referred her to a neurosurgeon because she started having symptoms of pain going down into her right arm. The neurosurgeon treated her with muscle relaxants and other medication for an additional six weeks and then based on his neurological examinations admitted her to the hospital for a myelogram. The myelogram was performed and it was determined that the patient had a slight posterior bulge at the C5–C6 level. He recommended surgery even though he offered the plaintiff the alternative of continued conservative therapy for the slight bulge. The plaintiff chose continued conservative therapy. At the time of the trial two years later she still had symptoms, although they were neither as severe nor as frequent as in the acute stage. Six months prior to trial the defendants had the plaintiff examined by a neurosurgeon of their choosing. That doctor found no muscle spasm, normal biceps and triceps reflexes, no atrophy, and a mild loss of sensation in the right upper extremity which did not follow any anatomical nerve root pattern. On the other hand, both the plaintiff's doctors had initially found severe muscle spasm and resulting limitation of motion. The neurosurgeon on several occasions had found the loss of sensation was in the C5–C6 dermatome pattern, that plaintiff had a decreased triceps reflex on the right side all of which was consistent, in his opinion, with a ruptured disc at the C5–C6 level. Under a Request for Production, the defendants obtained the films of the myelogram performed by the neurosurgeon a year earlier and although both he and the hospital radiologist read the films as being positive, the defense doctor was of the opinion that the myelogram was negative. He therefore concluded that he could find no basis for the plaintiff's continued complaint and that in his opinion she did not have neurological findings suggestive of a ruptured cervical disc and no further treatment was indicated. The following example is the cross-examination of the defense doctor:

. . .Counselor, you may cross-examine.

Q. [Counsel approaching witness and standing between witness and jury.] Good morning Dr. Levi, it is nice to see you in court again. Can you tell the court and this jury whether or not you have ever examined patients and rendered reports to Mr. Abramson, the defense counsel, previously?

A. Yes, I have on a few occasions over many years.

Q. Doctor, I did not ask you how often you had done it, I asked you whether or not you had done it, and we can establish that fact, can't we, that you have examined for Mr. Abramson previously?

A. Yes, but I thought it was important to bring out. . . .

Q. [Interrupting.] Doctor, I think this cross-examination could move along much more easily and fluently if you will simply listen to my questions and answer my questions. If anything needs to be added it is up to defense counsel to ask you about that on redirect examination.

COURT: Counselor, do not argue with the witness, just ask questions.

Q. Yes, your honor; it is true, is it not, Dr. Levi, that about 40% of your annual income comes from examining individuals for various defense counsel in this city and rendering reports as opposed to seeing patients whom you intend to treat?

A. Yes, I believe that is the estimate I gave you in my deposition.

Q. Doctor, you did review the X-rays of my client taken in the emergency room the evening of the incident?

A. Yes.

Q. And when you reviewed those X-rays, you did notice that the alignment of the cervical spine was straight with the head in a neutral position?

A. Yes, I saw that the neck was straight, but it was my opinion that the chin was tilted down slightly.

Q. But, you do agree, do you not, that this lady had a flattened lordosis?

A. Yes.

Q. And you do agree that it is quite possible, considering the history of a severe hyperextension injury earlier that evening that this flattened lordosis or loss of normal curvature of the spine was due to muscle spasm?

A. Yes, that is a possibility.

Q. Therefore, if this lady went to Dr. Newman the next day, and Dr. Newman clinically found the presence of muscle spasm, you would have no reason to disagree with that finding, isn't that true?

A. Yes.

Q. In fact, Dr. Levi, isn't it true that when people do suffer hyperextension injuries one would clinically expect muscle spasm to be present.

A. Yes.

Q. And isn't it true, Dr. Levi, that one would expect this muscle spasm to be present only in the early stages of the injury when it was in what the physicians call the acute stage?

A. Yes.

Q. And thereafter, one would expect the muscle spasm not to be present on an ongoing basis, but for it to come and go?

A. Yes.

Q. So one would expect, six months, a year, or a year and a half later that one could have an injury and one would not be expected to have muscle spasm necessarily?

A. Yes, that is true, but if one has a ruptured disc one often finds muscle spasm.

Q. Dr. Levi, you would agree, would you not, that one would not expect muscle spasm with a minimal disc rupture if at the time of the examination the symptoms from that disc rupture were not present?

A. I don't know about that.

Q. [Plaintiff's counsel turning and looking incredulously to the jury.] You don't know about that? You do not know about that part of medicine?

A. I am not sure what you are saying.

Q. Remember, doctor, when you gave your deposition in this matter, about two months ago?

A. Yes.

Q. And, doctor, calling your attention to page 34 of the deposition, and I now hand you a copy of that deposition, opened at page 34, and I ask you to follow me and see whether or not I am reading the question and answer accurately, starting on line 2. [The attorney faces the jury and starts reading the question]:

> "Q. Is it not true even if you have a ruptured disc that in the chronic stage, that is, after six months or a year, the muscle spasm comes and goes, and that you don't find it present every day or every examination?
>
> "A. Yes, that is usually true."

Q. Now, doctor, you remember giving that testimony back then?

A. But, I did not understand that was what you were asking, if that is what you were asking I agree with you.

Q. So, doctor, you do agree that one can have a ruptured disc and when a physician makes an examination a year and a half later, one would not necessarily expect to find muscle spasm on that date?

A. Yes.

Q. So the fact, doctor, is that when you examined this patient, a year and a half later, with this one examination, in order to render a report to defense counsel in this matter, the fact that you did not find muscle spasm does not rule out the possibility that she has a ruptured disc?

A. No, it doesn't rule it out.

Q. Doctor, in your experience, is it true that neurological findings often vary betweeen two qualified neurosurgeons depending on the cooperativeness of the patient, the stage of the patient's symptoms, and various factors between two different neurosurgeons, including to some degree the skill of the neurosurgeon himself, and the relationship that neurosurgeon has with the patient?

A. Yes, to some degree that is true.

Q. So, you would agree that it is perfectly probable in medical circles that one doctor can find loss of sensation to fit a particular dermatome pattern one day, and then on another day another doctor can examine the patient and the dermatome findings aren't clear?

A. Well, they should be consistent.

Q. Yes, doctor. But is it not true, in your experience, that sometimes two examiners often disagree on whether or not findings fit a particular dermatome pattern?

A. Yes, that is often disputed.

Q. But, doctor, you can't say, can you, that Dr. Jones was wrong when on three different occasions he felt that the loss of sensation in this lady's case fit the C5–C6 dermatome pattern?

A. No, I do not dispute his findings.

Q. Doctor, is it also true, this is with muscle spasm, depending on the degree of irritation that a disc is causing on an irritated nerve root on a particular day, that on some days you can have loss of a triceps reflex and on other days the triceps reflex will not be decreased?

A. Yes.

Q. So that would explain, doctor, why on your examination, and even on some examinations by Dr. Jones, this lady's treating neurosurgeon, that on some days the triceps was normal and on some days it was not?

A. Yes, one finds this to happen.

Q. So you would agree, doctor, would you not, that you did not find muscle spasm and the fact that you felt that the loss of sensation did not fit the C5–C6 nerve root and you found a normal triceps reflex does not rule out the possibility that this lady has a ruptured disc, does it?

A. It doesn't rule it in or rule it out.

Q. But, you would agree doctor, that if you would have seen her on a number of occasions and if you would have come to the conclusions that Dr. Jones did, that is, that if on some occasions you would have found an absent triceps reflex and after a number of examinations you were able to determine that the loss of sensation fit the C5–C6 dermatome pattern, then you would be more willing to say that this lady had a ruptured disc?

A. Hypothetically, if I had those findings I would be more suspicious of a ruptured disc, but I don't think that I would make a diagnosis on that basis.

Q. Well, let me ask you this doctor, you would agree, would you not, if you had personally made those findings, a decreased triceps reflex, muscle spasm, and loss of sensation over the C5–C6 dermatome pattern in the right arm, that you would be much more suspicious of the possibility that this lady had a ruptured disc?

A. Yes, that would increase my suspicions, but I do not have those findings.

Q. Yes, doctor. But, if you assume for a minute that you had those findings, those findings if present, and you were satisfied with them would increase your suspicion that this patient had a ruptured disc?

A. Yes.

Q. And, you would agree, would you not, that if you are more suspicious of a ruptured disc one would place more significance on the indentation in the dye column in the myelogram of my client's neck that you reviewed?

A. Yes, if you had those symptoms it might take on some added significance.

Q. So, when you say that you interpret the myelogram as negative, and you find that the bulge, the little indentation in the dye column is not significant it is based in part on the fact that you found no positive neurological findings on your physical exam?

A. Yes.

Q. In other words doctor, one always relates the radiologic findings to the clinical findings in order to have it make sense?

A. Yes.

Q. And, what you are really saying about the myelogram is that since this indentation in the dye column is slight, in your opinion it just could be an anomoly in the way the dye was filling the nerve roots, and of no significance?

A. Yes.

Q. But, it is also true doctor, that even if you have a negative myelogram, that in twenty percent of the cases you can have a false negative myelogram. That is, the myelogram can be negative and you can still have a ruptured disc?

A. That has been reported in the literature. My experience is more like ten percent.

Q. Okay, doctor, I will not argue with you, but you would agree that in at least ten percent of the cases in your experience you could have a myelogram like this lady has and even though it is interpreted as negative the lady could still have a ruptured disc.

A. Yes.

Q. So, then in your opinion doctor, there is at least a possibility that this lady had a ruptured disc in her neck?

A. You are asking about this particular lady?

Q. Yes, doctor, I am asking about this particular lady. You certainly admit that it is medically possible, do you not, that she had a ruptured disc?

A. No, I don't believe that is medically possible.

Q. [Attorney turning, facing the jury, and scratching the back of his head quizzically.] Doctor, didn't we just have a series of questions establishing that your lack of neurological findings and your interpretation of the myelogram does not absolutely rule out that my client has a ruptured disc?

A. I don't believe that it is possible that this lady had a full blown ruptured disc. No, sir, I just can't accept that.

Q. Oh! So what we are quibbling about here, doctor, is terminology?

A. I am not sure what you mean?

Q. Well, doctor, when you use the term ruptured disc, what you mean by ruptured disc is that not only has the annulus fibrosis been damaged, but that there is actual leakage of the nucleus pulposus out of the disc which is impinging directly on the spinal canal. In other words, it is a piece of the disc material posterior to the disc which is back in the spinal canal, irritating the spinal canal and its nerve roots?

A. Yes, that is the definition of a ruptured disc.

Q. And, doctor, when you have injury to the annulus fibrosis, and the annulus fibrosis is bulging you do not consider that a ruptured disc?

A. Yes, that is not what I call a ruptured disc.

Q. But, is it not true, that in the literature some physicians would call this a disc rupture, that this is just a question of labeling?

A. Yes, I suppose that you could look at it that way.

Q. Then, you do agree doctor, that the mechanics of a rear end collision can cause injury to the annulus fibrosis?

A. Yes, that has been reported.

Q. And, that the annulus fibrosis can be injured enough for it to bulge backwards, a defect but without the nucleus pulposus actually coming out of the disc?

A. Yes, that can happen, but I do not call that a ruptured disc.

Q. All right, doctor, but you do agree that in this case, even though you had negative findings, that it is possible that this lady could have an injury to the annulus fibrosis where it is bulging backwards?

A. Yes, but that does not usually produce symptoms.

Q. But, if the bulge is in the right spot, if it is bulging backward and laterally to the right side, while such a bulge will not cause symptoms by irritating the spinal column, if it is in exactly the right spot it can bulge in such a fashion so as to irritate one single nerve root?

A. Yes, I suppose that is possible.

Q. And, if that occurs, is it not true that the picture you would see clinically of someone with those symptoms is that of pain radiating down the right arm?

A. Yes.

Q. And, that pain would also be accompanied by loss of sensation that would fit the C5–C6 dermatone pattern?

A. Yes.

Q. And, that with this type of irritation you would find a decreased triceps reflex and a normal biceps reflex on the right side, and normal reflexes on the left side?

A. Yes, that would be the clinical picture.

Q. [Attorney now facing jury and indicating facially that he does not care about the answer of Dr. Levi.] And you have read the medical reports in this case, and are not those the exact findings of Dr. Jones, the treating neurosurgeon in this case; are those not the findings that he had, and is it not true therefore, doctor, that Dr. Jones with those findings is justified in saying that this lady has an injury to the annulus fibrosis?

A. I was not present to know what Dr. Jones found.

Q. Doctor, I am not asking whether or not you were present. What I am asking you, doctor, is that if Dr. Jones had those findings he would be clinically justified in saying that this lady had a ruptured disc at the C5–C6 level and that she may eventually need surgery, would he not?

A. Yes, with those findings he could say that and I would possibly say it.

Q. Then all you are saying is that on the one occasion you examined her those findings were not present?

A. Yes, that is all I can report.

Q. But, it is also true that she can have a ruptured disc and on some days not have those findings, and on other days they could be present, and in order to know whether or not she has a ruptured disc you would have to examine her on more than one occasion?

A. Yes, I suppose you could say that.

Q. And, if you can say that, and if this lady was asymptomatic, she had no symptoms, before this occurrence and if she has the bulge in the disc, would you not admit it is quite possible then that all of this by way of history would be related to the trauma of December 1982 in your opinion, isn't that correct?

A. Yes, that is what I told you in my deposition, so I suppose so.

Q. No further questions doctor. . . . Thank you very much.

It is difficult to evaluate the effectiveness of cross-examination or to understand the techniques of the cross-examination when it is just the written word. The effectiveness of the impression formation during the cross-examination has a great deal to do with the nonverbal communication that is taking place. It is the cues that the attorney is giving on a nonverbal level, the vocal cues, and the rhythm of the cross-examination itself that creates the overall favorable impression and drives home key points and underscores the information obtained. The point is that the cross-examination must be carried out in a logical order, a starting point followed by a logical sequence that works towards a conclusion which reaches some kind of climax.

II. Diminishing Credibility Through Mismatch

§ 9.03 The attack position: standing between the witness and the jury

Normally counsel does not want to interfere with the flow of information from a witness to the jury; that is, on direct examination counsel should not be in a position where he is physically blocking the witness or using his body as a barrier between that witness and the jury. This visibly and nonverbally interferes with the flow of information. On the other hand, jurors expect the trial counsel to be good at cross-examination. They expect the cross-examination to consist of an attack and for counsel to "score some points" with the witness. If trial counsel does not fulfill that preconceived stereotype, the jurors will see the witness as having won the battle and possibly even the war, i.e. the verdict, in favor of your opponent.

As stressed numerous times, remember that the information emanating from the trial lawyer, the communicator, is being sent on all three levels: verbally, vocally, and nonverbally. Therefore, it is important when conducting a cross-examination to express nonverbally through gestures, positioning, and facial expressions that the trial lawyer is master of the situation. Show that you are forcing agreements from the witness that he does not want to make, that you are in control of the situation, and have, to some degree, contempt for the witness' testimony. This impression is also conveyed by vocal cues, the rapidity with which the questions are asked, and the tone or pitch of voice. All of these factors play a part in creating the impression that this cross-examination is effective. Thus, when it is stated that the attorney should assume the attack position when preparing to begin a cross-examination, it means more than him placing his body between the witness and the jury. He needs to remain in that position, for the most part, when asking his questions. Of course, on occasion when he wants to show the witness a document or he wants to impeach the witness, he may approach the witness or take a position nearer to the witness stand. But, at all other times, and when allowed by the judge, position yourself between the witness and the jury. When asking your questions look at the witness, but while listening to his answers turn and look at the jury. Do not forget for a moment that the jury is sitting there evaluating you and when making your key point, be sure that you look those jurors in the eye. Be sure that when summarizing the witness' testimony or reaching a dramatic point of the cross-examination, that you are neither playing to the witness nor looking at him. At that point you need to be looking directly at the jury, making eye contact with them, and letting them read your face so that they know that you are in control, that you have mastered this witness. All of this is part of the vocal, verbal, and nonverbal cues that the attorney projects and which form part of the jury's perceptions regarding his cross-examination. They will be impressed with the cross-examination itself and the overall effect far more than the wording of any particular answer. Of course, there are some cases in which a particular answer is devastating and the words are so critical that they alone could have a significant effect. However, with respect to the average cross-examination, it is the overall impression perceived by the jurors that counts, not the individual answer or the particular admission obtained. This overall impression is most effectively communicated when the cross-examining attorney projects in his cross-examination that he is controlling, that he is in the attack position, and that he is accomplishing his goal of creating a favorable impression—i.e., that the witness agrees with him.

§ 9.04 Mismatching communication channels to create pressure

Communication Principle 4: People use stereotypes to organize their perceptions and Principle 6: People attempt to maintain their original perceptions regardless of contradictory information, are applicable during cross-examination. Jurors have a preconceived stereotype or perception of a dishonest witness; that is, one who fidgets, hesitates, pauses, sweats, or squirms in his chair. The trial attorney can successfully create this impression of the witness by the skillful use of mismatching. If it is created early during the cross-examination, the jurors will attempt to maintain their original perception regarding this witness' less than truthful nature regardless of opposing counsel's attempts to rehabilitate the witness by presenting contradictory information. While he is standing between the jury and the witness in the attack position, it is essential that the trial attorney understand and use the technique of mismatching the witness so as to create the perception in the jury's mind of hesitancy in the witness' testimony.

The witness is engaging in a communication process between himself and the attorney. First, the witness is generally more uncomfortable than the attorney is because the attorney is in his natural habitat, the courtroom. Most witnesses are nervous and fidgety. Indeed, they have been nervous about this cross-examination for days, always wondering what you were going to ask, how you were going to ask it, and how uncomfortable the trial attorney will make them feel. Therefore, there is a certain amount of nervousness and mismatching inherent in the situation. This inherent nervousness is increased by mismatching the witness vocally. If the witness is speaking rapidly, the attorney should speak slowly, using a voice tone and style of questioning which do not match the witness' answer. Mismatching his body movements and gestures is also important; shy and slow movements demand gregarious and rapid movements in return. Whatever the witness does, attempt to do the opposite. It is always more effective if the attorney can mismatch the witness verbally. That is, each witness tends to communicate through one of three major channels, either kinesthetic (feeling), visual (seeing), or auditory (hearing). A person's primary channel can be identified by listening to his language and reading the witness' eye patterns.[4] For example, a person who is primarily visual in nature will talk about the way he sees things and the way other people look at situations. Therefore, when questioning that witness, use kinesthetic or auditory words. This successfully creates a hesitancy in the speech pattern of the witness. The witness is accustomed to communicating primarily through the visual channel, but now he is forced to communicate in a different channel because of the nature of your questions. He must use kinesthetic or auditory words and this creates a hesitancy in his speech pattern. The hesitancy is identified by the jurors, mostly in the unconscious mind, as pauses and delayed answers. It is also identified by disruption of the actual words he uses, as well as his choice of words and phraseology. This technique can be used to disrupt the witness' pattern of thought and speech. As hesitancy increases, the attorney's facial expressions, tone of voice, and the rapidity of his speech pattern should indicate to the jury the importance of the question and the "worthlessness" of the answer, regardless of whatever response this particular witness offers. The hesitancy communicates to the juror's unconscious mind an uneasiness or an untrustworthiness about this witness' testimony. Some jurors, usually not all of them, may even consciously pick up on some of the vocal and visual cues created by the disfluency. They may well interpret this nonverbal behavior as an indication that the witness is being less than honest. Remember that this will be a juror's perception even if it is not the truth. This relates to Communication Principle 1: Communication is based on perception. Thus, through the use of mismatching in cross-examination, you have the opportunity at least to create significant vocal and nonver-

---

[4]*See generally supra* Chapter 2, *Persuasive Strategies in the Courtroom*.

bal cues in the witness which may be interpreted either on the unconscious or, in some cases, on the conscious level as dishonesty on the part of the witness.

§ 9.05 Asking questions where does not counsel care about the answer

Some situations call for counsel to close his cross-examination dramatically by asking a question which amounts to a speech to the jury. In that situation, the question, because of its considerable content and logical impact, is the important thing and not the answer. This is a question which should be used at the tail end of the cross-examination and should be asked in a dramatic fashion. It is usually a question that makes a statement. In some instances, the question can be so framed that it is almost an argument. The attorney's back should be to the witness and he should give a definite indication nonverbally that he does not care about the answer. Be sure, however, that the question is one to which you clearly do not care what the witness says.

An example of such a situation often arises in a medical malpractice case. Often the attorney tries medical malpractice cases involving a physician who, in the performance of a hysterectomy, will accidentally sever the ureter, the connection between the woman's kidney and her bladder. Severe consequences result if this is not diagnosed and corrected immediately. The defense often takes the position that severing the ureter is a risk of the procedure and can occur even when the physician is as careful as possible. It is just one of those risks that happen occasionally and it is nobody's fault. Frequently, the defendant will bring in the head of the department of the local hospital, often a friend of the defendant himself, to testify that this conduct meets the standard of care and that this can occur even if the doctor is as careful as possible. Discovering that this physician has never severed a ureter even though he has performed a thousand or more hysterectomies provides an opportunity to use the following questions to close the cross-examination:

Q. Doctor, you told us, have you not, that you are an expert in this procedure.

A. Yes.

Q. And you have performed this procedure on a number of occasions; could you tell the jury how many times you have done this?

A. Over my fifteen years as a practising gynecologist-obstetrician I must have performed two thousand hysterectomies.

Q. [Attorney now turning to face the jury.] And, doctor, you have performed that same operation two thousand times, then, haven't you?

A. Yes.

Q. [Attorney now fully facing the jury.] Then it is true, doctor, is it not, that when you performed that operation two thousand times, that never on one single occasion did your scalpel slip and did you ever cut a ureter, is that not true?

A. Yes, that is true. . . .

Q. [Rapidly cutting off any further answer.] And that is true, doctor, because when you do this particular surgery you are always careful? [Attorney shows disregard for the answer in keeping back to witness, then turns and walks back to counsel table.]

A. . . . .

Q. [After the witness presents his explanation as to how a ureter can be cut while carefully performing a hysterectomy, the lawyer looks over to the jury with a disgusted expression on his face and says:] I have no further questions of this witness!

§ 9.06 Using prior statements to impeach

In most cases, there is a limited amount of evidence available to impeach the credibility of the witness. When there is a prior statement or other document that can be used in some fashion to impeach the witness' credibility, the trial attorney has to make a decision regarding its use. In making that decision, remember that the cross-examination is judged by jurors not on its verbal content as much as the overall impression created by the cross-examiner. The lay witnesses have preconceived generalizations about the attorney's power during cross-examination which must be taken into account. Laymen see trial attorneys as "word magicians"; they believe the shrewd way in which the attorney phrases his questions can trip up unskilled witnesses. The preconceived notion that the attorney is equipped with some magical skill in cross-examination and that it is unfair for him to use that skill is clearly more applicable to lay witnesses than to experts, but it does apply in some degree to both. Hopefully, by the time you have reached cross-examination, the jury will have a trust relationship with you. They will have perceived you as always being fair because your voir dire questions indicated that you wanted both sides of the question answered and you wanted to be fair. Do not ruin that image by appearing to be the bully. More harm than good could result if you appear to be badgering the witness, particularly one of the opposite sex or one who is smaller or belongs to a minority group. Do not be seen as taking unfair advantage during cross-examination.

The personalized generalization that exists in most laymen's minds regarding the clever skills of the trial attorney makes thorough and well-planned cross-examination questions regarding impeachment mandatory. If you are going to attempt to impeach a witness, you must be prepared to make it an effective impeachment. An unsuccessful attempt at impeachment can lose the case on that one tactical error alone. If the jury knows you are attempting to impeach a witness, particularly a lay witness, and they perceive you as being unfair, an unsuccessful attempt to impeach that witness' credibility will cause the jurors to resent the attack.

COMMENT: Remember that the jurors do not possess the clever skill of cross-examination. They do not identify with the trial attorney; rather, in their minds they identify with the witness. After all, this type of unfair advantage could someday happen to them.

The trial attorney must be sure he has unshakable documents (or other strong evidence) which will result in a solid impeachment. If your impeaching evidence is a prior inconsistent statement, be sure the statement cannot be explained away. Analyze the statement and discuss it with other attorneys in the office to see whether they feel this is really something that impeaches the credibility of the witness and has a devastating effect. If it does not, do not use it, do not gamble, and do not let the jury feel that you are a crafty and clever lawyer who tried to take unfair advantage of the unsuspecting witness.

After the decision to use a document for impeachment has been made, the cross-examination must be constructed so as to close all the doors before attempting to spring the trap. If you are going to saw the limb off and let the witness crash to the ground, make sure that you are sitting on the trunk side of the limb. Failing to close all the doors gives the witness the opportunity to explain away the document that is being used for impeachment. This is particularly true when a prior inconsistent statement is contained in a deposition. The jurors understand that the witness was under pressure at the deposition. The witness could easily have made a mistake. A critical admission made only once in a deposition and/or is in any way equivocal in its wording may not successfully impeach a witness. As discussed previously, it is strongly recommended that a question yielding an important admission which can be used at trial be rephrased differently later on in the deposition to obtain the same answer several times.[5] The exact location of these answers needs to be worked into the cross-examination outline because a witness confronted with one prior inconsistent statement will attempt to get off the hook by saying things like: (1) "That is not exactly what I said"; (2) "The court reporter made a mistake taking it down"; (3) "What I meant by that was. . . ."; (4) "If you read the entire page and take the statement in context, it means. . . ." On the other hand, it is much more difficult to explain that three statements were misinterpreted or the same mistake was made three times.

§ 9.07 —Sample cross-examination—impeaching witness' credibility (unequivocal impeaching evidence)

For example, assume that in an auto collision case the defendant stated in a deposition that as she approached the intersection she was "going at 40 miles an hour" and was approximately 20 feet from the intersection when a car suddenly came in front of her. Obviously, considering time, speed and distance, and particularly reaction time, the defendant would have to have been several hundred feet from the intersection when the car she struck entered that intersection. At trial the defendant will find it necessary, in order not to conflict with the physical evidence, to change her testimony regarding the distance from the intersection and/or the speed at which she was traveling. She can successfully do that by saying she was just guessing, that it was just an estimate, that, in essence, she did not mean what she said. She can do that successfully if the statement is made only once in the deposition. If the statement has been made two or three different ways and in response to two or three different questions, the witness can be impeached with the prior inconsistent statement.

On direct examination at trial, the witness has testified to driving at a lower speed and changed the distance from the intersection. You must

[5] *See generally supra* Chapter 5, *Preparing for Effective Courtroom Communication*, and specifically § 5.67.

now decide whether to attempt to impeach her with the prior inconsistent statements made at deposition. What judgments would you make regarding this type of impeachment? This would be an impeachment based on a different version of the facts which could easily be argued away as a simple mistake. Certainly it is not impeachment which tends to raise the specter of any dishonesty of the witness. Therefore if this is to be attempted at all, the attorney must appear to be entirely fair in his use of the documents. Always be polite. This is particularly true if the witness is of the opposite sex. In other words, the tenor of the presentation of the impeachment document is related directly to two factors: (1) the skill and status of the witness being attacked, i.e., is this a witness who could easily be taken advantage of by the attorney? and (2) the nature of the impeaching document, i.e., does it deal with factual matters which could be explained away as a prior mistake in memory and ability to estimate or is it an impeachment where the witness was actually forging documents? Having decided to proceed with the impeachment attempt, the questioning could go something like this:

Q. Ms. Jones, you do remember coming to my office about a year ago and giving some testimony in a deposition at that time?

A. Yes, sir.

Q. And, you do remember at that time I asked you, before your deposition, if you were nervous and whether there was anything we could do to make you more comfortable?

A. Yes, I believe I remember you saying something like that.

Q. And, at that time, do you remember we offered you coffee and you had a cup?

A. Yes, I think I remember that.

Q. And at that time we asked you just to give the best honest answers you could?

A. Yes, sir, that is what I tried to do.

Q. You stated today in court that you were going 20 miles an hour and were 150 feet from the intersection when Barbara's car first came into the intersection?

A. Yes, sir.

Q. Now, Ms. Jones I would like to hand you that deposition and call your attention to page 29 so that you can read along with me what you said to questions about speed and distance at that point in the deposition.

A. Yes, sir.

Q. And, we asked you back on April 29th, 1981, a year ago:

> "Q. And, can you tell us how fast you were going at the time?
>
> "A. I am sure I was going about 40 miles an hour.
>
> "Q. How do you know that?
>
> "A. I had looked at my speedometer shortly before the accident and it was right between 35 and 40 miles an hour.
>
> "Q. And you had not reduced your speed any from the time you looked at your speedometer until you saw the plaintiff's car coming into the intersection and slammed on your brakes?
>
> "A. I had not reduced my speed any substantial degree.
>
> "Q. So, your speed had remained constant, about the same 35 to 40 miles an hour, from the time you looked at the speedometer until you slammed on your brakes?
>
> "A. Yes, sir, about that.
>
> "Q. And how far were you from the intersection when you slammed on your brakes?
>
> "A. I was only about 30 feet, maybe even less."

Q. Now, I did hear correctly when you testified for your lawyer a few minutes ago that you now say you were going about 20 miles an hour and that you were 150 feet away when my client's car first came into the intersection?

A. Yes, sir, but I have had a chance to think about it and I thought about it a lot after the deposition and I just could not have been going that fast and been that close to the intersection.

Q. Okay, ma'am, now that is what you said on page 29, lines 1 through 14, of your deposition, which we just read, is that correct?

A. [Looking at the deposition.] Yes, sir.

Q. Now, I would like to call your attention to page 42, lines 12 through 14. Ma'am, would you read the testimony that you gave, the questions and answers contained in the deposition.

A. [Witness reading from deposition.]

> "Q. And you say that you looked at your speedometer a few minutes before this and you know you were going 40 miles an hour and you were only 20 or 30 feet away from the intersection when you first saw the car?
>
> "A. That is the way I remember it."

Q. Now, ma'am, you did give that answer on page 42, did you not?

A. Yes, sir, I guess that was my best estimate then, I have just changed it now.

Q. Ma'am, would you look at page 102 of the deposition and read from lines 14 through 18?

A. [Witness reading from deposition.]

> "Q. And you say you looked at the speedometer and you weren't guessing, you hadn't reduced your speed, you knew that you were going 40 miles an hour, and certainly at the very least 35 miles an hour, is that not so?
>
> "A. Yes, sir."

Q. Now, ma'am, did you give that testimony?

A. Well, it is written here so I suppose I did.

Q. But is it not true that at no place in your deposition in all three instances where you discuss your speed did you tell us then that you were estimating the speed, you told us you looked at the speedometer and you knew what the speed was?

A. Yes, sir, I must have been wrong in remembering that. It could not have been correct.

Q. And, it wasn't correct, ma'am, when you said that you were only 20 feet from the intersection, you were further back?

A. Yes, sir.

Q. And, if you were further back and going slower and had been watching, ma'am, is it not true that you would have had ample time in which to stop your car and bring it under control before it broadsided my client?

A. I suppose you could argue that, but that is not the way I remember it happening.

Q. And, you remember it happening differently today, though, than you did when you gave your deposition in my office about a year and a half ago?

A. Yes, sir, I suppose you could say that.

[End of cross-examination]

Note how the cross-examination emphasizes that the witness gave a completely different account of how the accident occurred at deposition than she gave at trial. Note the tactic of setting up the questioning by showing the courtesy extended to the witness at the deposition. Also, you should not appear to be badgering the witness now. It may well be that she was not adequately prepared when she gave the original estimate at her deposition. She may have honestly, but incorrectly, given her original estimate as she remembered it, but which had to be in conflict with the physical facts. It is something that can be used to an advantage, but it is not a "stake" to be driven through "the heart of Count Dracula." It is to be used gently and with tact. It can be used to make a point and it can later be argued that this witness' memory of the events cannot be relied upon, but it is not a document that impeaches the honesty of the witness.

§ 9.08 —Impeaching witness who denies prior inconsistent statement

A different situation arises when the information which could be used to impeach a witness, while contradictory and having some effect on the witness' credibility, is an impeachment document which has some equivocal quality about it. In most cases, the witness should be able to explain away the inconsistency with ease. But sometimes the witness' inability to properly handle the impeachment information allows what should be an ineffective impeachment to become an effective impeachment.

In one case, a defendant general practitioner had failed to diagnose eclampsia (toxemia of pregnancy), a disorder of pregnancy with potentially disastrous results. The warning signs are high blood pressure, weight gain, and protein in the urine. In this particular case, the defendant doctor had done the crucial urinalysis by rubbing the dipstick on the patient's wet pubic hair rather than into a sample of the patient's urine to test for protein. This contaminated the stick and made the urinalysis unreliable. The physician had testified in his deposition that he had taken her blood pressure and it was 140 over 95, and that he considered this to be high blood pressure. In actuality, in many standard textbooks 140/95 is not considered necessarily high enough to be an indication of pending eclampsia. Rather than using these texts to show lack of high blood pressure, he closed his eyes on the stand and remembered that he had never used the words "high blood pressure" in his deposition. He insisted that the court reporter made an error when the testimony was transcribed. When confronted with the words "high blood pressure" at another place in his deposition, he was again insistent that the court reporter made another error, that he never called that "high blood pressure" because in his opinion 140 over 95 was not high blood pressure but simply a borderline pressure. He absolutely refused to admit that he said "high blood pressure" in the deposition. After his testimony, the deposition court reporter was called to testify and read his original notes to the jury. He testified that the doctor had said exactly what was typed in the deposition and that he had not made a mistake. Thus, this particular witness impeached himself by taking a position on a prior statement which was not necessarily inconsistent at all. It would have been far better for this defendant to admit that he called 140/95 high blood pressure, and that the inconsistency between high blood pressure and borderline pressure was simply his own mistake in terminology.

§ 9.09 —Sample cross-examination—"closing the door" on the witness before impeachment

On the other hand, on those rare instances when the trial attorney truly has a "smoking gun," he is dealing with a piece of evidence that goes directly to the witness' credibility and, to some degree, not only impeaches what the witness said or did previously, but shows that he is attempting to be dishonest. The caveat again, however, is to be sure that all the doors have been closed before you spring the trap. Make sure that the witness is out on the tip of the limb before you saw it off.

In an admitted liability case tried in Jackson, Mississippi, in the days before listing witnesses was required, the issue was whether the plaintiff had suffered permanent tunnel vision due to an injury to the optic chiasma. The optic chiasma is that point behind the eyes where the two optic nerves join in a plexus before they branch out to various areas of the brain. Plaintiff was able to call two treating neurosurgeons who testified that her lack of symptoms for four months after the accident was a normal clinical pattern to be expected in closed head trauma cases with injuries to the optic chiasma, particularly where the patient is not knocked unconscious. They testified that it takes three to four months for the resulting optic nerve atrophy to occur and that this was the reason for the delay in diagnosis.

Since the defendants had admitted liability and never had an "independent medical exam" performed, plaintiff's counsel did not anticipate the defendant calling any witnesses. Yet, the morning after the plaintiff had rested his case, defense counsel called a neurosurgeon from the Jackson area. He testified on direct examination that he had been practicing neurosurgery and teaching at the University of Mississippi Medical School in Jackson, Mississippi, for twenty years. He testified that he was board qualified in neurosurgery. After his qualifications were given to the jury, the defense attorney read the other medical reports to this witness and asked his opinion. During the opinion testimony, he emphasized over and over again that he came from the same community as did the jurors, unlike the neurosurgeons from Texas and Louisiana who had testified that this blow to the plaintiff's head had caused injury to the optic chiasma. He then went to a blackboard, drew a circle which he labeled the skull, sketched in the eyes, and drew the optic chiasma. He then explained emphatically that this nerve was completely surrounded by the bone of the skull, that it is in the middle of the head, and that there was no way to injure the chiasma with closed trauma to the head that did not also fracture the skull. Fortunately plaintiff's counsel had researched the medical factors of the case even though he was not specifically prepared to do a cross-examination. The fact that this injury usually occurs with a closed head trauma and that the trauma did not have to be severe to injure the skull in order to damage the optic chiasma was documented in a well-known textbook. But in order to make that cross-examination effective, all the doors had to be closed. The stage had to be set before this witness, who was obviously lying, could be impeached. The transcript of the cross-examination reads as follows:

Q. Doctor, you are familiar, are you not, with Dr. Homer Jones, who is a neurosurgeon on the staff of Ochsner Foundation Hospital and is a member of the medical staff of Tulane University Medical School?

A. Yes, I have heard of the man.

Q. And, you know that he is a competent board certified neurosurgeon?

A. Yes, sir.

Q. And, his report and deposition was read to you in this case, before the jury, was it not?

A. Yes.

Q. And, is it true that you directly dispute him and disagree with his conclusion that based on a history of the head trauma and of the client while not being knocked unconscious but only being disoriented for an hour or two, that based on this history the automobile accident was the cause of the injury to my client's optic chiasma and the resulting atrophy of the optic nerve resulting in a permanent partial blindness and tunnel vision?

A. Yes, sir, as I have said before I just have to disagree with Dr. Jones in that regard. As I explained to the jury [looking at them], I think that this atrophy of the nerves was due to some congenital defect of long-standing or some type of virus, but it was strictly coincidental and in no way related to the trauma. The trauma was not severe enough, the plaintiff was not knocked unconscious.

Q. So, you disagree with Dr. Jones.

A. Yes.

Q. You also read a medical report given to you by defense counsel of Dr. Bill Smith from the University of Texas Medical School in Dallas, Texas. Do you remember reading that?

A. Yes, sir.

Q. And, you would agree that Dr. Bill Smith, who is at the Southwest Medical Center, a nationally known regional medical center, and he is chairman of the department of neurosurgery there, that his opinion disagrees with yours?

A. Yes, sir. As I explained before. . . .

Q. Don't explain it again, doctor, we understand your position. I just wanted to establish that you disagree with both of these neurosurgeons, the one from Texas and the one from Louisiana.

A. Yes, sir.

Q. And, doctor, you are familiar with these men and as far as you know they are board certified neurosurgeons?

A. Yes, sir, as far as I know.

Q. Now, doctor, you say you teach at the University of Mississippi Medical School?

A. Yes, sir, as I said before, I have been teaching there for over twenty years.

Q. Yes, sir, we heard you say that many times. And, at that Medical School do they have a major medical library like they have at Tulane University Medical School in New Orleans?

A. Yes, sir! We have a very large medical library.

Q. And, in that medical library do they have a book by Dr. Brock, entitled *Injuries to the Brain and Spinal Cord*?

A. Yes, sir, they have that book, in fact I have a personal copy of it in my office.

Q. And, do you rely on that book and use it when you are teaching your students over at the University of Mississippi Medical School?

A. Yes, sir, I have relied on that book.

Q. And, by the way, have you ever met Dr. Brock, or do you know Dr. Brock.

A. Yes, I know him very well. I have met him at several medical conventions.

Q. Then you would agree, would you not, that Dr. Brock is a nationally known authority in the field of neurosurgery with particular specialty in the subject of his book, injury to the brain and spinal cord, that he lectures on that and teaches on that subject a lot?

A. Yes, sir, I heard him lecture in a medical convention in Biloxi, Mississippi, about five years ago on that very subject.

Q. You would certainly agree, would you not, that Dr. Brock's book is an accepted authoritative medical text on which doctors rely regularly?

A. Yes, sir, as I said, I have it in my library and use it often.

Q. [Counsel walking back to counsel table and picking up a briefcase on the floor with his back turned to the doctor.] Doctor, do you know what I have here in my briefcase? [Keeping back turned to build drama.]

A. No, sir, I don't have any idea.

Q. Doctor, I have a copy of the book we have been discussing, Brock's *Injuries to the Brain and Spinal Cord*.

A. Oh, you have it here? [nervously.]

Q. Yes, doctor, I have it here and I'm going to give it to you. [Counsel stands between the doctor and the jury, but faces the jury.] Doctor, would you open that book to page 104 and read aloud to the jury, if you don't mind, the sentence in Brock's textbook that's underlined in red on the paragraph that is entitled in black captions above it *Injuries to the Optic Chiasma*?

A. What page was that?

Q. Page 104. Doctor, do you need me to find it for you?

A. No, I have it.

Q. Would you read it?

A. [Fidgeting and nervous.] Right now?

Q. Yes, sir, out loud to the jury if you don't mind, would you read what it says in Brock on page 104?

A. [Doctor reading aloud:]

> "The unusual thing about injuries to the optic chiasma is that they normally occur with only slight trauma to the head with a period of disorientation but no unconsciousness. It sometimes takes three or four months for the resulting optic nerve atrophy and symptoms to occur."

Q. Now doctor. . . .

A. [Angrily interrupting attorney while slamming book shut.] Well, I agree with Dr. Brock with everything else he's got in his book but this. I disagree with Dr. Brock with regard to this.

Q. So we have now established that you also disagree with Dr. Brock. Is that correct?

A. [Indignantly.] Yes, sir, definitely. He's wrong. As I explained before, you have to have a severe trauma. The optic chiasma is in the middle of the head.

Q. [Lawyer still facing jury.] So, you disagree then with Dr. Brock. If you look in the front of the book, I believe you will find that Dr. Brock is a Board Certified Neurosurgeon?

A. I don't have to look, I know he is.

Q. And you disagree with Dr. Homer Jones from Ochsner Foundation Hospital who is a board certified neurosurgeon.

A. That's right.

Q. And you disagree with Dr. Bill Smith from the University of Texas Medical School and Head of the Department at the Southwest Medical Center in Dallas who is also board certified?

A. Yes, sir.

Q. [Attorney now gambling.] And, doctor, you told us on qualification that you have been teaching at the University of Mississippi Medical School here in Jackson, Mississippi for twenty years?

A. [Witness now squirming, looking eyes downcast.] Yes, sir.

Q. And, doctor, you did tell us that you are only board qualified—that you are not board certified in neurosurgery?

A. Yes, that's right.

Q. And to be board certified doctor you have to take a national exam and pass it, do you not?

A. Yes, yes, yes, that's right.

Q. [Lawyer looking all 12 jurors directly in the eyes with back now completely turned to doctor.] Doctor, you are not going to tell us, are you, that you took your exams and that you flunked them?

A. Well, I passed part of them.

Q. [Taking book from doctor and walking back to counsel table with it.] No further questions, doctor.

A. [Physician now nervously looking at jury and all twelve are staring at ceiling.] But you have to understand, ladies and gentlemen, I tried to explain it to you, the optic chiasma is in the middle of the head. . . .

> JUDGE: Doctor, we have heard enough testimony from you. You can step down now and get off the witness stand. You don't need to explain that answer any further.

Note how the doors were closed and how he was lead in by trial counsel to emphasize the fact that the other physicians with whom he vehemently disagreed were all board certified. Note how the door was closed by the use of the medical textbook. He was set up to admit that it was an authoritative text and, therefore, it could be used to impeach him.

This was, of course, a devastating cross-examination that resulted in a substantial judgment for the plaintiff. It actually occurred in the early 1960's in Jackson, Mississippi. However, opportunities today to conduct this type of devastating cross-examination occur more rarely because at that time an attorney was not required to file pretrial orders and to list witnesses. Now it is necessary to list witnesses in all federal courts and in almost all state courts or they cannot be called. While some state courts hold that rebuttal witnesses need not be listed, it is very cloudy as to how a judge will rule regarding rebuttal witnesses and rebuttal testimony. Therefore, most lawyers list all of the witnesses and thus sometimes lose a very effective tool in the search for the truth. Full broad discovery does not necessarily always lead to the truth. In some cases, it can lead to a better prepared witness who can defend any and every position he happens to need to defend during a particular case.

COMMENT: As discussed previously, we emphasize that you generally do not use all the medical texts and your medical quotes on the defendant's expert at the pretrial discovery deposition.[6] Always save some ammunition for trial, something which will catch him by surprise. It is this element of surprise which allows for the effective impeachment of credibility on cross-examination. If he knows every detail of the forthcoming cross-examination, he will be well prepared by opposing counsel regarding the answer he is to give to avoid the trap. Remember, if you intend to spring a trap, it must actually be a trap. It must be a surprise and you must have closed all the doors prior to springing the trap.

---

§ 9.10 —Sample cross-examination—"closing the door" (altered medical document)

Another example of how to close all the doors and effectively spring the trap can be seen in the illustration of an actual cross-examination where a defendant nurse had changed critical times in a medical record by merely writing over the original times. This type of information, i.e., an altered signature or a change in the record, is an obvious attempt to cover up. It is surely some form of dishonesty and it allows for effective impeachment of credibility on cross-examination. Such changes and alterations are to be scrutinized in every case that involves documents such as hospital records, wills, and so forth.

The case that we are using to illustrate impeachment with an altered document involved a young man who was brought to the hospital with a cut on his leg. Three hours later he was dead. Two years of discovery finally lead to a lay witness who indicated that the problem had occurred after the man was returned to his room from surgery. He was transferred to the care of an LPN Charge Nurse before he had adequately

[6] *See generally supra* Chapter 5, *Preparing for Effective Courtroom Communication*.

reacted from one of the anesthetic drugs. The administration of most general anesthetics includes the positioning of an endotracheal tube between the anesthesia machine and the patient's lungs. This is accomplished by administering a potent muscle relaxant after the patient is asleep, following which the tube is placed, via the mouth or the nose, between the vocal cords and into the lungs. Proper breathing can then be maintained mechanically. Sometimes, as a complication of the muscle relaxant drug, sufficiently shallow respirations may result in fluid in the lungs, also called pulmonary edema. This is a known complication of the relaxant drugs and is reversible by giving other drugs to counteract their effects and by maintaining the patient's breathing with mechanical ventilation. However, ignoring this anesthetic complication leads to pulmonary edema which ultimately decreases the oxygen supply to the heart and cardiac arrest ensues. However, even at this point the patient may be resuscitated if the code team is called and responds within a minute or so of the cardiac arrest. Failure to promptly start cardio-pulmonary resuscitation generally leads to death.

In the case at hand, the patient was brought to the room at 2:00 a.m. He was monitored in the room by the charge nurse, an LPN named Riley and a nurse's aide. The patient developed pulmonary edema but neither Riley nor the aide knew the significance of the pink bubbly froth which they dutifully suctioned from the patient's mouth as he slowly drowned. Finally, the aide could not obtain a blood pressure. She went out into the hallway and called the charge nurse who entered the room and tried to take the patient's blood pressure on the other arm. She finally sent the nurse's aide to get the RN who was down the hall. Only after all of this had occurred did the RN come to the room and finally put in an emergency call. Unfortunately, it was too late. Nurse Riley, a defendant in the case, denied that this happened and testified that the nurse's aide who had testified for the plaintiff had been discharged by the hospital and was simply trying to get even by not telling the truth.

During discovery, plaintiff's counsel noticed that although no alteration was apparent on the photostatic copy of the record, the original record looked as though a critical time had been written over. The original record indicated that the patient had suddenly stopped breathing at 2:40 a.m. and that the code team had arrived at 2:45 a.m. (*See* Figure 9–1). Testimony of the nurse's aide indicated that it took close to 15 minutes from the time the patient stopped breathing until the time the code team reached the patient. The critical change involved writing over the 2:30 a.m. time so that it now said 2:40 a.m. Plaintiff's counsel, saying that he wanted to use blowups of the records at trial, asked for permission to take photographs of the original record. To prevent defense counsel from recognizing the significance of any particular page, forty pages of records were photographed. These negatives were then blown up under ultraviolet light and when the enlargement was printed, the handwriting expert could clearly show that the time originally written was 2:30 a.m. not 2:40 a.m. (*See* Figure 9–2). Counsel therefore had a "smoking gun" with which he could impeach a key defense witness and show that actually the nurse's aide, now a plaintiff's witness, was telling the truth. An excerpt from the trial transcript showing how that piece of information was actually used to impeach Nurse Riley follows.

Counsel first established with Nurse Riley that the patient was not reactive from the anesthesia when she received the patient back to her ward. This was an act of negligence by the hospital and the nurse anesthetist which occurred because the operation was performed at midnight and the recovery room was not open during the night shift. Instead, the patient ought to have been monitored for forty-five minutes to an hour in the operating room by the nurse anesthetist. However, the nurse anesthetist had brought the patient directly back to the ward without waiting for the patient to adequately react from the anesthetic. Therefore, and contrary to good practice, this patient was turned over to Nurse Riley, an LPN charge nurse, in a condition where he could have a complication from the anesthetic while in the care of inexperienced hands. Counsel for plaintiff clearly established the patient's unreactive condition and the fact that he should not have been turned over to Nurse Riley in order to establish the negligence of the nurse anesthetist and the hospital. After that, the following cross-examination of Nurse Riley occurred:

Q. Now, Nurse Riley, is it true that both you and the nurse's aide, at approximately 1:00 a.m., started to notice pink bubbly froth coming from the patient's mouth?

A. Yes, sir.

Q. And is it also true that since you and the nurse's aide had never worked in anesthesia or in the recovery room, you did not think this was significant and thought that it was something that just needed to be cleared out of his mouth?

A. Yes, sir, I had never experienced that before and thought that it was a normal complication of the anesthetic and that all we had to do was maintain an airway.

Figure 9–1
Twenty-Four Hour Nurse's Notes

PO = Oral R.D. = Righ[illegible]ltoid Abd = Abdominal Wall L.L.T. = Left lateral thigh
R = Rectal L.D. = Left [illegible]toid L.G. = Left Gluteal R.M.T. = Right midanterior thigh
V = Vaginal R.G. = Right Gluteal R.L.T. = Right lateral thigh L.M.T. = Left midanterior thigh

DATE:	7 – 3								3 – 11								11 – 7							
Medication – Treatment	7	8	9	10	11	12	1	2	3	4	5	6	7	8	9	10	11	12	1	2	3	4	5	6
Dr. Visited (Initials)																								
Signature of Med. Nurse									[illegible]															
TIME																								
BLOOD PRESSURE																								
PULSE																								

DIETS		
Time	Type	Remarks

INTAKE	7 – 3	3 – 11	11 – 7
ORAL			
I.V.			
Totals			
24 HR. TOTAL			

OUTPUT	7–3	3–11	11–7
VOID			
CATH			
Suction			
Emesis			
Totals			
24 Hr. Total			

Time	Nurses Notes (includes I.V.s and PRN Treatments)	Time	Nurses' Notes (Continued)
1:30	[illegible]	2:00	[illegible] frequent suction
	[illegible]	2:15	BP 110/[illegible] P 78 R 24
	[illegible]	2:40	Pt's breathing became slow
	[illegible]		Suddenly. No BP detected
	[illegible]		No pulse detected. Cardiac
	[illegible]		Heart Called. Cardiac massage
	[illegible]		started immediately, mouth
	[illegible]		to mouth breathing started
	BP 110/[illegible] P 70 R 22	2:45	[illegible]
1:55	BP 108/70 P 74 R 20		Nurses Notes Continued on Reverse Side [ ].

DATE 7-13-70

NAME: LAST · FIRST	HOSP. No.
Knighton, Rodger	420442[illegible]
ADM TO SERVICE OF DR. Slaccari	ROOM NO. 241

FORM 25 24 HOUR NURSE'S NOTES 0-1

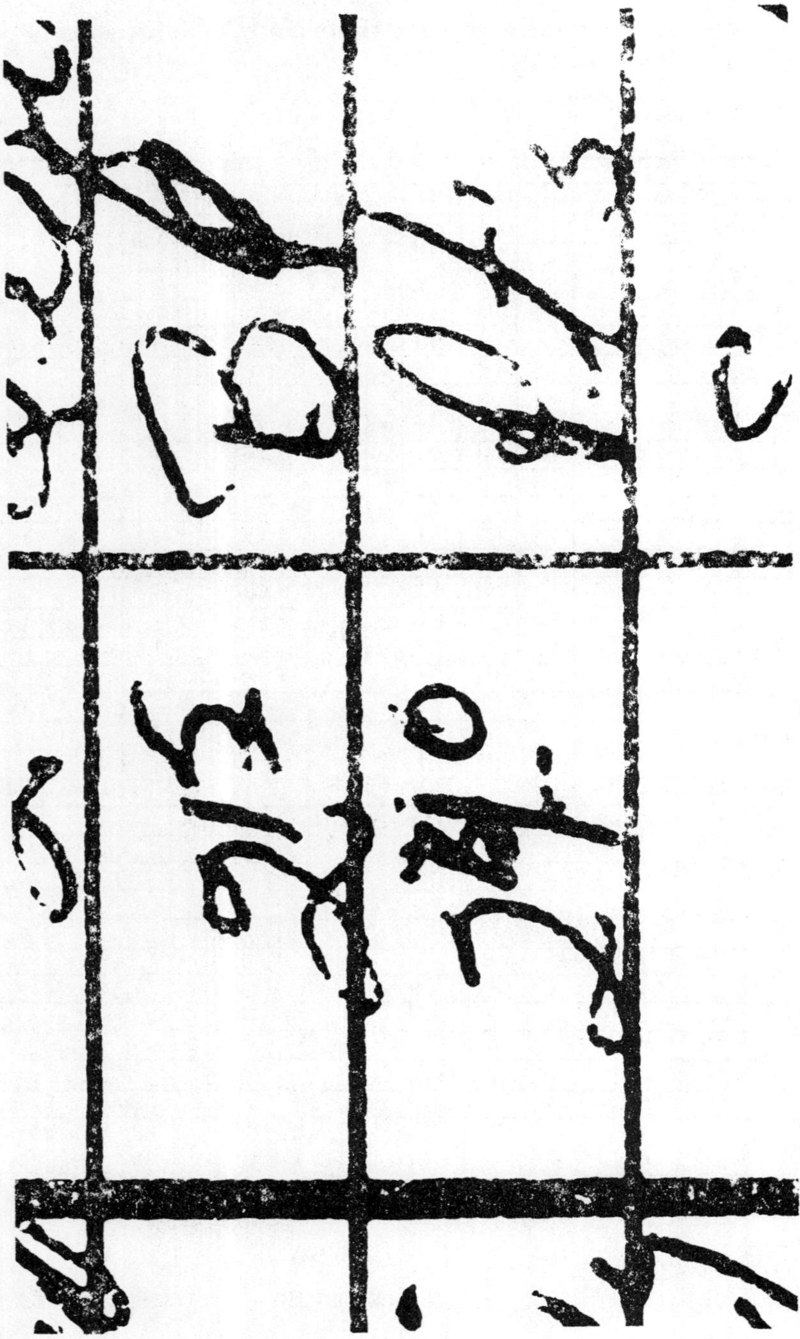

Figure 9–2
Enlarged Portion of Nurse's Notes Showing Alteration

Q. So all that both you and Nurse's Aide Jones did under your direction was to suction the pink froth out of the patient's mouth and to maintain his airway?

A. Yes, sir.

Q. But during the half hour that this was going you did nothing further in terms of calling anybody to check this patient or doing anything to see what was the cause of the pink bubbly froth coming out of his mouth?

A. As I told you, not having worked recovery room, I thought that this was simply a normal complication of coming out of anesthesia and that all we had to do was maintain an airway.

Q. And for that reason you didn't call anybody?

A. Yes, sir.

Q. It is true, as Nurse's Aide Jones testified, isn't it, that after a half hour she couldn't get a blood pressure on the man and when she told you that, it's your testimony that you immediately called a code because at that point you certainly knew that the man probably had had a cardiac arrest for some reason and that he needed to be revived immediately?

A. Yes.

Q. [Handing the witness the original record.] And according to the record, that occurred at 2:40 a.m., did it not?

A. I believe it was that time.

Q. Go ahead and look at your original record and see if that's the time that this occurred.

A. [Witness looking at record.] Yes, sir, it says here 2:40 a.m., that's the time that it occurred.

Q. Yes, and as soon as that occurred, and you went in there you immediately called a code. Is that right?

A. Yes, sir, that's what I testified to.

Q. And the code team was there in a very short period of time?

A. Yes, sir. According to the record the code team arrived at 2:45 a.m. But I really think it was quicker than that. The times were just estimates.

Q. Yes, ma'am. But it was certainly less than, not more than, fifteen minutes, wasn't it?

A. Oh, surely.

Q. Now you were present and you remember the testimony of Nurse's Aide Jones when she says that after the man stopped breathing you came in, took the blood pressure cuff off one arm, tried it on the other arm, and took quite a bit of time before you sent for the RN and that the RN was the one that finally came in and said "My God, this man's dead, call a code!" And this time was the only time that you called the code, you remember that?

A. Yes, sir, she was not correct in that. That did not occur.

Q. What I am asking you Nurse Riley is, do you remember her testimony that all of this took about 15 minutes, and your testimony that she is not accurate either because her memory is faulty or because she has tried to get even with the hospital for firing her?

A. Yes, sir, that's what I testified to on questions from the hospital's lawyer.

Q. Yes, I remember and I am sure the jury remembers your testimony in that regard. Is it still your position under oath today that your testimony is correct and that you are sure that you immediately called a code and that the code team was there in less than five minutes?

A. Yes, sir.

Q. And you are sure that this record is correct when it says that the man suddenly stopped breathing at 2:40 a.m. and that the code team was there at 2:45 a.m.?

A. Yes, sir, that is correct. [Witness again looking at records.]

Q. Now, ma'am, is it true that you have been a charge nurse with St. Mary's Memorial Hospital for the last ten years and have worked as an LPN for this hospital for a total of fifteen years?

A. Yes, sir, I've been with St. Mary's for a long time.

Q. And during the fifteen years that you've been with St. Mary's Memorial Hospital you are aware that they have certain nursing manuals and other specialized manuals that set out the procedures in the hospital as to how you are supposed to do things?

A. Yes, sir, I am familiar with that.

Q. I hand you now a manual. Are you familiar with it and have you seen it before? It's the St. Mary's Memorial Hospital Administrative Manual which is marked for identification, Plaintiff 70? [Handing witness manual.] And in fact you have used this manual in the past?

A. Many times. I have referred to it to get information.

Q. In fact, as a charge nurse you teach other nurses, do you not? You help train them?

A. Yes, sir.

Q. And in training these nurses, do you use this administrative procedure manual along with the nursing policy manual and other manuals regularly?

A. Yes, sir.

Q. And as a good nurse you rely on what's in those nursing manuals and procedure manuals both when you practice nursing yourself and when you teach other nurses how to do things. Isn't that true?

A. Yes, sir, that's true.

Q. Now, Nurse Riley, I'd like to turn your attention, if I may, to page 48 of the nursing procedure manual. Would you open the book that you have in your lap to that page?

A. Yes, sir.

Q. And it is true, is it not, that this is the section of the administrative procedure manual that deals with hospital records and how hospital records are to be handled and maintained and how things are to be recorded in hospital records?

A. Yes, sir, that appears to be on that page.

Q. And it is true, is it not, that this manual says that if a nurse makes an error and writes something wrong in a hospital record, she is supposed to put a line through that entry, right the word error above or below it, initial it, and then write the correct entry in the chart. Isn't that true?

A. Yes, sir, that's what it says and that's what I do all the time.

Q. And it would be wrong and a violation of your training and what's in this administrative procedure manual of St. Mary's Memorial Hospital if you made a mistake in a record and then simply wrote over or changed it?

A. That's correct.

Q. Have you ever done that, ma'am?

A. Done what?

Q. Have you ever violated the policy manual and written over in a record, or do you always if you make a mistake, put a line through it and put error down and initial it and then write the correct entry?

A. Yes, sir, if I make a mistake that's what I always do.

Q. Have you ever been in a hurry and just written over or anything like that?

A. No, sir, I know better than that.

Q. So you wouldn't do that, you wouldn't write over an incorrect entry. It would be wrong to do that. Is that right, ma'am?

A. Yes, sir.

Q. And you were the one that made the entries contemporaneously in the record, that is, you wrote down what was going on and you were the only one that made all of these nursing notes in the record about Roger Johnson and what went on that night in the hospital. You wrote that. That's your handwriting?

A. Yes, sir, I wrote all the entries.

Q. Ma'am, did you write them as these things were happening?

A. Yes, sir.

Q. And you looked at the clock and you know these times are accurate? And when you wrote these times down, you were writing down accurate times. Is that right?

A. Yes, sir.

Q. So that you know that the time written down at 2:40 a.m. (patient suddenly stopped breathing) is an accurate time?

A. Yes, sir.

Q. And you were looking at the clock when you wrote that?

A. I looked at either the clock or my watch, but it was right at 2:40 a.m. when that occurred.

Q. And that didn't occur at 2:30 a.m. and it didn't take fifteen minutes for the code team to get there until 2:45 a.m.?

A. No, sir, that did not occur. Nurse's Aide Jones is wrong about that.

Q. [Counsel approaches witness and hands witness magnifying glass.]

Ma'am, I am now handing you a magnifying glass and I'm going to ask you to look through that magnifying glass and look at the time written there 2:40 a.m.?

A. [Witness fidgeting.] . . . What do you want me to do?

Q. I want you to look through the magnifying glass and look at that record and I want to ask you a question?

A. What for?

Q. Well, if you will just look through the magnifying glass, [Attorney now turns his back to witness and looks directly at jury] I believe you will find that the time originally written there by you was 2:30 a.m. and not 2:40 a.m.?

A. [Witness now sobbing.] I don't know what you are talking about. There must be some mistake . . . there must be some mistake. . . .

JUDGE: Let me see that record. [Judge takes magnifying glass and record from witness.] "It looks to me like Mr. ______ is correct. This was originally 2:30 and it has been changed to 2:40."

LAWYER: That's correct, your Honor. We have a handwriting expert who has blown up the record and you can see it more clearly and he will follow this witness.

[Witness sitting on the stand, sobbing quietly.]

JUROR: Your Honor, may we see the record.

JUDGE: Mr. ______?

LAWYER: Judge, counsel for plaintiff asks permission to show the original page from record with the magnifying glass to the jurors.

JUDGE: Permission granted.

Q. [While jurors are looking at record.] Isn't it true that when you originally made your notes in this record, you wrote down the correct time? That it was 2:30 a.m. when Roger stopped breathing; that it was 2:45 a.m. when the code team got there and that later on when you realized you shouldn't have delayed that long, that you took too long to call the code, that you went back and wrote over the record?

A. My pen must have slipped and I must have changed it and didn't realize I did it.

Q. You made a mistake?

A. Yes, sir.

Q. And you made a mistake when you didn't call the code team promptly?

A. No, sir, I called them promptly.

Q. So you are still maintaining that when you say you called them promptly you're telling the truth and that Nurse's Aide Jones is the one that is not being accurate in her testimony?

A. I don't know what to say. Yes, sir, I guess so.

Q. And when Nurse Elliott, the RN from down the hall, says that when she got to the room you hadn't called the code and that she was the one that said "My God, this man is dead! Call a code, Riley," she's not accurate in that either? And those two people are inaccurate in their testimony. Is that correct, ma'am?

A. I don't know. Yes . . . yes, I guess that's what . . . happened.

Q. That's all I have.

JUROR: Your Honor, may we take a recess.

LAWYER: [Counsel for plaintiff:] I don't mind taking a recess now, Judge, so long as this witness is instructed while she is still on cross-examination and redirect examination that she doesn't talk to anyone, particularly her lawyer, about the subject matter that we just went into or about anything.

JUDGE: I am instructing you that you are not to talk to anyone during the break. You understand that ma'am?

A. Yes, sir.

WHEREUPON A RECESS OCCURRED.

During the recess, plaintiff's counsel and two court officials saw defense counsel huddling with the client and discussing the situation prior to going back into the courtroom.

BACK ON THE RECORD.

JUDGE: Mr. ______, you may proceed with your redirect examination if you have any.

Q. Yes, sir, your Honor. Now, Nurse Riley, I want to call your attention to the hospital record and I want you to explain to the jury why it looks as if 2:30 was changed to 2:40 a.m. in that entry by the words "suddenly stopped breathing"?

A. Well, sir, I think what happened was I started to write 2:30, realized it was wrong and my pen didn't leave the page. I then tried to make it 2:40.

MR. ______ [Plaintiff's counsel]: Your Honor, we object and move that this last answer from this witness be stricken from the record. We move for that on the basis that contrary to the instructions of the Court, counsel for defendant, Mr. ______, and his witness had a conference about all of this during the break and that this was contrary to the instructions of your Honor and I am sure that this answer is what they were discussing.

JUDGE: Mr. ______, did you talk to this lady during the break?

MR. ______ [sheepishly]: Yes, sir, your Honor, I didn't hear you say anything about my not talking to her. I thought you meant the other lawyers.

JUDGE: Mr. ______, you know what I meant. I'll see both counsel in my chambers.

A lengthy discussion in chambers yielded a settlement quite favorable to the plaintiff. Of course, the offer of settlement resulted from the very effective use of a piece of impeaching information.

It should also be noted that the tone of the two impeachment cross-examinations illustrated above is entirely different. In the first case, the tone of voice, the facial expressions, and the manner of questioning is much softer. When there is an indication of dishonesty, i.e., the witness may have altered a record which is crucial to the case, a somewhat different tone is projected.

A harsher tone of voice, facial expressions, and gestures nonverbally indicating distrust of the witness and a more rapid sequence of questions is appropriate. Such a cross-examination style would not be appropriate in the situation where a witness may have simply made a mistake while giving the deposition.

During the impeachment cross-examination, and almost at all other times, a lawyer tries to place himself between the jury and the witness. As his cross-examination builds to its climax, the lawyer spends more time facing the jury and turning his back to the witness.

Such a positioning is a nonverbal indication to the jury that the witness is not trustworthy and, therefore, is not to be believed. As the witness fidgets and squirms and winces with the questioning, the attorney increases his time spent facing the jury. Further dissonance is created by mismatching the witness' language patterns and nonverbal actions.

Combining mismatching with the nonverbal techniques just described produces an excellent tool for the effective impeachment of a witness using a written document.

III. Listening to Witness' Answer; Observing Witness Reaction

§ 9.11 Interpreting and using facial expressions

Facial expressions alone are not an indicator of any specific feeling. However, facial expressions may be an indicator of a change from baseline behavior, actually an indication that some reaction is taking place.[7]

Jurors' feelings are primarily affected by their perceptions. Communication Principle 1 states that communication is based on perception. One factor is facial expressions. A favorable edge can be gained with the lay jury if the attorney is able to cause the witness to project unusual facial expressions such as grimaces or shifting of the eyes.

Some jurors may actually interpret these facial expressions as signs of deceit. Therefore, the attorney should watch the witness' facial expressions, searching for the opportunity to react to any change. It is quite possible that a change may indicate that further questioning along this particular line may yield good results.

§ 9.12 Interpreting and using body movements and positions

As with facial expressions, body movements are not necessarily an absolute indicator that the witness is ill at ease or is being deceitful. However, some body positions do project the witness' attitude towards the cross-examiner. For example, it is apparent that a witness sitting in the chair with his back stiff and in a rigid body mode is resistant to the cross-examiner. Note that as he gives in to the cross-examiner, his shoulders will slump forward, he will not be as stiff, and he will visibly "cave in."

As with facial expressions, body movements may indicate a change in mood and a reason to probe deeper on a particular subject. Similarly, body movements, particularly fidgeting, can be perceived by jurors as indicating a lack of reliability. If the attorney notices that a particular trigger causes the witness to become fidgety, he should repeat the trigger frequently. Thus, while not subject to absolute interpretation, it can be

---

[7] *See supra* §§ 3.19 and 5.04, for a discussion of the accuracy of interpreting nonverbal cues.

an indication of change which can be used effectively to create a nonverbal appearance that the witness is being less than candid with the jury.

The attorney's body position and movements during cross-examination are a key factor in creating certain effects. The position of the lawyer in the courtroom may even psychologically affect the witness' answer. For example, if the lawyer is asking for an estimation of distance, his position in the courtroom relative to the witness will affect the amount of the estimate. The further away the lawyer stands from the witness, the longer the estimate of the distance, while the closer he stands to the witness, the shorter the estimate of the distance.

Estimates of time can be affected not only by the position of the lawyer relative to the witness but also by the rapidity with which the lawyer asks the question. If the question is asked very rapidly with the lawyer standing close to the witness, the estimate of time will be much shorter than if the lawyer asks the question slowly while standing away from the witness.

Additionally, the positioning of the lawyer in relation to the witness can undermine credibility. The lawyer, during cross-examination, should always interpose his body between the witness and the jury. He wants to block off bodily the information coming from the witness, to intercept it if you will and, therefore, to effectively control it. He wants to appear to be in control and to be dominating the witness. This is accomplished by standing between the jury and the witness.

Further, the effect of certain questions can be emphasized, particularly those questions directly challenging the credibility of the witness, by the lawyer turning his back on that witness. "Turning your back" on what someone says indicates nonverbally that what they are saying is not worthy of belief. It is a very effective technique to turn your back on the witness at the high point of the cross-examination and talk directly to the jury while momentarily ignoring the witness.

All of these techniques regarding body movement and positioning tactics must be used sparingly and with good judgment. In addition, the attorney's body position and movement during cross-examination must relate to some degree to the actual impeachment of credibility of the witness that is going on.

COMMENT: The trial lawyer who attacks a perfectly believable witness without substantial reason or uses the nonverbal language of turning his back on that witness will simply hurt his own image. On the other hand, if he has a document or other evidence which in some way impeaches the testimony, then it is time to use body position to underscore the witness' lack of credibility.

---

§ 9.13 Interpreting and using verbal and vocal cues

As with facial expressions, and body position and movements, verbal and vocal cues project information and can be used to create the impression that the witness' testimony lacks credibility. The verbal content can play a role and be significant for two reasons: (1) it is the substance of the information, and (2) it reflects the phraseology that the witness has chosen to use. If the witness uses weak language, such as "I think . . .," "maybe," or "possibly," he can be made to look less credible. What a witness thinks or believes to be true is verbally not as credible to lay jurors as are the facts that are stated simply and plainly. The trial lawyer should listen for such weak language, then repeat it during his next question. By repeating the weak language, he reinforces it. For example, "I believe that it's correct" or "I think it's correct," is rephrased in the next question to become "Now what you believed took place here was. . . ." The question which then follows begins with, "But isn't it true that . . .", and ties in a new fact or begins a new issue.

Vocal cues also relate to credibility. A witness who speaks very slowly and uses many pauses and "errs" can be made to appear less credible if the attorney reinforces the witness' choice of vocal cues. Listen to the witness. If the witness uses vocal cues that indicate uncertainty, then as with the verbal cues, repeat the vocal cue in some fashion and underline it. The next question should mimic that verbal cue so the jury understands, at least on a nonverbal level, that you think the slow responses and pauses are significant and affect the witness' credibility. Witnesses who speak rapidly, unless their speech becomes indistinguishable, are generally perceived as being more believable. During cross-examination, pace the witness to slow down his rate of speech. This is particularly important if he is a very strong witness who normally speaks rapidly. If the attorney succeeds in pacing the witness to a slower rate of speech, this witness' credibility will suffer.

§ 9.14 Use of filled and unfilled pauses

In addition to the verbal and vocal cues used above, there are filled and unfilled pauses which form part of the witness' testimony. Also, there are pauses which the attorney can use during cross-examination.

A filled pause is a break in thought that is filled with pause words. Pause words are words which have no actual meaning and are simply used to fill a pause. Pause words include "ah", "uhm", "yes", or "uhum".

An unfilled pause then is literally a break in the sentence structure with no words. There is a period of complete and awkward silence. It is not there for any reason. A witness who uses filled and unfilled pauses will have a reduced impact on the jury and will project reduced credibility. If an attorney is cross-examining a witness and that witness has a habit of using unfilled pauses during the testimony, the attorney should not fill in the pause for him. Don't start the next question during the pause. Let him either fill the pause or let it pass as an unfilled pause. Either way, it will reduce his credibility.

There is one exception to the general rule that pauses, either filled or unfilled, reduce credibility. An unfilled pause at the right moment can increase credibility. An attorney who wants to make a dramatic point during cross-examination can then use an unfilled pause and even couple it with an anchor.[8] The pause then is used to heighten the effect and to allow for the attorney to move to his anchoring position. This pause causes the jury's listening behavior to become more attentive. Then when the anchoring position is reached and the next question is asked, the answer will have a more lasting impact on the jurors.

§ 9.15 Use of reframing during cross-examination

Remember that witnesses are testifying through and using their own personalized generalizations and stereotypes. Therefore, Communication Principles 4 and 6 apply here. These principles deal with the use of stereotypes to shortcut the impression formation process and that once these stereotypes are formed, they are usually not dislodged by just presenting contradictory information. Rather, the attorney must identify those stereotypes and personalized generalizations, link to them, and then change the stereotypes. Reframing is the application of these two communication principles.

---

[8] *See supra* §§ 4.34–4.37, for a discussion of anchoring techniques.

Reframing is a process by which we cause a change in an individual's point of view or perspective. What a witness says, whether it is a fact or an opinion, is directly tied to the reference frame through which he perceives any subject. If the attorney can identify the witness' underlying reference frame and then approach the subject differently, he essentially changes the way in which the witness views the situation and can, in all probability, affect his testimony as well.

Reframing is necessary, for example, in a medical malpractice case when a physician expert witness has himself been a defendant in a medical malpractice case which he perceived as frivolous. Since that time, his frame of reference is that all attorneys who represent plaintiffs are dishonest and that all medical malpractice cases are without merit. This is the frame of reference through which he will testify that almost any conduct meets the standard of care. You will not be able to change his testimony to any degree regarding the subject until you change his frame of reference. He needs to see things differently by taking a different approach to the subject of medical malpractice cases. The attorney gains an edge by gaining a reframing-type admission from the witness.

Q. Doctor, I read in the newspaper the other day that there was a case in California involving a young man in his 30's who was taken to surgery with a cancerous kidney and a perfectly good kidney. They put the X-ray up backwards and because they misread the X-ray, they removed the good kidney and left in the cancerous kidney. They had to go back and remove the cancerous kidney and now the man will spend the rest of his life on dialysis. Certainly, doctor, you would agree that this case does not meet the standard of care?

A. Yes, I would certainly have to admit it in that case.

Q. And, doctor, I read in another newspaper the next day about a lady in Florida who was pregnant and was undergoing an operation to have a cancer removed. And someone in the operating room put an unlabeled bottle of formaldehyde on the anesthetic tray. And by mistake, the formaldehyde was put into the spinal canal and the lady was irreversibly brain damaged. They are just keeping her alive now in order to deliver the baby. Certainly, doctor, you would agree that this situation does not meet the standard of care?

A. Yes, I would.

Q. So, doctor, you would agree, would you not, that there are some instances in which doctors make mistakes and in which conduct by health care providers doesn't meet the standard of care?

A. I suppose that's true.

Q. And you would agree, doctor, would you not, that sometimes there are two different standards of care?

A. What do you mean?

Q. Doctor, what I mean by that is that sometimes there is a high standard of care that is set out in a textbook or a manual. But as a practical matter, that is not the way medicine is practiced. Isn't that true?

A. Yes, I can think of some situations like that.

Q. So that in some situations textbooks set forth a high standard of care, while in actuality, as a matter of practice, physicians choose, in some cases, not to follow what is in the textbooks and to practice a lower standard of care as a matter of reality?

A. I would think most physicians live up to what is in textbooks.

Q. Well, now, Doctor, getting particular to this case. . .? [And then the cross-examination would go on to show how the defendant violated standards set forth in textbooks.]

In summary, reframing the witness' point of view will allow the attorney to obtain certain admissions. If the doctor in the above example can be made to admit that not all malpractice cases are evil and that not all plaintiffs' attorneys are the devil reincarnated, he will reframe or change his point of view regarding malpractice cases and plaintiffs' attorneys. This self-admission will cause him to soften his rigid position and allow the attorney to conduct a cross-examination regarding textbook authority and to obtain certain admissions not otherwise obtainable.

Reframing is a technique that can also be successfully employed to show your own witness and even your client a different point of view. Again, identify each person's point of view, that is, identify "where that person is coming from." This information, once obtained, can be used to direct the frame of reference in a new area.

There are some standard reframing questions which can be used to cause a change in perspective. Some of these are: (1) What stops you? (2) What would happen if you did? (3) What is the worst thing that would happen? (4) What would happen if you didn't? (5) Who specifically?

Another technique for use during cross-examination is the "challenging trigger." The language pattern of each individual includes "triggers." These cause the individual to talk in generalizations or comparisons or perhaps to display resistance.

Certain "triggers" in a question can cause a witness to use generalizations which can then be shown to be inaccurate. Such trigger words include "always" or "never." The witness says he has either "never" done or generally that he "always" does. . . . Such trigger word responses to overbroad generalizations should trigger in the attorney's mind that there is now an opportunity to show that this is inaccurate.

There are always triggers of resistance. These triggers include: (1) "no way," (2) "forget it," and (3) "I can't do it." After the trigger is used and the witness picks up on the trigger, the attorney can show that there is missing information, unrefined information, or deleted information. Use of trigger words is a way of leading the witness into positions which can be later shown to be inaccurate.

§ 9.16 Proper questioning techniques

Always use leading questions. If there is any rule that is absolutely axiomatic during cross-examination, it is that the cross-examiner must always use leading questions. His series of questions must always cry out for and demand a "yes" or "no" answer. Never ask an opposing witness a "why" or "how" question. A "why" or "how" question provides this witness, who is on the stand in opposition to your position, to repeat what he has already said on his direct examination. He will explain again why his response is the correct answer or how the "facts" he has presented explain the issue accurately. If the attorney does not ask only leading questions, he will provide the opposition with a splendid opportunity to reiterate and reinforce their position.

Just as there are certain so-called "crutches" to use to avoid an objection to a leading question on direct examination, there are "crutches" which are used to phrase the question as a leading question. The use of this or similar phraseology to precede a question generally allows the attorney to ask purely leading questions. The diligent use of these types of crutches will result in the asking of only leading questions during cross-examination. With time, the conscious use of these verbal crutches will decrease and the attorney will eventually reach a level of unconscious competence with regard to the asking of leading questions on cross-examination.[9] Some of these crutches are: "the truth . . .", and "you would agree, would you not, that . . .", and "it is a fact that . . .".

§ 9.17 Developing a rhythm during cross-examination

Developing cross-examination techniques, like bicycle riding, swimming, or horseback riding, is an acquired skill with a certain rhythm to it. A break in that rhythm tends to have a disruptive effect on the examination. This occurs when the attorney unintentionally hesitates during the questioning. The rhythm is that feeling and expectation that goes on during the cross-examination. It relates to the rapidity and manner in which the questions are asked which forces the witness to move right along answering the questions without having time to think of or alter the answers. In other words, the questions should follow one another not only logically but rapidly as well. The questions must fit into the rhythm of the cross-examination so that the witness is compelled to rapidly respond, one logical point followed by the next, always being faced with a question that cries out for a "yes" or "no" answer. Although the witness may be aware of what the next question will be, truly leading questions paced in an appropriate rhythm and sequence will compel the witness to give an answer that is more or less a "yes" or "no" answer. In fact, the phraseology and the leading nature of the question appropriately paced set the questioning up so that any response other than a "yes" or "no" answer will be perceived as a rude interruption in the anticipated rhythm. Cross-examination rhythm should be such that only a very experienced witness could effectively break the rhythm and still not alienate the lay jurors.

The attorney who conducts an effective cross-examination using leading questions and proper timing and rhythm leaves the jury the impression that this witness is in agreement with the attorney. The jury clearly sees that you are controlling the questions and forcing the agreement. They subconsciously perceive you as competent and trustworthy and, therefore, someone in whom they can have confidence. This image is significantly reinforced when the witness must stretch to find a reason to say "yes, but . . ." or to say "I can't answer that question as asked," or indeed to make some other excuse to break the rhythm.

It should be noted that the rhythm of the cross-examination subtly increases from beginning to end. The tempo of the questioning is slower

---

[9] *See generally supra* Chapter 1, *Impression Formation in the Courtroom*, for a discussion of "unconscious competence."

at the beginning. As the first few "yes" or "no" admissions are obtained, the rhythm increases slightly with the next question being asked a little more rapidly. The rhythm or tempo of the examination is increased with each succeeding series of questions. The rhythm definitely becomes more rapid as the witness is further pinned. The questions should come in increasingly rapid fashion climaxing at the end of the cross-examination when the intense urgency of the attorney's voice combined with a rapidly paced rhythm yields leading questions which will not be satisfied with any answer less committing than a "yes" or "no".

§ 9.18 Prestructuring the cross-examination with a strong close

Every cross-examination should be prestructured to have a strong close. If the lawyer has engaged in thorough discovery and proper preparation, he will know what testimony this witness will offer at trial. He will use the weak points and the strong points to build to a strong conclusion. The attorney should use a cross-examination outline or worksheet.

The cross-examination worksheet should not exclusively consist of prewritten questions. As the attorney gains experience and skill at cross-examination, the need to write out the questions decreases. Unfortunately, questions which are written out in advance encourage the attorney to read the questions verbatim, thus essentially negating any effective rhythm. Therefore, it is highly recommended that the cross-examination worksheet be an outline of topics or a listing of key phrases which set up a series of questions. The worksheet should include an indication of the document or deposition page where the information relative to the topic or phrase can be readily found should it be necessary for use for impeachment purposes. With a thoroughly prepared cross-examination worksheet, the attorney can adequately control the witness. The first time a witness wanders or attempts to contradict a question provides the trial attorney with the opportunity to immediately reach for the deposition, open it to the correct page, and cross-examine him about his prior inconsistent testimony. (*See* Figure 9–3 for a cross-examination outline.)

An example of a cross-examination outline follows, dealing with a case involving the death of a six-year-old child who fell at a football game on a Friday evening and injured her kidney.

Defendant physician, Dr. Peter James, admitted the child to the hospital for observation. On Saturday morning, the physician wrote an order "repeat IVs" after the nurse had already given almost 2000 cc of fluid.

This was the order that caused the nurses to give fluids in excess, which drowned the child. She died about twenty-four hours after admission to the hospital. He admitted that the injured kidney did not kill her.

After two years of discovery, plaintiff finally determined that the child died because she was given over 4000 cc of fluid in a twenty-four hour period. The maximum fluid that should have been given the child for this period was 1800–2000 cc. She was therefore given double the amount of fluids that her little body could tolerate and she drowned.

Figure 9–3
Cross-Examination Outline

Atkinson v. St. James Memorial Hospital

Cross-Examination of Dr. Peter James

I. Treatment of Child in ER
  1. IVP performed in ER under defendant's supervision;
     depo p. 7—suspicious IVP not normal;
     depo p. 10, 11—however, after death radiologist read IVP normal (see hospital record);
  2. fluids started by defendant in emergency room;
     p. 12—infusion running at 28 drops per minute;
     p. 14—mother available in emergency room and talked with her;
     p. 15—estimated child's weight, 20 to 25 kilos or 40 to 50 pounds on admit;
     p. 84—defendant responsible for IV's and orders regarding IV's;

II. Fluids Actually Given
  1. Cover admit orders from hospital record;
  2. Show IV fluids given, first 500 R/L then 500 D5W;
  3. Go through fluids given on intake and output sheet;
  4. Show fluids given at 25–30 drops per minute; show 2000 cc first 12 hours; show order repeat IV's; show 2000 cc second 12 hour period (all as per medical records);
  5. Show defendant physician's order—have him note nurses not told over what period of time IV fluids to be given;
  6. Have defendant admit 30 drops per minute is approximately 2 cc per minute—equals 120 cc per hour—approximately 1500–2000 cc in 12 hours;

7. Have defendant admit he intended 2000 cc over 24 hours or did not know what he intended;
8. See if defendant knows difference between rate for adult drip and pediatric drip;

III. Order of Events Next Day

1. 10:00 a.m. next morning ordered repeat IV's (see physician's orders);
2. Output in first 12 hours—378 cc (see I/O sheet);
3. Have defendant estimate fluid loss through child vomiting . . . he estimated very small amount—10 cc or less—depo p. 71;
4. Saw child again 5:00 p.m.—Adam not descended; child lethargic; child has possible respiratory problem;
5. Arterial blood gases available in hospital—depo p. 52;
6. No arterial blood gases ordered—depo p. 53;
7. Child's respiratory status unevaluated—depo p. 64;

IV. Head Injury Ruled Out

1. Check child's eyes and neurological status on entry to hospital—normal (depo pp. 16 and 17);
2. Conclusion—no head injury;
3. Lack of head injury further confirmed by note in hospital record (see p. 6); "neck supple"; he admits no indication of any type of brain damage (depo pp. 20 and 21);

V. Sequence of Events That Evening

1. Defendant can't say specifically what time he arrived at hospital (depo p. 47);
2. When he arrived at 5:00 p.m., he thought child was having phenolthizine reaction;
3. Prescribed suppository for phenolthizine;
4. At 5:00 p.m., blood pressure 90/60; child was a little shocky (depo p. 95);
5. At 5:00 p.m., did not assess child's respiratory status (depo p. 40; p. 70; p. 182; p. 202);
6. Agrees clinical picture of child suffering shock from blood loss (depo p. 80, p. 92);

VI. P.M. Insertion of Naso-Gastric Tube

1. Nasogastric tube ordered and inserted at 5:00 p.m.;
2. Nasogastric tube's purpose—prevent aspiration (depo p. 30, p. 82, p. 96);
3. When he put tube in all he got out of stomach was brown fluid;

4. After inserting nasogastric tube at 5:00 p.m. on Saturday, went home (depo p. 80, p. 162);

VII. EVENTS AFTER 5:00 P.M. VISIT

1. 9:00 p.m., nurse called him at home; said child still very ill—did not come to the hospital (depo p. 55, p. 105, p. 162);
2. 9:20 p.m., nurse called again—said that paramedal movements or convulsions worse (depo p. 56, p. 64)—still did not come to the hospital (depo p. 57, p. 65);
3. 9:50 p.m., nurse called again; child had convulsed again; blood pressure was unobtainable with a pulse of 64 and respirations of 20, still did not come to the hospital (depo p. 82, p. 98, p. 148);
4. 9:50 p.m. prescribed Demarol and Phenabarbitol to calm child (depo p. 87);
5. GO BACK HERE AND STRESS THREE CALLS BETWEEN 9:00 AND 10:00 P.M. AND DEFENDANT DID NOT COME TO THE HOSPITAL TO SEE VERY SICK CHILD;

VIII. GO THROUGH AUTOPSY

1. Talk defendant through blowup of autopsy and discuss findings;
2. Make him admit that between 10 and 10:30 p.m.—according to autopsy child had (1) pulmonary edema; (2) hypoxia; (3) would have had poor arterial blood gases if they had been done;

IX. CONTINUATION OF SEQUENCE OF EVENTS

1. Notified at 10:30 p.m. that child worse (depo p. 104, p. 162);
2. Arrives at hospital at 11:00 p.m. (nurse's note);
3. 11:10 p.m., tries to intubate child—couldn't get tube in;
4. ER doctor called 11:20 p.m.—child intubated (depo p. 67, p. 68);
5. When he arrived at hospital at 11:00 p.m., child had forced respiratory sounds (depo p. 69);
6. Admits that at 11:00 p.m., child probably had pulmonary edema (p. 69, p. 108);
7. When he arrived at hospital, child's heart stopped—epinephrine given to no avail (p. 108);
8. 12:05 p.m.—after many efforts child pronounced dead (depo p. 71, p. 72);

X. CAUSE OF DEATH

1. Already established not head trauma (see previous cross-examination) (depo. p. 50, p. 102);

2. No indication of aspiration, food, or gastric content in stomach or lungs (depo p. 54, p. 103);
3. Autopsy protocol (depo p. 74, p. 75, p. 182, p. 184);
4. Death not due to respiratory suppression—due to drugs (depo p. 80, p. 84, p. 190);
5. Agrees that kidney injury and bleeding did not cause death (depo p. 90, p. 30, p. 148);
6. Death not due to lack of fluid volume because 500 cc is all that is lost from kidney; (depo p. 192);
7. Agrees that direct cause of death was pulmonary edema and that the child died a respiratory death—i.e., stopped breathing and then heart stopped (depo p. 74, p. 186, p. 192);
8. Agrees that the administration of excess fluids will cause death by pulmonary edema forming in lungs (depo p. 88, p. 89);
9. Can't rule out that this death was not caused by excess fluids (depo p. 148, p. 202);
10. Have Him Agree that Pulmonary Edema of This Magnitude Occurred Over Some Length of Time—estimates of this time would be more in the expertise of pediatric surgeons and pulmonary specialists;
11. Agrees that pulmonary edema could have been there as early as 10:00 p.m. (depo p. 150);
12. Pulmonary edema probably there at 10:30 p.m. (depo p. 155);
13. When called at 9:00 p.m., child had significant indications of respiratory problems (depo p. 182, 183);
14. Admits that if he would have come to the hospital when first called around 9:00 p.m., he may have intubated child (depo p. 186, p. 202);
15. Admits that despite calls from nurses between 9:00 p.m. and 11:00 p.m. (until he got there) nothing was done for child who had respiratory problem during that time (depo p. 186, p. 204);

XI. 4,000 cc in 24 Hours Excessive

1. Nelson's *Textbook of Pediatrics* authoritative (depo p. 205);
2. Show him Nelson's;
3. Nelson's chart p. 186 says six-year-old child of the kg. weight should receive 1800–2000 cc (not 4000 cc) over 24 hours;
4. Have him admit that he was taught at LSU Medical School;
5. Show him chart from LSU Medical School materials entitled pediatric handbook;

6. Have him admit that this chart recommends for a six-year-old child no more than 1500 cc of fluid over 24 hours;
7. Have him admit that his administration of cc's of fluid over 24 hours into this child violated the basic textbook, Nelson's, and the pediatric handbook of his own medical school.

As is evident from the cross-examination outline in Figure 9–3, the examination is preplanned to conclude with a strong close. This does not mean that variance is not possible. Frequently, as the attorney listens to the answer, a new line of questioning develops which could yield an effective area of cross-examination. At that point, by all means abandon the outline and develop the new line. Exploration of the witness' testimony may reveal an answer so startling and significant that a strong close has been reached. If this occurs, then stop the cross-examination. Do not be married to the outline. All the questions do not have to be asked. Remember, something can go wrong with the best laid plans. If, during cross-examination, a line of questioning reaches a strong, favorable answer, then stop there. Having reached the pinnacle, the only direction remaining is downward.

Cross-examination is a question of impression in the jury's mind. A terrible impression remains when a cross-examination is ended with the opposing lawyer objecting, the judge ruling against the cross-examiner, and the cross-examiner sitting down in apparent defeat. The cross-examiner must always have one strong point to make and after that point is made, it is time to close the cross-examination. It ends on a high note with the lawyer saying, "that's all I have" or "no further questions of this witness" in a voice projecting at least subtle sarcasm. The lawyer then sits down as though he has devastated that witness. The lawyer's nonverbal communication to the jury is that "I've won this battle," "I've proved my point," "I've gotten everything that can be gotten out of this witness." It is with an air of confidence that he then sits down at the counsel table and allows the witness to walk from the stand in apparent defeat. The strong close is thus properly executed.

Chapter 10

SUMMATION: A TIME FOR MOTIVATING JURORS

KLUWER LITIGATION LIBRARY REFERENCES

JEANS, LITIGATION: Chapter 16, *Summation*.

JOYE & LOVETT, DRUNK DRIVING: THE TRIAL WORKBOOK, THE TRIAL SOURCEBOOK, THE TRIAL NOTEBOOK: Chapter 113, *Final Argument*.

PREISER & PREISER, HANDLING SOFT TISSUE INJURY CASES: Chapter 17, *Summation*.

I. The Function of Summation

§ 10.01 Goals of summation

A trial attorney's goal in summation is to capitalize on the chain he has forged, hopefully, throughout the trial; now is the time to use that chain to pull the jury over to his side. Never forget that a chain is only as strong as its weakest link. Interspersed throughout the other chapters are the basic goals of each stage of the trial. Voir dire has multiple goals; in opening statement, the attorney seeks to capitalize on the psychological principle of primacy and convince the jurors that he ought to win; the goal of direct examination is to present the evidence with impact, while in cross-examination the attorney retains control of the case by creating an impression that the witnesses called by the opposition have not seriously damaged the case.

If these goals have been accomplished, the chain has been forged and you are ready to move to that portion of the trial where the attorney's powers of persuasion are paramount. The jury must now be motivated to take action in favor of the client. However, this does not imply that summation is the part of the trial wherein the liability issue is won. By the time the jury is ready for the summation, each juror has, to a varying degree, made up his mind as to which party should prevail. Prior to summation, the plaintiff will have attempted to establish the presentation of the evidence with impact so that the winning edge gained during the opening statement will not be lost. On the other hand, the defense counsel will have attempted to establish enough confusion and doubt concerning the plaintiff's case to allow the jurors to entertain a verdict for his client. The same reasoning applies to a criminal trial. The State hopes that the jury is ready to convict while the defense believes that there is or should be a reasonable doubt in the minds of the jurors. Thus, although the liability issues are not won on summation, the attorney must reinforce the facts relating to liability so as to bolster those specific pieces of evidence which support the plaintiff's theory of liability. Abundantly clear liability as in a rear-end collision case with no special defenses requires a very short period of time devoted to liability while a complex products liability or malpractice case warrants that a more extensive period of time be spent on the liability issue. However, the goal is not to win the liability issues, but to reinforce favorable jurors with evidence that will enable them to persuade the remaining "doubting Thomases" that your client should be awarded damages in a civil case or be acquitted in a criminal matter.

When considering the summation goal, it is essential to remember Communication Principle 21: Jurors seek to render a verdict which they perceive as equitable. The key word in this communication principle is "perceive," and a key factor of perception is the individual juror's system of preexisting beliefs. The summation presents the attorney with the opportunity to again identify those beliefs, link to those beliefs, and use them in such a fashion as to allow the juror to perceive the equity of his client's case. In essence, the jury must feel that the only fair thing to do is to decide for your side, and if it is a civil case, to decide for your side in a big way.

§ 10.02 The lawyer's role

The lawyer's role in summation is to bring all the pieces of evidence together in one whole and consistent picture. The picture is designed so as to achieve the primary goals discussed previously.[1] In a civil case, the attorney should paint word pictures which pull together the pieces, thereby reinforcing the other party's liability, but should primarily concentrate on encouraging the jury to award adequate damages by tapping their reason and empathy for people who are injured or maimed. The defense lawyer in a civil case has a goal of maintaining absolute objectivity, that is, to take away the impact of the plaintiff's summation, and to demand a cold hard analysis of the evidence, including the rejection of the injured and maimed plaintiff by the jury. It is his role to motivate the jury to resist the emotional appeal he knows is coming.

II. Nonverbal and Vocal Considerations

§ 10.03 Anchoring

Anchoring is a technique of establishing a pattern of behavior to communicate with the listener's unconscious mind. It is an organized means of verbally communicating with the conscious mind while nonverbally communicating with the unconscious mind.[2] Anchoring is first used to establish the case theme in opening statement. At some point in the beginning of the summation, again anchor the case theme. That is, return to the language which sets out the case theme, say it in the same manner with the same gestures and from the same position in the courtroom. In addition to anchoring the case theme, anchor those impact words and phrases which are crucial to the case. For example, when trying a cervical injury case, a good impact phrase is "neck cripple." Anchoring the impact phrase "neck cripple" includes repeating that phrase while standing in the same spot of the courtroom, using the same tone of voice, and making the same gestures and movements each time. Anchors ideally are used throughout every phase of the trial. To be effective, they must be used consistently and precisely.

§ 10.04 Mood transference

Several years ago a great trial attorney presented a hypothetical summation during a seminar to approximately three hundred lawyers, most of whom were brought to tears by his powerful and moving summation. However, when that seminar was viewed on videotape, the same emo-

---

[1] *See supra* § 10.01, *Goals of summation*.

[2] *See supra* Chapter 7, *Opening Statement: Getting the Jury Committed*.

tional impact was not felt by the audience. The same words and phrases said the same way did not have the same effect.

Following extensive discussions, it was realized that while the attorney put himself in a morose mood by thinking of a tragic personal experience, he was not able to communicate his personal emotion via videotape. He had used a form of method acting to transfer his morose mood to those attending the original lecture, however, his mood was not as apparent on the videotape. The lawyers in the original live audience admitted that the summation had been very effective and that had it been a real case supported by evidence, they would have decided the case in favor of the plaintiff and would have given the widow an adequate award. In essence, they were motivated by effective mood transference.

Another great trial attorney preparing to try a case for a man who suffered the loss of one arm spent a week with one of his arms tied behind his back. The attorney said he needed to know how his one-armed client felt in order to get a "feel" for the case. The attorney needed to feel the loss. When the attorney feels the loss, he can effectively represent the client. The plaintiff's attorney must understand the extent of plaintiff's loss and its emotional impact in order to be able to transfer those feelings to the jury. On the other hand, the defense lawyer seeks to transfer to the jury a mood of calm and cold reason. He wants to rationalize away the evidence of fault and call for "reason" in the award which he interprets as a "small award." Defense lawyers do not make emotional appeals to the jury because it does not fit the evidence available to them.

§ 10.05 The use of behavioral cues

What was described in the previous section is nothing short of Stanislavsky-like method acting. This great teacher would instruct actors as to how to create a particular mood in the audience by creating that particular mood within themselves. Feeling any mood strongly with enough force allows the actor to transfer his mood to the audience. How is this mood transferred? Moods are not transferred by magic or illusion. There are still only three levels of communication: verbal, vocal and nonverbal. As discussed earlier, it is important to understand that these three levels are all used in the creation and transfer of any mood.

Well-trained actors can create a mood by their use of verbal, vocal and nonverbal cues. The words they choose to use and how those words are used, combined with eye movements and gestures, can be an effective method of mood transference. Good actors repeatedly create a mood every night while doing a Broadway show. They do not go through the emotional turmoil of "feeling" that mood night after night, rather, they create the mood by pure acting.

When first lecturing about the use of mood transference in summation, one particular attorney used to read a very emotional piece from the newspaper about the death of a child. The morose subject coupled with the speaker's ability to put himself into a morose mood prior to reading the article produced a very effective demonstration of mood transference. Almost every member of the audience felt sad and were close to tears by the end of that reading. Every time he read the piece, the audience was brought to tears. This occurred because the attorney had learned and internalized the appropriate verbal, vocal and nonverbal cues; that is, as he read the piece his voice would tremble and project emotion at the appropriate time, the verbal content was morose in and of itself, and he had learned the appropriate facial gestures, and eye and body movements to convey the feeling of the loss. He was able to transfer the mood by the application of his personal association with the loss. This is different from acting. Attorneys should not be actors. If the jury believes that the attorney is acting or is attempting to act, the attorney will be perceived as phony and will lose credibility and thus will be totally rejected.

COMMENT: There is no doubt that verbal, vocal and nonverbal cues communicate our mood to others. We definitely can and do transfer our moods. While the trial attorney should not act, he should be aware that he does transfer his moods, both the one he actually feels and the one the jury actually perceives, regardless of the attorney's personal mood.

The plaintiff attorney's nonverbal cues during summation usually are aimed at conveying a mood of sadness. He is trying to have the jury understand how seriously the client was injured. Appropriate cues for conveying sadness include lowering the eyes toward the left side while gesturing downward with that hand. This motion causes the juror to lower his eyes toward his lower right hand corner. As discussed earlier, studies show that this eye position indicates greater accessibility to kinesthetic communication; that is, greater vulnerability for experiencing feelings.

Making emotional statements affects the breathing patterns of the communicator. The more depressing the news, the more slowly the rate of breathing. Therefore, conveying a sad mood requires that the attorney slow his breathing rate while breathing more deeply. On the other hand, indignation or anger about a person's conduct is best conveyed by more rapid, shallow breathing.

§ 10.06 Pacing the jury

In addition to using verbal, vocal and nonverbal cues to create the appropriate mood for your case, it is necessary to pace the jury during summation. The attorney has paced the individual juror during voir dire and he has watched the jurors closely during trial. The attorney knows which jurors relate to one another, which jurors like humor, and what cues elicit desired responses, and what phraseology and verbiage to use. He also has some information regarding their background. Pacing in summation is based on weaving that information into the phraseology and nature of the summation. The nature of the summation is based on the intensity of the emotional impact to be conveyed to the particular jury type that you are facing. A conservative upper class jury will not be persuaded by a summation loaded with emotional impact. On the other hand, a blue-collar-type jury is more likely to react favorably toward an emotional summation containing a strong theme, pictures, and impact words and phrases. All of these factors should be considered when pacing the jury in summation.

§ 10.07 The use of unfilled pauses

Pauses can be used effectively during summation. However, as during cross-examination, never fill an unfilled pause. Counsel should note that filled pause includes the use of disinfluencies such as "ah", "umm", and so forth.

The unfilled pause, if not used at a logical point, reduces the credibility of the speaker while its use at an opportune moment greatly increases that individual's credibility. It is used to create a moment of silence which sets the dramatic stage before the use of an anchoring sentence by the attorney. It is also used when the attorney is reaching the close of the summation and is attempting to establish a moment of great emotional impact. Its use underscores what has just been said or what is going to be said and allows the jury to absorb the facts of the statement. After an unfilled pause, jurors reflect not only on what was said, but the vocal and nonverbal cues as well. After an unfilled pause, listening behavior increases and the jurors become more attentive.

§ 10.08 Movements and gestures

Movements or gestures form part of the style of summation. The more flamboyant the attorney's style of delivery, the more movements and gestures are used. Some movements and gestures are essential. An effective summation cannot be given by standing in one spot, rigid and stiff. On the other hand, too much uncontrolled movement is distracting. The speaker who paces back and forth in an uncontrolled fashion, like a caged lion, actually distracts the jurors with his movements and gestures.

No attorney should use gestures or movements with which he is totally uncomfortable. A background in some type of public speaking is helpful in developing appropriate movements and gestures. Most communities have toastmaster clubs or other such clubs where the neophyte attorney can develop important speaking skills. He will find that the practiced gestures become more natural as he learns to use his movements to correctly emphasize important points.

An effective means of developing gesturing skills is by the use of videotaped practice sessions. This allows an individual to learn about his own style and gestures and how to use them most effectively. If we attempt to communicate through the nonverbal channel with inappropriate and improperly timed gestures, jurors will perceive a lack of authenticity, at least on the subconscious level. Generally, most of the attorney's movements during summation ought to be restricted to the upper torso. He can move from side to side, but generally should be stationary for many moments at a time, never appearing to be nervously pacing. Movements of the upper torso appear more like gestures of nervousness if made too close to the body. Arm and hand movements need to be full and robust, and certainly at no time should the attorney stand with his hands in his pockets. Nor should his hands be clasped tightly behind his back as such movements are distracting and definitely affect credibility. The only object which should be held during summation is one you intend to use, i.e., a piece of evidence to be shown to the jury or a pointer of some type used as an extension of your arm. A collapsible-type pointer is recommended because it looks more professional and projects an air of authority and competence.

§ 10.09 Touching the client

The jury searches for and is impressed by an apparent relationship between the attorney and the client. This is particularly true where the attorney is representing an individual rather than a corporation or some other nonpersonal entity. If the attorney is representing an individual in a personal injury claim, some physical touching of the client is essential during the course of the trial and during summation because touching is interpreted as a sign of affection. Although it is nonverbal, it will surely be picked up by the "Sherlock Holmes" of the jury. It is a nonverbal cue that can only be narrowly interpreted. It projects the attorney's belief in the client and the warm relationship that exists between them. Touching projects that the attorney, like the juror, has feelings about and empathy for human beings and their suffering.

The caveat regarding touching the client is that it must always be appropriate and almost incidental. The sex and age of the client and the attorney must be considered to avoid all sexual connotations potentially associated with the touching. The young male attorney should never touch a young female personal injury client, nor should a young male client be touched by a young female attorney. An older fatherly-type attorney may appropriately put his arm around or touch the client of either sex. An older female attorney can be seen as mothering a younger client by her touch. The touching of older clients by younger attorneys, regardless of the sex, is usually permissible as long as the touch can be interpreted as indicating that "I believe in this client," or "I have feelings for this client."

§ 10.10 Dressing for summation

As the trial progresses, the attorney's dress should become progressively more conservative. An attorney representing a seriously injured client in a civil case will be making a somber summation emphasizing the serious injuries and damages suffered by the client. Appropriate dress for the delivery of such a somber message approximates the visual image of the minister who has come to the house to tell the widow that her husband died in an accident. The attorney wants to be identified with the archconservative banker-type, dressing in dark blue or gray. As discussed previously, the attorney's dress obviously varies according to the sex and personality of the attorney.[3]

[3] *See supra* §§ 1.16–1.32.

COMMENT: As the plaintiff's lawyer works his way toward the summation in a serious injury or death case, his dress should become more conservative. On the first day of trial he may wear a light gray. The second day requires a dark gray, while the third day demands a navy blue.

III. Verbal Considerations

§ 10.11 The use of embedded commands

As discussed earlier, the unconscious mind can be reached while communicating with the conscious mind by the use of embedded commands. Embedded commands use a particular phrase to open a channel to the unconscious mind. Essentially, any phrase that asks whether or not someone possesses a particular capability is the type of preface which is used to instill an embedded command. The preface sets up a definite affirmative answer. While not telling the conscious mind what to do, it asks the conscious mind whether or not it could really do it. It is important to simplify a message and to repeat the simplified message often throughout the trial.[4] An embedded command is the embodiment of Communication Principle 19 which recognizes that decisions are made based on emotion. This is best accomplished when a change in the voice pattern occurs between the phrase used to create the embedded command and the actual communication.

An embedded command reaches through the conscious and attempts to reach the unconscious mind. With the proper use of a pause and a change in voice level and other nonverbal cues, it motivates the juror to take certain actions. Embedded commands start with such phrases as "I know you were wondering . . .", or "I know that you are thinking . . .", or "This must be on your mind . . .". Embedded commands in summation can tie into the juror's physical and mental condition or to specific pieces of evidence.[5]

---

[4] *See supra generally* §§ 3.27, 3.28.

[5] *See supra* §§ 4.15–4.19, for a complete discussion of embedded commands.

For example, in summation you might say to the jurors "I know the trial has been long, and I know that you are tired; and for that reason I promise not to take long with what I have to say, but there a few things that I need to say before you go out to decide this case and deal with the requirements of justice." Of course, the lawyer then discusses the requirements of justice and uses that phrase throughout the summation. He motivates the jury to act on the embedded command "to do justice" for his client; doing such will alleviate the situation that existed in their minds at the beginning of the summation, that is, that it had been a long trial and they are tired.

Another type of embedded command deals with the establishment of evidence. This is accomplished using the phraseology, "I knew then what you know now." The use of this particularly effective command works to reconfirm the evidence in the juror's mind. The following is an example of an attorney using embedded commands in a simple rear-end collision case.

> "At the beginning of this case you were wondering why I was asking questions about whether or not you could be fair and (pause) *return a verdict for a large amount of money*. You know now what I knew then. You know now that even though this was a simple rear-end collision it caused serious injury. You know now what I knew then. You know now that this injury is serious because there was ripping and tearing of the muscles and fibers and ligaments of my client's neck, and that this resulted in hemorrhage and ultimately in scar tissue. You know now what I knew then. You know now that she will suffer with this condition, with the scar tissue in her neck for the rest of her life, and that is a long time. And, you know now what I knew then, that the damages were going to take place over her lifetime, and that she has a life expectancy of forty years. So now you know why, at the very outset and even though I am sure you were wondering why at the time, that I had to ask you if you could *return a serious amount of money damages for this type of injury*.

§ 10.12 The use of analogy

Analogy is one of the most powerful tools used in summation. Summation is the one time during the trial when the advocate is afforded the opportunity to argue his client's position to the jury. The most effective way to explain a position is through the use of an analogy. Using an analogy refers to telling a story to illustrate the point. Parables are often used in the Bible to make a point. There is no more effective way to make a point and argue the case to the jury than by the use of an analogy.

Analogies are used for aspects of the case including, the illustration of injuries, emphasis of important facts, explanations of case theory, or points of law. Sometimes one analogy can cover more than one point. The following is an example of an analogy which illustrates facts as well as a point of law. Assume the attorney is arguing a case with preexisting osteoarthritis which has been made symptomatic by the superimposition of a cervical sprain. The jury needs to understand the significance of the facts of the case and why the defendant is liable for all of the damage even though his negligence caused only a cervical injury and not the osteoarthritis:

> Ladies and gentlemen of the jury for just a minute I would like you to forget that this is a rear-end collision case involving a lady stopped at a traffic light in New Orleans, Louisiana. Let's assume for a minute that you have a case in the country. Instead of the lady's car that is stopped at a traffic light, let's assume it is a farmer's truck. I want you to assume that it is a farmer's truck that has stopped on the roadway and that this farmer's truck is loaded with eggs. It is parked on the side of the roadway and the farmer was on his way to the market to sell the eggs. The same defendant, the Continental Bus Company, comes along and rear ends the farmer's truck parked on the side of the road. It's a hot July day just as it was in this case. And the impact throws the eggs all over the highway. In fact, it is so hot that a couple of eggs start to fry right there.
>
> Would you have any trouble, if you were a jury in that case up in the country, in awarding a judgment which pays for the fenders and the broken windshield on the farmer's truck? Of course not! Just as you won't have any trouble awarding the farmer monetary damage for the loss of his eggs? Of course you wouldn't! That would be no problem. It would simply involve some simple mathematics. You would find out the wholesale price of the eggs, because after all he wasn't going to sell them retail, he was going to sell them wholesale. Then you would find out how many eggs were broken or damaged and figure out how much was owed. In that case in the country, wouldn't you be astounded if the defense lawyer got up and said:

"Ladies and Gentlemen of the jury, my defense is that the truck should not have been loaded with eggs, it should have been loaded with Ping-Pong balls so that when they hit the highway they bounced, we could have collected them back up and there would have been no problems?" Why, you say, that's ridiculous.

Well, ladies and gentlemen, that's the defense that is being presented in this case. They are saying that my client's neck should have been resilient. It should have been like Ping-Pong balls and not eggs. The neck should not have been fragile and should not have had a preexisting condition in it. And the judge is going to tell you that they are liable for any activation or aggravation of a preexisting condition. You listen for those words. And what he means by that is that it is no defense to stand up here and say that my client should have had a rubber resilient neck like the Ping-Pong balls. The fact is that she had a neck that was like an egg. It was fragile; it was breakable—just like the eggs. And they are liable for all the damage done and cannot be heard to come in and complain that she did not have a young strong neck.

COMMENT: Note how the analogy, the telling of the story, makes a difficult point clear. It is through the use of this analogy that counsel can really make the jury understand what all the lawyers and the judge are talking about in terms of the defendant being liable for any activation or aggravation of a preexisting condition. Those legal words are really not understood by laymen. The analogy argues the point of law more effectively than can be done by simply telling the jury that the defendant is liable for any activation or aggravation of preexisting conditions and that this is the law and they must follow it. They will have difficulty following a law they don't understand, and they may not understand the law unless it is explained effectively through the use of an analogy.

Analogies are also used to illustrate a case theory. In a medical malpractice case, your case theory should be that the standard of care you are describing is a reasonable one under all circumstances and that the defendant should be held to this standard of care and not be allowed to practice sloppy medicine. In these cases, the defendant argues a lower standard of care and attacks the plaintiff's experts for testifying that the defendant should live up to a high standard of care. It is important to make the jury understand that it is their role to set the standard of care and this can effectively be done with the following analogy:

> Ladies and Gentlemen: When you enter the juryroom you will decide whether this defendant has violated the standard of care. I know you are wondering if that decision can really cause good medicine to be practiced in the community. (Pause) If you decide for the plaintiff, the answer is yes! By your decision, you are saying what kind of medicine you, the members of this community, want practiced in this city. You, by your verdict, select and actively set the standard of care. You listen to the experts but then you have to choose the standard of care. Which standard of care should you choose? What is the standard of care that is required under the circumstances?
>
> Well, suppose for a minute, this was an automobile case and the defendant was driving down the interstate highway at the posted speed limit of 55 miles per hour. Under those circumstances, you would probably find that the driver of that car, since he was going the posted speed limit, was obeying the law and was not negligent. He had not violated the standards of care. But, let's change the facts a little. Now, same highway, same posted speed limit, but assume instead of driving a passenger car that the defendant was driving a truck. And assume that this truck was loaded with nitroglycerine. How do you drive a nitroglycerine truck?
>
> The one thing we all know is you don't drive a nitroglycerine truck at the posted speed limit of 55 miles per hour. You drive a nitroglycerine truck at 5 miles an hour, with a police escort, being very careful not to go over any bumps in the highway. Why are you required to be more careful with a nitroglycerine truck? You are more careful because there is a greater risk of harm. One bump and you can not only blow up the interstate but half of the town that you are passing through as well. Because there is a greater risk of harm, you must be much more careful with a nitroglycerine truck. You can't drive at the posted speed limit and use ordinary and reasonable care. You have to use extraordinary care whenever you are engaged in a business where there is a great risk of harm.

Well, the defendant in this case is an anesthesiologist. When you really understand what he does for a living, you know that he poisons people close to death and then brings them back. He gets paid a lot of money to do this because it is a very dangerous, high risk business. He has to be very careful. Isn't an anesthesiologist in his work more like the nitroglycerine truck driver? Do you want to say that anesthesiologists in this community can use ordinary reasonable care? Is he really like the passenger car driver?

So, understand that when you enter that jury room, you are selecting the standard of care under which all of us will be treated. You are choosing either a high standard of care under which the anesthesiologist must be very careful in monitoring the patient and must watch for signs of anoxia so as not to allow the patient to become brain damaged, or a standard of care that has been espoused by the defendant's friends in the local community which allows him to be sloppy, to let a patient under spinal anesthetic to develop hypoxia and not know it is happening. The standard they espouse says those things happen and it is nobody's fault. The high standard of care as espoused by Dr. Jones, the plaintiff's expert, is that those things shouldn't happen if we are careful, if the anesthesiologist is watching the patient as he should. If the anesthesiologist is using the kind of care he should be using, if he's driving with the same care as a nitroglycerine truck driver, these things don't happen.

An analogy can also be used to illustrate simply a point of law. For example, the plaintiff in a civil case may want to illustrate the difference between the burden of proof in the civil versus the criminal case; that is, a proponderance of the evidence versus beyond a reasonable doubt standard. Various analogies can be used to illustrate that point. Using the baseball score analogy, tell the jury that this is a civil case and it's like a baseball game. The winner only needs to score one run more than the loser. If the score is 11 to 10, we win. Another analogy is that all the plaintiff is required to do is to carry the burden of proof is a passing grade. The plaintiff is not required, as in a criminal case to get an "A", to have an almost perfect proof. All that is required is that we get a "C", which is passing.

Perhaps one of the best analogies used to illustrate the quality of proof needed in a civil liability suit is to argue that it is like the ordinary business judgment which we each make every day. It is what we do when we go out and buy a car. We look at a few cars, go to a couple of dealerships and make up our minds. We don't go out and study every car in the city for four months before making a decision. It is ordinary reasonable judgment under all of the circumstances.

To illustrate a point concerning your client's impairments and injuries, be sure to use analogies. One analogy used for this purpose is termed the "watch analogy." The defendant has stressed the fact that the plaintiff has only suffered a "5% disability." However, our client was a millwright and must use his back to make a living. He was 5% impaired, but he cannot work anymore. In that situation you might use the following analogy:

> Ladies and gentlemen of the jury: The defendant will emphasize that my client, according to both doctors, only suffered a 10% impairment in the function of his spine. But remember, there is a difference between impairment and disability. A person can suffer a small impairment and still be totally disabled. That's because of the type of impairment combined with the nature of his job. Let's assume for a minute that the watch you own is not working properly. It only loses about 60 seconds out of every hour. By the end of the day, it's 24 minutes off. As a watch, it doesn't keep accurate time anymore. As a watch, though it's only off a little, it is totally useless. You can't depend on it. The time it keeps is not accurate.
>
> Well, my client's employability as a millwright was like the requirements for a watch. He had to be able to do the job. He had to be able to rely on his back to do the heavy lifting. It may be that he is only 5% impaired, but like the watch, he is totally disabled. He can't work as a millwright anymore and because of his education, age and status in life, he is not really employable anyplace else. You have heard the evidence to that effect. His skills as a millwright are about as marketable as a watch that doesn't work. He is a millwright and he can't work. His skills are about as marketable in the labor market as a broken watch is in a jewelry store.

§ 10.13 The use of rhetorical questions

Another common verbal technique used during summation is the rhetorical question. The question is rhetorical when the answer is so obvious that it does not require an answer. Rhetorical questions will work only if the attorney is absolutely sure of how the jury will respond to the question. The theory behind the use of the rhetorical question is that juror who answers that question in his own mind then becomes an advocate for that point of view in the jury room. That answer becomes his own. He defends it because it is not a statement that has been made by the trial lawyer who, after all, is an advocate.

Some rhetorical questions ask such things as: (1) "Is that fair?", (2) "Is that what justice demands?", (3) "Would you want to be treated that way?", (4) "Do you believe that?", (5) "That's supposed to be the truth?"[6]

An example of particularly effective use of rhetorical questions to emphasize key points during summation is as follows: The case involved the failure to diagnose eclampsia in a woman who is nine months pregnant. Eclampsia is a toxemia or poisoning that may develop in the female body during pregnancy and can cause convulsions and death if it goes undiagnosed and untreated.

In this case, on that fatal day, the patient was complaining of severe neck pain, nausea, inability to focus her eyes, and borderline high blood pressure. There was clinical evidence that she was developing a rapid form of eclampsia, that she could being convulsing, and that she needed to be hospitalized. The treating physician saw her, he listened to the fetal heart tones which at that point were still normal, and then did a urinalysis to test for albumin content. However, he performed the test by rubbing the dipstick on her wet pubic hair rather than dipping it into an actual sample of her urine. Incredibly, the defendant doctor claimed that the urinalysis was negative for albumin and that therefore she would not have had eclampsia. He also said he did not know what caused her death. The defendant's experts testified that because albumin was not present in the urine, the patient did not have eclampsia. One defendant's expert, a urologist, actually testified that this was an acceptable procedure to do a urinalysis.

Plaintiff's attorney contended that it was gross malpractice to perform the urinalysis in this manner; that this failure to do a proper urinalysis led to the misdiagnosis; that in fact the lady had died from eclampsia; that if the diagnosis had been made properly and if she had been hospitalized and treated with magnesium sulfate, she and the baby would still be alive. In fact, the physician had sent her home and was treating her for a neck sprain when she began having seizures. Both she and the unborn child died at home. The defense urologist attempted, on direct examination, to demonstrate that a reading of albumin in the urine can be

[6] *See supra* § 10.11, *The use of embedded commands*, for additional examples of the use of rhetorical questions.

obtained by rubbing the dipstick in the lady's vaginal area. He took pure albumen (the white of an egg), placed it on his wrist, and then rubbed the area with a dipstick to demonstrate that he could get a positive reading. Every time he tried it, the hair on his arm contaminated the dipstick, and a positive reading was not obtainable.

At the time the case was tried, Louisiana was still laboring under the antiquated Locality Rule. However, the plaintiff's expert, a nationally known urologist, testified that this method of doing a urinalysis violated the standards of good medicine in every state in the union and even in "the mountains of Tennessee." During summation, the ridiculousness of the attempt to defend this method of doing a urinalysis was highlighted by use of the rhetorical question. A portion of the summation follows:

> You know, ladies and gentlemen, that you are about to render a verdict in this case. The word verdict is taken from the Latin word *veritos* which means truth. So you've got to determine what's the truth here. Let's talk about that for a minute.
>
> What's the truth here? We know that the whole argument in this case is whether the diagnosis of eclampsia should have been made and everyone agrees that if she had had a high degree of albumin in the urine, a diagnosis of eclampsia could have been made and you could say today that she died from eclampsia. But we don't know whether the high albumin was present because of the way the test was done. A simple test, merely dipping a chemically treated dipstick into a sample of her urine would have provided an answer. Why don't we have the answer? You know why we don't have the answer. You heard the testimony didn't you? The defendant, Dr. Jones, told you how he did the urinalysis. It was incredible, wasn't it? He took the dipstick and rubbed it between her legs. That's what he said. That's what he said in his deposition and that's what he said here in court.
>
> Where's the truth? He said that's the way he did it. He said it was alright to do a urinalysis like that because you could get an accurate reading.
>
> You remember that? You remember Dr. Smith, the urologist called by the defendants? He came in here and said it was alright to do a urinalysis like that. And our expert, a top urologist, Dr. Brown, told you that they wouldn't do a urinalysis like that in the mountains of Tennessee. You remember that?

> And you remember what happened when Dr. Smith tried to demonstrate to you that he could get an accurate reading of albumin. Remember he sat right up there on the witness stand and took an egg and a syringe, with a big long needle on it, it was very dramatic . . . you remember he drew the white of the egg out with the syringe . . . and you remember that none of us knew for a minute what he was going to do with that syringe and that egg, you remember that don't you? Then he pulled the white of the egg out of the syringe onto his wrist and he tried to pick up the white of the egg with a dipstick and get a reading of albumin. Remember that? And you remember that the plaintiff introduced those dipsticks into evidence because every time the defendant's expert did it, he contaminated the dipstick, an accurate reading was not obtainable. All of you remember that? The evidence is right here. The dipsticks are plaintiff's exhibits 27 through 34 [holding them up]. Can you believe it? He tried it six times and it didn't work once. Can you believe that? Well in a few moments you'll go and do what is your duty. You'll reach the truth; you'll reach a verdict. Where's the truth here? Can you plausibly say that this is the way a urinalysis should be done? Can you say that this is an accurate urinalysis? Can you say, based on that kind of urinalysis, that she didn't have albumin in the urine? Can you say, based on that kind of urinalysis, that while we don't know what she died from, that it wasn't eclampsia? Isn't it more likely that, in fact, she did have albumin in the urine since she had all the other signs of eclampsia? Is that the way you want medicine practiced here in your community . . . a way that they wouldn't practice it even in the mountains of Tennessee? What's the truth here? I am sure your verdict will answer those questions.

Note in the foregoing illustration that the use of rhetorical questions during summation reinforces the obvious answers. Here was a situation where the defendants had truly overreached in trying to defend this as an accurate way to do a urinalysis. When they had actually tried to demonstrate that you could do a urinalysis that way, it did not work six times. Therefore, the answers to the questions were obvious. Rather than stand up before the jury as an advocate and state the obvious, however, it was more effective to put the obvious in the form of rhetorical questions. This allowed the jury to answer the questions for themselves. The answers become their answers and therefore they believe those answers more strongly and will defend those beliefs more strongly than if the answers had been supplied by the trial lawyer advocating his client's position.

§ 10.14 Understanding understatements

Another verbal technique which is used in summation which is similar in nature to the rhetorical question technique is the application of understatements. The principle of understatement simply means that it is far better, in terms of impact of testimony, that the obvious not be belabored. A piece of dramatic evidence of disability or injury should speak for itself. Do not harp on that evidence or belabor it because it surely will lose its impact.

A few years ago two young and inexperienced lawyers began trying a quadriplegic case. The client was brought into the courtroom and remained on her stretcher during voir dire and opening statement. Her counsel, discussing the case with an experienced trial lawyer later that day said that he anticipated a big verdict because the jury would be overwhelmed by the sight of this quadriplegic client. The experienced lawyer correctly predicted that there would be a verdict for the defendants. Ten days later, the jury wasted little time in returning a defense verdict. The young lawyer went back to the more experienced lawyers and asked how he knew it would be a defense verdict. The explanation was simple. The inexperienced trial counsel had failed to apply the technique of understatement to the case. The most dramatic piece of evidence was the quadriplegic client. They were hoping that the severity of the injury would overcome the liability problems of the case. Sometimes it does, but by overexposing the jury to the horrors of the plaintiff's injury day after day, the jury became accustomed to the sight rather than being persuaded by the horror. A more successful approach could have been understating the evidence. Viewing the quadriplegic plaintiff briefly, combined with a viewing of a-day-in-the-life film, will cause the jurors to retain the shock of seeing your client.

Properly applied understatement lets the jury use its imagination, and often the horrors that can be unleashed by the imagination are worse than what the actual evidence could show. This is illustrated by the emergence of modern television, which allows the graphic depiction of violence. The horror movies today do not have nearly the impact of the horror movies of twenty or thirty years ago. What we imagine in our minds is far more horrible and devastating than reality. The most significant example of this is Orson Welles' 1938 radio show about an invasion from Mars, which caused the imaginations of millions of Americans to run wild while the whole nation panicked.

Another startling example of the application of understatement in summation can be illustrated by the effective application of that principle by the late Moe Levine of New York. He was trying a case for a man who had lost both arms. The defendants, the judge, and everyone connected with the case expected a long summation from Mr. Levine about a life with no arms. In fact, his summation was short, simple, and to the point. It was a masterpiece of understatement and resulted in one of the largest verdicts in the history of the State of New York at the time it was given. That brief summation, as paraphrased by Moe Levine himself, is:

> "Your Honor, eminent counsel for defense, ladies and gentlemen of the jury: as you know, about an hour ago we broke for lunch. And I saw the bailiff came and took you all as a group to have lunch in the juryroom. And then I saw the defense attorney, Mr. Horowitz and his client decided to go to lunch together. And the judge and the court clerk went to lunch. So, I turned to my client, Harold, and said why don't you and I go to lunch together, and we went across the street to that little restaurant and had lunch. [Significant pause.]
>
> "Ladies and gentlemen, I just had lunch with my client. He has no arms. He eats like a dog! Thank you very much."

Sweet, short, simple, and to the point. It described the horrible injuries in that admitted liability case and emphasized them far greater by the application of understatement than if Mr. Levine had engaged in a long dialogue about what it is like to have no arms. A point can always be made more effectively and with greater impact when the principle of understatement is applied.

§ 10.15 Impact words and phrases

During the summation always try to use impact words and phrases. For example, during summation never talk about the client being involved in an "accident." "Accident" is not an impact word and even implies that the incident was no one's fault. Instead, the incident should be described using impact words and phrases. "My client was involved in a horrendous crash which propelled her vehicle forward almost fifty feet after it was struck from the rear."

Scientists have been attempting to understand the neurophysics of memory for years and as yet have no definitive answers. They theorize that memory is a chemical process within the brain's cortex. On a psychological level, we know that there are two kinds of memory: long-term memory and short-term memory. Long-term memory refers to the recordation in the brain of almost everything that goes on in our lives through a process we do not understand. Short-term memory refers to the ability to recall names and facts we have observed just one or two hours before. We know that short-term memory can be severely affected by some brain injuries, while long-term memory functions perfectly. Memory is really the ability to recall. It is a known fact that we can recall those things which make a vivid impression upon us. It is much easier to recall things that we have seen. Therefore, if one can paint word pictures in each juror's mind so that the juror can visualize what is happening or what is being theorized to have happened, they will have a much easier time recalling it in the juryroom and it will have more of a persuasive impact.

Understanding the reason for the use of impact words and phrases is important. We use impact words and phrases because they most graphically describe events. They conjure up mind pictures. The things we picture in our "mind's eye" have more of an impact on us and are more easily remembered. They are more persuasive because we can actually see the event occurring in the way it is described. If you have ever seen an auto fatality, you can remember the scene because it left a substantial impression.

The most effective means of memorizing new information is by creating mind pictures. It is very difficult to memorize in the abstract. This principle was utilized by Harry Lorraine to develop a memory system called mnemonics. He has published two books which present a system whereby feats of memory can be performed. Using mind pictures even allows a person to remember people's faces or names for years. This principle of mnemonics is now being taught to grammar school students to improve their ability to master school material. A basic system of mnemonics works as follows:

> Take the numbers 1 through 20 and associate a key word with each number. Then, associate a picture of that key word with the number. The picture you have in your mind is then altered by the new item you are trying to remember. It is a striking feat of memory which anyone can do with a little practice.

The following is a list of key words for the numbers 1 through 20:

— 1 Won
— 2 Shoe
— 3 Tree
— 4 Gore
— 5 Dive
— 6 Kicks
— 7 Heaven
— 8 Bait
— 9 Dine
—10 Hen
—11 Football
—12 Hell
—13 Thirsty
—14 Guarding
—15 Sifting
—16 Sorting
—17 Leveling
—18 Dating
—19 Piling
—20 Plenty

With each number develop a simple picture which illustrates the key word. For example, with the number 1 and the key word Won, pin a blue ribbon on the item you wish to associate with number 1. The picture should always be something graphic. With the number 10, picture a hen about to lay an egg and then replace the egg with the object to be associated with the number. With a little practice you will be able to ask friends to write down a list of objects next to the numbers 1 to 20. The objects are called out to you and you never see the written list. Without ever looking at the list, you will be able to instantaneously recall the objects in association with the number.

This is not magic, it is the proper use of memory. Understanding how this works and why it works illustrates the importance of impact words and phrases. The pnemonic system works because we remember those things which have impact and which we can picture in our "mind's eye." Therefore, if we describe the facts of the case that are favorable to us with impact so as to paint word pictures, the jury will not only remember them but will be persuaded by the impact of the facts. In essence the jury should be able to see an incident happening in their "mind's eye."

The painting of word pictures should begin during opening statement.[7] In closing argument, we should return to those word pictures and reinforce them. We should bring the jury back to the scene of the incident momentarily to make them see the little child being run over once more. During summation we might not necessarily want to reinforce all of the word pictures painted in opening statement. For example, in a rear-end collision case we might not want to describe in detail the occurrence of the crash again. Instead we may want to stress the medical theory that the plaintiff now has permanent scar tissue. We do this by reinforcing the medical theory which was laid out in the opening statement.[8] In closing argument counsel could also use embedded commands to reinforce the word picture painted previously in the opening statement. That portion of the closing argument could sound something like this:

> Can you remember the opening statement where we told you what really happened to Mary's neck? (Pause) Mary's neck hemorrhaged and formed scar tissue. Just as Mary didn't understand what was happening when it happened, you could not understand either when we gave the opening statement. I know you were wondering if we could prove it to you. Well, you know now that we have proved it. You know what the medical evidence shows.
>
> The medical evidence showed that when Mary was rammed from the rear and knocked into the car ahead of her, the muscles in her neck, and particularly the sternoclaidomastoid muscles, were ripped and torn. And you know that they hemorrhaged causing her pain and spasm in the neck, and the doctors told you that this is why her neck was stiff originally and this is why she had to wear that neck collar for several months. She needs to splint her neck just like you splint a broken arm so that the ripped and torn muscles would have time to heal. In essence, the collar splints her neck so she would not use her muscles so they could heal. And all the physicians testified, didn't they (pause), that when the muscles healed, they formed the scar tissue? Scar tissue is thick and will never be as flexible as normal tissue. And, because she has scarred muscles in her neck, she is going to have problems with her neck for the rest of her life.
>
> That is what the medical evidence shows. Dr. Jones, her treating physician, told you that. He told you it was his option that the scar-

---

[7] *See supra* § 7.10, *Painting word pictures*; § 7.13, *Telling the "story" of the case*; and § 7.16, *Introducing the medical theory of the case*, for examples of word pictures.

[8] *See supra* § 7.16, *Introducing the medical theory of the case*.

ring was permanent and that with weather changes and overuse she would have pain and disability on a daily basis for the rest of her life. And you remember they sent her to Dr. Smith who carried out one examination and you remember the cross examination of Dr. Smith. I have had that cross examination typed up. Let me read it to you.

> "Q. [Lawyer visible picking up transcript and reading it to jury.] It is true is it not, Dr. Smith, that there have been studies performed on monkeys, both here at Tulane University, and at other medical centers where the monkeys were rear ended and after the rear-end injuries to the monkey's neck had healed they sacrificed the monkeys and in autopsy they were able to find the presence of scar tissue?
>
> "A. Yes, that is true. Sometimes it was only present microscopically, sometimes visibly.
>
> "Q. And, Dr. Smith, is it also true that the medical studies we discussed earlier show that a significance percentage of 10% to 20% of people who suffer these types of injuries, even after they have settled their cases, continue to have permanent symptoms of the neck?
>
> "A. Yes, those studies say that. I don't know whether the percentages are that high, but they could be that high.
>
> "Q. Then you do agree Dr. Smith that if Mary is telling the truth about the symptoms she has, then she has scar tissue in her neck and she falls within the 10% to 20% that is going to have permanent symptoms from a rear-end collision for the rest of her life, that is certainly a medical possibility?
>
> "A. That is true, it could be the case."

And those are the words of the doctor who was chosen by the defendant for an "independent" medical examination. He, in essence, on cross-examination agreed with our doctor. So you can stop wondering. You do not have to wonder about the proof anymore. You have seen it and you know now what we knew when we gave the opening statement. You know now that in fact Mary, more probably than not, has scar tissue present in her neck. You know now that Mary has this scar tissue in her neck because of the rear-end collision in which her muscles were torn and ripped in her neck and bled and that when they healed, they healed with scar tissue. You know now that Mary not only suffered with that since the incident, as she has told you and her friends have told you, but that she is going to suffer with it for the rest of her life. The rest of her life is about 40 years. That is the evidence. So you know now we have delivered all our proof. We have accomplished what we promised in opening statement. And now you must take the action you promised Mary during voir dire. You promised to give a just amount of damages if we could show you that this was a serious and permanent injury. You remember promising that and the court reporter taking it down? Each of you gave that promise. We have taken the action that we were suppose to take. Mary has delivered the proof. Now is the time for you to go in the jury room and take the necessary action to do justice in this case.

IV. Structuring the Argument

§ 10.16 Structuring the argument generally

Communication Principle 15 is applicable when structuring an argument. "People are influenced by the way the message is structured and delivered." There can be little doubt as to the accuracy of this principle. The message must be delivered with powerful and not powerless words. It must be kept simple and consistent and it should be repeated frequently. It should be presented with enough impact and intensity so that the points made are retained. Whether the trier of fact is a judge or jury, the points made in final argument should have a great deal of impact so they will be recalled during the decision-making process.

The first rule of structuring arguments can be called the "climax-anticlimax" rule. While some people believe that one should argue "anticlimax-climax," that is, save the best for last, this is simply not true. One should always structure an argument so that the strongest points are presented first. Attorneys should always argue their cases with the climax-anticlimax rule in mind.

The reasoning behind the "climax-anticlimax" rule is related to Communication Principle 6: People attempt to maintain their original perceptions regardless of contradictory information. In psychological terms this is called the rule of primacy. First impressions count. And once those impressions are made it is very difficult to reverse them. First impressions are colored by preexisting belief systems, personalized generalizations, and stereotypes.[9] They include the impressions that were made about you and your client during voir dire as well as the first impression stage of the trial.

Thus one cannot afford to make a weak first impression by structuring an argument in an anticlimax-climax fashion. For if the judge or jury does not buy the first argument, the chance of them believing the second argument, even if it is stronger, is greatly reduced. By the time one reaches a third or fourth point under the anticlimax-climax approach, the presenter's credibility is so weakened that the strongest argument, which is being presented later, will be rejected out of hand.

COMMENT: For the same reasons that you want to make a strong impression at the beginning of the trial, so too should you want to make a strong impression during the beginning portion of the closing argument. For this reason, you should always structure the argument so the strongest point is presented first. Once you have favorably impressed the jury and/or the judge by the strong argument, it becomes easier to sell the weaker arguments. Generally, the weaker arguments should link to the stronger arguments and they should be tied together as a chain of reasons why your client should prevail.

This rule is violated frequently. The disastrous effects of violating the climax-anticlimax rule are apparent in rules and/or motion parts in any court in the country.

The rule of recency applies to structuring a final argument. Primacy related to the intensity of belief one has in a particular argument. Recency relates to the ability to recall a particular argument.[10] Recency says we remember those things better that we heard last. Therefore, when structuring the argument, place points that we want the jury to remember at the end of your argument. Usually that means that counsel

[9] *See generally supra* Chapter 1, *Impression Formation in the Courtroom*.

[10] *See supra* § 1.52, for a discussion of the reasons why primacy is important and how primacy and recency link together.

should return to his strongest point at the close of the final argument. The jury is going to be more impressed with, or at least remember better, the last things we say in a final argument. Not only should these closing words contain what is logically the argument's strongest point, but the message should contain much emotional impact. Remember Communication Principle 19 which embodies the concept that basic decisions are made on a gut level in the unconscious mind and then verified with logic by the conscious mind. Our closing sentences must be persuasive. To be persuasive, a message must communicate with the unconscious mind while engaging the conscious mind. In other words, the message must have an emotional element to be fully effective.

It should, therefore, be clear to the trial attorney that both the opening and closing remarks during the closing argument are crucial. The first two minutes and the final five minutes are controlling in terms of the impact and persuasiveness that any final argument is going to have.

Finally, in structuring any closing argument, remember that Communication Principle 15 states that people are influenced by the way the message is structured and delivered. If the message is too complex, the jurors will not doubt their ability to understand the message. Instead, they will, in essence, blame it on the trial attorney. They will believe that they did not understand the message, not because of their own lack of intelligence or ability, but because the message was not properly presented. Therefore, if the message delivered in closing argument is too complex, you run the risk of seriously damaging your credibility as an attorney. The jurors will see the complex message which they do not understand as an inability on the part of the trial attorney to adequately communicate with them.

COMMENT: A final general rule regarding the structure of a final argument is the old salesman's rule of KISS. This phrase is summarized in most sales motivation courses as "Keep It Simple Stupid."

---

§ 10.17 Capitalizing on voir dire commitments

We have previously discussed at length the power of commitments and the need of individuals to be consistent with their commitments.[11] The various psychological studies cited clearly indicate that once a commitment is made, particularly if that commitment is public and if it is in writing, that there is an overwhelming need for the individual to be consistent with that commitment.

In addition, we previously discussed voir dire techniques and we demonstrated the power of commitment and how to obtain and reinforce those commitments.[12] This material stressed that you should obtain a specific commitment from the jurors concerning key issues. You should then reinforce these so called "red flag" answers by pointing out that they were being transcribed. Make sure that individual answers are given by each juror in front of other jurors. We now turn to the techniques of using those voir dire commitments in summation so that the jurors will be compelled to be consistent with their prior commitments.

In trying a light impact rear-end collision case, counsel should obtain from each juror a commitment during voir dire that if the evidence shows a light impact can cause serious permanent injury, he will vote in favor of a significant damages award for your client. It was pointed out at the time of this positive individual answer that the court reporter was transcribing the answers. The attorney could then obtain a transcript of those voir dire questions and the individual answers of the jurors in writing for use during summation. Counsel could then project these vital voir dire answers on an overhead projector so each juror can see in writing his public commitment with those answers showing in the background. The summation could proceed as follows:

> Ladies and Gentlemen: You remember what each of you promised Mary and I. That despite the fact this was only a light impact, because of the mechanics of this type of injury one could receive a serious injury and the evidence showed exactly that, didn't it? We showed you that even though there was a light impact it was sufficient to jolt the car forward and to snap Mary's neck back and to cause Mary serious injury. And I am sure each of you remember the promise you made Mary and I at the beginning of this trial. You remember we asked you several questions during what the

[11] *See supra* § 2.04.

[12] *See supra* § 6.05, *Obtaining commitment*.

> judge told you was voir dire? You remember when we asked you about a light impact. (Pause) You promised that even with a light impact you could return a substantial verdict. Do you remember that? And you remember that I pointed out the court reporter was taking it down when you made the promise to Mary and I?
>
> Well, here it is. [Flip projection on screen for overhead projector showing answers.] And as you can see on the screen, it's right there! It's written down what each of you promised! You promised that if the evidence showed that even though this was a light impact it could cause serious injury and that if Mary suffered a serious injury you could give an adequate verdict. The time has now come for you to look at the evidence realistically and to do what is fair. It's time to do what is right. It's time to do as you promised on voir dire. It's time to go through the grisly accounting of this injury and what happened to Mary's neck, how she suffered in the past and will suffer in the future because of this severe injury.

From this point on, you would go on to discuss the nature of the injury in detail and the resulting monetary damages.

This is what is meant by capitalizing on the voir dire commitment in summation. You should remind the jurors emphatically of the individual, specific commitment they made that they would not be swayed by the "red herring" of light impact. Whenever you have a specific crucial issue, it can be handled in this manner.

Whatever the specific problem, the need for the jurors to be consistent with a public commitment which was transcribed can be overwhelming. It is always a good technique to capitalize in summation on the commitment obtained in voir dire and thereby use the methods of persuasion discussed previously.[13]

§ 10.18 Opening line: reestablishing rapport and anchoring the case theme

How should counsel start a summation? Everyone has heard the old show business axiom: "Every act should have a flashy, attention-getting opening and a strong close." We also know that the jury's attention, in terms of all twelve jurors, is the highest when the curtain is raised at the beginning of summation. It is a dramatic moment in the trial. The attorney should begin the summation by saying something which will link to

[13] *See supra* §§ 2.53–2.67.

the juror's model of the world. In this fashion, counsel reestablishes the rapport that has hopefully been building throughout the trial. As soon as this goal is accomplished, hopefully within the first two minutes, the attorney needs to reanchor the case theme. Remember Communication Principle 20: People more easily retain information which is anchored.[14] In essence, the trial lawyer's opening lines in the summation should be good theatre. He should use emotion to both establish rapport and remind the jury why his client should prevail.

In the past, many noted trial lawyers had standard opening lines they used to accomplish these goals in summation. A standard opening line can be used as a crutch and can help a lawyer overcome the natural tension and nervousness at the beginning of the summation. If it's standard and is memorized, the lawyer will not have to think about what he is saying. He can then concentrate on the nonverbal aspects of the message.

When the court says to the trial lawyer: "Counselor, you may proceed with summation," it is one of the most dramatic moments in the courtroom. It is expected that you should follow the traditional ritual of recognizing the court, opposing counsel and the jury before beginning. The court expects this ritual to take place, and so does the jury. Remember, however, that this is the opening overture to your show. It's the curtain going up on what you are about to present. Do not raise that curtain sloppily. Do not say "May it please your Honor, or "May it please the court" while you are looking down fumbling through papers. Do not mumble the line. Rather let your voice fill the courtroom so its resonant ring will fill the jury's ears as you say: "May it please your Honor" and then turning to opposing counsel, "Eminent counsel for defense" and then turning to the jury, "and Ladies and Gentlemen of the Jury." You would then say the first few sentences of your opening two minutes.

The late Moe Levine had several standard opening lines which he used to build rapport and to set an emotional tone for the summation which would follow. In a serious personal injury case he would open every summation with the following standard lines:

> Man, born of woman, comes into this world in pain and begins to die the very minute that he is born and who knows what lies in the hours ahead? There are those things that are born of the will of God and those things that are born not of the will of God but of the will

---

[14]*See supra* §§ 4.07 & 4.34–4.37, for a discussion of Communication Principle 20.

of man. Those things born of the will of God must and should endure. But those things born not of the will of God but born of the carelessness of man, the law says we need not endure.

And life is not made up of days, minutes or hours. Our life is measured in moments. And we work to fill our lives with moments that are filled with pleasure and my client's life has become a life filled with nothing but moments of pain.

And in a wrongful death case, Levine would set the emotional stage with the following opening line:

The Bible tells us that there is a time for joy and a time for sorrow. That there is a time for living and a time for dying. May 26, 1967 was Harold Jones' day for dying and, Mary, our widow's day for crying. On that day, Mary lost all the joy of living.

Note how these standard openings, through the emotional content of the language, plus the vocal cues and nonverbal behavior that were given during their presentation set a serious emotional tone. They gained attention with sufficient impact so that the jury would pay attention to what followed.

On the other hand, an equally successful, famous trial lawyer from New York started all of his opening summations by proclaiming that he was not about to give an opening argument. Rather he would invite the jury to come into his living room, sit down, and over a cup of imaginary coffee, discuss the case with him. He told them that he was not about to argue with them but simply to discuss what the evidence had shown. This folksy presentation established great rapport and was just as effective as the emotional openings of Moe Levine.

For this reason, we think it is wise to try and combine both approaches. That is, the opening of the summation should in some way link the mental state of the jury to what is going on in the courtroom, and should involve the use of embedded commands.[15] The appropriate opening line prior to summation might begin something like this:

I know it's almost lunch hour. I know you are wondering how long I am going to be. I promise you that I will be as short as possible but I must say those things that are necessary for me to adequately represent my client who has been seriously injured; a client who has been badly burned and is scarred for the rest of his life. I know

---

[15] *See supra* § 10.11, *The use of embedded commands*.

when the case began, each of you must have thought [pause—then use embedded command] that we would prove to you through the evidence [here anchoring case theme by standing in the same spot, using the same gestures and tone of voice as used in opening statement and throughout the trial when these words are mentioned] that ABC Construction Co. contracted to build an oil refinery. Instead of building an oil refinery, they built a bomb. They did not know who it was going to kill, but they surely knew it was going to kill somebody.

Harold and I fulfilled the promise made to you in opening statement. The evidence showed that the valves on this pump violated every basic standard of safety and made this pump so dangerous that sooner or later they had to know it was going to seriously burn someone. The only thing they didn't know was when and who. It turned out that the who was my client Harold. Harold has fulfilled his burden of proof. He has proved it to you and now it's time for you to fulfill the promise you made during voir dure that you would give fair and adequate compensation for serious injuries even if the amount required by those injuries is large.

§ 10.19 Covering the evidence

Every summation should cover the evidence. This is the "meat and potatoes" of the summation. In covering the evidence, however, one has to be careful not to bore the jury to death. Certainly the testimony of each witness should not be reviewed in detail. Such a detailed review will lack interest and impact and will not be persuasive. Remember, we are interested even when covering the evidence in talking to the conscious mind but communicating with the unconscious. The attorney should still be trying to work through the perceptions of the jurors and link to their model of the world. Certainly, by the time we reach summation, the jurors are both impatient and anxious. They are impatient for the summation to be over and anxious to begin deciding the case. During the summation, you should talk about what the evidence shows as a whole rather than talking about what each witness said and how each issue was proved. Most jurors have already made a preliminary decision about liability by the time of summation. Therefore, a review of the evidence in detail is probably not going to change the minds of the jurors against you. On the other hand, a concise statement covering the key points will reinforce those jurors in your favor and arm them with arguments to persuade fellow jurors during deliberation.

COMMENT: To reiterate, when covering the evidence, counsel should cover only the most salient portions of evidence and, in essence, summarize the crucial points.

In one actual case, a defendant physician failed to do a spinal tap to check for bacterial meningitis. As a result, the mother took the child home to die. This was true despite the fact that all the clinical indications were that the child had spinal meningitis. It was the classic clinical picture except the child did not have a stiff neck. It was too early in the progress of the disease. Plaintiffs brought in one nationally recognized pediatrician who was also board certified in emergency medicine and pediatrics who testified that there was sufficient evidence, even in the absence of a stiff neck to indicate the necessity of a spinal tap to rule out spinal meningitis. He further concluded that if a spinal tap had been done the probability is that the proper diagnosis would have been made. The defense brought in three local pediatricians who all testified that the child died of spinal meningitis, but the failure to make the diagnosis, while unfortunate, met the standards of care because the child didn't have a stiff neck. Without a stiff neck, there was no necessity, under the standards of care espoused by the defendants, to do a spinal tap despite the fact that all other clinical signs of spinal meningitis were clear. Even the family thought the child had it and mentioned it to the pediatrician in the emergency room. In that case, the evidence in summation should be covered in the following fashion:

> Ladies and Gentlemen: The evidence in this case clearly shows that there are two different standards of care being espoused. One standard of care says that even though there is not a stiff neck, where one even suspects spinal meningitis, because the chance of death is so real, one should do a spinal tap. This was the testimony of plaintiff's expert, Dr. Miller. He is well qualified and he espoused a standard of care that does apply and should apply throughout the nation. When a physician even suspects spinal meningitis, and the defendant in this case admitted suspecting it, a spinal tap ought to be done. Nowhere in the textbooks does it say that one does not

need to do a spinal tap unless the child has a stiff neck. In fact, the textbooks state the contrary. You remember the direct quote from *Principles of Internal Medicine*, a standard textbook for all doctors, it said on page 523 [quote shown on overhead projector]:

> "The sudden onset of high fever and/or severe headache of unknown etiology is an indication for an immediate spinal tap."

That is the standard of care in the medical textbooks and that is the standard of care that Dr. Miller testified to.

Opposing that standard of care is the testimony of three local doctors, all of whom knew the defendant before, three friends of the defendant. They espoused a standard of care that says that even though you have a severe headache and a high fever of unknown origin, if you don't have a stiff neck you don't have to do a spinal tap.

What we have here are two standards of care. A reasonably high standard of care for good safe medicine and a standard of care espoused by the defendants which amounts to nothing more than sloppy statistical medicine. The defendant's standard says it is alright to take a chance with a child's life. That's what the evidence shows and only you can choose between the two standards of care.

Notice how neatly and precisely the evidence was covered in that case. It is simplified but all the key issues were raised despite the many collateral issues and red herrings that could have confused the jurors.

§ 10.20 Simplifying the issues

A jury trial is not a law school exam. One does not get a passing grade based on the number of issues raised. In fact, counsel can get a failing grade if he goes about analyzing the facts of the case and trying to see how many legal issues can be raised. The attorney should keep the final argument simple. If you represent the plaintiff in a civil suit or the State in a criminal case, your final argument is first. Therefore, you should not only simplify the issues but pick only one or two major issues. Be sure and pick your strongest issues to ensure success in the case.

Notice in the preceding case how the analysis of the evidence simplified the case down to one issue. There were many collateral issues that could have been discussed during summation. For example, there was an issue in the case that even if they had done the spinal tap, it was too early to get a positive result and they would have sent the child home anyway. However, that was a collateral issue. The central issue in the case was the failure to practice good safe medicine. Once the jury realized that they had to choose between safe medicine and sloppy medicine, they were not about to turn this childless mother away on a collateral issue of causation. That's why the theme in the case had to be good safe medicine versus sloppy statistical medicine. That is why the case was simplified into one issue. This should be done in every case. No matter how complex the case is, it can be boiled down to one or at the most two issues.

In a products liability case, the issue may be whether you want to allow defendant manufacturer to put profits ahead of safety. In a slip and fall case, the issue may be that the one making money from the patrons has to provide them with a safe place to shop.

COMMENT: Boil the case down to a simple issue. Make sure it is a winnable issue and it becomes central to your case theme. You must tie the case together in order for the summation to be effective.

---

§ 10.21 Covering the theories of liability

In a more complex case, you must sometimes spend time in summation reexplaining the case's theory of liability. For example, if you are trying a diethylstilbestrol (DES) case, certainly the evidence concerning culpability and causation needs to be covered. The case theory deals with the relationship between the facts and the law and theoretically why the plaintiff should prevail when the two are applied together. The products liability law in most states follows Restatement of Torts § 402A. Therefore, the diethylstilbestrol cases are generally defended on the theory that the manufacturer, at the time diethylstilbestrol was put on the market (around 1947), had no indication that it could cause cancer and did not and could not know it at that time. Plaintiff's theory of strict liability is that the manufacturer cannot ignore the fact that it was known in the 1930's that estrogen caused cancer in animals. Therefore, reasonable testing should have been required to see if there was a relationship between estrogen-induced cancer in animals and whether this could be applied to humans. This was not done before DES was marketed. The manufacturer could have and should have known of the dangers.

Thus, in the diethylstilbestrol case, you would have to cover precise jury instructions and explain in detail to the jury plaintiff's theory as to why he should recover even though the manufacturers in fact, as they claim, did not know in 1947 that estrogen would cause cancer in human beings. In summation, one would have to explain to the jury very emphatically that actual knowledge is not the test. Manufacturers cannot insulate themselves from liability simply by refusing to look at what they should have looked at before a drug is put on the market.

One would then cite the literature from the 1930's showing that all forms of estrogen, including synthetic estrogen, caused various forms of cancer in animals. In particular, cancer in the genital tracts of mice was reported. Yet this literature was not cited to the Federal Drug Administration and no animal tests were done prior to a massive amounts of diethylstilbestrol being sold to Americans as a preventor of miscarriages. The jury must be made to understand that before such a massive profit-motivated scheme can be put into effect the safety and efficacy of a drug needs to be tested.

Summation must then go into a description of the testing that was done and compare it to the double blind testing that was ultimately done showing that the drug was nonefficacious, that is, that it served no useful purpose. Not only did it serve no purpose, but, in fact, DES caused clear cell adenocarcinoma of the cervix and vagina in the female offspring of mothers who ingested the drug. One should then cover the evidence on causation showing the statistical relationship between DES and cancer based on the cases reported in the Herbst registry.

In order to refute the defense attack you know is coming on causation, as you cover the theory of such a case, you should explain to the jury that the drug industry sells almost every drug they make based on a statistical study which shows the drug works. Very few drugs are understood, even by the drug industry, to the extent that the industry can "explain precisely why the drug has its therapeutic effect." The efficacy of most drugs is established solely by a significant statistical link between the drug and its alleged therapeutic effect. Therefore, it is not fair to require the plaintiff in a case like this to have a burden which no one can carry for any drug. It is true the plaintiff cannot show specifically why estrogen causes the cancer. Clearly, however, there is an overwhelming statistical association between the drug and cancer of the vagina in female offspring. You must try to prove the relationship as a probability.

You would then explain that this is all that is required under the law as set out in the jury charges.

The foregoing analysis of a diethylstilbestrol case is an example of what is meant by covering the theory of the case. The theory of the case does not necessarily have to be covered in detail in less complex litigation. But in every case, there has to be some medical theory in order to show injury and the permanency thereof. For example, in a soft tissue case, the case theory may simply be that the ripping and tearing of the muscles caused hemorrhaging in the muscles and that the tears healed with permanent scar tissue.

§ 10.22 Covering the damages issues

Once you have discussed the theories of liability, you should turn to the damages issues. By covering damages, we mean that you should show the effects of the injury upon the plaintiff and then thoroughly discuss the monetary ramifications thereof.

In covering damages, remember to use embedded commands.[16] In every case during voir dire, counsel should have obtained the commitment that if the evidence showed serious and permanent injury to the plaintiff, the jurors are committed to awarding a significant amount of money. Therefore, Communication Principle 8 would come into play. The jurors would have an inherent need to be consistent with that commitment. You should couple the discussion of damages with that commitment and remind the jurors of their commitment made during voir dire. You should then apply the techniques described previously to enforce this commitment by having the request go through the conscious mind into the unconscious mind.[17] That is, one should link back to the wording used to mark the embedded command in voir dire and opening statement and repeat that language with regard to damages.

An example of the language that can be used to cover damages can be taken from the cervical sprain case of Mary that we have discussed throughout this text.

> My client and I were wondering if you could follow the law (pause) and give substantial damages where the evidence showed that the defendant caused a serious injury. I know that each of you remember making that commitment. [You may or may not show

---

[16] *See supra* § 10.11, *The use of embedded commands*.

[17] *See supra* § 4.17.

the jury the commitment in a written form from the transcript.] I suppose you were wondering how we could possibly prove such serious consequences could occur that from a simple bump in the rear.

But now you are wondering no longer. Now you know what the evidence showed. It is clear from the evidence that when Mary's car was rear-ended her neck snapped forward down on her chest and that as a result of this light impact severe mechanics took place. That when this happens the muscles in the neck are ripped and torn. When they are ripped and torn, they bleed and hemorrhage. And that when they heal, they heal with scar tissue. And that the scar tissue is thick and not as pliable as normal tissue. These muscles are therefore weak and susceptible to pain and spasm when they are overused and when the weather changes. And what did the evidence show in this case? Mary and her friends answered that for you. Not only did the physicians tell you that she had permanent scar tissue but her friends told you the effects. This is the damage. Whenever the weather changes, whenever she stands too long, whenever she tries to play a sport or to do some of the things she used to do, Mary suffers pain and has to go to bed. It's that simple. It recurred repeatedly over the last three years. And Mary's treating physician, Dr. Jones, told you that it is going to continue to occur on a regular basis in the future for the rest of her life and that is all the result of the defendant, Mr. Harry James, not watching out and hitting her in the rear.

Oh, I know they say it's a light impact, but remember that's all it takes for the muscles to be torn and ripped and scar tissue to occur. And you were wondering how we could prove it was serious? (Pause) Well we proved it even through the words of the defense doctor who examined Mary and sent a written report back to the defense counsel in this case. You remember his testimony on cross-examination he was asked this question (casually reading from transcript):

> "Q. Doctor, wouldn't you agree that there have been significant studies on animals, particularly monkeys, that show that when an animal suffers this type of cervical injury as a result of the hemorrhaging in the animal's neck, the presence of microscopic scar tissue in the fibers in his neck has been seen on autopsy?
>
> "A. Yes.

"Q. Doctor, so you agree that there is a possibility or even a probability, concerning what happened to Mary's neck in this rear-end collision, if you accept the fact that she can have scar tissue in the neck?

"A. That's certainly a possibility."

So even their expert does not emphatically deny it. It is there. It is permanent and she is going to live with it the rest of her life. You have to compensate her not only for the three years that occurred in the past but for the balance of her life. And she is only 22-years-old and the balance of her life is in excess of fifty years. And you were wondering how we could show a serious injury that would require you giving serious damages? But I know you are wondering no longer. Because we have proved to you that the plaintiff's pain and suffering is going to last better than fifty years into the future. No matter what amount of money you find reasonable to live with this pain and disability in the future, on a day by day basis, it comes to a lot of money when you add it up over fifty years.

Fifty years is a long time and numbers can literally roll off your tongue with ease. But let's assume that you move fifty years in the past. It would be 1935. If we were trying this case in 1935, how adequate would your verdict have been? It is only when we look at the case as though it was being tried in 1935 can we get a perspective of what it is going to be like to live fifty years in the future. An awful lot took place in those fifty years. In 1935, World War II had not occurred and most of us here were not yet born. It's a long time. That's what you are going to have to deal with in the jury room if you are going to be fair and follow the law and the evidence as you promised Mary and I you would do.

From here, you might use a damages chart and actually mention a dollar amount. However, in a cervical sprain case, you may choose not to recommend a specific amount and simply let the jury do the rest. If you become too locked into a per diem argument in a cervical sprain case, it may result in a severe case of overreaching.

COMMENT: In covering the damages, return to the commitments given on voir dire and to the commands that were embedded at that time. If you do that, you can then let the jury make an adequate award. For no matter how small an amount they choose to award per year, it's going to be a substantial sum when multiplied by the life expectancy of the injured party.

---

§ 10.23 Using standard arguments

There is a whole series of time-tested standard arguments which can be used to structure summations. You need to be aware of these standard arguments and learn to use them effectively. Such standard arguments, are a form of good verbal communication. This verbal communication can effectively be woven into the vocal and nonverbal techniques that are discussed elsewhere in this text.[18]

An example of a standard argument is the one commonly used to cover plaintiff's burden of proof in a civil case by relating it to a baseball score. That argument follows:

> We realize ladies and gentlemen, Mary has what the law calls the burden of proof in this civil case. But listen to only his Honor when he reads you his civil law charge. He will tell you this being only a civil and not a criminal case we have to prove the case by a preponderance of the evidence. That is to prove what is more probably true than not true. That means a slight tipping of the scales is all that is required. It's kind of like a baseball score. You don't have to win the World Series by 10 runs or 20 runs. If the Yankees win the 7th game of the World Series by only one run, that's sufficient, they still win. Well, if when you put all the evidence together on a particular point in this case, if the score is simply 9 to 8, if the plaintiff leads by only 1 point, he still wins. And you promised to follow the law. Don't require Mary to eliminate doubts and prove her case beyond a reasonable doubt. That's for a criminal case! Require Mary only to carry the burden that the law puts on her and to win her case by only a single point. If that's all she won it by, you still have to decide it in her favor.

The following standard argument is concerned with handling contributory negligence of the plaintiff. It compares contributory negligence or if applicable, comparative negligence, to a grade on a report card.

---

[18] *See supra generally* Chapter 7, *Opening Statement: Getting the Jury Committed*.

> Ladies and gentlemen, the defendants have the burden of proving the negligence of the plaintiff. But when talking about contributory negligence of the plaintiff, as opposed to the gross misconduct of the defendant, Mr. Jones, one should consider it like a report card. Mary is not required to get 100 to pass. She is not required to have an A+. She is not required to have a B+. She is not required to have a C. She can even have a D. As long as the grade is above a 70, she passes. Her conduct in this case may not be perfect. In the juryroom you can criticize the way she drove the car and the way she stopped the car. Some can say she didn't get a 100. But other people would act that way. All she did was drive the car like an average person and bring it to a stop like an average person would when faced with a sudden emergency of a fire engine coming into the intersection. It may be that all she gets is a 70 or 80 but as long as she gets a passing grade, she was not negligent.

There are, of course, hundreds of other standard arguments. The point is that one should know these standard arguments and use these verbal concepts and mold them to the facts of each individual case. Using standard arguments is part of good advocacy. It's part of being persuasive.

§ 10.24 The closing line

The closing line of a summation has been referred to by one famous trial lawyer as "the final five minutes." There can be no doubt about its importance. This last few moments speaks directly to the psychological principle of recency or the ability of the jury to recall what you said in the summation. It is an important five minutes in which you make a final attempt to motivate the jury to decide the case in favor of your client. The final few minutes of the summation are critical to all parties concerned with the case.

This is a time for using linguistic techniques that create moving images in the mind.[19] This is also the time for pacing the jury so that we transfer not only words and information but a feeling about our client and his cause.[20] In a serious personal injury case, plaintiff's counsel should be attempting to transfer a feeling of empathy or tragedy for his client to the jurors. On the other hand, defense counsel should be using complimen-

[19] *See supra* § 4.31.

[20] *See supra* §§ 2.49–2.52, for a textual discussion concerning the techniques for transferring feelings.

tary pacing insisting that the jurors maintain a very logical and detached perspective about the evidence.[21]

On the other hand, while the plaintiff's attorney will be using techniques designed to aid in transferring feelings, he will be attempting to create a mood of empathy and a feeling about how serious and tragic the plaintiff's injuries really are. This is the point in the summation where you should use a slower rate of speech and a lower voice tone. In addition, you should use dramatic pauses which should be accompanied by a lowering of your eyes to the right, and gestures down to the left, thereby causing jurors to drop their eyes to the lower right in an attempt to access the kinesthetic state of the jurors' minds. In most instances, you are attempting to increase the jurors' association with your client through emotional imagery. This is the point in the summation where the emotional appeal should take place. This is what the closing line is all about.

The closing of the summation involves communicating on all three levels, verbally, vocally and nonverbally. Nonverbally, of course, includes both visual (what the jurors see you do) and nonverbal feelings that are transferred to the jury. The closing should create in each juror a strong feeling that to render a verdict in your client's favor is to do what the jurors perceive and feel is right and equitable. This relates to Communication Principle 21: Jurors seek to render a verdict which they perceive as equitable.

Each closing line, in terms of emotional content, must be in balance on whole with the nature of the case. In a cervical sprain case, too much emotional content, i.e., content out of proportion to the nature of the injury, will cause a loss of credibility and therefore a definite drop in the persuasiveness of the message. On the other hand, when one is dealing with catastrophic injury, disability, death or disfigurement, the emotional content of your closing lines can be proportionally increased. Whatever the appropriate degree of emotional content, there is no question but that the closing line of the summation should have some emotional impact and should motivate the jury to take action in your client's favor.

Following is an example of a closing line from a summation given several years ago in a case involving the death of a fetus. This closing line, given with appropriate vocal cues and nonverbal communications, had a significant impact on the jurors and even the defense counsel. It was

---

[21] *See supra* § 2.50, for a discussion of how to successfully transfer an unattached state of mind to the jurors (aid the jurors in being detached).

instrumental in the jury's awarding the highest verdict ever given for the death of an unborn child in Louisiana.

The actual case involved gross medical malpractice. It involved the death of a mother and her unborn fetus due to the failure of the defendant to do a proper urinalysis which resulted in the failure to diagnose the impending eclampsia. Everyone had thought that the death of the fetus along with the wife was not important as an element of damages. Everyone thought that the death of the wife of an immigrant from South America was the primary damage factor in the case. Applying Communication Principle 21, however, counsel for the plaintiff realized that the most innocent victim under the facts was the unborn child. It was decided that the jury's attitude towards this particular plaintiff, an unborn child, would be unquestionably favorable, and that its death was a horrible injury. Therefore the equity factor in the case made this an area where emotional impact could be maximized. This was where the jury could maximize their sense of outrage at the defendant's actions and the need for justice for the injured party. Therefore, plaintiff's counsel wisely saved the arguments concerning damages for death of the fetus for last. Discussion of that loss was the closing line of the hour-long summation. The closing line of the summation follows:

> We have been talking now for over an hour about the unnecessary death of Marguerite. We have talked to you about what that means to Jose and the economics of that loss in terms of the hundreds of thousands of dollars it's going to take to replace Marguerite. But at the end we must talk about the most horrible aspect of the damage.
>
> That's the death of Jose Jr. You remember the defendant on that fateful day when he did that improper urinalysis he told the mother he knew by the heartbeat that it was going to be little boy. And Jose told you that's what he was hoping for. It was going to be his first-born American son. He was to be Jose's first natural born American citizen. Jose was so proud of that.
>
> That's the real injury here. It's little Jose, his nine-month-old baby, who was about to be born. He never saw the light of day! At least the mother, Marguerite, had a chance to drink half of the rich cup of the wine of life before it was spilled by the negligence of Dr. Aguillard. But little Jose didn't have a chance to taste the first sip of the cup of the wine of life. He never got to exist and yet he was real, he was there in his mother's womb, the fetus that was fully grown,

ready to be born, when her life was snuffed out by gross negligent misconduct.

He may have been ordinary or he could have been another Simon Bolivar. Jose will never know what Jose Jr. would have been like. Nor will our community. Society has been robbed of the bright promise of a life that now can never be fulfilled. A bright hope for the future has been wiped out. Not only has Jose lost his helpmate for life, he has lost all hope. He has lost Jose Jr., who never came out of his mother's womb, who died trapped in there while gasping and struggling to exist.

And if by your verdict you could undo this hurt and correct this terrible wrong, I am sure that Jose would forget about the rest of the damages and go home. Never mind about the loss of his wife, Marguerite, he could tolerate that if he could have Jose Jr. If you, by your verdict, could cause those doors in the back of the courtroom to swing open and little Jose could come running in here now . . . (pointing to the door) he'd be four-years-old. . . . And if he could run up to his father, throw his arms around his neck and hug him and kiss him and say "Hi, Dad, I'm glad to know you," my client, Jose, would be so proud and happy, that even though full justice would not be done, he would be satisfied.

But you can't even do that. You can't, by your verdict, restore even Jose Jr. You must express both of these terrible hurts in the inadequate remedy of dollars. But just because you as a jury cannot restore little Jose and Marguerite to life does not mean that your verdict should not in dollars and cents express full and complete justice. Your verdict should, in equity, express an amount which says that this was a terrible hurt, that this was a terrible wrong. And my client Jose and I will be here waiting for your verdict knowing that it will express full justice not only for the loss of Marguerite but for the loss of this baby that never was, for the loss of this young man who never had a chance to fulfill his bright promise of life, for the loss of Jose Jr. Thank you very much.

Note how the closing line of that summation took what most thought to be the weak point of the case and hammered it home as the strongest. The equity of the situation was what made the loss of the fetus so effective. Note how the closing line painted an imagined event in the jury's mind's eye. This visualization of an imagined event caused an emotional impact which motivated the jurors to give a very adequate award for the death of a fetus whose life they could not restore. The closing lines of this summation also involve moving the jurors across time and space lines and transference of a mood through association as described previously.[22]

COMMENT: Closing lines with sufficient emotional impact motivate and persuade jurors to take action that is both appropriate and favorable to your client.

---

§ 10.25 Structuring the emotional appeal in summation

There is no doubt that a summation should create a message that has high emotional impact.[23] The bottom line is that a message, in order to be retained, in order for it to be effective, in order for it to motivate people, must have strong emotional content.

The question then raised in summation is that if a message is going to have emotional impact, to which of the jurors' emotions should there be an appeal. Basically there are only two emotions to which a message can appeal, either anger/hate or kindness/love. When choosing what emotion the message should have, it is important to remember that the emotion of love and kindness is much more permanent, lasting, and persuasive than hate and anger. We tend to avoid situations where hate and anger are involved. We cross the street in order to avoid a confrontation or a fight. On the other hand, we naturally seek out messages or anything else that involves love and kindness.

Therefore, in almost all cases, the attorney should appeal to the emotion of love. This emotion portrays a feeling of kindness, not only for the injured party in a civil suit, but also for the person who committed the wrong, for the victim in a criminal action, and even for the person accused of the crime. Generally, we can be more persuasive when we approach either a criminal or civil case with arguments relating to love, kindness, and generosity. This is a much more long lasting emotion. Consider the fact that religions built on love have lasted for thousands of years. Those empires throughout history that have been based predomi-

[22] *See supra* §§ 2.49–2.52, for a discussion of mood transference.

[23] *See supra* § 3.26, for a discussion of how to create strong emotional impact.

nantly on hate have not lasted very long. We simply cannot expect a jury to be angry and hate the other party on a long term basis. Those emotions don't stay with them in the jury room. Therefore, the bottom line is that the emotion that should be appealed to in almost every case, is one of love, kindness and giving. This ties in with Communication Principle 21 that jurors want to do with their verdict what they perceive as equitable and just.

In some situations, however, the attorney might properly want to appeal to the jurors' sense of righteous indignation. Certainly this is true when one is seeking punitive damages. In the case of the improperly installed automobile gasoline tanks where the evidence clearly showed that the manufacturer was more interested in saving dollars and paying off a few burn victims, counsel could properly call for righteous indignation. In that kind of a situation, counsel may want to appeal to the emotion of anger and hatred for a defendant who balanced profit against public safety. The same has been true in the asbestosis cases. Large verdicts for punitive damages have resulted from those cases because lawyers have been able to show that one of the manufacturers of asbestos, Johns-Manville, had a great disregard for the health of their employees. They literally hid the information from everyone that asbestos would cause lung cancer. They knew it for decades and fought to keep this information secret. The manufacturer never kept their employees apprised of this information even though it was well known to the manufacturer. This situation is the exception rather than the rule. It is one where the jury has just grounds to be angry with and dislike the defendant. In most cases, however, you should appeal to the jury to love the plaintiff and even to forgive the defendant while doing full justice for your client.

VI. Developing a Summation Style

§ 10.26 Technique as opposed to style

In order to develop a style of summation one has to distinguish between summation style and techniques. Summation techniques involve such verbal concepts as the use of analogies and rhetorical questions. They involve using appropriate vocal cues and nonverbal messages. Summation techniques are varied. Techniques are something that all lawyers use. The difference between technique and style can best be understood if we look at the distinction with reference to artists and their various artistic works.

The style of painting of the Renaissance painter, Michelangelo, and of the subrealistic Picasso, are vastly different. Yet they used the same techniques to accomplish different styles. They both used certain mixtures of colors to create certain effects. They both held the brush a certain way and painted with certain strokes to create the illusion of light coming out of the background. They used the same techniques, but the style of their creations was completely different and opposite.

The same is true of trial lawyers. Their style of delivery is personal and unique to each one of them. Yet all great trial lawyers use the same techniques. To some trial lawyers, the techniques are a natural extension of their personalities. Others have learned the techniques and use them in a conscious, selective manner. You must be able to distinguish between style and technique. This book attempts to teach techniques through which we can communicate effectively on the verbal, vocal and nonverbal levels, as well as techniques used to establish rapport by pacing the jurors and anchoring themes. These are techniques that all lawyers can use. The style with which a particular theme is anchored in a particular case is unique to the individual attorney.

§ 10.27 —The logical delivery style

Some trial lawyers are very effective persuaders, with a low keyed, even handed style of delivery. These lawyers are low self-monitors.[24] The low self-monitor, as part of his natural personality, has a style of delivery which is basically logical. His style of delivery will have some, but not a great deal, of emotional content. The persuasiveness of his style of delivery is that it is so clearly based on logic, one cannot help but believe it. It is simple and direct. Using this style, the case is put forward in a simple fashion by saying simply that 2 + 2 must and should always equal 4. The case is built one logical brick at a time so that there can be no question but that your client will prevail.

§ 10.28 —The emotional delivery style

The antithesis of the logical style of delivery is the emotional delivery style. This style emphasizes changes in voice pitch and varies the rapidity with which the words are delivered. This style creates high emotional content and impact. This is the delivery style of the high self-monitor.

---

[24] *See supra* § 2.66, for a comparative discussion of low and high self-monitors.

The bravado of the message simply sweeps one away with its emotional content. The problem with the emotional delivery style is that when the smoke clears, the person giving the message is not perceived as being very credible. The persuasiveness of this style generally does not have a very long-lasting effect. A juror may feel a particular emotion when he is receiving the message, but when he goes to the jury room he may not be able to recall that emotion. Therefore, the emotional delivery style must be tempered by some of the characteristics of the low self monitoring style. That is, while a lot of flag waving can be very persuasive initially, that persuasiveness will be short-lived unless it is also firmly based in logic. Therefore, the lawyer who gravitates towards the emotional style has to be very careful that his arguments are also based on logic. The points he makes must be sound. He has to work towards creating the perception of a low self-monitor while delivering a persuasive message in the style of a high self-monitor.

§ 10.29 —A combination style of delivery

The best style of delivery, for most lawyers, is a combination of the logical delivery style and the emotional delivery style. In essence, most people, when given the high self-monitor test, neither fall in a range of a high self-monitor nor a low self-monitor. They have characteristics of both. For those who are neither low nor high self monitors, this means that there is a balanced style of delivery which can be most effective. Their arguments are based predominantly on logic. They do not openly display much emotion yet their message has a subtle emotional element which can be very persuasive.

On the other hand, the unique thing about developing a style is that the style of delivery must be true to the personality of the lawyer involved. If one is truly a low self-monitor, a combination style will not work. Likewise, if one is truly a high self-monitor, an attempt to use a combination style will not be effective. But whatever style of delivery one ultimately develops, it must be well thought out and planned. It must be practiced frequently so that the style of delivery becomes natural.

§ 10.30 —Adopting as opposed to adapting styles of delivery

In the final analysis one must work on developing a style of delivery. Ultimately each lawyer will develop a unique style of delivery. The basic point however is that in developing a style of delivery, lawyers can see the delivery styles of experienced trial lawyers in the courtroom or on a lecture platform.

The trial lawyer must understand that he cannot adopt the style of others. He may directly adopt the techniques of others. A style itself, however, is something that is unique and personal unto each trial lawyer.

COMMENT: Therefore, you may look at styles and try them out. Eventually, you must develop your own unique style, although you should never adopt or copy directly another attorney's style. You must take all of the information and adapt it over to your own personality and to your own limitations and talents. When we adopt something, we take something that really belongs to another and use it as our own. When we adapt something, we change it in some way so that it truly becomes our own.

INDEX

[References are to sections and tables.]

—A—

[References are to sections and tables.]

[References are to sections and tables.]

[References are to sections and tables.]

Index

[References are to sections and tables.]

[References are to sections and tables.]

[References are to sections and tables.]

[References are to sections and tables.]

[References are to sections and tables.]

[References are to sections and tables.]

[References are to sections and tables.]

CREDIBILITY IN THE COURTROOM—Continued

CRIMINAL CASES

CROSS-EXAMINATION

[References are to sections and tables.]

[References are to sections and tables.]

[References are to sections and tables.]

Index

[References are to sections and tables.]

[References are to sections and tables.]

Index

[References are to sections and tables.]

[References are to sections and tables.]

—E—

[References are to sections and tables.]

EXPERT WITNESS—Continued

Index

[References are to sections and tables.]

[References are to sections and tables.]

INITIAL INTERVIEW WITH CLIENT—Continued

[References are to sections and tables.]

[References are to sections and tables.]

[References are to sections and tables.]

[References are to sections and tables.]

[References are to sections and tables.]

[References are to sections and tables.]

Index

[References are to sections and tables.]

[References are to sections and tables.]

OPENING STATEMENT

[References are to sections and tables.]

[References are to sections and tables.]

[References are to sections and tables.]

[References are to sections and tables.]

PERSUASIVE COURTROOM STRATEGIES—Continued

[References are to sections and tables.]

[References are to sections and tables.]

[References are to sections and tables.]

[References are to sections and tables.]

—R—

[References are to sections and tables.]

—S—

Index

[References are to sections and tables.]

[References are to sections and tables.]

[References are to sections and tables.]

[References are to sections and tables.]

[References are to sections and tables.]

[References are to sections and tables.]

[References are to sections and tables.]

[References are to sections and tables.]

[References are to sections and tables.]

[References are to sections and tables.]

—W—

[References are to sections and tables.]

Courtroom Communication Strategies

Edited by Kenneth R. Gesser, J.D., and Jerome Nates, J.D.

Index by Lucille Boorstein

Text design by Benjamin Y. Lee

Cover and title page design by David Merrill Design

Composition, printing, and binding by Joe Christensen, Inc., Lincoln, Nebraska. Text set in 11 on 13 Times Roman on the Datalogic system; printed on 50 lb. Hammermill Cream Eggshell; bound in Library Buckram with 90 lb. White Scott Vellum endsheets.